Teaching English as a Second or Foreign Language

THIRD EDITION

MARIANNE CELCE-MURCIA

EDITOR

HEINLE & HEINLE

THOMSON LEARNING

UNITED STATES · AUSTRALIA · CANADA · MEXICO · SINGAPORE · SPAIN · UNITED KINGDOM

HEINLE & HEINLE

TM

THOMSON LEARNING

Teaching English as a
Second or Foreign Language, Third Edition
Marianne Celce-Murcia, Editor

Vice President, Editorial Director ESL: Nancy Leonhardt
Acquisition Editors: Eric Bredenberg/Sherrise Roehr
Developmental Editor: Sarah Barnicle
Production Editor: Eunice Yeates-Fogle
Marketing Manager: Charlotte Sturdy

Manufacturing Coordinator: Mary Beth Hennebury
Composition: Dewey Publishing Services
Project Management: Tünde A. Dewey
Cover/Text Design: Carole Rollins
Printer: Von Hoffmann Graphics

For more information contact Heinle & Heinle, 25 Thomson Place, Boston, MA   02110   USA, or you can visit our Internet site at http://www.heinle.com

For permission to use materials from this text or product contact us:
Web: www.thomsonrights.com
Fax: 1-800-730-2215
Tel: 1-800-730-2214

ISBN: 0-8384-1992-5

Library of Congress Cataloging-in-Publication Data
Teaching English as a second or foreign language/Marianne Celce-Murcia, editor–3rd ed.
    p. cm.
  Includes bibliographical references (p. 553) and index.
  ISBN 0-8384-1992-5 (alk. paper)
   1. English language–Study and teaching–Foreign speakers. 2. Second language acquisition. I. Celce-Murcia, Marianne

PE1128.A2 T44 2001
428'.0071–dc21

2001024061

ASIA (excluding India)
Thomson Learning
60 Albert Street #15-01
Albert Complex
Singapore 189969

AUSTRALIA/NEW ZEALAND
Nelson/Thomson Learning
102 Dodds Street
South Melbourne
Victoria 3205 Australia

CANADA
Nelson/Thomson Learning
1120 Birchmount Road
Scarborough, Ontario
Canada M1K 5G4

LATIN AMERICA
Thomson Learning
Seneca, 53
Colonia Polanco
11560 México D.F. México

SPAIN
Thomson Learning
Calle Magallanes, 25
28015-Madrid
España

UK/EUROPE/MIDDLE EAST
Thomson Learning
Berkshire House
168-173 High Holborn
London, WC1V 7AA, United Kingdom

à Maryse et Gabriel

Text Credits

We are grateful to the following publishers for permission to reproduce their materials in the following chapters:

"Teaching Pronunciation," Janet Goodwin:
pp. 135 and 137: "Sagittal Section Diagram" (p. 43) and Fig. 4.1 "The Vowel Quadrant" (p. 95). From M. Celce-Murcia, Brinton, D. M., and J. Goodwin. 1996. *Teaching Pronunciation: A Reference for Teachers of English to Speakers of Other Languages.* Cambridge: Cambridge University Press. Reprinted with the permission of Cambridge University Press.

"Developing Children's Listening and Speaking in ESL," Sabrina Peck:
p. 141: Graham, Carolyn (1979). "You Did It Again" (p. 25). From *Jazz Chants for Children.* New York: Oxford University Press. Reproduced by permission of Oxford University Press.
p. 144: Graham, Carolyn (1988). Extract from "The Three Bears" (p. 4). From *Jazz Chants Fairy Tales.* New York: Oxford University Press. Reproduced by permission of Oxford University Press.

"Teaching Children Literacy Skills in a Second Language," Anne M. Ediger:
p. 164: TESOL (1997). ESL Standards for Pre-K–12 Students (pp. 9–10). Alexandria, VA: Author. Reprinted with permission. For more information, or to obtain a copy of the full Standards volume, please contact TESOL Publications, Tels. 1-888-891-0041 (toll free) or 1-301-638-4427; E-mail tesolpubs@tasco1.com.
p. 165: Board of Education in the City of New York. New York City Edition, New Standards Performance Standards for English Language Arts, English as a Second Language, and Spanish Language Arts. Reprinted with permission from the Board of Education of the City of New York.

"Experiential and Negotiated Language Learning," Jan Eyring:
pp. 342–344: Legutke, Michael and Thomas, Howard (1991). Process and Experience in the Language Classroom. Reprinted by permission of Pearson Education Limited ©Longman Group U.K. Limited.

"When the Teacher is a Non-native Speaker," Péter Medgyes:
p. 441: Davies, Alan (1996). Selection (pp. 27–29) from "What Second Language Learners Can Tell Us About the Native Speaker: Identifying and Describing Exception." Presented at the 1996 American Association of Applied Linguistics (AAAL), Chicago, IL. Reprinted with permission.

"Computers in Language Teaching," Maggie Sokolik:
p. 484: Liang, Jeff (1998). Description entitled "The Garage" of MOO space written for College Writing 108. Reproduced by permission of student author Jeff Liang (5/4/99).
p. 484: Rodriguez, Veronica (1998). Description entitled "The Sultan's Room" of MOO space written for College Writing 108. Reproduced by permission of student author Veronica Rodriguez (5/1/99).

Every effort has been made to trace all sources of illustrations/photos/information in this book, but if any have been inadvertently overlooked, the publisher will be pleased to make the necessary arrangements at the first opportunity.

Contents

 *Foreword*

The purpose of this third edition of *Teaching English as a Second or Foreign Language*, also known as "The Apple Book," remains the same as the first (1979) and second (1991) editions: to produce a comprehensive introduction to the profession of teaching English to speakers of other languages. The goal has been to maintain a balance between theory and practice—between providing necessary background information and relevant research, on the one hand, and offering many classroom suggestions and resources for teachers, on the other. This edition covers the areas I believe to be critical to successful language instruction: knowledge of past and present teaching approaches, background on and techniques for teaching the language skills, various options for integrating the skills, awareness of important learner factors, and information that is useful for the classroom teacher's everyday performance and professional growth. I have tried to produce an introduction to the field that would be of sufficient depth and breadth to be suitable for students with some previous teaching experience, yet straightforward enough not to needlessly bewilder the novice.

This third edition covers more topics and has more contributing authors than the previous ones:

- First edition (1979): 31 chapters, 27 contributors
- Second edition: 32 chapters, 36 contributors
- Third edition: 36 chapters, 40 contributors

Nineteen of the thirty-six authors who contributed to the second edition have also contributed to this volume (often—but not always—on the same topic). Sixteen of the chapters appearing in this edition are revised and updated versions of chapters in the second edition and, in most cases, the revisions have been substantial. Ten chapters have been completely rewritten; the remaining ten chapters represent topics that appear as chapters for the first time in this edition (the author's name is in parentheses):

- Communicative Language Teaching for the Twenty-First Century (Savignon)
- Syllabus design (Nunan)
- Developing Children's Listening and Speaking Skills (Peck)
- Cognitive Approaches to Grammar Instruction (Fotos)
- Bilingual Approaches to Language Learning (McGroarty)
- When the Teacher Is a Non-Native Speaker (Medgyes)
- Facilitating Cross-Cultural Communication (Hinkel)
- Action Research, Teacher Research, and Classroom Research (Bailey)
- Reflective Teaching (Murphy)

I am most grateful to all forty contributors to this third edition for their splendid work.

Many of the new topics in this edition were originally suggested by colleagues who anonymously reviewed the second edition for Heinle & Heinle. I am very grateful for their input, which I have used along with my own judgment to create this volume. The reviewers also helped to convince me that a revised and updated third edition was necessary, and they encouraged me to once again undertake the daunting task of preparing a comprehensive textbook for use in methods courses designed to prepare ESL/EFL teachers.

As in both previous editions, each chapter concludes with discussion questions, suggested activities, and a number of suggestions for further reading. These supplementary materials show how the authors feel their chapter can be used in methodology courses to stimulate critical thinking, further reading on a topic, and application of knowledge. The new feature in this edition is the listing of useful websites at the end of most chapters to make teachers in training aware of the vast array of resources available to them via the World Wide Web if they have access to a computer, even if they are working in remote areas.

Although designed primarily as a textbook for a preservice TESL/TEFL methods course, I feel that this volume will also be a useful reference and guide for those who are teaching ESL or EFL without having had specific training and for practicing teachers who received their training some years ago.

In trying to make the text comprehensive, I admit to having made it too long for one course. Thus I would advise instructors who plan to use this book to be selective and to focus on the chapters most relevant to the preparation of their students as teachers. One colleague has written that he prefers to emphasize Units I, IV, and V in his methods course, whereas another colleague informs me that she uses Units II and III as the core of her class. I even know of one setting where Units I, IV, and V constitute one course and Units II and III a second course. Different instructors and different training programs emphasize different topics and organize courses differently. This is understandable.

I personally like to give students options when I assign chapters to read. For example, after everyone has read and discussed the five chapters in Unit I, students can select the chapter(s) that best meet their current or anticipated needs:

- Read one of the two chapters on listening
- Read two of the three chapters on speaking, reading, and writing and so on

Another approach I have used is to ask everyone in a class to skim a particular unit of the book (or subsection in Unit II). Then I ask students to form pairs or small groups that are responsible for presenting and leading discussions on individual chapters. (The instructor must of course provide a model and explicit guidelines for what is expected in such a presentation.) The textbook chapters that are not covered in a course as a result of needs analysis and careful selection then become useful reference materials for the teacher in training, whose interests and needs and target students may well change after completion of the methods course and the training program. Also, if one goes to another region or country or works in a remote area, it is useful to have a single, comprehensive reference for language methodology—just as it is useful to have a comprehensive dictionary and a comprehensive reference grammar. This volume is my attempt to compile and edit such a reference for language methodology.

I welcome comments and feedback on this edition. In our role as teachers, we all have much to learn from one another.

–Marianne Celce-Murcia, editor

Acknowledgments

Many colleagues, students, and friends have been of invaluable assistance in the preparation of this volume. My greatest debt is to all the colleagues who graciously accepted my invitation to write chapters for this edition. The breadth and depth of their expertise make this collection truly unique.

I am especially indebted to Brent Green, my research assistant, who helped to prepare the cumulative list of references and the index. I could not have finished this book without his and Jo Hilder's assistance and offer them my heartfelt thanks.

Many people at Heinle & Heinle have helped in the shaping and production of this large volume. I had my initial discussions with Erik Gundersen, then had further discussions and signed the contract with Eric Bredenberg, who then turned the project over to Sherrise Roehr. I received much help and support from Sherrise Roehr, Sarah Barnicle, and Eunice Yeates-Fogle of Heinle & Heinle in the completion of the manuscript and once again had the pleasure of working with Tünde A. Dewey of Dewey Publishing in the final phase of production. My warm and sincere thanks to everyone mentioned in this paragraph.

Finally, I would like to note that I have incorporated into this edition many suggestions for improving the second edition that readers, students, and colleagues have graciously shared with me over the years. I offer special thanks to the anonymous reviewers who completed Heinle & Heinle's questionnaire, designed to elicit suggestions for revision and improvement. The responsibility for the choices made and for any critical omissions is mine alone.   –MCM

UNIT I

Teaching Methodology

In this first section, Celce-Murcia's chapter gives the reader a historical perspective and outlines the principal approaches to second and foreign language teaching that were used during the twentieth century. Then Savignon's chapter goes into detail in describing the components of communicative language teaching, the currently dominant approach. In their chapter, Crookes and Chaudron discuss classroom research and its implications for developing a principled approach to language teaching. The following chapter by Johns and Price-Machado introduces the reader to the English for Specific Purposes movement, which has had a profound influence on all English language teaching. Finally, Nunan's chapter gives the reader an overview of the syllabus design process, bringing us full circle, since the syllabus ideally goes hand-in-hand with the materials and approaches used in the language classroom.

Language Teaching Approaches: An Overview[1]

MARIANNE CELCE-MURCIA

In "Language Teaching Approaches: An Overview," Celce-Murcia gives some historical background, then outlines the principal approaches to second and foreign language teaching that were used during the twentieth century. She previews the book as a whole and projects some trends for language instruction in the new millennium.

INTRODUCTION

The field of second (or foreign) language teaching has undergone many fluctuations and shifts over the years. Different from physics or chemistry, in which progress is more or less steady until a major discovery causes a radical theoretical revision (Kuhn 1970), language teaching is a field in which fads and heroes have come and gone in a manner fairly consistent with the kinds of changes that occur in youth culture. I believe that one reason for the frequent swings of the pendulum that have been taking place until fairly recently is the fact that very few language teachers have a sense of history about their profession and are thus unaware of the historical bases of the many methodological options they have at their disposal. It is hoped that this brief and necessarily oversimplified survey will encourage many language teachers to learn more about the origins of their profession. Such knowledge will ensure some perspective when teachers evaluate any so-called innovations or new approaches to methodology, which will surely continue to emerge from time to time.

Pre-twentieth-Century Trends: A Brief Survey

Prior to the twentieth century, language teaching methodology vacillated between two types of approaches: *getting learners to use* a language (i.e., to speak and understand it) versus *getting learners to analyze* a language (i.e., to learn its grammatical rules).

Both the classical Greek and medieval Latin periods were characterized by an emphasis on teaching people to use foreign languages. The classical languages, first Greek and then Latin, were used as lingua francas. Higher learning was conducted primarily through these languages all over Europe. They were used widely in philosophy, religion, politics, and business. Thus the educated elite became fluent speakers, readers, and writers of the appropriate classical language. We can assume that the teachers or tutors used informal and more or less direct approaches to convey the form and meaning of the language they were teaching and that they used aural-oral techniques with no language textbooks per se, but rather a small stock of hand-copied written manuscripts of some sort, perhaps a few texts in the target language, or crude dictionaries that listed equivalent words in two or more languages side by side.

During the Renaissance, the formal study of the grammars of Greek and Latin became popular through the mass production of books made possible by the invention of the printing press. In the case of Latin, it was discovered that the grammar of the classical texts was different from that of the Latin being used as a lingua franca—the latter subsequently being labeled vulgate Latin, i.e., Latin of the common people. Major differences had developed between the classical Latin described in the Renaissance grammars, which became the formal object of instruction in schools, and the Latin being used for everyday purposes. This occurred at about the same time that Latin began to be abandoned as a lingua franca. (No one was speaking classical Latin anymore, and various European vernaculars had begun to rise in respectability and popularity.) Thus, in retrospect, strange as it may seem, the Renaissance preoccupation with the formal study of classical Latin may have contributed to the demise of Latin as a lingua franca in Western Europe.

Since the European vernaculars had grown in prestige and utility, it is not surprising that people in one country or region began to find it necessary and useful to learn the language of another country or region. Thus the focus in language study shifted back to utility rather than analysis during the seventeenth century. Perhaps the most famous language teacher and methodologist of this period is Johann Amos Comenius, a Czech scholar and teacher, who published books about his teaching techniques between 1631 and 1658. Some of the techniques that Comenius used and espoused were the following:

■ Use imitation instead of rules to teach a language.
■ Have your students repeat after you.
■ Use a limited vocabulary initially.
■ Help your students practice reading and speaking.
■ Teach language through pictures to make it meaningful.

Thus Comenius, perhaps for the first time, made explicit an inductive approach to learning a foreign language, the goal of which was to teach use rather than analysis of the language being taught.

Comenius's views held sway for some time; however, by the beginning of the nineteenth century, the systematic study of the grammar of classical Latin and of classical texts had once again taken over in schools and universities throughout Europe. The analytical Grammar-Translation Approach became firmly entrenched as a method for teaching not only Latin but, by extension, modern languages as well. It was perhaps best codified in the work of Karl Ploetz, a German scholar who had a tremendous influence on the language teaching profession during his lifetime and afterwards. (He died in 1881.)

However, the swinging of the pendulum continued. By the end of the nineteenth century, the Direct Method, which once more stressed the ability to use rather than to analyze a language as the goal of language instruction, had begun to function as a viable alternative to Grammar-Translation. François Gouin, a Frenchman, began to publish in 1880 concerning his work with the Direct Method. He advocated exclusive use of the target language in the classroom, having been influenced by an older friend, the German philosopher-scientist Alexander von Humboldt, who had espoused the notion that a language cannot be taught, that one can only create conditions for learning to take place (Kelly 1969).

The Direct Method became very popular in France and Germany, and has enthusiastic followers among language teachers even today (as does the Grammar Translation Approach).

In 1886, during the same period that the Direct Method first became popular in Europe, the International Phonetic Association was established by scholars such as Henry Sweet, Wilhelm Viëtor, and Paul Passy. They developed the International Phonetic Alphabet (IPA) and became part of the Reform Movement in language teaching in the 1890s. These phoneticians made some of the first truly scientific contributions to language teaching when they advocated principles such as the following:

■ the spoken form of a language is primary and should be taught first;
■ the findings of phonetics should be applied to language teaching;
■ language teachers must have solid training in phonetics;
■ learners should be given phonetic training to establish good speech habits.

The work of these phoneticians focused on the teaching of pronunciation and oral skills, which they felt had been ignored in Grammar-Translation. Thus, although the Reform Movement is not necessarily considered a full-blown pedagogical approach to language teaching, its adherents did have an influence on future approaches, as we shall see.

Quite apart from the work of the Reform Movement, the influence of the Direct Method grew; it crossed the Atlantic in the early twentieth century when Emile de Sauzé, a disciple of Gouin, came to Cleveland, Ohio, in order to see to it that all foreign language instruction in the public schools there implemented the Direct Method. De Sauzé's endeavor, however, was not completely successful (in Cleveland or elsewhere) since there were too few foreign language teachers in the United States. who were fluent speakers of the language they taught. Later, the Modern Language Association of America, based on the Coleman Report (Coleman 1929), endorsed the Reading Approach to language teaching, since given the skills and limitations of most language teachers, all that one could reasonably expect was that students would come away from the study of a foreign language able to read the target language—with emphasis on some of the great works of literature and philosophy that had been produced in the language.

The Reading Approach, as reflected in the work of Michael West (1941) and others, held sway in the United States until the late 1930s and early 1940s, when World War II broke out and made it imperative for the U.S. military to quickly and efficiently teach foreign language learners how to speak and understand a language. At this time, the U.S. government hired linguists to help teach languages and develop materials: the Audiolingual Approach (Fries 1945), which drew heavily on structural linguistics (Bloomfield 1933) and behavioral psychology (Skinner 1957), was born. In Britain the same historical pressures gave rise to the Oral or Situational Approach (e.g., Pittman 1963), which drew on Firthian Linguistics (codified in the work of Firth's best-known student, M. A. K. Halliday [1973]) as well as drawing on the experience of Britain's language educators with oral approaches to foreign language teaching. Although somewhat influenced by, but less dogmatic than, its American counterpart (the Audiolingual Approach), the Oral or Situational Approach advocated organizing structures around situations that would provide the learner with maximum opportunity to practice the target language, with "practice"

nonetheless often being little more than choral repetition. Some historians of language teaching (e.g., Howatt 1984) believe that the earlier Reform Movement played a role in the development of both Audiolingualism in the United States and the Oral-Situational Approach in Britain.

Nine Twentieth-Century Approaches to Language Teaching

In addition to the Grammar-Translation Approach, the Direct Approach,[2] the Reading Approach, the Audiolingual Approach, and the Oral-Situational Approach—whose historical development I have sketched above briefly—there are four other discernible approaches to foreign language teaching that developed and were widely used during the final quarter of the twentieth century. Thus, there are nine approaches altogether that I shall be referring to:

1. Grammar-Translation
2. Direct
3. Reading
4. Audiolingualism (United States)
5. Oral-Situational (Britain)
6. Cognitive
7. Affective-Humanistic
8. Comprehension-Based
9. Communicative

However, before listing the features of each approach, I would like to digress a moment to clarify some terminology that is crucial to this discussion. Namely, what do we mean by the terms *approach, method,* and *technique*? Are these terms synonymous? If not, how do they differ? Anthony (1963) has provided a useful set of definitions for our purposes. An *approach* to language teaching is something that reflects a certain model or research paradigm—a theory, if you like. This term is the broadest of the three. A *method,* on the other hand, is a set of procedures, i.e., a system that spells out rather precisely how to teach a second or foreign language. It is more specific than an approach but less specific than a technique. Methods are typically compatible with one (or sometimes two) approaches. A *technique* is a classroom device or activity and thus represents the narrowest of the three concepts. Some techniques are widely used and found in many methods (e.g., dictation, imitation, and repetition); however, some techniques are specific to or characteristic of a given method (e.g., using cuisinaire rods = the Silent Way [Gattegno 1976]).

The most problematic of Anthony's three terms is *method*. Methods proliferated in the 1970s. They were typically very specific in terms of the procedures and materials that the teacher, who required special training, was supposed to use. They were almost always developed and defined by one person. This person, in turn, trained practitioners who accepted the method as gospel and helped to spread the word. Some methods and their originators follow:

- Silent Way (Gattegno 1976)
- Community Language Learning (Curran 1976)
- Total Physical Response (Asher 1977)
- Suggestology, Suggestopedia, or Accelerated Learning (Lozanov 1978)

However, the lack of flexibility in such methods led some applied linguists (e.g., Richards 1984) to seriously question their usefulness and aroused a healthy skepticism among language educators, who argued that there is no such thing as the best "method":

> the complex circumstances of teaching and learning languages—with different kinds of pupils, teachers, aims and objectives, approaches, methods, and materials, classroom techniques and standards of achievement—make it inconceivable that any single method could achieve optimum success in all circumstances. (Strevens 1977, p. 5).

At this point I will outline each of the nine approaches listed above. In addition, I will note any special proficiency or role that the teacher is expected (or not expected) to fulfill.

1. Grammar-Translation Approach (an extension of the approach used to teach classical languages to the teaching of modern languages)

a. Instruction is given in the native language of the students.
b. There is little use of the target language for communication.
c. Focus is on grammatical parsing, i.e., the form and inflection of words.
d. There is early reading of difficult texts.
e. A typical exercise is to translate sentences from the target language into the mother tongue (or vice versa).
f. The result of this approach is usually an inability on the part of the student to use the language for communication.
g. The teacher does not have to be able to speak the target language.

2. Direct Approach (a reaction to the Grammar-Translation Approach and its failure to produce learners who could communicate in the foreign language they had been studying)

a. No use of the mother tongue is permitted (i.e., the teacher does not need to know the students' native language).
b. Lessons begin with dialogues and anecdotes in modern conversational style.
c. Actions and pictures are used to make meanings clear.
d. Grammar is learned inductively.
e. Literary texts are read for pleasure and are not analyzed grammatically.
f. The target culture is also taught inductively.
g. The teacher must be a native speaker or have nativelike proficiency in the target language.

3. Reading Approach (a reaction to the problems experienced in implementing the Direct Approach; reading was viewed as the most usable skill to have in a foreign language since not many people traveled abroad at that time; also, few teachers could use their foreign language well enough to use a direct approach effectively in class)

a. Only the grammar useful for reading comprehension is taught.
b. Vocabulary is controlled at first (based on frequency and usefulness) and then expanded.
c. Translation is once more a respectable classroom procedure.

d. Reading comprehension is the only language skill emphasized.

e. The teacher does not need to have good oral proficiency in the target language.

4. Audiolingualism (a reaction to the Reading Approach and its lack of emphasis on oral-aural skills; this approach became dominant in the United States during the 1940s, 1950s, and 1960s; it draws from the Reform Movement and the Direct Approach but adds features from structural linguistics [Bloomfield 1933] and behavioral psychology [Skinner 1957])

a. Lessons begin with dialogues.

b. Mimicry and memorization are used, based on the assumption that language is habit formation.

c. Grammatical structures are sequenced and rules are taught inductively.

d. Skills are sequenced: listening, speaking—reading, writing postponed.

e. Pronunciation is stressed from the beginning.

f. Vocabulary is severely limited in initial stages.

g. A great effort is made to prevent learner errors.

h. Language is often manipulated without regard to meaning or context.

i. The teacher must be proficient only in the structures, vocabulary, etc. that he or she is teaching since learning activities and materials are carefully controlled.

5. Oral-Situational Approach (a reaction to the Reading Approach and its lack of emphasis on oral-aural skills; this approach was dominant in Britain during the 1940s, 1950s, and 1960s; it draws from the Reform Movement and the Direct Approach but adds features from Firthian linguistics and the emerging professional field of language pedagogy)

a. The spoken language is primary.

b. All language material is practiced orally before being presented in written form (reading and writing are taught only after an oral base in lexical and grammatical forms has been established).

c. Only the target language should be used in the classroom.

d. Efforts are made to ensure that the most general and useful lexical items are presented.

e. Grammatical structures are graded from simple to complex.

f. New items (lexical and grammatical) are introduced and practiced situationally (e.g., at the post office, at the bank, at the dinner table).

6. Cognitive Approach (a reaction to the behaviorist features of the Audiolingual Approach; influenced by cognitive psychology [Neisser 1967] and Chomskyan linguistics [Chomsky 1959, 1965])

a. Language learning is viewed as rule acquisition, not habit formation.

b. Instruction is often individualized; learners are responsible for their own learning.

c. Grammar must be taught but it can be taught deductively (rules first, practice later) and/or inductively (rules can either be stated after practice or left as implicit information for the learners to process on their own).

d. Pronunciation is de-emphasized; perfection is viewed as unrealistic and unattainable.

e. Reading and writing are once again as important as listening and speaking.

f. Vocabulary instruction is once again important, especially at intermediate and advanced levels.

g. Errors are viewed as inevitable, to be used constructively in the learning process.

h. The teacher is expected to have good general proficiency in the target language as well as an ability to analyze the target language.

7. Affective-Humanistic[3] Approach (a reaction to the general lack of affective considerations in both Audiolingualism and the Cognitive Approach; e.g., Moskowitz 1978 and Curran 1976).

a. Respect is emphasized for the individual (each student, the teacher) and for his or her feelings.

b. Communication that is meaningful to the learner is emphasized.

c. Instruction involves much work in pairs and small groups.

d. Class atmosphere is viewed as more important than materials or methods.

e. Peer support and interaction are viewed as necessary for learning.

f. Learning a foreign language is viewed as a self-realization experience.

g. The teacher is a counselor or facilitator.

h. The teacher should be proficient in the target language and the student's native language since translation may be used heavily in the initial stages to help students feel at ease; later it is gradually phased out.

8. Comprehension-Based Approach (an outgrowth of research in first language acquisition that led some language methodologists to assume that second or foreign language learning is very similar to first language acquisition; e.g., Postovsky 1974; Winitz 1981; Krashen and Terrell l983)

a. Listening comprehension is very important and is viewed as the basic skill that will allow speaking, reading, and writing to develop spontaneously over time, given the right conditions.

b. Learners should begin by listening to meaningful speech and by responding nonverbally in meaningful ways before they produce any language themselves.

c. Learners should not speak until they feel ready to do so; this results in better pronunciation than if the learner is forced to speak immediately.

d. Learners progress by being exposed to meaningful input that is just one step beyond their level of competence.

e. Rule learning may help learners monitor (or become aware of) what they do, but it will not aid their acquisition or spontaneous use of the target language.

f. Error correction is seen as unnecessary and perhaps even counterproductive; the important thing is that the learners can understand and can make themselves understood.

g. If the teacher is not a native (or near-native) speaker, appropriate materials such as audiotapes and videotapes must be available to provide the appropriate input for the learners.

9. Communicative Approach (an outgrowth of the work of anthropological linguists [e.g., Hymes 1972] and Firthian linguists [e.g., Halliday 1973], who view language first and foremost as a system for communication; see Savignon's chapter in this volume)

a. It is assumed that the goal of language teaching is learner ability to communicate in the target language.

b. It is assumed that the content of a language course will include semantic notions and social functions, not just linguistic structures.

c. Students regularly work in groups or pairs to transfer (and, if necessary, negotiate) meaning in situations in which one person has information that the other(s) lack.

d. Students often engage in role play or dramatization to adjust their use of the target language to different social contexts.

e. Classroom materials and activities are often authentic to reflect real-life situations and demands.

f. Skills are integrated from the beginning; a given activity might involve reading, speaking, listening, and also writing (this assumes the learners are educated and literate).

g. The teacher's role is primarily to facilitate communication and only secondarily to correct errors.

h. The teacher should be able to use the target language fluently and appropriately.

To sum up, we can see that certain features of several of the first five approaches arose in reaction to perceived inadequacies or impracticalities in an earlier approach or approaches. The four more recently developed approaches also do this to some extent; however, each one is grounded on a slightly different theory or view of how people learn second or foreign languages or how people use languages, and each has a central point around which everything else revolves:

Cognitive Approach: Language is rule-governed cognitive behavior (not habit formation).

Affective-Humanistic Approach: Learning a foreign language is a process of self-realization and of relating to other people.

Comprehension Approach: Language acquisition occurs if and only if the learner comprehends meaningful input.

Communicative Approach: The purpose of language (and thus the goal of language teaching) is communication.

These four more recent approaches are not necessarily in conflict or totally incompatible since it is not difficult to conceive of an integrated approach which would include attention to rule formation, affect, comprehension, and communication and which would view the learner as someone who thinks, feels, understands, and has something to say. In fact, many teachers would find such an approach, if well conceived and well integrated, to be very attractive.

A Note on Approach, Method, and Syllabus Type

We now understand that an approach is general (e.g., Cognitive), that a method is a specific set of procedures more or less compatible with an approach (e.g., the Silent Way), and that a technique is a very specific type of learning activity used in one or more methods (e.g., using colored rods of varying lengths to cue and facilitate language practice in the Silent Way). Historically, an approach or method also tends to be used in conjunction with a syllabus, which is an inventory of objectives the learner should master; this inventory is sometimes presented in a recommended sequence and is used to design courses and teaching materials.

What sort of syllabuses have been used with the approaches discussed above? Most of them have used—implicitly or explicitly—a structural syllabus, which consists of a list of grammatical inflections and constructions that the teacher is expected to teach and the learner is expected to master. The Grammar-Translation Approach, the Direct Approach, the Audiolingual Approach, the Cognitive Approach, and even some methods following the Comprehension Approach have all employed a structural syllabus. In other words, teachers and textbook writers following these approaches have organized their language courses and language-teaching materials around grammar points, with Audiolingualism also specifying pronunciation points and the Oral-Situational Approach often specifying vocabulary objectives in additional to grammar.

In contrast to the structural syllabus, the Reading Approach is text-based; this kind of language course is organized around texts and vocabulary items with only minor consideration given to grammar.

In the Oral-Situational Approach, there is often a dual-objective syllabus in which various situations are specified for instruction (e.g., the post office, a restaurant, a bus, the doctor's office, etc.), along with some of the structures and the vocabulary that one might need to produce the language needed in these situations.

In the Communicative Approach, one type of syllabus is organized around notions (meanings such as spatial location, time, degree) and functions (social transactions and interactions such as asking for information or complimenting someone). In this syllabus format, grammar and vocabulary are secondary, being taught not as ends in themselves, but only insofar as they help express the notions and functions that are in focus. Many adherents of the Communicative Approach, however, reject any sort of atomistic syllabus, whether structural or notional-functional. They advocate instead a communicative syllabus (i.e., a process-based or task-based syllabus) in which real-world tasks and authentic materials are used to design language courses (Yalden 1983).

The Affective-Humanistic Approach has produced the most radical syllabus type—the learner-generated syllabus. Thus, in methods like Community Language Learning (Curran 1976) and Project Work (see Eyring's chapter in this volume), the learners decide what they want to learn and what they want to be able to do with the target language. For a fuller discussion of syllabus design, see Nunan's chapter in this volume.

CONCLUSION

What is the solution for the ESL/EFL teacher, given the abundance of past, current, and future approaches? The only way to make wise decisions is to learn more about the various approaches and methods available and to find out which practices have proved successful (see the chapter by Crookes and Chaudron in this volume). This chapter has just scratched the surface. Further information is available in the remainder of this volume and in many other books, in journal articles, at professional conferences and workshops, and on the World Wide Web.

There are also five other things the teacher should do to make good decisions concerning the choice of an approach, a method (or methods), and finally techniques and materials:

1. Assess student needs: Why should they be learning English? For what purpose? (See Johns and Price-Machado's chapter in this volume).
2. Examine instructional constraints: time (hours per week, days per week, weeks per term); class size (nature of enrollment); materials (set syllabus and text, or completely open to teacher?); physical factors (classroom size, AV support). Then decide what can reasonably be taught.
3. Determine the attitudes and learning styles (see Oxford's chapter in this volume) of individual students to the extent that this is possible, and develop activities and materials consistent with the findings.
4. Identify the discourse genres, speech activities, and text types that the students need to learn so that you can incorporate them into materials and learning activities.
5. Specify how the students' language learning will be assessed (see Cohen's chapter in this volume.)

Having done all these, the teacher will be in a position to select the most useful techniques or principles and to design a productive course of study by drawing from available approaches, syllabus types, and existing research findings. Clifford Prator, a former professor and colleague of mine, summed up the professional ESL teacher's responsibility nicely (personal communication):

Adapt; don't adopt.

Teachers are certainly in a better position to follow Prator's advice if they are familiar with the history and the state of the art of our profession. Some suggestions for further reading are provided below to aid the reader in attaining these objectives.

In fact, all of the chapters in this volume end with discussion questions, suggested activities, suggestions for further reading, and, where relevant, useful Web sites. Section 1 of this volume discusses topics in language methodology, Section 2 focuses on teaching the individual language skills, Section 3 presents some integrated approaches to language teaching, Section 4 focuses on specific groups of learners, and Section 5 provides language teachers with background information and skills that will help them become more knowledgeable and skillful practitioners.

DISCUSSION QUESTIONS

1. What has been the attitude toward the teaching of (a) pronunciation, (b) grammar, and (c) vocabulary in the nine approaches discussed in this chapter? Has there been a swinging of the pendelum? Why or why not?
2. What changes have occurred regarding the position of spoken language and written language in the various approaches? Why?
3. Which of these approaches have you personally experienced as a language learner? What were your impressions and what is your assessment of the effectiveness of the approach(es)?
4. Which approach(es) do you, as a teacher, feel most comfortable with? Why?

SUGGESTED ACTIVITIES

1. Select an integrated skills ESL/EFL text that you have used or expect to use. Examine its contents to determine which approach it seems to follow most closely. Support your decision with examples. Discuss any mixing of approaches that you observe.

2. Examine any English language proficiency test, standardized or otherwise. See if you can detect a methodological bias in the test. Support your conclusion(s) with examples.

3. What kinds of language learners do you teach (or expect to teach)? Be as specific as possible. Which approach(es) would serve such a population best? Why?

 FURTHER READING

Teachers interested in the history of the language teaching profession should consult:

Howatt, A. P. R. 1984. *A History of English Language Teaching.* Oxford: Oxford University Press.

Kelly, L. G. 1969. *Twenty-Five Centuries of Language Teaching.* New York: Newbury House.

Teachers interested in the current state of the art in language teaching methodology should consult:

Larsen-Freeman, D. 2000b. *Techniques and Principles in Language Teaching.* 2d ed. New York: Oxford University Press.

Richards, J. C., and T. S. Rodgers. 1986. *Approaches and Methods in Language Teaching.* New York: Cambridge University Press.

Stern, H. H. 1983. *Fundamental Concepts of Language Teaching.* Oxford: Oxford University Press.

ENDNOTES

1 Precursors to this chapter were published in the *Mextesol Journal* (Celce-Murcia 1980) and *Practical English Teaching* (Celce-Murcia 1981). This is a revised and updated version based on these and several other sources, notably Kelly (1969), Madsen (1979), Blair (1991), and Prator with Celce-Murcia (1979), and Celce-Murcia (1991b).

2 The term *Direct Method* is more widely used than *Direct Approach*; however, the former is a misnomer, since this is really an approach, not a method, if we follow Anthony's (1963) terminology.

3 The term *humanistic* has two meanings. One refers to the humanities (i.e., literature, history, philosophy). The other refers to that branch of psychology concerned with the role of the socio-affective domain in human behavior. It is the latter sense that I am referring to here. However, see Stevick (1990) for an even broader perspective on humanism in language teaching.

Communicative Language Teaching for the Twenty-First Century

SANDRA J. SAVIGNON

In "Communicative Language Teaching (CLT) for the Twenty-First Century," Savignon identifies five components of a communicative curriculum. She sees the identification of learner communicative needs and goals as the first step in the development of a teaching program that involves learners as active participants in the interpretation, expression, and negotiation of meaning.

You may not loiter downtown in ice cream stores. You may not ride in a carriage or automobile with any man unless he is your father or brother. You may not dress in bright colors. You must wear at least two petticoats. You must start the fire at 7 A.M. so the school room will be warm by 8 A.M.

Rules for teachers,
Goodland, Kansas (1915)[1]

What do you think of the above *1915 Rules for Teachers*? Do they seem somewhat strange or outdated? Do they make you smile? If you had been a talented new teacher in Goodland, Kansas, in 1915, you most likely would have found these rules to be the mark of a school system with high standards. No doubt the standards set for students were as high as those set for teachers. Teachers in Goodland could count on students to be respectful and diligent. In turn, teachers were expected to set a good example.

Teachers have always been expected to set a good example for learners, to provide a model of behavior. But as the 1915 rules for teachers so clearly remind us, the model can and does change. What seems a good example in one time or place, a given *context of situation*, may seem quite strange or inappropriate in another time or place. And so it is with language teaching. As this volume's introductory chapter by Marianne Celce-Murcia shows, teachers have found many ways or methods for teaching languages. All have been admired models in some time or place, often to be ridiculed, perhaps, or dismissed as inappropriate in yet another. Times change, fashions change. What may once appear new and promising can subsequently seem strange and outdated.

Within the last quarter century, communicative language teaching (CLT) has been put forth around the world as the "new," or "innovative," way to teach English as a second or foreign language. Teaching materials, course descriptions, and curriculum guidelines proclaim a goal of *communicative competence*. For example, *The Course of Study for Senior High School*, guidelines published by the Japanese Ministry of Education, Science, and Culture (Mombusho) state the objectives of ELT: "To develop students' ability to understand and to express themselves in a foreign language; to foster students' positive attitude towards communicating in a foreign language, and to heighten their interest in language and culture, thus deepening international understanding" (Wada 1994, p. 1). Minoru Wada, a university professor and a senior advisor to Mombusho in promoting ELT reform in Japan, explains the significance of these guidelines:

The Mombusho Guidelines, or course of study, is one of the most important legal precepts in the Japanese educational system. It establishes national standards for elementary and secondary schools. It also regulates content, the standard number of annual teaching hours at lower level secondary [junior high] schools, subject areas, subjects, and the standard number of required credits at upper level secondary [senior high] schools. The course of study for the teaching of English as a foreign language announced by the Ministry of Education, Science, and Culture in 1989 stands as a landmark in the history of English education in Japan. For the first time it introduced into English education at both secondary school levels the concept of *communicative competence*. In 1989, the Ministry of Education, Science, and Culture revised the course of study for primary as well as secondary schools on the basis of proposals made in a 1987 report by the Council on the School Curriculum, an advisory group to the Minister of Education, Science, and Culture. The basic goal of the revision was to prepare students to cope with the rapidly occurring changes toward a more global society. The report urged Japanese teachers to place much more emphasis on the development of communicative competence in English.

Parallel efforts are underway in nearby Taiwan for similar reasons. Based on in-depth interviews of expert teacher educators, Wang (in press) reports on the progress (see also Wang 2000):

> Much has been done to meet the demand for competent English users and effective teaching in Taiwan. Current improvements, according to the teacher experts, include the change in entrance examinations, the new curriculum with a goal of teaching for communicative competence, and the island-wide implementation in 2001 of English education in the elementary schools. However, more has to be done to ensure quality teaching and learning in the classrooms. Based on the teacher experts' accounts, further improvements can be stratified into three interrelated levels related to

teachers, school authorities, and the government. Each is essential to the success of the others' efforts.

This chapter looks at the phenomenon of communicative language teaching (CLT). What is CLT? How and why did it develop? What are the theoretical underpinnings of this approach to language teaching? How has CLT been interpreted and implemented in various contexts? Keeping in mind the needs and goals of learners and the traditions of classroom teaching, what are some ways for teachers to shape a more communicative approach to ELT in the context of their own situation?

WHAT IS CLT?

Not long ago, when American structural linguistics and behaviorist psychology were the prevailing influences in language teaching methods and materials, second/foreign language teachers talked about communication in terms of four language skills: listening, speaking, reading, and writing. These skill categories were widely accepted and provided a ready-made framework for methods manuals, learner course materials, and teacher education programs. Speaking and writing were collectively described as *active* skills, reading and listening as *passive* skills.

Today, listeners and readers no longer are regarded as passive. They are seen as active participants in the negotiation of meaning. *Schemata, expectancies*, and *top-down/bottom-up processing* are among the terms now used to capture the necessarily complex, interactive nature of this negotiation. Yet full and widespread understanding of communication as negotiation has been hindered by the terms that came to replace the earlier active/passive dichotomy. The skills needed to engage in speaking and writing activities were described subsequently as *productive*, whereas listening and reading skills were said to be *receptive*.

While certainly an improvement over the earlier active/passive representation, the terms "productive" and "receptive" fall short of capturing the interactive nature of communication. Lost in this productive/receptive, message sending/message receiving representation is the *collaborative* nature of making meaning. Meaning appears fixed, to be sent and received, not unlike a football in the hands of a team quarterback. The interest of a football game lies of course not in the football, but in the moves and strategies of the players as they punt, pass, and fake their way along the field. The interest of communication lies similarly in the moves and strategies of the participants. The terms that best represent the collaborative nature of what goes on are *interpretation, expression,* and *negotiation* of meaning. The communicative competence needed for participation includes not only grammatical competence, but pragmatic competence.

The inadequacy of a four-skills model of language use is now recognized. And the shortcomings of audiolingual methodology are widely acknowledged. There is general acceptance of the complexity and interrelatedness of skills in both written and oral communication and of the need for learners to have the *experience* of communication, to participate in the negotiation of meaning. Newer, more comprehensive theories of language and language behavior have replaced those that looked to American structuralism and behaviorist psychology for support. The expanded, interactive view of language behavior they offer presents a number of challenges for teachers. Among them, how should form and function be integrated in an instructional sequence? What is an appropriate norm for learners? How is it determined? What is an error? And what, if anything, should be done when one occurs? How is language learning success to be measured? Acceptance of communicative criteria entails a commitment to address these admittedly complex issues.

HOW AND WHY DID CLT DEVELOP?

The origins of contemporary CLT can be traced to concurrent developments in both Europe and North America. In Europe, the language needs of a rapidly increasing group of immigrants and guest workers, as well as a rich British linguistic

tradition including social as well as linguistic context in description of language behavior led the Council of Europe to develop a syllabus for learners based on notional-functional concepts of language use. Derived from neo-Firthian *systemic* or functional linguistics that views language as *meaning potential* and maintains the centrality of context of situation in understanding language systems and how they work, a Threshold Level of language ability was described for each of the major languages of Europe in terms of what learners should be able to *do* with the language (van Ek 1975). Functions were based on assessment of learner needs and specified the end result, the *goal* of an instructional program. The term *communicative* attached itself to programs that used a functional-notional syllabus based on needs assessment, and the language for specific purposes (LSP) movement was launched.

Other European developments focused on the *process* of communicative classroom language learning. In Germany, for example, against a backdrop of social democratic concerns for individual empowerment, articulated in the writings of the contemporary philosopher Jürgen Habermas (1970), language teaching methodologists took the lead in the development of classroom materials that encouraged learner choice (Candlin 1978). Their systematic collection of exercise types for communicatively oriented English language teaching were used in teacher in-service courses and workshops to guide curriculum change. Exercises were designed to exploit the variety of social meanings contained within particular grammatical structures. A system of "chains" encouraged teachers and learners to define their own learning path through principled selection of relevant exercises (Piepho 1974; Piepho and Bredella 1976). Similar exploratory projects were also initiated by Candlin at his then academic home, the University of Lancaster in England, and by Holec (1979) and his colleagues at the University of Nancy in France. Supplementary teacher resource materials promoting classroom CLT became increasingly popular during the 1970s (e.g., Maley and Duff 1978).

Meanwhile, in the United States, Hymes (1971) had reacted to Chomsky's (1965) characterization of the linguistic competence of the "ideal native speaker" and proposed the term *communicative competence* to represent the use of language in social context, or the observance of sociolinguistic norms of appropriacy. His concern with speech communities and the integration of language, communication, and culture was not unlike that of Halliday in the British linguistic tradition (see Halliday 1978). Hymes's communicative competence may be seen as the equivalent of Halliday's meaning potential. Similarly, his focus was not language learning, but language as social behavior. In subsequent interpretations of the significance of Hymes's views for learners, methodologists working in the United States tended to focus on native speaker cultural norms and the difficulty, if not impossibility, of authentically representing them in a classroom of nonnative speakers. In light of this difficulty, the appropriateness of communicative competence as an instructional goal was questioned (e.g., Paulston 1974).

At the same time, in a research project at the University of Illinois, Savignon (1972) used the term "communicative competence" to characterize the ability of classroom language learners to interact with other speakers, to make meaning, as distinct from their ability to recite dialogs or perform on discrete-point tests of grammatical knowledge. At a time when pattern practice and error avoidance were the rule in language teaching, this study of adult classroom acquisition of French looked at the effect of practice on the use of *coping strategies* as part of an instructional program. By encouraging learners to ask for information, to seek clarification, to use circumlocution and whatever other linguistic and nonlinguistic resources they could muster to negotiate meaning and stick to the communicative task at hand, teachers were invariably leading learners to take risks and speak in other than memorized patterns. The coping strategies identified in this study became the basis for subsequent identification by Canale and Swain (1980) of *strategic competence* which—along with grammatical competence and sociolinguistic competence—appeared in their three component framework for communicative competence. (The original Canale and Swain framework with subsequent modifications is discussed below.) Test results at the end of the instructional period showed conclusively that learners who had practiced communication in lieu of laboratory pattern drills performed with no less accuracy on discrete-point tests of grammatical structure. On the other hand, their *communicative competence* as measured in terms of fluency, comprehensibility, effort, and amount of communication in unrehearsed oral communicative tasks significantly surpassed that of learners who had had no such practice. Learner reactions to the test formats lent further support to the view that even beginners respond well to activities that let them focus on meaning as opposed to formal features.

A collection of role plays, games, and other communicative classroom activities were subsequently developed for inclusion in adapting the French CREDIF[2] materials, *Voix et Visages de la France*. The accompanying guide (Savignon 1974) described their purpose as that of involving learners in the experience of communication. Teachers were encouraged to provide learners with the French equivalent of expressions that would help them to participate in the negotiation of meaning such as "What's the word for . . . ?" "Please repeat," "I don't understand." Not unlike the efforts of Candlin and his colleagues working in a European EFL context, the focus here was on classroom process and learner autonomy. The use of games, role play, pair work, and other small-group activities has gained acceptance and is now widely recommended for inclusion in language teaching programs.

CLT thus can be seen to derive from a multidisciplinary perspective that includes, at a minimum, linguistics, psychology, philosophy, sociology, and educational research. Its focus has been the elaboration and implementation of programs and methodologies that promote the development of functional language ability through learner participation in communicative events. Central to CLT is the understanding of language learning as both an educational and a political issue. Language teaching is inextricably tied to language policy. Viewed from a multicultural *intra*national as well as *inter*national perspective, diverse sociopolitical contexts mandate not only a diverse set of language learning goals, but a diverse set of teaching strategies. Program design and implementation depend on negotiation between policy makers, linguists, researchers, and teachers. And evaluation of program success requires a similar collaborative effort. The selection of methods and materials appropriate to both the goals *and* context of teaching begins with an analysis of socially defined learner needs *and* styles of learning.

HOW HAS CLT BEEN INTERPRETED?

The classroom model shows the hypothetical integration of four components that have been advanced as comprising communicative competence (Savignon 1972, 1983,1987, in press; Canale and Swain 1980; Canale 1983a; Byram 1997). Adapted from the familiar "inverted pyramid" classroom model proposed by Savignon (1983), it shows how, through practice and experience in an increasingly wide range of communicative contexts and events, learners gradually expand their communicative competence, consisting of *grammatical competence, discourse competence, sociocultural competence,* and *strategic competence.* Although the *relative* importance of the various components depends on the overall level of communicative competence, each one is essential. Moreover, all components are interrelated. They cannot be developed or measured in isolation and one cannot go from one component to the other as one strings beads to make a necklace. Rather, an increase in one component *interacts* with other components to produce a corresponding increase in overall communicative competence.

Grammatical competence refers to sentence-level grammatical forms, the ability to recognize the lexical, morphological, syntactic, and phonological feature of a language and to make use of these features to interpret and form words and sentences. Grammatical competence is not linked to any single theory of grammar and does

not include the ability to state rules of usage. One demonstrates grammatical competence not by *stating* a rule but by *using* a rule in the interpretation, expression, or negotiation of meaning.

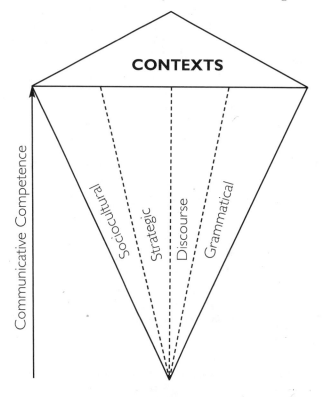

Figure I. Components of Communicative Competence

Discourse competence is concerned not with isolated words or phrases but with the interconnectedness of a series of utterances, written words, and/or phrases to form a text, a meaningful whole. The text might be a poem, an e-mail message, a sportscast, a telephone conversation, or a novel. Identification of isolated sounds or words contribute to interpretation of the overall meaning of the text. This is known as *bottom-up processing.* On the other hand, understanding of the theme or purpose of the text helps in the interpretation of isolated sounds or words. This is known as *top-down processing.* Both are important in communicative competence.

Two other familiar concepts in talking about discourse competence are text *coherence* and *cohesion.* Text coherence is the relation of all sentences or utterances in a text to a single global proposition. The establishment of *a global meaning,* or topic, for a text is an integral part of both expression and interpretation and makes possible the interpretation of the individual sentences that make up the text. Local connections or *structural links* between individual sentences provide cohesion. Halliday and Hasan (1976) are well-known for their identification of various cohesive devices used in English, and their work has influenced teacher education materials for ESL/EFL (for illustration, see Celce-Murcia and Larsen-Freeman 1999).

Sociocultural competence extends well beyond linguistic forms and is an interdisciplinary field of inquiry having to do with the social rules of language use. Sociocultural competence requires an understanding of the social context in which language is used: the roles of the participants, the information they share, and the function of the interaction. Although we have yet to provide a satisfactory description of grammar, we are even further from an adequate description of sociocultural rules of appropriateness. And yet we use them to communicate successfully in many different contexts of situation.

It is of course not feasible for learners to anticipate the sociocultural aspects for every context. Moreover, English often serves as a language of communication between speakers of different primary languages. Participants in multicultural communication are sensitive not only to the cultural meanings attached to the language itself, but also to social conventions concerning language use, such as turn-taking, appropriacy of content, nonverbal language, and tone of voice. These conventions influence how messages are interpreted. Cultural *awareness* rather than cultural knowledge thus becomes increasingly important. Just knowing something about the culture of an English-speaking country will not suffice. What must be learned is a general empathy and openness towards other cultures. Sociocultural competence therefore includes a willingness to engage in the active negotiation of meaning along with a willingness to suspend judgement and take into consideration the possibility of cultural differences in conventions or use. Together these features might be subsumed under the term cultural flexibility or *cultural awareness*.

The "ideal native speaker," someone who knows a language perfectly and uses it appropriately in all social interactions, exists in theory only. None of us knows all there is to know of English in its many manifestations, both around the world and in our own backyards. Communicative competence is always *relative*. The coping strategies that we use in unfamiliar contexts, with constraints due to imperfect knowledge of rules or limiting factors in their application such as fatigue or distraction, are represented as *strategic competence*. With practice and experience, we gain in grammatical, discourse, and sociocultural competence. The *relative* importance of strategic competence thus decreases. However, the effective use of coping strategies is important for communicative competence in all contexts and distinguishes highly competent communicators from those who are less so.

By definition, CLT puts the focus on the learner. Learner communicative needs provide a framework for elaborating program goals in terms of functional competence. This implies global, qualitative evaluation of learner achievement as opposed to quantitative assessment of discrete linguistic features. Controversy over appropriate language testing measures persists, and many a curricular innovation has been undone by failure to make corresponding changes in evaluation. Current efforts at educational reform favor essay writing, in-class presentations, and other more holistic assessments of learner competence. Some programs have initiated portfolio assessment, the collection and evaluation of learner poems, reports, stories, videotapes, and similar projects in an effort to better represent and encourage learner achievement.

Although it now has a new name and is enjoying widespread recognition and research attention, CLT is not a new idea. Throughout the long history of language teaching, there always have been advocates of a focus on meaning, as opposed to form, and of developing learner ability to actually *use* the language for communication. The more immediate the communicative needs, the more readily communicative methods seem to be adopted. In her book *Breaking Tradition*, Musumeci (1997) provides a fascinating account of language teaching reform efforts dating back to the Middle Ages when Latin, not English, was the lingua franca. *Breaking Tradition* is a favorite reading of my students. They find it a refreshing and reassuring reminder that discussions of methods and goals for language teaching predate the twentieth century by far.

Depending upon their own preparation and experience, teachers themselves differ in their reactions to CLT. Some feel understandable frustration at the seeming ambiguity in discussions of communicative ability. Negotiation of meaning may be a lofty goal, but this view of language behavior lacks precision and does not provide a universal scale for assessment of individual learners. Ability is viewed as variable and highly dependent upon context and purpose as well as on the roles and attitudes of all involved. Other teachers who welcome the opportunity to select and/or develop their own materials, providing learners with a range of communicative tasks, are comfortable relying on more global, integrative judgments of learner progress.

An additional source of frustration for some teachers are second language acquisition research findings that show the route, if not the rate, of language acquisition to be largely unaffected by classroom instruction. First language cross-linguistic studies of developmental universals initiated in the 1970s were soon followed by similar second language studies. Acquisition, assessed on the basis of expression in unrehearsed, oral communicative contexts, appeared to follow a describable morphosyntactic sequence regardless of learner age or context of learning. Although they served to bear out teachers' informal observations, namely that textbook presentation and drill do not ensure learner use of taught structures in learners' spontaneous expression, the findings were nonetheless disconcerting. They contradicted both grammar-translation and audiolingual precepts that placed the burden of learner acquisition on teacher explanation of grammar and controlled practice with insistence on learner accuracy. They were further at odds with textbooks that promise "mastery" of "basic"

English, Spanish, French, etc. Teacher rejection of research findings, renewed insistence on tests of discrete grammatical structures, and even exclusive reliance in the classroom on the learners' native or first language, where possible, to be sure they "get the grammar," have been in some cases reactions to the frustration of teaching for communication.

SHAPING A COMMUNICATIVE CURRICULUM

In recent years, many innovations in curriculum planning have been proposed that offer both novice and veteran teachers a dizzying array of alternatives. Games, yoga, juggling, and jazz have been proposed as aids to language learning. Rapidly increasing opportunities for computer-mediated communication, both synchronous—online chat rooms—and asynchronous—the full spectrum of information and interactions available on the Internet as well as specialized bulletin boards and e-mail—hold promise for further integration of communicative opportunities for learners worldwide.

In attempting to convey the meaning of CLT to both pre-service and in-service teachers of English as a second or foreign language in a wide range of contexts, I have found it helpful to think of a communicative curriculum as potentially made up of five components. These components may be regarded as thematic clusters of activities or experiences related to language use and usage, providing a useful way of categorizing teaching strategies that promote communicative language use. Use of the term *component* to categorize these activities seems particularly appropriate in that it avoids any suggestion of sequence or level. Experimentation with communicative teaching methods has shown that all five components can be profitably blended at all stages of instruction. Organization of learning activities into the following components serve not to sequence an ELT program, but rather to highlight the *range of options* available in curriculum planning and to suggest ways in which their very interrelatedness benefit the learner.

- Language Arts
- Language for a Purpose
- My Language Is Me: Personal English Language Use
- You Be, I'll Be; Theater Arts
- Beyond the Classroom

Language Arts, or language analysis, is the first component on the list. Language Arts includes those things that language teachers often do best. In fact, it may be *all* they have been taught to do. This component includes many of the exercises used in mother tongue programs to focus attention on formal accuracy. In ELT, Language Arts focuses on forms of English, including syntax, morphology, and phonology. Spelling tests, for example, are important if writing is a goal. Familiar activities such as translation, dictation, and rote memorization can be helpful in bringing attention to form. Vocabulary expansion can be enhanced through definition, synonyms, and antonyms as well as attention to cognates and false cognates when applicable. Pronunciation exercises and patterned repetition of verb paradigms and other structural features can be useful in focusing on form, along with the explanation of regular syntactic features, rules of grammar. There are also many Language Arts games that learners of all ages enjoy for the variety and group interaction they provide. So long as they are not overused and are not promoted as the solution to all manner of language learning problems, these games can be a welcome addition to a teacher's repertoire.

Language for a Purpose, or language experience, is the second component. In contrast with language analysis, language experience is the use of English for real and immediate communicative goals. Not all learners are learning English for the same reasons. Attention to the specific communicative needs of the learners is important in the selection and sequencing of materials. Regardless of how distant or unspecific the communicative needs of the learners may be, every program with a goal of communicative competence should give attention to opportunities for meaningful English use, opportunities to focus on meaning rather than on form.

In an ESL classroom where English is the language of instruction, there is an immediate and natural need for learners to use English. Where this happens, Language for a Purpose is a built-in feature of the learning environment. In an EFL setting where the teacher may have a language other than English in common with learners, special attention needs to be given to providing opportunities for English language experience. Exclusive use of English in the classroom is an option. In so-called *content-based* instruction, the focus is other than the English language. The *content*, for example history, music, or literature, is taught through the *use* of English. *Immersion* programs at the elementary, secondary, or even university level where the entire curriculum is taught in English offer a maximum amount of Language for a Purpose (see Snow's chapter in this volume). In addition, *task-based* curricula are designed to provide learners with maximum opportunity to use Language for a Purpose (see chapters by Nunan; Johns and Price-Machado; and Chaudron and Crookes in this volume).

Learners who are accustomed to being taught exclusively in their mother tongue may at first be uncomfortable if the teacher speaks to them in English, expecting them not only to understand but, perhaps, to respond. When this happens, teachers need to take special care to help learners realize that they are not expected to understand every word, any more than they are expected to express themselves in nativelike English. Making an effort to get the gist and using strategies to interpret, express, and negotiate meaning are important to the development of communicative competence. For learners who are accustomed to grammar translation courses taught in their mother tongue with an emphasis on grammar and accuracy, the transition will not be easy. Kiyoko Kusano Hubbell (in press), a Japanese teacher of English in Tokyo, recounts some struggles in her determined effort to teach communicatively:

> Many Japanese students have been taught that they have to really know every word in a sentence or a phrase

in order to understand a foreign language. They are not taught to use the strategies that they already use in their native Japanese, that is, to guess the meaning from the context. When the blackboard is full of writing and I am busy in class, I ask a student, "Please erase the blackboard!", handing him an eraser and pointing to the dirty blackboard. If he does not move, it is not because he is offended. He just did not recognize the word "erase," and to him that means he did not understand me. If he is willing to accept the ambiguity, he gets up and cleans the board.

With encouragement and help from their teacher in developing the strategic competence they need to interpret, express, and negotiate meaning, learners express satisfaction and even surprise. Kusano Hubbell goes on to report the positive reactions she receives at the end of the term. (All comments have been translated from Japanese by the author.)

> "Completely different from any class I've ever had!"

> "I have never expressed my own ideas in English before. Work was always to translate this section, to fill in the blanks or read. It was all passive."

> "In my career of English education from Jr. High to Cram School there was no teacher who spoke English other than to read the textbooks."

My Language Is Me: Personal English Language Use, the third component in a communicative curriculum, relates to the learner's emerging identity in English. Learner attitude is without a doubt the single most important factor in learner success. Whether a learner's motivations are integrative or instrumental, the development of communicative competence involves the whole learner. The most successful teaching programs are those that take into account the affective as well as the cognitive aspects of language learning. They seek to involve learners psychologically as well as intellectually.

In planning for CLT, teachers should remember that not everyone is comfortable in the same role. Within classroom communities, as within society at large, there are leaders and there are those who prefer to be followers. Both are essential to the success of group activities. In group discussions, there are always some who seem to do the most talking. Those who often remain silent in larger groups typically participate more easily in pair work. Or they may prefer to work on an individual project. The wider the variety of communicative, or meaning-based, activities, the greater the chance for involving all learners.

My Language Is Me implies, above all, respect for learners as they use English for self-expression. Although Language Arts activities provide an appropriate context for attention to formal accuracy, Personal English Language Use does not. Most teachers know this and intuitively focus on meaning rather than on form as learners express their personal feelings or experiences. However, repeated emphasis on structural accuracy in textbooks or on tests may cause teachers to feel uncomfortable about their inattention to non-nativelike features that do not impede meaning. An understanding of the importance of opportunities for the interpretation, expression, and negotiation of meaning in CLT and of the distinction between Language Arts and My Language Is Me can help to reassure teachers that the communicative practice they are providing is important for their learners.

Respect for learners as they use English for self-expression requires more than simply restraint in attention to formal "errors" that do not interfere with meaning. It includes recognition that so-called "nativelike" performance may not, in fact, even be a goal for learners. Language teaching has come a long way from audiolingual days when "native" pronunciation and use was held up as an ideal. Reference to the terms "native" or "nativelike" in the evaluation of communicative competence is inappropriate in today's postcolonial, multicultural world. As observed earlier, we now recognize that native speakers are never "ideal" and, in fact, vary widely in range and style of communicative abilities.

Moreover, as the English language is increasingly used as a language of global communication, so called "non-native" users of its many varieties overwhelmingly outnumber so-called "native speakers." The decision of what is or is not one's "native" language is arbitrary and irrelevant for ELT and is perhaps best left to the individual concerned. Chenny Lai, a graduate MATESL candidate studying in the United States, expresses his views:

> As to the definition of "native" or "first" language we discussed in today's class, I came up with the idea that we have no say about whether a person's native language is this one or that one. It is the speaker who has the right to FEEL which language is his native one. The native language should be the one in which the speaker feels most comfortable or natural when making daily communication, or more abstractly, the one in which the speaker does all his thinking. There are two major languages spoken in Taiwan: Mandarin and Taiwanese. I don't have any slightest problem using either of them since I use both every day in equal proportion. But when I do my thinking, considering things, or even kind of talking to myself, my "mental" language is Mandarin. Because of this, I would say that my native language is Mandarin. . . . we probably can say that a person's native language can actually "switch" from one to another during stages of his life.

Since a personality inevitably takes on a new dimension through expression in another language, that dimension needs to be discovered on its own terms. Learners should not only be given the opportunity to say what they want to say in English, they also should be encouraged to develop an English language personality with which they are comfortable. They may feel more comfortable maintaining a degree of formality not found in the interpersonal transactions of native speakers. The diary entry of a Japanese learner of English offers important insight on the matter of identity:

> I just don't know what to do right now. I might have been *wrong* since I began to learn English; I always tried to be better and wanted to be a good speaker. It was *wrong, absolutely wrong*! When I got to California, I started imitating Americans and picked up the words that I heard. So my English became just like Americans. I couldn't help it. I must have been funny to them, because I am a Japanese and have my own culture and background. I think I almost lost the most important thing I should not have. I got California English, including intonation, pronunciation, the way they act, which *are not* mine. I have to have *my own* English, be myself when I speak English (Preston 1981, p. 113).

On the other hand, learners may discover a new freedom of self-expression in their new language. When asked what it is like to write in English, a language that is not her native tongue, the Korean writer Mia Yun, author of *House of the Winds* (1998), replied that it was "like putting on a new dress." Writing in English made her feel fresh, see herself in a new way, offered her freedom to experiment. When expressing themselves in a new language, writers are not the only ones to experience the feeling of "putting on a new dress." My Language Is Me calls for recognition and respect for the individual personality of the learner. (We will return to the matter of the "native/non-native" distinction with respect to users of English later when discussing sociolinguistic issues.)

You Be, I'll Be: Theater Arts is the fourth component of a communicative curriculum. "All the world's a stage," in the familiar words of Shakespeare (*As You Like It*, II, viii; 139). And on this stage we play many roles, roles for which we improvise scripts from the models we observe around us. Child, parent, sister, brother, employer, employee, doctor, or teacher—all are roles that include certain expected ways of behaving and using language. Sociocultural rules of *appropriateness* have to do with these expected ways. Familiar roles may be played with little conscious attention to style. On the other hand, new and unfamiliar roles require practice, with an awareness of how the meanings we intend are being interpreted by others. Sometimes there are no models. In the last half of the twentieth century, women who suddenly found themselves in what had been a "man's world," whether as firefighters, professors, or CEOs, had to adapt existing models to ones with which they could be comfortable. And the transition is far from complete. With the exception of Great Britain, no major world power to date has had a woman head of state. By the end of the twenty-first century there no doubt will be numerous models from which to choose.

If the world can be thought of as a stage, with actors and actresses who play their parts as best they can, theater may be seen as an opportunity to experiment with roles, to try things out. Fantasy and playacting are a natural and important part of childhood. Make-believe and the "you be, I'll be" improvisations familiar to children the world over are important to self-discovery and growth. They allow young learners to experiment and to try things out, such as hats and wigs, moods and postures, gestures and words. As occasions for language use, role-playing and the many related activities that constitute Theater Arts are likewise a natural component of language learning. They allow learners to experiment with the roles they play or may be called upon to play in real life. Theater Arts can provide learners with the tools they need to *act*, that is, to interpret, express, and negotiate meaning in a new language. Activities can include both scripted and unscripted role play, simulations, and even pantomime. Ensemble-building activities familiar in theater training have been used very successfully in ELT to create a climate of trust so necessary for the incorporation of Theater Arts activities (see Savignon 1997). The role of the teacher in Theater Arts is that of a coach, providing support, strategies, and encouragement for learners as they explore new ways of being.

Beyond the Classroom is the fifth and final component of a communicative curriculum. Regardless of the variety of communicative activities in the ESL/EFL classroom, their purpose remains to prepare learners to use English in the world beyond. This is the world upon which learners will depend for the maintenance and development of their communicative competence once classes are over. The classroom is but a rehearsal. Development of the Beyond the Classroom component in a communicative curriculum begins with discovery of learner interests and needs and of opportunities to not only respond to but, more importantly, to *develop* those interests and needs through English language use beyond the classroom itself.

In an ESL setting, opportunities to use English outside the classroom abound. Systematic "field experiences" may successfully become the core of the course, which then could become a workshop in which learners can compare notes, seek clarification, and expand the range of domains in which they learn to function in English. Classroom visits to a courtroom trial, a public auction, or a church bazaar provide introductions to aspects of the local culture that learners might not experience on their own. Conversation partners, apprenticeships, and activities with host families can be arranged. Residents of nearby retirement communities can be recruited as valuable resources for a range of research projects. Senior citizens often welcome the opportunity to interact with international visitors or new arrivals and offer a wealth of knowledge and experience. They could be interviewed about noteworthy historical events, child rearing in earlier decades, or their views on politics, health care, or grandparenting.

In an EFL setting, on the other hand, the challenge for incorporating a Beyond the Classroom component may be greater, but certainly not insurmountable, and is essential for both teacher and learners. As a child, I looked forward to receiving letters from my pen pals. They would arrive bearing colorful stamps from France, Wales, Japan, Taiwan, and Australia. I had yet to learn a second language, so our correspondence was all in English. However, this regular exchange of letters put a small town midwestern American girl in touch with other places around the globe and with other users of English. Technology has since brought the whole world much closer. English language radio and television programs, videos, and feature length films are readily available in many EFL settings, along with newspapers and magazines. English speaking residents or visitors may be available to visit the classroom. The Internet now provides opportunities to interact with English speaking peers on a variety of topics, to develop grammatical, discourse, sociocultural, and strategic competence. These opportunities for computer-mediated communication (CMC) will increase dramatically in the years ahead. The following except from an e-mail exchange between classes of secondary school students in Germany and the United States on the topic of the death penalty reveals the potential for developing sociocultural and strategic skills in addition to grammatical and discourse competence (Roithmeier and Savignon in press):

GER 1:   Death Penalty—an *inhuman* punishment
GER 3:   . . . Finally, I think nobody has the right to kill other people but to kill a person because of mercy is *inhuman* and should never be a law in certain democratic states or countries. . . .
USA 2:   . . . I can see both sides of the death penalty. I believe when discussing this *inhuman* treatment you must think about the victims of these people.
USA 4:   . . . Basically, I think the death penalty is wrong and *inhumane.*
USA 6:   The death penalty is *inhumane* . . .

Examples such as the above provide strong support for the claim that members of a discussion group are strongly influenced by prior postings and that the language they use is influenced by what they read from participants. In addition to prearranged exchanges, learners can check World Wide Web sites for a range of information, schedules, rates, locations, descriptions, and the like.

PUTTING IT ALL TOGETHER

How do we put it all together? Is there an optimum combination of Language Arts, Personal Language Use, Language for a Purpose, Theater Arts, and Beyond the Classroom? These questions must be answered by individual language teachers in the context in which they teach. Cultural expectations, goals, and styles of learning are but some of the ways in which learners may differ from each other. To the complexity of the learner must be added the complexities of teachers and of the settings in which they teach. Established routines, or institutional belief about what is important, weigh heavily in a teacher's decisions as to what and how to teach and often makes innovation difficult (see Sato in press; Wang in press). Finally, the need for variety must be taken into account. Learners who are bored with rule recitation or sentence translation may just as easily lose interest in games or role play, if these are allowed to become routine. Difficult as it is, the teacher's task is to understand the many factors involved and respond to them creatively.

Teachers cannot do this alone, of course. They need the support of administrators, the community, and the learners themselves. Methodologists and teacher education programs have a responsibility as well. They should provide classroom teachers with the perspective and experiences they need to respond to the realities of their world, a changing world in which the old ways of ELT may not be the best ways. The optimum combination of the analytical and the experiential in ESL/EFL for a given context is a focus of ongoing research. However, a now well-established research tradition in second/foreign language learning/teaching has clearly shown the importance of attention to language use, or experience, in addition to language usage, or analysis. But the overwhelming emphasis in most school programs is on the latter, often to the complete exclusion of the former.

WHAT ABOUT GRAMMAR?

Discussions of CLT not infrequently lead to questions of grammatical or formal accuracy. The perceived displacement of attention to morphosyntactic features in learner expression in favor of a focus on meaning has led in some cases to the impression that grammar is not important, or that proponents of CLT favor learner self-expression without regard to form. While involvement in communicative events is seen as central to language development, this involvement necessarily requires attention to form. The nature of the contribution to language development of both form-focused and meaning-focused classroom activity remains a question in ongoing research. The optimum combination of these activities in any given instructional setting depends no doubt on learner age, nature and length of instructional sequence, opportunities for language contact outside the classroom, teacher preparation, and other factors. However, for the development of communicative ability, research findings overwhelmingly support the *integration* of form-focused exercises with meaning-focused experience. Grammar is important, and learners seem to focus best on grammar when it relates to their communicative needs and experiences.

Communicative competence obviously does not mean the wholesale rejection of familiar materials. There is nothing to prevent communicatively-based materials from being subjected to grammar-translation treatment, just as there may be nothing to prevent a teacher with only an old grammar-translation book at his or her disposal from teaching communicatively. What matters is the teacher's conception of what learning a language is and how it happens. The basic principle involved is an orientation towards collective participation in a process of use and discovery achieved by cooperation between individual learners as well as between learners and teachers.

SOCIOLINGUISTIC ISSUES

Numerous sociolinguistic issues await attention. Variation in the speech community and its relationship to language change are central to sociolinguistic inquiry. As we have seen above, sociolinguistic perspectives on variability and change highlight the folly of describing native speaker competence, let alone non-native speaker competence, in terms of "mastery" or "command" of a system. All language systems show instability and variation. Learner language systems show

even greater instability and variability in terms of both the amount and rate of change. Moreover, sociolinguistic concerns with identity and accommodation help to explain the construction by bilinguals of a "variation space" that is different from that of a native speaker. This may include retention of any number of features of a previously acquired code or system of phonology and syntax as well as features of discourse and pragmatics, including communication strategies. The phenomenon may be individual or, in those settings where there is a community of learners, general. Differences not only in the code itself but in the semantic meanings attributed to these different encodings contribute to identification with a speech community or culture, the way a speech community views itself and the world. This often includes code mixing and code switching, the use by bilinguals of resources from more than one speech community.

Sociolinguistic perspectives have been important in understanding the implications of norm, appropriacy, and variability for CLT and continue to suggest avenues of inquiry for further research and materials development. Use of authentic language data has underscored the importance of context, such as setting, roles, and genre, in interpreting the meaning of a text. A range of both oral and written *texts in context* provides learners with a variety of language experiences, which they need to construct their own "variation space" and to make determinations of appropriacy in their own expression of meaning. "Competent" in this instance is not necessarily synonymous with "nativelike." Negotiation in CLT highlights the need for interlinguistic, that is, *intercultural,* awareness on the part of all involved (Byram 1997). Better understanding of the strategies used in the negotiation of meaning offers a potential for improving classroom practice of the needed skills.

Natives and Foreigners

We might begin by asking ourselves whose language we teach and for what purpose. What is our own relationship with English? Do we consider it to be a *foreign, second,* or *native* language?

Webster's New International Dictionary, 2nd edition, published in 1950, a time when language teaching in the United States was on the threshold of a period of unprecedented scrutiny, experimentation, and growth, provides the following definitions of these terms we use so often with respect to language. *Foreign* derives from Middle English *forein, forene,* Old French *forain* and Latin *foras,* meaning *outside.* Related words are *foreclose, forest, forfeit.* Modern definitions include "situated outside one's own country; born in, belonging to, derived from, or characteristic of some place other than the one under consideration; alien in character; not connected or pertinent," etc.

Those identified as teaching a foreign language, perhaps even in a Department of Foreign Languages, should ask, "Why?" What does the label "foreign" signal to colleagues, learners, and the community at large? Today we are concerned with global ecology and global economy. And English has been describe as a "global language" (Crystal 1997). Nonetheless, one might object, "foreign" is still a useful term to use in distinguishing between teaching English in, say, Pattaya, Thailand, and teaching English in Youngstown, Ohio. In Youngstown, English is taught as a second language whereas in Pattaya it is a foreign language. The contexts of learning are not the same, to be sure. Neither are the learners. Nor the teachers. But do these facts change the nature of the language? And what about the teaching of Spanish in Chicago, in Barcelona, in Buenos Aires, in Guatemala City, in Miami, or in Madrid? In what sense can Spanish in each of these contexts be described as "foreign" or "second"? And what are the implications of the label selected for the learners? For the teachers?

Having taught French in Urbana, Illinois, for many years, I can easily identify with the problems of teachers of English in Pattaya. More so, perhaps, than those who teach ESL in Urbana with easy access to English speaking communities outside the classroom. On the other hand, teaching French in Urbana or English in Pattaya is no excuse for ignoring or avoiding opportunities for communication, both written and oral. The potential of computer-mediated negotiation of meaning for language learning and language change in the decades ahead will be increasingly recognized, both inside and outside language classrooms.

What may be a problem is the teacher's communicative competence. Is he or she a native speaker? If not, does he or she consider him- or herself bilingual? If not, why not? Is it a lack of communicative competence? Or, rather, a lack of communicative confidence? Is he or she intimidated by "native" speakers? *Native Speaker* is the title of a moving first novel by Chang-rae Lee, an American raised in a Korean immigrant family in New Jersey. It documents the struggle and frustration of knowing two cultures and at the same time not completely belonging to either one. As such, it serves as a poignant reminder of the challenges of bilingualism and biculturalism. How does one "belong"? What does it mean to be bilingual? To be bicultural? To be a native speaker?

Again, the example of English is important. Such widespread adoption of one language is unprecedented. English users today include those who live in countries where English is a primary language—the United States, the United Kingdom, Canada, Australia, and New Zealand; those who live in countries where English is an additional, *intra*national language of communication—for example, Bangladesh, India, Nigeria, Philippines, and Tanzania; those who use English primarily in *inter*national contexts—countries such as China, Indonesia, Japan, Saudi Arabia, and Russia. By conservative estimates the number of non-native speakers of English in the world today outnumbers native speakers by more than 2 to 1, and the ratio is increasing. Models of appropriacy vary from context to context. So much, in fact, that some scholars speak not only of varieties of English but of *World Englishes,* the title of a new journal devoted to discussion of descriptive, pedagogical, and other issues in the global spread of the English language. As we have seen above, depending on the context as well as learner needs, "native" speakers may or may not be appropriate models (see also Kachru 1992).

WHAT CLT IS NOT

Disappointment with both grammar-translation and audiolingual methods for their inability to prepare learners for the interpretation, expression, and negotiation of meaning, along with enthusiasm for an array of alternative methods increasingly labeled *communicative*, has resulted in no small amount of uncertainty as to what are and are not essential features of CLT. Thus, this summary description would be incomplete without brief mention of what CLT is not.

CLT is not exclusively concerned with face-to-face oral communication. The principles of CLT apply equally to reading and writing activities that involve readers and writers engaged in the interpretation, expression, and negotiation of meaning; the goals of CLT depend on learner needs in a given context. CLT does *not* require small-group or pair work; group tasks have been found helpful in many contexts as a way of providing increased opportunity and motivation for communication. However, classroom group or pair work should not be considered an essential feature and may well be inappropriate in some contexts. Finally, CLT does *not* exclude a focus on metalinguistic awareness or knowledge of rules of syntax, discourse, and social appropriateness.

The essence of CLT is the engagement of learners in communication in order to allow them to develop their communicative competence. Terms sometimes used to refer to features of CLT include *process oriented*, *task-based*, and *inductive*, or *discovery oriented*. Inasmuch as strict adherence to a given text is not likely to be true to its processes and goals, CLT cannot be found in any one textbook or set of curricular materials. In keeping with the notion of context of situation, CLT is properly seen as an approach or

theory of intercultural communicative competence to be used in developing materials and methods appropriate to a given context of learning. Contexts change. A world of carriages and petticoats evolves into one of genomes and cyberspace. No less than the means and norms of communication they are designed to reflect, communicative teaching methods designed to enhance the interpretation, expression, and negotiation of meaning will continue to be explored and adapted.

DISCUSSION QUESTIONS

1. If you had to choose three adjectives to describe CLT, what would they be?
2. What might be some obstacles encountered by teachers who wish to implement a communicative approach to language teaching? How might these obstacles be overcome?
3. Do you feel English to be a *foreign*, *second*, or *native* language? How might your feelings influence your classroom teaching?
4. Of the five described components of a communicative curriculum, which are the most familiar to you as a language learner? As a language teacher?
5. Who sets the norm for English language use in your particular context of situation? How? Why?

SUGGESTED ACTIVITIES

1. Request permission to observe two or three different introductory level ESL or EFL classes. Note the interaction between the teacher and the learners. Who does most of the talking? How much of the talking that you hear is in English? Why?
2. Interview some language learners for their views on why they are learning a foreign or second language.

3. Look at the inverted pyramid diagram of communicative competence on page 17. Do you agree with the proportions drawn? Draw your own diagram to show the relationship between the four components of communicative competence.

4. Select one of the five components of a communicative curriculum described in this chapter. Make a list of corresponding learner activities or experiences that you would like to use in your teaching.

 **FURTHER READING**

Breen, M., and C. Candlin. 1980. The essentials of a communicative curriculum in language teaching. *Applied Linguistics* 1(1):89–112.

Byram, M. 1997. *Teaching and Assessing Intercultural Communicative Competence.* Clevedon, UK: Multilingual Matters.

Holliday, A. 1994. *Appropriate Methodology and Social Context.* Cambridge: Cambridge University Press.

Nunan, D. 1989a. *Designing Tasks for the Communicative Classroom.* Cambridge: Cambridge University Press.

Savignon, S. J. 1997. *Communicative Competence: Theory and Classroom Practice.* New York: McGraw Hill.

ENDNOTES

[1] The author copied this passage many years ago while visiting the Union School, a country school building that was moved to the city of Goodland, Kansas, by the Sherman County Historical Society. It is owned and operated as a school museum by the Society.

[2] CREDIF is the acronym for Centre de Recherche et d'Etude pour la Diffusion du Français. It was an institution specializing in French as a foreign language and functioned in association with the École Normale Supérieur de Saint-Cloud from 1959 to 1996.

Guidelines for Language Classroom Instruction[1]

GRAHAM CROOKES • CRAIG CHAUDRON

In "Guidelines for Language Classroom Instruction," Crookes and Chaudron review research and practice in both second and foreign language contexts. The main areas of classroom instruction described are: presentational modes and focus on form, types of activities and parameters of tasks and interaction, classroom organization, teacher control of interaction, and corrective feedback.

1. INTRODUCTION

What goes on in the language classroom between the teacher and students is obviously the core area of information pertaining to formal second language (SL) teaching and learning. "Out-of-class" knowledge of language teaching in areas such as needs analysis, curriculum design, lesson planning, materials design, and evaluation is, of course, necessary for a truly professional operation, but so long as there is a teacher working with a group of students, the essence of classroom SL teaching resides in the nature of instruction and interaction between teachers and students.

In this chapter we identify and discuss some of the more important characteristics and principles of this interaction.[2] Our conception of the teacher is someone with a great number of decisions to make at every moment of classroom instruction. In some cases, research findings can guide those decisions. In others, research can inform professional judgment, but decisions must be based on experience and intuition rather than knowledge. However, decisions will be aided by a knowledge of the range of instructional alternatives available, as well as by an awareness of the cultural context and personal values of the teacher and students.

When a second language is taught, a number of major steps must be taken. First, elements of the language or its use, or skills such as learning strategies, must be brought into the classroom and presented or highlighted. The teacher and,

under certain learner-centered conditions, the students select elements of the SL in this phase.[3] Second, that which has been selected and presented must be learned; the teacher has to arrange matters and events to bring this about. Third, the teacher must provide knowledge of results, that is, correction or feedback, to the students.

We should not ignore that these processes take place in a social milieu, and that because of the way language functions between individuals, these processes cannot be totally separated from the social climate which develops among students and between teacher and students, though space does not permit us to address this important point here. Finally, let us note that conscientious SL teachers usually come out of a class asking themselves how the class went—in other words, engaging in a process of self-evaluation. We believe that this is a vital process for professional self-development, and one which needs to be explicitly structured into SL teachers' routines. See Murphy's chapter on reflective teaching in this volume, for a full discussion.

2. LANGUAGE PRESENTATION

2.1 Meta-Planning for Lesson Objectives

Which elements of language are undertaken depends on the objectives a teacher has in mind for the lesson. They are then the result of lesson planning and the general syllabus for the course (see the chapters by Jensen and Nunan in this volume). Despite considerable variation, generally the first element of a lesson is the first component of the traditional "present-practice-evaluate" sequence, which constitutes many teachers' understanding of basic lesson structure.

Let us assume for present purposes that a teacher has selected a particular element of language, or aspect of language learning, to be focused on as the first major stage of a class period. There are then two types of choices to be made: those concerning the physical characteristics of the presentation, that is, materials, use of audiovisual (AV) equipment, etc.; and those concerning the deductive or inductive procedures that learners will be engaging in in order to acquire rules, items, analogies, and other aspects of the target language. The former are considered in the following section, the latter in section 2.3.

2.2 Modalities (Materials, AV)

While not espousing any particular approach in this chapter, we feel that many professionals recognize the importance of practice in the acquisition of any cognitive skill. There is increasing recognition[4] of SL learning as a process of skill acquisition (O'Malley, Chamot, and Walker 1987), which implies the importance of practice, or output, rather than mere input (cf. Pica et al. 1996; Swain and Lapkin 1995). Teachers thus need to remain aware that they are not in the classroom to fill up the time with the sound of their own voices, but to arrange matters so that their students do the talking (or writing, or listening). Particularly in EFL rather than ESL situations, class time is so valuable that we believe the teacher should move on to practice phases of a lesson as soon as possible in a manner consistent with an adequate presentation of material and the giving of clear instructions for some practice exercises.

Assuming that the instructor decides that a given teaching objective calls for some support in the way of materials, what then? The major resource is of course the textbook. In addition, other teaching aids fall into two categories (Celce-Murcia 1979): nontechnical aids and technical aids (not counting the students themselves, who can of course play a stimulating role in the presentation stages of a lesson). The former include the chalkboard, realia, flashcards, magazine pictures, and charts. The latter include the overhead projector, audio and video recordings, CD-ROM, and Internet. Both types of aids are considered elsewhere in this book (see chapters by Brinton and Sokolik in this volume).

Despite increasing research into some media, the range of classroom and cultural contexts for TES/FL means that deciding whether or not to use AV aids is usually a matter for individual teacher judgment, supported by general considerations. Does their use in a given circumstance aid comprehension? Do they stimulate more student talk than would have otherwise occurred? Above all, does their use constitute an efficient use of class time, particularly taking into account the teacher time required to produce them or the logistics of setting up and removing any necessary equipment? This is an area in which careful teacher investigation and reporting of successes and failures in practice would benefit the profession.

Perhaps because of the complexity of the question, a surprisingly small amount of research informs teachers of how to use a textbook (but see Tomlinson 1997). For the untrained teacher, a good textbook can stand in for a syllabus and training program, while an experienced teacher can use the text as an aid, adopting some parts, adapting others (Stevick 1971), or can even dispense with it completely. The utility of the average textbook for a typical present-day ESL/EFL course is normally unquestioned (but see Allwright 1981 and O'Neill 1982 for positions on both sides of this point). Nonetheless, we urge teachers to remember that most textbooks in a given period of time are often very much alike (Ariew 1982); they are the product of the pressures of the market, as imperfectly interpreted through the publisher and materials writer, and can often run counter to legitimate educational pressures. What sells may not be what works; what works may not necessarily have a format which book publishing companies can utilize or produce. Above all, therefore, a critical stance is called for (see Byrd's chapter in this volume).

Some general points can be made about the presentation stage of a lesson. First, the instructor is, in fact, rather free from constraints despite the various procedures suggested by the teachers' notes typically accompanying the text. Texts designed for beginning and intermediate learners still commonly present the material of each unit via a dialogue, and the teacher is often instructed to have the students work with the dialogue. In many traditional classroom settings (especially EFL settings), this involves having the class repeat the dialogue in unison, possibly moving next to partial memorization. Yet, an equally efficient procedure for some classes would be to have students pair off and read the dialogue aloud while the teacher circulates and checks individual performance. The point is that teachers have the right and responsibility to utilize the material in whatever way seems appropriate, hopefully making use of the findings that SL research suggests.

For example, an increasingly well-established line of work has stressed the role of attention and awareness in SL learning (Schmidt 1990, 1995) and the importance of drawing the learner's attention to certain characteristics of the language which might otherwise be missed (referred to as "input enhancement"; see Rutherford 1987, Doughty and Williams 1998a). It follows, therefore, that the teacher should usually present the text or illustrative material with an immediate focus on the target points. On the other hand, research over the last two decades has made clear that SL learning does not take place in a simple linear fashion with one linguistic element being added to the next. In the syntactic domain, learners proceed at different speeds through fairly regular sequences (Pienemann and Johnston 1987). It is unlikely that structural target points will be internalized by many in a class after one exposure.[5] Consequently, the particular aspect of language to be learned should almost certainly come up on other occasions, in other lessons. The fact that SL learning involves the learning of a cognitive skill implies that the first stage of use (the

"cognitive stage") will be errorful and difficult for the learner. Movement towards automaticity will require a great deal of active, realistic practice in the use of the target language, which may not be susceptible to general error correction. Finally, at the presentation stage, it is relevant to consider what little is known about the learner's development of control over the pragmatic aspects of the SL. An emphasis on realistic, communicative language use in the classroom from an early stage is therefore justified, as is the development of the metalinguistic terms needed to talk about language use (Henriksen 1988).

As a final comment, although we have used the generally accepted term *textbook* throughout this section, it is clear that sole reliance on a textbook within the classroom is becoming less common in richer countries or more well-resourced schools. Developments in technology have made the creation and almost immediate use of in-house materials increasingly possible. The advantages of personalization and localization of materials are clear. In addition, of course, the ease of access to all kinds of supplementary resource materials and stimulus materials via the Web has helped teachers supplement textbooks while at the same time raising students' expectations.

2.3 Rule Presentations and Explanations

A great deal of research in the 1960s was concerned with whether and when to present explicit second language grammar rules to students (Levin 1972; see recent discussion of the issue in Borg 1999). The upshot of those studies was that explicit grammar instruction was not consistently superior in the long run to other practices. As a result, the various communicatively oriented language teaching methods and prescriptions developed after this time de-emphasized the use of explicit grammar rule presentation and even questioned the use of grammatically based materials.

However, subsequent research on second language acquisition has increasingly established the legitimacy of a focus on form (see most recently Doughty and Williams 1998a, 1998b; and

Norris and Ortega 2000), while still questioning the desirability of a persistent focus on correctness at all times in a syllabus or course of study. (These issues are dealt with in more detail in the chapters by Larsen-Freeman and Fotos in this volume.)

Based on the claims of most theorists that some focus on form can be required by learners or by a given classroom sequence, it is reasonable for teachers to be aware of options in how to make a rule explicit or not; whether or not to isolate a rule; whether an explanation should involve a deductive or inductive presentation; who should give the explanation—the teacher, the text, or another student; whether the language is abstract or not; and whether the explanation is provided orally or in writing. Teachers must ensure the clarity and sufficiency of their explanations by checking student comprehension, preferably not merely by solicitation of a "yes" or a nod.

Following the approach of Chaudron's (1982) description of teachers' vocabulary elaboration, Yee and Wagner (1984) developed a discourse model of teachers' vocabulary and grammar explanations. Their model contains several major segments (a framing stage, a focusing stage, the explanation itself, and a restatement), with several subcategories as optional features (e.g., with or without mention of the topic item, metastatements, teacher solicits of students, examples, etc.). At each stage, they point out that comprehension checks by the teacher are optional. An example of their model in a brief grammar explanation follows:

TEACHER: Can we say "these" in a tag? *Focus + solicit*

STUDENT: You can't use the word "these" in a tag. *Explanation + explicit rule*

TEACHER: What do we need to use? *+ solicit*

Taking a functional approach to analysis of rules and explanations, Faerch (1986) found that a typical sequence in teacher rule presentation involved (1) a "Problem-formulation"; (2) an "Induction" with the teacher eliciting student opinions; and (3) the teacher's "Rule-formulation"; followed optionally by (4) "Exemplification" by the teacher or students. Alert teachers will adapt this typical pattern to their circumstances, either shortening the sequence if a rule is judged to be quickly learned, or developing more student-generated ideas and interaction if the students have difficulty.

3. TASKS

The next major step in executing classroom lessons involves practice and "learning" of the material. In this section we will identify the primary units of classroom teaching and evaluate the components of those that most influence learning. To aid discussion and communication among teachers (as well as for the sake of comparative research), it is useful to have a set of terms to describe similar teaching procedures. Over several decades of classroom research, standard terminology for what ought to be the basic units for planning and executing lessons has been lacking. In the following sections we will utilize the words *activity* and *task*, and attempt to show how these can be more systematically classified, described, and analyzed for their contribution to instruction.

3.1 Subsections of a Lesson— The Activity

Probably the most commonly used and general term for the parts of a lesson is *activity*. Most teachers will use this word in discussing their lesson plans and behaviors, although specific activities often have particular names. In much recent analysis of SL classrooms, materials, and syllabi, the term *task* has been used to discuss those less-controlled activities which produce realistic use of the SL (Crookes and Gass 1993a, 1993b). This term has also characterized certain communicative approaches[6] whose upsurge marks the current era of SL teaching. In fact, the widespread use of the label *task-based* has in many cases simply replaced the older term *communicative*. In discussing both controlled and freer types of classroom learning procedures, we will utilize *activity* as a broader term; *task* will apply to a separable element of a lesson that is primarily geared to practicing language presented earlier (or otherwise learned), usually involving students working with each other, to achieve a specific objective.

It is often said that for each specific learning point, learners need to develop from more controlled and mechanical to freer and communicative behaviors. Therefore, a classification of activity types along such a continuum provides the options from which the teacher can select a given sequence within a lesson. Valcárcel et al. (1985) have developed a tentative list of activity types. We have grouped this list according to four phases of instructional sequencing in lessons (see Edelhoff 1981, p. 57): Information and Motivation (in which learners' interest, experience, and relevant language knowledge are aroused); Input/Control (in which learners are involved in deepening their understanding by close attention to detail); Focus/Working (in which individual linguistic and thematic difficulties can be isolated and examined in depth); and Transfer/Application (in which new knowledge and the learner's refined communicative abilities can be put to active use). Teachers should be familiar with each of these activity types and pay attention to the various discussions in the literature of their benefits and disadvantages.

Information and Motivation Phase

Warm-up: mime, dance, song, jokes, play, etc.; the purpose is to get the students stimulated, relaxed, motivated, attentive, or otherwise engaged and ready for the classroom lesson; not necessarily related to the target language.

Setting: focus is on lesson topic; either verbal or nonverbal evocation of the context that is relevant to the lesson point; teacher directs attention to the upcoming topic by questioning, miming, or picture presentation, or possibly a tape recording.

Brainstorming: free, undirected contributions by the students and teacher on a given topic to generate multiple associations without linking them; no explicit analysis or interpretation is given by the teacher.

Story telling: oral presentation by the teacher of a story or an event as lengthy practice, although not necessarily lesson-based; it implies the use of extended discourse; it usually aims at maintaining attention or motivation and is often entertaining.

A propos: conversation and other socially oriented interaction/speech by teacher, students, or even visitors on general real-life topics; typically authentic and genuine.

Input/Control Phase

Organizational: managerial structuring of lesson or class activities; includes reprimanding of students and other disciplinary action, organization of class furniture and seating, general procedures for class interaction and performance, structure and purpose of lesson, etc.

Content explanation: explanation of lesson content and grammar or other rules and points: phonology, grammar, lexis, sociolinguistics, or whatever is being "taught."

Role play demonstration: use of selected students or teacher to illustrate the procedures(s) to be applied in the following lesson segment; it includes brief illustration of language or other content to be incorporated.

Recognition: students identify a specific target form, function, definition, rule, or other lesson-related item, either from oral or visual data, but without producing language as a response (e.g., checking off items, drawing symbols, rearranging pictures, matching utterances with pictures, underlining significant information from a text.)

Language modeling: presentation of new language by the teacher through isolated sentences with the help of visuals, drawings on blackboard, realia, miming, recorded material, etc.; involves students' participation in the form of repetition, question-answer display, translation, etc.; it usually aims at checking correct pronunciation and syntax, or meaning comprehension.

Dialogue/Narrative presentation: reading or listening passage in the form of dialogue, narration, song, etc., for passive reception (students become familiar with the text without being asked to perform any task related to the content); it usually implies students' listening to a tape or the teacher reading aloud while students follow with or without the text.

Question-answer display: controlled activity involving prompting of student responses by means of *display questions* (teacher or questioner already knows the response or has a very limited set of expectations for the appropriate response); these are distinguished from *referential questions* by means of the likelihood of the questioner knowing the response and the speaker being aware of the questioner knowing the response.

Review: teacher-led review of previous week/ month or other period; a formal summary and assessment of students' recall and performance.

Focus/Working Phase

Translation: student or teacher provides L1 or L2 translations of given text.

Dictation: students write down orally presented text.

Copying: students write down visually presented text.

Reading aloud: student(s) read aloud from a given text—distinguished from *dialogue presentation* in that the focus is on pronunciation and rhythm.

Drill: typical language activity involving fixed patterns of students and teacher responding and prompting, usually with repetition, substitution, and other mechanical alterations; typically with little meaning attached.

Dialogue/Narrative recitation: students recite a passage or dialogue which they have previously learned or prepared; either in unison or individually.

Cued narrative/dialogue: students build up a dialogue or a piece of narrative following cues from miming, cue cards, pictures, flow charts, key functional requests, or other stimuli related to narrative or dialogue (e.g., filling empty bubbles, cued dialogues, completing a dialogue or a text, discourse chains, etc.).

Meaningful drill: language activity involving exchange of a limited number of fixed patterns

of interaction; distinguished from *mechanical drills* in that students have to make a choice with respect to the meaning conveyed.

Preparation: students plan the subsequent activity (in pairs, individually, or in groups) by means of rehearsing, making notes, or simply thinking.

Identification: students pick out and produce/ label or otherwise identify a specific target form, function, definition, or other lesson-related item.

Game: organized language activity that has a particular task or objective and a set of rules which involve an element of competition between players (e.g., board games, hangman, bingo, etc.); it usually implies entertainment and relaxation.

Referential question-answer: activity that involves prompting of responses by means of referential questions (the questioner does not know beforehand the response information); distinguished from *information exchange* in that the information obtained is not meant to achieve a task or solve a problem.

Checking: teacher guides the correction of students' previous activity or homework, providing feedback as an activity rather than within another activity.

Wrap-up: brief teacher- or student-produced summary of points or items that have been practiced or learned.

Transfer/Application Phase

Information transfer: students extract information from a text (oral or written) which they apply to another mode (e.g., visual ➡ written; oral ➡ written, etc.); it implies some transformation of the information by filling out diagrams, graphs, answering questions, etc., while listening or reading; distinguished from *identification* in that students are expected to reinterpret the information.

Information exchange: activity that involves one-way or two-way communication such as information gap exercises, in which one or both parties must obtain information from the other to achieve a goal; distinguished from *meaningful drill* in that the pattern of exchange is not limited to a fixed set or order of structures; distinguished from *information transfer* in that the information is not reinterpreted; and distinguished from *referential questions* in that obtaining the information is critical for the resolution of the task.

Role play: students act out specified roles and functions in a relatively free way; distinguished from *cued dialogues* by the cuing being provided only minimally at the beginning, not during, the activity.

Report: prepared oral exposition of students' previous work (books or stories read, project work, etc.) and elaborated on according to students' own interpretation; it can also be students' reports on information obtained from a previous activity as long as it can be considered as preparation (i.e., students report back with the help of data obtained during the activity).

Narration: students' lengthy exposition of something which they have seen (film, video program, event, etc.), read (news, books, etc.), or experienced (events, story, etc.); narrated in their own words and without previous preparation; distinguished from *cued narrative* because of lack of immediate stimulus.

Discussion: debate or other form of group discussion of specified topic, with or without specified sides/positions prearranged.

Composition: written development of ideas, story, dialogues, or exposition; akin to *report* but in the written mode.

Problem solving: students work on an activity in which a problem and some limitations on means are established; it requires cooperative action on the part of participants, in small or large groups, in order to reach a solution; only one outcome—sometimes among other possible solutions—is allowed per group.

Drama: planned dramatic rendition of play, skit, etc.

Simulation: activity that involves complex interaction between groups and individuals based on simulation of real-life actions and experiences.

Borderline Activity

Testing: formal testing procedures to evaluate students' progress; considered borderline because it could be included in any phase, depending on the content to be tested.

3.2 Task Types and Parameters

A number of the labels from this list of activities have entered into the research and pedagogical literature on "tasks." Currently there is considerable experimental work being conducted on factors that differentiate learning tasks with respect to their parameters and their influence on learners' production in terms of fluency, complexity, and accuracy. Some of these factors are summarized in this section (see also the seminal collection of studies in Crookes and Gass 1993a, 1993b).

Below are three commonly applied definitions of tasks, falling on a continuum from the notion of "real-world" tasks to specifically focused pedagogical activities:

> [a] piece of work undertaken for oneself or for others, freely or for some reward . . . examples . . . include painting a fence, dressing a child, buying a pair of shoes . . . by "task" is meant the hundred and one things people do in everyday life, at work, at play, and in between (Long 1985, p. 89).

> a task is taken to be an activity in which meaning is primary; there is some sort of relationship to the real world; task completion has some priority; and the assessment of task performance is in terms of task outcome (Skehan 1996, p. 38).

> the smallest unit of classroom work which involves learners in comprehending, manipulating, producing, or interacting in the target language. Minimally, tasks will contain some form of data or input (this might be verbal, e.g., a dialogue or reading passage, or nonverbal, e.g., a picture

sequence). The task will also have (implicitly or explicitly) a goal and roles for teachers and learners.(Nunan 1989a, p. 5).

Almost anything can be used as the basis of a task, such as dialogues, public announcements, newspaper headlines, telephone directories, or picture strips (Nunan 1989). In many SL teaching situations, use of a variety of texts (written and spoken) is justified, since part of developing learners' skill is ensuring that they become familiar with as wide a range of text types as possible.

Current research is focusing on ways and means to establish a priori the relative complexity of tasks. This will aid task selection as well as support the development of task-based syllabuses. Robinson (2000) has recently proposed a distinction between task *complexity*, task *conditions*, and task *difficulty*, which can be compared with schemas for the analysis of task factors and dimensions proposed in earlier work, such as that of Nunan (1989), Pica, Kanagy, and Falodun (1993), and Skehan (1996). Robinson includes in task *complexity* only those factors that affect learners' cognitive resources for attention and processing of information and therefore affect the accuracy, fluency, and complexity of their production. These characteristics are viewed as continua, with end points represented by the presence or absence (±) of features: ± few elements, ± here-and-now reference (vs. there-and-then), ± reasoning demands, ± planning, ± single task, and ± prior knowledge. There are several studies which have demonstrated, for example, that allowing for planning in the performance of tasks leads to improvements in either accuracy, fluency, or complexity or combinations of these positive outcomes (Crookes 1989; Ortega 1999). Similarly, less complex tasks favor the more positive end of each continuum. As complexity increases, fluency and accuracy tend to drop.

What Robinson proposes as task *conditions* have often been examined in the literature with respect to their effects on amount of learner production, interaction, and feedback. Thus, "participation variables" such as open and closed tasks, one-way and two-way tasks, and convergent and divergent tasks have been shown to have substantive effects on interaction. Some of these are discussed briefly below. Likewise, "participant variables" such as gender similarities or differences, familiarity among learners, and power relationships can have an influence on task outcomes.

Finally, Robinson makes an important distinction between those factors that can be described for specific tasks and the learner-internal factors that influence the *difficulty* that different learners will have in ability to perform on any given task. These include learners' motivation, anxiety, confidence, aptitude, level of attained proficiency in the L2, and intelligence. Skehan (1996) has also pointed out the importance of various pressures on learners (e.g., time pressures) that can affect how successfully they perform on tasks.

It is important to note that whatever approach one takes to the task analysis, it must be embedded in an analysis of the effects of task *sequencing*. That is, as suggested in the listing of activities within phases in the previous section, implementation of tasks in pedagogically rational sequences can accomplish a great deal toward ensuring learner success on a given task. Skehan's model (1996, p. 57) of task implementation, for instance, suggests ways in which pre-tasks help establish target language or reduce cognitive load through consciousness-raising or practice, and post-tasks help learners to restructure and integrate target forms or functions, increasing the integration of learning goals as further similar tasks are performed.

3.2.1 Relevant Characteristics

Several of the characteristics to be discussed are among the "task conditions" proposed by Robinson (2000). Although they may not affect complexity per se, they have been shown to affect the nature of the language used in tasks. The main focus of such language has been on the provision of comprehensible input as indicated by markers of interactional modification. It has been argued that language which is comprehensible to the SL learner and is at an appropriate level will be of high utility for learning purposes, and that indicators of such discourse are those deviations from normal talk which are used to clarify misunderstandings or problems in communication (Long 1980). The role of practice in SL development has also been emphasized, and Swain (1985) has referred to this as the *output hypothesis*. This suggests that valuable task characteristics would require learners to produce more complex constructions than they would otherwise use (Crookes 1989; Duff 1986; for further discussion see Crookes 1986; Pica, Kanagy, and Falodun, 1993).

A typical task condition which was heavily investigated was "information structure" (an aspect of "information transfer" activities—see section 3.1). Information gap tasks may be designed so that each participant holds different information which must be shared verbally in order for the task to be successfully completed. Such a "two-way task" can be compared with one in which verbal information transfer is also necessary for task completion, but where the information is allocated solely to one participant, who is required to convey it to the other. Classic work of this type (Long 1980) showed that two-way tasks produced more interactional modification (repetitions, expansions, confirmation checks, etc.) than did one-way tasks for native speaker/non-native speaker (NS-NNS) dyads.

A second set of task characteristics, in a sense complementary to the one-/two-way distinction, is shared assumptions. Some studies suggest that the extensive shared background information available in some two-way tasks may work against calling forth more negotiation of meaning. It may be, as Gass and Varonis (1985) argue, that if both participants in an information-gap task have a very clear idea of the structure of one another's information, there will be less likelihood of partial or complete meaning breakdowns. Similarly, as Gaies (1982) suggests, if both participants are well acquainted with each other, they will be able to manage communication difficulties without the need for the extensive negotiation that is probably useful for language acquisition. This may also apply to the availability of visual support for a task. In an investigation of the degree to which three

different tasks produced changes in learners' interlanguages (IL), Crookes and Rulon (1988) found that of two problem-solving tasks, the one in which observable IL development was less evident was the one in which the task provided visual support to both members of the dyad. Even though the pictures used were not identical, they were versions of the same picture, differing only in certain limited features (often called "Spot the Difference").

A third feature which has been posited as likely to be relevant is recycling. If the discourse generated by a task requires the same linguistic material to be used repeatedly, such a conversation would be potentially more useful to the NNS than one in which many items occurred once only (see Gass et al. 1999).

A fourth possible factor is convergence, which derives from the work of Duff (1986). Many communicative tasks available on the ESL materials market require participants to "reach a mutually acceptable solution" (Duff 1986, p. 150), often in solving some values clarification problem. Also quite common now are materials which require students to take a stand on one side of an issue and argue their positions (e.g., Alexander, Kingsbury, and Chapman 1978). The former may be termed a "convergent task type," the latter a "divergent task type" (Duff 1986, p. 150). Duff found that convergent tasks lead to frequent exchange of turns and more communication units, whereas divergent tasks lead to longer turns of greater syntactic complexity. If convergent tasks produce more questions and shorter turns, one may assume that more comprehensible input is available in the discourse which accompanies their performance. Alternatively, if output and the role of practice are emphasized, divergent tasks may be more highly valued, although

> the extended discourse (long turns) in [divergent tasks] reduces opportunities for negotiation of input . . . coupled with the greater syntactic complexity of [discussion], this reduces . . . the amount of comprehensible input available (Duff 1986, p. 170).

We hope that by being aware of the factors which have been investigated, as well as the factors for which no evidence can legitimately be claimed (despite publishers' promotional claims), teachers will find it easier to make the best possible decisions when designing or selecting SL tasks.

4. FACILITATION

A major role of the instructor is to arrange matters so the material presented gets used and thereby learned. This may be far more critical in the learning of a cognitive skill, in which practice assumes major dimensions, than in the learning of most school subjects, in which declarative knowledge (Anderson 1982; O'Malley, Chamot, and Walker 1987) is being presented and clear presentation may be sufficient in itself to ensure learning (cf. West 1960). We need, therefore, to give some consideration to such matters as the overall organization of the classroom, the nature and dynamics of teacher-student and student-student interaction, and the interface between these matters and the selection of classroom learning tasks.

4.1 Class Organization

The key participants in classroom organization are the teacher, the teacher aide or trainee, the individual student and groupings of students, the class as a whole, the language presentation materials used (e.g., textbook, AV media), and any visitors or outsiders. Combinations of these result in particular structures in class organization and effects on language learning processes.

The dominant view of second language classroom processes today favors student-centered learning instead of the traditional teacher-dominated classroom (Nunan 1988b). The teacher-dominated classroom ("teacher-fronted") is characterized by the teacher speaking most of the time, leading activities, and constantly passing judgment on student performance; in a student-centered classroom, students typically will be observed working individually or in pairs and small groups, each on distinct tasks and projects.

Learner-centered instruction has the benefits of greater individualization of learning objectives, increased student opportunities to perform using the target language (whether receptively or productively), and increased personal sense of relevance and achievement, thus relieving the teacher of the need to constantly supervise all students. Students often will pay more attention and learn better from one another since their performances and processes of negotiation of meaning are more closely adapted to one another's level of ability. Teachers should thus be prepared to develop fewer teacher-dominated activities and tasks, while remaining conscious of their students' need for guidance in setting objectives, for appropriate models of and feedback about the target language, and for constructive and supportive evaluation of their progress.

In general, the most appropriate and effective classroom organization is pair and group work. Traditional teachers still harbor negative views of the outcomes of learner-dominated activities, but a small amount of important classroom-centered research has demonstrated that when students have more opportunities to employ the target language, they manage to perform equally successfully in terms of grammatical accuracy as when the teacher is leading the discussion (Doughty and Pica 1984; Pica and Doughty 1985; cf. discussion in Chaudron 1988, pp. 151–152).

Group work has been shown to result in many advantages for SL learners (see, for example, Long et al. 1976; Pica and Doughty 1985; Pica et al. 1996): learners speak more frequently and with longer stretches of speech; they produce more interactional modifications directed at one another; and they utilize a wider range of language. An especially important effect related to cultural differences is that the observable inhibitions to speak in larger classes tend to disappear in small group work.

It should also be recognized that group work results in diversity of performance between groups. This suggests that just as individuals contribute to a group, the different groups in a classroom can be linked through different tasks, roles, and shared responsibilities to generate whole-class tasks and objectives. Although competitive models can be employed in this way (as described in Kagan 1986), many favor whole-class cooperative learning projects.

4.2 Aspects of the Teacher-Fronted Class

Although we emphasize the relative productivity of the small group over the teacher-fronted class, teachers sometimes need to operate in a "lock-step" mode. We will discuss two general characteristics of teacher-student interaction which can fairly easily be manipulated under these conditions to the advantage of SL learning: question type and wait time.

4.2.1 Question Types

Studies (Brock 1986; Long and Sato 1983) have shown that ESL teachers' classroom questioning patterns are typically different from those used by native speakers conversing casually with adult non-native speakers. SL teachers ask more display questions (those to which the questioner already knows the answer) than do ordinary NSs talking to NNSs. The latter usually use referential questions (those to which the questioner does not already know the answer). This difference may be because teachers tend to act as if the SL were information which they must transmit to students, testing whether it has been understood by using display questions.

There are reasons to be concerned about this. First, it is generally accepted that the model of the target language provided by the teacher in the classroom should not deviate greatly from that likely to be encountered in real life. Second, if teacher-student interaction is predominantly through display questions, relatively little real communication is going on. As Long and Crookes observe,

> Display questions by definition preclude students attempting to communicate new, unknown information. They tend to set the focus of the entire exchange they initiate on accuracy rather than meaning. The teacher (and usually the student) already

knows what the other is saying or trying to say, so there is no meaning left to negotiate (1987, p. 181).

Without negotiation of meaning it is questionable whether students addressed by a teacher are actually receiving useful input, in terms of appropriateness to their current level of comprehension and/or language development. Furthermore, less complex language is likely to be produced by learners who know that the teacher is only asking the question to check their knowledge, rather than really wanting a proper and complete answer to a real question.

A further distinction is relevant: closed referential questions versus open referential questions. The former are questions to which the speaker does not know the answer, but to which there is either only one or a very limited set of possible answers; the latter are questions to which the speaker does not know the answer and to which a large variety of answers are possible (see the the distinctions among activity types in Section 3.1). Long et al. (1984) found that open referential questions produced more complex student responses than did closed referential questions, with complexity measured by number of words per student turn.

4.2.2 Wait-Time

Wait-time refers to the length of the pause which follows a teacher's question to an individual student or to the whole class. This lasts until either a student answers or the teacher adds a comment or poses another question. It can also apply to the period between one student's answer to a question and the response of the teacher or another student. A number of investigations in general education have found that wait-times can be altered by teachers but tend to be short, around one second (e.g., Rowe 1969; for a review see Tobin 1987). When wait-time is increased to three to five seconds, there is improvement in learning and in the quality of classroom discourse. The principal SL study of wait-time (Long et al. 1984) found that increased wait-time after teacher questions resulted in longer SL student utterances. It did not result in more utterances per student turn, however, which may have been due to the low proficiency level of the students in the study or possibly to an interaction between cognitive level of questions and wait-time. When asking "harder" questions, teachers tended to wait longer, but the difficulty of such questions was not always compensated for by proportionately longer wait-time. We advance the matter of wait-time here as an example of a classroom procedure which is easy to manipulate and which warrants further classroom investigation. Teachers might want to try the effects of simply waiting longer as they interact with their SL students, knowing that their findings, if communicated, could aid their colleagues and further substantiate (or perhaps disprove) the potential of increased wait-time in SL teaching.

5. CORRECTION AND FEEDBACK

In Section 2.3 we noted that a focus on formal aspects of the SL has again become a concern of methodologists and practitioners. Error correction and feedback have typically been considered to be part of such a focus. As Chaudron notes in his review of feedback in language teaching

> In any communicative exchange, speakers derive from their listeners information on the reception and comprehension of their message. . . . From the language teacher's point of view, the provision of feedback . . . is a major means by which to inform learners of the accuracy of both their formal target language production and their other classroom behavior and knowledge. From the learners' point of view, the use of feedback in repairing their utterances, and involvement in repairing their interlocutors' utterances, may constitute the most potent source of improvement in both target language development and other subject matter knowledge (1988, pp. 132–133).

While there is no reason to associate feedback and correction solely with a formal focus, approaches to language teaching will vary in the degree to which the teacher is expected to be the source of "correcting" behavior. A traditional notion is that the teacher or materials provide a correction of every (important) learner error, while a more current view emphasizes the importance of learners obtaining feedback (and possible correction) only when the meanings they attempt to convey are not understood; even then, the feedback should be a natural outcome of the communicative interaction, often between learners. Even in the most learner-centered instruction, learners need feedback in order to differentiate between acceptable and unacceptable target language use. (See the chapters by Larsen-Freeman and Fotos in this volume for further discussion.)

The provision of feedback, or even "corrections," does not mean that the information provided must be stated in formalized grammatical or other descriptive terms. The teacher has many options available, from simply indicating lack of comprehension or otherwise signaling the occurrence of an error and getting the learner to self-correct, to the most elaborate grammatical explanation and drill of correct forms.

Teachers frequently make the mistake of thinking that by providing a correct "model," by repeating student statements with some slight change in the grammatical form, learners will perceive the correction and incorporate it into their developing grammars. This is the form of feedback known as "recasts," which is a relatively implicit focus on form (see Long, Inagaki, and Ortega 1998). As Chaudron (1977) notes, and Lyster (1998a) argues further, such feedback is likely to be perceived by the learner not as a formal change, but rather as a confirmation, rephrasing, or clarification of the functional meaning. For example:

STUDENT: I can no go back home today early.
TEACHER: You can't go home early today?
STUDENT: No.

If there is in fact reason to provide formal feedback in such a case, it helps to focus on the specific correction by emphasizing and isolating the modeled forms (Chaudron 1977): *I can't go home*, or *early today*. But it appears evident from studies of recasts that they are in fact effective 20-25 percent of the time. This effectiveness may be because they occur when the learner has reached a stage of grammatical competence that allows him or her to perceive the slight difference in use.

In some recent research on French language immersion classrooms in Canada, Lyster and Ranta (1997; see also Lyster 1998a, 1998b) illustrate a wide variety of feedback events, frequently in the middle of content-based exchanges. They argue that their data illustrate the positive value of explicit correction and negotiated feedback in guiding learners' to the correct use of target forms, since "uptake" of correct grammatical forms occurred more frequently following such corrective moves. It should be noted that a considerably higher rate of uptake of pronunciation and lexical errors occurred in their data when the teachers provided only implicit feedback in the form of recasts.

On the other hand, such practices may be less effective than encouraging learners to self-correct (see Tomasello and Herron 1988) or having other learners assist in corrections. Peer correction has the potential advantage of being at the right level of development in the learner's interlanguage grammar.

As we noted in Section 2.3, an important limitation on the effectiveness of feedback and correction, especially with respect to grammatical development, is the natural order of acquisition of a given structure or function. Ultimately, teachers must remain current with findings of research in SL acquisition, to better understand when it might be useful to correct.

6. CONCLUSION

This introductory review of SL classroom teaching as an area of study and professional practice could be extended; indeed, many other chapters of this volume continue the discussion of key areas for classroom practice. Nonetheless, it is evident that teachers still encounter many areas

of ignorance where ideally there should be knowledge. On the one hand, teachers should know what relatively firm information does exist, and where there is room for investigation. This should aid their decision making. As the SL profession develops, more teachers are qualified to conduct their own research or to collaborate with researchers.[7] On the other hand, teaching will always be a series of judgment calls; its real-time cognitive complexity means it will never be just a science, and will always remain something of an art (cf. Clark and Lampert 1986; Leinhardt and Greeno 1986). We have tried here to help the judgment calls be educated, informed ones through the teacher's combined use of knowledge and educated professional reflection.

DISCUSSION QUESTIONS

1. Why should ESL teachers be concerned about keeping up with the results of classroom research and second language acquis-ition research?
2. Do you agree that teachers should make their lesson objectives clear to their students? Can you think of situations in which this would be inappropriate? Why?
3. How much place do you think presentation, explanation, and discussion of rules for language use have in the SL classroom? What underlying view of language and language learning supports your view?
4. Discuss the ways in which one might investigate the most effective way of giving feedback (or correction). What data would you collect, and how would you identify successful correction?

SUGGESTED ACTIVITIES

1. Prepare (individually) and compare (as a group) a mini-lesson. Select a specific point of language form or function, rule of conversation, or other social use of English. Individually develop a sequence of activities that you might use to present, develop, and

evaluate this point, and then compare your suggestions in a group. Develop a jointly agreed-upon way of teaching this point and practice it with one another.

2. A useful alternative way of practicing the first activity is for each person to teach a point in a language unknown to the others in the group. Discuss your feelings on once again being a second language learner.

3. Working with a partner, discuss ways in which a teacher with a multicultural group of students can best maintain a positive classroom climate, promoting student interest and motivation.

 FURTHER READING

Bailey, K. M., and D. Nunan, eds. 1996. *Voices from the Language Classroom.* Cambridge: Cambridge University Press.
An extensive and accessible collection of recent classroom SL studies, illustrating the range of current work of a more qualitative nature.

Burns, A. 1999. *Collaborative Action Research for English Language Teachers.* Cambridge: Cambridge University Press.
A practical introduction to teacher research in SL contexts based on actual investigations by a team of SL teachers in Australia.

Chaudron, C. 1988. *Second Language Classrooms.* Cambridge: Cambridge University Press.
A comprehensive survey of earlier SL classroom research.

Crookes, G., and S. M. Gass, eds. 1993. *Tasks in a Pedagogical Context: Integrating Theory and Practice.* Philadelphia, PA: Multilingual Matters.
An illustrative collection of studies of pedagogical applications of the concept of "task" in SL teaching.

Lynch, T. 1996. *Communication in the Language Classroom.* Oxford: Oxford University Press.
A useful introduction to basic processes of classroom interaction and teacher talk, with clear examples.

ENDNOTES

1. We are grateful to many people named for their assistance with the previous version (Crookes and Chaudron 1991) of this paper, and we wish to continue acknowledgement of Marisol Valcárcel, Mercedes Verdú, and Julio Roca, of the Universidad de Murcia.

2. Our discussion is traditional to the extent that we will not deal with approaches to SL teaching that involve going outside the classroom (e.g., Ashworth 1985; Auerbach 1996; Fried Booth 1986).

3. What "size" the elements are is not at issue here. That is to say, we are not concerned with whether the units presented are structural or functional, or if the language of a given pedagogical task is an unanalyzed whole.

4. Though the idea is not a new one—see, e.g., West (1960).

5. This is, of course, a problem for the syllabus designer to be aware of and to resolve by proper choice of learning targets (see Long and Crookes 1993).

6. We should point out that we deliberately avoid the word "method" here; we do not accept its general validity as a term of analysis (cf. Richards 1984).

7. This is particularly clear in the increased recognition of the importance of action research in the area of SL teaching (Burns 1999; Crookes 1993; Freeman 1998).

English for Specific Purposes: Tailoring Courses to Student Needs— and to the Outside World

ANN M. JOHNS • DONNA PRICE-MACHADO

In "English for Specific Purposes," Johns and Price-Machado argue that all good teaching is 'specific purpose' in approach. Using Vocational ESL and other examples, this chapter covers key questions such as "Who are the stakeholders?" and "What is authenticity in the classroom?" which are addressed using needs and discourse analysis. Various program models demonstrate how ESP values are realized in different contexts.

WHAT IS ESP?

English for Specific Purposes (ESP) is a movement based on the proposition that *all* language teaching should be tailored to the specific learning and language use needs of identified groups of students—and also sensitive to the sociocultural contexts in which these students will be using English. Most of the movement's practitioners are teachers of adults, those students whose needs are more readily identified within academic, occupational, or professional settings. An increasing number of ESP practitioners live and work in English-speaking countries, teaching in programs offering vocational ESL (VESL) or English for Occupational Purposes (EOP) programs for new immigrant and refugee populations or in contexts emphasizing academic (EAP) or business language (English for Business Purposes). However, ESP continues to be even more common in English as a *Foreign* Language (EFL) contexts, where an increasing number of adult students are eager to learn business English or academic English in order to pursue their careers or study in English-medium educational institutions. One remarkable example of the explosion of ESP programs in EFL contexts has taken place in China, where foreign trade has risen from 10 percent to 45 percent of the Gross National Product over the last thirty years and the need to speak English in international trade is urgent (Huang 1999). Many employers and educational institutions throughout the world are searching for ESL/EFL teachers with solid ESP backgrounds.

ESP Categories

The main interests of the ESP movement can be categorized in a number of ways (see, for example, Dudley-Evans and St. John 1998, p. 6). For the purposes of this discussion, we have created a set of categories as shown in Figure 1 on page 44.

Because of their current importance, a few of these categories will be highlighted in this chapter: English for Occupational Purposes, particularly VESL and English for Business Purposes (EBP), and English for Academic Purposes (EAP). It is important to note, however, that this chart is far from exhaustive; there is a remarkable array of ESP courses offered throughout the world. In various cities in Italy, for example, there are project-oriented curricula for white-collar workers in the tourist industry (English for Tourism). In Morocco, Hasan II University devotes many of its EAP courses to specific graduate majors such as agronomy. In some nations, learning English to contribute to the development of a community or region is a central goal (Gueye 1990). As the prison population grows

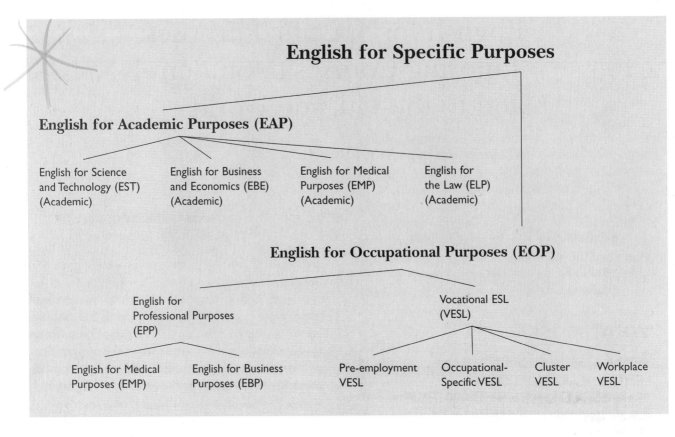

English for Specific Purposes

English for Academic Purposes (EAP)

English for Science and Technology (EST) (Academic)

English for Business and Economics (EBE) (Academic)

English for Medical Purposes (EMP) (Academic)

English for the Law (ELP) (Academic)

English for Occupational Purposes (EOP)

English for Professional Purposes (EPP)

Vocational ESL (VESL)

English for Medical Purposes (EMP)

English for Business Purposes (EBP)

Pre-employment VESL

Occupational-Specific VESL

Cluster VESL

Workplace VESL

Figure 1. Classification of ESP Categories

in the United States, there are ESP courses in computer repair and other areas of computer language and technology for the incarcerated. This remarkable diversity of situations and curricula highlights one of the virtues of ESP: the programs are adapted to the contexts and needs of particular groups of students.

CENTRAL ESP COMPONENTS

Although the modern ESP movement has evolved in many directions since it was founded in the mid 1960s (see Swales [1988] for an excellent overview), several components have remained relatively constant throughout its history. In 1988, Peter Strevens provided the following overview of ESP and its features.

The claims for ESP are that it is

- focused on the learner's need and wastes no time

- relevant to the learner
- successful in imparting learning
- more cost-effective than "General English."[1]

An ESP definition needs to distinguish between four absolute and two variable characteristics:

1. Absolute characteristics: ESP consists of language teaching which is

- designed to meet the specified needs of the learner
- related to content (i.e., in its themes and topics) to particular disciplines, occupations, or activities
- centered on the language appropriate to these activities in syntax, lexis, discourse, semantics, and the analysis of this discourse
- in contrast to "General English."

2. Variable characteristics: ESP may be, but is not necessarily

- restricted to the language skills to be learned (e.g., reading only)
- not taught according to any preordained methodology.

The "absolute characteristics" of the movement, in particular, have provided guidance in the design of ESP curricula and teaching over the years. Thus, they are important for understanding how ESP practitioners distinguish themselves from other ESL/EFL teachers in professional organizations, such as TESOL, and elsewhere. Each characteristic will be discussed later in this chapter.

First, however, it is necessary to lay a foundation, to consider those issues that ESP practitioners must address as they plan programs and develop curricula.

ISSUES ADDRESSED IN ESP PROGRAM PLANNING

ESP programs are developed because there is a demand, because teachers, supervisors, government agencies, professionals, students, or others see a need for language courses in which certain content, skills, motivations, processes, and values are identified and integrated into specialized, often short-term, courses. As ESP practitioners approach course development, they must consider a multitude of factors—and some essential questions—before, and during, project initiation.

1. Stakeholders in the Class or Project What are the sources of demand for this ESP program? Who are the clients? An employer, an agency, a government, a more traditional educational institution, or the students themselves? What do the stakeholders view as the essential elements of the ESP program they desire?

These are the first questions posed—for a number of reasons, one of which is funding: Stakeholders generally provide the money for courses and curriculum development. Another reason is mandates: Governments and institutions

throughout the world require specialized language training or education for certain employees and students.

Sometimes mandates, funding, and government recommendations create a intricate web of requirements, responses, and oversight. For example, vocational ESL (VESL) programs in the United States[2] have been developed as complex responses to welfare reform and the needs of funding agencies such as the Adult Education and Family Literacy Act.[3] Many VESL programs, in their attempt to meet current requirements, are informed by the U.S. Department of Labor's SCANS Report[4], though no funding for VESL comes directly from this agency.

The SCANS Report established two levels of criteria for workplace skills (see, for example, Marshall 1997). At the first level, the Foundation Skills include *basic components* (reading, writing, active listening, quantitative operations, interpreting, organizing information and ideas), *thinking skills* (learning and reasoning, thinking creatively, making decisions, solving problems), and *personal qualities* (responsibility, self-esteem, sociability, integrity, self-management). At the second level, the Workplace Competencies include *resource management* (organizing, planning, etc.), *interpersonal skills* (working in teams, teaching others, negotiating, working effectively within culturally diverse settings, etc.), *information management* (acquiring and evaluating facts and data, using computers, etc.), *systems management* (understanding social organization and technological systems), and *technology* (selecting equipment and tools, applying technology to tasks, etc.). Because of the influence of this report, many VESL textbook writers and teachers have used SCANS as the basis for their curricula (see, for example, Price-Machado 1998).

In other contexts, the stakeholders are the students themselves, particularly in private ESL/EFL schools throughout the world which professionals attend to upgrade their language skills. These students are often very precise about what they want to learn and achieve. Even if the students do not, or cannot, initiate or direct an ESP project, there has been considerable attention given to ways in which they should be empowered to participate within it. Somerville (1997, p. 92), working in Australia, argues that we must be asking questions such as the following if we are to design workplace literacy curricula that are learner-centered:

- Who are the participants in workplace literacy programs?
- How do the *workers* experience the programs?
- How do programs change worker participation in workplace culture?
- (What happens to the workplace during and after workers' participation in the program?)

Other major stakeholders are educational institutions, particularly universities involved in academic-purposes programs, and private companies that need focused English language and skills training for their professional employees.

An example of combined government and institutional stakeholder influence has taken place in recent years in Tunisia. This country's president, with his entourage, made diplomatic and trade-related trips to countries such as South Africa where English plays a central role. Although the president's major advisors and business people spoke French and Arabic, they did not have sufficient command of business or diplomatic English to be successful. As a result, he has required all institutions of higher learning in Tunisia to step up their teaching of the English language.[5]

2. Available Teachers   A central issue to be considered is the nature of the teachers who will be involved in an ESP program. What content, skills, and literacies will they be expected to teach? How much teacher training have they completed? Are they linguistically sophisticated, i.e., can they discuss how English works and analyze specialized discourses? What types of curricula and approaches are they most comfortable with? All of these questions are central to design. Inexperienced or "traditional" teachers cannot work within an experimental ESP context, for example. In many EFL contexts, the ESP teacher is not a native speaker of English (See Medgyes's chapter in this volume); this, too, will influence the type of ESP curriculum designed.

ESP teachers face challenges that other instructors may be able to circumvent. One challenge relates to ESP *content:* discerning the particular vocabulary, discourses, and processes that are essential to the ESP training of students within a specialized context. What does the teacher have to know about electrical engineering and its practices to assist students to write a research paper in that discipline? What does a teacher have to know about the language of welding, or tourism, to address the needs of students who have chosen these vocations? Many ESP practitioners argue that if they can analyze language and discourses and study language use, they do not need specialist expertise. Others argue that at least some familiarity with the students' discipline or vocation is valuable.

In all cases, the teacher/practitioner conducts some research in the form of needs assessment and target situation analysis before designing the curriculum—and often, throughout the course. In English for Academic Purposes programs, practitioners often analyze the discourses of the students' discipline, visit classes, talk to faculty, and study the strategies and language that students use to succeed. In business or diplomatic English, as discussed in the Tunisian example above, the practitioner may have to accompany a delegation to an English-speaking country in order to understand the required language for that context. In VESL, this needs analysis research often includes interviewing vocational instructors or employers and attending vocational classes. In Fairfax County (Virginia) Adult ESL Programs, for example,

> [The VESL teacher attends vocational classes], taking notes on troublesome vocabulary, idioms, slang, concepts, cultural differences, and then s/he addresses these things in the ESL class. This makes up most of the content of the ESL class with additional practice in the development of reading, listening, speaking, writing and problem solving skills (Schrage, personal communication, 2/26/00).

Another challenge for ESP teachers involves attaining the necessary breadth of understanding about successful communication within a context that they, and their students, need to develop. How is a good working and communicative relationship established among professionals from different cultures who are negotiating or presenting papers in English? What kinds of problems and relationships exist between L2 workers and their supervisors? How should a person use language to be polite, give orders, or perform other English language functions within the target context? Or, to give one very specific purpose area, how does a pilot establish contact with and give clear messages to air traffic controllers? These are subtle and not-so-subtle communications issues that can make or break businesses and affect safety and good working relationships.

3. Authenticity Issues Because ESP involves special Englishes and contexts, not "General English," efforts to achieve maximum linguistic, strategic, and situational authenticity are made in designing curricula. One of the most advantageous "authentic" possibilities is provided by courses offered wholly, or in part, on site in the target location: at a workplace, such as a factory or shipyard, or within specific academic contexts, such as an engineering or biology department. On-site ESP provides opportunities for an accurate and rich needs assessment and ongoing training and evaluation, as well as for input from the stakeholders involved. In universities, on-site language training may occur in adjunct courses or other types of content-based arrangements that permit students to experience language and literacies in their natural contexts (see Johns 1997).

If on-site courses cannot be offered, practitioners search for other ways to provide students with authenticity. There is a long and sometimes contentious history of introducing into the classroom written or oral discourses that are central to, but removed from, the target situation in which the students will eventually be using English. Many curriculum designers analyze and segment these discourses so that they can be studied within a curriculum. However, some experts argue that when practitioners import into the classroom target situation texts (or "genres") taken out of their original settings, these texts lose their authenticity of context, audience, and other factors:

> a traditional belief that now appears problematic is that genres for use in one context—history lessons or office work—can be straightforwardly taught in a different context such as the English lesson. . . . Producing an example of a genre is a matter not just of generating a text with certain formal characteristics but of using generic resources to *act* effectively on a situation through a [written or spoken text] (Freedman and Medway 1994, p. 11).

Supporting this claim, some practitioners argue that authenticity should relate to the *transferability* of strategies or activities rather than to spoken or written texts from target contexts. Thus, for example, if students practice politeness strategies in the target language, they may be able to use these approaches in a variety of somewhat unpredictable contexts. In the following quote, which continues to influence ESP curricula, Widdowson argues the following:

> [a] process-oriented approach accepts from the outset that the language data given to the learner will not be preserved in store intact, but will be used in the mental mill. Hence the language content of the course is selected not because it is representative of what the learner will have to deal with after the course is over but because it is likely to activate strategies for learning as the course progresses (1981, p. 5).

Efforts at activating strategies and processes in ESP classrooms can take many forms. For example, after researching the target EFL situation, Souillard (1989, p. 24) found certain oral activities for French students to be relevant and transferable to their disciplinary classrooms in which English was the medium of instruction: dictating calculations, describing a geometric figure, giving instructions for a procedure, describing a plant site, preparing a schedule, and describing a graph or flowchart.

4. Curricular Decisions Other chapters in this volume address the issues of curriculum. (See especially those by Nunan, Snow, Eyring, and McGroarty.) All of those issues must also be addressed in ESP. In making curricular decisions, ESP practitioners have been influenced over the years by trends in applied linguistics and general ESL/EFL teaching, when relevant to their students, moving through the methodological variations, from grammar-based to communicative, to process-based, and to genre-based curricula. But whatever the current trends, it is a basic responsibility of an ESP practitioner to be context- and student-sensitive. Thus, in several EFL contexts, only ESP reading is taught, often using methods such as intensive reading that are most amenable to local student learning. In other contexts, the concentration is upon oral/aural skills. (See Lazaraton's chapter in this volume.) The purpose of any ESP curriculum, then, is to meet the specific linguistic and pragmatic needs of students as they prepare for identified English-medium contexts. No texts and discourses and no tasks or activities should be extraneous to student needs and the requirements of the target context.

Of course, this makes the selection of off-the-shelf textbooks very difficult, as Swales (1980), among others, has noted. Should a textbook be "wide-angled" and inclusive, such as many English for Business texts are, losing some of the specificity of local student needs? Should textbooks be "narrow-angled," addressing some of the focused needs of the learner? State-of-the-art ESP classes often must also include the integration of computer technology. How this technology is used, and which skills are integrated, will again depend upon the specific needs of the students. Kappra (2000), for example, makes these suggestions for integrating SCANS/VESL and computer technologies:

a. Have students keep computer records of their progress and assess that progress by completing reports,
b. Assign computer-related tasks such as distributing disks and trouble-shooting,
c. Use problem-solving activities that require basic computer skills (p. 14).

Whether practitioners choose published textbooks or develop their own materials, revision and updating must occur constantly in ESP. In "adjunct" EAP classes in universities, for example, the ESP teachers must consult frequently with the content instructors to adjust or renegotiate their assignments. In EOP/VESL programs, job shadowing can be used to update curricula. VESL programs are also frequently revised and new modules created to reflect the language and other skills needed for jobs that become available in the community.

5. Assessment All ESL/EFL teachers must consider issues of assessment, discussed in the chapter by Cohen in this volume. What is particularly challenging in ESP programs is that students and their sponsors, governments, or academic institutions are anxious to see immediate and focused assessment results that address specific objectives. Thus, the demands of assessment, both in terms of formative and summative evaluation, are great. In a work on ESP testing, Douglas (2000) points out the following:

> [a] specific purpose language test is one in which test content and methods are derived from an analysis of the characteristics of a specific target language use situation, so that test tasks and content are authentically representative of the target situation, allowing for an interaction between the test taker's language activity and specific purpose content knowledge, on the one hand, and the test tasks on the other. Such a test allows us to make inferences about a test taker's capacity to use language in the specific purpose domain (p. 19).

ESP assessment must also be appropriate to the instructional context. In VESL programs, for example, interviewing supervisors or the students themselves about language, content, and task proficiency can be more effective than any traditional oral examination or reading and writing test. Some ESP experts, particularly in large VESL and EAP programs, are now testing students on-line to encourage the development of computer skills and to make testing more efficient. In EAP programs, there is a long history of attempting to design discipline-sensitive examinations at institutions such as the University of Michigan.

PREPARING AN ESP CURRICULUM

After this discussion of the questions and topics that must be addressed before a curriculum is prepared, we now turn to the "absolute characteristics" mentioned by Strevens (1988) and their application to curriculum design. Though ESP shares much with "General English" curricula and overlaps with content-based designs, there are certain features which distinguish it from other approaches.

Needs Assessment In every genuine ESP course, needs assessment is obligatory, and in many programs, an ongoing needs assessment is integral to curriculum design and evaluation. In performing an assessment, practitioners attempt to determine as closely as possible what students will need to do—and how they will need to do it—in English language contexts or with English language literacies. Over the years, methods of assessing learner needs have become increasingly sophisticated and process-based. Here are a few of those employed, often for the same curricular design:

1. Questionnaires and surveys: These can be given to the students themselves, their employers or supervisors, or the audiences to whom they will be writing or speaking. They can be administered as "precourse questionnaires" (Dudley-Evans and St. John 1998), throughout the course, or after it is completed.
2. Interviews of experts, students, and other stakeholders: Particularly useful for academic English are some of the interviews about uses and functions of specific linguistic items in discourses, a practice that has become increasingly popular after a land-

mark study of the uses of the passive published in *The ESP Journal*.[6] (Tarone et al. 1981).

In VESL (Vocational ESL) and Business English, interviewers tend to rely upon the supervisors and experts within the target situation in which the students would be working, as well as the workers/students themselves.

3. Observation, job-shadowing, and analysis: These approaches can take place on the job, in academic contexts while students are reading and writing (i.e., "processing") texts, while individuals are speaking, working in groups, etc. ESP needs assessments have been greatly influenced by recent qualitative research, specifically ethnography. Much of the current work is "thicker" in terms of description than that of the past, so careful observation tends to be integrated with other forms of needs assessment.

   Job-shadowing is very valuable to VESL teachers, who explore the linguistic, cultural, and pragmatic experiences of workers as they experience a typical day on the job.
4. Multiple intelligence and learning style surveys of the students: ESP practitioners use standard instruments as well as other methods for determining student approaches to learning and text production such as protocols and interviews (see St. John 1987).
5. Modes of working: Working in teams is another aspect of job performance that is common in many VESL contexts as well as in some academic classes. A needs assessment may thus include analysis of how teams work in the target context, breakdowns in negotiation in culturally mixed groups, and other factors that may inhibit or enhance success.
6. Spoken or written reflections by the students—or their supervisors—before, during, or after instruction: In reflection, stakeholders are able to look back on what they have experienced with an ESP program. Reflections can be used to determine how a current program should be revised or future programs should be designed.

There is important literature distinguishing between student *needs, wants,* and *lacks* (see, for example, Hutchinson and Waters 1987, p. 55), and for adults, these are important distinctions. Readers interested in exploring these issues are encouraged to consult the considerable literature in both ESP and job training programs on needs assessment for curriculum design.

From the established needs, specific objectives for students are written, and from these objectives, the classroom tasks and methods for assessment of the program and its students are determined and revised as the course progresses.

Relating to Content (of Occupations, Disciplines, etc.) Since 1988 when Strevens wrote his ESP overview, there has been an explosion of research and theory on content (see, for example, Snow's chapter in this volume), as well as on the ways in which values established within communities of workers and practitioners influence the manner in which content is approached and visually displayed. Berkenkotter and Huckin (1995, p. 14), discussing academic content, argue that "what constitutes true . . . knowledge . . . is knowledge of appropriate topics and relevant details." One example from the literature may show how understanding the uses of content influences students' success in universities. Giltrow and Valiquette (1994) asked teaching assistants from psychology and criminology to read their students' papers and critique their ability to manage the knowledge of their respective disciplines. The teaching assistants found that successful student papers were quite different, depending on the field. In psychology, students were required to demonstrate how they could manage details in texts by including some information and excluding other topics. In criminology, on the other hand, the most important skill involved relating concepts to examples, again making the content work within a disciplinary framework.

What does this mean about content selection for curricula? It tells us that in all ESP situations, practitioners must continuously assess what types of content are central, how content is used and valued, and the relationships between vocabulary and central concepts. Another essential element of successful curriculum design is selecting content that motivates students: those topics that these important stakeholders want to address. In a volume on adult participatory literacy instruction and VESL, Auerbach et al. (1996) argue the following:

> very often, [adult students] are immersed in the struggles of adjusting to a new culture, separation from families, preoccupation with the political situation in their home countries, trying to find work, and so on. Rather than seeing these preoccupations as obstacles to learning, a participatory approach allows them to focus on them as part of learning . . . [and they are] more engaged in content (p. 158).

Identifying and Analyzing Essential Language and Discourses Since ESP can be considered a subdiscipline of applied linguistics, practitioners have made effective use of the trends in this area to analyze, for curricular purposes, the language and discourses (genres) of the target situations in which their students will be studying, living, or working. In the 1960s, language analysis tended to center on the particular grammatical or lexical features (i.e., "registers") of discourses. Thus, researchers found that certain verb forms predominated in scientific discourses (Barber 1966), that a limited group of cohesive devices are found in business letters (Johns 1980) and that abbreviations are characteristic of telexes (Zak and Dudley-Evans 1986). Now, of course, much business and academic communication takes place via e-mail, so practitioners are researching the registers of e-mail communication in order to develop more authentic curricular materials (see, for example, Gimenez 2000).

As communicative syllabus design (especially Notional Functional syllabi) became popular, the types of discourse analyses conducted relied more upon language *function* than upon counts of specific linguistic items. Matsunobu (1983), for example, found that university business professors used three major types of speech acts in their lectures: informatives, metastatements, and discourse markers; thus, she developed a listening curriculum in which these acts were the focus. As it has matured, research into communicative functions has drawn increasingly from pragmatics, showing, for example, that the ways in which individuals are polite to each other depend upon their disciplines and upon their relative status. Hyland (1998) found that when published authors in the sciences write to their peers, they tend to "hedge" their conclusions, making comments such as, "The data appear to show . . ." or "Perhaps this indicates . . . "

Not surprisingly, computers are now used to determine the grammatical features shared by large numbers of spoken or written discourses within certain genres (Biber 1994). A related approach, more typical of the British ESP specialists, is concordancing (Johns 1989), a method for determining lexical collocations in a large number of spoken and written texts. In concordancing, practitioners determine what language most commonly surrounds a word in authentic discourses. They might explore a common word such as *take,* and through examining a large number of written and spoken discourses from particular situations, they can determine the linguistic environments in which *take* appears. This work is a boon to ESP, of course, since teachers organize their curricula according to the most common contexts of central vocabulary.

Concordancing and corpus linguistics tend to be most concerned with bottom-up studies of texts, measuring the nature and interactions of various grammatical and lexical features. Other ESP practitioners have concentrated upon the macro features of texts—and their contexts—by studying the relationships between the structure and language of written texts and the situations in which these texts appear. John Swales's *Genre Analysis: English in Academic and Research Settings* (1990) set the tone for ESP research of this type, and many others have followed his lead.

Drawing from earlier work in applied linguistics, ESP specialists have studied genres from a variety of occupational and academic communities such as the law (Bhatia 1993) and business (Eustace 1996). Though using curricula in which genres are central has been characteristic of EBP for a number of years (Johns 1987), these approaches have only recently influenced the teaching of reading and writing in academic settings, particularly at the graduate level (see Swales and Feak 1994).

PROGRAM MODELS

What do ESP programs look like? It should be clear from this discussion that there is a wide range of courses and programs in a wide range of locations, always keyed to the language needs, skills, content, and processes required. Perhaps one of the best articulated and widespread sets of program models in ESL contexts falls under the VESL rubric. It includes the following:

Preemployment VESL This is a modified version of a "general" ESL class in that the content is devoted to job readiness and general "soft" job skills as outlined in the SCANS Report. Students practice general job functions such as responding to complaints, making requests, and answering the phone. They may also prepare for job interviews and other initial job skills.

Occupation-Specific VESL Here, the content is related to a particular job such as nursing assistant or electronics assembler. It can be taught either as preparation for, or concurrently with, a vocational program. An example might be a three-hour class, three days a week, in which students study vocabulary and other skills they will need for an electronics assembly class that also enrolls native speakers of English. After the VESL class, they attend the regular electronics assembly class—or they may attend both concurrently. There is frequent communication between the VESL and vocational instructors.

Cluster VESL These classes include students from different vocations in one classroom. Students study all four "skills" (listening, speaking, reading, and writing), often in a theme-based program (e.g., "The World of Work"). In one class, for example, students read about how to meet people and make small talk in the workplace. Then, they meet in pairs or teams answering jigsaw comprehension questions or completing a problem-solving or writing exercise. Later, students work on individualized modules devoted to their chosen professions and are assessed on this work. (Note: Because of the attendance requirements in many adult schools, this is probably the most common type of program.)

Workplace VESL This term applies to skills and content of a specific workplace. It can be job-specific, such as for electronics assembly, or it may have a broader emphasis. Often, the employer pays for some or all of the course, and employees are excused during their workday to attend (Thomas, Bird, and Grover 1992, p. 108).

English for Business programs are the most popular in the English as a Foreign Language world. Businesses, or individuals, require classes in negotiation, correspondence, bid and report writing, and in supervising bilingual and ESL/EFL workers. Not surprisingly, program design comes in many shapes and sizes depending upon the large variety of contexts and students served. (See the special Business English issue of *English for Specific Purposes*, 15(1), 1996.)

English for Academic Purposes also has a long history of program specialization, particularly in science and technology areas at advanced levels (see Swales 1988). Some excellent research and curricula (see, for example, Swales and Feak 1994) have been developed for graduate students in the areas of research paper analysis and advanced academic writing. Unfortunately for many ESL contexts, the EAP tradition at the undergraduate level has been clouded with controversy. There is little agreement on how, or what, EAP should consist of for those students who have not yet advanced into their academic majors.

ESP and the Future There is no question that ESP is well established, particularly in EFL academic and business contexts and in VESL programs in English-speaking countries. Our largest professional organization, TESOL, has an active ESP Interest Section whose members represent a wide variety of EFL and ESL contexts. There is considerable demand for ESP teachers who can perform a variety of needs assessment tasks, such as collecting authentic discources and analyzing them, making appropriate observations, and consulting various stakeholders—and then produce curricula sensitive to the students and context. There is also a need for discourse analysis research, particularly in English for Business and VESL contexts. In addition, there is a growing demand for specialists who can develop computer-based curricula and more authentic tests. Teachers with professional training in these areas find themselves in great demand internationally—and often they are leaders in adult school sites within their home countries.

In the future, ESP may include much more study of genres, particularly the "homely" genres of the workplace and community. It may lead to the development of more sophisticated, learner-centered or team-oriented curricula, particularly in VESL and professional programs. There may also be greater involvement of ESP in economic development and nation building.

Whatever its directions, ESP will remain central to ESL and EFL teaching throughout the world.

DISCUSSION QUESTIONS

1. How can a VESL teacher (or any ESP teacher, for that matter) integrate the essential areas of sociability, teamwork, and self-esteem into his or her teaching?
2. Your supervisor has decided that you will initiate a VESL class (an ESP program) at your school. What are some of the questions you need to ask and things you need to do to prepare for that class?
3. What areas of ESP appeal to you most? Why? If you were to teach a class in the most appealing area, what would its focus be? Why?
4. How can a person effectively assess the results of an ESP program? After consulting the chapter by Cohen in this volume or the work by Douglas (2000), discuss some possibilities for assessment.
5. Throughout this chapter, the authors juxtapose "General English" and ESP. What is "General English" in your view? To whom should it be taught?

SUGGESTED ACTIVITIES

1. Design a "triangulated" needs assessment for a particular class, which includes obtaining the same data in different ways. Consider questionnaires, observation, interviews, and discourse analysis.

2. Where does communication breakdown occur? Where do ESL/EFL students face the most difficulty in using English in target situations? Observe a class, a lab, bilingual workers on-line or at a construction site. Decide what the areas of breakdown are (e.g., question-posing skills) and how you might teach them.

3. Using information from needs assessments or other sources, develop some group activities that rely upon either strategies for achieving ends (e.g., negotiation) or essential linguistic features (e.g., hedging). Assign these activities to a class.

4. What are the features of a particular genre that students will need to read or write? Classify some of these features and discuss how you might present them to a class.

5. If available, survey the three "wide-angled" VESL textbooks listed below. Make a list of similarities and differences among these volumes that considers:

   a. the use and weighing of the SCANS competencies,

   b. the text's organization,

   c. central activities.

   Does one textbook seem more appropriate for certain groups of students? Why?

   ■ Price-Machado, D. (1998). *Skills for Success.* New York: Cambridge University Press.

   ■ Magy, R. (1998). *Working It Out.* Boston: Heinle & Heinle Publishers.

   ■ *English ASAP* (1999). Austin, TX: Steck-Vaughn.

 ## FURTHER READING

Douglas, D. 2000. *Assessing Languages for Specific Purposes.* New York: Cambridge University Press. This is the first volume devoted exclusively to assessment, a central issue in ESP and in other specific purposes languages (LSP). A text that is accessible to nonexperts, it includes a variety of actual test tasks taken from a number of LSP areas.

Dudley-Evans, T., and M. J. St. John. 1998. *Developments in ESP: A Multi-Disciplinary Approach.* Cambridge: Cambridge University Press. This is a very good text for those new to ESP. It includes discussions and examples of all the "absolute characteristics" of the movement and provides a variety of examples from EAP and English for Occupational Purposes (both professional and VESL).

English for Specific Purposes: An International Journal (formerly *The ESP Journal*). Founded in the early 1980s, the journal includes articles on all of the "absolute characteristics" of ESP (needs assessment, discourse analysis, etc.) as well as discussions of research and the practical issues of curriculum design. Also included are more informal discussions of ESP issues and book reviews.

Gillespie, M. 1996. *Learning to Work in a New Land: A Review and Sourcebook for Vocational and Workplace ESL.* Washington, D.C.: Center for Applied Linguistics. This text examines the role of immigrants in the workforce, the status of English language learning in vocational and workforce education, and the ways the educational and governmental systems can enhance opportunities and productivity for the English language learner.

Grognet, A. 1997. *Integrating Employment Skills into Adult ESL Education.* (A project in adult immigrant education, PAIE). Washington, D.C.: National Clearinghouse for ESL Literacy Education. [Sponsoring agency: Office of Educational Research and Improvement, Washington, D.C.] (ERIC PRODUCT, 071). This question and answer text discusses how employment preparation can be integrated into an English as a Second Language curriculum, whether in a workplace or general ESL program.

Johns, A. M., and T. Dudley-Evans. 1991. English for specific purposes: International in scope, specific in purpose. *TESOL Quarterly*, 26(2): 297–314. Commissioned for TESOL's twenty-fifth anniversary, this article provides a short overview of the ESP movement and its history.

ENDNOTES

[1] "General English" is enclosed by quotes throughout this chapter because the authors do not believe that such a language exists. All language and language classes are specific to the learner, the context, and the content.

[2] The authors would like to thank Gretchen Bitterlin, ESL Resource Teacher, San Diego Community College District; and Brigitte Marshall, Educational Programs Consultant, Adult Education Office, California Department of Education, for their assistance in the VESL discussions found in this chapter.

[3] As Title II of the Workforce Investment Act (WIA).

[4] Secretary of Labor's Commission on Achieving Necessary Skills.

[5] The authors are indebted to Mohamed Daoud, one of Tunisia's foremost ESP experts, for this anecdote.

[6] Now called *English for Specific Purposes: An International Journal.*

Syllabus Design

DAVID NUNAN

In "Syllabus Design," Nunan describes and evaluates a range of syllabus types including grammatical, notional-functional, content-based, task-based, and integrated. he also sets out and illustrates key procedures for developing syllabuses. These include needs analysis, goal and objective setting, and the development of competencies.

OVERVIEW

In order to define syllabus design, we need to start with the broader field of curriculum development. *Curriculum* is a large messy concept which can be looked at in a number of ways. A very broad definition is that it includes all of the planned learning experiences of an educational system. The field of curriculum development was first systematized by Tyler in 1949, who articulated four fundamental questions that must be answered by any curriculum developer:

1. What educational purposes should a school seek to attain?
2. What educational experiences can be provided that are likely to attain those purposes?
3. How can the educational experiences be effectively organized?
4. How can we determine whether these purposes have been attained?

In the context of language teaching, the first two questions have to do with syllabus design, the third with language teaching methodology, and the fourth with assessment and evaluation. Syllabus design, then, is the selection, sequencing, and justification of the content of the curriculum. In language teaching, content selection will include selecting linguistic features such as items of grammar, pronunciation, and vocabulary as well as experiential content such as topics and themes. This selection process is guided by needs analyses of various kinds. Needs analysis provides the designer with a basis both for content specification and for the setting of goals and objectives.

In 1976, David Wilkins published an influential book called *Notional Syllabuses,* in which he argued that the point of departure for syllabus design should not be lists of linguistic items, but a specification of the concepts that learners wish to express (notions such as time and space), and the things that learners want to do with language (functions such as complimenting or apologizing). More recently, there have been calls for the adoption of a process approach, in which the point of departure is not lists of linguistic or notional-functional content, but a specification of communicative and learning processes. This has resulted in proposals for task-based syllabuses. Another significant trend, particularly in second as opposed to foreign language contexts, has been the emergence of content-based syllabuses. Most recently, an integrated approach has been called for. In such an approach, all or most of the elements and processes described above are incorporated into the syllabus.

In this chapter, I will elaborate on the concepts and processes described in the preceding paragraph. Where appropriate, the concepts will be illustrated with extracts from syllabuses of different kinds.

Grammatical Syllabuses

Traditionally, the point of departure for designing a language syllabus has been to select and sequence lists of grammatical items, and then integrate these with lists of vocabulary items. Lists of phonological items have sometimes been thrown in for good measure.

Grammatical syllabuses are still very popular today, although they were at their most popular through the 1960s, when virtually all syllabuses were crafted in grammatical terms. The assumption underlying these syllabuses is that language consists of a finite set of rules which can be combined in various ways to make meaning. The task for the language learner is to master each rule in the order presented by the syllabus before moving on to the next. The whole purpose of the grammatical syllabus was to control input to the learner so that only one item was presented at a time. This created a dilemma, which became more and more pressing with the advent of Communicative Language Teaching: How could one control input at the same time as one is providing learners with exposure to the kinds of language they would encounter outside the classroom?

This problem can be addressed in a number of ways. One solution is to abandon any attempt at structural grading. Another is to use the list of graded structures, not to determine the language to which learners are exposed, but to determine the items that will be the pedagogic focus in class. In other words, learners are exposed to naturalistic samples of text which are only roughly graded, and which provide a richer context, but they are only expected formally to master those items which have been isolated, graded, and set out in the syllabus (Nunan 1988a, p. 30).

During the 1970s, the grammatical syllabus came under attack on two fronts. In the first place, the linear sequencing entailed in grammatical syllabuses did not represent the complexity of language. Secondly, evidence from the field of second language acquisition showed that learners did not necessarily acquire language in the order specified by the grammatical syllabus. For example, Dulay and Burt (1973) and Bailey, Madden, and Krashen (1974) showed that certain grammatical items appeared to be acquired in a predetermined order, and that this order appeared to be impervious to formal instruction. This led Krashen (1981, 1982) to argue that we should abandon grammatically structured syllabuses completely in favor of a "natural approach" to language learning. In the natural approach, grammatical grading is eschewed,

replaced by communicative activities that promote subconscious acquisition following the "natural" order rather than conscious learning based on classroom instruction.

An alternative explanation for the lack of congruence between the input provided by grammatical syllabuses and the language actually used by learners at different stages of development has been provided by Pienemann and Johnston (1987). These researchers argue that the order in which learners acquire a particular item will be determined, not by the grammatical complexity of the item, but by its speech processing complexity. Their hypothesis predicts that the third person singular verb inflection (present tense) s, which is grammatically simple but complex in terms of speech processing, will be acquired relatively late in the language acquisition process, and this is indeed what we find. Third person s is one of the first grammatical morphemes to be taught, but for many learners it is one of the last items to be acquired. In fact, some learners never acquire it.

The speech processing theory predicts that the following items will be acquired in the order below, and that this is therefore the order in which they should be introduced in the syllabus:

What's the time?/What's your name?
How do you spell X?/Are you tired?
Where are you from?/Do you like X?

Pienemann and Johnston (1987) argued that the structural syllabus should be retained. However, the ordering of items in the syllabus should follow a very different sequence—that established by their research as being "learnable." Thus, wh-questions with do would not be taught until learners had mastered wh-questions with be.

The problem with this proposal, particularly in light of Communicative Language Teaching, is that many of the items that are required for communication are "late acquired"—for example, wh-questions with do. Teachers working with such a syllabus would be able to use few communicative tasks in the early stages of learning. Critics of the Pienemann and Johnston proposal have argued that "unlearnable" structures can be introduced, but they should be presented as holistic formulae. In other words, learners would be taught question forms such as *What do you do?* and *Where does she live?* as single "chunks" for use in communicative tasks such as role plays, information gaps, and so on. They would not be expected to break these down into their constituent parts immediately; this would happen gradually over time. In fact, some second language acquisition researchers argue that this process of learning strings of language as unanalyzed chunks and then later breaking them down is a key psycholinguistic mechanism in the acquisition process (Ellis 1994).

THE "ORGANIC" APPROACH TO GRAMMAR

Underlying the traditional linear syllabus is the notion that learning is a process of mastering each item perfectly one at a time. In fact, when the structural syllabus was at its height of popularity, mastery learning was an important movement within educational psychology. In metaphorical terms, it was believed that a language develops in the same way as a building is constructed—one (linguistic) brick at a time.

However, the complexity of the acquisition process revealed by a growing body of second language acquisition (SLA) research led some syllabus designers to argue that language development is basically an organic process. According to this metaphor, a new language develops in a way that is more akin to plants growing in a garden rather than a building being constructed. Learners do not acquire each item perfectly, one at a time, but numerous items imperfectly, all at once.

NEEDS ANALYSIS

With the advent of Communicative Language Teaching (CLT) in the 1970s, a very different approach to syllabus design was proposed by a number of linguists. This approach began, not with lists of grammatical, phonological, and lexical features, but with an analysis of the communicative needs of the learner. A set of techniques and procedures, known as needs analysis, was developed to assist designers adopting such an approach. While needs analysis was a crucial tool for those working in the areas of English for Specific Purposes (ESP) and English for Academic Purposes (EAP), it was also widely used in General English syllabus design.

The appearance of needs analysis in language education (it had existed in other areas of educational planning for many years) was thus stimulated by the development of Communicative Language Teaching (CLT). Proponents of CLT argued that it was neither necessary nor possible to include every aspect of the target language in the syllabus. Rather, syllabus content should reflect the communicative purposes and needs of the learners. Language-for-tourism syllabuses will contain different content from syllabuses designed for teaching academic English. (See Johns and Price-Machado's chapter in this volume).

Needs analysis includes a wide variety of techniques for collecting and analyzing information, both about learners and about language. The kinds of information that syllabus designers collect include biographical information such as age, first language background, reasons for learning the language, other languages spoken, time available for learning, and so on. The most sophisticated instrument for doing a needs analysis was developed by Munby (1978). Called the *communicative needs processor*, it involved specifying the following:

- participant (biographical data about the learner);
- purposive domain (the purposes for which the language is required);
- setting (the environments in which the language will be used);
- interaction (the people that the learner will be communicating with);
- instrumentality (the medium: spoken versus written; the mode: monologue or dialogue, face-to-face or indirect);
- dialect;
- target level (degree of mastery required);
- communicative event (productive and receptive skills neded);
- communicative key (interpersonal attitudes and tones required).

Brindley (1984, 1990) draws a distinction between "objective" needs and "subjective" needs:

> Objective needs are those which can be diagnosed by teachers on the basis of the analysis of personal data about learners along with information about their language proficiency and patterns of language use. . . . whereas the "subjective" needs (which are often "wants," "desires," "expectations" or other psychological manifestations) cannot be diagnosed as easily, or, in many cases, even stated by learners themselves (Brindley 1984, p. 31).

Objective needs analyses result in content derived from an analysis of the target communicative situations in which learners will engage, as well as an analysis of the kinds of spoken and written discourse they will need to comprehend and produce. Such analyses were fundamental to the development of an important and enduring movement within language teaching—that of language for specific purposes.

Needs-based course design, particularly when it results in tightly specified learning outcomes, has been heavily criticized. Widdowson (1983), for example, claims that such courses are exercises in training rather than in education because learners can only do those things for which they have been specifically prepared. He argues that learners should be to able to do things for which they have not been specifically prepared. However, the extent to which learners are able to transfer learning from one context to another is basically a methodological issue rather than a syllabus design issue. Syllabus designers can facilitate learning transfer by building into the syllabus opportunities for recycling.

Another criticism of needs-based course design is that, while it might be relevant in second language contexts, it is often irrelevant in foreign language contexts, where learners have no immediate, or even foreseeable, need to communicate orally. In such contexts, subjective needs, relating to such things as learning strategy preferences, may be more relevant than objective needs.

Goal and Objective Setting

Needs analysis provides a basis for specifying goals and objectives for a learning program. Goals are broad, general purposes for learning a language. At the broadest level, Halliday (1985) argues that individuals use language

- to obtain goods and services,
- to socialize with others, and
- for entertainment and enjoyment.

These very broad goals can be elaborated and refined, as the following goal statements illustrate:

Instruction should enable learners to

1. participate in conversation related to the pursuit of common activities with others;
2. obtain goods and services through conversation or correspondence;
3. establish and maintain relationships through exchanging information, ideas, opinions, attitudes, feelings, experiences and plans;
4. make social arrangements, solve problems, and come to conclusions together;
5. discuss topics of interest;
6. search for specific information for a given purpose, process it, and use it in some way;
7. listen to or read information, process it, and use it in some way;
8. give information in spoken or written form on the basis of personal experience;
9. listen to or read, and/or view a story, poem, play, feature, etc., and respond to it personally in some way (Clark 1987, p. 186).

Having established the goals of a learning program, the syllabus designer articulates a set of objectives designed to realize the goals. Objectives are therefore much more specific than goals, and numerous objectives will be specified for any given goal. Formal performance objectives have three elements: a "task" or performance element, a standards element, and a conditions element. The task element specifies what the learner is to do, the standards element sets out how well the performer is to carry out the task, and the conditions element establishes the circumstances under which he or she is to perform.

The following examples illustrate just how specific performance objectives are:

1. In a classroom role play (condition), students will exchange personal information (performance). Three pieces of information will be exchanged (standard).

2. When listening to a taped weather forecast (condition), students will extract information on minimum and maximum temperatures and other relevant information such as the likelihood of rain (performance). All key information will be extracted (standard.)

In the field of general education, the objectives approach has been criticized over the years. One criticism that is relevant to language education is that truly valuable learning outcomes cannot be accurately specified in advance. (This belief is captured by the aphorism, "Education is what's left when everything that has been taught has been forgotten.") In language teaching, our aim is to help learners develop the ability to communicate meanings, attitudes, and feelings that can only be prespecified in a very general sense. Proficiency requires creativity, and proficient language users know multiple ways of achieving communicative ends through language. Identifying objectives a priori may therefore be problematic. Another criticism is that the prespecification of precise and detailed objectives prevents the teacher from taking advantage of instructional opportunities occurring unexpectedly in the classroom.

COMPETENCE-BASED LANGUAGE TEACHING (CBLT)

According to Richards (in press), competency-based training developed as an alternative to the use of objectives in program planning, although there are many similarities between the two approaches. As with the objectives movement, CBLT focuses on what learners should be able to do at the end of a course of instruction. As with objectives, competencies are concerned with the attainment of specified standards rather than with an individual's achievement in relation to a group. They are therefore criterion- rather than norm-referenced and this is the major difference between the two approaches.

Example of a competency statement:

The learner can negotiate complex/problematic spoken exchanges for personal business and community purposes. He or she

- Achieves purpose of exchange and provides all essential information accurately
- Uses appropriate staging, for example, opening and closing strategies
- Provides and requests information as required
- Explains circumstances, causes, consequences, and proposes solutions as required
- Sustains dialogue, for example, using feedback, turn taking
- Uses grammatical forms and vocabulary appropriate to topic and register; grammatical errors do not interfere with meaning
- Speaks with pronunciation/stress/intonation that does not impede intelligibility
- Is able to interpret gestures and other paralinguistic features (Adult Migrant Education Service 1993).

The competency-based approach has had a major influence on syllabuses in particular sectors of the educational systems in most English-speaking countries, including Australia, New Zealand, the United Kingdom, and the United States.

CBLT first emerged in the United States in the 1970s and was widely adopted in vocationally oriented education and in adult ESL programs. By the end of the 1980s, CBLT had come to be accepted as the "state-of-the-art" approach to ESL by national policymakers and leaders in curriculum development (Auerbach 1986).

If we look at the sample competency statement provided above, we will see that it has several points of similarity with the objectives described in a previous section. It contains a "task" statement and a number of "how well" or standards statements ("achieves purpose of exchange," "provides all essential information accurately," "uses appropriate staging," "errors do not interfere with meaning," "pronunciation does not impede intelligibility").

THE STANDARDS MOVEMENT

The most recent manifestation of performance-based approaches to syllabus design, in the United States at least, is the standards movement. Throughout the 1990s, there was a concerted push for national education standards. This push was seen at all levels of government, and it resulted in legislation mandating the development and implementation of standards. For example, the Adult Education Act and the National Literacy Act of 1991 require adult basic education programs in all states to develop indicators of program quality and to attach performance standards to these quality indicators (see website at the end of chapter).

In many ways, just as the competency movement was a repackaging of concepts from the objectives movement, the same is true of the standards movement. "Objectives/competencies" are redefined as standards, which can also be used in work done in other areas such as math and language arts. For example, the National Council of Teachers of English (NCTE 1997) standards document for English language arts states, "By content standards, we mean statements that define what students should know and be able to do" (p.1–2).

In ESL, the TESOL organization has commissioned several sets of standards in areas such as pre-K–12, adult education, and workplace education. The most fully developed of these are the pre-K–12 standards (Short et al. 1997). These are framed around three goals and nine standards. The standards are fleshed out in terms of descriptors, progress indicators, and classroom vignettes. The nine content standards "indicate more specifically [than the goals] what students should know and be able to do as a result of instruction" (p.15). Descriptors are "broad categories of discrete, representative behavior" (p.15). Progress indicators "list assessable, observable activities that students may perform to show progress towards meeting designated standards. These progress indicators represent a variety of instructional techniques that may be used by teachers to determine how well students are doing" (p.16).

The following example from the *ESL Standards* illustrates the different components of the standard. It is written for grades pre-K–3.

Goal:
- To use English to communicate in social settings

Standard:
- Students will use English to participate in social interactions

Descriptors:
- Sharing and requesting information
- Expressing needs, feelings, and ideas
- Using nonverbal communication in social interactions
- Getting personal needs met
- Engaging in conversations
- Conducting transactions

Sample Progress Indicators:
- Engage listener's attention verbally or nonverbally
- Volunteer information and respond to requests about self and family
- Elicit information and ask clarification questions
- Clarify and restate information as needed
- Describe feelings and emotions after watching a movie
- Indicate interests, opinions, or preferences related to class projects
- Give and ask for permission
- Offer and respond to greetings, compliments, invitations, introductions, and farewells
- Negotiate solutions to problems, interpersonal misunderstandings, and disputes
- Read and write invitations and thank you letters
- Use the telephone

(Short et al. 1997, p. 31)

Unit I Teaching Methodology

NOTIONAL-FUNCTIONAL SYLLABUSES

The broader view of language as communication that emerged during the 1970s was taken up by syllabus designers. As indicated earlier, an important figure here was Wilkins (1976), who argued for syllabuses based on notions and functions. Notions are general conceptual meanings such as time, cause, and duration, while functions are the communicative purposes that are achieved through language such as apologizing, advising, and expressing preferences.

Like most syllabus proposals, notional-functionalism was not impervious to criticism. Early versions of notional-functional syllabuses ended up not being so very different from the grammatical syllabuses that they replaced. Instead of units entitled "simple past," we find units entitled "talking about the weekend." Widdowson (1983) also pointed out that simply replacing lists of grammatical items with lists of notional-functional ones neither represented the nature of language as communication nor reflected the way languages were learned any more than grammatical syllabuses did.

When syllabus designers began turning away from grammatical criteria as the point of departure in designing their syllabuses, selection and grading became much more problematic. As soon as one looks beyond linguistic notions of simplicity and difficulty, the number of criteria begins to multiply. These criteria include situational, contextual, and extralinguistic factors. There are no objective means for deciding that one functional item is more complex than another. In addition, most functions can be expressed in many different ways and at many different levels of complexity. Apologizing, for example, can range from *Sorry* to *I really must apologize—I do hope you can forgive me.*

The relative arbitrariness of selecting and sequencing can be seen in the following list of functional components from a well-known EFL course:

1. Ask and give names; say hello; ask and tell where people are from
2. Say hello formally and informally; ask about and give personal information
3. Describe people; tell the time
4. Describe places; give compliments; express uncertainty; confirm/correct information
5. Describe houses and apartments; make and answer telephone calls
6. Express likes and dislikes; ask about and describe habits and routines
7. Ask and tell about quantity
8. Ask for and give directions; ask for and tell about physical and emotional states
9. Talk about frequency; express degrees of certainty
10. Describe people's appearances; write simple letters; give compliments

(Swan and Walter 1984)

CONTENT-BASED SYLLABUSES

Content-based instruction (CBI) comes in many different guises (see Snow's chapter in this volume). However, all variants share one characteristic—language is not presented directly, but is introduced via the content of other subjects. In school settings, this content is typically the regular subjects in the curriculum such as science, geography, and mathematics. Learners acquire the target language in the course of doing other things. The approach draws strongly on the experiential view of learning, that is, that active engagement in communicating in the language is the most effective means of acquiring it.

As we saw at the beginning of this chapter, the three core tasks for the syllabus designer are selecting, sequencing, and justifying content. In CBI, the justification comes from the content area itself. For example, if the content area is general science, the topic of photosynthesis would be introduced on the grounds that it is a core topic in the field.

A recent book on content-based instruction presents teaching suggestions in the following categories:

- *Information management:* Here learners sift data into different categories, or are given categories and are required to find examples to fit these categories.

- *Critical thinking:* Learners go beyond classifying to evaluate or analyze data, for example, by determining a point of view or arguing from a given stance.
- *Hands-on activities:* These involve manipulating data through games, experiments, and other experiential activities.
- *Data gathering:* These tasks involve learners in scanning for specific information and/or collecting and assembling facts, data, and references.
- *Analysis and construction:* This final category involves "(a) breaking a text into its component parts, elucidating its rhetorical pattern, and examining text flow (cohesion and coherence) or (b) applying knowledge of oral and written discourse conventions to create a specifically patterned text with the goal of increasing fluency, accuracy, or both" (Master and Brinton 1997, p. vi).

TASK-BASED SYLLABUSES

Task-based syllabuses represent a particular realization of Communicative Language Teaching (Nunan 1989, see also Crookes and Chaudron's chapter in this volume). Instead of beginning the design process with lists of grammatical, functional-notional, and other items, the designer conducts a needs analysis, which yields a list of the communicative tasks that the learners for whom the syllabus is intended will need to carry out. In syllabus design, a basic distinction is drawn between target tasks and pedagogical tasks. A target task is something that the learner might conceivably do outside of the classroom. Examples of target tasks include

- Taking part in a job interview
- Completing a credit card application
- Finding one's way from a hotel to a subway station
- Checking into a hotel

Pedagogical tasks are unlikely to be deployed outside the classroom. They are created in order to "push" learners into communicating with each other in the target language, on the assumption that this communicative interaction will fuel the acquisition process.

The following is a fairly common example of a pedagogical task:

> In pairs, students complete an information gap task to get instructions on how to get from one's hotel to the nearest subway station. Student A has a map of the town center with the hotel marked. Student B has the same map with the subway marked.

Having specified target and pedagogical tasks, the syllabus designer analyzes them in order to identify the knowledge and skills that the learner must have in order to carry out the tasks. The next step is to sequence and integrate the tasks with enabling exercises designed to develop the requisite knowledge and skills. One key distinction between an exercise and a task is that exercises will have purely language-related outcomes, while tasks will have nonlanguage-related outcomes, as well as language-related ones.

Examples of exercises:

- Read the following passage, from which all prepositions have been deleted, and reinstate the correct prepositions from the list provided.
- Listen to the dialogue and answer the following true/false questions.
- Rearrange these questions and answers to form a conversation, and practice the conversation.

Example of a task:

- Listen to the weather forecast and decide what to wear. (Such a target task might be carried out in the classroom by having students circle pictures of clothing and accessories such as jackets, shorts, umbrellas, and sunglasses.)

TYPES OF TASKS

Another way of distinguishing between tasks is to divide them into *reproductive* and *creative* tasks. A reproductive task is one in which the learner is reproducing language following a model provided by the teacher, textbook, tape, or other source. A task is reproductive if the language that the learner is to use is largely predetermined and predictable. This does not mean that such tasks are necessarily noncommunicative. Many communicative tasks, such as the following, are of this type.

Class survey. Find someone who likes/ doesn't like the following:

	likes	doesn't like
Eating chilis	_____	_____
Playing tennis	_____	_____
Watching sci-fi movies	_____	_____
Doing homework	_____	_____

This task is reproductive because we know that if the students are doing it right, they will be saying, "Do you like eating chilis?" "Do you like playing tennis?" etc. It is communicative in that the person asking the question does not know whether the classmate's answer will be *yes* or *no*.

Creative language tasks, on the other hand, are less predictable. Learners must assemble the words and structures they have acquired in new and unpredictable ways. Here is an example of a creative task.

Pair work. Who is the best person for the job?

Read the following résumés, and decide who the best person is for the following jobs:

- ■ School building supervisor
- ■ Receptionist
- ■ Librarian
- ■ Bookstore clerk

In this task, the language used by the students is much less predictable. If we were to eavesdrop on the task, we might predict that we would hear utterances such as:

> "I think . . . "
> "We should . . . "
> "This person might . . . "

However, there is no way of predicting precisely the language that will be used.

AN INTEGRATED APPROACH TO SYLLABUS DESIGN

In this chapter, I have outlined the major trends and developments in syllabus design over the last twenty years. In my own work, I have tried to embrace an integrated approach to syllabus design in which all of the elements and options discussed above are brought together into a single design. The following example illustrates one way in which this might be done.

1. Identify the general contexts and situations in which the learners will communicate.
2. Specify the communicative events that the learners will engage in.
3. Make a list of the functional goals that the learners will need in order to take part in the communicative events.
4. List the key linguistic elements that learners will need in order to achieve the functional goals.
5. Sequence and integrate the various skill elements identified in steps 3 and 4.

In developing integrated syllabuses, I find that cross-reference planning grids are very useful, because they enable me to map out and coordinate the different elements in the syllabus. Here is a cross-reference grid integrating functions and structures for the first few units in a syllabus underpinning a textbook series for younger learners. Not only does the grid help guide me in selecting which items to teach when, it also shows me where and when recycling is necessary. I can also see if there are gaps in the syllabus.

CONCLUSION

In this chapter, I have provided an introduction to the field of syllabus design. I suggest that syllabus design is that part of curriculum development which is concerned with selecting, grading, integrating, and justifying the content of the curriculum. Different types of syllabuses, from grammatical to task-based, are introduced, described, and critiqued. The key theoretical and empirical

	Structures					
Functions ↓	Simple present tense + *be*	What questions	Demonstratives: *this, that*	Where questions	Prepositions: *on, in, under*	Simple present tense + *have*
Introduce yourself	✗	✗				
Identify ownership		✗	✗			
Introduce people			✗			
Talk about where things are				✗	✗	
Talk about likes and dislikes	✗					✗

(*Source:* Nunan 1999a)

influences on the field are also introduced. In the last part of the chapter, I argue for an integrated syllabus which draws on and incorporates all of the key experiential and linguistic elements discussed in the body of this chapter.

DISCUSSION QUESTIONS

1. What do you see as the role of the classroom teacher in syllabus design?
2. What do you see as the advantages and disadvantages of an objectives-based syllabus?
3. What do you think that content-based and task-based syllabuses might have in common? How might they differ?
4. If you were asked to design a syllabus for a new ESL or EFL course, what are some of the first things you would do as preparation?

SUGGESTED ACTIVITIES

1. Look at the "Course Overview" in Appendix B of Jensen's chapter on lesson planning in this volume. Is this a syllabus? Explain your answer.
2. Design a needs analysis questionnaire for a specified group of learners.
3. Compare the selection and sequencing of functional and grammatical components in several general ESL/EFL textbooks. What similarities and differences are there? Is there a "common core" of elements across the textbooks?
4. Identify a target group of learners and carry out the five planning tasks suggested in the section on the integrated syllabus on page 64. Develop a cross-reference grid similar to the one set out in the chapter.
5. Design four three-part performance objectives for the group of learners in Activity 4 above.

FURTHER READING

Dubin, F., and E. Olshtain. 1986. *Course Design*. Cambridge: Cambridge University Press.

This book is designed for teachers who have the planning and development of courses as part of their duties. It covers what the authors call the "fact-finding" stage—establishing realistic goals, surveying existing programs, realizing goals through instructional plans, selecting the shape of the syllabus—and the considerations involved in constructing communicative syllabuses.

Brown, J. D. 1995. *The Elements of Language Curriculum*. Boston, MA: Heinle & Heinle.

Although it is a book on curriculum, and therefore deals with issues that go beyond syllabus design, it also provides an accessible introduction to syllabus design issues.

Graves, K., ed. 1996. *Teachers as Course Developers*. Cambridge: Cambridge University Press.

This book contains six interesting case studies of teachers as course developers and syllabus designers. The narratives of these teachers, who work in very different contexts worldwide, illustrate the process of course development from the perspective of the teacher.

Nunan, D. 1988a. *Syllabus Design*. Oxford: Oxford University Press.

This book explores the principles involved in selecting, grading, and integrating the various components of a language syllabus and demonstrates how teachers can go about analyzing the syllabuses in use in their own classrooms. It offers analytical tools and techniques for evaluating, modifying, and adapting syllabuses.

WEBSITES

Both the U.S. National Literacy Act of 1991 and the U.S. Adult Education Act of 1991, along with related policy resources, are available on-line at

www.nifl.gov/lincs/collections/policy/resource. html

UNIT II A

Language Skills

Listening

Until quite recently, listening comprehension had been neglected with regard to both its place in second or foreign language teaching methodology and the development of techniques and materials for use in the classroom. As Morley's chapter points out, listening comprehension is now felt to be a prerequisite for oral proficiency as well as an important skill in its own right. She offers guidelines for developing activities and materials, including the development of a self-access, self-study listening program. In Peterson's chapter, the acquisition of listening skills in a second or foreign language is explained with reference to a cognitive processing model. She presents a taxonomy of exercises and activities, showing how at each stage of learning, students can be assisted in developing bottom-up and top-down listening strategies and skills.

Aural Comprehension Instruction: Principles and Practices

JOAN MORLEY

In "Aural Comprehension Instruction: Principles and Practices," Morley first traces the changing patterns of second language listening instruction, outlines four generic instructional models, and discusses some of the psycho-social dimensions of listening. She then goes on to present suggestions for developing activities and materials for coursework, including detailed guidelines for developing a self-access self-study listening program.

INTRODUCTION

During the past thirty years, theory and practice in language learning and language teaching have changed in some fundamental ways. In retrospect, the four themes that dominated the Second AILA (International Association of Applied linguistics) Conference in 1969 (Cambridge, England) seem to have been prophetic in pointing the way toward trends in second/foreign language (S/FL) education during the last quarter of the twentieth century. They heralded new views on the importance of

1. individual learners and the individuality of learning;
2. listening and reading as nonpassive and very complex receptive processes;
3. listening comprehension's being recognized as a fundamental skill;
4. real language used for real communication as a viable classroom model.

Every facet of language study has been influenced by these trends, but none more dramatically than listening comprehension. In the 1970s, the status of listening began to change from one of neglect to one of increasing importance. Instructional programs expanded their focus on pragmatic skills to include listening as well as reading, writing, and speaking. During the 1980s special attention to listening was incorporated into new instructional frameworks. Prominent among these were formats that featured functional language and communicative approaches. Throughout the 1990s, attention to listening in language instruction increased dramatically. Aural comprehension in S/FL acquisition became an important area of study.

Although aural comprehension is now well recognized as an important facet of language learning, much work remains to be done in both theory and practice. Unfortunately, as Brown (1987) observed, a significant number of published courses on listening comprehension and classroom practices in many schools in many countries continues to demonstrate that listening is still regarded as the least important skill.

The first three parts of this chapter discuss general aspects of listening and language learning. (See Peterson's chapter in this volume for additional information.) The last three sections outline principles and guidelines for developing and/or adapting listening comprehension activities and materials. Lesson suggestions are given for class, small-group, and pair work and for individualized self-study using equipment in the classroom, at home, or in a language laboratory setting.

TRACING THE HISTORY: LISTENING AND LANGUAGE LEARNING

Today the centrality of listening in language learning is well established. An appropriate aural comprehension program that targets learner listening at all levels of instruction is an essential for second language competence. Aural comprehension establishes a base for the development of oral language within the "speech chain" of listening and speaking (Denes and Pinson 1963, p. 1). It is important to note that multiple benefits accrue to the learner beyond the obvious improvements in listening skills. In particular, listening comprehension lessons are a vehicle for teaching elements of grammatical structure and allow new vocabulary items to be contextualized within a body of communicative discourse.

Making the Case: The Importance of Listening in Language Learning

It has taken many years to bring the language teaching profession around to realizing the importance of listening in second and foreign language learning. As observed by Rivers, long an advocate for listening comprehension, "Speaking does not of itself constitute communication unless what is said is comprehended by another person. . . . Teaching the comprehension of spoken speech is therefore of primary importance if the communication aim is to be reached" (1966, pp. 196, 204). The reasons for the nearly total neglect of listening are difficult to assess, but as Morley notes, "Perhaps an assumption that listening is a reflex, a little like breathing—listening seldom receives overt teaching attention in one's native language—has masked the importance and complexity of listening with understanding in a non-native language" (1972, p. vii).

In reality, listening is used far more than any other single language skill in normal daily life. On average, we can expect to listen twice as much as we speak, four times more than we read, and five times more than we write (Rivers 1981; Weaver 1972).

Emerging Recognition of the Importance of Listening in Second/Foreign Language Study

It is easy for us to take listening for granted, often with little conscious awareness of our performance as listeners. Weaver commented on the elusiveness of our listening awareness: "After all, listening is neither so dramatic nor so noisy as talking. The talker is the center of attention for all listeners. His behavior is overt and vocal, and he hears and notices his own behavior, whereas listening activity often seems like merely being—doing nothing" (1972, pp. 12–13).

Much of the language teaching field also has taken listening for granted until relatively recent times (but see Gouin 1880; Nida 1953; Palmer 1917; Sweet 1899). Modern-day arguments for listening comprehension began to be voiced in the mid-1960s and early 1970s by Rivers (1966) and others. Newmark and Diller underscored "the need for the systematic development of listening comprehension *not only as a foundation for speaking, but also as a skill in its own right* . . ." (1964, p. 20). Belasco expressed his concerns as follows: "I was rudely jolted by the realization that it is possible to develop so-called 'speaking ability' and yet be so virtually incompetent in understanding the spoken language. . . . [Students] were learning to audio-comprehend certain specific dialogues and drills, but could not understand [the language] out of the mouths of native speakers" (1971, pp. 4–5). Morley decried the fact that "virtually no specialized textbook materials exist in the area of intermediate and advanced listening" (1972, p. vii), and Blair (1982) observed that special attention to listening just didn't "sell" until recent times.

Four Perspectives—Four Models of Listening and Language Instruction

In the English language teaching programs of the 1940s, 1950s, and 1960s, neither the British Situational Approach to language teaching nor the American Audiolingual Approach paid much attention to listening beyond its role in grammar and pronunciation drills and learners' imitation of dialogues. The language learning theories of those times attributed little importance to listening beyond the sound discrimination associated with pronunciation learning. Listening, along with reading, was regarded as a "passive" skill and was simply taken for granted.

However, slowly and steadily, more attention has been given to listening comprehension. Today, the role of listening and the purpose of listening comprehension instruction in the S/FL curriculum, can be one of four different perspectives. A generic instructional model for each perspective that reflects underlying beliefs about language learning theory and pedagogy is outlined below.

Model # 1 Listening and Repeating

Learner Goals To pattern-match; to listen and imitate; to memorize.

- *Instructional material:* Features audiolingual style exercises and/or dialogue memorization; based on a hearing-and-pattern-matching model.
- *Procedure:* Asks students to (a) listen to a word, phrase, or sentence pattern; (b) repeat it (imitate it); and (c) memorize it (often, but not always, a part of the procedure).
- *Value:* Enables students to do pattern drills, to repeat dialogues, and to use memorized prefabricated patterns in conversation; enables them to imitate pronunciation patterns. Higher level cognitive processing and use of propositional language structuring are not necessarily an intentional focus.

Model # 2 Listening and Answering Comprehension Questions

Learner Goals To process discrete-point information; to listen and answer comprehension questions.

- *Instructional material:* Features a student response pattern based on a listening-and-question-answering model with occasional innovative variations on this theme.

- *Procedure:* Asks students to (a) listen to an oral text along a continuum from sentence length to lecture length and (b) answer primarily factual questions. Utilizes familiar types of questions adapted from traditional reading comprehension exercises; has been called a *quiz-show* format of teaching.
- *Value:* Enables students to manipulate discrete pieces of information, hopefully with increasing speed and accuracy of recall. Can increase students' stock of vocabulary units and grammar constructions. Does not require students to make use of the information for any real communicative purpose beyond answering the questions; is not interactive two-way communication.

Model # 3 Task Listening

Learner Goals To process spoken discourse for functional purposes; to listen and do something with the information, that is, carry out real tasks using the information received.

- *Instructional material:* Features activities that require a student response pattern based on a listening-and-using (i.e., "Listen-and-Do") model. Students listen, then immediately do something with the information received: follow the directions given, complete a task, solve a problem, transmit the gist of the information orally or in writing, listen and take lecture notes, etc.
- *Procedure:* Asks students to (a) listen and process information and (b) use the orally transmitted language input immediately to complete a task which is mediated through language in a context in which success is judged in terms of whether the task is performed.
- *Value:* The focus is on instruction that is task-oriented, not question-oriented. The purpose is to engage learners in using the informational content presented in the spoken discourse, not just in answering questions about it. Two types of tasks are (a) language use tasks, designed to give students practice in listening to get meaning from the input with the express purpose of

making functional use of it immediately and (b) language analysis tasks, designed to help learners develop cognitive and metacognitive language learning strategies (i.e., to guide them toward personal intellectual involvement in their own learning). The latter features consciousness raising about language and language learning.

Model # 4 Interactive Listening

Learner Goals To develop aural/oral skills in semiformal interactive academic communication; to develop critical listening, critical thinking, and effective speaking abilities.

- *Instructional material:* Features the real-time/real-life give-and-take of academic communication. Provides a variety of student presentation and discussion activities, both individual and small-group panel reports, that include follow-up audience participation in question/answer sessions as an integral part of the work. Follows an interactive listening-thinking-speaking model with bidirectional (two-way) listening/speaking. Includes attention to group bonding and classroom discourse rules (e.g., taking the floor, yielding the floor, turn taking, interrupting, comprehension checks, topic shifting, agreeing, questioning, challenging, etc.). (See Morley 1992 and 1995.)
- *Procedure:* Asks students to participate in discussion activities that enable them to develop all three phases of the speech act: speech decoding, critical thinking, and speech encoding. These phases involve (a) continuous on-line decoding of spoken discourse, (b) simultaneous cognitive reacting/acting upon the information received (i.e., critical analysis and synthesis), and (c) instant-response encoding (i.e., producing personal propositional language responses appropriate to the situation).
- *Value:* The focus here is instruction that is communicative/competence-oriented as well as task oriented. Learners have opportunities to engage in and develop the complex array of communicative skills in the four

competency areas: linguistic competence, discourse competence, sociolinguistic competence, and strategic competence (Canale and Swain 1980).

SOME PSYCHOSOCIAL DIMENSIONS OF LANGUAGE AND THE LISTENING ACT

The Dynamic Process of Communicative Listening: Active, Not Passive

Listening, along with reading, has been labeled a "passive" skill. Nothing could be further from the truth. Anderson and Lynch (1988) reject a conceptualization of listening as a passive act, calling it a "listener-as-tape-recorder" explanation. They argue that such a perspective fails to account for the interpretations listeners make as they hear the spoken text according to their own purposes for listening and their own store of background knowledge.

Implications for Instruction One of the obvious implications for instruction is to bring students to an understanding that listening is not a passive skill, but an active receptive skill which needs special attention in language study. This goal can be accomplished gradually as a part of listening skill-building activities. Learners can be guided to realize that achieving skill in listening requires as much work as does becoming skilled in reading, writing, and speaking in a second language.

Listening in Three Modes: Bidirectional, Unidirectional, and Autodirectional

If we consider the roles we play in our listening interactions, we can identify three specific communicative listening modes: bidirectional, unidirectional, and autodirectional.

Bidirectional Listening Mode The obvious mode is two-way or *bidirectional* communicative listening. Here the reciprocal speech chain of speaker/listener is easily observed (Denes and Pinson 1963). Two (or more) participants take turns exchanging *speaker role* and *listener role* as they engage in face-to-face or telephone verbal interaction.

Unidirectional Listening Mode A second mode is one-way or *unidirectional* communicative listening. Auditory input surrounds us as we move through the day. The input comes from a variety of sources: overheard conversations, public address announcements, recorded messages (including those on telephone answering machines), the media (e.g., radio, television, films), instructional situations of all kinds, and public performances (e.g., lectures, religious services, plays, operas, musicals, concerts). As we hear speakers but are unable to interact, we often talk to ourselves in a reactive or self-dialogue manner as we analyze what we hear. We may subvocalize or even vocalize these responses.

Autodirectional Listening Mode The third communicative listening mode is *autodirectional.* We can think of this as *self-dialogue communication* in which we may not be aware of our *internal roles* as both speaker and listener/reactor *in our own thought processes.* Sometimes we re-create language internally and "listen again" as we retell and relive communicative interludes. Sometimes we simply attend to our own internal language which we produce as we think through alternatives, plan strategies, and make decisions—all by talking to ourselves and listening to ourselves.

In all of these communicative listening modes, notice that listening is *not* a passive experience. Each listening mode is a highly active, clearly participatory, verbal experience.

Implications for Instruction S/FL learners need to have instruction and practice in both the *bidirectional* communicative listening mode and in the *unidirectional* mode. In addition, *self-dialogue* in the *autodirectional* communicative listening mode *should not be ignored.* It is an important feature of language behavior which should be discussed with students. Autodirectional "talk" is something which learners should be led to develop as a skill in its own right, as well as a tool to be used in connection with bidirectional and unidirectional listening.

Psychosocial Functions of Listening: Transactional Listening and Interactional Listening

Brown and Yule (1983a) suggest dividing language functions into two major divisions: language for transactional purposes and language for interactional purposes. They note that transactional language corresponds to Halliday's notion of *ideational,* while interactional language corresponds to his term *interpersonal* (Halliday 1970, p. 143).

Transactional Language Function Transactional language is *message oriented* and can be viewed as "business-type" talk with the focus on content and conveying factual or propositional information. Transactional language is used for giving instructions, explaining, describing, giving directions, ordering, inquiring, requesting, relating, checking on the correctness of details, and verifying understanding. The premium is on message clarity and precision. Speakers often use confirmation checks to make sure what they are saying is clear; they may even contradict the listener if he or she appears to have misunderstood.

Interactional Language Function The most important difference between the two types of language use is that interactional language is "social-type" talk; it is *person oriented* more than message oriented. Its objective is the establishment and maintenance of cordial social relationships. Brown and Yule comment that a great deal of casual conversation contains phrases or echoes of phrases which appear to be intended more as contributions to a conversation than as instances of information giving. Important features of interactional language are those of identifying with the other person's concerns, being nice to the other person, and maintaining and respecting "face."

Implications for Instruction Teachers need to provide practice experiences in both transactional talk and interactional talk. While the contrast between the two types of talk is usually clear, sometimes it is not so obvious in an interaction where the two functions may be intertwined. Students need instruction and listening practice to help them recognize when one of the two functions is operating and how they can respond appropriately.

Psychological Processes: Bottom-Up and Top-Down Listening Schemata

In accounting for the complex nature of listening to understand spoken language, it is hypothesized that two different modes work together in a cooperative process. One is the externally based bottom-up mode while the other is the internally based top-down mode. (See Peterson's chapter in this volume for more information.)

Bottom-Up Processing The bottom-up mode of language processing involves the listener playing close attention to every detail of the language input. *Bottom-up* refers to that part of the aural comprehension process in which the understanding of the "heard" language is worked out proceeding from sounds to words to grammatical relationships to lexical meanings. That is, the meaning of the message is arrived at, bottom to top, based on the incoming language data.

Top-Down Processing On the other hand, the top-down facet of listening involves the listener's ability to bring prior information to bear on the task of understanding the "heard" language. This internal resource includes a bank of prior knowledge and global expectations about language and the world. It is used by the listener to make predictions about what the incoming message is expected to be at any point, and how the pieces fit into the whole. Chaudron and Richards (1986) note, "Top-down processing involves prediction and inferencing on the basis of hierarchies of facts, propositions, and expectations, and it enables the listener or the reader to bypass some aspects of bottom-up processing" (pp. 114-115).

Implications for Instruction Teachers need to provide students with practice in both kinds of language processing. Many published materials focus heavily on one or another of these processes, without necessarily labeling them as *top-down* or *bottom-up*.

Taking dual perspectives into account, Richards (1990) proposes a model of materials design for second or foreign language listening comprehension that combines language functions (interactional and transactional) and language processes (top-down and bottom-up). He observes that the extent to which one or the other process dominates is determined by (a) whether the purpose for listening is transactional or interactional, (b) what kind of background knowledge can be applied to the task, and (c) what degree of familiarity listeners have with the topic. He concludes:

> Too often, listening texts require students to adopt a single approach in listening, one which demands a detailed understanding of the content of a discourse and the recognition of every word and structure that occurs in a text. Students should not be required to respond to interactional discourse as if it were being used for a transactional purpose, nor should they be expected to use a bottom-up approach to an aural text if a top-down one is more appropriate (p. 83).

Richards's Functions/Processes Chart Richards combines the functions and the processes into the following very useful chart. It provides teachers with a way to construct a listening lesson which can be cross-classified according to the demands of both the listening *function* involved and the listening process which can be expected to be most prominently involved.

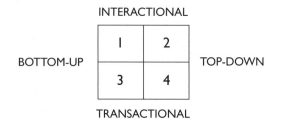

Richards gives an example for each of the four cells as follows.

In the bottom-up mode:

Cell #1: Listening closely to a joke (interactional) in order to know when to laugh.

Cell #3: Listening closely to instructions (transactional) during a first driving lesson.

In the top-down mode:

Cell #2: Listening casually to cocktail party talk (interactional).

Cell #4: Experienced air traveler listening casually to verbal air safety instructions (transactional) which have been heard many times before.

Other examples of transactional uses are instructions, descriptions, lectures, and news broadcasts. Other examples of interactional uses are greetings, small talk, jokes, and compliments. Richards notes that in many situations both interactional and transactional purposes are involved and suggests that effective classroom participation requires both.

1. Interactional—to interact with the teacher and other students while accomplishing class tasks (i.e., "classroom" talk).
2. Transactional—to assimilate new information, construct new concepts, and acquire new skills.

AFFECT AND ATTITUDES

In developing activities and materials for listening instruction, it is essential to consider the *affective domain,* which includes attitudes, emotions, and feelings. Here the focus is on (1) the ways attitudinal and emotional information may be conveyed, both *linguistically* and *nonlinguistically,* and (2) some of the attitudinal language functions that second language learners need to experience via instructional listening materials.

Linguistic and Nonlinguistic Cues to Affect

As the old saying goes, it's not *what* you say, it's *how* you say it! But how can ESL and EFL listeners learn to recognize and interpret aspects of the *how* as well as the *what* in two-way and one-way oral communication? How can they become skilled at processing both *nonlinguistic* and *linguistic* affective information?

In bidirectional interactive communication, messages are conveyed in at least three ways: *linguistic* (i.e., the words and their meanings), *paralinguistic* (i.e., vocal meaning) and *extralinguistic* (i.e. the meaning transmitted through various aspects of body language). In unidirectional communication, the visual cues of extralinguistic information may be missing, and the listener must then rely on only the linguistic and paralinguistic information

Linguistic Messages (the Words) Meanings begin in people. But sometimes meanings don't come across clearly, and we hear speakers protest, "But that's not what I *meant.*" In an attempt to convey an intended meaning, speakers choose words and arrange them into sentences or partial sentences, groups of sentences, and larger pieces of monologue or dialogue discourse.

Both the words chosen, and their intrasentential and intersentential arrangements, map *affect* (i.e., feelings) onto the linguistic information. As speakers do this, they may or may not be conscious of either the nature or the strength of the affective coloring; on the other hand, they may use it deliberately, with careful design.

Examples:

That was an (interesting/excellent/ good/fair/so-so/terrible) movie.

I like him a lot but . . .

Even though she's my best friend, I must tell you that . . .

Clearly, affective interpretation must be a part of listening comprehension activities. This means that instructional experiences must be contextualized and must reflect real-world situations and feelings.

Paralinguistic Messages (Vocally Transmitted Meaning) The very way the voice is used in speaking transmits meaning. That is, the way words, sentences, and groups of sentences in spoken language are programmed *vocally* enables them to carry information about how they are to be interpreted. Although the speaker may not be aware of it, the *speaker's attitude toward what he or she is saying* is transmitted by vocal features. In the important realm of intonation, the work by Brazil, Coulthard, and Johns (1980) and Brown, Currie, and Kenworthy (1980) has explored a variety of aspects of intonational meaning in oral discourse. The vocal elements that map affective information onto the linguistic message are those beyond the neutral patterns of basic stress, rhythm, and intonation. Nuances of meaning can be transmitted by subtle changes in tone quality, rate, rhythm, stress, and many other features.

Extralinguistic Messages (Meaning Transmitted through Body Language) Speakers also convey meaning through body language. That is, simultaneous physical messages are being transmitted with the words and vocal information and must be interpreted by the listener. Once again, the speaker may or may not be fully aware of this aspect of his or her communication. Elements involved include body postures, body movements, body and hand gestures, facial expressions, facial gestures, eye contact, and use of space by the communicators. It is important to help students learn the meanings of specific features of body language in the second language; they also need to recognize that body language differs greatly between languages and between cultures.

Intellectual, Emotional, and Moral Attitudes

As noted above, an important part of communication is the expression and comprehension of attitudes. Van Ek (1976) lists six basic language functions, including three which are attitudinal: intellectual, emotional, and moral attitudes.

Intellectual Attitudes These include expression and comprehension of agreement/disagreement; confirming/denying; accepting/declining; forgetting/remembering; possibility/impossibility; capability/incapability; uncertainty; obligation, permission; and more (pp. 45-47).

Emotional Attitudes Included in this area are expressing pleasure/displeasure; interest/lack of interest; surprise; hope; fear; worry; satisfaction/dissatisfaction; disappointment; preference; gratitude; sympathy; intention; wants and desires; and more (pp. 47–48).

Moral Attitudes Moral attitudes are expressed in the language of apologizing; expressing approval/disapproval; appreciation; indifference; regret; and more (p. 48). (For additional information see Munby 1978; Wilkins 1976).

DEVELOPING LISTENING COMPREHENSION ACTIVITIES AND MATERIALS

This second section focuses on instructional considerations, while keeping in mind the following three important points about listening as a language act.

1. Information Processing Listening comprehension is an act of information processing in which the listener is involved in *bidirectional* communication, or *unidirectional* communication, and/or *autodirectional* communication.

2. Linguistic Functions Broadly speaking, real-world spoken communication can be viewed as serving two linguistic functions: *interactional* and *transactional*.

3. Dimensions of Cognitive Processing The cognitive processing of spoken language appears to involve simultaneous activation of both *top-down* and *bottom-up* engagement in order for listeners to construct what they believe to be the intended meaning of the spoken message.

With these features of listening as a language act in mind, we begin with a discussion of three important principles of materials development. Next, we outline six kinds of communicative outcomes, with lesson suggestions for each. In the final section we present some suggestions for creating a self-access, self-study listening center. Central to the underlying belief system reflected in this chapter is a communicative language teaching perspective which values meaningful tasks and communicative activities. (See Savignon's chapter in this volume.)

Principles

In order to get learners' attention, to keep them actively and purposefully engaged in the task at hand, and to maximize the effectiveness of listening/language-learning experiences, three materials development principles are suggested: *relevance, transferability/applicability,* and *task orientation*. These three principles are important in making choices about both language content (i.e., the information presented) and *language outcome(s)* (i.e., the way the information is put to use).

1. Relevance

Both the listening lesson *content* (i.e., the information) and the *outcome* (i.e., the nature of the use of the information) need to be as relevant as possible to the learner. This is essential for getting and holding learner attention and provides a genuine motivational incentive. Lessons need to feature content and outcomes that have "face validity" for students. The more that lessons focus on things with real-life relevance, the more they appeal to students, and the better the chance of having learners' wanting to listen. And if students really want to listen, we have accomplished at least part of the task which Strevens (1988) calls *encouraging the intention to learn.*

Relevance is easy to control in self-created classroom listening activities. However, when using published materials, it is necessary to choose those lessons with topics that are relevant to one's students. It may be necessary to modify both the way the material is presented and the way students are asked to use the information. Richards suggests some ways to adapt materials, including modifying the objectives; adding prelistening activities; changing the teaching procedures for class presentation; and devising postlistening activities (1983, pp. 237–238).

2. Transferability/Applicability

Whatever is relevant is also likely to have potential for transferability. Insofar as possible, at either the *content* level or the *outcome* level, or both, listening lessons need to have transferability/applicability value, internally (i.e., can be used in other classes), externally (i.e., can be used in out-of-school situations), or both. In order to foster transfer of training, the best listening lessons present in-class activities that mirror real life. For example, the use of radio or television news broadcasts in adult classes can provide not only a real experience in listening comprehension, but such lessons also contain content that can be applicable outside of class as a source of conversation topics.

3. Task Orientation

In formal language classes for teenage and adult students and in language activity lessons for children, it is productive to combine two different kinds of focus: (1) language use tasks and (2) language analysis activities.

Notions of *task* have developed out of communicative teaching and materials production. Johnson defines task-oriented teaching as teaching which provides "actual meaning" by focusing on tasks to be mediated though language, and in which success is judged in terms of whether the tasks are performed (Brumfit and Johnson 1979, p. 200). Maley and Moulding focus on instruction which is *task-oriented* not *question-oriented*, providing learners with *tasks* which *use the information* in the aural text, rather than asking learners to "prove" their understanding of the text by answering questions (1979, p. 102). Candlin and Murphy note, "The central process we are concerned with is language learning, and tasks present this in the form of a problem-solving negotiation between knowledge that the learner holds and new knowledge. This activity is conducted through language in use, which may, itself, be seen as a negotiation of meaning" (1987, p. 1).

3a. Language Use Tasks The purpose here is to give students practice in listening for information and then immediately doing something with it. This kind of lesson features *specific* Listen-and-Do communicative outcomes such as these:

- Listening and performing actions (e.g., command games and songs such as "Do the Hokey Pokey," "May I?" "Simon Says").

- Listening and performing operations (e.g., listening and constructing a figure, drawing a map).

- Listening and solving problems (e.g., riddles, intellectual or logic puzzles, real-life numerical, spatial, or chronological problems).

- Listening and transcribing (e.g., taking telephone messages, writing notes).

- Listening and summarizing information (e.g., outlining, giving the gist of a message either verbally or in writing).

- Interactive listening and negotiating of meaning through questioning/answering routines (e.g., questions for repetition of information, questions for verification, questions for clarification, questions for elaboration).

These listening and language use tasks help students to build the following two things:

(i) A Base of Content Experiences This will help them to develop expectancies, increase their vocabulary, and build a repertoire of familiar top-down networks of background knowledge in the second language. This, in turn, increases predictive power for future communicative situations, including *schemata* (i.e., the larger-order mental frameworks of knowledge) and *scripts* (i.e., the situation-specific mental frameworks that allow us to predict actors, events, action sequences, and alternative outcomes). These include formulaic speech routines and assumed elements in the physical setting.

(ii) A Base of Operational Experiences This will help learners to acquire a repertoire of familiar information-handling operations in the second language that are applicable to future communicative encounters in that language.

3b. Language Analysis Tasks The purpose here is to give students opportunities to analyze selected aspects of both language structure (i.e., form) and language use (i.e., function) and to develop some personal strategies to facilitate

learning. (See Peterson's chapter in this volume.) The goal is consciousness raising about language, which can be accomplished through what Wendin and Rubin (1987) term *awareness-raising* tasks. Some language analysis tasks can be designed to help students become knowledgeable about how language works. Activities can focus on one or two points at a time and can include attention to a variety of features of grammar, pronunciation, vocabulary, and discourse as well as sociolinguistic and strategic features (Canale and Swain 1980). Specific activities can include:

- Analysis of some features of "fast speech"; tasks can help students learn to deal with the rapid patterns of contextualized speech.

- Analysis of phrasing and pause points; attention to the ways the grouping of words into functional units (ones that "follow" grammar) can be used to facilitate listening; "chunking" the input into units for interpretation.

- Analysis of both monologues and dialogue exchanges, with attention to discourse organizational structures.

- Describing and analyzing sociolinguistic dimensions, including participants and their roles and relationships, settings, purpose of the communicative episodes, and expected outcomes.

- Describing and analyzing communicative strategies used by speakers to deal with miscommunication, communication breakdowns, distractions, etc.

Recordings of real-life conversations, talks, and discussions can be used to introduce listening analysis tasks. (See Morley 1984 and 1985.) Lynch (1983), Ur (1984), Davis and Rinvolucri (1988), and Mendelsohn (1995) all give a variety of language analysis tasks.

Communicative Outcomes: An Organizing Framework

It is clear by now that a Listen-and-Do format—that is, information gathering and information using—is recommended for listening instructional activities in the ESL or EFL curriculum. Listening comprehension in today's language curriculum must go far beyond a 20-minute tape a day or a paragraph or two read aloud followed by a series of "test" questions about the factual content.

Listen-and-Do in the listening comprehension context implies an outcome "objective." The purpose of oral communication in the real world is to achieve a genuine outcome; it may be very simple (e.g., enjoying sociable conversation) or it may be very complex (e.g., understanding intricate instructions), but an outcome is achieved. This same attention to outcome must be a part of any listening comprehension activity planned for use in the second language learning context.

Minimum requirements for two-way oral communication are two active participants and an outcome. Participants alternate roles of speaker-sender and listener-receiver. One-way communication requires one active participant (a listener-receiver), one long-distance participant (a speaker-sender), either "live" or recorded, and an outcome.

What is an *outcome*? According to Sinclair (1984), an outcome is a realistic task that people can envision themselves doing and accomplishing something. An outcome is an essential component in both two-way and one-way communication listening comprehension activities.

Six broad categories of outcome are discussed below. Each, of course, can be subdivided into more narrowly focused specific outcomes, which can be modified to suit a given student group. Lesson outcomes can be graded toward gradual expansion of difficulty, complexity, and increasing performance expectations for students.

A lesson may contain more than one outcome, although too many outcomes for a given activity may be overwhelming. Any outcome can be used at any age, as long as it is a part of a task that is appropriate to the age, interests, and language proficiency level of the learners.

There is overlap between some outcome categories, and no attempt is made here to make them mutually exclusive. They are presented as an organizing framework for consideration by teachers in developing class or listening library materials.

Outcome 1. Listening and Performing Actions and Operations

This category includes responses to things such as directions, instructions, and descriptions in a variety of contexts. Examples include listening and

- Drawing a picture, figure, or design.
- Locating routes of specific points on a map.
- Selecting a picture of a person, place, or thing from description.
- Identifying a person, place, or thing from description.
- Performing hand or body movements as in songs and games such as "Simon Says" or "Do the Hokey Pokey."
- Operating a piece of equipment such as a camera, a recorder, a microwave oven, or a pencil sharpener.
- Carrying out steps in a process such as a math problem, a science experiment, or a cooking sequence.

Outcome 2. Listening and Transferring Information

Two kinds of information transfer are featured: *spoken-to-written* (i.e., hearing information and writing it) and *spoken-to-spoken* (i.e. hearing information and transmitting it in speech).

Spoken-to-written   The following are some activities for spoken-to-written practice.

- Listening and taking a message (in person or by telephone) by transcribing the entire message word for word if it is very short or by writing down a list of the important items if it is long; the purpose is to give another person a clear sense of the message.
- Listening and filling in blanks in a gapped story game in order to complete the story.
- Listening and completing a form or chart in order to use the information for a later purpose, such as making a decision or solving a problem.
- Listening and summarizing the gist of a short story, report, or talk in order to report it to a third person.

- Listening to a "how to" talk and writing an outline of the steps in the sequence (e.g., how to cook something, how to use a piece of equipment, how to play a game) in order to carry out the action.

- Listening to a talk or lecture and taking notes in order to use the information later for some a purpose.

A popular activity called *jigsaw listening* is suggested by Geddes and Sturtridge (1979). In one form of jigsaw listening, small groups of students listen to different parts of a set of information and write down the important points of their portions. Then they share their information with other groups so that a story or a sequence of actions can be completed, a problem solved, or a decision made.

Spoken-to-spoken Jigsaw listening also can be used with a spoken-to-spoken transfer of information. Other activities in this mode are the following:

- Listening to directions, then passing them along to a third person who must use the information to carry out a task.

- Listening to part of a story and repeating it to others.

(For examples see Davis and Rinvolucri 1988, pp. 29–30 and Morley 1984, pp. 68–69.)

Outcome 3. Listening and Solving Problems

Many kinds of activities for either groups or individuals can be developed in this category. One is games and puzzles:

- Word games in which the answers must be derived from verbal clues.

- Number games and "story" arithmetic problems.

- Asking questions in order to identify something, as in "Twenty Questions" or "Animal, Vegetable, or Mineral."

- Classroom versions of "Password," "Jeopardy," or "Twenty Questions" in which careful listening is critical to the successful completion of the game.

- Minute mysteries in which students, listening to the teacher or a tape, read a very short mystery story; this can be followed by small group work in which students formulate solutions.

- A jigsaw mystery in which each group listens to a tape which provides one of the clues. Groups then share information with everyone in order to solve the mystery.

More demanding varieties of problem solving are found in riddles, logic puzzles, and other intellectual problem-solving activities.

Real-world problems can include:

- Comparison shopping tasks using recorded conversations for practice (e.g., asking for prices from several rental car agencies, florist shops, or barber shops, then choosing the best bargain), followed by similar field trips.

- Short descriptions of court cases, with listeners asked to make a decision and defend it.

Field trips can be assigned in which pairs of students go out to do comparison shopping for products or services, then report back to the entire class.

Outcome 4. Listening, Evaluating, and Manipulating Information

These outcomes are intellectually challenging ones in which the listener evaluates and/or manipulates the information received in some manner. Lesson activities for individuals, pairs, or small groups can take many directions, including the following:

- Writing information received and reviewing it in order to answer questions or solve a problem.

- Evaluating information and reviewing it in order to make a decision or develop a plan of action.

- Evaluating arguments in order to take a position.

- Evaluating cause-and-effect information.

- Making predictions from information received.

- Summarizing or giving the gist of information received.
- Evaluating and combining or condensing information.
- Evaluating and elaborating or extending information.
- Organizing unordered information into a pattern of orderly relationships: chronological sequencing, spatial relationships, cause-and-effect, or problem-solution.

Field trips are challenging and useful for intermediate and advanced learners. Students can be assigned fact-finding, information-gathering tasks for panel presentations or use in a project. At more advanced levels, preparing for and carrying out a debate or discussion assignment on current local, national, or international issues can use both aural and written information and involves the student in evaluating and manipulating information.

Outcome 5. Interactive Listening-and-Speaking: Negotiating Meaning through Questioning/Answering Routines

Here the focus of the outcome is on both the *product* of transmitting information and the *process* of negotiating meaning in interactive reciprocal listener/speaker exchanges. Initially, in small groups, (i.e., four to ten students), one student can give a brief presentation such as a short set of locally relevant announcements, a five-minute "how-to" talk, a personal story or anecdote, or an explanatory talk using visual aids. (See Morley 1992.)

Either during or immediately after the presentation, each listener is required to ask at least one question in a questioning/answering routine. At first listeners can be given a card listing a question type and assigned the responsibility for asking that kind of question. The listener-questioner must continue with follow-up questions as necessary until both participants are satisfied that clear meaning has been negotiated. This means that the speaker is also a listener and

must keep questioning the listener-questioner to make sure of the nature and intent of the his or her questions. Videotape or audio recordings of these class sessions with subsequent viewing and discussion of selected segments quickly demonstrates the importance of negotiation of meaning and how much time and energy must sometimes be expended in order to arrive at a consensus on meaning.

A wide variety of question types can be used in this kind of activity, but for each lesson it is useful to have only a limited number of question types used. Some examples are the following:

- **Repetition**—questions asking only for verbatim repetition of information ("Could you repeat the part about xx?").
- **Paraphrase**—questions asking only for restatement in different words, often words that are simpler and easier to understand ("Could you say that again?" "I don't understand what you mean by xx.").
- **Verification**—questions seeking confirmation that the information was understood correctly by the listener ("Did I understand you to say that xx?" "In other words, you mean xx." "Do you mean xx?").
- **Clarification**—questions seeking more details or an explanation of an item ("Could you tell me what you mean by xx?" "Could you explain xx?" "Could you give us an example of xx?").
- **Elaboration**—questions that ask for additional information on a point introduced in the presentation ("Could you tell us more about xx?").
- **Extension**—questions that ask for information on a new point, one that was not introduced in the presentation ("What about xx?" "How is this related to xx?").
- **Challenge**—questions that challenge points given or conclusions drawn ("What did you base xx on?" "How did you reach the conclusion of xx?" "How did you xx?" "Why did you xx?").

Outcome 6. Listening for Enjoyment, Pleasure, and Sociability

Tasks with this outcome can include listening to songs, stories, plays, poems, jokes, anecdotes, or, as suggested by Ur, "general interesting chat improvised by the teacher" (1984, p. 29). Some of the activities in this category come under the heading of interactional listening, different from the previous outcome categories, which by and large are focused on transactional outcomes.

For these tasks, Ur notes that setting any outcome other than enjoying, for instance, may become superfluous or even harmful to the completion of the outcome of just enjoying.

Ur makes an especially good case for informal "teacher-chat" as an excellent source of listening material and observes that it serves as a relaxing break from more intensive work. She suggests "teacher-talk" on personal topics (e.g., your favorite hobby, plans for the future, your opinions on topical or local issues) (pp. 62–63). She notes that this, in turn, may lead naturally to "student-talk" on similar subjects for loosely structured and comfortable communicative classroom interludes, ones that afford student "practice" opportunities in both listening and speaking.

SELF-ACCESS/SELF-STUDY LISTENING AND LANGUAGE LEARNING

The purpose of a self-access/self-study resource is to provide an inviting listening center within a conventional language laboratory or a broader language resource center. This self-study facility needs to offer a wide choice of appealing audio and video materials on a variety of topics and at a range of proficiency levels. Books to accompany tapes are useful, of course. However, in addition to (or in place of) commercial books, a library of listening materials might also include carefully designed worksheet materials that present listening tasks for self-study, pair-study, or small-group study, both on the school premises and for checkout and home use.

Materials for free-listening time (like free-reading time) can be provided and students can be given a chance to self-select from a listening library that includes stories and poems, talks and lectures, plays and literary classics, participatory games, puzzles, riddles, and read-along or sing-along stories, songs, and games. Commercial audio- and videotapes can easily be adapted for listening library use. More innovatively, a collection of local audio or video recordings of conversations, songs, music events, lectures, or panel discussions can be compiled. Home videos can be an appealing addition to a listening library. Such locally produced auditory materials have a special *relevance* and *applicability* potential that commercial materials lack.

Setting Up a Self-Access/Self-Study Listening Resource Center

A self-access/self-study listening resource center can be started with a modest listening library of audio and video recorded material and the teacher-time needed to put materials into self-study packets or modules.

Ideally, listening materials can be made available to students in a special language learning center or multipurpose study room that also features reading and writing materials and has a teacher or monitor present at all times to guide students in the selection and use of materials and equipment.

Alternatively, self-access self-study materials can be used in a more conventional language laboratory setting. Whatever the setting, the most important point is that the individual learner has complete personal control over the materials. It is essential that students be able to control the source of input so that they can pace it—stop it, start it, replay it—at will. Such control allows students to regulate their own schedules of study, rather than having a rate and volume of auditory input imposed on them. This helps reduce the anxiety and pressure that many students, particularly beginners, seem to experience when listening in the second or foreign language. Some materials might be made available for checkout and home study. However, a study facility often has fewer distractions than a home or dormitory environment, and its atmosphere is usually more conductive to the self-discipline necessary for concentrated listening in the second or foreign language.

The procedures for using self-access self-study materials might be organized in the following way:

1. Students check out a listening packet or module that contains the audio- or video-tape, prelistening introductory material, worksheets (and perhaps some visuals), answer key (and perhaps a script), instructions, and postlistening tasks.
2. Students play the tape on their own schedule of starting, stopping, and replaying.
3. Students check their work themselves for verification of comprehension.
4. Students consult the teacher or monitor when necessary.

Self-access listening materials can be organized into self-study packets or modules of manageable lengths. They can be cross-referenced in a variety of ways to meet the needs of individual students or groups of students (i.e., content or topical groups, notional categories, functional categories, situational or activity categories, level-of-difficulty groupings, specific listening-task groupings, English for Specific Purposes groupings).

Modules that feature up-to-date, locally relevant, authentic aural texts are especially effective and are recommended wherever possible. In addition, segments from selected commercial listening materials can be adapted to fit into this format.

Guidelines for Developing Self-Access/Self-Study Listening Materials

In addition to relevance, transferability, task orientation, and the communicative outcomes framework, the following guidelines are suggested as a reference in preparing self-access self-study listening practice materials:

1. A focus on listening as an active process with instant or only slightly delayed manipulation of the information received.
2. A focus on purposeful listening (a) in order to process information and immediately do something with the information, by performing a task of some nature, and (b) in order to analyze particular features of the message (i.e., linguistic features, sociolinguistic features, discourse features, strategic features), and (c) in order to build a base of *content experiences* and *outcomes experiences*.
3. A focus on a variety of practice materials that includes a mix of authentic, semi-authentic, and simulated language activities.
4. A focus on internal communicative interaction, as the listener receives language input (aurally and visually), restructures it, and makes a response that is either a reformulation of some of the information or an analysis of some of its features.
5. A focus on providing learners with verification of comprehension (i.e., immediate or only slightly delayed feedback) with self-check answer keys or scripts as needed.
6. A focus on encouraging guessing and following "hunches" when in doubt.
7. A focus on selective listening, ignoring irrelevant material, and learning to tolerate less than total understanding.
8. A focus on self-involvement with an emphasis on self-study and taking responsibility for one's own work and pride in one's accomplishments.
9. A focus on providing learners with less threatening listening/learning experiences; a self-study listening mode where students have the freedom to regulate their own work and can stop the tape, rewind, and replay as they wish.
10. A focus on integrating auditory and visual language by combining listening, reading, and writing, and observing relationships between spoken forms and written forms.
11. A focus on gradually increasing expectations for levels of comprehension (i.e., encouraging students to challenge themselves and to move themselves along toward increasingly demanding expectations).
12. A focus on the fun of listening!

FINAL COMMENTS

Since the 1960s, the importance of listening comprehension in language learning and language teaching has moved from a status of incidental and peripheral importance to a status of significant and central importance. Whereas only a few instructional materials were available in the 1970s, today there are many texts and tape programs to choose from and, in general, materials are becoming more carefully principled, with serious attention to theoretical considerations. Each year more diverse materials are developed, and many now focus on the narrowly specified listening needs of particular groups of learners, including English for Specific Purposes.

Finally, it is important to emphasize that the S/FL listening curriculum cannot focus only on buying the right books and tapes. Skill building in listening comprehension is not something that can be accomplished in a half-hour lesson three times a week, nor can attention to listening be limited to language laboratory tapes. Listening, the language skill used most in life, needs to be a central focus—all day, every day—limited only by the availability of the target language in the school, the community, and the media. Listening instruction needs to include both *two-way* interactive listening activities and tasks and *one-way* reactive Listen-and-Do activities and tasks. Materials developers should pay careful attention to principles of design, communicative outcomes, language functions, language processes, and affective considerations.

DISCUSSION QUESTIONS

1. Characterize each of the three communicative listening modes: bidirectional, unidirectional, and autodirectional. From your own personal experience, give examples of each of these three kinds of communicative listening.
2. Discuss why listening has been called "the neglected skill" of language teaching.
3. For three days, keep a record of how much time you spend each day in each of the four skill areas: listening, speaking, reading, and writing. In small groups, make a composite of the times recorded for each of the four language skills.
4. Review the three principles of materials development discussed in this chapter. Give examples of ways they can be implemented in listening lessons.
5. Discuss the differences between interactional language use and transactional language use. Give examples from your personal experience and compare them with those given by others in your class.

SUGGESTED ACTIVITIES

1. Ask permission to observe two or three ESL or foreign language classes. Observe the nature of the interactions in the class. Note the amount of time in which students are engaged in listening and the amount of time they are engaged in speaking, reading, or writing.
2. Write a lesson plan that focuses on two or three ways to include specific listening opportunities in a class where the central focus is on another aspect of language learning.
3. Working in pairs, use the Richards matrix (Richards 1990) and come up with two or three examples for each of the four cells.

 **FURTHER READING**

Anderson, A., and T. Lynch. 1988. *Listening.* Oxford: Oxford University Press.
    This book stands back from the surface detail of comprehension materials and provides an overall perspective on listening as a communicative activity and as a language learning activity. It includes a research design focus.
Brown, G., and G. Yule. 1983. *Teaching the Spoken Language.* Cambridge: Cambridge University Press.
    Using an approach based on the analysis of conversational English, this book examines the nature of spoken language and presents principles and techniques for teaching spoken production and listening comprehension.

Nunan, D., and L. Miller. 1995. *New Ways in Teaching Listening Comprehension.* Alexandria, VA: TESOL.
A very useful compendium of activities for planning language lessons with a listening focus.

Mendelsohn, D., and J. Rubin. 1995. *A Guide for Teaching Second Language Listening.* San Diego, CA: Dominie Press.
An excellent collection of diverse topics in teaching second language listening. Contains may practical examples and suggestions for lesson development.

Morley, J. 1999. Current Perspectives on Improving Aural Comprehension. *ESL Magazine* 2 (1): 15–19.
This is an easy-to-read article for the beginning TESL/TEFL student. It presents current perspectives in the area of ESL/EFL aural comprehension instruction.

Ur, P. 1984. *Teaching Listening Comprehension.* Cambridge: Cambridge University Press.
Analyzes real-life listening characteristics and the problems encountered by language learners. Presents a wide range of exercise types, ranging from elementary to advanced, and appropriate for both adults and children.

Special periodical issues devoted to listening comprehension:

Applied Linguistics 7 (2), Summer 1986.

ELT Documents Special, "The Teaching of Listening Comprehension," 1981.

Foreign Language Annals 17 (4), September 1984.

JALT Newsletter 19 (4), 1982.

TESOL Newsletter 19 (6), December 1985.

Skills and Strategies for Proficient Listening

PAT WILCOX PETERSON

In "Skills and Strategies for Proficient Listening," Peterson offers a developmental view of second language listeners at beginning, intermediate, and advanced levels. She describes the comprehension processes of proficient listeners as being both top-down and bottom-up in nature, and offers exercises for building listening skills and strategies at all proficiency levels.

INTRODUCTION: THE IMPORTANCE OF LISTENING IN LANGUAGE LEARNING

Teachers who want to provide the most effective classroom experience for their second language students should consider this: No other type of language input is as easy to process as spoken language, received through listening. At the beginning stages of language study, before students have learned to read well, it is by listening that they can have the most direct connection to meaning in the new language. Through listening, learners can build an awareness of the interworkings of language systems at various levels and thus establish a base for more fluent productive skills.

At the intermediate level, when students are refining their understanding of the grammatical systems of their second or foreign language, listening can be used to stimulate awareness of detail and to promote accuracy. At advanced levels, when students are able readers and written language has become a viable source of input, listening should still occupy a central place in their language use. A regular program of listening can extend learners' vocabulary and use of idioms and build their appreciation for cultural nuances. Moreover, successful academic study in English requires a mastery of the listening demands in formal lectures as well as in the interactive exchanges which are common to seminar settings and conversational lecture styles.

There is such a wide range of listening tasks for different purposes and for all proficiency levels that teachers can find listening activities to promote learning at every stage. This chapter will present a brief developmental view of listening skills: how people learn to listen and how listening promotes learning. Sample exercises will be given to facilitate listening at beginning, intermediate, and advanced stages of language development.

THEORIES OF LANGUAGE COMPREHENSION

The following ideas about the listening process had their beginnings more than forty years ago and have recently gained wide acceptance in the field.

Listening Is the Primary Channel for Language Input and Acquisition

Proponents of comprehension approaches recognize the primacy of listening in the processes of comprehension, retention of information in memory, and acquisition of second language competence. Nida (1957) describes the language learning experience of people in Africa, where multilingualism without formal instruction is a common phenomenon. People simply go to a place to live and work, they listen without attempting to speak, and quite soon they find that they can "hear" the language. Only after internalizing some part of the language do they try to speak. Nida concludes, "Learning to speak a language is very largely a task of learning to hear it" (p. 53).

This emphasis on the primacy of listening contrasts dramatically with audiolingual practices of the 1960s and 1970s, which promoted early intensive oral practice. In an essay entitled "Why not start speaking later?" Postovsky (1977) called for an extended period of listening with delayed oral production. Asher's (1969) Total Physical Response approach featured a long preproduction phase in which students listened, followed commands, and demonstrated their comprehension through nonverbal actions. The Natural Approach (Krashen and Terrell 1983) also set a prespeech period for listening only, to be followed by an early production phase in which students gave answers in single words or short phrases. The prespeech period could last for a few hours in the case of adult students, or for up to six months with children.

According to Nord (1981), reception should precede production because reception enables production. While it is possible to learn to understand without speaking, it is not possible to learn to speak without understanding. Premature production has several negative effects: Lacking L2 competence, students are forced back on L1 production habits and may make many L1 transfer errors. The need to produce utterances may interfere with the ability to comprehend the language completely, and thus interfere with learning and memory. The overload of task demands on the learner produces anxiety, which further inhibits learning.

Listening Comprehension Is a Multilevel, Interactive Process of Meaning Creation

When good listeners involve themselves with any type of spoken discourse, a number of processes work on various levels simultaneously to produce an understanding of the incoming speech. The higher level processes (top-down) are driven by listeners' expectations and understandings of the context, the topic, the nature of text, and the nature of the world. The lower level processes (bottom-up) are triggered by the sounds, words, and phrases which the listener hears as he or she attempts to decode speech and assign meaning.

The acoustic signal itself carries few cues to the meanings that are encoded within it; the listener must use his or her knowledge of the language to recognize meaningful sound units, to determine syllable boundaries, and to identify words. This phase of comprehension is known as *perceptual processing* (Anderson 1985). Next the listener works with the words and phrases he or she has decoded to form meaningful units, which are stored in short-term memory. This is the *parsing* phase. Finally, the listener searches long-term memory for ideas that relate to the new information; when a match is made between old and new information, comprehension occurs. This is the *utilization* stage.

With higher levels of language proficiency, the listener works more efficiently and is able to maintain activity on all levels simultaneously. At beginning proficiency levels, perceptual (bottom-up) operations require great amounts of conscious attention, so that little capacity remains for higher level operations. Later, after lower level skills have been rehearsed many times, they can be performed automatically, and the learner's attention can be freed up for top-down operations (McLaughlin, Rossman, and McLeod 1983).

In proficient listeners, top-down and bottom-up processes interact, so that lack of information at one level can be compensated for by checking against information at the other level. For example, advanced listeners may use their knowledge of lexis and topic to interpret the confusing sounds in the speech stream and to aid in word recognition. On the other hand, they may also use their basic decoding skills to check the progress of the argument and to determine whether the discourse is going in the direction they had predicted. Listening in their native language, people never hear all the information in a message, and they do not need to; proficiency in comprehension is the ability to fill in the gaps and to create an understanding that meets one's purpose for listening.

Rost (1990) credits the contributions of second language reading research for pointing to the importance of the student's prior knowledge in making sense of incoming linguistic data. This general comprehension model has been extended to listening as well. There are many terms for the meaning structures in the mind; they have been called *frames* (Minsky 1975), *scripts* (Schank 1975), and *schemata* (Rumelhart 1980). We will use Rumelhart's terminology. He defines a schema as "a data structure for representing generic concepts stored in memory" (p. 34). Carrell and Eisterhold (1983) suggest that background information in the reader's mind is of two kinds: content schemata and formal schemata. Content schemata include cultural knowledge, topic familiarity, and previous experience with a field. Formal schemata have to do with people's knowledge of discourse forms: text types, rhetorical conventions, and the structural organization of prose. Both content and formal schemata can aid the reader (and the listener) in comprehending text (Floyd and Carrell 1987).

Models of the Comprehension Process

One view of listening comprehension describes comprehension of a speaker's message as the internal reproduction of that message in the listener's mind, so that successful listening reproduces the meaning much as the speaker intended (Clark and Clark 1977). This is the information processing view of listening. A second view (Rost 1990) places more emphasis on the goals and internal meaning structures of the listener; in this view, the listener does not receive meaning, but rather constructs meaning. The constructed message differs somewhat from the intended message and is influenced by context, purpose for listening, and the listener's own prior knowledge. Both views acknowledge the complexity of the listening process and the importance of both top-down and bottom-up operations.

Nagle and Sanders (1986) offer a model of comprehension that incorporates the distinction between controlled and automatic processing as well as the active role of the listener in attention and monitoring. They propose an executive decision maker that decides how to deal with input, and a feedback loop that allows the listener to monitor ongoing comprehension. Their model is specifically intended to describe comprehension in a second language. They make the point that while comprehension is not exactly the same thing as learning, successful comprehension makes material available for learning.

Principles for Listening Comprehension in the Classroom

The above findings suggest a set of principles for teaching listening in the second language classroom.

Increase the amount of listening time in the second language class. Make listening the primary channel for learning new material in the classroom. Input must be interesting, comprehen-sible, supported by extralinguistic materials, and keyed to the language lesson.

Use listening before other activities. At beginning and low-intermediate levels, have students listen to material before they are required to speak, read, or write about it.

Include both global and selective listening. Global listening encourages students to get the gist, main idea, topic, situation, or setting. Selective listening points student attention to details of form and encourages accuracy.

Activate top-level skills. Give advance organizers, script activators, or discussions which call up students' background knowledge. Do this before students listen. Encourage top-down processing at every proficiency level.

Work towards automaticity in processing. Include exercises which build both recognition and retention of the material. Use familiar material in novel combinations. Encourage overlearning through focus on selected formal features. Practice bottom-up processing at every proficiency level.

Develop conscious listening strategies. Raise students' awareness of text features and of their own comprehension processes. Encourage them to notice how their processing operations interact with the text. Promote flexibility in the many strategies they can use to understand the language. Practice interactive listening, so that they can use their bottom-up and their top-down processes to check one against the other.

Skills and Strategies

Before proceeding with a developmental description of listening proficiency, it is helpful to differentiate between the following terms: listening process, listening skill, and listening strategy. The models in the preceding section present a view of some simultaneous, interactive operations which are hypothesized to constitute the successful comprehension *process*. These operations are made up of various subprocesses: chunking input into syllables, recognizing words, recalling relevant schemata, and matching key words to the semantic structure of the text. These subprocesses are the *skills* of the competent listener. If these skills are practiced enough, they become automatic and are activated much more quickly. When things are going well, the listener is not conscious of using skills at all. At the point when the comprehension process breaks down for some reason, the listener becomes aware of the need for repair and seeks an appropriate *strategy* for comprehension.

A major difference between skills and strategies is that strategies are under the learner's conscious control; they are operations which the learner chooses to use to direct or check his or her own comprehension. Chamot explains:

> Wh's desirable for basic cognitive skills to become automated, the same is not true for strategies, which need to be controlled consciously if learners are to maintain awareness of different learning conditions and select the strategies most appropriate for specific tasks (1995, p.16).

Competent listeners tend to monitor their comprehension rather steadily and, when necessary, to select appropriate strategies for the task at hand. Field (1998) points out the compensatory nature of strategies in that they make up for a lack of linguistic skill or topic knowledge. As the listener's ability improves, strategies may be used less frequently (or may develop into unconscious skills).

Students may not immediately see the benefits of strategy use or they may feel that strategy instruction takes time away from the practice of language skills. According to MacIntyre and Noels (1996), teachers can motivate students by showing them how and when to use strategies. Teachers must also show students how effective strategy use can be through successful experiences. Mendelsohn (1995) calls for strategy instruction to be delivered gradually, over an extended period of time, and in a manner appropriate to the learners' proficiency level. Strategy training does not replace language practice, but rather is interspersed with practice throughout a course.

In fact, untutored students use strategies anyway, but they do not always choose wisely. Eastman (1991) points out that students sometimes use ineffective strategies such as on-line translation. Translation of single words may be the only strategy that beginning listeners think to use, but it restricts listeners to the surface features of the language and uses up all of their available processing capacity. The urge to translate is so natural at lower proficiency levels that students must be explicitly encouraged to avoid it. Teachers can help their students to practice more productive strategies such as attending to longer chunks of language and relating new information to what they already know.

Types of Strategies

Taxonomies of learning strategies have been proposed for second language use in general (Oxford 1990). Strategies specific to listening comprehension are based on these general lists and include the categories of metacognitive, cognitive, and socioaffective strategies.

Metacognitive strategies involve planning, monitoring, and evaluating comprehension. Cognitive strategies are used to manipulate information. Examples of cognitive strategies are rehearsal, organization, summarization, and elaboration. Socioaffective strategies have been less studied but are thought to be particularly important when the listening is two way and meaning can be negotiated between speaker and listener, as in conversations. Examples of socioaffective strategies are cooperative learning, questioning for clarification, and managing one's emotions in the learning situation. A complete list of strategies would be quite lengthy, since it would have to describe all the possible actions that a learner could take in the face of widely different texts and tasks.

Strategy use varies with proficiency, and so the relationship between strategy use and proficiency level is an important one. More advanced learners use a greater number of strategies than beginners do, and they also use them with more flexibility, choosing strategies to fit a specific situation. O'Malley, Chamot, and Kupper (1989) found that effective learners select strategies appropriate to the processing phase. In the perceptual phase, they use focused, selective attention; in parsing, they prefer top-down strategies; and in the utilization phase, they draw on personal experience and world knowledge. Several studies have found that advanced learners are able to process larger chunks of information and to draw on linguistic and world knowledge simultaneously in building meaning (Rost and Ross 1991; Vandergrift 1998).

In contrast, beginning and low-intermediate listeners rely too much on information at one level, either at the top or at the bottom, and fail to check one level against the other. They may come to the listening experience with a fixed idea of what they will hear, and be unwilling to change their idea as the text comes in. They are less able to revise their schemata when faced with contradictory information and either ignore the contradiction or shift their conceptual frameworks too frequently. Alternately, such learners may be bound to surface features of the data, making all their inferences at the local level and lacking any overall schema for understanding (Vandergrift 1998).

A DEVELOPMENTAL VIEW OF LISTENING SKILLS

Profile of the Beginning-Level Student in Listening

True beginners in a second language lack adequate bottom-up processing skills because they have not yet developed the linguistic categories against which the language must be heard. They perceive the new language as undifferentiated noise. They are not yet able to segment the speech stream into word units—to tell where one word begins and another ends. The new phonemic system is an unbroken code: Sounds which native speakers consider similar may be perceived and classified as different; sounds which native speakers consider different may be

perceived and classified as the same. If the stress patterns of words differ from those in the L1, true beginners may have trouble identifying L2 word boundaries. They have no idea about phonological rules that change sounds in certain environments or cause reductions of sound. To decode the sensory data as a native speaker would, learners must first build a linguistic structure of important sound distinctions and categories. Beginners' structural competence also places limitations on their bottom-up processing skills. They are not familiar with rules for word formation, inflections, or word order. Their vocabulary store is practically nonexistent.

The novice stage is of very short duration. Almost immediately upon hearing the new language, learners begin to sift and sort the acoustic information by forming categories and building a representation of the L2 system. If the teacher follows principles of comprehension training, learners will have many opportunities to work with a limited amount of language that is focused on clearly illustrated subjects. The simplified code that is used in the classroom at this point helps learners direct their attention to the important features of the message. After a few hours of instruction, the learners know a tiny bit of the language very well and can use their emerging understanding of linguistic categories to decode new utterances.

Despite its brevity, the novice stage is important for the development of positive attitudes toward listening. Learners should be encouraged to tolerate ambiguity, to venture informed guesses, to use their real-world knowledge and analytical skills, and to enjoy their success in comprehension. The world outside the classroom asks, *Do you speak English?* and ignores the very formidable accomplishment of skilled comprehension. Rarely does anyone ask, *Do you understand English?* Teachers can help correct this situation by attaching value to students' progress in listening skills.

True beginners are found in beginning classes for immigrants to English-speaking countries and in EFL classes abroad. Many of the teachers in the second setting are not native speakers themselves, and some may lack the confidence to provide students with the kind of global listening experiences they need (see Medgyes's chapter in this volume).

Yet, considering the great value of exposure to spoken English, all teachers should attempt to provide this important input. The following suggestions are meant to encourage such teachers.

1. Global listening selections should be short—one to three minutes in duration.

2. The teacher does not have to speak as if he or she were addressing colleagues at a professional meeting. Teachers' monologues are most effective at beginning levels if they are delivered in a simplified code. Such language involves short, basic sentences, clear pronunciation, repetition of ideas, limited vocabulary, and visual or situational support for new words.

3. It is best to add new material (vocabulary and structures) gradually. Experience with recombinations of familiar material builds learners' confidence and lessens the amount of totally new texts the teacher must prepare.

4. Global listening exercises such as short teacher monologues can be given to large classes, which are often found in the EFL setting where it is more difficult to provide speaking activities for the same number of students. Students should be kept active with a task to perform while listening, so the teacher can be sure that he or she is using class time wisely.

5. Selective listening exercises, which focus on structures or sounds in contrast, are relatively easy to prepare. Most EFL teachers have come through educational systems where grammar was emphasized and are quite comfortable with this kind of task. Listening discrimination tasks can focus on tenses, singular/plural differences, word order, or new vocabulary; there are many possibilities.

Techniques for Global Listening One important use of global listening is the presentation of new material. Until students are skilled readers, it is best to present new material orally. The teacher may select any part of the lesson for a global listening experience, or he or she may write a text based on the lesson. Introduction of new material through global listening is common to many of the newer comprehension approaches, yet the technique is not described in language textbooks. Once the teacher has mastered a few simple principles and routines, he or she can use the technique daily.

Texts for global listening should be short, and preceded by a prelistening activity. Wherever possible, the theme and situation of the story should be presented visually by drawing on the chalkboard, overhead projector, or a large poster. If the new material is a dialogue, draw the participants and tell their ages and relationships to each other. Setting the scene in this way activates the learners' background knowledge and encourages them to make predictions about the text. New vocabulary can be used in short, illustrative sentences before learners hear it as part of the lesson. If possible, use new vocabulary in a personal way, supported by the context of the classroom, so its meaning is clear. Descriptive words, colors, numbers, sizes, shapes, action verbs, and spatial relations are easy to model and to support with tangible examples.

The prelistening stage should develop learners' curiosity about how all the phrases and words they have heard will fit together in a context. The new text should be modeled at normal speed, but with pauses between natural phrase groups. Teachers should not slow their speech, because the students' short-term memory capacity is too limited to remember sentences when they are extended by slow speech. The psycholinguistic processing model described above indicates that short phrases can be held in working memory until the next pause; during the pause, the phrase is analyzed, interpreted, related to the rest of the message, and comprehended.

If objects and actions are demonstrated clearly and if the message contains a clear dramatic structure, even beginners will soon begin to perceive patterns of sound. Vocabulary from the prelistening phase will stand out especially clearly from the rest of the speech stream, providing listeners a pleasant experience of recognition. Working with a few content words, learners can use top-down processing to fill in the gaps and guess the general meaning of the text. Comprehension of every function word and grammatical marker is really not necessary when the goal is simply to get the gist.

It should be clear from this description of global listening that comprehension at the beginning stage is not total—rather real-life comprehension does not depend on understanding every word. Students on the first day of class will be able to understand some words of the story through use of these techniques. They will not remember the words or be able to produce them, but they will quite likely recognize the words when they hear them again in a familiar context. At the least, they have been exposed to three to five minutes of the new language with its own distinctive sound system, intonation patterns, pause system, and word order. Comprehension theorists such as Nida (1957) point out that during this time a great deal of active processing has been going on just below the students' level of conscious awareness.

Selective Listening Techniques   The other half of the listening plan is to bring some of the new contrasts and patterns into conscious awareness through selective listening exercises. Here are the listening goals for beginners with exercise types.

The classification of exercises as bottom-up or top-down does not indicate that only one kind of cognitive activity can occur during each exercise, but rather that some foster predominantly bottom-up responses, and some exercises promote predominantly top-down processing. An exercise is classified as bottom-up if focus is on form and the exercise deals with one of the structural systems of English. Alternately, this designation may indicate selection of specific discrete items from the listening text such as listening for details. An exercise is classified as top-down if the focus is on meaning and the listener uses global listening strategies. Alternately, this designation may indicate a reliance on extralinguistic skills which the learner brings to the listening task. All listening is to some degree interactive due to the nature of the processing mechanism. An exercise is classified as interactive if the listener must use information gained by processing at one level to check the accuracy of his or her processing on another level.

Bottom-Up Processing Goals and Exercise Types, Beginning-Level Listeners

Goal: Discriminate between intonation contours in sentences
- Listen to sentences with either rising or falling intonation and mark them with appropriate punctuation for statements (.),

questions (?), surprise (??), or excitement (!) (Rost and Uruno 1995, p. 54).
- Listen to pairs of sentences spoken by a driver and a policeofficer. In each case the police officer's words are the same as the driver's. Use the intonation pattern of the policeofficer to determine whether he is repeating or questioning what the driver said (Foley 1994a, p. 83).

Goal: Discriminate between phonemes
- Listen to the teacher read pairs of words. Each pair differs by one sound. Then listen again as the teacher reads only one of the words in each pair and circle the word you hear (Benz and Dworak 2000, p. 126).
- Listen to three words and determine which word is different from the other two (Rost and Uruno 1995, p. 55).

Goal: Listen for morphological endings
- Listen to a number of verbs that end in *-s* or *-es*. For each verb, note the pronunciation /s/, /z/, or /əz/ (Benz and Dworak 2000, p. 189).
- Listen to sentences and decide if the verb is in the present tense or the past tense. Then listen to a list of verbs that end in *-ed* and note the pronunciation /t/, /d/, or /əd/ (Benz and Dworak 2000, p. 226).

Goal: Recognize syllable patterns, number of syllables, and word stress
- Listen to a short radio commercial. In each word, count and note the number of syllables, and underline the stressed syllable. Then practice reading the commercial aloud to your partner, preserving the stress pattern (Benz and Dworak 2000, pp. 47–48).

Goal: Be aware of sentence fillers in informal speech.
- Listen to sentences and identify sentence fillers such as: "well," "I mean," "like," "you know" (Foley 1994b, p. 82).

Goal: Select details from the text
- Listen to a recorded telephone menu about the movies playing, the theaters, and the show times. Circle the number that you must press at each point to work down the menu (Benz and Dworak 2000, p. 69–70).
- Listen to some conversations about sickness. Refer to a list of symptoms and check

those symptoms which are mentioned in the conversation (Benz and Dworak 2000, p. 112).

Top-Down Processing Goals and Exercise Types, Beginning-Level Listeners

Goal: Discriminate between emotional reactions
- Listen to a statement about a vacation and decide whether or not the speaker enjoyed the vacation (Richards 1995, p. 29).

Goal: Get the gist or main idea of a passage
- Listen to a dialogue and decide what type of weather is being described. Find the picture that shows the weather (Benz and Dworak 2000, p. 80).
- Listen to a series of short conversations and for each one mark a picture that shows where the conversation took place (Rost and Uruno 1995, p. 49).
- Listen to a number of short biographies and for each one write a title that expresses the main idea of the passage (Benz and Dworak 2000, pp. 142–143).

Goal: Recognize the topic
- From a list of possible topics predict the topics that people will discuss when they don't know each other well. Listen to a series of short conversations in different settings and note which topics are actually discussed (Benz and Dworak 2000, pp. 71–72).
- Listen to a series of process descriptions, telling how to do something and mark a picture that tells the topic of the description (Rost and Uruno 1995, p. 78).

Interactive Processing Goals and Exercise Types, Beginning-Level Listeners

Goal: Use speech features to decide if a statement is formal or informal
- Look at five pictures which show people meeting each other. Based on extralinguistic information such as setting, age, and professions of the people, predict whether the language will be formal or informal. Listen

to the short dialogues to confirm your prediction. Analyze features of the speech (tone, speed, word choice) to determine what makes an introduction more formal (Benz and Dworak 2000, pp. 5–6).

Goal: Recognize a familiar word and relate it to a category
- Review the names of objects that are sold in different stores. Listen to statements that tell what people want to buy and select a picture of the store they will visit. Then mark the picture of the item they will buy (Rost and Uruno 1995, p. 41).

Goal: Compare information in memory with incoming information
- Read a sentence and then listen to a sentence on tape to decide if the meaning is the same or different (Foley 1994a, p. 71).
- Listen to a passage that describes a dramatic event such as a natural disaster. Then listen to a sentence from the passage and remember its meaning. On a worksheet, read two sentences and decide which sentence would best follow the sentence you heard (Foley 1994b, p. 107).

Goal: Compare information that you hear with your own experience
- Listen to statements about recycling in the United States Compare them with recycling in your country. Tell whether your country is the same or different (Foley 1994b, p. 116).

Profile of the Intermediate-Level Learner

Intermediate-level learners continue to use listening as an important source of language input to increase their vocabulary and structural understanding. Although they have internalized the phonemic system of the language fairly well, they may have little understanding of the complexities of phonological rules that govern fast speech: reductions, elisions, assimilation, and so forth. They need practice in word recognition, in discriminating fine differences in word order and grammatical form, in registers of speaking, and in emotional overtones.

Intermediate-level learners have moved beyond the limits of words and short phrases; their memory can retain longer phrases and sentences. They can listen to short conversations or narratives that are one or two paragraphs in length. They are able to get the gist, to find the main idea and some supporting detail (ACTFL Proficiency Guidelines 1988). They are ready to practice more discourse level skills: predicting what will happen next and explaining relations between events and ideas.

Techniques for Global Listening At the intermediate level, it is no longer necessary to provide learners with simplified codes and modified speech. Indeed, learners need to hear authentic texts with reduced forms, fast speech features, false starts, hesitations, errors, some nonstandard dialects, and a variety of different voices.

There are several definitions of authenticity in materials. Porter and Roberts (1987) state that authentic texts are those "instances of spoken language which were not initiated for the purpose of teaching . . . not intended for non-native learners" (p. 176). Rogers and Medley (1988) use the term *authentic* to refer to all language samples which "reflect a naturalness of form, and an appropriateness of cultural and situational context that would be found in the language as used by native speakers" (p. 468). With this definition, very good teacher-made or adapted materials may qualify as authentic.

Techniques for Selective Listening At the intermediate-level, students need a well-organized program of selective listening to focus their attention on the systematic features of the language code. Accuracy in discriminating grammatical features is very important at this level. If learners cannot hear certain unstressed endings, articles, inflections, and function words, they are less likely to incorporate them into their grammatical competence. Intermediate-level students who were trained with simplified codes and with clearly pronounced models may not recognize the same words and phrases in normal fast speech. Gilbert (1995) suggests that some pronunciation training has an important place in the listening class—to draw students' conscious attention to the features of natural speech.

Finally, the intermediate level is an appropriate time to teach explicitly some strategies of interactive listening: how to use one's knowledge of formal grammar to check the general meaning of a speaker's statement and how to use one's background knowledge to predict and direct the process of comprehension.

Bottom-Up Processing Goals and Exercise Types, Intermediate-Level Listeners

Goal: Differentiate between content and function words by stress pattern

■ Read a series of sentences and predict which words will be stressed (content words) and which will be reduced (function words.) Listen to the sentences and confirm your predictions (Hagen 2000, p. 8).

Goal: Find the stressed syllable

■ Listen to a list of multisyllable words. Repeat each one and check whether the stress is on the first, second, or third syllable. Note which syllables were more frequently stressed (Carlisi and Christie 2000, pp. 153–154).

Goal: Recognize words with reduced vowels or dropped syllables

■ Listen to a series of statements about sports activities and use word stress to determine whether the speakers are saying "can" or "can't" (Gill and Hartmann 2000, p. 81).

■ Read a list of polysyllabic words and predict which syllabic vowel will be dropped. Listen to the words and confirm your predictions (Hagen 2000, pp. 6–7).

Goal: Recognize words as they are linked in the speech stream

■ Listen to a series of short sentences with consonant/vowel linking between words. Mark the linkages on the answer sheet (Hagen 2000, p. 16).

Goal: Recognize pertinent details in the speech stream

■ Listen to a short dialogue between a boss and a secretary regarding changes in the daily schedule. Use an appointment calendar. Cross out appointments that are being changed and write in new ones (Schecter 1984, p. 36).

- Listen to a short telephone conversation between a customer and a service station manager. Fill in a chart which lists the car repairs that must be done. Check the part of the car that needs repair, the reason, and the approximate cost (Schecter 1984, p. 26).

Top-Down Processing Goals and Exercise Types, Intermediate-Level Listeners

Goal: Discriminate between registers of speech and tones of voice

- Listen to sentences with either flat or varied intonation and determine whether the speaker is enthusiastic, friendly, or sincere by the amount of pitch change and energy in the voice (Gill and Hartmann 2000, pp. 120–123).

Goal: Listen to identify the speaker or the topic

- Listen to four short conversations with people making small talk and match each to a picture of the speakers and the setting (Gill and Hartmann 2000, pp. 10–11).
- Read the headlines for five different news stories on the topics of environment, health, and lifestyle. Listen to the news stories and match each one with the appropriate headline (Gill and Hartmann 2000, pp. 187–189).

Goal: Find main ideas and supporting details

- Listen to a short conversation between two friends. On your answer sheet are scenes from television programs. Find and write the name of the program and the channel. Decide which speaker watched the program (Schecter 1984, p. 22).

Goal: Make inferences

- Listen to a woman and a man ordering dinner in a restaurant. Based on the food choices they make, tell which person is more conscious of health concerns (Gill and Hartmann 2000, p. 72).

Interactive Processing Goals and Exercise Types, Intermediate-Level Listeners

Goal: Use word stress to understand the speaker's intent

- Listen to a series of statements about money problems. In each statement, circle the words that are emphasized. With a partner, discuss what is important to the speaker and how the speaker feels about it (Carlisi and Christie 2000, p. 116).

Goal: Recognize missing grammar markers in colloquial speech and reconstruct the message

- Listen to a series of short questions in which the auxiliary verb and subject have been deleted. Use grammatical knowledge to fill in the missing words: "(Have you) got some extra?" (Hagen 2000, pp. 9–10).
- Listen to a series of questions with assimilated verb auxiliary and subject, and use grammatical knowledge to identify the missing verb (*does it/is it*). Example: "Zit need more salt?" and "Zit OK?" (Hagen 2000, p. 17).

Goal: Use context and knowledge of the world to build listening expectations; listen to confirm expectations

- Based on your knowledge of other cultures, predict whether their topics of conversation in an academic setting will be personal or impersonal, direct or indirect. Then listen to a newcomer describe his experience in that culture and note what kind of culture shock actually occurred. After listening, discuss with a partner whether your initial idea was correct and how you have to revise your ideas because of your added knowledge (Carlisi and Christie 2000, pp. 40–42).

Profile of the Advanced Learner

There is evidence that in the learning continuum, somewhere between high-intermediate and advanced levels, a qualitative shift occurs in the learner's processing style (Cummins 1981). Cummins notes that truly proficient bilinguals are able to use their second language skills fully to acquire knowledge: They have cognitive and academic language proficiency (CALP). Advanced students are no longer simply learning to listen or listening to learn the language. They are listening in the language to learn about the content of other areas. To build toward this level, curriculum and program planners have established courses in English for Specific Purposes (ESP), English for Academic Purposes (EAP), and adjunct courses in which mainstream content classes offer language support (see chapters by Johns and Price-Machado, and Snow in this volume).

The ACTFL Proficiency Guidelines (1988) list the following competencies for advanced listeners: They can listen to longer texts such as radio and television programs and academic lectures. Their vocabulary includes topics in current events, history, and culture; they can deal with a certain degree of abstraction. The listeners begin to fill in gaps and can make inferences when the text is incomplete or their background knowledge is lacking. However, their understanding of the language remains on a fairly literal plane, so that they may miss jokes, slang, and cultural references.

Academic lectures in English-speaking countries may employ a much less formal delivery style than the lectures that international students know from their home countries. Instead of the read-aloud lecture, American lectures tend to be conversational and even interactive (Flowerdew 1994). Professors may include jokes, cultural references, asides, and digressions; they may allow interruptions from students who ask questions, which they then go on to weave into the information structure of their lecture. The non-native listener needs to determine what is relevant and what is not. Rost (1994) suggests strategies for learning from lectures, including formulating questions to ask the lecturer, searching lecture notes for logical relationships, and building a list of key terms to form a lexical base.

Many advanced learners are more skilled at reading than they are at listening. This is particularly true of students who have learned their English in a foreign language context and whose training has emphasized grammar, vocabulary, and reading. Such students may learn to comprehend spoken discourse more easily if they can activate their knowledge by completing the assigned reading before the lecture (Mason 1994). Some experts also suggest judicious use of lecture transcripts in listening classes as a means of using students' familiarity with written text to make an explicit connection with the spoken form of the language (Lebauer 2000).

For many international students, reductions in normal speech present a major comprehension problem. Listening classes at the advanced level may need to include a systematic program of exposing learners to reduced speech. A review of stress, pause, pitch, and intonation patterns can serve to unlock mysteries of discourse structure and point students toward recognition of organizational markers, cohesive devices, and definitions in context.

For listening to fit the interactive model of the skilled native speaker, both top-down and bottom-up processes must be learned. The following recommendations for advanced listeners assume an international student population that needs to develop cognitive and academic language proficiency for effective study in English.

Bottom-Up Processing Goals and Exercise Types, Advanced-Level Listeners

Goal: Use features of sentence stress and intonation to identify important information for note taking

■ Listen to a number of sentences and extract the content words, which are read with greater stress. Write the content words as notes (Lim and Smalzer 1995, p. 50).

Goal: Recognize contractions, reduced forms, and other characteristics of spoken English that differ from the written form

■ Listen to sentences containing reduced forms and write the sentences as they would appear without reduction in formal, written English (Leshinsky 1995, pp. 1–6).

Goal: Become aware of common performance slips that must be reinterpreted or ignored

■ Listen to and look at sentences that contain fillers (hesitation phenomena such as "uh," "er," and "um") and phrases such as "I mean," "you know," "sort of," and "like." Rewrite the sentences without the fillers;

omit any words that don't add to the information (Leshinsky 1995, pp. 6–8).

Goal: Become aware of organizational cues in lecture text

■ Look at a lecture transcript and circle all the cue words used to enumerate the main points. Then listen to the lecture segment and note the organizational cues (Lebauer 2000, pp. 14–15).

Goal: Become aware of lexical and suprasegmental markers for definitions

■ Read a list of lexical cues that signal a definition; listen to signals of the speaker's intent such as rhetorical questions; listen to special intonation patterns and pause patterns used with appositives (Lebauer 2000, pp. 52–54).

Goal: Identify specific points of information

■ Read a skeleton outline of an interview about youth gangs and neighborhood watch clubs in which the main categories are given but the specific examples are left blank. Listen to the interview and take notes on the information which belongs in the blanks (Numrich 1995, p. 51).

Top-Down Processing Goals and Exercise Types, Advanced-Level Listeners

Goal: Use knowledge of the topic to predict the content of the text

■ Before listening to a conversation about food, write a description about the way that food is prepared and eaten in your culture; share this information with others. Use your ideas to write questions that you think may be answered in the listening text (Leshinsky 1995, pp. 27–28).

Goal: Use the introduction to the lecture to predict its focus and direction

■ Listen to the introductory section of a lecture. Then read a number of topics on your answer sheet and choose the topic that best expresses what the lecture will discuss (Lebauer 2000, pp. 49–51).

Goal: Use the lecture transcript to predict the content of the next section

■ Read a section of a lecture transcript. Stop reading at a juncture point and predict what will come next. Then read on to confirm your prediction (Lebauer 2000, pp. 18–20).

Goal: Find the main idea of a lecture segment

■ Read a skeleton outline for a lecture about American work habits, noting the number of main ideas and digressions. While listening to the lecture, fill in the outline and identify the main points and digressions (Lim and Smalzer 1995, pp. 24–25).

Goal: Recognize point of view

■ Take notes on a debate about whether or not it is ethical to keep dolphins in captivity. Afterwards, organize your notes under two headings: the arguments for keeping dolphins and the arguments against keeping them (Leshinksy 1995, p. 95).

Interactive Processing Goals and Exercise Types, Advanced-Level Listeners

Goal: Use knowledge of phrases and discourse markers to predict the content in the next segment of the lecture

■ Identify the lecturer's intention by his choice of discourse markers and predict the kind of information that will follow (Bame 1995, pp. 221–224).

Goal: Make inferences about the text.

■ Listen to a conversation about restaurants, ethnic cuisine, and good food. Read a number of statements about people's food preferences and decide if they are possible inferences based on the text (Leshinsky 1995, p. 22).

Directions for Future Research

Recent reviews of research in the field of listening comprehension have pointed to the need for additional research in a number of areas. A common theme is the link between proficiency level and strategy use. We need to know more about what good listeners do and how they learn their strategies. Introspection, self-report, and interview methods show great promise in this elusive area. Rubin (1994) calls for a prioritization of the importance of elements in bottom-up and top-down processing that affect listening at each proficiency level.

Since the selection of strategies can also be influenced by factors other than proficiency level, it seems important to investigate some of these variables as well: learning style, personality type, previous educational experience, task constraints, and text type. Much of the research to date has concentrated on schema use and top-level processing. However, given the importance of automaticity in perceiving and parsing, it would also be helpful to know about the effects of more intensive classroom practice on bottom-up processing.

One of the difficulties of comparative studies with low and high proficiency groups is that there is no commonly accepted measure of proficiency in ESL listening. Thus, it is difficult to compare the results of studies; some use TOEFL®, CELT,[1] or MLA test scores, some use teacher assessment, and some use the ACTFL Oral Proficiency Interview as a global measure. Rubin (1994) reports that ACTFL and the Interagency Language Roundtable are working on tests that may serve as a standard in future listening comprehension research.

Other research areas include the effect of social, cultural, and affective factors on listeners. We need to know more about the demands placed on students by formal and informal classroom styles, interactional teaching styles, and group work. As multimedia resources become more available, and as we come to value the visual element in listening comprehension, a study of the effects of video and other visual media is of growing interest (Rubin 1995).

Finally, it would be very instructive to replicate a study done by Berne (1998) in which she asked practicing foreign language teachers about their areas of research interest. The list from teachers only partly overlaps with the topics given by academic researchers. Teachers wanted guidelines for setting appropriate goals for different levels of proficiency; for using the appropriate amount of repetition; for incorporating support materials such as visual aids and physical activities into listening tasks; for choosing the L1 or L2 in assessing comprehension; for reducing the amount of mental translation that students do; for assessing the level of difficulty of a listening text; for incorporating authentic and culturally relevant texts; and for combining listening with other skills. How many of these issues would emerge from a similar survey of ESL/EFL teachers and what additional issues would the responses of ESL/EFL teachers raise?

SUMMARY

ESL/EFL teachers have several responsibilities with respect to the listening skill. First, they must understand the pivotal role that listening plays in the language learning process in order to utilize listening in ways that facilitate learning. Second, they must understand the complex interactive nature of the listening process and the different kinds of listening that learners must do in order to provide their students with an appropriate variety and range of listening experiences. Finally, teachers must understand how listening skills typically develop in second language learners—and must be able to assess the stage of listening at which their students are—so that each student can engage in the most beneficial types of listening activities given his or her level of proficiency.

DISCUSSION QUESTIONS

1. In a group, recall the stages that you went through in listening when you learned a second language. What elements did you hear first? What elements took a long time to hear? What part did memory play in your listening at each stage?

2. In your opinion and based on your experience, what is the most effective relationship between teacher talk and student talk in the L2 classroom?

3. Describe the differences in texts with simplified codes and authentic language. What purpose does each text type have in the L2 classroom?

4. The learner proficiency profiles given in this chapter are loosely based on the ACTFL Proficiency Guidelines for listening. The profiles assume a certain learning context, one in which the target language is not spoken outside the classroom (similar to an EFL context).

Discuss ways in which context variables might lead to a different learner proficiency profile at each level. (Consider class size, age of learners, amount of exposure to the language, length of instruction, and similar factors.)

5. Review the results of Berne's study, listed in the last section of this chapter. Survey your classmates and/or colleagues and find out whether these issues are of interest to ESL/EFL teachers. Do your classmates and colleagues have other issues to add to the list?

SUGGESTED ACTIVITIES

1. Prepare a presentation of new material from an ESL/EFL text. Choose a short dialogue or narrative passage. Plan a prelistening phase in which you use visual and situational support to teach the new words and concepts. Then present the text orally. Your presentation should last no longer than three to five minutes.

2. Prepare a selective listening exercise which focuses on language form and guides students to discriminate between structural features.

3. Choose a listening comprehension text that has been published in the last five years. Select a typical chapter and analyze the cognitive processing demands of its exercises. How many are top-down? How many are bottom-up? Interactive? What is the plan for sequencing the exercises?

4. Record one or two minutes of authentic text from the radio or television. Develop a framework of language support for the text and show how you could use it in an intermediate-level class.

5. With a partner, conduct an experiment to discover your (or your partner's) preferred listening strategies. One of you will act as the investigator and the other will serve as the consultant. Choose a language which you both know but which is not native to the consultant. The investigator will prepare a one- to three-minute tape in that language and transcribe it, noting junctures where there are natural pauses (approximately every two or three sentences). The investigator will play the tape, pausing at the junctures, and ask the consultant to report what he or she is doing mentally to comprehend the tape. Make note of all the listening strategies mentioned and classify them as cognitive, metacognitive, or socioaffective. What does this tell you about your listening strategies? What have you learned about doing this kind of research?

FURTHER READING

Blair, R., ed. 1982. *Innovative Approaches to Language Teaching*. New York: Newbury House.
"Learning to Listen," the third chapter of Nida's (1957) book, is reprinted in Blair, pp. 42–53. Also, this anthology includes representative articles by Asher, Postovsky, Nord, and Krashen.

Nagle, S., and S. Sanders. 1986. Comprehension Theory and Second Language Pedagogy. *TESOL Quarterly* 20(1):9–26.
Presents the information-processing model of listening comprehension with suggestions for classroom applications.

Flowerdew, J., ed. 1994. *Academic Listening: Research Perspectives*. Cambridge: Cambridge University Press.
A collection of chapters by experts in the field of English for Academic Purposes, with insights into the structure of various types of lectures and information on how students understand.

Joiner, E. 1997. Teaching listening: How technology can help. In M. D. Bush and R. M. Terry, eds., *Technology Enhanced Learning* (pp. 77–120). Lincolnwood, IL: National Textbook Company.
Describes the kinds of technology that are available for teaching listening (audio, video, radio, computers, videodisc, multimedia workstations) and how to use them.

Mendelsohn, D., and J. Rubin., eds. 1995. *A Guide for the Teaching of Second Language Listening*. San Diego, CA: Dominie Press.
An excellent collection of articles on the full range of listening issues, with consideration of teaching and assessment.

Vandergrift, L. 1998. Constructing meaning in L2 listening: Evidence from protocols. In S. Lapkin, ed., *French as a Second Language in Canada: Recent Empirical Studies*. Toronto: Toronto University Press.
Presents the methodology for a study of listening strategies and includes a lengthy taxonomy of types of listening strategies.

ENDNOTE

1 CELT is the Comprehensive English Language Test by Harris and Palmer (1986).

UNIT II B

Language Skills

Speaking

This section focuses on how ESL/EFL teachers can facilitate their students' acquisition of oral skills. Lazaraton's chapter draws on current practice in oral skills pedagogy to show teachers how to develop the speaking skills of their students through appropriate course design and materials development. The chapter by Goodwin describes a principled and systematic approach to pronunciation, recognizing that intelligible pronunciation is critical for effective oral communication. She treats the skills needed for comprehension, self-expression, and monitoring. Peck's chapter discusses the teaching of listening and speaking skills to young learners, emphasizing how children differ from adults when learning aural-oral skills in the classroom. According to Peck, these differences require the use of special resources and activities.

Teaching Oral Skills

ANNE LAZARATON

In "Teaching Oral Skills," Lazaraton discusses current practice in oral skills pedagogy in terms of how to structure an oral skills class and determine its content, along with implementing a variety of classroom activities that promote skills development, and understanding issues related to classroom evaluation of speaking skills and testing via large-scale oral examinations.

INTRODUCTION

For most people, the ability to speak a language is synonymous with knowing that language since speech *is* the most basic means of human communication. Nevertheless, "speaking in a second or foreign language has often been viewed as the most demanding of the four skills" (Bailey and Savage 1994, p. vii). What specifically makes speaking in a second or foreign language difficult? Brown (1994) mentions a number of features that interact to make speaking as challenging a language skill as it is. To start, fluent speech contains reduced forms, such as contractions, vowel reduction, and elision, so that learners who are not exposed to or who do not get sufficient practice with reduced speech will retain their rather formal-sounding full forms. The same can be said for the use of slang and idioms in speech: Without facility in using these ubiquitous features of spoken language, learners are apt to sound bookish. Students must also acquire the stress, rhythm, and intonation of English, a complicated task for many (see Goodwin's chapter on teaching pronunciation in this volume). Perhaps the most difficult aspect of spoken English is that it is almost always accomplished via interaction with at least one other speaker. This means that a variety of demands are in place at once: monitoring and understanding the other speaker(s), thinking about one's own contribution, producing that contribution, monitoring its effect, and so on.

This is one reason why many of us were shocked and disappointed when we used our second or foreign language for the first time in real interaction: We had not been prepared for spontaneous communication and could not cope with all of its simultaneous demands. That is, speaking is an "activity requiring the integration of many subsystems. . . . all these factors combine to make speaking a second or foreign language a formidable task for language learners. . . . yet for many people, speaking is seen as the central skill" (Bailey and Savage 1994, p. vi–vii).

Oral skills have not always figured so centrally in second and foreign language pedagogy. In classes that utilize comprehension-based approaches to language teaching, listening skills are stressed before speaking, if speaking is stressed at all (see the section on listening skills in this volume). Even in a production-based approach such as the Silent Way, student speech is carefully controlled for structure and content. And while audiolingualism stressed oral skills (evidenced by the amount of time spent in the language laboratory practicing drills), speech production was tightly controlled in order to reinforce correct habit formation of linguistic rules.

But with the advent of the theory of communicative competence (Hymes 1972) and the practice of communicative language teaching (see Savignon's chapter in this volume), the teaching of oral communication skills as a contextualized sociocultural activity has become the focal point in many ESL classrooms. Briefly,

Canale and Swain's (1980) adaptation of Hymes's theory of communicative competence proposes that the ability to communicate in a language comprises four dimensions:[1] *grammatical competence* (including rules of phonology, orthography, vocabulary, word formation, and sentence formation), *sociolinguistic competence* (rules for the expression and understanding of appropriate social meanings and grammatical forms in different contexts), *discourse competence* (rules of both cohesion—how sentence elements are tied together via reference, repetition, synonymy, etc.—and coherence—how texts are constructed), and finally, *strategic competence,* (a repertoire of compensatory strategies that help with a variety of communication difficulties).

The impact of communicative competence theory on second and foreign language teaching cannot really be overstated; few ESL materials published in the last decade or so fail to claim that their materials reflect "the communicative approach." What features of this theoretical approach are relevant to teaching oral skills? Perhaps the most obvious way in which oral skills pedagogy has evolved as a result of this theory is that it is no longer acceptable to focus *only* on developing the grammatical competence of our students, as was the case with a number of language teaching methodologies which were popular in the past. Today, teachers are expected to *balance* a focus on accuracy with a focus on *fluency* as well. According to Hedge (1993, pp. 275–276) the term *fluency* has two meanings. The first, which is "the ability to link units of speech together with facility and without strain or inappropriate slowness or undue hesitation," is what is commonly understood as fluency in language teaching materials and in language assessment procedures. But Hedge proposes a second, more holistic sense of fluency, that of "natural language use," which is likely to take place when speaking activities focus on meaning and its negotiation, when speaking strategies are used, and when overt correction is minimized. This second, broader definition is certainly consistent with the aims of many ESL classrooms today where the negotiation of meaning is a major goal.

A second implication is that multiple skills should be taught whenever possible. In fact, Murphy (1991) believes that oral skills teachers should always connect speaking, listening, and pronunciation teaching although the focus in any one class or activity may highlight one or another. More broadly, oral skills classes may use reading and writing activities as the basis or follow-up for speaking activities.

Training learners to use strategies and encouraging strategy use is another prominent feature of today's oral skills classroom. Books such as *Language Learning Strategies: What Every Teacher Should Know* (Oxford 1990) discuss this topic in detail; while the utility of teaching "communication strategies" is a debated theoretical issue (see Dörnyei 1995), it is clear that language learners must become competent at using strategies, such as circumlocution, hesitation devices, and appeals for help, and that the oral skills teacher should at least advocate and model their use.

A final feature which characterizes the current ESL classroom is that students are encouraged to take responsibility for their own learning. No longer is learning seen as a one-way transfer of knowledge from teacher to student; today we understand that students learn from teachers, from classmates, and from the world outside the classroom, and the more the learner seeks these opportunities, the more likely he or she will learn to use the language. In the oral skills classroom, students should be allowed and encouraged to initiate communication when possible, to determine the content of their responses or contributions, and to evaluate their own production and learning progress.

The Oral Skills Class

In deciding how to structure and what to teach in an oral skills class, questions such as the following should be considered: Who are the students? Why are they there? What do they expect to learn? What am I expected to teach?

One basic consideration is the level of the students and their perceived needs. Level may be determined by a placement test administered by the institution or by a diagnostic test given by the teacher. Information on learner needs can be obtained by means of a student information sheet on which they report the amount of time they spend speaking English, their future goals, their goals for the course, and their assessment (perhaps a four-point scale from "poor" to "excellent") of their overall speaking ability, confidence in speaking English, their pronunciation, social conversation, and listening ability.

With low level adults, the teacher may need to find L1 speakers to help him or her get information on student experiences, educational background, and needs. It will be especially important with this student group to build on their experiences, to share expertise, and to use realia in order to keep learning as concrete as possible. More often than not, oral skills courses for nonacademic adults focus on survival English and basic communication functions based on a strong structural component.

On the other hand, academic learners will need practice with different sorts of activities. Based on survey responses from university faculty, Ferris and Tagg (1996a, 1996b) suggest that, in general, what academic ESL students need most is extensive authentic practice in class participation, such as taking part in discussions, interacting with peers and professors, and asking and answering questions. In fact, these students may be facing some sort of exit examination at the conclusion of the course that will determine whether or not they are competent to teach in English, to take other academic courses for credit, and so on. As a result, these learners take their course work seriously and have high expectations of the teacher. Yet even these students can probably benefit from (and may even ask for) some instruction on the more interpersonal aspects of oral communication.

Nowadays, oral skills classes at all levels are often structured around functional uses of language. In a nonacademic context, these might involve basic greetings, talking on the telephone, interacting with school personnel, shopping, and the like. In *New Vistas: Getting Started* (Brown 1998), a multiskills book for beginners, students learn to introduce themselves and greet other people; give and request personal information,

directions, and prices; talk about family members; tell time; give and accept invitations; describe clothing; and give and accept compliments.

With academic adults, practice in activities such as leading and taking part in discussions and giving oral reports is needed to be done. For example, in *Speaking of Business* (England and Grosse 1995), a text for high-advanced learners in business fields, students learn to plan and conduct business meetings, give speeches, make oral presentations, participate in conferences, and socialize with colleagues. With (prospective) international teaching assistants, course activities may be even more specific—simulations of teaching a lab section, holding office hours, or interacting with regular faculty.

In more informal conversation courses, the content can be structured around *speech acts*, which are actions such as greeting and apologizing that are encoded in language in "routinized" forms (e.g., "hi" and "hello" for greeting, "sorry" for apologizing). One of the standard textbooks for this purpose is *Speaking Naturally: Communication Skills in American English* (Tillitt and Bruder 1985), which has chapters covering opening and closing a conversation, introducing and addressing people, giving invitations, expressing thanks, apologizing, complimenting, getting attention and interrupting, agreeing and disagreeing, controlling the conversation, and getting information.

Teachers may, or may not, be given textbooks or materials for teaching the oral skills class. Buyer beware: Not all materials live up to their claims about what they promote or teach in terms of language content, teaching methodology, and textual/task authenticity. In an analysis of a number of ESL speaking texts published between 1976–1995, Lazaraton and Skuder (1997) found that even the most recent texts fell short on the authenticity criteria used (formality, turn taking, quantity of talk, etc.). For this reason, teachers need to become critical consumers of published materials by asking questions such as the following: Is the text appropriate for the level/audience being taught? What sorts of content/topics are used, and are they appropriate for this group of students? Is the focus on authentic communication? Does the text integrate speaking, listening, and pronunciation? More often than not, teachers will decide to pick and choose activities from a variety of sources and create some of their own materials as well.

Activities

There are many ways to promote oral skills in the ESL/EFL classroom. The discussion below centers on the major types of speaking activities that can be implemented: discussions, speeches, role plays, conversations, audiotaped oral dialogue journals, and other accuracy-based activities.

Discussions

Discussions are probably the most commonly used activity in the oral skills class. Typically, the students are introduced to a topic via a reading, a listening passage, or a videotape and are then asked to get into pairs or groups to discuss a related topic in order to come up with a solution, a response, or the like. Teachers must take care in planning and setting up a discussion activity. First, planned (versus random) grouping or pairing of students may be necessary to ensure a successful discussion outcome. While there is no one "right way" to group students, considerations such as gender, ethnicity, background, talkativeness, etc. may come into play. Second, students need to be reminded that each person should have a specific responsibility in the discussion, whether it be to keep time, take notes, or report results; these decisions can, and should, be made by the group members. Finally, students need to be clear about *what* they are to discuss, *why* they are discussing it, and *what outcome* is expected. In other words, it is insufficient to tell students, "Get in groups and discuss this topic." There should be guidance beforehand and follow-up afterward. Think about how *success* or *completion* can be defined for the activity and observed in the groups. Green, Christopher, and Lam (1997) believe that students will be more involved with and motivated to participate in discussions if they are allowed to select discussion topics and evaluate their

peers' performance; this idea is in line with the principle of students taking responsibility for their own learning.

Books such as The *Non-stop Discussion Workbook* and *Let's Start Talking* (Rooks 1988, 1994) contain many excellent ideas for interesting and provocative discussions that can be modified to suit learners at different ability levels. A well-known example is the "Desert Island" discussion activity, where students are presented with the task of choosing five survivors out of a group of ten possible candidates to start a new civilization after a nuclear war. Once groups reach a consensus, they must present their choices to the other groups and argue for them if the groups disagree.

A creative variation on the discussion is the "Cocktail Party" activity (Lester 1994), where an actual social occasion is simulated. Students are given new identities, which they commit to memory. Then they try to find their partner, through introductions and questions, without revealing their own identity (for example, Bill and Hillary Clinton; a vegetarian and a manager of McDonald's). After partners are located, the students can write a dialogue consistent with their identities.

Speeches

Another common activity in the oral skills class is the *prepared speech*. Topics for speeches will vary depending on the level of the student and the focus of the class, but in any case, students should be given some leeway in determining the content of their talks. In other words, the teacher can provide the structure for the speech—its rhetorical genre (narration, description, etc.) and its time restrictions—while the students select the content. For example, asking students to "tell us about an unforgettable experience you had" allows them to talk about something that is personally meaningful while at the same time encourages narration and description.

Speeches can be frightening for the speaker and, after a while, boring for the listeners, so it is a good idea to assign the listeners some responsibilities during the speeches. This is an excellent time to require peer evaluation of a classmate's speech. Generally, one or two students can be assigned beforehand the responsibility for evaluating a certain speech, using guidelines created by the teacher or—with more advanced students—by the learners themselves. Who better to decide what is or is not important when listening to a peer's speech? At the speech's conclusion, the evaluators can be asked to summarize its content, note strengths or weaknesses, or relate the speech topic to a personal experience.

Videotaping of speeches allows all evaluators (the speaker, peers, and teacher) to do a more in-depth critique at a later time with the videotape. For self-evaluation, students themselves can come up with their own evaluation guidelines, use teacher-made criteria, or a combination of the two. Students are usually surprised to see how they appear and sound on the tape and can often come up with their own ideas about how to improve their performances. If the speeches are audiotaped or videotaped, some of the language analysis activities described below can be used to encourage learners to become aware of their individual problems with pronunciation, grammar, vocabulary, and fluency.

Teacher evaluation of speeches can also benefit from the availability of videotapes since they allow for more sustained attention to both the overall speech and to the details of performance than real-time evaluation does. Of course, the evaluation criteria used should be consistent with the goals of the class: categories of performance that may be considered include *delivery* (Was the volume loud enough? Was the speed appropriate? Did the speaker stay within the time limits?), *interaction/rapport with audience* (How were the visual aspects of the presentation—eye contact, posture, gestures, nervousness?), *content and organization* (Was it easy to locate and understand the main event or main point of the talk? Was there an appropriate introduction and conclusion?), and *language skills* (Were there any particular problems with grammar, fluency, vocabulary, or pronunciation?).

A second type of speech is the *impromptu speech*, which can serve several purposes in an oral skills class. Of course, this activity gives students more actual practice with speaking the language, but it also forces them to think, and speak, on their feet without the benefit of notes or memorization. A variation on this activity can be part of a lesson on using hesitation markers, such as *um, eh, well, sort of,* and *like.* Students are told that using hesitation markers is a speaking strategy that is an acceptable, if not preferred, alternative to silence, which can cause embarrassment and confusion and can also permit other people to take over a conversation. After going over a list of hesitation markers and letting students practice their pronunciation and intonation, each learner is assigned a topic he or she is likely to know little about. For example, in university academic English classes, topics such as finding a derivative in mathematics or describing the molecular structure of carbon are likely to be unfamiliar to at least some members of the class. With nonacademic learners, describing how a camera works or explaining how to preserve fruit or to change spark plugs in a car may be suitable topics. Once students understand the task and are familiar with the markers, they are given a strip of paper with the topic on it just before being asked to speak. They are then asked to give a one-minute, unprepared response in which they should keep talking using the hesitation markers—not be silent, and give as little actual information as possible. This is actually a quite a humorous activity that students enjoy; it can be expanded by having students who *do* know the topics give a short explanation of their own after each attempt.

Role Plays

A third major speaking activity type is the role play, which is particularly suitable for practicing the sociocultural variations in speech acts, such as complimenting, complaining, and the like. Depending on student level, role plays can be performed from prepared scripts, created from a set of prompts and expressions, or written using and consolidating knowledge gained from instruction or discussion of the speech act and its variations prior to the role plays themselves. Olshtain and Cohen (1991) recommend several steps for teaching speech acts. First, a diagnostic assessment is useful for determining what students already know about the act in question.

A model dialogue, presented aurally and/or in writing, serves as language input, after which the class is encouraged to evaluate the situation so as to understand the factors that affect the linguistic choices made in the dialogue. Students can listen to and practice prototypical phrases used in the speech act, and then perform a role play (after considering appropriate information about the participants and their ages, genders, relationship, etc.) as a final practice.

Because sociocultural factors are so crucial in the production of speech acts, Lee and McChesney (2000) suggest that discourse rating tasks, in which students rate dialogues or scenarios on various continua of formality and the like, can raise awareness about language and can help transfer this knowledge to production activities such as role plays. Additionally, requiring students to observe native speakers interacting can supplement in-class production activities such as role plays. For example, when teaching a unit on complaints, one assignment might be to have students go to places where complaints might be common (the return desk at a discount store, for example). There, they can listen carefully for how complaints are stated and responded to, perhaps using a checklist that the students themselves create for observing that particular speech act.

Conversations

One of the more recent trends in oral skills pedagogy is the emphasis on having students analyze and evaluate the language that they or others produce (see, for example, Riggenbach 1999). In other words, it is not adequate to have students produce lots of language; they must become more metalinguistically aware of the many features of language in order to become competent speakers and interlocutors in English. One speaking activity which is particularly suited to this kind of analysis is conversation, the most fundamental form of oral communication. Almost all ESL/EFL students can benefit from a unit on[2] and practice with informal conversation, but few students report having either the opportunity or the confidence to engage in unplanned conversations with native speakers. A conversation assignment can be helpful in this regard.

One way to approach this activity is to assign students to find a native speaker (or near-native speaker) they know—a friend, roommate, or colleague—and arrange to taperecord a 20- to 30-minute interaction with this person. Of course, not all of the discourse that results from this encounter will be truly "natural conversation"—the native speaker may fall into the role of "interviewer" and ask all the questions while the non-native speaker merely responds; therefore, the instructor may want to encourage the learner beforehand to come up with a few questions to ask the native speaker. In any case, the resulting interaction will provide a sample of spontaneous production from (and for) the learner to analyze.

The next step is for the students to transcribe a portion of their interaction. Transcription involves a faithful reproduction of what was said on the tape onto paper and can provide a genuine awareness of what speech is really like. One can "see" speech the way one can "see" writing, and students may be surprised to discover that native speaker speech is far from "perfect."

Students are shown an example of a transcript and its notation before starting, and are reminded that transcription is tedious and frustrating for native speakers, too. There is no need to require a very detailed transcript although some students may want to use phonetic symbols for their pronunciation. Students should be warned *not* to correct grammar or pronunciation mistakes, and to include all the hesitation markers, false starts, and pauses.

Once the transcript is produced, there are various activities that can be pursued. One that works well is to have students find several instances of "communication difficulties." They can be asked to define and exemplify the ones, on their own tapes and then ask them to determine what happened, why, and how the difficulty could have been avoided or repaired. In a class where students feel comfortable with each other, tapes can be switched and critiqued, or the teacher can use critical incidents from each for a group or whole-class activity on communication breakdown and repair. Additionally, the teacher can highlight several interesting sections in each student transcript and then ask the students to analyze the interaction and determine why the teacher pointed them out as interesting.

In a variation of the conversation assignment, learners are required to tape-record an *interview* with native speakers on a topic of their choice and then report the results to the class. For example, students can brainstorm some controversial issues (abortion, gun control, illegal immigration), choose the topic that most interests them, and then alone, in pairs, or in groups, survey native speakers about their opinions. The results of the survey can then be presented in the form of an oral presentation which in turn can be audiotaped and/or videotaped for self-, peer, and teacher evaluation.

Audiotaped Oral Dialogue Journals

The activities discussed so far have emphasized fluency and meaning negotiation rather than accuracy. One activity that lends itself well to both concerns is the oral dialogue journal (Allan 1991; Foley 1993). Like written journals, which are used extensively in writing classes, the oral dialogue journal has much to offer both the teacher and the students in the oral skills classroom. Oral dialogue journals are one format where practice with fluency and attention to accuracy can be accomplished at the same time. Ordinarily, the student gives an audiocassette tape to the teacher, who starts the oral journal on the tape by giving some directions for the assignment and perhaps suggesting a topic, such as *Tell me about your first day in the United States*. Be sure to remind students to speak extemporaneously and explain why; some students will want to write their entries and read them, or turn the tape recorder on and off so that they can sound "perfect." Remind them that the purpose of the activity is to work on unplanned speaking; also give them some guidance as to the expected length of their responses.

The tape is then returned to the student, who reacts to the teacher prompt, and then returns the tape to the teacher, who can respond in various ways. It is always nice to make some com-

ments about the content of the response to reinforce that *what* is said is as important as how it is said. Nevertheless, these audiotapes are an excellent resource for the teacher to provide individual feedback and instruction on pronunciation or grammar problems since the student has a recording of speech to which he or she can refer.

In a small class, it is not unrealistic for the teacher to listen to all the tapes on a regular basis: perhaps five or six times a semester. A large class, on the other hand, makes this unfeasible, so several variations are possible. The tapes can be turned in on a rotating basis, some one week, and some the next. Or students can switch tapes with each other and provide feedback, given some guidance from the instructor. Even in a small class, this sort of peer exchange can be useful. Lucas-Uygun (1994) describes an activity called "Secret Audio Pals," in which students are paired anonymously and exchange tapes for several weeks before trying to guess who their partners are. She suggests that the activity can be extended to students from other classes, or to exchanges of videotapes. Finally, a graduate student may be willing to respond to the student tapes in order to have access to them for research purposes (Marianne Celce-Murcia, personal communication, 8/1/00).

Other Accuracy-Based Activities

Still other classroom activities can be used for accuracy practice.[3] In the past, speaking activities that focused on accuracy invariably involved drills (commonly uncontextualized pattern practice exercises), which have, for the most part, fallen out of favor in language teaching. Brown (1994) recommends that if drills *are* to be used, they should be short, simple, and snappy, they should be used sparingly, and they should lead to more authentic communication activities. In the activities described below, a drill using the particular structure may prove useful as the first step towards more communicative output.

Activities that promote students' getting acquainted with each other lend themselves to practice with specific structures but in a realistic context. For example, Wong (1994) recommends an activity called "Two-Minute Conversations: "If I

Were . . ." in which students become acquainted with each other by taking on the identity of various foods, animals, buildings, etc. using the structure "If I were (a/an) ____, I would be (a/an) _____ because . . . ." More advanced students would be expected to produce more than just the structure; lower-level students would probably benefit from some preteaching of the vocabulary, and all students could benefit from some instruction on the present unreal conditional!

Another early course activity is a structured interview in which students talk to their classmates using an interview form which requires the use of *wh-* and/or yes-no questions. A variation on this is an activity in which students need to "Find someone who . . . ." Here, they are given a sheet of habits or characteristics (smokes a pipe, runs marathons, has a tattoo) and must find at least one other classmate who can answer *yes* to the question "Do you . . . ?" The first student to "find someone who" can answer each question wins the game.

Before closing this section, a word about error correction is in order. In the meaning-centered activities discussed here, explicit error correction will probably be out of place because it disrupts the communication that is going on. Teachers may note errors that occur at these times for some later instruction to the class as a whole or to individual students, as necessary. *During* accuracy-based activities, the basic decision to be made is whether to treat any actual error or to ignore it, which will depend on several factors, including the error being made and the context in which it occurs. In the unreal conditional activity above, it may be instructive, if not necessary, to correct errors in the conditional form, but not errors in subject-verb agreement. Some teachers choose to correct only those errors which impede communication (such as incorrect word order) and ignore less serious errors (such as third person singular *-s* or phoneme confusion). Teachers must determine, perhaps in consultation with their students, how these errors should be corrected, and by whom. Brown (1994) presents some useful guidance on the topic of error correction, but he stresses that teachers should strive for "optimal feedback," which shows that learner contributions are valued

in their own right rather than representing imperfect native speaker speech that needs remediation (see also Pica 1994 for a summary of research on error correction and language learning).

Teaching Oral Skills in an EFL Context

This chapter is primarily written with the ESL teacher in mind, teaching a heterogeneous (by native language and ethnicity) class of learners in an English-speaking environment. However, homogeneous EFL classes, where all students speak the same first language and English is not used outside the classroom, present certain additional challenges for the teacher. In a survey of EFL teachers, Nunan (1993) found the biggest challenges in the EFL classroom to be lack of motivation, getting students to speak (a cultural issue for some where speaking in class is prohibited except when called on), and the use of the first language. In addition, large classes are often the norm overseas, limiting both student opportunities to talk and teacher opportunities to provide feedback. Other problems may arise if the curriculum does not stress speaking skills or views them solely as an avenue to grammatical accuracy; furthermore, if the teacher is a nonnative speaker of English, he or she may not be competent or confident in speaking English.

While solutions to these problems are beyond the scope of this chapter, some general suggestions can be made. When teaching speaking skills, EFL teachers need to be particularly adept at organizing class activities that are authentic, motivating, and varied. The use of authentic, engaging materials should be the basis for in-class activities. If the necessary technology is available, showing movies or recorded television programs and playing audiotapes of programs can be enjoyable for students and can provide them with authentic practice in listening to native speaker speech. The teacher can also assign out-of-class learning activities, such as watching and/or listening to an English-language film, television show, or radio program. This material then becomes input for subsequent in-class activities such as oral reports or discussions. Students can be encouraged or assigned to go to English-speaking businesses or embassies/consulates to find native speakers to observe or interact with. They can also be encouraged to start an English club or to find a English-speaking conversation partner. Finally, the teacher can invite native English speakers to the class to give speeches, talks, or presentations, followed by questions from the students; learners can also be assigned to interview or interact with the guest speakers.

Assessment

The oral skills teacher may be required to make decisions about two kinds of oral assessment. The first, evaluation of classroom performance, has been discussed above along with various oral skills class activities. Brown and Yule (1983) make several useful recommendations for classroom oral assessment. First, whenever possible, extended chunks of speech that have a purpose and that are structured or organized should be elicited. This means that isolated sentences, spontaneous production with no planning time, and decontextualized tasks do not make for the best performance. A second important suggestion is that the input given to students, whether it be visual (e.g., a picture for description), aural (e.g., a directive to "tell me about the most exciting day you have had"), or interactive (e.g., questions in an interview), be consistent for all examinees. This can be especially problematic in an interview situation where the interviewer must respond to the turn-by-turn interaction taking place and, in the process, may inadvertently deviate from the interview agenda (see Lazaraton 1996 for more on this issue). Finally, the results of oral assessment should be reported using terms that are clearly defined for and understandable to students. For example, terms such as *communicative effectiveness* don't mean much unless they are operationalized in ways that are consistent with course goals, the student level, and the speaking task itself. Note the difference in specificity between "generally effective communication" and "can answer questions about home, family, and work with a range of simple vocabulary and accurate linguistic structures with confidence and can find other ways of expressing

meaning through paraphrase." Obviously, learning how to write these operational definitions, to create assessment procedures which test such constructs, and to elicit language which demonstrates this communicative ability takes a great deal of training (but see Cohen's chapter on language testing in this volume and Underhill's [1987] useful guide to oral testing techniques).

A second assessment situation with which the oral skills teacher may be confronted is preparing students to take—interpreting results from—large scale oral examinations, successful performance on which has become increasingly common as a requirement for admission to universities, as a minimum standard for teaching assistantships, and as a qualification for various types of employment. Oral skills examinations from four international testing organizations are described here; interested readers should consult the websites for more information.

The University of Cambridge Local Examinations Syndicate (UCLES; www.cambridge-efl.org) offers two large-scale speaking tests (which are independent parts of larger test batteries in other language skills). One is the Oral Interaction test in the *Certificate in Communicative Skills in English* (CCSE), in which candidates take part in three task-based interactions, lasting about 30 minutes: an interview with the examiner, a presentation with another candidate, and a discussion with the examiner and the second candidate. The test can be taken at one of four levels; at any given level the test taker is awarded a *Pass* or *Fail* based on the degree of skill in five areas: accuracy, appropriacy, range, flexibility, and size of contributions. The second test is part of the *Business Language Testing Service* (BULATS), a language assessment procedure for businesses and organizations to assess the English language skills of their employees, job applicants, or trainees. The 12-minute face-to-face speaking test, consisting of an interview, a presentation, and a discussion, is conducted by a trained examiner and then rated by the examiner and another assessor. Results are reported on a five-point scale of overall speaking ability and are supplemented with a detailed ability profile which describes what the candidate should be able to do in English in the workplace.

The Educational Testing Service, who administer the TOEFL® (Test of English as a Foreign Language; www.toefl.org), offers the *Test of Spoken English* (TSE), a test of overall speaking ability, whose scores can screen potential international teaching assistants and health professionals, among other uses. The 20-minute test is conducted and recorded on audiotape and is composed of 12 speech-act based tasks that are presented in a printed test booklet and on the audiotape. Candidates are given some time to plan what to say, and then given 30–90 seconds to respond to each task. The test answer tapes are scored independently by two trained raters using the five-point TSE rating scale of communicative effectiveness; each point contains descriptions of functional ability, response appropriacy, cohesion and coherence features, and linguistic accuracy. Results are reported to candidates as a single score on a scale of 20 to 60. The Educational Testing Service also provides institutions with the *Speaking Proficiency English Assessment Kit* (SPEAK), an "off-the-shelf" version of the TSE, that can be administered and scored by institutional staff.

A third large-scale oral examination, administered by the American Council on the Teaching of Foreign Languages (ACTFL; www.actfl.org), is the *ACTFL Oral Proficiency Interview*. The interview can be used to assess the language competence of teachers, workers, and students in a number of languages, including English. The 10- to 30-minute tape-recorded interview is administered (either over the telephone or face-to-face) by a trained Oral Proficiency Interview (OPI) tester who carefully structures the interaction to elicit the best possible performance from the candidate. The interviewer and a different tester independently rate the tapes by comparing the speech performance with the *ACTFL Proficiency Guidelines—Speaking* (Revised 1999); (Breiner-Sanders et al. 2000), which define proficiency at ten levels, from Superior to Novice Low. Each level in the *Guidelines* is accompanied by an extensive description of what the speaker can do in various settings and with various tasks.

Finally, a relatively new spoken English test is PhonePass (www.ordinate.com), which provides an assessment of English speaking and listening ability that can be used to place students in ESL courses, screen international teaching assistants, and judge the English language ability of (potential) employees in the health care, hospitality, and information technology industries. The 10-minute test, which is given over the telephone and graded by a computer system, presents the candidates with a number of interactive tasks, such as reading aloud, repeating sentences, producing antonyms of cue words, and answering questions. An overall summary score on a two- to eight-point scale is reported, along with subscores in listening vocabulary, repeat accuracy, pronunciation, reading fluency, and repeat fluency.

Conclusion/Future Trends

Oral skills are not only critical for communication in the ESL classroom, they are necessary for communication in, and with, the English-speaking world. As a result, all ESL/EFL teachers will want to do whatever they can to promote the development of speaking, listening, and pronunciation skills in their students. This chapter has given an overview of the theoretical basis for teaching oral skills communicatively, described some features of the oral skills class, detailed a number of speaking activities that promote oral skills development, and discussed some considerations that go into oral assessment and some large-scale oral examinations that ESL/EFL students may be required to take at some point in their learning.

While it is difficult to predict with certainty what the future holds for language teaching in general, and oral skills pedagogy in particular, it is reasonable to assume that the focus on the sociolinguistic and sociocultural dimensions of oral communication will continue. As we learn more about how people behave in real life and how this behavior is encoded in speech (by accumulating research on speech acts and different varieties of English, for example), we will be in a better position to teach and design materials based on authentic language and communication patterns.

Content- and task-based teaching seem certain to remain important aspects of oral skills pedagogy as well. In particular, teaching materials for specific speaking contexts will likely become more prevalent. For example, Tarone and Kuehn

(2000), in their study of non-native speaker (NNS) performance in a social services oral intake interview, found that the NNS used little or no backchanneling (*uh huh, right*) and fewer responses, suggesting lack of understanding. They point out that misunderstandings in this context can have potentially serious consequences, such as the applicants' failing to receive needed funds, or in the worse case scenario, inadvertently committing welfare fraud. They suggest developing teaching materials for this specific context, which might include a description of the purpose and the nature of the encounter, actual forms used during the interview, audiotapes and transcriptions of sample interactions, and exercises based on these materials. Clearly, these suggestions can be applied to other special purpose situations as well and we can expect more such teaching materials and courses to suit the special needs in these interactional contexts.

But perhaps the most profound impact on language teaching will come from the never-ending developments in technology. Video technology allowed the Czech and German EFL learners in Gersten and Tlusty's (1998) study to undertake student-generated video exchange projects, which promoted learning in a number of areas including practice with self- and peer evaluation, fluency in using English, and increased cultural sensitivity. Various forms of technology have also made recording and analyzing large corpora of spoken English more easily accomplished. As a result, we have a much better idea of what "spoken grammar" is like (see, for example, McCarthy [1998] for a corpus-based account of spoken English grammar). How will we as ESL/EFL teachers deal with this spoken grammar? Should we teach it alongside our rules of written grammar? Will features of written grammar be seen as incorrect in speech as features of spoken grammar are in writing today? Furthermore, because recorded sound can now be transmitted over the Internet, it will be possible for learners to communicate with teachers and other learners without having to use audiotapes. Distance learning courses already permit teaching, learning, and interaction with others who are not present in the actual classroom. And it is probably not too far in the future that speech recognition software will allow actual oral communication between a student and a computer to take place. As language educators, we must remain open to these new developments in order to provide the best possible instruction for our students.

DISCUSSION QUESTIONS

1. Think about a foreign or second language class you have taken. How were oral skills addressed? How do you judge your speaking ability as a result of the class? How could the class have been improved so that your ultimate attainment might have been better?

2. What are the advantages and disadvantages of having (a) a native English speaker or (b) a non-native English speaker as the teacher in an oral skills class (see Medgyes's chapter in this volume)?

3. What role, if any, should the first language play in the ESL oral skills class? Would your answer change if the class were in an EFL context?

4. What would you tell a student who asks you to correct all of his or her oral language errors (pronunciation, grammar, lexical choice) in all of his or her oral production work?

5. What considerations go into grouping or pairing students for speaking activities?

6. How would you prepare your students to take any one of the large-scale oral examinations mentioned in this chapter?

SUGGESTED ACTIVITIES

1. You teach an ESL oral skills class where some students, perhaps due to their personalities and/or cultural backgrounds, are the most talkative and dominate class discussions, while others never speak up in class and, even when called on, merely agree or claim they have no opinion. Develop a set of contingencies you can draw on to equalize opportunities for class participation.

2. Imagine that you have access to audiotapes and transcripts of authentic native speaker/native speaker and native speaker/non-native speaker conversation, such as the excerpts from taped

telephone closings shown below. What sorts of activities could be developed based on this type of material?

(1) Brother and sister (native speakers of American English); Telephone

1 B: okay Viola. I'm gonna get going.
2 S: okay.
3 B: alright?
4 S: alright.
5 B: see you this evening.
6 S: okay bye bye.
7 B: bye.
8   ((clicks))

(2) MATESL student (NS) and university ESL course student (NNS); Telephone (Bargfrede 1996)

1 NS: right. right. well it'll come. don't worry.
2 NNS: okay. thank you. (.5) oh alright. I will (.8)
3   finish my conversation.
4 NS: okay
5 NNS: okay? uh have a good time.
6 NS: okay
7 NNS: bye bye
8 NS: bye
9   ((clicks))

3. You suspect that the classroom text that you have been assigned to use in your ESL/EFL oral skills class presents dialogues containing stilted, awkward language. How could you test this assumption? In other words, what criteria would you use to evaluate *dialogue authenticity*?

4. Imagine you have been assigned to teach a university-level oral skills class for international teaching assistants. You are required to cover material specifically tailored to their future teaching needs, but you find that nearly all the students need practice with and ask for material on informal conversation. What should you do in such a situation?

Ask at least two experienced ESL/EFL teachers what they would do. Did you offer similar solutions?

5. You have been hired to tutor two rank beginners, married women who are highly educated in their native languages but have almost no ability in English. They want to learn how to make travel plans over the telephone for an anticipated trip to Disney World in Florida with their families. How would you go about teaching oral skills to these learners? Prepare a course outline for this teaching situation.

 **FURTHER READING**

Bailey, K. M., and L. Savage., eds. 1994. *New Ways in Teaching Speaking*. Alexandria, VA: TESOL.
A useful "how-to" book containing over 100 speaking activities developed by professional teachers which focus on fluency, accuracy, pronunciation, and speaking in specific contexts.

Murphy, J. M. 1991. Oral communication in TESOL: Integrating speaking, listening, and pronunciation. *TESOL Quarterly* 25(1):51–75.
One of the most comprehensive journal articles on teaching oral communication. The "conceptual framework" Murphy proposes is accompanied by an extensive list of activities that focus on accuracy and/or fluency for beginning- to advanced-level ESL students.

Riggenbach, H. 1999. *Discourse Analysis in the Language Classroom. Volume 1. The Spoken Language*. Ann Arbor, MI: University of Michigan Press.
This book is designed to assist ESL/EFL teachers in becoming familiar with discourse analysis as a body of knowledge and as a language analysis technique. It presents various student activities that focus on many aspects of spoken language.

Underhill, N. 1987. *Testing Spoken Language: A Handbook of Oral Testing Techniques*. Cambridge: Cambridge University Press.
A practical, teacher-friendly guide to the testing process which covers numerous testing techniques and suggests how to elicit and rate spoken language and how to evaluate tests themselves.

ENDNOTES

[1] Canale and Swain's model did not include discourse competence until Canale (1983a), and it has since been modified and/or expanded; see, for example, Bachman (1990) and Celce-Murcia, Dörnyei, and Thurrell (1995).

[2] Of course, students can also benefit from some explicit instruction about the structure of conversation. Markee (2000) presents a theoretical overview of the nature of conversation and its relevance to SLA theory and research; Dörnyei and Thurrell (1994) highlight the basics of conversational structure and suggest some ways these issues can be covered in the ESL/EFL classroom.

[3] A number of useful resources are available for teaching grammar in contextualized, interesting ways; see Rinvolucri and Davis (1995) and the end-of-chapter "Teaching Suggestions" in Celce-Murcia and Larsen-Freeman (1999); Celce-Murcia, Brinton, and Goodwin (1996) contains many valuable and innovative techniques for teaching pronunciation.

Teaching Pronunciation

JANET GOODWIN

In "Teaching Pronunciation," the goal of instruction is threefold: to enable our learners to understand and be understood, to build their confidence in entering communicative situations, and to enable them to monitor their speech based on input from the environment. To accomplish these goals, Goodwin describes the tools we need to teach pronunciation in a systematic and principled way.

"I feel that I am judged by my way of talking English. In other classes, teachers often treat me as inferior or academic disability because of my muttering English."

Undergraduate student in an ESL pronunciation course

"Sometime when I speak to native American, I guess because of my Chinese a sense or mispronunciate the word, they ask me what did you say, can you repeat, or I beg your pardon. Sometime my face turn red, and become so embarrassed in front of them. I remembered once my tears were in my eyes."

Graduate student in an ESL pronunciation course

INTRODUCTION

The above quotes highlight why the teaching of pronunciation is so crucial to our students. Pronunciation is the language feature that most readily identifies speakers as non-native. It is a filter through which others see them and often discriminate against them. When we witness otherwise proficient learners who are barely intelligible while speaking, we can understand their frustration and the hope they place in us.

In the past, pronunciation instruction usually focused on the articulation of consonants and vowels and the discrimination of *minimal pairs*.[1] In recent years, the focus has shifted to include a broader emphasis on *suprasegmental*[2] features, such as *stress* and *intonation*. However, many teaching materials still do not make clear that pronunciation is just one piece of the whole communicative competence puzzle. As Seidlhofer (1995) states, "pronunciation is never an end in itself but a means of negotiating meaning in discourse, embedded in specific sociocultural and interpersonal contexts" (p. 12). Indeed, pronunciation instruction needs to be taught as communicative interaction along with other aspects of spoken discourse, such as pragmatic meaning and nonverbal communication.

THE SEGMENTAL/ SUPRASEGMENTAL DEBATE

Pronunciation instruction historically has emphasized mastery of individual sounds. With the advent of Communicative Language Teaching (see Savignon's chapter in this volume), the focus shifted to fluency rather than accuracy, encouraging an almost exclusive emphasis on suprasegmentals. However, just as ESL teachers have acknowledged that an emphasis on meaning and communicative intent alone will not suffice to achieve grammatical accuracy, pronunciation has emerged from the segmental/suprasegmental debate to a more balanced view, which recognizes that a lack of intelligibility can be attributed to both micro and macro features. It is clear that learners whose command of sounds deviates too broadly from standard speech will be hard to understand no matter how targetlike their stress and intonation might be. Thus, it is no longer a question of choosing between segmentals and suprasegmentals but of identifying which features contribute most to lack of intelligibility, and which will be most useful in the communicative situations in which our learners will need to function.

SETTING REALISTIC GOALS

Morley (1999) has outlined four important goals for pronunciation instruction: functional intelligibility, functional communicability, increased self-confidence, and speech monitoring abilities.

For our purposes, intelligibility is defined as spoken English in which an accent, if present, is not distracting to the listener. Since learners rarely achieve an accent-free pronunciation, we are setting our students up for failure if we strive for nativelike accuracy. Eradication of an accent should not be our goal; in fact, some practitioners use the term *accent addition* as opposed to *accent reduction* to acknowledge the individual's first language (L1) identity without demanding it be sublimated in the new second language (L2).

Functional communicability is the learner's ability to function successfully within the specific communicative situations he or she faces. By examining the discourse our students will need to use in real life, we can see which features of pronunciation might be particularly important for them to master. Ideally, this entails observing or videotaping the target communicative situation(s), be it a bank transaction, a friendly conversation with neighbors, a patient-doctor interview, or some other situation. At the very least, it is useful to distribute a survey to students at the beginning of instruction that elicits their needs and interests. This information guides us both in the features we choose to emphasize and in the content into which the pronunciation practice should be embedded.

Dalton and Seidlhofer list six communicative abilities related to pronunciation:

- Prominence: *how to make salient the important points we make*

- Topic management: *how to signal and recognize where one topic ends and another begins*
- Information status: *how to mark what we assume to be shared knowledge as opposed to something new*
- Turn-taking: *when to speak, and when to be silent, how (not) to yield the floor to somebody else*
- Social meanings and roles: *how to position ourselves vis-à-vis our interlocutor(s) in terms of status, dominance/authority, politeness, solidarity/separateness*
- Degree of involvement: *how to convey our attitudes, emotions, etc.* (1994, p. 52)

If we teach learners how to employ pauses, pitch movement, and stress to achieve the above communicative goals, then they will have attained a great deal of "functional communicability."

As our students gain communicative skill, they also need to gain confidence in their ability to speak and be understood. To accomplish this, we can design our materials around the situations learners will actually face, move carefully from controlled to free production in our practice activities, and provide consistent targeted feedback.

By teaching learners to pay attention to their own speech as well as that of others, we help our learners make better use of the input they receive. Good learners "attend" to certain aspects of the speech they hear and then try to imitate it. Speech monitoring activities help to focus learners' attention on such features both in our courses and beyond them.

A DESCRIPTION OF THE SOUND SYSTEM OF ENGLISH

Traditionally, the sound system has been described and taught in a building block fashion:

sounds ➡ syllables ➡ phrases and thought groups ➡ extended discourse

Though this may make sense from an analytical point of view, this is not how our learners experience language. As speakers, we don't usually think about what we're saying sound by sound, or even syllable by syllable unless communication breaks down. So the *bottom-up* approach of mastering one sound at a time and eventually stringing them all together is being replaced by a more *top-down* approach, in which the sound system is addressed as it naturally occurs—in the stream of speech. In this more balanced approach, both suprasegmental and segmental features can be addressed through a process akin to that of a zoom lens. Global aspects are addressed first; yet whenever the "picture" of speech is unclear, we "zoom in" to examine it at a more micro level. This approach recognizes that all features of the sound system work in tandem.

Thought Groups

In natural discourse, we use pauses to divide our speech into manageable chunks called *thought groups*.[3] Just as punctuation helps the reader process written discourse, pausing helps the listener to process the stream of speech more easily. Learners understand the concept of pausing but do not always manage to pause at appropriate junctures. In fact, the most common error of less fluent speakers is pausing too frequently, thereby overloading the listener with too many breaks to process the discourse effectively.

Since thought groups usually represent a meaningful grammatical unit, the sentence below could be divided up like this:

I was speaking to him / on the phone yesterday.

but not like this:

I was speaking to / him on the / phone yesterday.

Sometimes utterances can be divided in more than one way. This is illustrated nicely by Gilbert (1987), who makes use of ambiguous phrases to show how pausing in different places can cause a change in meaning. Read these examples aloud to yourself. Can you figure out who is stupid?[4]

1. *Alfred said/the boss is stupid*
2. *Alfred/said the boss/is stupid*
   (Gilbert 1987, p. 38)

Thought group boundaries are also influenced by the speaker's speed—faster speakers pause less frequently and have fewer but longer thought groups. Public speakers, such as politicians and members of the clergy, tend to pause more frequently in order to emphasize their ideas more strongly and make them easier to process. In a speech, a politician might utter as a conclusion:

My fellow citizens/this/is/our/moment.

Or a frustrated parent might say to a recalcitrant child:

Come/here/right/now!

In each case, the speaker has a clear communicative reason for wanting to emphasize each word.

Prominence[5]

Within each thought group, there is generally one *prominent* element, a syllable[6] that is emphasized, usually by lengthening it and moving the *pitch* up or down:

I was SPEAKing to him/on the PHONE yesterday.

The prominent element depends on context but generally represents information that is either

  a. new:
     *(I got a postcard from Sue.)
     She's in MEXico.*

  b. in contrast to some other previously mentioned information:
     *(Are you leaving at five thirty?) No,
     SIX thirty.*

  c. or simply the most meaningful or important item in the phrase:
     He's studying ecoNOMics.

Keep the following phrase in your mind for a moment: "I am reading." Now, answer these questions:

What are you doing?   *I am reading.*
Who's reading?   *I am reading.*
Why aren't you reading?!!   *I am reading.*

What word did you emphasize most in each reply? It should have been *reading, I,* and *am* respectively. Each question provided a context for the reply. Since the speaker chooses the prominent element based on the communicative context, this feature should be presented and taught *only* in context.

Intonation

Thus far, we have looked at how speech is divided up into thought groups marked by pauses, and how within each thought group one prominent element is usually stressed. Each thought group also has another distinctive feature, namely its intonation—the melodic line or pitch pattern. The interplay of these pronunciation features becomes evident as we note that the pitch movement within an intonation contour occurs on the prominent element:

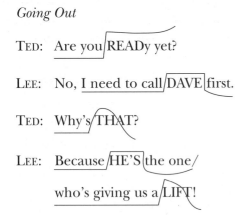

Going Out

TED: Are you READy yet?

LEE: No, I need to call DAVE first.

TED: Why's THAT?

LEE: Because HE'S the one / who's giving us a LIFT!

Intonation patterns do vary but certain general patterns prevail.[7] General rules about intonation patterns are not meant to deny the regional and individual variation of authentic speech. Still, by offering our learners at least some generalized patterns for specific contexts, we give them *an* appropriate option, if not the *sole* appropriate one. Certainly, it is crucial to provide continued exposure to real speech for listening analysis so that students can be aware of the contextual meaning of intonation choices.

Although intonation certainly carries meaning, it is dangerous to make one-to-one associations between a given emotion and an intonation contour. Often, intonation is one factor among many that communicate an attitude. Word choice, grammatical structure, the situational context, facial expressions, and body movement all contribute to infusing an utterance with emotion.

Rhythm

Just as longer and shorter notes make up a musical measure, longer and shorter syllables occur in speech. This alternating of longer (stressed) and shorter (unstressed) syllables can be appreciated in poems read aloud. Even if not as noticeable as in poetry, regular spoken English has rhythm as well. English speech rhythm is usually referred to as *stress-timed*, i.e., with stresses or beats occurring at regular intervals:

•   •   •

She would've liked to have gone to the movie.
(11 syllables but only 3 beats)

This contrasts with so-called *syllable-timed* languages, such as French and Japanese, in which each syllable receives roughly the same timing and length.

In reality, natural English speech is not perfectly stress-timed and the "one syllable, one beat" explanation for syllable-timed languages is also an oversimplification. Nonetheless, the highlighting of certain syllables over others in English through syllable length, vowel quality, and pitch is a crucial road map for the listener.

How can a learner of English predict which words should be stressed and which unstressed? In general, *content words* (words that carry more meaning, such as nouns, main verbs, adjectives, and some adverbs) are stressed whereas *function words* (structure words, such as articles, pronouns, auxiliary verbs, and prepositions) are not.

A point of clarification should be made here. Rhythm, or sentence stress, refers to ALL the syllables that receive stress in a thought group, typically the content words. Prominence refers to ONE of those stressed elements, the one which receives the most emphasis within the thought group:

•   •   ●

She attends the University of MARyland.
(of the three stressed syllables, the third is prominent)

Traditionally, pronunciation materials have included analytical exercises in which learners look at written utterances and carefully analyze the part of speech of each word in order to determine which syllables will be stressed and which unstressed. Although such an exercise can help an analytical learner understand the concept of rhythm, the speaker does not have time to do this during a conversation.

Chela Flores (1998) recommends that teachers help learners develop an awareness of rhythm by highlighting rhythmic patterns apart from words and meaning. To represent rhythm graphically, she uses written dots and dashes to emphasize the short and long syllables. To introduce a new pattern orally, she uses spoken nonsense syllables, such as *ti* for unstressed syllables, *TA* for stressed syllables, and *TAA* for the prominent element in a thought group. Here are two possible four-syllable patterns a teacher might present:

	Pattern A	Pattern B
Teacher writes on board:	. __ . .	__ . . __
While clapping or stretching a rubber band, the teacher says:	"ti TAA ti ti"	"TA ti ti TAA"

First, the teacher pronounces one of the two patterns that students distinguish by pointing to it on the board. Once students are able to hear and also reproduce the selected patterns themselves using the nonsense syllables, they can try to distinguish actual phrases (adapted from Chela Flores 1998):

Listen and circle the pattern you hear.

Student hears:	*Student circles:*	
1. (A little one)	a. . __ . .	b. __ . . __
2. (Lots to be done)	a. . __ . .	b. __ . . __
3. (It's marvelous)[8]	a. . __ . .	b. __ . . __

By first divorcing rhythm from its context and content, we can draw the learners' attention to it, help them internalize it, and then, finally, practice meaningful phrases with it.

Reduced Speech

When we speak in thought groups in a rhythmic way, we find ways to highlight important syllables and to de-emphasize others. Learners will have less difficulty stressing syllables than they will *un*stressing them. One way to weaken unstressed syllables is to shorten them. Another is to relax the mouth when articulating the vowels and to use less energy or muscular tension. Because we are not spreading our lips so widely or letting the jaw drop so far, these *reduced vowels* can be spoken more quickly, helping us to maintain a more or less regular interval between stressed syllables.

The most common reduced vowel is called *schwa* /ə/. This is the vowel you make when your mouth is completely relaxed with no particular effort to raise or lower your jaw or to spread or round your lips. Examples include the unstressed vowels in the words b<u>a</u>nan<u>a</u> and p<u>o</u>lice.[9]

Since many function words are unstressed, they have both a *citation* form (also known as full, strong, or stressed) and a *reduced* form (unstressed or weak). Here are two examples:

	Citation Form	Reduced Form
HAS	He <u>has</u>? /hæz/	What <u>has</u> he done now? /əz/
TO	Do you want <u>to</u>? /tuw/	a ticket <u>to</u> Tucson /tə/

The reduced form of *has* exhibits two types of reduction: (1) loss of full vowel quality (the vowel /æ/ has been reduced to a *schwa* /ə/) and (2) loss of a sound, the initial *h*. In the second example, *to*, only the vowel /uw/ has been reduced.

Linking

Words that non-native listeners can comprehend easily in isolation can sometimes be unrecognizable to them in connected speech. The boundaries between words seem to disappear. Linking is a general term for the adjustments speakers make between words in connected speech. Say to yourself: *Why don't you find out?* When you say *find out*, it probably sounds a lot like *fine doubt*. In other words, you have linked the syllables together (and made them easier to pronounce) by shifting the final consonant of *find* to the next syllable, which begins with a vowel. Some speakers, particularly in North American English, also pronounce *don't you* so that it sounds like *don-chew*.

In this form of linking, sounds blend together to form a third sound.

Morphological information (plurals, verb form and tense, possessive, etc.) can be conveyed by endings, which are often easier to pronounce and become more salient to the listener when linked:

> *She change-dit* is easier to pronounce than *She changed-it.*

If learners simply leave off an ending, important information can be lost. Instead, we need to focus learners' attention on the linked sound, which, in the examples below, provides the listener with the distinction between present and past:

Present   *They live in Miami.*

          (The *v* should be linked clearly between *live* and *in*)

Past   *They live-din Miami.*

          (The *d* should be linked to the next syllable *in*)

We need to make learners aware that all of these pronunciation features (thought groups, prominence, intonation, rhythm, reduced speech, linking) work together to package our utterances in a way that can be processed easily by our listeners. So, rather than being more comprehensible by speaking each word separately, our learners actually become less fluent and less intelligible.

Consonants

Consonant sounds are characterized by *place* of articulation (where the sound is made), *manner* of articulation (how the sound is made), and *voicing* (whether the vocal cords are vibrating or not). These three dimensions are commonly illustrated in a consonant chart (see Appendix 1). The place of articulation is usually illustrated in a diagram called a *sagittal section* diagram, often referred to as "The Organs of Speech" (see Appendix 2).

To teach consonants, we first need to decide whether phonetic symbols are necessary. In most cases, the orthographic letter is the same as the phonetic representation. However, for certain sounds (th̲is, th̲umb, sh̲op, deci̲sion, bu̲tcher, pag̲eant, lon̲g), a single letter that represents the most common spellings is not available. The International Phonetic Alphabet uses the following symbols for these sounds:

> th̲is /ð/, th̲umb /θ/, sh̲op /ʃ/, deci̲sion /ʒ/, bu̲tcher /tʃ/, pag̲eant /dʒ/, lon̲g /ŋ/

A complete phonetic alphabet for English can be found in Appendix 3.

A second consideration is that the articulation of a consonant varies, depending on its environment. For example, the sound /p/ occurs twice in the word *paper*, but the first /p/ is accompanied by a small puff of air called *aspiration* while the second /p/ is not. This and other examples of *positional variation* reflect sound system rules that native speakers have command of but rarely any conscious knowledge of until it is pointed out to them.

Clustering is a third feature of English consonants that presents a challenge to our students. Since many other languages never allow two, much less three or four, consonants in sequence, learners from such a language background struggle with words like *strengths* or *texts*. Our learners need to know how consonant clusters function in English and also that there are acceptable *cluster reductions* for some forms. For example, in the phrase: *The facts of the case are . . . ,* many speakers would pronounce *facts* as *fax*, omitting the /t/ without any loss of intelligibility.[10]

Learners will usually have difficulty with sounds that don't exist in their L1, such as the two *th* sounds or the *l* and the *r* sounds. Despite these isolated difficulties, instruction should always focus on sounds *in context*. How a particular sound is articulated in real speech, or how crucial it is to intelligibility, will become evident only when embedded in spoken discourse.

Vowels

Whereas consonant sounds in English occur at the beginning or end of a syllable, vowel sounds are the syllable core, the sound within the syllable that resonates and can be lengthened or shortened.

In fact, a vowel can even constitute a syllable or a word, as in *eye*. Unlike consonants, vowels are articulated with a relatively unobstructed airflow, i.e., there is usually no contact between articulators. As a result, vowels are often defined in relation to one another rather than to some fixed point. They are distinguished by tongue position (front/central/back), tongue and jaw height (high/mid/low), degree of lip rounding and the relative tension of the muscles involved (tense versus lax vowels). Some of this information is conveyed in a vowel chart, representing the space within the oral cavity (see Appendix 4).

What are the challenges in teaching vowels? First, English has more vowels than many other languages. Japanese has 5 vowels; English has 14 (or 15, if you include the *r*-colored vowel sound in b<u>ir</u>d). Also, there is a great deal of variation in vowels between dialects (*Oh, you pronounce the vowel in "doll" and "ball" differently? I pronounce it the same!*). Unlike the "pure" vowels of many other languages, several English vowels are accompanied by a glide movement. Try saying *eye* slowly. Do you notice how your jaw glides upward? This glide feature is especially important for English *diphthongs*.[11]

Another challenge for learners is the fact that most vowels can be spelled in many different ways. Learners who are used to a strict sound/spelling correspondence in their L1 will often be misled by English spelling. For EFL learners, who often depend more on the written text than on what they hear, this can cause many pronunciation errors (see Olshtain's chapter in this volume).

Finally, vowel sounds are usually reduced in unstressed syllables; notice the difference in the pronunciation of the two *a*'s in *madam* or the two *o*'s in *motor*. In both cases, the first syllable is stressed and the second is not. As a result, the first vowel has its full vowel quality, so the first syllables sound like *mad* and *moat*, respectively. The second vowel in each word is reduced so the second syllables do NOT sound like *dam* and *tore* (as they would if they were stressed) but instead like *dumb* and *ter*. As mentioned earlier, the process of reducing or weakening a vowel involves a relaxing of the articulators, i.e., using less effort to raise or lower one's jaw or to round or spread one's lips.

The following phrases from Morley (1979, p. 116) help learners initially associate each vowel with a key word rather than a phonetic symbol:

SEE	IT	SAY	YES	a FAT	BIRD
/iy/	/ɪ/	/ey/	/ɛ/	/æ/	/ɜʳ/
1	2	3	4	5	6

a BUS	STOP	TWO	BOOKS
/ʌ/	/ɑ/	/uw/	/ʊ/
7	8	9	10

NO	LAW	MY	COWBOY	
/ow/	/ɔ/	/ay/	/aw/	/ɔy/
11	12	13	14	15

Together, students should rhythmically repeat these phrases until they can remember them. The teacher can also attach a number to each key word (as shown above) without introducing any phonetic symbols at all. It is easier to refer to the "it" vowel or the #2 vowel rather than the /ɪ/ vowel, since many listeners will not be able to distinguish /iy/ and /ɪ/ when hearing either sound in isolation.

Word Stress

The discussion of vowels provides a good foundation for understanding word stress. Just as thought groups can have more than one stressed syllable but only one prominent element, multisyllabic words can also have more than one stressed syllable, but only one of those syllables receives primary stress (●). The other(s) receive secondary stress (•) or almost no stress (·):

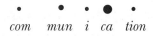

This can be compared to the cognate word in French where the stress is more equal, not alternating, with slightly more stress on the final syllable:

·   •   ·   ·   •
com mun i ca tion

English word stress patterns are somewhat complex and can depend on several factors: the historical origin of a word, the part of speech, and affixation.[12] In very general terms:

1. Stress falls more often on the root or base of a word and less often on a prefix:

   beLIEVE, preDICT, comPLAINT

2. Compound nouns tend to take primary stress on the first element and secondary stress on the second:

   AIRPLANE, BUS STOP, comPUter DISK

3. Suffixes can either
   a. Have no effect on stress

BEAUty	→	*BEAUtiful*
deLIVer	→	*deLIVerance*
perFORM	→	*perFORMer*

   b. Take the primary stress themselves (many of these are from French):

   picturESQUE, trusTEE, enginEER, balLOON

   c. Cause the stress pattern in the stem to shift to a different syllable:

PERiod	→	*periODic*
SEquence	→	*seQUENtial*
ORganize	→	*organiZAtion*

While our students may still need to look up the stress of an unfamiliar word in the dictionary, these basic rules will aid them in understanding how the system of word stress can function in English.

A COMMUNICATIVE FRAMEWORK FOR TEACHING PRONUNCIATION

Celce-Murcia, Brinton, and Goodwin (1996) present a framework for the sequencing of activities within pronunciation instruction. Their five teaching stages include description and analysis, listening discrimination, controlled practice, guided practice, and communicative practice.[13]

These stages are similar to a presentation, practice, and production sequence. Keeping such a framework in mind helps us to plan lessons that move the students forward in a principled way, building the foundation for more intelligible spontaneous production.

1. Description and Analysis

Initially, the teacher presents a feature showing when and how it occurs. The teacher might use charts (consonant, vowel, or organs of speech) or he or she might present the rules for occurrence either inductively or deductively. For example, the teacher can either present the rules for *-ed* endings or provide multiple examples and ask the learners to figure out the rules themselves.[14]

2. Listening Discrimination

Listening activities include contextualized minimal pair discrimination exercises such as the following from Gilbert (1993, p. 20). The speaker (who may be the teacher or another student) pronounces either sentence *a* or *b*. The listener responds with the appropriate rejoinder.

a.	*He wants to buy my boat.*	*Will you sell it?*
b.	*He wants to buy my vote.*	*That's against the law!*

In another discrimination activity, the student listens for either rising or falling intonation in utterances where either is possible.

Instructions: *Circle the arrow which corresponds to the intonation you hear at the end of the utterance, either rising or falling:*

	Rising	Falling
The plane's leaving	↗	↘
Sam finished it	↗	↘
You can't	↗	↘

Using a transcript with a short listening passage, learners can mark the pauses and/or circle the prominent elements they hear. In general, the listener's task should be clearly defined and focused on only one or two features at a time. At this stage, we want to focus learners' attention directly on a feature that they might not be recognizing yet.

The three final stages, which involve practice and production, actually progress on a continuum. It is less important to define an exercise as strictly controlled, guided, or communicative. Rather, it is important to sequence our oral production activities so that they move forward systematically.

3. Controlled Practice

At the beginning, in more controlled activities, the learner's attention should be focused almost completely on form. Any kind of choral reading can work if the learner's attention is clearly focused on the target feature. Poems, rhymes, dialogues, dramatic monologues—all of these can be used if the content and level engage a learner's interest. When performed with student partners, contextualized minimal pair activities (as mentioned above) are a combination of controlled practice for the speaker and listening discrimination for his or her partner.

4. Guided Practice

In guided activities, the learner's attention is no longer entirely on form. The learner now begins to focus on meaning, grammar, and communicative intent as well as pronunciation. Teachers need to develop a continuum of bridging activities, which shift attention gradually to a new cognitive task while the learner attempts to maintain control of the pronunciation target. As an example, Hewings and Goldstein (1998, p. 127) make use of a memory activity while practicing -s endings. Students are instructed to study a picture containing a number of common objects for one minute (two bridges, three suitcases, four glasses, etc.). With the picture hidden, they then try to recite the correct number of each item, while concentrating on pronouncing the plural -s correctly.

5. Communicative Practice

In this stage, activities strike a balance between form and meaning. Examples include role plays, debates, interviews, simulations, and drama scenes. As the activities become gradually more communicative, the learner's attention should still be focused on one or two features at a time. It is overwhelming to suddenly monitor all pronunciation features at once. Set an objective, which can be different for different learners, and let students know it in advance. For example, "When performing this role play, Marco, pay special attention to linking between words." Feedback should then be focused on the stated objective.

SOME TEACHING TECHNIQUES

A wealth of good material has been published for teaching pronunciation. This is not an exhaustive list of techniques; instead, just a brief overview of possibilities with sources for the teacher to investigate.

Contextualized Minimal Pair Practice

Bowen (1975) was one of the first to stress the importance of teaching pronunciation in meaningful contexts. Rather than just distinguishing *pen* and *pan* as isolated words, Bowen embedded these minimal pair contrasts into contextualized sentences and rejoinders:[15]

> *This pen leaks.*   *Then, don't write with it.*
> *This pan leaks.*   *Then, don't cook with it.*
>   (p. 17)

Contextualized minimal pair drills include more than individual sound contrasts as shown, for example, in *Clear Speech* (Gilbert 1993):

Word stress

Is it elementary?   *No, it's advanced.*

Is it a lemon tree?   *No, an orange tree.*
                              (p. 69)

Prominence

*I didn't know
she was <u>out</u> there.*

*I thought she
was inside.*

*I didn't know
<u>she</u> was out there.*

*I thought it
was just him.* (p. 117)

Cartoons and Drawings

Cartoons and drawings can be used to cue production of particular sentences or an entire story as well as for showing language in context. *Rhythm and Role Play* (Graham and Aragones 1991) uses humorous cartoon stories to illustrate short plays to practice rhythm in English. In the description and analysis stage of teaching a particular feature, cartoons can be shown on an overhead for the students to read and analyze: *What's going on here? What's funny?*

Gadgets and Props

To help learners understand the rhythmic patterning of stressed and unstressed syllables, Gilbert (1994) suggests using a thick rubber band. The teacher holds the rubber band between two thumbs. While pronouncing words or phrases, the teacher stretches the rubber band widely apart for the stressed syllables and lets it relax for the unstressed ones. As kinesthetic reinforcement, students each use a similar rubber band to stretch while speaking, first at the word level and then with phrases.

Gilbert (1994) also recommends using kazoos to highlight intonation patterns. Since learners can have difficulty attending to intonation, the teacher can speak into a kazoo, which focuses the learners' attention on the melody of speech rather than the meaning.

Cuisenaire rods, often used in the Silent Way, can illustrate various pronunciation features. These rods (each color is a different length) can illustrate rhythm by using longer rods for stressed syllables and shorter rods for unstressed syllables. Linking between syllables can be shown by moving the rods next to each other. For tactile learners, manipulating objects provides a powerful learning tool.

Rhymes, Poetry, and Jokes

Nursery rhymes, limericks, and many poems all have strong patterns of stressed and unstressed syllables that help our learners hear (and to a certain extent *feel*) the rhythm of English. One well-known use of rhythmic chants is Graham's *Jazz Chant* series. These short, easy to learn chants have a strong beat and can be used with adults as well as children.[16]

Vaughan-Rees (1991) has devised poems to illustrate and reinforce some of the basic spelling rules in English. Since English spelling is usually presented as complex, he deliberately presents examples where pronunciation and spelling are predictable so that learners can begin to internalize these associations:

"What's the matter!" said the Hatter
to his mate by the gate.
"The cat ate my hat
and now it's made me very late." (p. 36)

Jokes can also be used in the pronunciation classroom. Noll (1997) suggests using knock-knock jokes to illustrate and practice linking and reduced speech:[17]

A: *Knock Knock.*
B: *Who's there?*
A: *Jamaica.*
B: *Jamaica who?*
A: *Jamaica mistake?*   (=<u>*Did you make a mistake?*</u>)

Drama

Drama is a particularly effective tool for pronunciation teaching because various components of communicative competence (discourse intonation, pragmatic awareness, nonverbal communication) can be practiced in an integrated way.

Stern (1980) proposes a method for using eight- to ten-minute scenes, usually involving two characters. Each pair of students receives the script to a different scene. Rather than memorizing the lines, they are simply to provide a dramatic reading—looking up frequently at their partner and reading with feeling. The teacher helps them prepare by modeling each line and having students repeat, drawing attention to aspects of pronunciation as they appear. After rehearsing, the pairs are videotaped performing the scene. Following this, the pair of students, remaining in character, are first interviewed by the audience and then perform a short improvisation based on the scene.

Kinesthetic Activities

"We speak with our vocal organs, but we converse with our whole bodies."

(Abercrombie 1968, p. 55)

One important way to effect change in pronunciation is through kinesthetic techniques. In addition to relaxation and breathing exercises, Chan (1987) makes use of basic hand gestures to teach pronunciation.[18] Syllables are shown by the number of fingers one holds up or by tapping out the number with one's hand. An open hand indicates stress while a closed hand shows a lack of stress. Linking thumb and forefingers between both hands illustrates linking. A sweeping hand motion for rising and falling pitch illustrates intonation. Once students are familiar with the gestures, the teacher can use them as silent correction techniques.

In the film, *The Wizard of Oz*, Dorothy, the Tin Man, and the Scarecrow walk arm in arm down the yellow brick road worriedly repeating the phrase, "**LI**ons, **TI**gers, and **BEARS**. Oh **MY**!" Grant (2000) suggests a technique in which learners stand up and take a step in synchrony with each stressed syllable while repeating the above phrase at least three times. In the next stage, learners create new phrases in the same four-beat pattern. For example:

1	2	3	4

HyENas and CROCodiles and PYthons oh MY

Learners should take steps at regular, natural intervals regardless of the number of syllables between beats. In this way, they begin to internalize the rhythm of English.

Acton (1984) makes the point that to "pronounce like a native one must move like a native as well" (p. 77). The technique of *mirroring* involves trying to imitate the body movements, gestures, and facial expressions of another speaker, whether face-to-face or on video. Acton recommends this approach for helping fossilized learners develop more acceptable rhythm patterns.

AN INTEGRATED WHOLE-BODY APPROACH TO TEACHING PRONUNCIATION[19]

Developed out of Isaac's (1995) spoken fluency approach and Stern's (1980) use of drama, the basis of this integrated approach is spoken interaction. Whether one is contributing to a class discussion, giving instructions to an employee, obtaining directions to the bank, or simply chatting, the intelligibility of one's pronunciation is measured by the *success of the interaction*.

This approach involves using short (60 to 90 second) videotaped interactions as the springboard for instruction. One possibility would be actual videotaped interactions of communicative situations your learners face. Otherwise, clips from film or television can be used (with copyright permission).

The class analyzes the video, first shown silently for general nonverbal cues and then with sound to confirm predictions about the content. Once a context has been established, each line is carefully analyzed (through repeated listening) for prosodic features, accompanying gestures, and pragmatic meaning. Students mark pauses, prominence, and intonation on a copy of the transcript and note gestures. This intensive listening focus is followed by intensive speaking practice in which learners try to imitate the pronunciation as well as the movements of each line. Choral and individual repetition of lines allows the instructor to provide feedback on errors. Individual practice is particularly effective in a computer lab using software that allows the learner to both hear each line and see a visual pitch trace of its intonation pattern. Learners compare both the sound of their utterance and the visual contour of it with the model. In the next stage, learners work in pairs to rehearse the interaction while the teacher monitors performance and provides more feedback. Then, the teacher videotapes each pair performing the interaction. Students review their performance outside of class (if a video lab is available) and fill in a guided self-analysis sheet. The performance is evaluated by the instructor, who makes decisions about what pronunciation features to cover in more depth. Finally, pairs are given role cards for a situation similar to the original interaction and asked to perform it without a script. This allows the instructor to see if learners can transfer what they have learned to a new but similar interaction.

MEDIA AND TECHNOLOGY

Audio

Audio recording is the most basic way to capture sound—either a model or the student's own speech—for the learner to review. Tapes from a variety of textbook series can be made available in a language laboratory, either for use in class with teacher supervision or as self-access.

Beyond commercial audio programs, learners should periodically record their homework on tape for the instructor to respond to. As a personal resource, learners can create a pronunciation tape log by bringing in a blank tape and a short written list of words and phrases they find hard to pronounce. The teacher or a tutor/aide then records each student's phrases (the teacher should embed any individual words the student requests into a phrase) onto the cassette. This motivates learners to make choices about what they want to learn and gives the instructor insight into learners' needs and interests.

If you hold office hours or if learners have access to pronunciation tutoring, encourage them to record the session. Tutoring can be very effective, but without a recording of the advice and corrections it will be nearly impossible for the learner to continue working with the feedback on his or her own.

Similar to written dialogue journals, students can record oral entries on an audiocassette in an exchange with the teacher. The entries can be structured by the teacher or left completely to the student's choice. Such oral journals can be an effective way of helping students to locate error patterns, review the instructor's feedback, direct their own learning, and note progress over time.

Video

A growing number of commercial videotape programs focus on pronunciation[20] and usually involve the author teaching pronunciation lessons or actors performing a scene with exercises. Such videotape programs serve as additional models that the instructor can bring into class; most lessons are no more than 15–30 minutes long.

As suggested earlier in this chapter, you can videotape local communicative situations that your learners might face. If you teach international teaching assistants (ITAs), tape skilled teaching assistants in the same disciplines at your university. If you are teaching recent immigrants, find out what their employment goals are and try to set up a mock job interview and record it. If you are teaching young adults in an intensive program, try to find a group of their "age-mates" from your area and record a conversation. Recordings can provide motivating peer target models for your learners.

Commercial films and off-air television recordings can be used to teach pronunciation but are subject to copyright law. The showing of short clips from a film to illustrate a point in a lesson is permissible if the instructor uses a purchased video and not an illegal copy. Off-air recordings for educational purposes are subject to a time limit from the date of recording. For more information on U.S. copyright code, check the following websites:

http://www.nolo.com/encyclopedia/articles/pct/nn72.html

http://www.law.cornell.edu/topics/copyright.html

A video camera is a wonderful tool for recording student performances. It allows the learner to see the entire communicative performance, not just the sound. The teacher can also evaluate the performance in more depth than would be possible from notes taken during the performance. In a class where students are videotaped regularly, class members can be trained to operate the camera.

Computer Software

A number of CD-ROM programs now exist that target pronunciation. These vary in scope, price, type of hardware needed, platform (Mac or Windows), and ease of use. Some programs focus primarily on sounds, whereas others visually display the length, pitch, and loudness of an utterance. Some programs have authoring systems in which the instructor can upload his or her own content to the program; others come with a stock set of utterances for the learner to practice.

In some cases, the visual feedback that is provided is hard for students to interpret or is inconclusive, i.e., even native speakers cannot match their pitch trace to the model. Most teachers who use computerized visual feedback stress that it is *not* necessarily useful in and of itself—the learner must be trained to make effective use of these visual representations of speech.

Other programs function much like a traditional language lab—students record their voice and then press a button to play it back—but they still use their own perception to hear the difference between their production and the model utterance.

An overview of many of the software programs available for teaching pronunciation has been compiled by Deborah Healey and can be found at this website:

http://osu.orst.edu/dept/eli/ june1998.html

This overview contains a brief description of each program with approximate cost and contact information.

Internet

The Internet offers a wide array of resources for both teachers and learners of pronunciation. While not replacing CD-ROM programs, the Internet provides a continually expanding number of websites which can be mined for pronunciation instruction. These include articles about teaching, lesson plans, charts, diagrams, audio and video listening tasks, dictionaries with pronunciation features, and so on. Brinton and LaBelle (1997) created an annotated list of pronunciation websites. It is available at:

http://www.sunburstmedia.com/ PronWeb.html

Using voice-encoding technology, the instructor can e-mail sound files back and forth with students. This type of software compresses the speech signal into a compact digital format.[21] For activities such as oral dialogue journals, the pronunciation log, and oral homework exercises, this option eliminates the need for exchanging audiocassettes.

One of the main stumbling blocks for our learners is access. Although we may have sophisticated computers and Internet connections where we teach, many of the new websites require extensive plug-ins. In general, the more interactive the site, the more powerful the hardware and plug-ins need to be. In addition to a fairly sophisticated computer with Internet capability, many sites will require a sound card, headphones, speakers, and a microphone.

ASSESSMENT

In this section we will examine three types of pronunciation assessment: diagnostic evaluation, ongoing feedback, and classroom achievement testing. (See Cohen's chapter in this volume.)

Diagnostic Evaluation

The most common forms of diagnosing a learner's production are the use of a diagnostic passage and a free speech sample. In the first, learners read a passage designed to contain a variety of features and sounds. In the second, learners are prompted by a topic, a series of questions, or an illustration. In order to obtain the truest sample of speech proficiency, learners should have time to formulate a thoughtful response—however, they should *not* write it out and read it aloud. Another possibility includes an oral interview recorded for later evaluation.

Ongoing Feedback

Feedback during instruction gives learners a sense of their progress and indicates where they need to focus their attention for improvement. With a growing awareness of progress, learners also gain confidence in their pronunciation. There are three main ways of providing ongoing feedback.

Self-Monitoring

One way to guide learners to self-correct is to point out their errors silently (rather than simply pronouncing it correctly for them). We can use various means to cue correction:

1. **Gestures** As mentioned earlier, hand gestures can represent different aspects of pronunciation (e.g., number of syllables, linking, rising or falling intonation, etc.).

2. **Pronunciation correction signs** Signs can be placed around the room, displaying the features that you have taught. Once learners understand what is meant by each sign, it becomes shorthand for error correction. One sign might say *-ed,* which cues a learner to think about past tense endings in his speech (which he might have either omitted or pronounced incorrectly). Other signs might say:

| -s | | Intonation | | linking | or | stress |

3. **Charts** If you have introduced a vowel chart (see Appendix 4) and have a large version of it hanging in the classroom, you can point to the vowel you hear the learners making and guide them toward the correct one. An understanding of the vowel chart can guide learners toward raising or lowering their jaw, gliding, or spreading or rounding their lips to better approximate a particular vowel.

A second way to encourage self-monitoring is to record student speech, in either audio or video format. Learners can monitor their own performance with the guidance of a self-analysis sheet. This is particularly effective if the learners' first task is to transcribe their speech (not phonetically, just regular orthography). Working with their transcript while listening to their tape, learners can monitor for a specific feature. For example:

> *Think about the rules we have learned concerning word stress. Listen carefully to your tape while looking at your transcript.* <u>*On the transcript,*</u> *underline any words that you think you stressed incorrectly and draw an arrow to the syllable that you should have stressed. Here is an example:*
>
> My name is Lee and I study <u>ecónomics</u>.

Peer Feedback

During a traditional minimal pair activity, rather than having students only work in pairs (one speaker and one listener who responds with the appropriate rejoinder), students can be placed in groups of four. In this scenario, the first speaker reads one of the two minimal pair options and the three other group members each mark what they hear. If only one listener is giving the feedback, it is less reliable and convincing to the speaker since that listener might have difficulty hearing that particular distinction.

If a role play between two students is recorded on tape, then the two can transcribe it together and also fill in the analysis form together. In this case, it would be good to pair students together who don't necessarily share the same pronunciation difficulties. Learning from someone who is only a little further along than you can be an effective alternative to instructor feedback alone.

Teacher Feedback

During class, the teacher can use gestures or pronunciation correction signs to provide feedback silently. Out-of-class feedback can be provided through audiocassettes or computer sound files in an e-mail exchange.

Which errors should we correct? Rather than overwhelming the student with feedback on every possible error, follow the guidelines below:

1. Errors which cause a breakdown in communication
2. Errors which occur as a pattern, not as isolated mistakes
3. Errors which relate to the pronunciation points we are teaching

This last point is not to be viewed as the least important; it is related to the first two in an integral way. It is *the errors that learners make* that guides us toward *what to teach*. Thus, what we attend to in our learners' speech is the feedback we must have in order to navigate our teaching in a targeted way.

Classroom Achievement Tests

Classroom achievement tests evaluate learners' progress according to what has been taught and are consequently more focused than diagnostic assessment. The testing tasks should resemble the classroom teaching tasks in order to reduce the effect of an unfamiliar format on learner performance.

Any oral performance to be evaluated for a grade should be recorded on tape. This is not only to make the teacher's evaluation of it easier (although this is the case); it also allows the learner to review and revise the tape before turning it in. In fact, since one of our goals is to help learners monitor their own speech, this step is crucial. Although our ultimate goal is intelligibility during spontaneous speech, for assessment purposes it is also critical to know whether learners can control their pronunciation during a communicative task when they are monitoring for specific features. This ability to determine what might have gone wrong in their pronunciation allows learners to recover from a communication breakdown in real life. In other words, when they notice the puzzled look or blank stare, they can mentally run through what they just said and in all likelihood, reformulate the same utterance intelligibly.

CONCLUSION

The discussion of assessment brings us full circle back to the goals we have set for ourselves and our learners. These goals are realistic—the ability of our learners to understand and be understood in the communicative situations they face, the confidence to enter these communicative situations with ease, and the ability to monitor their speech in order to make adjustments and improvements

based on input from the environment. If we consider the frustration expressed by the learners quoted at the beginning of this chapter, we now have tools to respond to their pronunciation needs in a systematic and principled way.

DISCUSSION QUESTIONS

1. Think about a foreign language you have learned. How good is your accent? What factors have contributed to how well you pronounce this language?
2. Think of one communicative situation you engage in every day. What kinds of language do you use? What aspects of pronunciation do you need to know to function well in this situation?
3. Who is better equipped to teach pronunciation—a non-native who speaks the L1 of her learners or a native English teacher who does not? Upon which factors might your answer depend?
4. Which aspect of pronunciation is the hardest to teach? Why?

SUGGESTED ACTIVITIES

1. Consult one of the references listed below that contain contrastive analyses and summarize the information for a language that you know well (other than English). What are the predicted pronunciation errors for learners from that language when learning English? How does this compare with your knowledge of the sound systems of the two languages?

Avery, P., and S. Ehrlich. 1992. *Teaching American English Pronunciation*. Oxford: Oxford University Press. (Chapter 8)

Deterding, D. H., and G. R. Poedjosoedarmo. 1998. *The Sounds of English: Phonetics and Phonology for English Teachers in Southeast Asia*. Singapore: Prentice Hall.

Swan, M., and B. Smith, eds. 2001. *Learner English*. 2d ed. Cambridge: Cambridge University Press.

2. Choose one pronunciation teaching point (e.g., word stress in compound nouns, /l/ versus /r/, one rhythm pattern). Develop one or two activities for each of the five stages of the communicative framework to teach this point.

3. Interview a non-native speaker of English who has a good accent. How did this person achieve good pronunciation?

4. Examine a textbook for teaching pronunciation and evaluate it in terms of

- *Layout:* Is it user-friendly? Are the diagrams, charts, and explanations clear?
- *Use of phonetic symbols*
- *Focus:* segmentals, suprasegmentals, or both?
- *Exercises:* logical progression from controlled to communicative? Are the instructions clear? Is the language authentic? (See Byrd's chapter in this volume as you do this activity.)

 FURTHER READING

Teacher References

Avery, P., and S. Erlich. 1992. *Teaching American English Pronunciation.* Oxford: Oxford University Press.

Celce-Murcia, M., D. Brinton, and J. Goodwin. 1996. *Teaching Pronunciation: A Reference for Teachers of English to Speakers of Other Languages.* Cambridge: Cambridge University Press.

Dalton, C., and B. Seidlhofer. 1994. *Pronunciation.* Oxford: Oxford University Press.

Morley, J., ed. 1987. *Current Perspectives on Pronunciation.* Washington, DC: TESOL.

———, ed. 1994. *Pronunciation Pedagogy and Theory.* Washington, DC: TESOL.

Student Texts

Dauer, R. 1993. *Accurate English: A Complete Course in Pronunciation.* Englewood Cliffs, N J: Prentice Hall Regents.

Gilbert, J. 1993. *Clear Speech.* 2d ed. New York: Cambridge University Press.

———, 2001. *Clear Speech from the Start.* New York: Cambridge University Press.

Grant, L. 2001. *Well Said: Pronunciation for Clear Communication.* 2d ed. Boston, MA: Heinle & Heinle.

Hewings, M. and S. Goldstein. 1998. *Pronunciation Plus: Practice through Interaction.* Cambridge: Cambridge University Press.

Miller, S. 2000. *Targeting Pronunciation.* Boston, MA: Houghton Mifflin.

Collections of Pronunciation Activities

Bowen, T., and J. Marks. 1992. *The Pronunciation Book: Student-Centered Activities for Pronunciation Work.* London: Longman.

Hancock, M. 1995. *Pronunciation Games.* Cambridge: Cambridge University Press.

 **WEBSITES**

TESOL Speech and Pronunciation Interest Section
Contains information about pronunciation issues, resources, activities, articles, and links to relevant sites.
http://www.public.iastate.edu/~jlevis/SPRIS

IATEFL Pronunciation Special Interest Group
An international site for teachers of English. Contains links, articles, bibliography, and information about SPEAK OUT! (the newsletter for this group).
http://members.aol.com/pronunciationsig/

Prolinks
John Murphy's list of sites related to phonology and teaching pronunciation. Includes Murphy's annotated list of resource books, journal articles, classroom texts, etc.
http://www.gsu.edu/~esljmm/ss/prolinks.htm

The Internet TESL Journal's pronunciation links
This site includes a variety of links for both learners and teachers.
http://www.aitech.ac.jp/~iteslj/links/ESL/Pronunciation/

Dave's ESL Café Web Guide for Pronunciation
Dave Sperling's source of annotated pronunciation links.
www.eslcafe.com/search/Pronunciation

Lessons
A nice selection of lesson ideas and links for both British and American English.
http://eleaston.com/pronunciation/

Pronunciation
Information and resources covering British as well as American resources. Well organized for learners and teachers.
http://esl.about.com/homework/esl/msub17.htm

ENDNOTES

1 A minimal pair is a set of two words that are alike except for one sound, e.g., *bet* and *bat*, or *great* and *crate*.

2 The term *segmentals* refers to the actual consonant and vowel sounds. The term *suprasegmentals* refers to the features which occur "above the segments," e.g., the stress, rhythm, and intonation.

3 Other terms for this include *tone units, breath groups*, and *intonation units*.

4 1. Alfred said, "The boss is stupid." 2. "Alfred," said the boss, "is stupid."

5 Other common terms for this include *nuclear stress, tonic syllable, focus word, emphasis*, and *primary phrase stress*.

6 When words of more than one syllable are prominent, it is only the syllable receiving primary stress that is prominent (e.g., SPEAKing, ecoNOMics).

7 See Bolinger (1986); Brazil, Coulthard, and Johns (1980); Celce-Murcia, Brinton, and Goodwin (1996) for descriptions of intonation patterns.

8 The correct answers are *a, b, a.*

9 In many North American learner textbooks, the schwa /ə/ symbol also represents the full stressed vowel /ʌ/, as in "bus." This pedagogical simplification thus describes the two vowels in the word "above" as being similar in quality if not in length.

10 See Celce-Murcia, Brinton, and Goodwin (1996), for further explanation of cluster reduction.

11 A diphthong is a sound that combines two vowel sounds in one vowel nucleus.

12 See Dickerson (1989), (1994) or Celce-Murcia, Brinton, and Goodwin (1996) for further explanation of word stress rules.

13 These stages are not necessarily meant to occur in one 50-minute lesson. They simply represent a pedagogical sequence which could take place over several lessons.

14 The *-ed* ending has three realizations in English, depending on the sound preceding the ending. Following any voiceless sound except /t/, the ending is pronounced /t/. Following any voiced sound except /d/, the ending is pronounced /d/ and following the sounds /t/ or /d/, the ending is an extra syllable: /əd/ or /ɪd/.

15 Good sources for minimal pair contrasts include Bowen (1975), Grate (1987), Henrichsen et al. (1999), and Nilsen and Nilsen (1987). A very thorough list of minimal pairs for British Received Pronunciation can be found at **http://www.stir.ac.uk/departments/human sciences/celt/staff/higdox/wordlist/index.htm**

16 The series includes: *Jazz Chants* (1978), *Jazz Chants for Children* (1979), *Grammarchants* (1993), *Small Talk* (1986), *Mother Goose Jazz Chants* (1994).

17 Noll has many more examples in her book, *American Accent Skills: Intonation, Reductions and Word Connections,* available at **http://www.ameri-talk.com/books.html**

18 Videos by Marsha Chan include "Using your hands to teach pronunciation" and "Phrase by Phrase," both available from Sunburst Media: **http://www.sunburstmedia.com**

19 I am indebted to Anne Isaac for a workshop she gave at UCLA in 1998. Her presentation, "An integrated approach to teaching spoken fluency" and the video "The rhythm of language" (1995) inspired my version of the approach described here.

20 These include *Phrase by Phrase* by Chan, *Pronunciation for Success* by Meyers and Holt, and *Breaking the Accent Barrier* by Stern.

21 One such technology is "PureVoice," available for download at **http://www.eudora.com/purevoice/**

APPENDIX I
Consonant Chart

MANNER OF ARTICULATION*	PLACE OF ARTICULATION						
	Bilabial	Labio-dental	Dental	Alveolar	Palatal	Velar	Glottal
Stop	p b			t d		k g	
Fricative		f v	θ ð	s z	ʃ ʒ		h
Affricative					tʃ dʒ		
Nasal	m			n		ŋ	
Liquid				l	r		
Glide	w				y		

Note: the voiceless sounds are in the top part of each box, voiced sounds are in the lower half.

MANNER OF ARTICULATION*
What happens to the air stream as the sound is articulated

Name	How the Sound Is Pronounced	Example
Stop	Air stream is blocked completely before it is released	/p/
Fricative	Air stream is compressed and passes through a small opening, creating friction	/z/
Affricative	Combination of a stop followed by a fricative	/tʃ/
Nasal	Air passes through the nose instead of the mouth.	/m/
Liquid	Air stream moves around the tongue in a relatively unobstructed manner	/r/
Glide	Sound is close to a vowel	/y/

APPENDIX 2

Organs of Speech

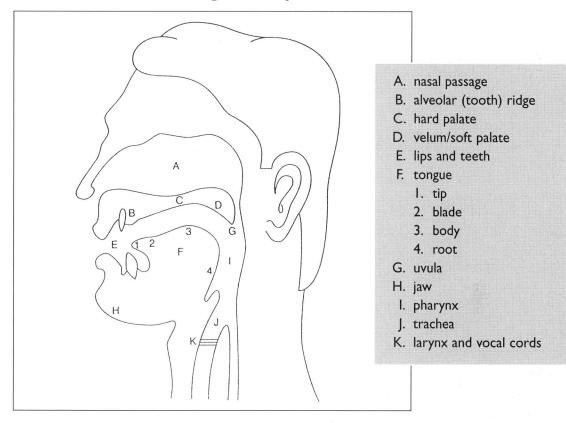

A. nasal passage
B. alveolar (tooth) ridge
C. hard palate
D. velum/soft palate
E. lips and teeth
F. tongue
   1. tip
   2. blade
   3. body
   4. root
G. uvula
H. jaw
I. pharynx
J. trachea
K. larynx and vocal cords

POINTS OF ARTICULATION
(from the front of the mouth to the back)

Name	Where the Sound Is Pronounced	Example
Bilabial	Two lips together	/b/
Labiodental	Lower lip and upper teeth	/v/
Dental	Tongue tip and inner edge of upper teeth	/θ/
Alveolar	Tongue tip on tooth ridge	/d/
Palatal	Body of tongue on hard palate	/ʃ/
Velar	Back of tongue on soft palate	/g/
Glottal	Throat passage	/h/

APPENDIX 3
The Phonetic Alphabet for English

The Consonants of North American English

1. /p/ pat, clap
2. /b/ boy, cab
3. /t/ tan, sit
4. /d/ dog, bed
5. /k/ cry, sick
6. /g/ go, beg
7. /f/ fine, safe
8. /v/ vein, glove
9. /θ/ thumb, bath
10. /ð/ this, bathe
11. /s/ sun, class
12. /z/ zoo, does

13. /ʃ/ shy, dish
14. /ʒ/ leisure, beige
15. /h/ his, ahead
16. /tʃ/ cheek, match
17. /dʒ/ just, bridge
18. /m/ me, trim
19. /n/ not, van
20. /ŋ/ sing(er), long
21. /l/ last, ball
22. /r/ rib, tar
23. /w/ win, away
24. /y/ yes, soya

The Vowels of North American English

1. /iy/ bee, seat
2. /i/ grin, fix
3. /ey/ train, gate
4. /ɛ/ set, then
5. /æ/ fan, mad
6. /ɑ/ hot, doll
7. /ɔ/ taught, walk

8. /ow/ code, low
9. /ʊ/ put, book
10. /uw/ boot, threw
11. /ay/ line, fight
12. /aw/ pound, foul
13. /ɔy/ noise, boy
14. /ʌ/ gun, but
15. /ɜʳ/ bird, curtain

APPENDIX 4
The Vowel Chart

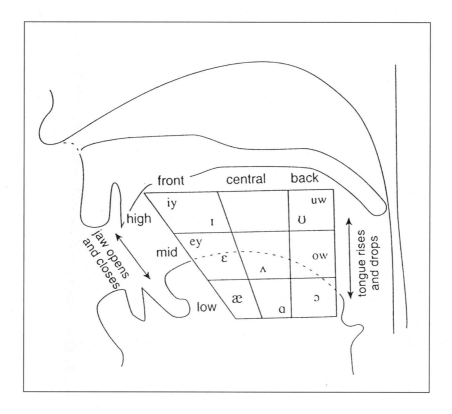

Developing Children's Listening and Speaking in ESL

SABRINA PECK

In "Developing Children's Listening and Speaking in ESL," Peck addresses teachers of adult ESL/EFL who are beginning to work with children. She outlines how children differ from adults as classroom learners of oral language. She also discusses how to make use of resources such as songs, chants, drama, and storytelling.

INTRODUCTION

Perhaps you have taught ESL or EFL before, but never to children. You may have some hunches about how child second language learners could differ from adults. In many ways, children who are learning ESL *are* different from adult students. Consider these anecdotes:

1. An ESL teacher instructs a group of 7 children every day for 45 minutes. They sing "I'm a Little Teapot" over and over again. Standing, they use one arm as the spout of the teapot. Bending, they use the other arm to show the tea pouring out. It feels like an eternity to the teacher: "I'm a little teapot, short and stout, here is my handle, here is my spout. When I get all steamed up, hear me shout, just *tip* me over and pour me out." And then the group starts again.

2. A kindergarten child, already in school for six months, still declines to speak in English. She hides under the table during group lessons. She speaks under her breath in Japanese to the other children, who speak English and/or Spanish.

3. In visiting the class of a noted and successful ESL teacher, you are struck that each activity lasts no more than ten minutes, that children are usually in movement—making something, holding something, moving their hands or walking somewhere. The class looks like an art class.

There are a few major contrasts that we can make between child and adult ESL learners. Children are more likely to play with language than adults are. Children can be more effectively engaged through stories and games. Younger children are less likely to notice errors or correct them. In general, children are more holistic learners who need to use language for authentic communication in ESL classes. In this chapter, I explain some ways in which children often differ from adults as developing listeners and speakers of a second language. I suggest listening and speaking activities and ways to focus on grammar within the authentic and communicative language of a children's ESL class.

HOW CHILDREN DIFFER FROM ADULTS AS LANGUAGE LEARNERS

In an ESL class for adults, the materials are books, papers, the blackboard, an overhead projector, and little else. In a children's class, all sorts of materials are used—magnets, hamsters, stuffed animals, art supplies, costumes, and so on.

Activities need to be child centered and communication should be authentic. This means that children are listening or speaking about something that interests them, for their own reasons, and not merely because a teacher has asked them to. Many authors (e.g., Enright

1991; Enright and Rigg 1986; Genesee 1994; Phillips 1993; Rigg and Allen 1989; McKeon and Samway 1993; Scott and Ytreberg 1990; Vale 1995) advise teachers to teach ESL holistically and to focus on the whole child. Several themes repeatedly come up:

- **Focus on meaning, not correctness.** Eight-year-olds, in groups, decide on themes for a class party: cowboys, dancing, or dinosaurs. Each group makes a poster and presents an argument for their theme. Children speak, write, listen, or draw according to their ability. The teacher does not correct errors.

- **Focus on the value of the activity, not the value of the language.** Advanced beginners each receive a potato. Each child has to name his or her potato, prepare an oral introduction (e.g., "This is my potato. Her name is Patricia."), and make a poster with an image of the potato that could be used if the potato were to get lost. (Activity described by Perros 1993.)

- **Focus on collaboration and social development.** Twelve-year-olds form groups in which they compare maps of North America that were drawn in different centuries. They discuss the comparison as a group, prepare an oral report, and do a written report. Each child has a role in the group.

- **Provide a rich context, including movement, the senses, objects and pictures, and a variety of activities.** Six-year-olds learn terms for community occupations such as doctor, teacher, and police officer. They wear appropriate hats, line up in order, follow directions by the teacher, act out brief scenes, and sing a song while moving and pointing. Note that in this way, teachers accommodate the kinesthetic and visual learning styles favored by most children (Keefe 1979).

- **Teach ESL holistically, integrating the four skills.** Seven-year-olds listen to the story of Little Red Riding Hood. Later, they repeat a refrain in the story and supply some missing words. They help the teacher retell the story, and discuss the qualities of each character. They label cards with the names of the characters and read aloud a version of the story written on word cards and sentence strips. Eventually, some will copy their own version of the story and make a small book to take home.

- **Treat learners appropriately in light of their age and interests.** At the end of an ESL content unit on volcanoes, eleven-year-olds play bingo using vocabulary and pictures from the unit.

- **Treat language as a tool for children to use for their own social and academic ends.** Eight-year-olds enjoy being part of a group as they sing and chant the same pieces in ESL class. They enjoy activities that allow them to work with friends in the class.

- **Use language for authentic communication, not as an object of analysis.** Eleven-year-olds in one class do not know the term *modal verb*, but enjoy making up role plays in which characters are polite to each other. (Activity from Ur 1988, p. 178).

Thus, the principles that underlie children's ESL classes are those of progressive education: that teachers adjust to the child's developmental level, use materials and techniques that appeal to children, and stress communication and the expression of authentic meaning. This progressive stance is not always carried out in schools.

HOW ESL CHILDREN APPROACH ORAL LANGUAGE

In some ways, children approach oral language differently than adults do. The role of language play within language learning is examined by Cook (2000). Children appear more likely than adults to play with language (Peck 1978) and may learn through language play (Peck 1980; Tarone 2000). They enjoy rhythmic and repetitive language more than adults do. They play with the intonation of a sentence, and most are willing to sing. They enjoy repeating a word or an utterance in a play situation. With less awareness of the ways in which languages can differ, children are more likely to laugh at the sounds of a second language, or to be reminded of a word in the first language. Young children such as kindergartners may comfortably talk to themselves, perhaps as part of a fantasy role play.

TECHNIQUES AND RESOURCES

Using Songs, Poems, and Chants

Given children's greater ability to play with language, teachers need to use songs, poems, and chants more than they would with adults. Many children do not tire of practicing a repetitive and rhythmic text several times a day, many days a week. They build up a repertoire of songs or chants and delight in reciting them, or playfully altering them. Often they incorporate gestures and movement into their songs and chants.

Some suggested poems are Mother Goose rhymes. Anthologies of children's poems from language arts anthologies for children are also useful (e.g., dePaola 1988). A guiding principle in choosing poems, chants, and songs is to pick the ones that you like, both as a teacher and as an individual. This is important because you will find yourself listening to them again and again!

Sometimes the line between poems and chants can be thin. In general, chants have a strong and catchy rhythm. Many are written for two parts, with a call and a response, such as for two groups or an individual and a group. Many reflect jazz or rap rhythms. Carolyn Graham originated the term *jazz chants* and has published several books of chants for children and for adults (among them, Graham 1978; 1979; 1993). Many current ESL materials for children, such as *Into English!* (Tinajero and Schifini 1997) include a chant (and a song and poem) in each thematic unit. In the following example, note the two voices or parts and how simple past forms of irregular verbs are practiced.

You Did It Again!

You did it again!
   What did I do?
You did it again!
   What did I do?

I told you not to do it, and you did it again!
   I'm sorry. I'm sorry.
You broke it!
   What did I break?
You took it!
   What did I take?
You lost it!
   What did I lose!
You chose it!
   What did I choose?
I told you not to do it, and you did it again!
   I'm sorry. I'm sorry.
You wore it!
   What did I wear?
You tore it!
   What did I tear?
I told you not to do it, and you did it again!
   I'm sorry. I'm sorry.

(Graham, *Jazz Chants for Children*, 1978, p. 25)

Written collections of children's folklore (for example, Opie and Opie 1959) are another source of chants. You will need to make sure that the values conveyed in a folk chant fit with your own values and the overall requirements of your school. Much of this folklore conveys rebellion against authority, put-downs of various ethnic groups, and joking about body parts and sexuality. Still, as you read Opie and Opie, you may remember less offensive rhymes from your own childhood that you will be able to use. Chants and jump rope rhymes overheard on your own school playground might also be used in ESL lessons. Printed versions of these chants may exist, but children usually learn them from their classmates. In the process, ESL students become familiar with the culture of their English-speaking classmates. Here are some examples from my childhood and from a child in the year 2000:

Made you look,
You dirty crook,
Stole your mother's pocketbook.
   (Massachusetts, USA, 1950s)

Down by the banks of the hanky panky
Where the bullfrogs jump from bank
   to banky

With an eeps, opps, soda pops,
Down by the lilies and I got you.

(California, USA, 2000)

Grandma, Grandma, sick in bed,
Called the doctor and the doctor said,
Let's get the rhythm of the head:
ding-dong [touch head],
Let's get the rhythm of the hands:
clap-clap,
Let's get the rhythm of the feet:
stomp-stomp.
Let's get the rhythm of the HOT DOG
[move hips].
Put 'em all together and what've you got?
Ding-dong, clap-clap, stomp-stomp,
HOT DOG.
Put it all backwards and what've you got?
HOT DOG, stomp-stomp, clap-clap,
ding-dong.

(California, USA, 2000)

Chants build children's proficiency in English in many ways. They build vocabulary. Learners hear pronunciation modeled and then they practice the same sounds repeatedly. Often the rhythm, intonation, and stress patterns of the chant exaggerate a typical pattern in English. Learners hear and produce the same grammar structures again and again. In addition, they are exposed to culture. For instance, in "You Did it Again," cited earlier, learners pick up the undesirability of breaking, tearing, or losing objects. They learn to apologize as well: "I'm sorry. I'm sorry."

A five- or ten-minute session of chanting or singing for an ESL class with varied levels can be fun and effective. The beginners may mostly listen. They will get the gist of the chant if you introduce the vocabulary and context clearly. Providing visuals and objects, and having other students role-play the chant will all help. The beginners will probably enjoy the rhythm of the language, and enjoy being part of a larger group. Intermediate and advanced children can participate fully if they desire. Many will take part in the chanting and singing, thus memorizing the text. Students that choose only to listen can still benefit.

There are several issues to consider when you choose songs for children's ESL instruction. First, you need to like the song yourself. For example, I could happily sing "The Eensy Weensy Spider" (also known as "The Itsy Bitsy Spider") or "Twinkle Twinkle Little Star" almost every day for an entire school year. Those songs speak to me of persistence and hope and of looking up to see beauty. But I quickly tire of "Old MacDonald Had a Farm" and have seldom taught this song to ESL learners. Your feelings about a song will carry over to the children, so it is important to consider your own likes and dislikes. After all, there are many songs available. You could also choose to set some new and appropriate words to a familiar tune.

You might choose songs because they fit with your ESL or interdisciplinary thematic focus. For instance, if your class is studying water, you may want to teach them songs featuring rivers, oceans, or the rain.

Rivers ("Shenandoah")

Oh, Shenandoah, I long to hear you
Away, you rolling river
Oh, Shenandoah, I long to hear you
Away, I'm bound away,
'Cross the wide Missouri.

(Boni 1947)

Oceans ("Skye Boat Song")

Speed, bonny boat like a bird on the wing,
Onward, the sailors cry.
Carry the lad who's born to be king,
Over the sea to Skye.

(Boni 1947)

Rain ("It's Raining, It's Pouring")

It's raining, it's pouring
The old man is snoring,
Went to bed with a cold in his head
And he couldn't get up in the morning.

(source unknown)

In the United States, a good source of folk songs is the *Wee Sing* series edited by Beall and Nipp. Each title includes a book and cassette tape. Some of the titles are *Wee Sing Children's Songs and Fingerplays* (1979), *Wee Sing Sing-alongs*

(1990), *Wee Sing Silly Songs* (1982), *Wee Sing Fun 'n' Folk* (1989), and *Wee Sing and Play: Musical Games and Rhymes for Children* (1981). A British source is *Jingle Bells* (Byrne and Waugh 1982), which includes a book of songs for children and an accompanying cassette.

Sometimes the language of a song or poem seems archaic or unusual ("the lad," "I'm bound away.") Some teachers do not teach songs with lines such as "Meat nor drink nor money have I none," and some teachers try to modernize the language, substituting "food" for "meat," for instance. Other teachers (and I am one) go ahead and teach songs with archaic language. In singing an unaltered folk song, children can pick up language, vocabulary, and culture in combination. Students usually sense that the archaic vocabulary is not appropriate in their own speech. For example, young children learn the nursery rhyme "Jack and Jill," but I have never heard a child complain that someone has broken his or her "crown." Children realize that the language of songs and nursery rhymes is not the language of everyday life. It is another register and not for use with family or classmates.

Choose songs with body movement and hand motions. Many children are kinesthetic learners: They learn best through lessons that involve movement. Just as Asher proposes with his Total Physical Response Approach (1969), they seem to learn language quickly and thoroughly when the brain and the body work together. You can find songs, particularly for young children, that have movements set to them (Beall and Nipp 1979), or you can make up the movements yourself.

One way of teaching a poem, chant, or song is to start with the context and vocabulary, and gradually move the students from listening to repeating to independent recitation or singing. This method is similar to traditional methods for introducing audiolingual dialogues. Here is a suggested sequence of steps:

1. Familiarize the children with the vocabulary and content by using pictures and objects. For instance, in teaching "The Farmer in the Dell," you could start with a picture of a farm, your own drawings, or dolls and stuffed animals representing the characters in the song. You might also ask children to wear hats or masks that correspond to the characters. Your goal here is for the children to understand the vocabulary while you use the visuals.

2. Recite the poem or chant. Sing or play a tape of the song. You may point to a poster or overhead transparency as you sing. The children listen.

3. Recite (sing, play) about one line at a time, and have the class repeat after you.

4. Recite the whole text with the class.

5. If the text has two parts, you now take one part, and the class takes the other.

6. Divide the class in two *groups* and have the children perform both parts on their own.

7. Practice the chants (poems, songs) for about five minutes a day.

8. Make costumes and props.

9. Have the class present the chants, poems, or songs to other children.

In summary, ESL teachers who have worked with adults need to keep in mind that many children enjoy playing with language and welcome the repeated and rhythmic language of songs and chants. Teachers need to choose texts with care and be prepared to work with them repeatedly over a long period of time.

Dramatic Activities

Children can be engaged in a lesson through drama more easily than through explanations or instructions. Some shy children will speak through a puppet but are reluctant to speak on their own. Dramatic activities can be beneficial for children whether they have a big or small part in the production. Even if a child has a non-speaking role, he or she may listen intently while silently playing the part of a tree or a river. All in all, children are more willing to take part in drama activities than are adults.

Commercially published skits and plays are available in magazines for children. Within the United States, a children's magazine called *Plays* and others such as *Cricket* and *Ladybug* are good sources.

Role plays can grow out of a story read or told in class. After the children are familiar with the story, assign them parts. Children might act out the story itself, or react in character to a situation that you describe for them.

Graham's *Jazz Chant Fairy Tales* (Graham 1988) are dramatic retellings of favorite fairy tales by a chorus and individual parts. They are suitable both for a mixed-level or a homogeneous class. Many are appropriate for younger children (e.g., "Little Red Riding Hood") and two ("Rumpelstiltskin," "The Fisherman and His Wife") have themes that appeal to children up to eleven or twelve years old. Before introducing the jazz chant fairy tale, the teacher needs to tell or read the traditional version so that everyone in the class is familiar with the tale.

Children enjoy the rhythmic language, the repetition, and the call and response structure of the dialogue. Many adults enjoy the jokes and productions. Graham has embroidered the fairy tales with her sense of rhythm. For instance, in "Goldilocks and the Three Bears," this chant details preparations for breakfast before the bears go for a walk:

Papa Bear:	I'll make the porridge.
Mama Bear:	I'll pour the milk.
Baby Bear:	I'll set the table.
	I'll set the table.
Chorus:	And they did (clap clap).
	And they did (clap clap).
	Baby set the table.
	Mama poured the milk.
	Papa made the porridge,
	And they all sat down.
Narrator:	Who set the table?
Chorus:	Baby set the table.
Narrator:	Who poured the milk?
Chorus:	Mama poured the milk.
	[continues]

(Graham 1988, p. 4)

Rehearsals of jazz chant fairy tales could take place over several weeks or months, so that the children can easily perform with notes or without. The class should make costumes, props, and perhaps a backdrop for the final production.

Reader's theater takes much less time and preparation. In reader's theater, children read aloud a story (usually from a children's book) that has been rewritten in play form. You can write your own reader's theater script by basing it on a children's book that is interesting to your students and at a suitable level for them. Your script can be almost the same as the book, except that you will have several narrators (for example, narrators 1, 2, and 3) to spread out the parts and give each child enough to read. A more difficult task is to use a story such as a Greek myth, a folktale familiar to your students, or an event that happened in the children's neighborhood. Then you will need to write out the story at the children's level, making sure to divide the narration among several children.

You might want to read the original story first with the class and then, if necessary, to read the script aloud to them. To include the whole class, groups of children can be assigned to each part. As a culmination, children can make costumes and perform the reader's theater for another class. You can purchase reader's theater scripts from Reader's Theatre Script Service (PO Box 178333, San Diego, CA 92177). Scripts are also available on some of the websites listed at the end of this chapter. Children can also make up their own skits orally or in writing. Some teachers assign groups to make up skits at the end of a unit. For instance, after the class has studied recycling, groups are asked to dramatize (1) an argument between people who want to recycle and those who don't, or (2) a neighborhood that learns about recycling.

Storytelling

Stories are a powerful means of language teaching. A skillful teacher can use stories to develop "more efficient listening, more fluent speaking and the ability to read and write easily and competently" (Garvie 1990, p. 161). Children usually enjoy hearing the same story many times. The teacher can easily vary the presentation. For instance, you can tell the story using a picture book, or a flannel board and movable characters. You can tell or read the story while children move puppets or dolls, or as they wear masks and act out the story. You can tell the story while children draw it. You can tell a version of a familiar story such as "Billy Goats Gruff" by a different author and illustrator. Children may listen to a tape-recorded story together or individually, using earphones. Many follow-up activities are possible. When they have heard a story several times, children can retell it, act it out, or write a script for the story.

As described by Donna Brinton (personal communication) and others, story activities can also be games. For example, the teacher chooses a brief story, such as a fable by Aesop, and rewrites it so that there is one sentence for each student to memorize. After the teacher checks each student's ability to recite his or her sentence, the students must first decide how to line up in order, and then recite the entire story. In another activity, three students leave the room, and the teacher tells a short anecdote or story to the remaining students. When members of the class are able to tell the story themselves, student X (who was in the hall) comes back to the classroom, and the other students tell him or her the story. Next, student Y rejoins the class and student X tells the story, and so on. Afterwards, the class can discuss how the story changed in the retelling.

Wright (1995) provides activities to use before, during, and after a story as well as stories and lesson plans for children of different ages. Ur and Wright (1992) describe brief activities that include stories, such as a chain story: One student begins a story and others take turns adding sentences, whether orally or in writing.

Gesture and Movement

Children need to move around more than adults do. As mentioned above, you can combine gesture and movement with songs, poems, or chants, with drama, and with stories. You can ask children to answer a question through movement: for instance, to say *yes* by raising one hand and *no* by looking at the floor. With young children, some teachers break up the lesson every five or ten minutes for a minute or two of physical exercise or dancing.

Total Physical Response (TPR)

The best known ESL approach involving movement is Total Physical Response (Asher 1969). In TPR, the teacher gives commands, models them, and gradually weans the student from watching the teacher's model. Soon students are able to carry out a variety of commands. They understand most of what is said, and in the process acquire receptive language, especially vocabulary and grammar. A lesson might start like this:

Teacher:	Stand up. (pauses, then stands up)
	Touch your shoulder. (pauses, then touches shoulder)
	Sit down. (pauses, then sits down)
	Stand up. (continues modeling)

Later, some students understand and follow the teacher's commands:

Teacher:	Touch your head.
Erika, José, Mahmoud:	(Touch heads)
Most other students:	(follow others and touch heads)
Teacher:	Good! Great job, Erika and José and Mahmoud!

TPR fits within comprehension-based approaches such as the Natural Approach (Krashen and Terrell 1983). Grammar is not overtly taught, the focus is on comprehension, and the input is supposed to be comprehensible.

While books of TPR commands are available, many teachers write their own commands, perhaps relating them to the topic of study. For instance, if children are studying the water cycle, commands such as *Touch/Point to/Pick up the Cloud/River/Raindrop* can be carried out using pictures or word cards. With a series of commands, teachers can ask students to carry out a simple process such as making a terrarium in which water will evaporate and condense: *Take the glass terrarium. Put water in the pool. Spray water on the sides Put plastic wrap on top. Put the terrarium by the window.*

Total Physical Response (TPR) Storytelling

TPR storytelling (Ray and Seely 1998; Seely and Romijn 1998) is a method of second or foreign language teaching that includes actions, pantomime, and other techniques. Much is taught through stories. The instructor begins by teaching the words of a story through associated gestures. Each word has its own gesture, perhaps a sign in American Sign Language (the language of the deaf in the United States) or perhaps a gesture that the teacher invents. Students then practice the vocabulary in pairs: One speaks and the other makes the gesture. After the vocabulary has been covered, the teacher tells a mini-story to the students, trying to incorporate the students' names and characteristics. After about a month of instruction, a teacher might tell a mini-story, such as the one below, much of which students would understand because of the previous stories, gestures, and pantomimes:

> Tammy has a cat in the chair. The cat runs away. Tammy looks everywhere for the cat. She comes back and sits down. Oh! The cat is asleep in the chair.
>
> (Seely and Romijn 1998, p. 42)

Later on, students are able to tell the story themselves, while others act it out. In the next step, the teacher tells a main story which students later retell and revise. Last, students create their own stories and tell them. Tests focus on vocabulary. In the second or third year, grammar is taught by telling the stories from another point of view, thus requiring the learner to change tenses, pronouns, and so on.

Teaching Grammar

Younger children are less likely to focus on the vocabulary or pronunciation errors of others, or to correct them. As children grow older, their metalinguistic awareness (ability to analyze language) grows, and they do tend to notice errors much the same as adults do.

As you work with children who are developing their oral language, you will notice many grammatical errors. How are you to respond? In EFL situations, where time is short and class is perhaps the only place where the child speaks English, many teachers are careful about noting errors, and plan lessons and homework in response. Some of the strategies and materials that Celce-Murcia and Hilles (1988) present for grammar lessons could be used with children. Ur's grammar practice activities (1988) are arranged by grammatical category (*adjectives, negative sentences*) and many can be used as is or adapted.

In the United States, where many teachers favor the Natural Approach, errors are often seen as indicators of the child's knowledge, but not as invitations to correct. Teachers of younger children (ages 5–10) often ignore errors. These teachers respond to the child's ideas, perhaps rephrasing the incorrect language in correct form.

All in all, when teachers notice errors in grammar, vocabulary, and pronunciation, they can choose from a range of strategies: ignore the error, make a mental note, rephrase the sentence, rephrase and expand, or present a lesson to a group or the whole class later on.

SUMMARY AND FUTURE DIRECTIONS

I have focused here on activities that are usually associated with ESL or EFL children's instruction: songs, poems, chants, drama, stories, gesture, movement, TPR, and TPR storytelling. At the same time, many activities associated with content classes can also give children oral language practice. Some examples are class discussions, pairwork, cooperative group work, oral reports, interviews and lectures.

The main point of this chapter is that children's ESL instruction needs to parallel their developmental levels. Since play is a child's successful work, the programs allow for many kinds of play, with talk built in. Since children learn from each other and crave interaction with peers, group activities are provided. Since children often enjoy language play, ample time is given for rhymes, chants, and jokes. Since children are restless and need to learn through movement, gestures and movement are incorporated into songs and games. In addition, TPR along with TPR storytelling are used. Children also move around as they work on experiments and art projects, and as they handle objects that relate to their topic of study. Stories, told with various kinds of visuals and sometimes supplemented with dramatic activities, provide children with a context for the language they are learning. These are examples for just some of the principles given at the beginning of this chapter. In addition, ESL materials published for children often reflect sensitivity to different learning styles (Peck 1995).

Since the 1960s, oral language has been emphasized more than written language in children's ESL. In the United States, children would often take part in listening and speaking activities in ESL classes, but would get most of their reading and writing instruction in English in a mainstream class.

Currently, in the schools of test-driven states such as California, reading seems to be the skill most taught and tested. Government agencies test children's reading and publicize scores. Publishers market "teacher-proof" materials such as *Success for All* and *Open Court,* asserting their usefulness with all children, including English-language learners. It is likely that publishers will decide that more work on oral language needs to go along with reading and writing activities. At the same time, materials such as *Into English!* may start to incorporate more written language. In all, the pendulum may swing back to oral language and then to an understanding of how all four skills can be taught so that they nourish each other.

Of current ESL methods, TPR storytelling seems ripe for further development and dissemination. When additional materials are produced and marketed—teachers' guides, student books, training videos—more teachers can learn to use this approach on their own, as well as through the existing training programs. Research may further document the success of an approach that relies on gesture, movement,

humor and stories. Perhaps other techniques will emerge in which students learn stories, act them out, retell, and vary them.

Teachers who move from ESL instruction for adults to ESL for children may find that their focus on the structure of English changes to a focus on the interests and characteristics of children. Teachers' knowledge of English grammar, of the children's native languages, of lesson planning, and of the contrasts between their own culture and the children's native cultures will stand them in good stead. They also may need to spend time observing some children, whether language learners or not, to become sensitive to children's classroom behavior and preferences. In a way, their task is to adapt tasks that children already enjoy (such as guessing games or jump rope rhymes) to the language classroom. They also can take advantage of some excellent published materials, as well as books and materials written for child native speakers of English.

So, if you are starting a new position as a teacher of ESL or EFL to children, you bring at least three resources: your knowledge of English, your experience with language teaching techniques, and your intuitions about children. As you learn more about children, you will see them more clearly as language students. You will note their learning styles, their need for work in listening and speaking, and their openness to language play; in the process, your work as a language teacher of children can be increasingly successful and enjoyable.

DISCUSSION QUESTIONS

1. Think of an incident when the oral language of a child surprised you. Write down, as far as you can remember, what the child said. Was there language play? How can you describe the unusual qualities of the child's language?
2. Are there other ways that you can think of in which children's oral language (both listening and speaking) differs from adults' language?
3. Games, such as jump rope rhymes and guessing games, can be used with children who are learning a language. In one game, children

line up according to the month and year in which they were born. Then each is invited to tell about his or her birthday. The teacher accepts correct responses and understandable ones: "I was born on March 23" is accepted as well as "Me, September." What oral language games did you enjoy as a child? Which ones could you use or adapt with child ESL learners?

4. Consider an oral language game such as "Simon Says" or "Mr. Wolf." How would you adapt it to a class, for instance, with beginners and intermediate learners?

5. What three stories would you most like to learn to tell to a class of ESL children? The stories could come from children's literature or be your own experiences. What visuals would you use?

SUGGESTED ACTIVITIES

1. Talk with some children between six and ten years old. Ask them to teach you their favorite board games. Examples might be "Clue," "Candyland," "Monopoly Jr." (United States), or "Parcheesi" and "Snakes/Chutes and Ladders" (worldwide). Tape record the players' language during one of these games. Write a paragraph or two explaining what ESL level(s) might play this game and why.

2. Choose a story, a poem, or song that tells a story. Obtain or make three sets of objects which you could use in presenting the story. Types of objects or visuals could include puppets, masks, dolls, pictures, posters, overhead transparencies, props, craft activities, art activities, and so on. Tell the story to your classmates, using each set of objects in turn.

3. Observe an intermediate- or advanced-level ESL class for children. Take special note of the grammatical errors in writing and in speaking. List them. Write a brief report listing the most frequent errors. Suggest two communicative activities that would be worthwhile to use in addressing the most common error.

4. Write a brief paper (one or two pages) about an adult's memory of studying a second or foreign language as a child. You may interview someone else or write about your own

memories. What feelings are remembered? How do you think learning occurred? In addition, how might a person's past experience influence his or her approach as a teacher?

5. Choose a story to teach to a group of children. Draw a picture or make a collage, using pictures from magazines and newspapers, that will help children to learn the story.

FURTHER READING

Each book can be adapted to an EFL/ESL context.

Claire, E. 1998. *ESL Teacher's Activities Kit.* Englewood-Cliffs, NJ: Prentice Hall.
   Experienced or inexperienced teachers can draw from this variety of games and activities. Directions and materials are clearly spelled out. Some unusual categories are Total Physical Response activities and activities in which students build social contacts.

Law, B., and M. Eckes. 2001. *The More-Than-Just-Surviving Handbook: ESL for Every Classroom Teacher.* 2d ed. Winnipeg, Canada: Peguis Publishers.
   This comprehensive guide covers all four skills and is useful for teachers who have two or three ESL students, or a whole class. The book is practical, concise, and filled with examples. The authors discuss how child ESL learners feel and how their language proficiency grows. Their discussion of assessment is practical and realistic.

Phillips, S. 1993. *Young Learners.* Oxford: Oxford University Press.
   Phillips provides children's EFL activities in several categories: listening, speaking, reading, writing, vocabulary and grammar, games, songs and chants, creative activities, and videos. The last chapter, "Putting It All Together," deals with the content and planning of lessons as well as with classroom management.

Scott, W. A., and L. H. Ytreberg. 1990. *Teaching English to Children.* London: Longman.
   A concise, practical and easy-to-read book about children's EFL. The authors also provide a helpful discussion of how young children differ from older people as language learners.

Ur, P. 1998. *Grammar Practice Activities: A Practical Guide for Teachers.* Cambridge: Cambridge University Press.

Communicative activities are provided to remedy grammatical errors in areas such as adjectives, interrogatives, and tag questions. Thirty-four areas are given, and Ur provides several activities for each one. While written with the needs of secondary and adult students in mind, many of the activities can be adapted to children.

 **WEBSITES**

Young Learners: Web Resources (Young Learners Special Interest Group, International Association of Teachers of English as a Foreign Language) (IATEFL)
This organization is based in the United Kingdom. The site contains more than 150 links to sites in several countries relating to ESL and EFL for young learners. This is the most detailed and complete site that I have seen relating to children's ESL.
http://www.countryschool.com/ ylresources.htm

TPRS (Total Physical Response Storytelling)
http://www.tprstorytelling.com/story.htm

This page is sponsored by Education World and shares a site with pages on foreign language resources.
http://www.education-world.com/ foreign_lang/classroom/esl.shtml

Aaron Shepard's Reader's Theater site.
http://www.aaronshep.com/rt/index.html

An index of websites dealing with reader's theater, drama, storytelling, etc.
http://falcon.jmu.edu/~ramseyil/drama.htm

E-mail Discussion Group

TESLK-12 (Teachers of English as a second language to children) is an e-mail discussion group (newsgroup) for teachers of children ages 5–18 (kindergarten through 12th grade).
To subscribe send a message to
LISTSERV@CUNYVM.CUNY.EDU

Or on BITNET to **LISTSERV@CUNYVM** with a message consisting of one line:

Subscribe TESLK-12 your name

UNIT II C

Language Skills

Reading

Teaching reading skills to non-native speakers of English involves unique problems and challenges at all conceivable levels of instruction. ESL/EFL teachers working with young children will be greatly assisted by Ediger's chapter, which provides background and review of issues and standards while also recommending many helpful teaching activities and techniques. The chapter by Weinstein is addressed to teachers of adult ESL learners; such teachers must start by understanding the special contexts in which adult literacy is taught. Weinstein synthesizes current curricula and pedagogical approaches, including a number of promising practices. In the final chapter of this section, Grabe and Stoller cover theory and practice as they apply to reading for academic purposes. After a discussion of curriculum-related issues, they recommend specific practices for facilitating effective academic reading.

Teaching Children Literacy Skills in a Second Language

ANNE EDIGER

"Teaching Children Literacy Skills in a Second Language" describes the background factors and issues influencing children's literacy development in a second language. Ediger brings together unique needs of child L2 learners, contributions of various instructional methods and recent ESL and English Language Arts literacy standards. She recommends a wide range of specialized approaches and techniques for teaching ESL/EFL reading and writing.

INTRODUCTION

In recent years, there has been increased focus on the teaching of reading and other literacy skills to children (Pre-K–6), both in North America and abroad. Part of this may relate to the recognition that reading is probably the most important skill for second language (L2) learners in academic contexts (Grabe 1991), and part of it may come from an increase in the numbers of children worldwide who are learning English as a second or foreign language (hereafter ESL or EFL). It may also be a result of the recent implementation of standards in much of public education in North America, a movement built upon the belief that basic literacy instruction should be a fundamental component of public education. In the last few years, many states and provinces in the United States and Canada have established literacy standards and implemented large-scale standardized testing of literacy skills.

Another possible factor contributing to an increased focus on literacy instruction to children in EFL contexts may be the growing numbers of countries that are moving toward making English language instruction mandatory from a younger age. For example, in Korea and Taiwan, English is now a required subject, beginning in the third grade. Given the portability of books and other reading materials (as well as the increasing availability of reading material over the Internet), reading is gradually being recognized as a valuable source of language input, particularly for students in learning environments (as in some EFL contexts) in which fluent speakers of English are generally not available to provide other kinds of language input.

Notions of literacy are expanding as well. Although many different definitions of literacy can be found in the literature on the subject, and reading still seems to be primary to most of them (see Urquhart and Weir 1998 for a discussion of this), the teaching of writing and oral skills is increasingly being integrated with reading instruction for both native English speakers (NES) and English language learners (ELLs). Many of the new standards, both for ELLs and NES children, also integrate expectations for the development of all four language skills—reading, writing, listening, and speaking (see examples of standards provided later in this chapter). In fact, increasingly, the large-scale standardized tests ask students to bring together all of these skills, requiring students to demonstrate competence in synthesizing information from multiple sources, or bringing information they have heard or read into written responses (see Board of Education of the City of New York 1997 for examples). This chapter, then, takes a similar approach: It investigates the development of L2 reading, addressing writing and oral skills to the extent that they are also involved in literacy development.

READING AS A COMPLEX, INTERACTIVE PROCESS

Various theories exist to explain what is involved when we read, and much of what we know about reading and literacy comes from research on first language (L1) learners. However, current research generally views reading as an interactive, sociocognitive process (Bernhardt 1991), involving a *text*, a *reader*, and a *social context* within which the activity of reading takes place. In reading, "an individual constructs meaning through a transaction with written text that has been created by symbols that represent language. The transaction involves the reader's acting on or interpreting the text, and the interpretation is influenced by the reader's past experiences, language background, and cultural framework, as well as the reader's purpose for reading" (Hudelson 1994, p. 130). However, our expectation and intent when we read is to make meaning, to comprehend what we read (Grabe 1991; Rigg 1986).

Within the complex process of reading, six general component skills and knowledge areas have been identified (Grabe 1991, p. 379):

1. Automatic recognition skills—a virtually unconscious ability, ideally requiring little mental processing to recognize text, especially for word identification
2. Vocabulary and structural knowledge—a sound understanding of language structure and a large recognition vocabulary
3. Formal discourse structure knowledge—an understanding of how texts are organized and how information is put together into various genres of text (e.g., a report, a letter, a narrative)
4. Content/world background knowledge—prior knowledge of text-related information and a shared understanding of the cultural information involved in text
5. Synthesis and evaluation skills/strategies—the ability to read and compare information from multiple sources, to think critically about what one reads, and to decide what information is relevant or useful for one's purpose
6. Metacognitive knowledge and skills monitoring—an awareness of one's mental processes and the ability to reflect on what one is doing and the strategies one is employing while reading

When fluent readers read, they bring together all of these components into a complex process. Exactly how they do this is something that is still the subject of great discussion and research; however, we know that all of these systems play a part in the process. Fluent readers recognize and get meaning from words they see in print, and use their knowledge of the structure of the language to begin forming a mental notion of the topic. They use the semantic and syntactic information from the text together with what they know from personal experience and knowledge of the topic to form hypotheses or predictions about what they are reading and what they are about to read. As they continue reading, they try to confirm or reject these predictions, asking, Does this make sense? Does what I'm seeing on the page fit the ideas in my head? If they are able to confirm their predictions, they read on. If not, they may reread the text, paying closer attention to the print, and reformulating their predictions. And thus the process of sampling text, making hypotheses, and confirming them continues. When some part of the process breaks down, and begins not to make sense, the reader often must re-examine the process being used, and must call upon strategies to try to repair the process and facilitate comprehension again. Some of the strategies may involve compensating for a lack of content or language knowledge by making more use of the print or of one's background knowledge; others may involve changing one's way of reading: slowing down, rereading part of the text, or looking for key words.

These are things fluent readers do. Similarly, for ELLs to read fluently, they must develop the ability to bring all of these elements together simultaneously and rapidly. However, sometimes there are gaps in their knowledge of the language or culture. Thus, it is the task of an effective reading program to provide information and practice in all of the systems which contribute to making the process work.

BECOMING LITERATE IN A SECOND LANGUAGE

There are many similarities in the process of learning to read for ELL and NES children, and as will be seen later in this chapter, similar approaches are often used in classes of both native and non-native readers; however, there are also some important differences (Hudelson 1994; Aebersold and Field 1997). Thus, while some researchers argue that L2 learners should not be segregated from L1 learners (Faltis and Hudelson 1994; Van den Branden 2000), teachers of ESL students need to be specially prepared and may need to adjust their instructional strategies in certain ways in order to teach L2 literacy skills effectively.

Oral Language Skills and Academic Literacy Skills

First of all, NES and ELL children often differ in terms of the language background they bring to the task of acquiring literacy. Children learning to read in their L1 generally are already fairly fluent in speaking and understanding the target language when they begin school, and can build on the oral language they already have. Often, words that they are learning to read are already present in their oral language vocabularies. ELLs, on the other hand, do not necessarily have oral ability in the L2 yet and generally cannot fall back on an oral knowledge of what they are learning to read or write. Thus, the language or vocabulary they encounter in reading is often completely new to them. At the same time, research shows that ELLs' informal oral language skills usually develop more quickly than their academic language and reading/writing abilities (Collier 1989). While teachers can build on this growing oral language ability, they need to keep in mind that some aspects of it are still developing. Furthermore, when initially assessing students' competence in reading and writing, particularly with children who are a little older, teachers must be careful not to assume that oral language proficiency is necessarily an indicator of reading and writing abilities. In other words, it is important to assess both oral and written language abilities independently in order to obtain a true understanding of a child's overall language proficiency level.

Research suggests, however, that even though ELLs are at a beginning level in their L2 development, they may not need to wait until they are orally fluent to begin learning to read and write. First of all, children living in English-speaking environments have been shown to be able to acquire a substantial amount of English from dealing with the English they are exposed to in their daily lives; they are often able to begin reading what they see in the environment around them. For example, children have been able to identify the meanings of words on packaged products, signs, and in comic books they have seen (Hudelson 1984). Also, children have shown that they are able to develop L2 knowledge from written language input, in addition to oral input (Elley and Mangubhai 1983), suggesting that

> [t]he relationships among listening, speaking, reading and writing during development, then, are complex relationships of mutual support. Practice in any one process contributes to the overall reservoir of L2 knowledge, which is then available for other acts of listening, speaking, reading, or writing. For this reason, it is important to provide abundant exposure to functional, meaningful uses of both oral and written language for all learners (Peregoy and Boyle 1997, p. 102).

The Role of the First Language in Literacy Development

Just as NES children bring valuable oral language knowledge to learning to read and write, the L1 and literacy background that ELLs may bring with them is a valuable asset to their L2 and literacy learning. Even if teachers cannot speak the L1(s) of their students, their acceptance of the child's L1 and support of its use can greatly benefit students learning the L2 (Lucas and Katz 1994; Faltis and Hudelson 1994).

Furthermore, although the research presents mixed findings on the transferability of specific L1 reading skills to L2 reading (Bernhardt 1991), there is clear evidence of a strong relationship between children's prior native language literacy and their development of English literacy (Lucas and Katz 1994; Cummins 1991). If children already understand the symbolic role of characters or letters or are familiar with some of the functions of print in society, this awareness can help them move to the next stages in their literacy development.

Varied Experiences, Background Knowledge, and Cultures of ESL Students

In ESL learning contexts, teachers must be cautious about making any assumptions about the cultural or language backgrounds of ELLs. In a single ESL class, students may have widely different L1 backgrounds, educational backgrounds, language proficiency levels, cultures, or prior experiences with literacy. This has several implications for teachers of ESL literacy. First of all, this may mean that ELLs bring differing world and background knowledge, as well as different degrees of topic familiarity, to the task of reading and writing, something that is likely to influence their comprehension of what they read (Steffensen and Joag-dev 1984). This variability of background in the classroom also suggests several things. First, teachers need to incorporate "responsive teaching" (Faltis and Hudelson 1994), by being prepared to employ a variety of teaching approaches and techniques with ELLs. It also suggests the importance of learning as much as possible about the students' cultural backgrounds and experiences. Furthermore, it means using various methods to activate the students' *schemata*, i.e., their knowledge of and beliefs about events, situations, and actions, based upon their experiences (Rumelhart 1980), through such activities as prereading discussions, pictures, diagrams, drawings, videos, or role-playing. Finally, it also suggests choosing (or having the children choose) reading material on topics that are familiar, which

they can identify with because they relate to their own cultures, backgrounds and present lives, or which are of high general interest (Faltis and Hudelson 1994; Day and Bamford 1998). (See Opitz 1998 for a list of multicultural children's books.)

First Language Literacy

ESL learners often come with very different prior experiences with literacy in their native cultures, and they may have experienced different values and functions ascribed to literacy. Or they may even have had very little exposure to literacy in the L1 and may be learning to read and write for the first time in their L2, English. Some may have had their formal schooling interrupted by war or the economic or political situation in their country, with the result that they first encounter learning to read and write as somewhat older students. Children who arrive at a young age may have an easier time fitting into a new environment than older children. There are several reasons for this. First, with younger ESL children, their NES peers are also developing literacy skills for the first time, and they have less far to go to "catch up" to their peers' level of academic language and literacy development in English (Hamayan 1994). Also, classes for younger children are usually oriented toward facilitating the natural emergence of literacy, whereas classes for older NES children tend to assume that some literacy background already exists and treat the learning of language more abstractly and more through the printed text than orally (Lucas and Katz 1994). However, older first-time literacy learners may bring greater cognitive development, more real-life experience, or even more maturity to the task of learning to read and write. For older beginning ELLs, then, it is important to provide reading materials that appeal to their age level and interests, even if they are at beginning levels of reading and writing ability. For this, it will be helpful to find reading materials at lower levels of difficulty, but which are not overly childish in their content. (See Hudelson 1993 for lists of low-level, high interest materials that are appropriate for these students.) Teachers need to be careful, though, not to assume that children with low-literacy backgrounds will come with the same understandings about literacy or print as they do. Children learning to read and write for the first time (including some beginning NES readers) may need assistance with developing an understanding of notions such as the following:

Some Assumptions We Make about Print

- Pictures go with text.
- We read from left to right, front to back, top to bottom.
- Words are written separately from each other.
- Quotation marks mean that someone is speaking.
- Punctuation marks separate notions or ideas from each other.
- Written language has different rules and conventions from oral language.

IS THERE AN OPTIMAL WAY TO TEACH READING AND WRITING?

Over the years, numerous approaches to teaching beginning reading have appeared. Weaver (1994) divides these approaches into two larger categories: *part-centered* (also called *code-emphasis* or *bottom-up*) approaches, which view reading instruction as moving from learning the "parts" and building up to the "whole"; and *socio-psycholinguistic* (also called *meaning-emphasis* or *top-down*) approaches, which emphasize the overall construction of meaning from connected or whole texts, and draw on the reader's and writer's schemata and personal experiences. Several of the more common approaches in each group are reviewed here.

Part-Centered (Code-Emphasis) Methods

Part-centered approaches include *phonics* approaches, so-called *linguistic* approaches, a *sight word* approach, and a *basal reader* approach.

A *phonics* approach generally emphasizes teaching children to match individual letters of the alphabet with their specific English pronunciations, with the idea that if children can "sound out" or "decode" new words, they will be able to read independently. In a phonics approach, children are explicitly taught sound-symbol patterns, and often the conscious learning of rules. The belief underlying this approach is that if children first learn individual sounds, they will be able to put them together into combinations, and then into words. Although phonics approaches vary, most teach the following basic concepts in approximately this order:

Consonants (C)

- for which there is a single sound
  b, d, f, j, k, l, m, n, p, r, s, t, v, z
- for which there is more than one sound
  c, g, h, w, y
- which occur in two-letter combinations, or "blends"
  with *l*: bl, cl, fl, gl, pl, sl
  with *r*: br, cr, dr, fr, gr, pr, tr
  with *s*: sc, sk, sm, sn, sp, st, sw
- which occur in three-letter blends
  scr, spr, str, squ
- which combine to form a new sound, or digraph
  ch, sh, th, wh, gh, -nk, -ng

Vowels (V)

long vowels	CV	be
	CVe	ate, like, rote
	CVVC	paid, boat
short vowels	VC or CVC	it, hot
r-controlled vowels	Vr or CVr	art, car, her
digraph/ diphthong	VV	saw, book; boil, out

Phonics, then, generally involves teaching students the sound-letter relationships used in reading and writing. A related type of knowledge, *phonemic awareness*, involves a student's understanding that speech is made up of individual sounds, including such things as the ability to tell if two words begin or end with the same sound, and the ability to focus on the form of speech apart from focusing on its meaning or content (Strickland 1998). Although there is some disagreement over which of these two kinds of awareness children really need, *phonemic awareness* is also considered important for literacy development and frequently taught with *phonics.*

A *linguistic* approach utilizes a scientific knowledge of language and exposes children to certain carefully selected words containing regular spelling patterns so that they can infer the letter-sound relationships in those words. For example, similar looking word groups such as *take-bake-lake-cake* or *went-cent-tent-bent* and common rhyme or word-ending patterns such as *-ate, -ell,* or *-ight* are used to teach the sound patterns. One linguistic approach uses a special alphabet (the i.t.a., or "initial teaching alphabet") containing 44 unique letters to represent the approximately 44 individual phonemes of the English language. It was believed that if children could be taught using a more regular sound-symbol system (with exactly one symbol for each sound), they could learn to read more easily. Books were printed using the i.t.a., and many children learned to read using this system.

A *sight word* or *look-say* method teaches children to recognize whole words, commonly using flash cards or other techniques to help children quickly identify such common words as *of, and,* and *the.* It is based upon the notion that if children can recognize about 100 of the most frequently occurring words, they will be able to read about half of the words they encounter in most texts. Teachers who use this method often do so because they believe that knowing the most frequent words will help students learn to read more efficiently. The *sight word* approach is often included with phonics approaches, with many proponents emphasizing rapid recognition or "decoding"; however, notions of comprehension are generally not addressed, possibly because it is assumed that once children can recognize words, comprehension takes care of itself.

A *basal reader* approach is based upon the notion that children should be taught to read through careful control and sequencing of the language and the sounds that they are exposed to.

As a result, basal readers are carefully graded, sequenced to present sounds, vocabulary, and individual skills at increasing levels of difficulty, and also to provide carefully controlled practice, recycling, and testing of the language and skills. In many cases, the reading texts are specifically written to have exactly the right combination of vocabulary, structures, and skill practice determined necessary for optimal learning at each level of ability. Present-day basal readers generally come in complete series which seek to provide a total reading approach from beginning to advanced levels. They are often "eclectic," including phonics, regularly patterned words, and basic sight words, and view reading as the mastery of individual reading skills.

Socio-Psycholinguistic (Meaning-Emphasis) Approaches

The *socio-psycholinguistic* methods included here are the *Language Experience Approach* (LEA), a *literature-based* approach, and the *Whole Language* approach.

The *Language Experience Approach* (LEA) builds upon the notion that if children are given material to read that they are already familiar with, it will help them learn to read. This method is based on two related ideas: that learning should move from the familiar to the unknown, and that readers whose world knowledge or schemata are similar to that underlying the text they are reading will be more able to make sense of the text. In fact, this approach goes one step further, proposing that if the actual language and content of the stories is familiar to readers, they should be able to learn to read it even more easily. The LEA accomplishes this by having students generate their own stories; transcripts of these stories then become their reading material. Typically, a class would follow a series of steps like this:

1. The student or class dictates a "story," usually based upon an experience they have had, that the teacher writes down on a large sheet of paper. The teacher tries to maintain the exact wording and expressions that the children

have dictated (if it contains errors, the children can correct them later as their proficiency increases).

2. The teacher then either reads the story to the class (if the children are beginning readers), or has the class read back the story they have composed, providing any help they need along the way to figure out individual words. This "reading" may be repeated several times, by different people or the whole class, until the children are familiar with what they have written. Eventually, the children should be able to read the story themselves.

3. Depending on their level of ability and needs, the class will then engage in various extended activities based upon the original story, including focusing on individual words, letters (e.g., those at the beginnings of words or rhyming endings), or meanings of various noteworthy parts. The children may also select some of the words to write on cards to practice later individually. In each case, the material comes out of, and is discussed within, the broader context of the original story. Additional exercises may also be constructed from the original reading, such as cutting the story up into sentence strips, or even into individual words, and having the children put them back in order.

4. Ultimately, the children are expected to move from the stories they have dictated toward being able to read those written by others. (See Dixon and Nessel 1983 for more about the LEA).

The LEA can be used with very beginning readers and writers because they only need to dictate the stories orally, and even this can be done collaboratively, bringing together the combined abilities of the entire class. Because it involves stories that are first dictated, the LEA allows children to see a direct link between oral and written language. In essence, it involves "writing to read." Because the children have "composed" the stories themselves, there is a close match between their knowledge or experience and the texts they read.

A *literature-based* approach is one that uses children's literature with the intention of focusing on meaning, interest, and enjoyment, while addressing individual children's needs in teaching them to read. In this approach, children often select their own books (generally, regularly published books) and read them on their own or with others. If the children are beginning or nonreaders, the teacher or a more proficient peer may read the book to them. Alternately, if the reading is done individually, the teacher may follow up by holding an individual conference with the child, asking the child questions about what he or she understood from the story or how he or she felt about the story. Children may also be asked to read portions of their stories aloud, and the teacher may take notes on the types of miscues they make as they read (as one method of diagnosing areas to address in the future). Some proponents of this approach maintain that individual skills should not be taught—they will emerge as the child reads. In any case, the overall focus is on the child's understanding of the story. Later, the same books may be used as springboards for writing, drama, or discussion activities, such as writing alternate endings to the story, role-playing parts of it, or describing one of the characters in more detail. Sometimes more than one book on the same theme or genre or multiple books by the same author (an "author study") may be read and compared. Use of this approach generally requires that students have access to a collection of books on a range of topics and at varying levels of difficulty (either in the classroom or in a library). Teachers who use a literature-based approach can greatly facilitate their students' success and skill development by helping them find books which best fit their interests and are either at or just slightly above their reading level. The idea is that if children find that they can be successful at reading, and their interest is held by the books they have selected, they will want to continue reading.

The *Whole Language* approach is a philosophy of learning. Proponents of Whole Language believe that they are not just teaching reading; rather, they are guiding and assisting learners to develop as independent readers, writers, and learners. They believe that language serves personal, social, and academic aspects of children's lives, and that children become literate as they grapple with the meaning and uses of print in their environments. Through such activities as storybook reading (being read to or reading the same stories multiple times) and writing their own texts, children become aware of storybook structure, and can identify (and use) the specific language typically used to tell stories. In fact, researchers have found that children go through a variety of developmental stages as they create their own written texts: (1) scribbling, and ascribing meaning to it (as if it were writing); (2) seeing print and drawing as the same; (3) using letters of the alphabet, often in continuous strings, without realizing that letters have a relationship to sounds; (4) using one or two letters (usually consonants), each representing a whole word (but still not segmented into words); (5) using letters to represent one or two of the sounds in a word, including vowels, and often applying a strategy of using names of letters instead of the sounds the letters make; (6) using transitional spelling, in which some words use conventional spellings and some do not; and finally, (7) using conventional spelling (Hudelson 1994; Gunderson 1991). LEA activities and literature, though described as separate approaches above, are often used along with other activities and content within the Whole Language approach. Whole Language incorporates all of the language skills, based on the belief that as stories are read to children, as children recount what they have heard (and hear others do so), and as they experiment with putting their ideas in writing, they wrestle with sound-letter correspondences and with the structure of written material. Through these activities, children figure out how written language works and how it relates to oral language; through these attempts at written language, in fact, they also learn how reading works. In Whole Language, the use of "authentic" texts from various genres is vital. This comes from the belief that only through encountering and attempting to deal with "real" texts and functions of literacy can children learn effective strategies and techniques for understanding and using them themselves. (See Heald-Taylor 1991 for more about Whole Language for ELLs.)

The Phonics/Whole Language Debate

Numerous studies have attempted to determine the relative effectiveness of many of these methods. Unfortunately, results have often been inconclusive or even contradictory. How does each approach work for ELLs? *Phonics* approaches presuppose that learners already know the sounds of the language, and that once a word is sounded out, they only need to match it up with a word they know. But ELLs don't yet know many of the words, even if they can sound a word out, they will still probably not understand what it means. Even more difficult, if they can't hear the difference between two sounds, for example, /ɪ/ in *hit* and /i/ in *heat*, they may have a hard time learning the letters that represent or distinguish these sounds. Phonics approaches have also been criticized because they don't address issues of comprehension. Rigg (1986) found that the children in her study who were most concerned about pronouncing words "right" showed less comprehension of what they had read. Another reason a pure phonics approach may cause difficulty for ELLs is that many of the most common words in English contain sounds and patterns which do not follow basic sound-symbol correspondences that the children may have been taught, e.g., *come*, or *through*.

A *sight word* approach to reading, like phonics, gives little focus to getting meaning from a text. As we can see from Grabe's (1991) six components of reading that were identified earlier, vocabulary recognition is but one small piece of what it takes to be able to read. Also, common words encountered in a sight word approach, e.g., *have*, *of*, or *do* don't provide learners much assistance, either with recognizing or with sounding out less frequently encountered words.

Criticisms of an *i.t.a.* approach include the finding that children who learned with this approach had difficulty making the transition to conventional spelling (Bond and Dykstra 1997), as well as the lack of sufficient material written in this alphabet (Gunderson 1991). *Basal readers* have primarily been criticized because in the process of sequencing all the language, vocabulary, and skills so carefully, many end up with boring and artificial readings; they contain stilted sentences, pieces of stories, and literature presented out of context.

Furthermore, they take a "one-size-fits-all" approach to the teaching of reading. As for individual *skills-based* teaching approaches, Strickland (1998) reports that teachers have found that their students have difficulty transferring skills learned in isolation to real reading and writing activities.

Some of the findings concerning these initial teaching approaches are promising, however. In the 1960s, the large-scale Cooperative Research Program in First-Grade Reading Instruction, comprising 27 studies comparing many of the methods and materials described above, was conducted. Among the conclusions Bond and Dykstra (1997) reached from their review of these studies were:

1. Regardless of what reading instruction approach is used, systematic emphasis and teaching of word study skills is necessary.
2. Eclectic programs produced better results than did orthodox approaches.
3. Not all reading programs work equally well in all situations. Within particular programs, factors such as teacher and learning situation characteristics rather than method may be more important to students' ultimate success in reading.
4. Children are able to learn to read by various methods and materials. With each approach, some students were successful, but others experienced difficulty. No single approach was so clearly better than the others that it should be used exclusively.
5. A writing component is likely to be an effective addition to a reading program.
6. "The relative success of the Nonbasal programs compared to the basal programs indicates that reading instruction can be improved. It is likely that improvements would result from adopting certain elements from each of the approaches used in this study" (p. 416).

In recent times, the debate over methods has concentrated mostly on the choice between the need for phonics instruction and/or phonemic awareness on one side and Whole Language on the other. Part of the difficulty in this debate lies in the fact that proponents of each side cite different kinds of research to support their method: Phonics supporters cite experimental studies assessing performance on standardized tests; Whole Language supporters cite basic research on how children learn to read and write, as well as classroom-based studies looking at long-term effects (Weaver 1994). Strickland (1998) concludes that "the debates about phonics and phonemic awareness have less to do with their value than with the amount and type of instruction they require" and suggests that even in this controversy, there are points of agreement. She explains,

> Educators on both sides of the phonics debate agree that, ultimately, reading and writing for meaning is paramount. Both sides are keenly aware of the importance of good literature in the lives of children and the need for responsive adults who support children's natural inclinations toward making sense of print. Needless to say, both sides recognize the importance of the alphabetic code in learning to read and write (p. 8).

Increasingly, the evidence seems to support addressing such a complex process as literacy with less simplistic solutions. Hamayan (1994) argues that because ESL students represent a very diverse group of learners, they require a range of approaches. Faltis and Hudelson (1994) say that teachers need to be flexible, taking their cues from students and adapting their pedagogies to meet students' needs. Other reading researchers (e.g., Weaver 1994; Strickland 1998) are increasingly advocating a more "balanced approach" or "whole-to-part-to-whole" approach—one that is engaging and rich with meaning, but focuses systematically on specific textual features so that children can draw their own conclusions about language and apply them to their reading and writing. Strickland provides the following instructional guidelines for such an approach:

1. Skills and meaning should always be kept together. Children need instruction focusing on the alphabetic code to be taught together with that which stresses comprehending, thoughtful responses to literature, and the creation of meaning in writing.

2. Instead of rigid, systematically predetermined instruction that is identical for all learners, such activities as word recognition skills and phonics, as well as invented spelling, can be systematically integrated into programs that take learner variability into account.

3. Intensive instruction on individual skills or strategies should only be provided to those children who demonstrate clear need for them.

4. Regular documentation and assessment of students' learning are still the best way to determine how skills should be addressed and to what degree.

5. Language arts instruction must be integrated with a school's or district's standards and the specific curricular objectives of the target grade level, as well as of the grades below and above it.

STANDARDS AND SECOND LANGUAGE LITERACY DEVELOPMENT

In recent years, as a measure designed to ensure accountability for learning and to set up uniformly high expectations for all learners, many states, provinces, school districts, and professional organizations have established standards for their students to attain. In setting up these standards, much has been accomplished simply through the very difficult process of bringing together stakeholders in the educational system to sit down and come to some agreement about what reasonable expectations might be. For many teachers, finally seeing a list of standards in writing has greatly helped to clarify the objectives toward which they should guide their students.

At the same time, while the establishment of these standards represents a very valuable first step in improving the overall quality of education for many students, they have also demonstrated that they are not the end point in the process of providing an equitable and uniform quality of education for everyone. First of all, many of the standards dealing with the various content areas covered in public education, including language arts, social studies, math, and science, have been developed with the assumption that students are able to understand and use English well enough to engage with their respective content. In fact, while some of them recognize that their students have extremely diverse cultural, ethnic, and linguistic backgrounds, many do not address the key role of language in the acquisition of content. The large-scale standardized tests that are often based on these standards and that document their achievement (or lack of it), make it difficult to obtain a true picture of the academic achievement of many ELLs because the tests do not take into account the interaction between content knowledge and language proficiency. In other words, if ELLs are not able to read, understand, write, or respond to the test questions and content, the test results will very likely not present an accurate picture of their true abilities. An incorrect answer on a test, for example, cannot distinguish whether the student did not know that concept, or whether he or she simply did not have the necessary language ability or test-taking strategies to answer correctly. As such, the current plethora of standards that now exist, while providing useful goals to aim for, may also lead to the unfair assessment or treatment of ELLs.

Second, although there are now finally some standards to teach to, the task of designing curriculum and instruction to meet them is still a complex task. This is partly because, depending on where one is, there are now multiple standards that one may be expected to meet simultaneously. For example, teachers of ELLs in New York City schools who wish to apply the Pre-K–12 ESL standards developed by the professional organization, Teachers of English to Speakers of Other Languages (TESOL), now must synthesize three different sets of standards because they must also teach to the standards of New York state and those of New York City as well (see Charts 1 and 2 (pp. 164–165) for the TESOL Standards and the English Language Arts Standards used in New York City schools).

One other issue relevant to the implementation of literacy standards for ELLs is the fact that many of the standards, because of their likely application to a wide variety of types and levels of students, do not specify in detail the level of competency needed for "meeting" the standard. This means that teachers who attempt to teach to them must still apply a great deal of judgment in identifying exactly to what degree of sophistication or accuracy a child must, for example, "[d]emonstrate a basic understanding of rules of the English language in written and oral work" (see Chart 2, English Language Arts Standards Used in New York City Schools, Standard E4a on p. 165). This is not to say that having the standards is not worthwhile; simply knowing the range of types of competence a child should be able to demonstrate is immensely useful. However, this raises serious questions about the degree to which assessments of the achievement of the standards are reliable (see Stotsky 1997 for a critical evaluation of 28 current standards documents).

Nevertheless, given the variety of standards relevant to the teaching of literacy skills to ELLs which are now available, a look at a few of these may be helpful here. One document which specifically addresses the needs of ELLs is the TESOL Standards for Pre-K–12 Students (TESOL 1997). These standards recognize the special needs of ELLs, providing a continuum of descriptors for documenting the development of all of the skills for students at beginning, intermediate, and advanced levels for each grade range (Pre-K–3, 4–8, and 9–12), as well as for those with limited formal schooling. The TESOL Standards are designed to provide educators with directions and strategies to assist ESL learners to attain the language they need for learning content. In other words, they are intended to be used as a "bridge" to other general education standards (See Chart 1 [p. 164] and TESOL 1997 for more information about the content and implementation of these standards). A number of states and districts also have established their own special standards for ELLs (see California Department of Education 1999 for an example of this). The use of special standards for ELLs varies: Some states and school districts use TESOL's standards, some have designed their own, building upon those from TESOL, and some have designed their own apart from TESOL's (see Short 2000 for more information on ways in which standards have been adopted by various states and school districts).

It is also helpful for ESL teachers to be familiar with the standards designed for NES learners, given the fact that many districts and states, at least for the time being, have opted to hold ELLs to the same English Language Arts standards expected of NES. Although many of these standards do not take into account the unique developmental needs of ELLs, ESL teachers nevertheless can benefit from knowing the kinds of expectations their ELLs will eventually be required to meet. One example is the New Standards Performance Standards—English Language Arts (Elementary), presently being implemented in New York City school districts (Board of Education of the City of New York 1997).

STRATEGIES TO FACILITATE SECOND LANGUAGE LITERACY DEVELOPMENT AND HELP STUDENTS ACHIEVE STANDARDS

The following strategies can help ELLs develop their literacy abilities as well as provide practice in some of the areas required by literacy standards.

Expose Students to the Many Uses of Print around Them

- *Label items in the room.* Have students (with or without help) make the labels themselves, in multiple languages, each in a different color.
- *Focus attention on the print around the classroom, school, or neighborhood.*
- *Manage aspects of classroom business in writing.* Include attendance lists, classroom chores, or charts showing the number of books read.
- *Establish a regular place to post announcements or messages.*
- *Record class discussions on chart paper; keep these posted as long as a theme is being studied.*
- *Create areas in the room for specific literacy purposes.* A reading, listening, or writing corner.

CHART 1
TESOL's Pre-K–12 ESOL Standards

Goals for ESOL Learners

Goal 1: To Use English to Communicate in Social Settings
Standards for Goal 1

Students will:

1. use English to participate in social interaction
2. interact in, through, and with spoken and written English for personal expression and enjoyment
3. use learning strategies to extend their communicative competence

Goal 2: To Use English to Achieve Academically in All Content Areas
Standards for Goal 2

Students will:

1. use English to interact in the classroom
2. use English to obtain, process, construct, and provide subject matter information in spoken and written form
3. use appropriate learning strategies to construct and apply academic knowledge

Goal 3: To Use English in Socially and Culturally Appropriate Ways
Standards for Goal 3

Students will:

1. use the appropriate language variety, register, and genre according to audience, purpose, and setting
2. use nonverbal communication appropriate to audience, purpose, and setting
3. use appropriate learning strategies to extend their sociolinguistic and sociocultural competence

(*Source:* TESOL 1997, pp. 9–10)

■ *Display different genres of reading and writing material or books.* Children's books, newspapers, magazines, downloaded messages or printed-out information from the Internet, and students' own writing—display everyone's work, not just the "best" papers.

CHART 2

English Language Arts Standards Used in New York City Schools

New Standards Performance Standards—English Language Arts (Elementary)

E1. Reading
E1a Read at least twenty-five books of the quality and complexity illustrated in the sample reading list.
E1b Read and comprehend at least four books on the same subject, or by the same author, or in the same genre.
E1c Read and comprehend informational materials.
E1d Read aloud fluently.

E2. Writing
E2a Produce a report of information.
E2b Produce a response to literature.
E2c Produce a narrative account (fictional or autobiographical).
E2d Produce a narrative procedure.

E3. Speaking, Listening, and Viewing
E3a Participate in one-to-one conferences with the teacher.
E3b Participate in group meetings.
E3c Prepare and deliver an individual presentation.
E3d Make informed judgments about TV, radio, and film.

E4. Conventions, Grammar, and Usage of the English Language
E4a Demonstrate a basic understanding of rules of the English language in written and oral work.
E4b Analyze and subsequently revise work to improve its clarity and effectiveness.

E5. Literature
E5a Respond to non-fiction, fiction, poetry, and drama using interpretive and critical processes.
E5b Produce work in at least one literary genre that follows the conventions of the genre.

(*Source:* Board of Education in the City of New York 1997, p. 23)

Provide Opportunities for Children to Read More Extensively on a Subject

Use content study as the context for literacy development; have students investigate topics of interest related to the content or theme being studied, writing up their findings or presenting them orally to the class. Extensive reading can also be very effective for increasing reading skills of children in EFL contexts (Mee and Moi 1999). Internet research and projects are excellent sources of extensive reading material.

Provide Authentic Purposes for Reading and Writing

Use students' natural urge to communicate when they need information for authentic purposes; set up genuine communication contexts involving e-mail messages, dialogue journals, or research projects, or develop class-to-class information exchanges through the Internet (see Ediger and Pavlik 2000 for more on this).

Provide Scaffolding for Learning

Scaffolding involves the setting up of "temporary supports, provided by capable people, that permit learners to participate in the complex process before they are able to do so unassisted" (Peregoy and Boyle 1997, p. 81). As students become able to do more complex language tasks, supports can be decreased or removed. Use predictable books; have children write their own stories using the same structure as one they have read in a book; provide sentences that students then complete or elaborate on (e.g., "I think (*character from book*) is (*adjective*). The parts of the book that make me think this are _____.")

Use Oral Skills to Support Reading and Writing Development

Van den Branden (2000) found that when children were allowed to "negotiate the meaning" of an original text they were reading, either through whole class discussion with facilitation by the teacher or with a peer of a different level of language proficiency, they were able to comprehend what they read better than if the text had been simplified for them to read on their own. Encourage cooperative groups of mixed-level students to work together to read or write various texts. Also, have students first explain orally what they will later be asked to write. Or, after working together in groups on a task, have students from each group report back to the class what their group discovered or accomplished. Then have them put the same information into written form.

Focus Students' Attention on Reading and Writing Strategies

First, call attention to any strategies students are already using, e.g., (1) thinking about what they already know about a topic; (2) asking, Are there any other words I know which are similar to this word in some way?; (3) looking backward and forward from a word or phrase they don't understand (using the context) to see if that can give them more information for comprehending what they are reading; (4) monitoring whether they understand what they are reading and, if not, changing *how* they are reading. Then, model some of these strategies for students by thinking aloud the thoughts going through your mind as you use them.

SUMMARY

This has been just a brief introduction to teaching literacy skills to ELLs. It has described three elements involved in reading: the text, the reader, and the context that the reading activity takes place in. It has also presented the various component knowledge areas which readers use, and which children learning to read in their L2 also need to master, as well as common characteristics of L2 readers and writers. In addition to understanding the reading process and common characteristics of their students, teachers need to be familiar with various approaches to teaching reading so that they can make wise choices about how to teach. It is ultimately the teacher's challenge to put together this information and what has been learned from research on literacy development with a knowledge of literacy standards and effective teaching strategies in ways that will allow the teacher to address the various needs of individual ESL students.

DISCUSSION QUESTIONS

1. As part of your assessment process for your second grade class, you have asked one child if she can read you a book she has chosen. When you sit down with her, she reads it very carefully and deliberately; you notice that she is able to read almost all of the words accurately. However, when you later ask her what the story was about, she has trouble explaining it to you. How would you account for this? How would you describe her overall reading ability? What are some other reading activities you might ask her to do in order to assess her ability more thoroughly?

2. If children who are taught to read using the Language Experience Approach are able to dictate the content of the story, have the teacher write it down for them, and assist them with reading it back, are they *really* reading and writing? Why? What is the *real* value of this method? What other learning concepts from this chapter does the LEA illustrate or make use of? If you were to use the LEA to write and then read something in a language you don't know very well, what do you think you would learn?

3. If teachers do activities to elicit students' background knowledge before they read a text, isn't the teacher merely helping them handle the particular text they are working on? Will this help students be able to read or handle the next text they encounter any more easily? What else could a teacher do to help students better handle future reading tasks?

4. Do you think having literacy standards can help teachers improve instruction in literacy?

Why? Look at the two examples of standards in this chapter. What kinds of special instruction or adaptations might a teacher use to help ELLs achieve these standards?

SUGGESTED ACTIVITIES

1. One way to familiarize children with different types of print is to show them that literacy serves a variety of functions in society (adapted from Halliday 1975), including:

   - Providing ways people learn about the world and share these experiences with others
   - Accomplishing various tasks of living
   - Establishing and maintaining communic-ation with others
   - Expressing differences and similarities among people
   - Reflecting and acting upon personal and social problems
   - Changing conditions in people's lives
   - Enjoying the beauty of language
   - Recognizing different people's cultural heritage
   - Understanding what it means to be human

   For each function, identify an activity or reading/ writing task which your students might be able to perform to learn more about that literacy function. For example, in order to teach students that literacy *"provides ways people learn about the world and share these experiences with others,"* you could have them read and discuss a news story, or have them write a report about a field trip they took recently. Can you think of some others?

2. For one or more of the following, select a book or story that you think would be particularly suitable for it, and which would allow you to develop a teaching lesson to illustrate that particular concept to your students. Then design the actual lesson. Explain why you think your chosen book/story is suitable, and why you designed the lesson in the manner that you did.

a. Scaffolding

b. Eliciting students' world knowledge

c. Identifying qualities that characterize a particular genre of text (Some possible genres: a letter, an invitation, a report, a description of a process, a film review, etc.)

d. Identifying the way a text is organized
   A story (narrative)
   A piece of non-fiction

3. Ask two beginning-level ESL/EFL children to write a story about an experience they recently had together. If they have difficulty writing, have them draw a picture to illustrate their experience, then have them dictate the story to you while you help them write it, using the Language Experience Approach. When they/you are finished, either ask them to read the story or read it for them, depending on their ability. What did you learn from this activity?

4. Read aloud a story to some children learning ESL, stopping at several points along the way to ask them to predict what will happen next. Do their predictions give you any evidence about whether they have understood the story so far? Then read further and ask them to tell you when they hear something in the story that confirms or disconfirms one of their predictions. Then discuss with them how well they were able to predict what would happen. Were the children able to make reasonable predictions? Were they able to identify information later in the reading which dealt with their prediction? Why or why not?

FURTHER READING

Day, R., and J. Bamford. 1998. *Extensive Reading in the Second Language Classroom.* Cambridge: Cambridge University Press.
Discusses the value of extensive reading and provides many ideas on incorporating such activities into literacy instruction.

Hudelson, S., ed. 1993. *Teacher Resource Guide for ESL.* Thousand Oaks, CA: Corwin Press.
Provides tremendously practical information about elementary ESL curriculum development and literacy teaching, lists of books, and an actual sample curriculum.

Crotchett, K. 1997. *A Teacher's Project Guide to the Internet.* Portsmouth, NH: Heinemann.
Provides many useful ideas for developing literacy projects using the Internet.

Fulwiler, T., ed. 1987. *The Journal Book.* Portsmouth, NH: Heinemann.
Explains ways to incorporate journals into literacy development.

O'Malley, J. M., and L. Valdez Pierce. 1996. *Authentic Assessment for English Language Learners.* Reading, MA: Addison-Wesley.
Describes classroom-based assessment of all skill areas; provides numerous samples of authentic assessment rubrics and methods of documenting literacy development.

WEBSITES

On-line Reading and Writing Opportunities

Intercultural E-Mail Classroom Connections
www.stolaf.edu/network/iecc/

E-Pals (electronic penpals)
www.epals.com

Global SchoolNet's Internet Projects Registry
Listing of collaborative Internet projects. Learn about ongoing projects or post your own ideas and invite collaboration.
http://www.gsn.org/pr/index.html

Children's Literature

The Children's Literature Web Guide
http://www.acs.ucalgary.ca/~dkbrown/

Internet Public Library
http://www.ipl.org/

Multicultural Book Review Homepage
www.isomedia.com/homes/jmele/homepage.html

Teacher Resources

Teaching with technology
http://ilt.columbia.edu/k12/livetext/
International Reading Association
http://www.ira.org

Kathy Schrock's Guide for Educators

A wonderful Internet site for teachers, with many project ideas and ways to use them in the classroom.

http://discoveryschool.com/schrockguide/

Language Arts/Literacy Standards

Information about ESL literacy and teaching; links to other related websites.

www.cal.org

Listserv for communicating with others about ESL standards. To subscribe, send an e-mail message to the above address. In the subject of the message, type "subscribe"; leave the remainder blank.

eslstds-request@caltalk.cal.org

Website providing a downloadable (.pdf) version of the 1999 California ELD (ESL) and Language Arts standards.

www.cde.ca.gov/statetests/eld/eld.html

ENDNOTE

I thank Evelyn Hatch and Barbara Hawkins for the ideas used here which originally appeared in their chapters in earlier editions of this book.

Developing Adult Literacies[1]

GAIL WEINSTEIN

In "Developing Adult Literacies," Weinstein invites readers to examine the role of language and literacies in learners' lives, examines critical contexts for ESL literacy instruction, and provides a synthesis of orientations to curriculum and teaching. She concludes with five "promising practices" that challenge both new and experienced teachers to reflect individually and collectively on their potentially life-transforming work.

INTRODUCTION

Profiles in Diversity and Strength

Socorro Tinajero was born in Mexico and is raising her children in the "borderlands" between Mexico and the United States. Described as an energetic and efficient woman, she works long hours in the family restaurant under difficult conditions. Her fatalism is quickly revealed: "A cada quien lo que toca" [Everyone has their lot in life]. Researcher Valdés tells us that this is a fairly common belief among those in Socorro's community—that life simply deals different luck to different people.

Socorro remembers with some nostalgia her days in Juarez, where neighbors were able to watch out for each other. Given her hard work and determination, one thing to which Socorro will not resign herself is that her children are being held back in school and are getting into trouble. She did not have an opportunity to go to school in Mexico. She wants to develop the language and literacy she needs to be able to intervene more successfully with their teachers (Valdés 1996, p. 91).

Pao Joua Lo was a retired soldier and was considered a war hero in his own community. Like 70,000 other Hmong refugees who resettled in the United States in the 1970s, he fled the hills of Laos in the throes of the wars of Southeast Asia. In his Philadelphia home, Pao Joua was often surrounded by his many grand-children and guests, and until his death in 1998, was considered both an elder and a leader by many Hmong throughout the United States.

Pao Joua had attended classes at the local community college but dropped out after only one semester. His English literacy skills, while minimal, allowed him to scan the newspapers for articles about Southeast Asia, which he then passed along to more literate men in the community. Besides keeping current on events in his homeland, Pao Joua was also interested in developing literacy skills to be able to record traditional Hmong courtship songs so that first his sons and later his grandsons could find desirable brides (Weinstein 1997).

Michela Stone works as an accountant at a community center serving immigrants from her native Byelorussia, as well as from the Ukraine and Lithuania. Many who frequent the center are university professors, businesspeople, doctors, or scientists who hope to be able to resume their professional lives when they have acquired the language needed in their new home. Michela teaches Russian on the side, both for some extra money and also for the chance to interact with Americans. She likes soap operas and reads *People* magazine. By reading up on movie stars, Michela figures she can start conversations with American friends and practice her English. Although she has little time to study between her two jobs and caring for her aging father, she hopes to prepare for American citizenship (Nesbit 1997).

Adults like these have different histories, circumstances, and purposes for wanting to develop and improve language and literacy skills. To understand the possibilities for language and literacy instruction, it is necessary to know something about learners, their resources, their needs, and their goals for learning English.

What is English as a Second Language (ESL) Literacy?

The learners described above bring different needs and resources to their desire to learn English language and literacy. Soccoro, who was born in Mexico, comes from a society with a rich literary tradition, but she herself has had little access to the formal education or native language literacy that others in her country may enjoy. Learners in this situation have been described in the literature as *nonliterate*. Pao Joua Lo, on the other hand, comes from a farming society where subsistence living posed very little need for print. In fact, the Hmong language did not have a written form until just a few decades ago, when missionaries created a writing system to teach the Bible. Learners in this situation are often called *preliterate*, because they come from a society that does not have a tradition with print. Michela illuminates yet another dimension of a complex linguistic picture, since she has highly developed literacy skills in her native language, but has not had prior experience with the Roman alphabet. She has many strategies for learning in formal settings, and is comfortable with the format and discourse of formal teaching situations. As she adds English to her repertoire, Michela will become *biliterate*, or proficient with print in two languages.

Until fairly recently, little attention was given to the role of native language literacy in learner acquisition of English. Research on second language learners either assumed native language literacy or did not investigate native language literacy as a factor in learner needs and strategies. In the 1970s, when a huge influx of Southeast Asian refugees found their way to our classrooms, teachers knew that this group was different. Rural Vietnamese, Khmer, Lao, and Hmong learners who were not literate in their native languages were not managing as well as their literate counterparts in the language classroom. Techniques that had been used in the past were no longer effective. In the 1980s, with the passage of the Immigration Reform and Control Act (IRCA), a second wave of undocumented learners flocked to our classrooms to qualify for "amnesty." These students had limited literacy in their native languages and could not access information the way we provided it, without first acquiring literacy. ESL classroom teachers were among the first to raise to national consciousness the unique characteristics of this group of learners.

Those of us who worked closely with these two groups of newcomers were struck by their resourcefulness. We learned that the Southeast Asian refugees had escaped through jungles, run through minefields, endured starvation, and crossed rivers on rubber tires at night with their children. In short, they were extraordinary survivors. We saw that most undocumented amnesty applicants had been living on the margins, managing to take care of their families while staying invisible from authorities who could deport them. We began to see the kinship and social networks that people relied on for solving problems and for helping one another navigate a new setting. While we became aware of these enormous resources, it was also clear that something critical was lacking—literacy skills that would provide these adults with access to the English language, and through English, to other information and education.

Many Learners, Many Literacies

While teachers of ESL were grappling with literacy issues face-to-face in their daily work, many changes were going on in the field of adult literacy (also called Adult Basic Education, or ABE) as well. Among these were attempts to move beyond the problematic notion of "grade level" in order to define and measure literacy in ways that were more informative and accurate for adults. The most comprehensive attempt in recent history to survey the literacy levels of adults in the United States was the National

Adult Literacy Survey (NALS). This instrument was designed to measure three areas of knowledge or skill:

- *prose literacy* (understanding texts such as news stories, poems, etc.),
- *document literacy* (locating and using information found in documents like job applications, transportation schedules, etc.), and
- *quantitative literacy* (applying arithmetic operations using numbers found in printed materials like order forms, etc. (Kirsch et al. 1993, p. 3).

The problem for English language educators was that this assessment tool could only measure English literacy—the results do not distinguish between the Cambodian peasant farmer who had never held a pencil and the Russian engineer with a Ph.D. who had not yet added the Roman to the Cyrillic alphabet in her repertoire of symbol systems.

The portraits of Socorro, Pao Joua, and Michela are the result of ethnographic studies in which the researcher seeks to make explicit how an individual or group makes sense of the world—in this case, with a focus on functions and uses of language and literacy in learners' lives. Ethnographic research can illuminate many forms of diversity among learners regarding their language and literacy resources. Many Asian foreign students in the United States, for example, are highly literate in their native language and have facility with written academic English, but have trouble communicating orally. In contrast, many Latino learners with fluent spoken English struggle with writing, particularly in academic genres. A new set of issues has begun to emerge with a growing population of immigrants who came to the United States as older children. Many of these young men and women do not speak "targetlike" (standard) English, yet are neither literate nor are they any longer orally proficient in the language of their parents. We do not yet have labels to neatly name what we see. Learners vary along dimensions of proficiency in English versus another language, spoken versus written proficiency, and academic versus social language, among other dimensions of literacy.

While there is not yet a universally accepted definition of literacy, there is a growing consensus that to be literate entails different things in different situations. All of us, including those of us who consider ourselves to be fairly literate, encounter situations in which we must master a new literacy genre, such as learning HTML for Web design, writing for a particular journal for the first time, or reading a paper from a different discipline. While there is no agreement on one definition of literacy, there is growing recognition that there are *many literacies,* and in the case of immigrant learners, there are potentially biliteracies with many dimensions.

CONTEXTS FOR LITERACY INSTRUCTION

Literacy for What?

In 1991 the United States Congress created a set of educational goals for the nation, including Goal 6 for Literacy and Lifelong Learning: "By the year 2000, every adult American will be literate and will possess the knowledge and skills necessary to compete in a global economy and exercise the rights and responsibilities of citizenship." To explore what this would entail, members of the Equipped for the Future Initiative asked adult learners what they hoped to gain from formal learning opportunities. From the responses of more than fifteen hundred adults, four themes or purposes for language and literacy learning emerged:

- *Access:* to information [as well as jobs and resources] so adults can orient themselves in the world;
- *Voice:* to be able to express ideas and opinions with the confidence they will be heard and taken into account;
- *Independent Action:* to be able to solve problems and make decisions on one's own, acting independently, without having to rely on others;
- *Bridge to the Future:* learning how to learn so adults can keep up with the world as it changes (Stein 1997, p. 7).

A National Literacy Summit followed by meetings throughout the United States resulted in the following Call to Action:

> By 2010, a system of high quality adult literacy, language and lifelong learning services will help adults in every community make measurable gains toward achieving their goals as family members, workers, citizens and lifelong learners (National Literacy Summit 2000, p. 1).

This section briefly provides models for instruction that currently speak to those roles and raises issues specific to each context that must be considered if this vision is to be achieved.

Basic Adult ESL/Literacy and Lifelong Learning

Adults have pursued their desire to improve language and literacy skills for personal, professional, or academic reasons through a wide range of venues such as adult schools, community colleges, community-based organizations, libraries, workplaces, or in their own homes through one-on-one volunteer programs. Nearly 50 percent of the learners enrolled in federally funded adult education programs are English language learners, and most adult education programs (70%) offer some ESL instruction (TESOL 2000).

Trends in immigration, attitudes toward immigrants, and educational and labor policies all have an impact on ESL/literacy instruction, no matter the context in which it occurs. In the 1990s, for example, the U.S. Congress began a series of efforts to cut, combine, and streamline federal programs. One result was a bill that combined literacy efforts with workforce training. Literacy initiatives for the first time were linked directly to adult employment, job training, and retraining. This bill has been followed by several legislative initiatives that place a heavy emphasis on job preparation. The cluster of initiatives popularly known as welfare reform, for example, places enormous pressure on families to get off welfare and find jobs. The results are felt not only in workplace programs, but also in general

ESL, family literacy, and other programs that are pushed to incorporate employment preparation into their curriculum and provide evidence of job outcomes to maintain their funding.

Family or Intergenerational Literacy

The terms *family literacy* and *intergenerational literacy* have been used to describe how literacy is valued and used in the lives of children and adults. These terms have also been used to describe educational programs designed to strengthen literacy resources by involving at least two generations for a variety of stated goals (Weinstein 1998). In the United States, the term *family literacy* has gained recognition through the growth of private initiatives such as the Barbara Bush Family Literacy Foundation and Toyota Families for Learning, as well as federal programs such as Head Start and Even Start.

Family Literacy Program Goals and Models

Many initiatives state that their goal is to support parents in promoting children's school achievement, with an emphasis on parental involvement with schools. Promising programs resist a model that is unilinear—that is, they recognize that it is not only that parents must understand and support schools, but also that school personnel have an obligation to understand and better respond to parents and families. With greater reciprocal connection as a goal, while parents learn about schools, teachers learn about families, and schools respond to the realities of the communities they serve (McCaleb 1994).

A second goal often found in family literacy programs is to foster a love of reading among both adults and children, or more specifically, to help adults transmit a love of reading to their children. In the case of immigrants, experience shows that parents are rarely in a position to know more English than their children, or thus to read comfortably to them in their newly developing language. Innovative programs may use a variety of ways to encourage reading and foster a love of literature while minimizing the stresses on adults. There is evidence, for example, that older children learn as much by reading aloud to their parents as by listening to their parents read. This allows adults to support their children's development without losing face. In other programs, Latino adults practice reading Spanish children's literature in order to read to their children, thus fostering native language literacy along with pride in the heritage language.

A third goal put forth for some programs is to provide literacy to support adults in addressing family concerns. These programs attend to the role of home language and culture, and include activities to enable adults to develop a critical understanding of schooling to "evaluate and rehearse appropriate responses and develop networks for individual or group advocacy" (Auerbach 1992, p. 35). Learners are supported in reflecting collectively on parenting, developing a voice in the education of their children, and in advocating for their families (Nash et al. 1992).

Finally, some programs aim specifically to reconnect the generations in positive ways. Children of immigrant families who have more exposure to English are often placed in a position of translating and solving other problems for parents, reversing traditional roles and creating additional stresses for all involved (Weinstein 1998). When the goal of intergenerational work is to restore channels for transmission of culture and values, children and adults can be resources for one another. In one family literacy class, for example, participants create a family Web page; adults provide stories of their past which children illustrate and input into the computer (Hovanesian 1999). Projects like these draw on the resources of children (for English and computer facility), while tapping the memories and knowledge of adults.

Issues and Agendas in Family Literacy

While the goal of many family programs is to improve children's school achievements, there is clearly more to family life than school success. The work of Valdés, cited at the beginning of this chapter, is one of many ethnographic studies that illustrate tensions when the culture of schooling violates the norms of family values. Other studies illustrate the ways in which teachers and other school personnel can inadvertently undermine parental authority—by valuing certain kinds of knowledge, while discounting the knowledge of the home culture.

Second, a majority of family literacy programs are designed in a way that seems to foster participation primarily of children and their mothers, to the exclusion of fathers or other significant caretakers who may be equally critical in children's lives. Elders continue to be an undertapped resource with a wealth of knowledge that can help to anchor children in their own culture and history at a time of enormous change and potential disconnection. Such grounding is especially critical at a time when children long for connection and belonging so that they do not need to seek it in other forms such as gang membership.

Finally, family literacy programs often grow from sources in early childhood education. If programs grew directly from the needs of adults and their own priorities as parents, how would they be different? When adults are asked about the family issues that concern them most, they rarely mention their toddlers—the targeted participants of most federally funded family literacy programs. Rather, uprooted adults tend to be most concerned about their older children who face the perils of adolescence, such as drugs, gangs, and other dangers associated with coming of age in modern times.

As funding and support continue to grow for family literacy programs, there will be many challenges ahead to ensure that programs strengthen families, honor the authority of parents, recognize and celebrate the wisdom of elders, and address the needs that adults themselves see in the challenging work they have to raise a family in a complex world.

PRE-EMPLOYMENT AND WORKPLACE LITERACY

In the 1970s, the influx of guest workers in west European countries caused British educators to reevaluate the efficacy of grammar-based and audiolingual methods and turn their focus instead to the linguistic tasks required on the job. At the same time, the United States was coping with an influx of almost 200,000 refugees who needed language and literacy for work more urgently than they needed bookish accuracy in producing carefully sequenced grammar structures.

This laid the groundwork for a growing shift toward employment-related ESL, which may be woven into a general ESL course or offered in pre-workplace classes on the job, by a union, or by a consortium of several partners. Programs generally entail a needs analysis of participants, an analysis of tasks entailed in a given job or setting, a plan for instruction, and an evaluation procedure (see chapter by Johns and Price-Machado in this volume).

Goals of Pre-employment and Workplace Programs

It has been suggested that there are goals for learners that cut across settings. By synthesizing literature from across the manufacturing, technical, service, and agricultural domains, Grognet (1997) proposed a set of competencies that are useful in any workplace setting. Below are examples of language functions associated with each of three goals.

To get a job:

- read want ads and complete application forms
- give personal information
- answer and ask questions (etc.)

To survive on a job:

- follow oral and written directions
- understand and use safety language
- ask for clarification (etc.)

To thrive on a job (and have job mobility):

- participate in group discussions
- give as well as follow directions
- state a position (etc.)

Other goals identified grow from research on skills required for the workplace. In 1992, the Secretary of Labor's Commission on Achieving Necessary Skills (SCANS) issued a report based on the collaborative work of business and education leaders. The Commission identified five competencies and three foundation skills needed for success in the workplace, which have been adapted to adult workplace curriculum in many settings. This framework is one that is supported and expanded upon by the Equipped for the Future initiative, which identifies skills needed by adults in their roles as workers, as well as those underlying areas of knowledge and skill that cut across roles and contexts (Stein 1997).

Issues and Agendas in Literacy for Workers: Workplace or Workforce Education?

In the two decades when workplace instruction was developing, the techniques used for needs assessment primarily involved surveys and interviews with employers, managers, and supervisors. Information from workers generally was gathered from the most successful employees to break down the functional and linguistic components of a given task or job in order to teach it more effectively to new workers. This implicit goal is to make employees more productive and efficient in meeting the needs of their employers (McGroarty and Scott 1993).

However, the agendas of workers may be different from that of their employers. Many workers want to improve their language and literacy skills to get out of low-paying or dead-end jobs, to get better jobs within an organization, or to better support their roles in family life. In addition, workers may need skills to cope with downsizing, layoffs, and other job dislocations in order to find new employment (Macias in press). The recognition of the needs of learners themselves has fostered a distinction between *workplace education,* to improve productivity in a given job, and *workforce education,* which is more oriented toward education of the whole person in his or her roles as a parent, community member, and even as a union member. This approach assumes that the workplace may be a good venue for addressing literacy needs, but that curriculum should be driven by the needs of the learner, whether for a particular job, for upward mobility, or for other personal goals as a learner and as a human being.

Clearly, those programs that prove most successful will be the ones that take into account the agendas of all constituencies and that create opportunities for those agendas to be negotiated. Employers need to see the value of programs to be willing to fund and support worker participation in them; workers need to feel that their own needs will be met if they are to participate and benefit from language and literacy instruction.

Civic ESL/Literacy Education

Civic education for newcomers is almost as old as immigration. Early in the twentieth century, for example, "settlement houses" were created to assist immigrants in assimilating to life in the United States and to prepare them for citizenship. What does it mean for any adult to be a "good citizen"? What skills, knowledge, or values should a person demonstrate to be accepted as a new citizen? These are questions that have been around as long as there have been neighbors and as long as there have been newcomers.

While it has long been required that new citizens be able to speak some English, it is a recent development that literacy was added to the list of requirements. In 1950, a reading and writing component was added to screening procedures for prospective new citizens. Today, the Immigration and Naturalization Service (INS) administers an examination that evaluates the applicant's knowledge of U.S. history and government by quizzing applicants from a list of 100 questions, as well as testing basic knowledge of spoken and written English (Becker 2000).

Goals of Civic ESL/Literacy Education

One goal of citizenship classes is simply to assist learners in preparing to take the naturalization exam. Public monies, as well as private support from sources such as the Soros Foundation's Emma Lazarus Fund, have made it possible to provide assistance to immigrants through education programs and community or social service

organizations. The classes may constitute distinct "citizenship" classes or they may be woven into the general ESL curriculum. Citizenship classes are sometimes taught bilingually, especially in community-based organizations.

Classes focusing on naturalization test preparation, according to Nixon and Keenan (1997), are most effective when they use a variety of materials, when they provide as much context for learners as possible, and when they use authentic materials and visual aids, especially for low-literacy learners. Classes may include traditional ESL activities geared to naturalization test preparation, such as:

- Question Division—learners arrange the 100 INS questions according to theme
- Information gap activities—learners match questions with answers
- Flash cards—learners create their own flash cards with questions on one side, answers on other to facilitate home study, etc. (Nixon and Keenan 1997, p. 2).

A second goal related to civic and citizenship education is to encourage learners who have been naturalized to exercise their newly earned franchise with the vote. *New Citizens Vote*, for example, is a voter education kit developed "to increase the skills and self-confidence of participants regarding voting and other local decision-making processes" (Northern California Grantmakers 1998). The kit, available in English, Chinese, Vietnamese, or Spanish from www.ncg.org, contains interactive exercises including, among others

- a mock election to illustrate the importance of each individual's vote;
- voting basics: eligibility requirements, registration, and voting procedures;
- how and where to find information about political parties, issues, and candidates.

A third goal focuses more broadly on many forms of civic participation. In *Civic Participation and Community Action Sourcebook* (Nash 1999), for example, a group consisting primarily of teachers share activities that move learners into action beyond voting. With this expanded notion of civic engagement, the sourcebook presents a range of tools that are aimed at helping readers

- examine their beliefs about community, citizenship, democracy, etc;
- identify and analyze issues that concern them; and
- build skills and strategies to take informed action(Nash 1999, p. ix).

These materials provide accounts by teachers of projects they have done, such as a group of formerly homeless women studying the history of welfare policy and then teaching others about the issue, or an ESL class that rallies to help a family that has been burned out of their home. The teacher-authors discuss the challenges of trying to incorporate community action into the culture of adult education.

Issues in Civic ESL Literacy Education

There are some poignant ironies that emerge in the conflict between preparing learners to be active, engaged citizens in their communities and the stresses of preparing learners for the INS naturalization test. This conflict is exemplified in SHINE, Students Helping in the Naturalization of Elders, a project I codirect in San Francisco. Through SHINE, we train and place volunteer university student "coaches" in citizenship classes to support older learners who are preparing for naturalization, as well as in other ESL literacy classes (Weinstein et al. in press).

We aim to incorporate learner-centered thematic units into our coaching curriculum through the "First Amendment Project," for which we collect narratives from learners and teachers about their personal experiences with freedom of expression. Our personal stories of standing up (or not) to parents, bosses, and other authority figures, participating in demonstrations, and suffering censorship cut to the core of civic engagement. We find enthusiasm for this initiative from participants across the ESL literacy and academic spectrum, *except for* participants in citizenship classes, whose overriding concern is to cram, as quickly and efficiently as possible, for the naturalization test. Given the high stakes, this comes as no surprise.

This schism illuminates the irony that the citizenship exam, as it is currently conceived and administered, does little to promote engagement for learners in the life of their communities. It continues to be a challenge for concerned ESL teachers to prepare learners for a test that has grave consequences for their lives, while also encouraging them to develop a voice and become informed and active members of their communities.

ORIENTATIONS TO CURRICULUM AND INSTRUCTION

There are a wide variety of approaches to ESL instruction, each with underlying assumptions about teaching and learning, as well as associated techniques and procedures. While it is problematic when a program pursues one approach with such rigidity that it precludes responding to learner styles or changing learner needs, Wrigley and Guth (2000) caution that there is equal cause for concern when programs become so "eclectic" that they have no philosophical coherence or unifying vision.

This section briefly examines two general orientations to ESL literacy instruction, as well as a variety of approaches and activities consistent with those orientations. A set of questions to investigate "what works" is provided, along with a set of dichotomies (or continua) for observing characteristics of ESL/literacy classrooms. Finally, the section concludes with a discussion of assessing learner success, and some of the challenges that face the field in terms of accountability in the decade ahead.

Mastery or Transmission of Knowledge

Most programs aim to help students learn facts, concepts, and skills (procedural knowledge) through guided and sequenced practice. In adult ESL, a "Mastery"-based orientation is exemplified by focus on linguistic structures, language skills, specific content, and/or competencies.

The teaching of *language structures* is as old as language teaching itself. From early techniques such as grammar translation to contemporary textbooks organized by verb tense and language form, mastery of language structures appears in most curricula to a greater or lesser extent. A glance at the table of contents of any ESL textbook will reveal the degree of prominence that language structures have in the organization of material that is taught.

Language skills are also featured in most curricula, with varying degrees of attention to the four skills of listening, speaking, reading, and writing. Focus on listening and speaking activities, according to the "What Works" study (Pelavin Research Center and American Institutes for Research 1999), constitute an *ESL Acquisition Model,* and may include vocabulary, pronunciation, language functions, and strategies to engage in oral communication with native speakers. In contrast, an *ESL Literacy Model,* according to this study, is constituted by reading and writing skills development. This may entail providing ESL literacy learners with opportunities to engage with print, skills and strategies for fluency in reading, and the goal of automaticity in decoding. Fluency skills include practicing letters of the alphabet, letter and word recognition, recognizing sound/symbol relationships, and blending sounds. Activities frequently associated with developing these skills include supported or choral reading and using "environmental" print (signs that surround us in daily life).

Content-based approaches to ESL literacy instruction are those in which the language and literacy curriculum is woven around specific subject matter. While this approach was initially developed to prepare refugee children for school subjects, there are many applications to adult contexts. Workplace literacy programs have long incorporated the specific vocabulary and language functions needed for a given job or profession into their curricula. Family literacy programs often provide language for teaching childhood development or an orientation to the structure of schools in the United States. Citizenship classes may provide English language vocabulary and skills in the context of the citizenship exam, such as the *Wh*-construction needed to understand the

"100 questions." Even the alphabet may be taught and practiced through key words in U.S. history (e.g., "*F* is for Flag"). (For more on content-based approaches, see Snow's chapter in this volume.)

Competency-based education (CBE) emerged in the late 1970s in a shift away from grammar-based curriculum when newly arriving refugees needed English for immediate application in their new lives. A competency is an instructional objective described in task-based terms such as "Students will be able to . . . ," ending with a verb phrase describing a demonstrable skill such as "find information in a bus schedule." During the period of intense refugee resettlement, this approach was aimed at helping learners use public transportation, shop, interact with a doctor, etc. The goal was not only to teach learners *about* language and grammar, but also to enable them to *use* language to accomplish a nonlinguistic end (Crandall and Peyton 1993). Competencies for early literacy might include items such as "can recognize letters of the alphabet" or "can write upper and lower case English letters."

Meaning-Making or Constructivism

A constructivist orientation to teaching and learning is one in which it is assumed that knowledge is not only transmitted to learners from teachers or books, but also that both meaning and knowledge can be created collectively by learners or by learners and teachers. A variety of approaches, methods, and techniques may be associated with this orientation. This section mentions a few, including participatory and whole language approaches, Learners' Lives as Curriculum (LLC), and project-based learning. These approaches have significant overlap, differing primarily in emphasis.

A *participatory, or "Freirian" approach,* to adult literacy education revolves around the tenet that education and knowledge have value insofar as they help people recognize and liberate themselves from the social conditions that oppress them. Paolo Freire was a Brazilian educator who helped initiate, develop, and implement national literacy campaigns in a number of developing countries. In his classic *Pedagogy of the Oppressed,*

Freire (1972) outlines an approach to teaching literacy in which researchers study the conditions in a community and identify generative words to describe situations familiar to learners, and then literacy teachers develop materials using these generative words to help learners decode the syllables as well as deconstruct their social conditions.

Most ESL educators who rely on a Freirian approach do not have the luxury of relying on social scientists to study learners' communities, nor do they focus on the analysis of syllables as the only way to attack the mechanics of language. However, those who ascribe to the primary tenets of participatory education (see Auerbach 1992), tend to agree on

- Use of generative words and themes drawn from learners' experiences
- The notion of teachers as facilitators rather than transmitters of knowledge
- Use of "problem-posing," a technique in which learners look at pictures or objects to discuss their situation and explore solutions to problems encoded in those situations. (see Auerbach 1992).

The *whole language approach*, a movement born in U.S. elementary classrooms, grows from a perspective on language learning and teaching in which language is seen as social, and is learned in interaction with other speakers, readers, and writers. In whole-language oriented classrooms, learners work together to read and write for and with each other and evaluate products together. While phonics or other bottom-up methods that break down language are not precluded, they are used in service of larger communicative events. As my colleague Carole Edelsky once explained to me, "You teach the sound 'h' not because it is 'H week,' but rather, because someone wants to write instructions for how to take care of the hamster." The *Language Experience Approach*, or LEA, a technique related to the whole language tradition, enables adult ESL literacy learners to engage with print from the outset by drawing on stories that they dictate to a teacher or more able classmate, either in the native language or in English. These stories become the basis for a language or literacy lesson (see Ediger's chapter in this volume).

An extension of the principles behind these techniques is found in a model called *Learners' Lives as Curriculum* (Weinstein 1999), in which learner texts (e.g., language experience, dictation, poem, story, folktale, or interview) are used as catalysts for discussing themes of interest or concern to learners. A *thematic unit,* according to this model, provides learners with personal stories of others like themselves, along with an opportunity to respond to those stories, generate their own narratives, and prepare for a collective project while learning specific language skills and structures. In a predesigned thematic unit on neighborhoods, for example, Tekola Beyene compares his new home in Virginia, where "houses are very far apart" and "people are afraid of me because I am a Black man" with his neighborhood in Ethiopia, where "my sons played in neighbors' houses every day. . . . if you needed help, someone was always there!" This narrative is used to invite discussion about the learners' own neighbors and neighborhoods, with a focus on the theme of giving and getting help. The unit leads toward a project in which learners compile a local community resource directory, invite a guest speaker from a service that is of interest to the group, and then create a classroom trading post to swap skills and services within their classroom community. According to LLC, thematic units include four main components:

- Narratives with a contextualized focus on themes and "hot topics" of interest to learners
- Language skills, structures, and competencies
- Opportunities to document current language use and monitor progress towards learner-selected goals
- Opportunities to build a classroom community in which learners get acquainted, solve problems together, and engage in authentic projects (Weinstein 1999)

Certain projects further illustrate the potential when learners are invited to collectively construct knowledge through telling stories for real readers or listeners outside the classroom. Mien hill tribe women work in groups to describe photos of village life in Laos. With help from a bilingual aide, they create a book that will be given to their children born in the United

States. Newly arrived immigrants at the city college develop a handbook for new(er)comers on how to survive the first semester in the United States, complete with a campus resource guide and tips for handling homesickness (Weinstein 1999). Students at El Barrio Popular investigate neighborhood problems that they themselves have identified, and compile their research for collective advocacy (Rivera 1999). In an Internet project that draws many "hits," English language learners from across the country contribute to a Web page for folk remedies, thus pooling their knowledge to the benefit of all. (Gaer, http://www.otan.dni.us/webfarm/emailproject/rem.htm).

These activities illustrate *project-based learning*, in which learners investigate a question, solve a problem, plan an event, or develop a product (Moss and Van Duzer 1998). Learners not only receive knowledge from a teacher or book, but also, they collectively share and create knowledge. Among the potential benefits are effective advocacy, support for problem-solving, and intergenerational transmission of culture. In addition, materials created by learners are often more powerful and compelling for future learners than anything the most dedicated materials writer can dream up.

What Works? Continua for Observation and Inquiry

English as a Second Language programs are the fastest growing component in federally funded adult education efforts. Notwithstanding a general sense of "promising practices" (Wrigley 1993), there is a dearth of empirical research about what works for whom and under what circumstances. The National Clearinghouse for ESL Literacy Education (1998) proposed an agenda for adult ESL literacy, including research on the efficacy of different approaches in different circumstances. The "What Works" study, mentioned earlier, systematically explores one set of contrasts within a Mastery orientation, that is, the efficacy of focusing on oral communication versus reading/writing skills in ESL literacy instruction. Other variables which the study seeks to investigate pose useful questions for

observation of ESL/literacy classes and food for thought for ESL literacy teachers both within and across orientations.

- What is the relative emphasis on reading, writing, listening, and speaking?
- How much emphasis is given to linguistic versus nonlinguistic outcomes?
- What is the extent of focus on structure versus meaning-making (i.e., on activities associated with mastery versus constructivist orientations)?
- What is the extent of "language practice" versus authentic communication?
- For how much time in the class do learners actually use language and literacy?
- Is curriculum predetermined or does it reflect evolving learner interests?
- To what extent do learners know the objectives of the lesson and have an opportunity for input?

Teachers (and teacher trainees) do not have the luxury of waiting for federal studies to come in with answers. With observation and reflective practice, these questions can guide our own inquiry, as we observe "what works" for different learners in different situations.

Setting Goals, Monitoring Progress

In any language or literacy program, there are several sets of "stakeholders," each of which want to know certain things about how things are going. Learners want to know how well they are doing vis-à-vis other students and if they are moving toward their own learning goals. Teachers want to know which methods work (and which ones don't) with various learners. Program staff need information in order to place learners in appropriate levels or classes, decide course offerings, plan the curriculum, and generally find out if they are meeting their program goals. Funders as well as taxpayers are interested in the return on investment of literacy dollars and may be interested in comparing learner achievement across programs. Policymakers want to know which practices are successful enough to replicate as guidelines for allocating future funds.

Stakeholders from the learner's community, family, and/or workplace may also want to know if the time spent by the learner is paying off, and if so, in what way (Van Duzer and Berdan 2000).

Assessing success has been very problematic in the fields of both ESL and adult literacy, partly because of the different information needs of the different stakeholders, and partly because of an absence of a coherent, comparable system. Such a system would require agreement on the nature of language and literacy, the goals of instruction, and a resulting agreement on a comparable way to measure progress toward those goals. None of these agreements is yet in place, which creates enormous challenges to programs for documenting progress in a way that is specific to the needs of stakeholders within their programs while providing information for funders that is comparable with other programs. The Equipped for the Future Initiative (EFF) has worked to build consensus around these areas in order to create a performance-based system which aligns student, program, and policymaker goals within one framework. With a growing emphasis on accountability, this is going to be a key area for the future of the field in the decade to come.

In general, there are two broad categories of assessment—general and program-based. *General assessments* are those that allow comparison across programs. Standardized tests such as CASAS or BEST[2] are commonly used, and have several advantages and limitations. Some *advantages* of standardized general assessments are that they

- Have construct validity and scoring reliability
- Are cost effective and relatively easy to administer
- Are accepted by funders for program accountability
- Allow for comparisons of learner progress within and across programs

Some *disadvantages* are that they

- Don't reflect what has been taught, or capture what has been learned
- Don't capture changes in language use and literacy practices beyond the classroom

- Don't discriminate well at the lower end of literacy achievement
- May be inappropriately used for "gatekeeping" purposes, especially in the workplace (Wrigley and Guth 2000, p. 135)

Program-based assessments, on the other hand, reflect the approach of the program and the content of the curriculum. They may be based on commercial materials used in the program (e.g., "Heinle & Heinle's *Collaborations* Assessment Package); or they may be developed by teachers through checklists of skills and competencies, surveys, teacher observation forms, as well as through learner writing, reading, and speaking logs. Some *advantages* of well designed program-based assessments are that they

- Reflect a program's underlying philosophy of instruction
- Are learner centered, reflecting strengths and goals of individual learners
- Are done "with" not "to" learners, who participate in setting goals, discussing interests, and reflecting on their accomplishments
- Involve a variety of tools, giving a more complete picture of each learner and his or her needs and progress (Van Duzer and Berdan 2000, p. 221).

Unfortunately, without guidelines and rigorous procedures, until a system is agreed upon, alternative assessments do not yet produce reliable hard data and are difficult to compare across programs. This is a serious drawback for funders, who are extremely important stakeholders.

PROMISING DIRECTIONS IN ADULT ESL LITERACY INSTRUCTION

Anyone who goes into adult ESL literacy instruction for the money or prestige is tragically misguided. Those who are adventurous, curious, able to tolerate ambiguity, anxious to make a difference, and willing to learn about the world from others' eyes, however, are in for an extraordinarily rich experience. For those who wish to take on the adventure, there are several promising directions for effective practice that can support if not transform all involved.

1. Take an Inquiring Stance

Practitioners who learn about learners are in the best position to help them address their evolving needs. If teachers do not have the luxury of meeting with learners on their home turf (by doing ethnographic research, visiting learners at home, attending community events, etc.), there are many tools for bringing inquiry into the classroom. Learners can talk about their practices, concerns, and needs (and successes!) using a variety of tools associated with any of the orientations and approaches outlined in this chapter. By identifying needs as learners themselves define them, practitioners can work to address those needs, either through the curriculum or, if necessary, between the cracks when institutional constraints make it impossible to do so directly. Those who make it a practice to learn about learners by observing and listening may be in for some inspiring surprises.

2. Balance Skills and Structures with Meaning-Making and Knowledge Creation

Those who were trained in structural linguistics or in competency-based approaches tend to be good at teaching language structures and functions but less practiced at starting conversations with students about things that they care about deeply. On the other hand, experienced participatory educators and community advocates tend to know how to engage learners in exploring "hot" issues, but may be less skilled in presenting the mechanics of language and literacy in a systematic way. To gain proficiency with language and literacy, it is necessary to have both the building blocks as well as the opportunity to use them for a deeper purpose. The linguists would do well to learn how to invite heart-felt conversation and collective problem-solving; the advocates and organizers need tools to help learners master the mechanics of language and literacy as an integral part of their project-based work. Practitioners can also learn from and collaborate with peers who have complementary strengths in skill-building and meaning-making—both essential parts of the language and literacy learning enterprise.

3. Develop "Vision-Making" Muscles

As we learn new techniques, follow new trends, or react to changing pressures, it is easy to forget what moved us to become teachers. We may settle into a mode of only reacting to outside mandates, losing track of the mandate that comes from our own vision. What is our purpose? What are we hoping to make happen for learners who enter our classrooms when they come in and after they've left? Articulating and pursuing a vision is, in my view, work that must be done on several levels. This happens in the daily fabric of lesson planning (What is the purpose of this lesson?); in providing input to the programs we work for (How should our curricula change?); in advocating for policies that support effective learning and effective teaching (What are the conditions that we and our learners need to pursue this vision?); as well as in how we assess the degree to which we are moving toward our vision. With too few full-time jobs and difficult working conditions, it can be challenging to remember and pursue such a vision and to be proactive rather than reactive to the day's circumstances. I believe that, as educators, we all need more practice and support in flexing our "vision-making" muscles.

4. Demand Mutual Accountability

With a growing emphasis on "accountability," it will become increasingly important for practitioners to have their own vision of what they are trying to accomplish through their literacy work and to seek ways of assessing the degree to which they are succeeding. Merrifield (1998) talks about a system of "mutually accountable" relationships in which every "player" would be both accountable to other players and held accountable by them. Learners would hold teachers accountable for meeting their learning needs, but teachers would hold learners accountable for attending and doing their work, while also holding program directors and funders accountable for providing them with adequate resources such as materials, space, or training.

While Merrifield's vision is far from the current reality, it is crucial for practitioners to know and articulate what they are trying to achieve, and to advocate for conditions they need to achieve it. Just as learners should not be asked to "wait" for meaningful communication until "after" learning the mechanics of language, practitioners must not wait for ideal conditions before engaging in vision-making work. Articulating our goals, inviting learners to articulate theirs, finding ways to measure how we are moving toward them, and fighting for conditions to make the process possible must be part of our ongoing practice in our classrooms, in conversations with our colleagues, and in wider arenas.

5. Create Communities of Learners and Communities of Teachers

In many of the orientations described in this chapter, attention is given to creating communities of learners who support one another in learning language and literacy while reflecting collectively (and sometimes taking resulting action) on their lives. Learner stories and experiences are the raw materials that can begin the conversation for planning such actions. Teachers who engage this way with the adults in their classes report enormous satisfaction when learners make individual or collective strides. Learners who have felt marginalized find strength and support in the safety of a nurturing classroom community. Technology provides new opportunities for learners to build communities both within the classroom as well as beyond its boundaries. The examples are numerous and continue to grow as learners collaborate to compile and create knowledge.

Teachers are also learners. They must constantly respond to new circumstances as the student population, legislative mandates, program constraints, and other conditions change. Like language and literacy learners, teachers must often manage despite difficult conditions. And like any learners, teachers also need time to tell stories of their teaching and to compare and analyze their experiences, both within programs and across them.

Instruction will be strongest where teachers are supported in taking time to discuss program goals, reflect collectively on their practice, frame questions, explore them systematically, and take action based on what they've learned. Such sharing may take many forms, whether it is through sharing lesson plans, peer observation, "study circles" about teaching issues, or collaboration on projects. In addition, national electronic lists such as those listed in the resource section below create opportunities for teachers to reflect collectively with a wider circle of colleagues without the constraints of in-person meeting time or the boundaries of geographic space. Communities of teacher-learners, whether in person or on-line, can provide support in one of the most challenging but rewarding endeavors imaginable—that of fostering and witnessing transformations that are associated with nurturing the development of adult literacies.

DISCUSSION QUESTIONS

1. Who are some of the ESL literacy learners in your community? What language and literacy resources do they bring, and what resources do they need or want? What are their goals for language and literacy learning?

2. What kinds of programs are available in your community for ESL literacy learners? Brainstorm a list of programs. You may wish to investigate such programs more fully as a term project.

3. What do you think the qualifications should be for teaching ESL literacy? What should be the salary and benefits? Find out about qualifications required and working conditions in programs in your community. Were there any surprises?

4. What are some of the debates that are currently on electronic literacy lists? Find a debate

or discussion and then summarize the key points from the current list or from the archives. What is your opinion about this issue?

SUGGESTED ACTIVITIES

1. Learn more about a bilingual family or community in your neighborhood. Investigate language use in a variety of ways—through interviews, observation, and/or attendance at community events. Write up a family or community profile, including patterns of who uses what language to whom and when.

2. Arrange to observe one or more classes in an adult school or ESL literacy instruction in a family, workplace, or community literacy context. Begin with a brief description of the setting, the students, and the course content. Note in nonjudgmental log format exactly what the teacher does and what the students do for the duration of the class. Write up the log, along with a discussion of the questions on page 181, or other questions you develop with your class. Interview the teacher when feasible. Find out as much as possible about the program and the funding and how they shape instruction.

3. Find examples of teachers and/or programs which
   - Have learner input at the classroom level (deciding topics, projects, etc.)
   - Have learner input at the program level (deciding curriculum, approaches, etc.)
   - Offer instruction in students' native language literacy
   - Engage in project-based work
   - Provide opportunities for community building among students and teachers

   What creates the conditions that enable these programs to engage in promising practices?

4. Imagine that the Paradise Foundation has granted you unlimited funds to design a program for the target group of your choice. Identify a group of ESL literacy learners in your community. Provide a description of their needs and resources. Describe the ideal program you would create to meet their needs, while tapping their resources.

FURTHER READING

Auerbach, E. 1992. *Making Meaning, Making Change: Participatory Curriculum Development for Adult ESL Literacy*. McHenry, IL: Delta Systems, Inc. and Center for Applied Linguistics.

Crandall, J., and J. Peyton, eds. 1993. *Approaches to Adult ESL Literacy Instruction*. McHenry, IL: Delta Systems, Inc. and Center for Applied Linguistics.

Weinstein, G., ed. 1999. *Learners' Lives as Curriculum: Six Journeys to Immigrant Literacy*. McHenry, IL: Delta Systems, Inc. and Center for Applied Linguistics.

Wrigley, H. S., and G. Guth. 2000. *Bringing Literacy to Life*. Rev. ed. San Mateo, CA: Aguirre International.

WEBSITES

The National Clearinghouse for ESL Literacy Education (NCLE) provides information on adult ESL literacy education to teachers and tutors, program directors, researchers, and policymakers interested in the education of refugees, immigrants, and other U.S. residents whose native language is not English. This site has scores of ERIC Digests, Q & As, annotated bibliographies, and other concise resources for ESL/literacy educators which can be downloaded for free. **http://www.cal.org/ncle**.

The National Institute for Literacy (NIFL) is the host of the Literacy Information and Communication System (LINCS), an information retrieval and communication network for the literacy community, also providing access to all published and unpublished literacy related materials and major literacy related databases. LINCS hosts several lists and collections, including

- the *NIFL-ESL list*, which focuses on topics such as instructional practices, program design, research, and policy. **http://www.nifl.gov/lincs/discussions/nifl-esl/about_nifl-esl.html**

- the *LINCS Adult ESL Special Collection*, which provides practitioners with curricular materials and resources, news in the field, and a forum for issues. **http://literacynet.org/esl/**

- *LINCS EFF Special Collection,* which features resources related to Equipped for the Future (EFF), NIFL's standards-based system reform initiative.
  http://www.nifl.gov/lincs/collections/eff/eff.html

NIFL also archives messages of the National Literacy Advocacy (NLA) list. The focus of this independent list, moderated by David J. Rosen, is national and state level adult literacy public policy information and advocacy, especially concerning legislation and funding.
http://www.nifl.gov/lincs/discussions/nifl-nla/nla.html

The National Center for the Study of Adult Learning and Literacy (NCSALL), according to their website, aims "to help the field of adult basic education define a comprehensive research agenda; to pursue basic and applied research under that agenda; to build partnerships between researchers and practitioners; and to disseminate research and best practices to practitioners, scholars, and policy makers." It contains an on-line version of Focus on Basics, which has many useful articles for practitioners.
http://gseweb.harvard.edu/~ncsall

Both the U.S. National Literacy Act of 1991 and the U.S. Adult Education Act of 1991, along with related policy resources, are available online at
www.nifl.gov/linc/collections/policy/resource.html

ENDNOTES

[1] I am grateful to Mary Ann Florez, Joy Peyton, Brigitte Marshall, Amanda Enoch, and Andy Nash for their helpful comments, and to David Rosen for pointing me to several useful resources. Any wrongheaded assertions or conceptual errors are strictly my own.

[2] CASAS is the acronym for the Comprehensive Adult Student Assessment System. BEST is the acronym for the Basic English Skills Test.

Reading for Academic Purposes: Guidelines for the ESL/EFL Teacher

WILLIAM GRABE • FREDRICKA L. STOLLER

Grabe and Stoller's chapter focuses on reading theory and practice as they apply to academic contexts. The authors outline central concepts underlying academic reading and their implications for instruction. They then highlight issues concerning the development of reading curricula including the analysis of needs and choosing appropriate texts and materials. They describe specific practices that build coherent and effective reading curricula.

INTRODUCTION

Many have argued in the past 15 years that reading is the most important academic language skill for second language students. Supporting these claims are several student and faculty surveys at post-secondary institutions that highlight the importance of reading for academic purposes. In academic settings, reading is assumed to be the central means for learning new information and gaining access to alternative explanations and interpretations. Reading also provides the foundation for synthesis and critical evaluation skills. In addition, reading is the primary means for independent learning, whether the goal is performing better on academic tasks, learning more about subject matter, or improving language abilities.

In this chapter, we describe how reading abilities can be developed and how teachers can guide student learning. The chapter opens with brief comments on the purposes for reading, a definition of reading, and implications for effective English for Academic Purposes (EAP) reading instruction. We then highlight major differences in first language (L1) and second language (L2) reading and consider curricular goals and instructional practices that support reading. The chapter concludes with our views of future trends in L2 reading practices.

Purposes for Reading

When we read, we read for a variety of purposes. We sometimes read to get the main idea but not much more (e.g., skimming a newspaper story), and sometimes we read to locate specific information (e.g., scanning for a name, date, or term). Commonly we read texts to learn information (i.e., reading to learn), and sometimes we are expected to synthesize information from multiple texts, or from a longer chapter or book, in order to take a critical position with respect to that information (i.e., reading to integrate and evaluate information). Perhaps most often, we read for general comprehension (i.e., reading to understand main ideas and relevant supporting information). We also read for pleasure, with the intention of being entertained or informed, but not tested.

In academic settings, almost every major purpose for reading comes into play. Thus, an EAP reading curriculum must account for how students learn to read for multiple purposes, including at least the reading

1. to search for information

2. for general comprehension

3. to learn new information

4. to synthesize and evaluate information

Although these purposes might give the impression that there are very different ways to read a text, these differing purposes actually depend on a stable set of processes and skills that underlies all reading, though in differing combinations of relative importance. Thus, we can still talk about reading in the singular and define it as such, as long as we recognize that processes and skills combine in differing ways depending on the reader's purpose (Grabe 1999a).

A Definition of Reading

The ability to read—taking general comprehension as the example—requires that the reader draw information from a text and combine it with information and expectations that the reader already has. This interaction of information is a common way to explain reading comprehension, though it does not reveal much about the specifics of reading. Recently, research on L1 reading has highlighted the need for readers to develop essential reading processes and abilities such as rapid word recognition, vocabulary development, text-structure awareness, and strategic reading (as opposed to learning individual strategies). Yet, all researchers recognize that the actual ability to comprehend texts comes about through reading, and doing a great deal of it, as the core of reading instruction.

A good way to understand reading is to consider what is required for fluent reading (see Grabe 1999b). Fluent readers, especially good L1 readers, typically do all of the following:

1. Read rapidly for comprehension
2. Recognize words rapidly and automatically (without seeming to pay any attention to them)
3. Draw on a very large vocabulary store
4. Integrate text information with their own knowledge
5. Recognize the purpose(s) for reading
6. Comprehend the text as necessary
7. Shift purpose to read strategically
8. Use strategies to monitor comprehension
9. Recognize and repair miscomprehension
10. Read critically and evaluate information

Using these characteristics of a fluent reader to create an expanded definition of reading reveals the multiple skills and strategies that L2 learners need in order to become fluent readers.

General Implications from Research for Reading Instruction

Based on these criteria for fluent reading and findings from reading research in L1 and L2 contexts, we see ten key implications for EAP reading instruction. Basically, EAP teachers can address the academic reading needs of their students by doing the following:

1. Helping students build a large recognition vocabulary
2. Providing explicit language instruction to help students build a reasonable foundation in the L2
3. Addressing the range of skills needed for successful comprehension
4. Introducing students to discourse-organizing principles through the use of graphic representations and other practices
5. Helping students become strategic readers by focusing on metacognitive awareness and strategy learning
6. Giving students many opportunities to read so that they develop reading fluency and automaticity
7. Making extensive reading and broad exposure to L2 texts a routine practice, in and out of class
8. Motivating students to read
9. Integrating reading and writing instruction
10. Developing effective content-based instruction for authentic integrated-skills tasks

Beyond these ten implications is the overarching principle that students become better readers only by doing a lot of reading. There are no shortcuts. All researchers agree on this principle.

L2 Readers and Sociocultural Factors in Learning to Read

Our definition of reading and the implications for instruction that emerge from current research reveal the complexity of reading and corresponding instruction. A more complete picture of EAP reading requires that we examine the differences between L1 and L2 readers and the ways in which these differences influence instruction. L2 readers generally have weaker linguistic skills and a more limited vocabulary than do L1 readers. They do not have an intuitive foundation in the structures of the L2, and they lack the cultural knowledge that is sometimes assumed in texts. L2 students may also have some difficulties recognizing the ways in which texts are organized and information is presented, leading to possible comprehension problems. At the same time, L2 students, working with (at least) two languages, are able to rely on their L1 knowledge and L1 reading abilities when such abilities are useful (as opposed to instances when L1 knowledge could interfere). Older academically oriented L2 students typically (but not always) have been successful in learning to read in their L1 and know that they can be successful with academic texts and tasks. L2 students also have certain resources for reading that are potentially strong supports: bilingual dictionaries, word glosses, mental translation skills, and the ability to recognize cognates (depending on the L1 and L2).

L2 students often come to class with a range of motivations to read that may be different from many L1 students' motivations. Another potential L1/L2 difference stems from students' social and cultural backgrounds. L2 students generally come from a variety of family, social, and cultural backgrounds. Some families read very little, have few reading materials available, and do not encourage independent reading. Some social settings do not encourage reading. For example, prior schooling may not have emphasized reading, other community institutions may not have encouraged reading, and libraries may have been scarce or inaccessible. Some cultures and social groups place more emphasis on spoken communication for learning, and reading plays a more limited role there. In some cases, educational and religious experiences may center more on the unquestioned truth of powerful texts, leading to the memorization of key text information rather than the evaluation of competing informational resources. Because such issues have

the potential to cause problems for students, teachers need to inform themselves about these issues and adjust their teaching accordingly to reach as many students as possible.

In addition to the varying linguistic and sociocultural factors that distinguish L2 readers from L1 readers, differences between ESL and EFL settings are worth mentioning. Prototypically, one thinks of ESL instruction as occurring in an L1 English-speaking country, typically with immigrant students in secondary schools and foreign students in post-secondary settings. In contrast, EFL students may be sitting in an English class in China, Morocco, or Belgium, learning to read English as part of a four-skills curriculum, with three to six hours of English instruction per week. In ESL and EFL settings such as these, goals for language instruction vary, levels of English proficiency differ, and expected reading outcomes are likely to be different.

The differences introduced here play major roles in establishing goals for reading instruction and specifying the levels of reading ability that constitute successful learning in a given curriculum. Each instructional setting defines somewhat different goals for reading achievement, purposes for reading, and uses of text resources. These are issues that all teachers must be sensitive to and that should guide the development of EAP reading curricula.

Goals for an Effective Reading Curriculum

In this section, we consider curricular issues that should be relevant across a wide range of EAP settings. We recognize, however, that we cannot anticipate every L2 reading context, and that recommendations must be adapted to teachers' individual situations. Nonetheless, we feel that there are at least six important goals that should be considered in planning any extended EAP reading curriculum:

1. Conduct needs analyses to interpret institutional goals and expectations for learning
2. Plan (or fine-tune) reading curricula in relation to specific goals, topics, texts, and tasks

3. Select appropriate text materials and supporting resources
4. Diversify students' reading experiences
5. Work with texts by means of a pre-, during-, and postreading framework
6. Recognize the complex nature of reading through meaningful instruction

These goals, discussed in more detail in the remainder of the chapter, offer a manageable structure for planning effective EAP reading instruction in almost any setting. Even where curricular guidelines are predetermined, exploration of these goals can significantly impact student learning outcomes.

Conducting Needs Analyses

Reading instruction, much like any instruction, needs to take into account institutional expectations in addition to students' goals, language abilities, and L1 and L2 reading experiences. It is especially important to examine students' motivations and attitudes toward reading in general, L2 reading more specifically, and the particular goals of the curriculum (e.g., topics to be covered, material to be read, means for assessment). In some settings, a certain amount of information can be collected by interviewing students' previous teachers and by becoming acquainted with institutional guidelines, assessment expectations, and reading resources (including textbooks).

Teachers also have a responsibility to gather information about students' goals, prior reading experiences, and attitudes toward L2 reading from other sources, most commonly the students themselves. One quick way to collect useful information is to conduct a short survey and have brief follow-up interviews with students. Questions can focus on how much reading students have done, what students like to read, what they have read, and when they read their last book and for what reason(s). Other questions can be directed at determining how students feel about reading and how successful they perceive themselves to be as readers. Even a simple set of questions gives teachers access to useful information that can be used to plan (or fine-tune) a reading curriculum.

Planning (or Fine-Tuning) Reading Curricula

After conducting a needs analysis, the goals of the curriculum can be spelled out (or interpreted) in more detail. Because there are many possible goals for a reading curriculum, curricular priorities need to be determined based on institutional goals, number of hours of instruction per week, available resources, and students' abilities, needs, and interests. (See Johns and Price-Machado's chapter in this volume.) Regardless of the number of student contact hours, all reading curricula should focus on comprehension of key texts, but they might also emphasize extensive reading, the development of strategic reading, a large increase in students' recognition vocabularies, greater fluency in reading, systematic analyses of difficult material, and the study of discourse-organization features. After goals and priorities are determined, texts and topics can be selected and tasks designed, with an eye toward creating a meaningful, motivating, and challenging curriculum.

Selecting Appropriate Text Materials and Supporting Resources

A reading curriculum is heavily dependent on the reading materials used: The choice of primary texts and textbooks, supporting resources, and classroom library materials have a major impact on students' motivations to read and their engagement with texts. Text materials should complement students' intellectual levels and be at appropriate levels of difficulty; potential sources of difficulty for L2 readers include assumed background knowledge, cultural assumptions, demanding topics, grammatical complexity, length of texts, new conceptual knowledge, organization, unusual formatting, and vocabulary. The text materials selected for EAP settings should be interesting and coherently linked (e.g., by topics, tasks, and overall themes) to simulate the demands of academic courses. Text materials and lessons should build in a degree of complexity through the introduction of new, though related, information and differing perspectives so that students feel some challenge and have the opportunity to develop some expertise and pride in what they are learning. Ideally, free-reading materials should be easily accessible, plentiful, attractive, and available for learner use beyond class time (Day and Bamford 1998).

Diversifying Students' Reading Experiences

Effective reading instruction should not be limited to activities done in the classroom. An ideal reading curriculum comprises reading in class, in a lab (see Stoller 1994a), in a library, and at home, in addition to reading for different purposes. As noted earlier, reading can develop successfully only if students read a large amount of material. A major task of a reading curriculum, then, is to guide students in doing as much reading as possible in the amount of time available. Silent reading should be part of every reading lesson; extended silent reading should be a major component of reading labs and library visits, and students must be encouraged to read at home.

Working with Texts by Means of a Pre-, During-, and Postreading Framework

If the heart of learning to read is the act of reading itself, then the heart of reading instruction is the set of tasks that students engage in to achieve learning goals. Countless instructional tasks are used in reading classes (Day 1993); some are more effective than others. Teachers' choices should be guided by instructional goals, student readiness, text resources, and implications from research and theory. One major implication from theory is a general framework based on pre-, during-, and postreading instruction (see Stoller 1994b, for practical applications).

Prereading instruction can serve five important purposes. It helps students access background information that can facilitate subsequent reading, provides specific information needed for successful comprehension, stimulates student interest, sets up student expectations, and models strategies that students can later use on their own. Some commonly used prereading activities include the following:

1. Previewing the text (by examining distinguishing features of the text such as the title, subheadings, illustrations and captions, and sections) to determine (or at least hypothesize) the general topic of the reading, relevant vocabulary, and possible challenges
2. Skimming the text or portions of the text (e.g., the first and last paragraphs) to decide what the main ideas of the text are
3. Answering questions about information in the text or formulating questions for which students want answers
4. Exploring key vocabulary
5. Reflecting on or reviewing information from previously read texts in light of the topic of the new text

During-reading instruction guides students through the text, often focusing on understanding difficult concepts, making sense of complex sentences, considering relationships among ideas or characters in the text, and reading purposefully and strategically. Some commonly used during-reading activities include the following:

1. Outlining or summarizing key ideas in a difficult section
2. Examining emotions and attitudes of key characters
3. Determining sources of difficulty and seeking clarification
4. Looking for answers to questions posed during prereading activities
5. Writing down predictions of what will come next

Postreading instruction typically extends ideas and information from the text while also ensuring that the major ideas and supporting information are well understood. Postreading activities often require students to use text information in other tasks (e.g., reading to write). Some commonly used postreading activities are

1. Completing a graphic organizer (e.g., table, chart, grid) based on text information

2. Expanding or changing a semantic map created earlier

3. Listening to a lecture and comparing information from the text and the lecture

4. Ranking the importance of information in the text based on a set of sentences provided

5. Answering questions that demonstrate comprehension of the text, require the application of text material, demand a critical stance on text information, or oblige students to connect text information to personal experiences and opinions

The pre-, during-, and postreading framework described here is easily adapted to different classroom contexts. All three components of the framework may be integrated into a single lesson (with a short reading passage on a familiar topic) or they may run across numerous lessons. The activities introduced in the upcoming sections of this chapter can also be integrated into the pre-, during-, and postinstructional framework.

Addressing the Complex Nature of Reading through Meaningful Instruction

Reading is a complex skill—as demonstrated by our definition of reading, the abilities of fluent readers, and the many purposes for which we read. Meaningful EAP reading instruction can account for this complexity by addressing the following: vocabulary development, careful reading of texts, awareness of text structure and discourse organization, the use of graphic organizers to support comprehension, strategic reading, fluency development, extensive reading, student motivation, and integrated-skills tasks. Because it is virtually impossible to develop each and every area with equal intensity, reading teachers need to decide which areas to focus more attention on, while not losing sight of the primary means for reading development: Students need to read extensively.

Vocabulary Development There is overwhelming evidence that vocabulary knowledge is closely related to reading abilities (Schoonen,

Hulstijn, and Bossers 1998). Students need to recognize a large number of words automatically if they are to be fluent readers. Some part of rapid word recognition skills comes from reading extensively and learning new words while reading. However, reading by itself does not provide full support for vocabulary development. In addition to reading extensively, students benefit from being exposed to new words through explicit instruction, learning how to learn words on their own, familiarizing themselves with their own word-learning processes, and becoming word collectors (see Graves 2000; Stahl 1999). (See also DeCarrico's chapter in this volume.)

With so many words for students to learn, a teacher needs to decide how many and which words to focus on. Inexperienced teachers may have difficulties selecting key words for instruction. Key words themselves should be the most important words for a text, the most useful for organizing and working with other vocabulary, and the most likely to be helpful to students beyond the text being read. Often textbooks highlight specific words for instruction; however, there may be other words that need attention. A useful approach for teachers is to preview the text to be assigned and identify words likely to be unfamiliar to their students. Words should be placed in one of three categories:

1. + + : Words that are critical for comprehending the text and useful in other settings

2. + − : Words that are necessary for comprehending the text, but not particularly useful in other contexts

3. − − : Words that are not necessary for comprehending the text, nor particularly useful in other contexts

Words that fall into the + + and + − categories should be considered for direct instruction. Yet, when texts are difficult for students, a teacher might identify 40 to 50 words in these two categories. The problem here is that trying to teach a large number of words directly at any one time is not an effective teaching strategy. In any given lesson, it is more efficient to focus on four to five key words, because that number of words is likely to be learned and remembered if used multiple times and in multiple ways. Many of the other useful and important words in a text can be built into exercises and activities (e.g., semantic maps, tables, word families) and explored as part of discussions about the text and what the text means. Ideally, key words can be used to build up sets of related words. For example, the word *computer* can bring up words such as monitor, electricity, software, printers, calculators, robots, e-mail, Internet, programming, writing, and graphics. A semantic mapping activity may place all of these words on a blackboard just by association with the key word. In this way, students gain exposure to other words without treating each one as a key word.

Many words that are difficult for students may be uncommon, specialized, unimportant for the text, or a name or place word. These can be addressed simply by providing glosses, good synonyms, or practice in guessing word meanings from context. More generally, teachers and students need to keep words active in the classroom environment through explicit instruction (see Figure 1) and the intentional recycling of words, and by putting words on walls (see Eyraud et al. 2000) and in notebooks, and incorporating them into larger learning projects.

- Analysis of word parts
- Associations
- Cognate awareness
- Definitions
- Dictionary activities
- Discussion of word meanings
- Flashcards
- Games
- Illustrations, drawings, realia
- Matching meanings and collocations
- Mnemonic techniques
- Parts of speech tables
- Semantic mapping and semantic grids
- Synonyms and antonyms
- Word family exercises

Figure 1. Sampling of Explicit Vocabulary Teaching Techniques

Students can also be taught how to learn words on their own, using, for example, a dictionary, word-part information, and context clues. Students can be encouraged to take responsibility for their own word learning by collecting words from texts (perhaps on index cards), recycling vocabulary from past texts, discussing words that they like, experimenting with words that have more than one meaning, and bringing new words to class to share with classmates.

Careful Reading of Texts   In academic settings, the careful reading of texts is a common task, one that requires readers to demonstrate a good understanding of details in the text, to learn information from it, and to use that information for other tasks. In EAP classrooms, careful reading activities typically center on questions that ask students to recognize main ideas and analyze supporting information, arguments, or details that explain the main ideas. Activities that require careful reading often focus on unraveling information in long and complex sentences, determining embedded definitions, exploring inferences that connect sets of information, distinguishing more important ideas from less important ones, examining the discourse structure of parts of the text, and using text information for other activities (e.g., filling in a table, writing a summary, comparing information from one text with another). Many of the postreading activities listed earlier can be used to promote careful reading; others include the following:

1. Filling in parts left blank in an extended summary
2. Determining the attitude of the writer, the intended audience, and the goal(s) of the writer and identifying clues in the text
3. Listing examples that appear in the text, adding other pertinent examples to the list, and explaining one's reasons for doing so
4. Matching information or evaluating possible true/false statements

In carrying out careful reading activities, there are some important guidelines to keep in mind. If a text is too difficult for students, additional support should be provided by, for example, putting students into groups to work out answers together. A second option is to provide some of the answers (and review strategies for how other questions can be answered), thereby making the remainder of the task easier. Students, when reporting answers or working on tasks, should occasionally be asked to explain how they arrived at their answers and point out where they found key information in the text. These confirming activities, though often quite time-consuming, help students sharpen their strategies for careful reading, give teachers insights into how texts are understood, and provide opportunities for discussions about strategic reading.

Awareness of Text Structure and Discourse Organization   Students in academic settings are often expected to learn new information from difficult texts. It is important that L2 students do not become confused by the larger organization of the texts (e.g., comparison-contrast, problem-solution, narrative sequences, and classification) and features of different genres (e.g., newspaper stories, letters to the editor, "how-to" procedures). A consistent effort to guide students to see the ways that texts are structured will help them build stronger comprehension skills. Activities that focus specifically on the ways in which discourse is organized and on specific aspects of text structure (e.g., transition phrases, words that signal patterns of text organization, pronoun references, headings, and subheadings) are often part of exercises that emphasize careful reading. Some of these activities use graphic organizers (discussed in the next section of this chapter), but there are many other ways to explore discourse organization and text structure:

1. Identifying the sentences that convey the main ideas of the text
2. Examining headings and subheadings in a text and then deciding what each section is about
3. Adding information to a partially completed outline until all key supporting ideas are included
4. Underlining transition phrases and, when they signal major sections of the text, describing what the next section covers
5. Explaining what a set of pronouns refers to in prior text

6. Examining an inaccurate outline and adjusting it so that it is correct
7. Reorganizing a scrambled paragraph and discussing textual clues used for decisions
8. Creating headings for a set of paragraphs in the text, giving a label to each, and discussing the function of each paragraph.
9. Identifying clues that indicate major patterns of organization (e.g., cause-effect, comparison-contrast, analysis)

These text-analysis activities, as representative samples of a larger set, help students understand that texts have larger patterns of organization beyond the sentence. Students benefit from being aware of these patterns when they read for academic purposes.

Use of Graphic Organizers to Support Comprehension and Discourse Organization Awareness
An effective way to carry out reading instruction that focuses on careful reading comprehension and discourse organization is through the use of graphic organizers (i.e., visual representations of text information). The main goal of graphic representations is to assist students in comprehending difficult texts. By using graphic organizers, students are able to see the key information in a text, the organization of text information, the ways that information is structured, and relationships among ideas presented in a text or a portion of a text. Graphic organizers are sometimes generic; at other times, they are tied to specific patterns of text organization. For example, outlines and semantic maps can be used across a large number of texts regardless of the way they are organized. As graphic representations, simple lines are versatile too, allowing students, for example, to chart events chronologically or rank characters' opinions on a continuum (Mach and Stoller 1997). Grids (or matrices) lend themselves nicely to comparison and contrast texts. Texts with causes and effects can be represented in two-column grids, but they can also be characterized by a series of unidirectional or bidirectional arrows, indicating causes and effects. A classification text (e.g., about different types of whales) might be sketched out with major categories to one side and descriptors across the top, with details in corresponding cells.

Graphic organizers come in many shapes and sizes (e.g., Grabe 1997; Parks and Black 1990, 1992; and websites listed at the end of this chapter). But not all graphics work with all texts. Thus, the teacher needs to read over the assigned text carefully and determine what types of graphic representations will assist students and what kinds of graphics-related activities will enhance learning and comprehension. There are many options for teaching with graphic representations, including:

1. Using a circle with arrows flowing in a circular direction to show an iterative process described in a text
2. Using a Venn diagram to highlight differences and similarities between characters, places, events, or issues in a text
3. Using a flowchart to trace events or steps in a process highlighted in a text

Activities such as these are effective means to help students improve their reading comprehension.

Strategic Reading   A major goal for academic reading instruction is the development of strategic readers (rather than the disconnected teaching of reading strategies). Strategic readers understand the goals of a reading activity, have a range of well-practiced reading strategies at their disposal, apply them in efficient combinations, monitor comprehension appropriately, recognize miscomprehension, and repair comprehension problems effectively. Strategic readers make use of a wide repertoire of strategies in combination rather than in isolated applications. Commonly used strategies include

- Previewing a text
- Predicting what will come later in a text
- Summarizing
- Learning new words through the analysis of word stems and affixes
- Using context to maintain comprehension
- Recognizing text organization
- Generating appropriate questions about the text
- Clarifying text meaning
- Repairing miscomprehension

The development of strategic readers requires a commitment to teaching strategies. The introduction of strategies, their practice, and their uses should be part of every lesson. Indeed, it is not difficult to talk about strategies in class if every session requires reading, focuses on text comprehension, and includes discussions about the text and how it is understood (see Janzen and Stoller 1998). Ultimately, the goal is to develop (a) fairly automatic routines that work to resolve more general reading comprehension difficulties and (b) a more elaborate set of problem-solving strategies that can be used when routine strategies do not work well.

One instructional approach that is particularly effective is known as *Transactional Strategies Instruction* (TSI) (Pressley 1998). TSI is typically characterized by the following tenets:

1. Strategy instruction requires a long-term commitment from teachers.
2. Teachers explain and model effective comprehension strategies. Typically only a few are emphasized at any time.
3. The teacher coaches students to use strategies as needed. Minilessons are given about when it is appropriate to use certain strategies.
4. Teachers and students model uses of strategies for one another, explaining aloud what strategies they are using.
5. The usefulness of strategies is emphasized continually and students are reminded frequently about the benefits of strategy use. Issues of when and where to use strategies are discussed regularly.
6. Strategy instruction is included in discussions about text comprehension, focusing on not only what the text might mean but also how students come to understand information in the text.

A similar approach, known as *Questioning the Author*, centers on the internalization of comprehension strategies through discussion focused on texts and their meanings (see Beck et al. 1997).

The goal of making every student a strategic reader is central to academic reading instruction. All reading instruction should be tied to reading strategies, their development, and their use in effective combinations. For any approach to strategy development, students need to be introduced to only a few strategies at a time. Each strategy should be discussed, explained, and modeled. From that point on, the strategies should be reintroduced on a continual basis through teacher reminders, discussions, wall charts, student modeling, and student explanations. Certain strategies, such as summarizing, suggest multiple activities. It is common practice to ask students to summarize a short text verbally. In instructional contexts where reading and writing are combined, summarizing takes on a larger role, integrating the two skills and leading to more demanding types of writing tasks.

Aside from discussions centered on text comprehension and strategy awareness, another approach to building strategic competence involves "elaborative interrogation." This instructional approach involves the addition of "why" questions to class discussions, after students have answered comprehension questions. The "why" questions oblige students to explain their answers and specify where the text provides appropriate support.

Fluency Development One of the most neglected aspects of L2 reading instruction is the development of reading fluency, even though research strongly argues that fluency is one of the central foundations for efficient reading. Fluency involves rapid and automatic word recognition, the ability to recognize basic grammatical information, and the rapid combination of word meanings and structural information to create larger meaning units. There are a number of reasons why fluency instruction is not promoted in L2 settings:

1. Reading fluency depends on knowing a fairly large number of words so that a reading task itself is not too difficult. Many L2 students do not recognize a large number of words quickly or easily, so they are very slow at initial efforts in fluency training. However, the best way to develop these skills is through methodical training in reading fluency.

2. Teachers sometimes feel that fluency training is too mechanical and not relevant to reading comprehension instruction. Other teachers question the benefits of fluency training because it requires a long-term commitment and students' reading gains are not immediately obvious. However, the development of rapid and automatic recognition of words is an essential component of skilled reading comprehension.

3. Fluency training often involves reading aloud and many teachers believe that they should never promote reading aloud in class. However, fluency training is one of the areas in which oral reading is a helpful support for reading development.

4. Teachers are typically given few guidelines for building reading fluency into reading curricula. There are, however, a number of ways to promote fluency without requiring a significant investment in resources.

Fluency activities—classified here as activities that develop overall fluency, rate, and word recognition—can be incorporated into any reading program regularly. Extensive reading (discussed more fully in the next section) helps students in all three areas. Activities that specifically target overall fluency include rereading practice and rereading for other purposes. Activities that promote reading rate include timed readings and paced readings. Activities that develop rapid recognition skills include word-recognition exercises, flashcard practice, teacher read-alouds (with students reading along silently), and rereading practice. Students benefit from hearing about the advantages of such activities and the need to work on them consistently to see long-range improvements. The use of progress charts assists students in visualizing their gradual improvement. One particular advantage of most fluency activities is that they take on a gamelike quality as students work against themselves rather than compete with other students. (See Anderson 1999; Samuels, Schermer, and Reinking 1992.)

Rereading practice involves reading aloud and should be done with texts that students can read without great difficulty or that have already been read and used for comprehension activities. Typically—though there are many variations—two students work together. The first student reads aloud from the beginning of a text while the second student keeps time and helps with any difficulties. After one minute, the first student stops and marks the place in the text where he or she stopped. The students may make a few very quick comments on the difficulties encountered. Then they switch roles. The second student reads from the beginning of the same text for one minute while the first student keeps time and helps with any difficulties. After one minute, the second student stops and marks the stopping point in the text. They switch roles again. At this point, the first student starts reading from the beginning of the text again for one minute with the goal of moving beyond his or her first stopping point. The second student again keeps time and helps if needed. The process is repeated for the second student. The students then note how many additional words they read the second time through the text and note their gains on a chart.

Rereading texts for new purposes provides another option for general fluency. After reading a text for comprehension purposes, a text may be reread to decide what the author's purpose is, to fill in a chart, or to compare the information with another source of information (e.g., a new text, a text read earlier in the course, or, for that matter, a video or lecture). In all forms of rereading, the goal is to give students enough time to actually read the text again, rather than simply skim the text to complete the follow-up exercise. When students reread a text that they are already familiar with, they often read more fluently, with higher rates of comprehension, thereby getting the feel for more fluent reading. They also extend their reading experiences by reading for different purposes.

Reading rates can be directly improved through two common techniques: timed readings and paced readings. In timed readings, students time themselves while reading a passage (typically not very difficult and of a reasonable length) from start to finish. Timed readings are usually followed by a set of fairly simple comprehension questions that can be answered and scored quickly. The results of timed readings are entered on a progress chart so that gradual gains in reading rate and comprehension are noticeable to students. Timed readings, when used as

part of a rate development program, need to be a consistent activity throughout the semester or year, usually once or twice a week. In this way, the cumulative practice leads to rate improvements as well as overall reading fluency (see Fry 2000).

Paced readings work on the same principle but oblige students to read at a specified pace (e.g., 120 words per minute) rather than at their own pace. Typically, paced readings are shorter than timed readings, about 400 words in length (though shorter passages can also be used for timed readings). Passages are of a consistent length, with marks of some sort (e.g., a check or dot) in the margin to indicate every 100-word segment. Thus, a 400-word text would have three marks, the first indicating the first 100 words, the second indicating the second 100 words, and so forth.

In a paced reading, students are directed to read at a pace specified (and maintained) by the teacher. For example, at 100 wpm, students would hear a signaling noise (e.g., a light tap on the desk by the teacher) at regular intervals, in this case every 60 seconds, indicating that they should either be at the first mark or move down to the first mark and continue reading from that point. When the signal is repeated again, at the next increment of time, students move to the second mark if they have not yet reached it. Again, simple comprehension questions appear after the text is completed. After answers are corrected, students enter results on a graph. Because paced readings are completed more quickly than timed readings, two or three are usually done in a row, sometimes with varying paces (e.g., the first at 150 wpm, the second at 110 wpm, and the third at 120 wpm). When students are familiar with the process, it is carried out quickly and three paced readings can be finished in less than 20 minutes. (See Spargo 1989, 1998; Stoller 1994a.)

Another way to develop reading fluency is through practice in word recognition under time pressure. Word-recognition exercises generally involve a set of about 20 key words or phrases down the left-hand side of a page, each one followed by a row of four or five words—one of which is identical to the key word, whereas the others are similar in shape or are morphological variations of the key word (see Figure 2). Students are asked to work as quickly as possible to mark the exact match for each key word. Upon completion, students check their work and record the number correct and the time spent on a chart. Typically, a word-recognition lesson includes three consecutive 20-word exercises and will take no more than 7–10 minutes total after students understand what is expected of them. (See Stoller 1993 for suggestions on creating recognition exercises and using them in class.)

Two other activities for improving the speed of word recognition involve (a) the use of flashcards for sets of key words that appear in readings for the week and (b) teacher read-alouds. Flashcard practice may seem very traditional, but recent research has shown that it works for fluency purposes (Nicholson and Tan 1999). Teacher and students make up 20 cards per text, and for 7–10 minute intervals, the teacher works with the class, or pairs of students work together, to read words aloud that are flashed very quickly, usually within one second. This flashcard practice should be done once or twice per text, or two to three times per week if time permits. Words that cause ongoing difficulty should be recorded in a notebook to be studied and used at later times in student pairs.

Extensive Reading Extensive reading, the practice of reading large amounts of text for extended periods of time, should be a central component of any course with the goal of building academic reading abilities. The sustained silent reading of level-appropriate texts is the single best overall activity that students can engage in to improve their reading abilities, though it is not sufficient by itself for an effective reading program. The point is simple. One does not become a good reader unless one reads a lot (see Anderson 1996; Elley 1991). Extensive reading, however, is typically not promoted in L2 reading courses. Teachers sometimes do not feel that they are teaching when students are reading silently in class; they think that extensive reading is something that should only be done at home. Sometimes there are limited re-sources for good class or school libraries. In some cases, schools have resources but they do not include books that interest students or they do not allow students to check out books to be read at home. There are cases in which teachers do not believe that reading large amounts of level-appropriate text is an appropriate goal for academic-reading development. Finally, some teachers would like to involve their students in extensive reading but do not know how to incorporate it into their lessons.

There are several ways to engage students in extensive reading, both in and out of class. We recognize that not every teacher has access to all possible resources for extensive reading, nor do they have unlimited time in their reading courses to promote as much extensive reading as should occur. Below we list ideal conditions for extensive reading, though we expect that any teacher can pursue only a subset of them.

1. Provide time for extended silent reading in every class session, even if it only involves reading from the textbook

2. Create opportunities for all types of reading

3. Find out what students like to read and why

4. Make interesting, attractive, and level-appropriate reading materials available

5. Build a well-stocked, diverse class library with clear indications of topic and level of difficulty for each text

6. Allow students to take books and magazines home to read, and hold students accountable for at-home reading in some simple way

Key word					
1. **direct**	directs	donate	direct	detect	desire
2. **trial**	cruel	serial	trail	trial	frail
3. **through**	through	though	thorough	borough	thought

Figure 2. Sample Word-Recognition Exercise Format

7. Create incentives for students to read at home
8. Have students share and recommend reading materials to classmates
9. Keep records of the amounts of extensive reading completed by students
10. Seek out class sets of texts (or at least group sets) that everyone can read and discuss
11. Make use of graded readers, provided that they interest students, are attractive, create sufficient challenge, and offer a good amount of extensive reading practice
12. Read interesting materials aloud to students on a consistent basis
13. Visit the school library regularly and set aside time for browsing and reading
14. Create a reading lab and designate time for lab activities

There are a number of specific instructional practices to consider when engaging students in extensive reading. In-class extensive reading is most often carried out by giving students 10–15 minutes of silent reading time. During this time, students may read a class reader; read a book or magazine of their choice while the teacher circulates to answer questions and offer assistance (free-reading); or engage in sustained silent reading (SSR). In SSR, the teacher does not circulate; rather he or she reads silently throughout the entire SSR period, serving as a role model of an engaged reader. (The teacher should not grade papers or plan future lessons during this time.) Students need to see that teachers really do read and that they enjoy it. After an uninterrupted SSR period, the teacher and students should take a minute or two to share ideas or make recommendations about their reading. Students may be asked to keep a simple log of what and how many pages they read so that a record of reading is built up over time. In SSR periods, there should be no evaluation, no instruction, and no interruptions.

Extensive reading, much like any new routine, is enhanced when the teacher discusses the goals with students and helps students find interesting and readable materials. The teacher should recognize that extended free-reading time or SSR may generate resistance from certain students. Over a number of sessions, with support from the teacher, students will become engaged and even look forward to extensive reading. Teachers also need to understand that extensive reading is not an occasional end-of-the-week, or end-of-the-day "reward." It is fundamental to the development of fluent reading abilities. If pursued as an instructional goal, it must be done consistently or students will not believe the teacher's rationale.

Extensive reading at school should be coupled with extensive reading at home, with as much reading as students can be persuaded to do. At a minimum, the books and magazines read at home should be discussed in class, with recommendations made to other students. There should also be an ongoing log of what is read, how long the student read, and how many pages were covered; this log should be checked regularly by the teacher. (See Day and Bamford 1998 for advice on promoting extensive reading.)

Student Motivation Motivation is another key to successful reading, one that is typically ignored in discussions of reading instruction. There is, however, a significant body of research that argues that motivation has an important impact on reading development. Motivation is a complex concept with many associated notions (e.g., interest, involvement, self-concept, self-efficacy). We discuss motivation here (following Guthrie et al. 1999) as an individual trait, related to a person's goals and beliefs, that is observed though task persistence and positive feelings toward an activity. The key idea for teachers is that motivation makes a real difference in students' reading development, and teachers need to consider how to motivate students to engage as actively as possible with class texts and in extensive reading.

There are a number of ways to develop positive motivation to read. First and foremost, teachers should discuss the importance of reading and the reasons for different activities used in class. Second, teachers need to talk about what interests them as readers and why. Students are often surprised to learn about what and why their teachers like to read. Likewise, teachers should invite students to share interests with classmates. Third, all class activities should be related to course goals to which students have been introduced. Fourth, all reading tasks (short and more extended) should have lead-ins (i.e., prereading activities) that develop initial interest. Fifth, teachers need to build their students' knowledge base so that students can manage complex ideas and develop a level of expertise on some topics. Sixth, teachers need to select texts and adapt activities with students' reading abilities and the inherent difficulties of the reading passages in mind. Seventh, teachers should nurture "a community of learners" among students, thereby ensuring that students learn to rely on each other effectively while working through complex tasks and associated reading materials.

Finally, teachers need to look for ways to help students encounter "flow" in their reading. Flow is a concept (developed by the psychologist Csikszentmihalyi [1990]) that describes optimal experiences. People encounter flow when they are engaged fully in activities in which their growing skills match well with task challenges. Commonly, the tasks have well-defined goals, the means for determining success are clearly understood, and the achievement of success is not easy but is possible. People having flow experiences typically lose track of time, do not get distracted, and lose any sense of personal problems. Csikszentmihalyi has consistently found (across many studies and hundreds of interviews) that a primary way to encounter flow is by becoming engaged in reading. Thus, flow experiences lead students to seek out reading as an optimal experience, resulting in intrinsic motivation to read regularly.

Integrated-Skills Instruction In academic settings, a common expectation of reading is that it is used to carry out further language- and content-learning tasks, most typically in connection with writing activities, though listening and speaking activities may also be linked to reading. Although integrated-skills activities take on greater significance as students move to higher language proficiency levels, a goal for EAP curricula should be the use of reading as a resource for integrated-skills tasks.

Taking reading and writing as a primary example, there are many ways in which these skills can be integrated and serve the development of reading, writing, and academic skills. The most obvious and generic options—such as summary writing, report writing, and outlining—should not be downplayed as too traditional. There is clear evidence that summary writing and outlining, when taught well, improve both reading and writing abilities (Grabe 2001). A number of other writing activities can be developed from reading resources:

1. Students keep journals in which reactions to readings are recorded and elaborated upon. Teachers collect journals periodically and add comments.

2. Students keep double-entry notebooks in which they summarize text ideas of particular significance on one side of the page. In later rereadings, students (and the teacher) write additional comments on the opposite side of the page.

3. Students write a simple response to some prompt (e.g., a minilecture, an object, a short video clip, a quick skim of the text to be read) to prepare themselves for the upcoming reading.

4. Students create graphic organizers to identify main ideas from the text, restructure information, or compare content from various texts. Students then write an explanation or critique of the reading(s) based on the graphic organizer.

5. Students connect new texts to previously read texts through speed writes, graphic organizers, or discussions.

6. Students determine the author's point of view in a text and then adopt a different point of view (not necessarily opposing). They develop the alternative point of view through an outline and consultation with other resources, and then write a critique of the text and the author's viewpoint.

7. Students make a list of ideas from the text, prioritize the list by level of importance, get into groups and prioritize a group list, and then develop a visual representation of their response (in the form of, for example, a diagram, outline, or figure) to be shared with classmates.

There are additional reasons for centering EAP reading instruction within an integrated-skills framework. Aside from the authenticity of integrated-skills activities for advanced students, integrated activities open up valuable opportunities for extensive reading (during which students search for additional information). Furthermore, integrated-skills activities engage students in complex tasks that complement their academic goals and require strategic responses. Finally, students inevitably learn a considerable amount of connected, coherent, and stimulating content knowledge from complex integrated tasks. The resulting mastery of a topic and sense of expertise often motivate them to learn even more. The most logical extension, then, from a reading course with integrated-skills activities is a reading course centered on a content- and language-learning foundation. In this way, academic reading instruction leads naturally into various types of content-based instruction.

CONCLUSION

This chapter has outlined components of effective academic reading instruction. When looking across the range of components (vocabulary, fluency, strategies, graphic representations, extensive reading, etc.), a natural response might be to say that all of these ideas cannot possibly fit into a reading course that is coherent and focused. Yet, over the past 20 years, we have become firmly convinced that all of these components can be drawn together coherently and effectively in an appropriately developed content-based instruction approach. (There is, we must add, nothing magical about content-based instruction; it needs to be grounded in the criteria discussed above, just like any other program or course in reading.)

In a content-based approach to reading, one can assume that reading multiple sources of information will be the norm and that there will be many opportunities for meaningful extensive reading. Vocabulary instruction should grow in complexity and there will be ongoing opportunities to recycle vocabulary as students explore sets of related content material. Similarly, there will be many occasions to reread texts for new tasks, for new information, for comparisons, and

for confirming information. Furthermore, students will have the chance to extend complex learning, carry out purposeful integrated-skills tasks, build expertise on a topic, and become more motivated. The more complex language and content learning that occurs in content-based classrooms will also open up opportunities to discuss comprehension and focus on the strategies that students use to build comprehension abilities. In brief, we see content-based instruction as providing the best foundation for academic reading instruction if it is planned and carried out well (Stoller and Grabe 1997). It is likely that the development of new ways to engage students through content-based instruction will be a major focus of advanced reading instruction for the coming decade. (See Snow's chapter in this volume.)

Before closing this chapter, we would like to address briefly three other future directions for reading instruction. First, we see technology as growing in importance, and related issues as centering on how to use technology to support reading development. At the moment, the options for computer-based reading instruction are not very advanced; in most cases, they involve little more than putting reading passages on the screen with a few tricks and gadgets. We expect that in the next five to eight years, this situation will change, and computer technologies and instructional software will create new options for reading instruction.

Second, we have not addressed reading assessment in any way, but it is an issue that cannot be ignored. Although assessment might not be considered a direct component of instruction, it certainly should be. Teachers need to know how to assess students' progress in addition to assessing the effectiveness of various practices in a reading course. What works and what does not work should not rest only with a teacher's subjective judgment but should be determined through both formal and informal assessment procedures. (Good sources on reading assessment include Alderson 2000; Hamayan 1995. See also Cohen's chapter in this volume.)

Third, in addition to assessing student progress, teachers need to evaluate course and teaching effectiveness. The most effective way to do this is through teacher-initiated inquiry (i.e., action research). Through systematic reflection and data collection, teachers can investigate aspects of their own reading classrooms to improve future instruction. They can investigate aspects of reading (e.g., rate, recognition, vocabulary, skimming) in relation to different instructional techniques or learning activities (e.g., the use of graphic organizers, strategy training, rereading) to determine their effectiveness, or classroom materials to ascertain their appropriateness, or a range of other issues. Action research provides teachers with a nonthreatening means for exploring what works best in their own teaching contexts (Grabe and Stoller in press).

Whether or not reading teachers design content-based courses, engage in action research, or use technology in reading classes in the future, we can be fairly certain that EAP instruction will continue to be important for L2 students. L2 teachers, whether they teach in ESL or EFL settings, owe it to their students to make the most of the time they have allotted for reading instruction. If teachers are obliged to use mandated materials, as most teachers are, they should evaluate them carefully, keeping in mind the complexities of fluent reading and effective reading instruction. The goal should be to augment and improve mandated materials so that students have the fullest reading development experience possible. For teachers who are in a position to create academic reading curricula and select materials on their own, this chapter provides many of the "ingredients" needed. It is up to the teachers to put them together to meet students' reading needs. Regardless of setting, teachers must remember that students most often rise or fall to the level of expectation of their teachers. Thus, teachers should set high expectations for their students and assist them in achieving those expectations by means of purposeful and principled reading instruction.

DISCUSSION QUESTIONS

1. How has your conception of reading changed since reading this chapter? Identify three ideas or concepts from the chapter that you think are important and rank order them. Provide a rationale for your decisions.

2. Consider the characteristics of a fluent L1 reader (page 188) as the ultimate goal for an L2 reading curriculum. What instructional practices would you incorporate into an L2 reading class to move your students toward that goal? What activities would you assign to address each characteristic or cluster of characteristics?

3. Reflect on your own experiences in reading for academic purposes. Which purposes for reading have been most important for you? What have you done to comprehend texts that have been challenging for you? What can you apply from your experiences to your teaching?

4. Consider the constraints that you might face if you were teaching reading for academic purposes in an instructional setting of your choice. What would you do to maximize the effectiveness of your reading instruction?

5. In this chapter, Grabe and Stoller assert that there is a difference between facilitating the development of strategic readers and teaching reading strategies. How would you explain the distinction they are making?

6. What is the relationship between content-based instruction (CBI) and reading development in L2 settings? How can CBI contribute to reading development?

SUGGESTED ACTIVITIES

1. Create a graphic organizer that depicts your current view of reading for academic purposes.

2. Select a short text (e.g., from a magazine, newspaper, textbook) that might be of interest to a class of L2 students.

   a. Analyze the text from the perspective of these L2 students. What aspects of the text might prove difficult to them?

   b. Identify 10–15 words in the text that might be unfamiliar to these students. Place each word into one of the following categories: + +, + –, – –. How would you introduce words falling into the + + category?

   c. Design three postreading tasks that will oblige students to engage in careful reading. Each task should focus on a different aspect of careful reading (e.g., recognizing main ideas; analyzing support information, arguments, or details that explain the main ideas; inferencing; unraveling information in complex sentences; determining author's attitudes; applying information). Be prepared to explain the aim of each task that you design.

3. Select three L2 reading textbooks. Examine them carefully to determine their effectiveness. Do they include motivating readings? To what extent are the following aspects of reading covered: strategy development, fluency training, opportunities for rereading, graphic organizers, vocabulary building activities, different purposes for reading, exercises on discourse organization and text structure, integrated-skills activities, pre-, during-, and postreading activities, etc.?

FURTHER READING

Aebersold, J. A., and M. L. Field. 1997. *From Reader to Reading Teacher: Issues and Strategies for Second Language Classrooms.* New York: Cambridge University Press.

Anderson, N. 1999. *Exploring Second Language Reading: Issues and Strategies.* Boston, MA: Heinle & Heinle.

Day, R. R., ed. 1993. *New Ways in Teaching Reading.* Alexandria, VA: TESOL.

Day, R. R., and J. Bamford. 1998. *Extensive Reading in the Second Language Classroom.* New York: Cambridge University Press.

Silberstein, S. 1994. *Techniques and Resources in Teaching Reading.* New York: Oxford University Press.

Urquhart, A. H., and C. Weir. 1998. *Reading in a Second Language: Process, Product and Practice.* New York: Longman.

WEBSITES

Repository for information on extensive reading:

> **http://www.kyoto-su.ac.jp/information/er/**

Inventory of graphic organizers, with multiple links:

> **http://www.graphic.org/goindex.html**
> **http://www.sdcoe.k12.ca.us/SCORE/actbank/torganiz.htm**
> **http://www.ncrel.org/sdrs/areas/issues/students/learning/lr1grorg.htm**
> **http://www.macropress.com/1grorg.htm**

Teacher guidelines for designing graphic organizers:

> **http://www.wm.edu/TTAC/articles/learning/graphic.htm**

UNIT II D

Language Skills

Writing

The ability to express one's ideas in writing in a second or foreign language and to do so with reasonable coherence and accuracy is a major achievement; many native speakers of English never truly master this skill. Olshtain's chapter shows how the teacher of even beginning-level ESL/EFL students can provide practice in writing that reinforces the language the students have learned while teaching the mechanics of writing (e.g., the Roman alphabet, penmanship, spelling, punctuation, formats) right from the start. Kroll's chapter gives the reader a comprehensive overview of current theory and practice in teaching writing to non-native speakers of English, with special focus on developing courses for teaching writing to these learners. Finally, Frodesen's chapter explores the problematic area of grammar (i.e., accuracy) in writing, which plagues so many non-native speakers even after they have more or less mastered the more global features of written English such as organization and coherence.

Functional Tasks for Mastering the Mechanics of Writing and Going Just Beyond

ELITE OLSHTAIN

Olshtain's chapter treats initial writing skills for low-level ESL/EFL learners. It starts with letter and word recognition, discrimination, and production and moves to basic rules of English spelling, punctuation, and capitalization. With focus on both content and accuracy, mastery of these skills then allows learners to perform more communicative tasks such as writing lists, messages, diary entries, and school assignments.

INTRODUCTION

Within the communicative framework of language teaching, the skill of writing enjoys special status—it is via writing that a person can communicate a variety of messages to a close or distant, known or unknown reader or readers. Such communication is extremely important in the modern world, whether the interaction takes the form of traditional paper-and-pencil writing or the most technologically advanced electronic mail. Writing as a communicative activity needs to be encouraged and nurtured during the language learner's course of study, and this chapter will attempt to deal with the early stages of ESL/EFL writing.

Viewing writing as an act of communication suggests an interactive process which takes place between the writer and the reader via the text. Such an approach places value on the goal of writing as well as on the perceived reader audience. Even if we are concerned with writing at the beginning level, these two aspects of the act of writing are of vital importance; in setting writing tasks, the teacher should encourage students to define for themselves the message they want to send and the audience who will receive it.

The writing process, in comparison to spoken interaction, imposes greater demands on the text, since written interaction lacks immediate feedback as a guide. The writer has to anticipate the reader's reactions and produce a text which will adhere to Grice's (1975) cooperative principle. According to this principle, the writer is obligated (by mutual cooperation) to try to write a clear, relevant, truthful, informative, interesting, and memorable text. The reader, on the other hand, will interpret the text with due regard for the writer's presumed intention if the necessary clues are available in the text. Linguistic accuracy, clarity of presentation, and organization of ideas are all crucial in the efficacy of the communicative act, since they supply the clues for interpretation. Accordingly, while the global perspectives of content and organization need to be focused on and given appropriate attention, it is also most important to present a product which does not suffer from illegible handwriting, numerous spelling errors, faulty punctuation, or inaccurate structure, any of which may render the message unintelligible.

The present chapter focuses on the gradual development of the mechanics of writing, which is a necessary instrumental skill without which meaningful writing cannot take place; the chapter then moves on to early functional writing, which can be carried out with a limited level of proficiency in the target language. It is important to remember that in the ESL/EFL context, writing, like the other language skills, needs to be dealt with at the particular level of linguistic and discourse proficiency that the intended students have reached (Raimes 1985). The proposed sequence of activities will start with primary focus on the mechanical aspects of writing, as the basic instrumental skill, and gradually move on to a combination of "purpose for writing" and language focus. Eventually, the communicative perspective will become more central to such writing activities. (For teaching writing in more advanced contexts, see Kroll's chapter in this volume.)

EARLY WRITING TASKS: COPING WITH THE MECHANICS

What Do We Teach?

The first steps in teaching reading and writing skills in a foreign or second language classroom center around the mechanics of these two skills. By *mechanics* we usually refer to letter recognition, letter discrimination, word recognition, and basic rules of spelling, punctuation, and capitalization, as well as recognition of whole sentences and paragraphs. These activities are for the most part cognitively undemanding unless the learners happen to come from a first language with a different writing system.

The interaction between reading and writing has often been a focus in the methodology of language teaching, yet it deserves even stronger emphasis at the early stages in the acquisition of the various component mechanics. In order to learn how to discriminate one letter from another while reading, learners need to practice writing these letters; in order to facilitate their perception of words and sentences during the reading process, they might need to practice writing them first. It is therefore the case that writing plays an important role in early reading—facilitating the development of both the reading and the writing skills. The importance of this early stage of reading and writing is emphasized in a study by Ke (1996) on the relationship between Chinese character recognition and production at the early stages of learning. With the English alphabet this stage is much simpler, yet it deserves appropriate attention for learners accustomed to other script types and for adult non-literate learners.

Sound–Spelling Correspondences

English presents the learner with a number of unique problems related to its orthographic rules, even in cases in which the learner comes from a first language that uses a version of the Roman alphabet. Students and teachers alike often throw their arms up in despair, ready to give up on finding reliable rules for English orthography; yet the English writing system is much more rule governed than many realize. In fact, English has a very systematic set of sound–spelling correspondences (Chomsky and Halle 1968; Schane 1970; Venezky 1970). These sound–spelling correspondences enable the second or foreign language teacher to combine the teaching of phonetic units with graphemic units and to give students practice in pronunciation along with practice in spelling (Celce-Murcia, Brinton, and Goodwin 1996).

The English Consonants The first rule to remember about English orthography is that students may tend to look for a one-to-one letter–sound correspondence and then discover that they get into a lot of trouble by doing this. For most of the 21 consonant letters, this type of rule works fairly well (if we disregard allophonic differences in pronunciation, such as an aspirated initial /t/ as opposed to a nonaspirated, unreleased final /t/ for monosyllabic words in English). Yet there are consonant letters whose sound depends on the environment in which they occur: Thus, the letter *c* can have the sound /k/ when followed by the vowel letters *a, o,* or *u* or by the consonant letters *l* or *r,* but it has the sound /s/ when followed by the vowel letters *e* or *i.* Although these rules may appear confusing to a learner coming from a first language with a simpler phoneme-grapheme correspondence system, they work quite consistently in English and need to be practiced from the very start. The story of the letter *c* is not finished, however, and now we come to the part that is less consistent. This is the case when *c* is followed by the letter *h* and can have the sound of /č/ (*chocolate*) or /k/ (*choir*). There is no help we can give our students in this respect but to tell them to pay special attention to such words and try to remember their sound according to the meaning of the word. The letter *c* also occurs in quite a number of common words followed by the letter *k* (not initially, but in the middle or at the end of words—such as *chicken* or *lock*). The sound in this case is /k/ and the correspondence should create no difficulty.

The letter *c* in English demonstrates that even for some of the consonants (such as *g* too) we need to alert students to the fact that the correspondence in English is not between letter and sound but between the letter and its immediate environment and the most appropriate sound. In many cases such correspondences are quite predictable, while in others the rules do not work as well.

A helpful generalization for English consonants is related to the letter *h*, which is very powerful in changing the sound of the consonant which it follows. Thus, the letter combinations *ch*, *sh*, and *th* represent distinct consonant sounds, and learners need to recognize these graphic clusters as such.

To summarize, when teaching consonant letters and their sound correspondences, it seems that for students whose own alphabet is similar to that of English, we need to focus only on the differences. Yet for students coming from a completely different writing system, such as Arabic, Hebrew, Chinese, Japanese, or Korean, it will be necessary to work carefully on the recognition of every consonant letter. Here learners might have difficulties similar to the ones encountered by young children who learn to read and write in English as their mother tongue, and they might need some special exercises for this purpose (see Appendix A).

The English Vowels   The vowel letters in English present more complex sound–spelling correspondences, but again there is much more consistency and predictability than many learners realize. Thus, learners need to be made aware of two basic types of environments that are very productive in English orthography: Consonant Vowel Consonant (CVC) (often known as the environment for short vowels) and CV or CVCe (the latter ending in a silent letter *e*) (known as the environments for long vowels). The terms *short* and *long* vowels are rather unfortunate, since for the second or foreign language learner it might, erroneously, become associated with vowel length rather than vowel quality. Thus, the main difference between the vowel sounds in the words *pin* and *pine* is not one of length (or production time) but one of phonetic quality. A difference in vowel length can be observed in the words *pit* and *pin*, where the quality of the two vowel sounds is similar but the one preceding the voiceless stop /t/ is shorter than the one preceding the voiced nasal /n/.

Although we often say that the 5 vowel letters of the English alphabet result in at least 11 or more vowel sounds (depending on the particular dialect), these sound–spelling correspondences are, at least in part, consistent and predictable. What teachers and learners need to take into account is the fact that in English we must consider both the vowel letter and the environment in which it occurs. The term *environment* might be delimited here to those features which may influence the quality of the vowel sound. Thus, the environment CVC is quite productive, and all 5 vowel letters *a, i, e, o,* and *u* will occur as simple lax (produced with relatively relaxed muscles), nondiphthongized vowel sounds, as in the words *pan, pin, pen, pot,* and *but*. However, the same 5 vowel letters occurring in the CVCe environment will all become tense and diphthongized, as in the words *pane, pine, Pete, rope,* and *cute*. Similarly, those vowels that can occur in the CV or V environment are also tense and usually diphthongized: *go, be, ma, I, Lu* (as in *Lulu*). Here again we have a very productive set of sound–spelling correspondence rules, yet not all of these patterns are equally frequent in English orthography. Thus, the letter *e* does not often occur as the vowel in the CVCe environment, and learners have to study the more common spellings as in *meet* and *meat* for the sound /iy/. In other words, there are some basic sound–spelling correspondences in English, knowledge of which can greatly facilitate the acquisition of these correspondences, but there are also quite a number of exceptions or expansions of these rules that need to be learned individually.

In teaching the basic sound–spelling correspondences in English, it is important to emphasize the rules which provide the learners with useful generalizations and which therefore help them become effective readers. Once students have assimilated and internalized the basic features of such correspondences—namely, the distinction between CVC and CV or CVCe syllables—this will work well not only for all monosyllabic words but also for polysyllabic ones, in which the stressed syllable can act as a monosyllabic environment for letter–sound vowel correspondences (e.g., *dispóse*).

Furthermore, some of the more advanced spelling rules related to English morphology can be facilitated by this knowledge. In polysyllabic verbs with the final syllable stressed, the spelling rules for adding the inflection *-ing* work in the same manner as for monosyllabic ones. Thus, learners who know the rule for consonant letter doubling when changing *sit* to *sitting* will be able to apply the same rule to any polysyllabic verb that ends with a stressed syllable having the form CVC. Therefore, the verb *begin*, since its final syllable is stressed, will undergo doubling of the last consonant in *beginning*, as opposed to the verb *open*, where the final syllable is not stressed and therefore the *-ing* form of *open* is spelled *opening*.

However, in spite of all that has been said so far, English orthography has a notorious reputation because, in addition to all these helpful and relatively reliable rules, we must account for various less productive rules. Some of these are quite predictable, such as the occurrence of the letter *a* in front of *l* or *ll*, which quite consistently is realized as the sound /ɔ/ as in *call*, or *a* in front of the letter *r*, which has the sound /a/ as in *car*. In general, the letter *r* affects the sound of the vowel preceding it and causes it to become more centralized, as in the words *world, bird, curd*. Furthermore, the vowel diphthongs have a variety of spellings, such as the following letter combinations, which all correspond to the same vowel diphthong /ow/: r*o*pe, b*oa*t, l*ow*, f*oe*. So, while it is true that there are quite a few cases in English which need to be remembered as individual words, there are far fewer than people imagine

(for good sources of rules on sound–spelling correspondences, see Schane 1970; Venezky, 1970).

In summing up this section dealing with the teaching points relevant to the mechanics of reading and writing, we should emphasize the fact that it is important for learners of English as a second or foreign language to realize from the start that English orthography is by no means a one-to-one letter–sound correspondence system; it has its own consistency embedded in the combination of letters with their immediate environments, resulting in what we tend to call sound–spelling correspondences. By practicing the proper pronunciation of sounds in relation to given spelling patterns, we can provide learners with a good basis for pronunciation as well as for the skills of reading and writing.

How Do We Teach Mechanics?

The stage devoted to the teaching of the mechanics of reading and writing aims at three different goals: (a) to enhance letter recognition—especially when learners come from a different writing system, (b) to practice sound–spelling correspondences via all four language skills, and (c) to help the learner move from letters and words to meaningful sentences and larger units of discourse.

Recognition and writing drills constitute the first steps in the development of effective reading and writing habits. However, in order to acquire active mastery of the sound–spelling correspondences, it is necessary for the learners to arrive at relevant generalizations concerning these correspondences. Such generalizations will lead to a better understanding of the systematic representation of sounds in English orthography, and will require learners to master some basic phonological rules in English and to develop an ability to recognize the distinctive features of each letter within a spelling pattern.

Three major types of recognition tasks are used at this early stage of reading and writing, each type incorporating a great variety of drills:

a. Matching tasks
b. Writing tasks
c. Meaningful sound–spelling correspondence practice

Examples of different *matching* tasks are given in Appendix A. These tasks enable the learners to develop effective recognition habits based on distinctive graphic features. Many of these have the form of games, puzzles, and other "fun" activities. Examples of different *writing* tasks are given in Appendix B; these start with basic letter formation and lead to meaningful writing of words and sentences. Examples of *sound–spelling* correspondence tasks are given in Appendix C. The common feature of all tasks in Appendix C is that they require the learner to focus on the pronunciation as well as the written shape of the spelling patterns.

An important feature of this early stage of writing is the need to accustom learners to correct capitalization in English and to basic punctuation rules. While practicing sound–spelling correspondences, students can be writing meaningful sentences (accompanied by pictures) with proper capitalization and punctuation, such as the following:

1. There is a cat on the mat and a cake on the plate.
2. The ball is near the tall boy next to the wall.

These sentences contain words which exemplify sound–spelling correspondences and, at the same time, they are words that students have probably just learned. They may not work out too well as a story or an interesting piece of discourse since our focus in this case is first and foremost on the sound–spelling correspondence. But eventually, discourse units will grow and incorporate more meaningful and interesting texts. The language knowledge the students gain can be the basis for developing more sophisticated and interesting texts, however.

At this early stage of writing, we need to give learners "plenty of opportunities for copying" (Byrne 1988, p.130). However, such copying activities can be cognitively more demanding if students are guided to search for the meaningful words and to create sentences in new contexts. Appendix B provides examples of this type of writing activity.

More Advanced Writing Tasks: Developing Basic Communication Tools

More advanced writing activities which start shifting their goal from the focus on the mechanics of writing to basic process-oriented tasks will need to incorporate some language work at the morphological and discourse level. Thus, these activities will enable focus on both accuracy and content of the message. In this chapter, since we are concerned with the beginning level, we will work with categories of practical writing tasks, emotive writing tasks, and school-oriented tasks (Nevo, Weinbach, and Mark 1987).

In order to develop and use these more demanding writing activities in the ESL/EFL classroom, we need to develop a detailed set of specifications which will enable both teachers and students to cope successfully with these tasks. Such a set of specifications should include the following:

Task Description: to present students with the goal of the task and its importance.

Content Description: to present students with possible content areas that might be relevant to the task.

Audience Description: to guide students in developing an understanding of the intended audience, their background, needs, and expectations.

Format Cues: to help students in planning the overall organizational structure of the written product.

Linguistic Cues: to help students make use of certain grammatical structures and vocabulary choices.

Spelling and Punctuation Cues: to help students focus their attention on spelling rules which they have learned and eventually on the need to use the dictionary for checking accuracy of spelling, and to guide students to use acceptable punctuation and capitalization conventions.

Practical Writing Tasks

These are writing tasks which are procedural in nature and have a predictable format. This makes them particularly suitable for writing activities that focus primarily on spelling and morphology. Lists of various types, notes, short messages, simple instructions, and other such writing tasks are particularly useful in reinforcing classroom work.

Lists can be of many types: "things to do" lists, "things completed" lists, or shopping lists. Each of these list types provides us with an opportunity to combine some spelling rules with morphological rules and with the logical creation of a meaningful message. "Things to do" lists are useful for practicing verb base forms and reinforcing various sound–spelling correspondences. When assigning such an activity, the teacher will have to indicate whether the list is personal or intended for a group. The content specification will have to indicate whether this is a list of things to do in preparation for some event or just a plan for someone's daily routine. For example, a list for a group of students who are preparing a surprise birthday party might look like this:

> *Things to Do*
> 1. Buy a present for Donna (Sharon).
> 2. Call Donna's friends (Gail).
> 3. Write invitations (Dan).
>   etc.

Following up on this type of list, we can easily move on to the "things completed" list, which specifies the things that have already been taken care of and is therefore useful for practicing past forms of verbs. As part of this activity, students will need to review the regular past tense formation of verbs where *-ed* is added and its exceptions in spelling are taught, such as the deletion of a final *e* before adding *-ed,* as in *lived;* the doubling of the last consonant in monosyllabic bases of the form CVC, as in *canned,* and the same doubling rule when the final syllable of a polysyllabic verb is stressed, such as in *occurred* but not in *opened;* the replacement of *y* with *i* when the base ends in C + *y,* as in *tried.* Such an activity also enables students to practice the spelling of irregular past-tense formations. For example, the above list might look like this when partially completed:

> *Things Completed*
> 1. Planned the games for the party.
> 2. Wrote the invitations.
> 3. Bought the present.
> 4. Called the friends.
> 5. Tried to call Donna's mother.

Shopping lists provide us with a very good opportunity to practice the spelling of the plural ending of countable nouns and the use of quantifiers. The sound–spelling correspondences here consist of the plural inflection with two of its three phonetic variants—/s/, /z/—which can be combined with the spelling pattern *s* as in *pens, pencils,* whereas in words like *brushes* or *oranges* the plural takes the phonetic form /əz/, an additional syllable, with such words ending in the spelling pattern *-es.*

Another type of practical writing task is notes and messages that are left for another person. These allow students to practice brief and simple sentences with proper punctuation and a meaningful message. To make the activity more interesting, students can design their own message headings and then fill them in. Here is an example:

> *Messages for My Little Sister*
> Wash the dishes in the sink.
> Feed the dog.
> Watch your favorite program on TV and
>   have a good time.

Other types of practical writing activities might include the filling in of forms and the preparation of invitations, "greetings" and "thank you" notes, and other such written communications. All of these activities, when carried out in class, will require the set of specifications mentioned above, with appropriate focus on orthographic, mechanical, and linguistic accuracy. (For various examples of such tasks see the appendices.)

Emotive Writing Tasks

Emotive writing tasks are concerned with personal writing. Such personal writing primarily includes letters to friends and narratives describing personal experiences, as well as personal journals and diaries. When dealing with letter writing, emphasis can be placed on format, punctuation, and spelling of appropriate phrases and expressions. When writing about personal experiences—usually done in a narrative format—spelling of past-tense forms can be reviewed and practiced. Entries in diaries and journals can take the form of personal letters and serve as a review of letter writing in general.

It seems that emotive writing, to serve the personal needs of the learners, has to be quite fluent. How can this be done in the early stages of an ESL/EFL course of study? The different types of emotive writing activities are, of course, suitable for the more advanced stages of the course, but they can be carried out, in a more limited manner, even at the initial stages. Thus, personal letters can be limited to the level of structural and vocabulary knowledge of the students at each point in time. Similarly, journal and personal writing activities can reflect the learner's proficiency level. It is important, however, in all cases to provide students with the specifications of the task, limiting it to their level of knowledge.

School-Oriented Tasks

One of the most important functions of writing in a student's life is the function it plays in school. It is still the case that much individual learning goes on while students are writing assignments, summaries, answers to questions, or a variety of essay-type passages. In most cases, the audience for these writing tasks is the teacher, but gradually students must learn to write to an unknown reader who needs to get the information being imparted exclusively via writing. Here again, at the early stages of ESL/EFL learning, the assignments might be short and limited. Answers might be single phrases or sentences, summaries (a listing of main ideas), and similar activities. However, all of these writing activities should be given attention, both at the linguistic-accuracy level and at the message-transmission level. It is the combination of content and organization with accepted formal features that will lead learners to better utilization of the writing skill in their future use of English.

Dialogue Journal Writing at the Early Stages

Dialogue journals enable students and teachers to interact on a one-to-one basis at any level and in any learning context. They are, therefore, also very useful communicative events at the early stages of learning to write in a new language. The dialogue journal enables the beginner to generate some personal input and receive the teacher's direct feedback on it.

According to Peyton and Reed (1990), both young children who are beginning writers in a second language and nonliterate adults can start a dialogue journal as soon as they are comfortable in the classroom. It can start out as an interactive picture book in which first the teacher and later the learners label the pictures and provide brief descriptions. Gradually, the texts become more detailed and the communication process is enhanced.

The dialogue journal, like any other type of writing activity, can be done via e-mail and the communication between students and teachers can take on this more modern form of interaction. Multimedia programs often include such correspondence, allowing learners to interact with the teacher, other learners, or a designated tutor.

CONCLUSION

It has been the objective of this chapter to encourage teachers to use a variety of writing tasks at all levels and particularly at the beginning level. Writing, in addition to being a communicative skill of vital importance, is a skill which enables the learner to plan and rethink the communication process. It therefore provides the learner with the opportunity to focus on both linguistic accuracy and content organization. It has been the major aim of this chapter to emphasize the fact that the mechanics of writing are particularly important at the initial stage of learning since they help students establish a good basis in sound–spelling correspondences, which are important for effective use of reading and writing skills and also for good pronunciation. A carefully planned presentation which combines the mechanics of writing with the composing process can serve the learner well during the early stages of a language course. This is especially true for children, but also true for adults whose native language uses a completely different writing system. And for preliterate adults, the more advanced activities suggested in Weinstein's chapter in this volume can be combined with some of the suggestions offered here to ensure that a proper foundation in writing is also established while such adults are learning to be better readers.

DISCUSSION QUESTIONS

1. How would you plan the early writing stage differently for students whose first language uses a Roman alphabet compared to students whose first language has a completely different writing system?
2. Identify an important sound–spelling correspondence in English that was not mentioned in the chapter and discuss how you might teach it.
3. How should we sequence the teaching of the various sound–spelling correspondences?
4. How can writing be used to ensure the interaction of all skills at the early stages of the ESL/EFL course of study? Give an example.
5. Give an example of how the teacher of beginning-level ESL/EFL students can combine elements of the composing process with elements of the mechanics of writing.

SUGGESTED ACTIVITIES

1. Prepare a game or a set of cards to practice the difference between the vowel sounds in the environment CVC and CVCe. Example: *hat, kit* versus *hate, kite*. Incorporate as many words as might be meaningful for the intended student population. You may have to use some new words that serve the sound–spelling correspondence but are not known to your students. What will you do to present the new words to your students before you practice the spelling patterns?
2. Design a lesson to focus on the different sounds associated with the letter *c*. First present the various environments and then develop some challenging activities to practice the relevant sound–spelling correspondences.
3. Find a picture or a number of pictures that depict various words with unusual spelling patterns. All of these should be useful words. Play a memory game with your students: They are allowed to look at the picture for two whole minutes, then the picture is taken away. The students write on a piece of paper all the words that they remember. How did this activity work?
4. Find pictures that can be used for simple descriptions. Develop a number of activities that will enable pairs and small groups to answer a set of questions about each picture. The questions should lead to a concise description of what can be seen in the picture.

FURTHER READING

Sources for Teaching Prereading and Early Writing Exercises

Byrne, D. 1988. *Teaching Writing Skills.* London: Longman.

Crittenden, J. 1978. *English with Solo.* Oxford: Oxford University Press.

Herman, M., and P. Sacks. 1977. *Tell Me How to Spell.* Tel Aviv: University Publishing Projects.

Johnson, K. 1983. *Now for English,* Course and Activity Books 1, 2, 3. Surrey: Thomas Nelson.

Llanas, A., and E. Taylor. 1983. *Sunrise 1.* Surrey: Thomas Nelson.

Olshtain, E., et al. 1970. *English for Speakers of Hebrew,* Prereader Workbook. Tel Aviv: University Publishing Projects.

Prince, E. 1990. *Write Soon! A Beginning Text for ESL Writers.* New York: Maxwell Macmillan.

APPENDIX A

1. Letter recognition activities:

   a. Find the ODD MAN OUT.

      h h (k)   n h n   f j j

      p b b   d b d

   b. Find the same letter.

      b: n d (b) c k

      k: j f k h i

      d: b p l d h

   c. Find all the *d*'s.   Find all the *h*'s.

      f k s n (d) j   s k j h n d

      s j d d b p   z k n b s d

      h f k s z m   m h n h s s

      f d k j n m   f g h k h b

   d. Underline the words that have *n*.

      <u>net</u>

      ben

      bed

      ten

   e. Underline the words ending in *ed*.

      <u>ned</u>

      bed

      dip

      net

2. Match capital letters with lower case. Connect the words beginning with the same letter.

   Pin   tin

   bib   pin

   Tin   Bin

   net   Net

APPENDIX B

I. Writing Practice: Tracing Letters, Words, and Sentences

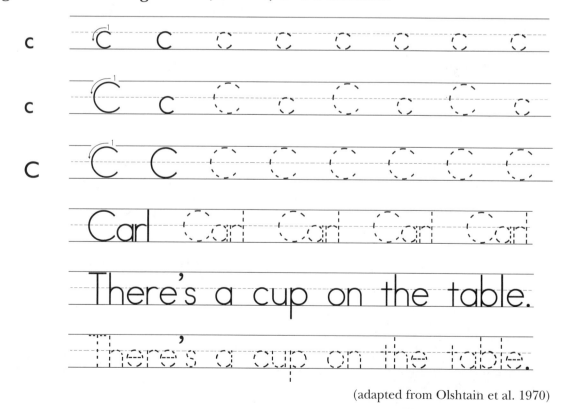

C

C

C

Carl

There's a cup on the table.

There's a cup on the table.

(adapted from Olshtain et al. 1970)

II. Meaningful Copying Activities

(Adapted from Olshtain et al. 1998, pp. 76, 85, and 157)

1. Read and decide.

Dan wants to win at tennis. He doesn't practice a lot, but when he goes to play he takes a lucky ring with him. He thinks it can help him win. What do you think?

□ It can help Dan.   □ It can't help Dan.

2. Read about Lucky the Rock Star in Exercise 3 below. Then answer these questions.

What is he wearing?

_____

_____

_____

What is he doing?

_____

_____

_____

3. Who is Lucky the Rock Star? Read and check (✔).

He is wearing 2 necklaces. He is wearing a funny hat. He is wearing huge sunglasses. He is wearing new black shoes. He is wearing old ugly jeans. He is holding a guitar. He is sitting on a black chair.

4. Read and decide. Where does he live? In South-Carolina or Canada?

He lives in _____ .
He doesn't live in _____ .

Where I live it rains a lot in winter, but there are also many sunny days. Sometimes it is cold, but it doesn't usually snow.

5. Write about today's weather. These sentences may help you.
It's very nice.   It's cloudy.   It's hot.   It's warm.
It's cold.   It's windy.   It's rainy.

_____

_____

_____

_____

_____

_____

_____

APPENDIX C

Practicing Sound–Spelling Correspondences

1. The letter *a* in *all* and *al*
   a. Read the following words out loud.

all	also
ball	always
call	almost
fall	although
wall	
tall	
hall	
small	

   but the sound is different in the word—
   shall

   b. Use the above words to write the missing letters and then read the sentence.

   __ l l   t h e   s m __ __ __

   __ __ l l s   f __ __ __.

2. Underline the word your teacher says.

a. Tin	**b.** tam	**c.** mit
tine	tame	mite
tan	time	mat

d. bad	**e.** hide	**f.** can
bade	hid	cane
bid	had	cap

Considerations for Teaching an ESL/EFL Writing Course

BARBARA KROLL

"Considerations for Teaching an ESL/EFL Writing Course" provides a general guide to shaping writing classes for English language learners. Among the topics addressed are syllabus design, techniques to help writers get started, assignment design, and teacher and peer responses to writing. It shows how the choices that teachers make are clues to their underlying philosophy of teaching.

INTRODUCTION

Teaching academic writing to both native and non-native speakers of English is an enterprise that unfolds in such a countless variety of settings and classrooms around the world that it is not hard to imagine considerable variation in how writing gets taught. Regardless of this variation, however, certain facts hold true for any classroom where the teaching of writing takes place: Students produce written texts that are expected to exhibit increasingly advanced levels of proficiency as the student writers progress through a curriculum, and teachers must make choices about how various learning experiences will promote this goal. Two of the components most central to any writing course are the writing assignments that students are asked to do to and the method(s) of feedback provided to learners on their evolving writing skills. To improve, writers must write; without feedback opportunities in a writing course, there is little reason for students to be there. These, then, are the constants of any writing course: teacher-planned lessons, presentation of writing assignments, student-written texts, and feedback on writing. How these components work together in any given classroom of English language learners (ELL), be they ESL or EFL[1] students, accounts for the many variations possible.

However, it is my belief that teachers cannot adequately serve their students armed simply with a general understanding of methods and materials. The strong teacher is a reflective teacher (see Murphy's chapter in this volume), and part of the necessary background preparation for becoming a teacher of writing is to recognize that every teacher brings to the classroom a philosophy of teaching and a set of beliefs about learning. To develop an approach with the goal of helping writers improve that is consistent with their philosophy and beliefs, teachers need to familiarize themselves, at least to a certain extent, with the field of composition studies and its interrelationship with ESL composition. Matsuda (1998, 1999) provides an extensive discussion of this topic.

BUILDING BACKGROUND KNOWLEDGE

Understanding current attitudes and practices in the teaching of writing requires some historical review so that teachers can have a richer awareness of how we have gotten to where we are today. Prior to the mid-1960s, teaching writing to native English speakers (NES) at the high school and college levels primarily focused on responding in writing to literary texts. Based on textbooks of the period, the model for teaching composition was fairly standard and included the following steps: (1) instruct the students in principles of rhetoric and organization, presented as "rules" for writing; (2) provide a text for classroom discussion, analysis, and interpretation (preferably a work of literature); (3) require a writing assignment (accompanied by an outline) based on the text; and (4) read, comment on, and criticize student papers prior to beginning the next assignment in this cycle. This approach is known as "the traditional paradigm" (Hairston 1982). Because teachers following this model tended to focus on evaluating student essays, the approach is also referred to as the "product approach," since the primary concern was really with the completed written product, not with the strategies and processes involved in its production or with the nature of any learning that might be required.

In the 1960s, ESL composition teaching in North America was dominated by a controlled composition model whose origins were in the oral approach promulgated in the 1940s by Fries (1945). While the written *product* was also the focal point of evaluation and concern as in first language (L1) writing, the approach for ELLs differed in that the stimulus for second language (L2) student writing was rarely a genuine text, and written tasks were not meant to elicit interpretive commentary on texts. That is, whatever writing took place was meant to serve primarily as reinforcement of language rules (and not, for example, for purposes such as addressing a topic or communicating with an audience), and the writing task was tightly controlled in order to reduce the possibility for error (hence the term "controlled" composition).

There were a number of forces that converged in the mid-1960s to change the way composition has come to be viewed and taught, starting with the call by Braddock, Lloyd-Jones, and Schoer (1963) for teachers or researchers to examine how writing is actually produced. In the late 1960s, Janet Emig pioneered the technique of the "think aloud" procedure[2] for collecting information about student writing processes; she is usually cited as the first researcher to call wide attention to the fact that the ways in which student writers produce text do not necessarily match the model that had been traditionally promulgated (Emig 1971). One of her watershed observations was the fact that writers do not, in general, produce text in the straightforward linear sequence that the traditional para-digm outlined, an observation which exposed the fact that much of what textbooks suggested in terms of a writing "process" was based on intuitions of textbook writers and not based on analyses of writers at work. The insights of process-based inquiry began to slowly but inexorably impact the teaching of first language writing, after which the field also came to have a profound influence on the teaching of composition to ELLs. Prior to the field of second-language composition teaching's developing its own body of knowledge, insights from L1 pedagogy tended to be imported directly into the second language classroom.

It has become commonplace to refer to the dominant trend in teaching writing today as the "process approach" or a "process classroom." This is true for both NES and ELL settings. When first used in the context of composition, this term contrasted the new classroom ideology with the "product approach." There was a great deal of emphasis in early L1 process courses on developing a personal voice in writing, especially as this promoted the idea of a learner-centered classroom. However, as the term has evolved, "process" no longer describes a single philosophy or any particular or specific curriculum (if it ever did). Rather, the "process approach" serves today as an umbrella term for many types of writing courses, each offering a curriculum shaped by other considerations (see Susser 1994). A writing course can focus on general academic writing, or on personal writing, or be linked to a so-called "content" course offered by another instructor; it can require students to do a greater or lesser amount of reading (if any) in genres as distinct as student-written texts, fiction, business communication, academic reports, or other varieties of nonfiction prose. Yet as radically different as the curriculum of such writing courses can be, nearly all writing courses provide for a "process" approach. What the term captures is the fact that student writers engage in their writing tasks through a *cyclical* approach rather than through a single-shot approach. They are not expected to produce and submit complete and polished responses to their writing assignments without going through stages of drafting and receiving feedback on their drafts, be it from peers and/or from the teacher, followed by revision of their evolving texts. This is what is truly meant by the "process" approach.

As the field of L2 composition studies established itself, researchers in ESL writing replicated many of the L1 research studies on the composing processes of student writers, often with a focus on pedagogical implications. Silva provides a review of a large number of studies comparing L1 and L2 writers. He points out that while there are many similarities between these populations, "they are different in numerous and important ways. This difference needs to be acknowledged and addressed by those who deal with L2 writers if [they] are to be treated fairly [and] taught effectively" (1993, p. 671). Such differences clearly call for curriculum and teaching choices that factor in the specific needs of the target population.

All of these research findings had profound impacts on curriculum. An early general shift in the teaching of ESL writing in North America changed the previous "focus on form" to a "focus on the writer" (Raimes 1991), dating perhaps from the mid-1970s, as an early interpretation of what *the* process approach meant. Raimes identifies two other pedagogical approaches that also came into prominence at about the same time in the mid-1980s: a focus on content-based instruction and a focus on a reader-dominated approach (Raimes 1991, pp. 410–413). It is important to recognize that as each new way of teaching writing evolves, the earlier focus does not necessarily disappear. Indeed, what we find today is that multiple approaches to teaching writing coexist, often presented by outspoken proponents with passionately held beliefs that greatly diverge from equally passionate claims presented by proponents of another camp. It is not into tranquil professional waters that the new L2 writing teacher steps. (Several of these issues are discussed in Grabe and Kaplan 1996; Raimes 1998; and Santos 2001.)

Thus, ESL/EFL writing teachers need to have solid scholarly training to develop their own approach to the teaching of writing, enabling them to choose methodologies and materials which arise from principled decisions

that they can articulate to others. Without a stance on how to promote student learning, teachers would have no choice but to make ad hoc decisions which may or may not be the best possible ones for their students or to rely on the choices of textbook writers, who certainly can't know the dynamics of every individual teacher's situation.

In this chapter, I discuss several key components in the ESL/EFL writing curriculum and the ESL/EFL writing class for teachers to consider as they develop their own approaches to teaching and their own philosophies of teaching. This will enable them to structure courses and programs to facilitate the improvement of student writing skills and to promote a variety of goals in whatever teaching situation(s) they find themselves.

THE WRITING CURRICULUM
Placement Considerations

Almost every institution that offers ESL/EFL writing courses sets up a number of different classes at various levels that are meant to reflect the range of skill levels of the students enrolled in that particular program. To establish a *writing* curriculum (as opposed to a general language skills curriculum) that can target specific principles to address in any one course of a given program, it is essential that students be given a placement test that includes asking them to produce one or more writing samples. Without a placement instrument that can sort students into levels of writing proficiency, it is not possible to establish clear curricular goals, since there is no way of assuring that students are grouped in classes that are relatively homogeneous, a necessary prerequisite for curriculum planning. And it is the curriculum of the writing program that designates the goals for each course and helps to distinguish one course from another. Although scoring writing placement tests is a complex and time-consuming procedure, indirect measures of writing, such as multiple-choice grammar tests, have proven to be undesirable as indicators of productive skills. Creating a placement instrument and scoring procedure appropriate to the goals of a particular program thus serves as a critical measure in providing teachers principled reasons for selecting the materials and the methodologies they will use in the ESL/EFL writing classroom.

Teachers in the program can score placement essays using either a global holistic scale, such as the six-point scale developed for the TOEFL® Test of Written English, which awards the top score of 6 to an essay that "demonstrates clear competence in writing on both the rhetorical and syntactic levels" and the bottom score of 1 to an essay that "demonstrates incompetence in writing" (*Test of Written English Guide* 1996), or a more detailed set of scoring guidelines, such as the widely used 100-point ESL English Composition Profile (developed by Jacobs et al. 1981), which has raters assign differentially weighted separate sub-scores in the five categories of content, organization, vocabulary, language use, and mechanics.

Despite the ease with which raters can be trained to agree on scores for placement essays, which creates a sense that students are being accurately slotted into courses at the appropriate level, sometimes students with different strengths and weaknesses do receive similar scores. Inevitably, students with midrange scores exhibit a wider range of actual writing skills than do student writers whose scores are at the higher and lower edges of the placement scoring scale. This is because it is extremely difficult to tease out the distinctions between a student whose writing might be quite strong at the level of language control while relatively weak at the level of discourse structure and vice versa. In setting up placement procedures suited to their specific institutions, curriculum planners and teachers need to recognize this reality.

Establishing Curriculum Principles

Once students are placed into classes, their particular skill levels will determine to a large extent the scope of writing activities they are able to undertake. While the ultimate goal of a writing curriculum in a postsecondary setting might be to have ELLs write essays that match the level of content and mastery of language skills required of NES students in a similar academic environment, it is not possible for beginning- or intermediate-level language learners to produce essays that exhibit such mastery. Writing activities that involve a variety of grammatical manipulations, the imitation of models constructed for teaching purposes, preparation of short texts using material supplied to the student writer, and practice in self-expression for its own sake certainly serve a function in helping students acquire familiarity with the nature of English-language texts and in laying the groundwork for more complex writing tasks to follow. However, for intermediate and advanced students, work on the creation of self-generated complete texts should constitute the bulk of their writing curriculum. (For discussions and examples of the types of writing activities appropriate for students with limited language skills, see Olshtain's chapter in this volume and Gebhard 1996).

Tasks that ask students to produce complete texts in response to a variety of writing stimuli, such as pictures, texts which have been read, or simply the presentation of some sort of "topic" to write about, can be referred to as "free" writing or open-ended writing tasks. The writer is free, in some sense, to work with the topic, and the reader/evaluator remains open to dealing with whatever product each writer generates. Helping students in an academic environment with the creation of open-ended, full-length texts is the focus of the following discussion.

THE WRITING CLASS

Regardless of how different any given writing class may be from others, each teacher works to carry out a somewhat predictable set of tasks. These involve designing and/or implementing a syllabus, structuring individual lessons, providing students opportunities for writing (typically in the form of assignments), and responding to that writing. While this listing of tasks may seem self-evident, *how* the tasks are actualized can vary quite widely and potentially marks a teacher as adhering to a particular point of view regarding optimal student learning. In the ongoing professional debate as to how best to serve our ELL student population in the writing course (see, for example, Santos 2001), it is through class planning that any teacher defines his or her stance as to the purpose of a given course.

Syllabus Design

A syllabus should be designed to take into account curricular goals and the particular students the teacher will face. The syllabus further reflects, whether intentionally or unintentionally, the philosophy of teaching writing that a teacher has adopted for that particular course in that particular institution. (See Nunan's chapter in this volume for a full discussion of syllabus design.)

One of the reasons why teaching writing is such a challenge is that most classes contain a mixture of students—those who have placed directly into a particular level of a course and those who have passed into that course in sequence from a previous one. While this might make it difficult to plan a rigidly outlined course in advance of the term, teachers need to consider at least the following aspects of course planning: (1) how much writing students are expected to complete during the term, divided into less formal work such as journals and more formal work such as assignments; (2) what the timelines and deadlines are for working on and completing papers; (3) how many of the formal writing assignments will be done in class as "timed" pieces; (4) what aspects of the composing process will be presented; (5) what aspects of English grammar and syntax, if any, will be directly addressed in class; (6) what will be seen to constitute "progress" in acquiring improved writing skills as the term moves along; (7) how much reading (and possibly which specific readings) will be covered; and (8) how the student's grade or a decision of credit/no credit will be determined.

In general, the teacher uses the syllabus to announce to students what he or she sees as important to the course as well as what is important to good writing. Without some informed sense of how he or she plans to use the class to foster individual growth in writing, the teacher will find it most difficult to devise any syllabus at all or to justify evaluation decisions.

Whether operating from a tightly organized or a fairly loose syllabus, the writing teacher needs to structure individual class sessions so that they allow students to learn and practice principles of good writing. Good writing results from a time-consuming process that cannot be reduced to formulaic rules, though many EFL students in particular, typically trained for years in classes that emphasized rigidly controlled grammatical exercises, will come to the writing class with the belief that there *are* rules to be learned which will yield fully conceived and problem-free essays.

The ESL/EFL writing class is perhaps best seen as a workshop for students to learn to produce academic essays through mastering techniques for getting started and generating ideas (discussed in more detail below), drafting papers which they will anticipate revising, and learning to utilize feedback provided by the teacher and other students in the class to improve the writing assignment at hand. The goal of every course should be individual student progress in writing proficiency, and the goal of the total curriculum should be that student writers learn to become informed and independent readers of their own texts with the ability to create, revise, and reshape papers to meet the needs of whatever writing tasks they are assigned.

Techniques for Getting Started

Regardless of the type of writing tasks the teacher might favor assigning, a good place to begin is to explore the prewriting stage, the stage prior to actual production of a working text. This is a topic well worth investing a lot of class time on because so many student writers fear the blank page. Not knowing where or how to begin causes inexperienced writers to waste time that could be better invested in working to improve a draft of a paper in progress; there can be no paper in progress, however, if the writer does not have a way into the topic or assignment.

Because there isn't *one* composing process, the goal of the teacher should be to expose students to a variety of strategies for getting started with a writing task and to encourage each student to try to discover which strategies work best for him or her. A few of the more popular heuristic devices[3] (or invention strategies) which can be explored in class for the purpose of providing students with a repertoire of techniques for generating ideas are presented below. Reid (1995), however, rightly cautions that some techniques may run counter to a given student's learning preferences; students should be asked to practice all techniques but should later focus on using those that clearly serve them best.

1. **Brainstorming** This is often a group exercise in which all students in the class are encouraged to participate by sharing their collective knowledge about a particular subject. It generates far more material than any one student is likely to think of on his or her own. Students can then utilize any or all of the information when turning to the preparation of their first drafts.

2. **Listing** Unlike brainstorming, listing can be a quiet and essentially individual activity. As a first step in finding an approach to a particular subject area, the student is encouraged to produce as lengthy a list as possible of all the main ideas and subcategories that come to mind as he or she thinks about the topic at hand. This is an especially useful activity for students who might be constrained by undue concern for expressing their thoughts in grammatically correct sentences.

3. **Clustering** Another technique for getting many ideas down quickly, clustering begins with a key word or central idea placed in the center of a page (or on the blackboard) around which the student (or the teacher, using student-generated suggestions) quickly jots down all of the free-associations triggered by the subject matter, using words or short phrases. Unlike listing, the words or phrases generated are put on the page or board in a pattern which takes shape from the connections the writer sees as each new thought emerges. Completed clusters can look like spokes on a wheel or any other pattern of connected lines depending on how the individual associations relate to each other. By sharing their cluster patterns with others in the class, students can be exposed to a wide variety of approaches to the subject matter, which might generate further material for writing.

4. **Freewriting** Suggested by Elbow (1973) for helping native speakers break through the difficulty of getting started, freewriting is also known by various other terms such as "wet ink" writing, "quick writing," and "speed writing." The main idea of this technique is for students to write for a specified period of time without taking their pen from the page (usually about three minutes for a first attempt and then typically for about five to eight minutes). For ESL/EFL students, this often works best if the teacher provides an opening clause or sentence for the students to start with to structure the freewriting. The writing generated from this technique often contains useful raw material for student writers to work with.

It is very important that students experiment with each of these techniques in order to see how each one helps generate text and shapes a possible approach to a topic. The purpose, after all, of invention strategies is for students to feel that they have several ways to begin an assigned writing task and that they do not always have to begin at the beginning and work through an evolving draft sequentially until they reach the end.

Using Readings in the Writing Class

The use of readings in the writing class is another topic that has generated a great deal of debate among those searching for methodologies which promote improvement in writing proficiency. Without a doubt, readings serve some very practical purposes in the writing class, particularly for ELLs who have less fluency in the language. At the very least, readings provide models of what English language texts look like, and even if not used for the purpose of imitation (where students are asked to produce an English language text to match the style of the model text), they provide input that helps students develop awareness of English language prose style. In class, close reading exercises can be done to draw students' attention to particular stylistic choices, grammatical features, methods of development, markers of cohesion and coherence, and so on. Such exercises help to raise student awareness of the choices writers make and the consequences of those choices for the achievement of their communicative goals. Further, readings help students develop and refine genre awareness (Johns 1997), an important criterion for being able to produce a wide range of text types.

On another level, there is ample evidence that writing tasks assigned by many professors require students to do a great deal of reading in order to synthesize and analyze academic material in particular content areas (Hale et al. 1996). Thus, the ESL writing class can incorporate lessons which assist students in preparing academic writing assignments by using readings as a basis to practice such skills as summarizing, paraphrasing, interpreting, and synthesizing concepts. More specifically, classes that have an English for Special Purposes (ESP) focus (see Johns and Price-Machado's chapter in this volume) are likely to put readings at the core of the writing curriculum. An examination of texts from a variety of different disciplines is likely to show how complex the learning task is. Lea and Street (1999), for example, point out that looking at how texts from different fields and disciplines contrast with each other not only shows how different such texts can be, but also reveals implicit distinctions disciplines make about what constitutes good writing.

Finally, many ESL students are not highly skilled readers, having had limited opportunities to read extensively in English; it is highly unlikely that anyone who is a nonproficient reader can develop into a highly proficient writer. For that reason alone, ESL/EFL writing teachers are well advised to include a reading component in their classes.

From another perspective, however, readings can be problematic if a teacher uses the topic or content area of the readings to turn a generic writing course into a class in the subject matter area of the readings, e.g., psychology or history or sociology, and loses sight of the focus on improvement of writing. Sometimes the intention of the class and the readings is precisely to focus student attention on issues related to the content area. (Snow's chapter in this volume discusses content-based instruction in more detail.) Multiple other contributions that reading material makes to writing courses are discussed in Carson and Leki (1993) and Johns (1997).

Writing Assignments

The writing assignment is the key component of all writing classes, lending it a rhythm that might be referred to as a "life cycle" (Kroll in press). In any given term, the writing course consists of a series of assignments that are targeted and undertaken in a sequence of steps followed by a similar round and a similar round until the timespan of the course is over. Since the object of any writing class is to have students work on their writing, all assignments and the topics they contain must be carefully designed, sequenced, and structured so that the teacher knows exactly what the learning goal of each paper is and the student gains something by working on any given assignment.

There are many factors to consider in selecting topics for writing, but even if not consciously aware of it, the teacher will be primarily influenced by a particular philosophy about teaching writing which he or she (or the textbook being followed) adheres to and which significantly shapes the approach to topic design. In fact, even when topics are chosen randomly, the teacher will probably select an assignment which seems appropriate on the basis of a felt inner sense of appropriacy, reflecting perhaps unconsciously how the teacher views the goals of the course, what he or she values as good writing, and the ways in which writers learn. For example, if the teacher wants the students to focus on standard organizational patterns common to English language writing, it is usually because the teacher values essays following discernible patterns and/or believes that training students to recognize and produce those patterns is an important goal of the course. If the teacher believes that writers learn best by writing about topics they can personally relate to and that the best essays are those that reveal the most about the writer's thinking or persona, then the assignments in that writing class will be designed to achieve those goals. If the teacher sees the writing course primarily as preparation for students to undertake writing tasks in other disciplines, then assignments will be focused on what the teacher sees as "real" academic requirements.

An assignment type that speaks to the first concern may fall within the realm of the "rhetorical patterns" approach. Assignments along these lines ask students to create or plug in content according to a specified manner of presentation, such as comparison and contrast or cause and effect. There is ample evidence that "real world" writing does not get produced in this fashion, which is one of the major criticisms leveled at textbooks that encourage these approaches. Not only do real writing tasks *not* begin with a particular form which merely lacks content to be complete, but content itself usually does not get generated without the writer first having a purpose for writing. However, I caution against abandoning the "rhetorical pattern" approach altogether, for there is evidence that many academic writing tasks outside of English departments or ESL/EFL classes *do* ask students to prepare papers which follow a particular format (Hale et al. 1996; Horowitz 1986) and the ability of ELLs to prepare papers that meet reader expectations has a definite value within such an academic environment.

A completely different philosophy of teaching leads to viewing writing as a vehicle of self-revelation and self-discovery, and assignments are presented in which students must reflect on and analyze their own personal experiences. Some examples ask students to write about being second language learners or to reflect on a lesson learned in childhood. The content in either case would arise from learners' personal biographies. This type of assignment has the potential of allowing writers to feel invested in their work. Perhaps more centrally, writing is seen as a tool for discovery of both meaning and purpose. Proponents of the "discovery approach" claim that the writing skills learned in practicing personal writing will transfer to the skills required to produce academic papers. However, there is no hard evidence

to support this claim. Further, many students from a range of cultural backgrounds do not believe it appropriate to share their personal thoughts with strangers (i.e., the teacher and fellow classmates), and therefore find personal writing far more challenging than academic, impersonal topics.

Regardless of the underlying philosophy of teaching that motivates the types of assignments presented to students, these assignments must be carefully constructed to assure their success and their contribution to promoting the goals of the course. The following set of six guidelines for the preparation of successful writing assignments (adapted from Reid and Kroll 1995) should prove helpful in reviewing the efficacy of any given assignment:

1. A writing assignment should be presented with its *context* clearly delineated such that the student understands the reasons for the assignment.
2. The *content* of the task/topic should be accessible to the writers and allow for multiple approaches.
3. The *language* of the prompt or task and the instructions it is embedded in should be un-ambiguous, comprehensible, and transparent.
4. The *task* should be focused enough to allow for completion in the time or length constraints given and should further students' knowledge of classroom content and skills.
5. The *rhetorical specifications (cues)* should provide a clear direction of likely shape and format of the finished assignment, including appropriate references to an anticipated audience.
6. The *evaluation criteria* should be identified so that students will know in advance how their output will be judged.

In sum, if one believes that students best learn to write by writing, then the design of writing tasks is perhaps the key component of curriculum design. It is in the engagement with and the completion of writing tasks that the student will be most directly immersed in the development of his or her writing skills; thus, a great deal of thought must go into crafting such tasks.

Responding

Responding to student writing—once seen as the main task of the writing teacher and certainly the most time-consuming one—is a complex process which also requires the teacher to make a number of critical decisions. Key questions to address include:

1. What are the general goals within the writing course for providing feedback to students?
2. What are the specific goals for providing feedback on a particular piece of writing?
3. At what stage in the writing process should feedback be offered?
4. What form should feedback take?
5. Who should provide the feedback?
6. What should students do with the feedback they receive?

Goal-Setting

Responding to student writing has the general goal of fostering student improvement. While this may seem to be stating the obvious, teachers need to develop responding methodologies which *can* foster improvement; they need to know how to measure or recognize improvement when it does occur. As with so many other aspects of teaching writing, there remains no easy answer to the question of what type of response will facilitate improved student mastery of writing. Therefore, in setting goals, teachers should focus on implementing a variety of response types and on training students to maximize the insights of prior feedback on future writing occasions. Students need to make the best use of commentary provided to them. Without training, it is possible that students will either ignore feedback or fail to use it constructively.

Shaping Feedback

Regardless of whatever repertoire of strategies teachers develop to provide feedback on student papers, students must also be trained to use the feedback in ways that will improve their writing, be it on the next draft of a particular paper or on another assignment. In two related case studies analyzing a very large number of marginal and end comments written by an experienced ESL composition instructor on first drafts, Ferris (1997) and Ferris et al. (1997) classified the teacher's comments into eight different categories. Ferris also further examined the second draft papers written by the same students to determine which type of comments led to change, and which changes appeared to improve the quality of individual papers. She concludes that most changes did improve the students' papers, and that the more specific and the lengthier the individual comments were, the more likely they were to lead to positive change (Ferris 1997, p. 330). The important thing to keep in mind is that students should be taught to process and work with a teacher's comments, whatever that teacher's commenting style is.

As with other issues discussed, the question of the teacher's philosophy is a key determinant of his or her approach to commenting. If teachers view themselves as *language* teachers rather than as *writing* teachers (see Zamel 1985), the nature of their comments and their feedback style will not promote growth in *writing*.

Forms of Feedback

Up to now we have been discussing feedback that is provided in writing by the teacher on various drafts of a student paper, a fairly traditional and time-consuming method, even for those teachers who do not respond to every draft as a finished product. But there are other ways for students to receive feedback on their writing that can and should be considered. Teachers should bear in mind that feedback can be oral as well as written, and they should consider individual conferences on student papers and/or the use of tape cassettes as two additional ways to structure their feedback. From another point of view, most writing teachers realize that they have many students in one class and they might also be teaching two or more writing classes, thus having a very limited amount of time to provide feedback to any one student. Teachers whose philosophies embrace the value of collaborative learning therefore may turn to the other students in the class to assist in the feedback process. Other students in the writing class can be taught to provide valuable feedback in the form of peer response, which serves to sharpen their critical skills in analyzing written work and also increase their ability to analyze their own drafts critically.

1. Oral Teacher Feedback

Because of potential communication problems, ELLs in a writing class need to have individual conferences with their teacher even more than native speaker students do. Conferences of about 15 minutes seem to work best and can provide the teacher an opportunity to directly question the student about intended messages which are often difficult to decipher by simply reading a working draft. Further, conferences allow the teacher to uncover potential misunderstandings the student might have about prior written feedback or issues in writing that have been discussed in class. Although a given student's cultural background can contribute to and potentially problematize the way that he or she processes what takes place in a conference (Patthey-Chavez and Ferris 1997), one benefit of conferences is that students can usually learn more in the one-to-one exchange than they can when attempting to decipher teacher written commentary on their own.

Some teachers provide all their feedback orally by asking students to submit a cassette tape with each draft. This method probably works best when the teacher reads over a student's paper and makes comments directly into the tape recorder while marking some accompanying numbers or symbols on the student's text. For ELLs, this method has the advantage of providing much more extensive feedback than is likely to be made in writing, even though it might take the teacher the same amount of time per paper. It also allows the student to replay the tape as many times as necessary to understand and benefit from the teacher's comments.

2. Peer Response

When the use of peer response became an early key component of teaching writing as a process in the L1 environment, many ESL/EFL teachers embraced the idea of having students read and/or listen to each other's papers for the purpose of providing feedback and input to each other as well as helping each other gain a sense of audience. But embracing a philosophy without understanding how to translate it to the L2 environment can often lead to rather disappointing results. That is, simply putting students together in groups of four or five, each with rough draft in hand, and then having each student in turn read his or her paper aloud, followed by having the other members of the group react to the strengths and weaknesses of the paper to indicate where their needs as readers have not been addressed, is *not* a format likely to work with even the most sophisticated class of ELLs. Because ELLs lack the language competence of native speakers who can often react intuitively to their classmates' papers, peer responding in the ESL/EFL classroom must be modeled, taught, and controlled if it is to be valuable.

One way to guide peer response is for teachers to provide a short list of directed questions that students address as they read their own or other students' papers. A first exercise of this type can involve giving students a short checklist of attributes to look for in their own papers, such as checking for a particular rhetorical feature that might have been discussed in class, e.g., topic sentences, or checking to assure no irrelevancies have been included. The checklist is submitted with the paper as a way for the student to assume responsibility for reading over his or her paper carefully. Next, students can be trained to read and respond to other students' papers by reviewing an essay written by a student in a previous class and working through, as a class, a peer response sheet that asks a few specific questions to elicit both a general reaction to the paper and suggestions for improvement. As the students gain practice in reading and analyzing each others' papers and their awareness of the conventions of writing increases, the questions can be made more complex and varied. Some typical questions to begin with might include: *What is the main purpose of this paper? What have you found particularly effective in the paper? Do you think the writer has followed through on what he or she set out to do?* Peer guidelines for students who have more practice in the technique might include the following step: *Find at least three places in the essay where you can think of questions that have not been answered by the writer. Write those questions in the margins as areas for the writer to answer in the next draft.*

In order to maximize the value of the feedback, responses should be written, providing practice in the valuable skill of text analysis for the student commenter. These written responses can be given to the student writer with or without the anonymity of the student reader preserved and/or used as the basis for oral discussion between reader(s) and writer. The teacher might also want to read the student feedback sheets to assess the analytical skills of the student readers.

Despite all the potential benefits of peer interaction, it is important to note that many studies conducted on L2 populations have indicated numerous problems in implementing peer response as a regular fixture in the ESL/EFL classroom. For example, one research study points to a tendency on the part of ELLs to focus on grammatical issues in their peers' papers despite training and instructions to the contrary (Leki 1990); some researchers have found that the purposes of collaboration are viewed differently in different cultures and participants in writing groups might operate at cross-purposes (e.g., Carson and Nelson 1994); and others have expressed reservations about the extent to which students in ESL classes believe they should put any credence in comments offered by their fellow students (e.g., Zhang 1995). These concerns should not be minimized, but should be factored into how teachers train their classes to work with peer response in a manner best suited to a particular classroom environment.

Error Correction

Regardless of which agenda the writing teacher sets and the number of drafts that students produce, the papers that ELLs write are likely to exhibit problems in language control. Still, the question of whether or not errors should be corrected at all and the role of overt grammar instruction as a way to help students avoid or lessen the presence of error in future writing undertakings are hotly debated (see especially Truscott 1996). However, I concur with Ferris and Hedgcock's claim:

> we proceed on the assumption—supported by the intuitions of many ESL writing teachers and certainly by those of their students—that grammar and editing feedback and instruction, when thoughtfully and carefully executed, can help many or most students improve the accuracy of their texts (1998, p. 202).

It is very important that the teacher not be swayed by the presence of language problems into turning a writing course into a grammar course. Rather, errors must be dealt with at an appropriate stage of the composing process, and this stage is best considered part of the final editing phase.

The role of editing, when seen as distinct from rewriting, is essentially working to eliminate grammatical problems and stylistic infelicities; this type of editing is certainly essential to the production of good prose, but is probably an activity that is best attended to when a text is considered complete in terms of having been shaped by content, organization, attention to the needs of the reader, and a consideration of its purpose. In fact, teacher editing of or correction of grammatical errors on first drafts can be a counterproductive activity, possibly exacerbating whatever insecurities students might have about their writing and drawing their attention away from the other kinds of revision that must be attended to. The long-term goal on the path to becoming a better writer is for students to develop techniques for learning to edit their own work (see Bates, Lane, and Lange 1993).

In addition to deciding *when* to correct errors, teacher must also decide *who* will correct the errors, *which* errors to correct, and *how* to correct errors. Besides the obvious role the teacher plays as a corrector of errors, the student writer and other students in the class can be called upon to provide feedback on errors as part of the peer feedback process. (For a discussion of activities for training students in error detection procedures, see Frodesen's chapter in this volume.)

The decision whether to address all or selected errors is a complex one, and probably depends a great deal on the level of writing the student is capable of producing. However, correcting all of a student's errors is probably rarely called for, unless there are very few errors present in the text. The teacher should probably concentrate instead on calling the student's attention to those errors which are considered more serious and/or represent a pattern of errors in that particular student's writing.

Lastly, the "how" of calling students' attention to their errors is also complex. Teachers can choose (1) to point out specific errors by using a mark in the margin or an arrow or other symbolic system; (2) to correct (or model) specific errors by writing in the corrected form; (3) to label specific errors according to the feature they violate (e.g., subject-verb agreement), using either the complete term or a symbol system; (4) to indicate the presence of error but not the precise location, e.g. noting that there are problems with word forms; or (5) to ignore specific errors. Most teachers use a combination of two or more of these methods, depending on what they perceive to be the needs of the student; studies of teacher feedback are inconclusive as to what the best methodology might be. The best approach to feedback on errors undoubtedly derives from considering the circumstances of the individual student coupled with the goals of the course and the stage of the composing process a particular draft reflects.

CONCLUSION

Producing a successful written text is a complex task which requires simultaneous control over a number of language systems as well as an ability to factor in considerations of the ways the discourse must be shaped for a particular audience and a particular purpose. Given that language use is both culturally and socially determined, it is no less the case that written texts are shaped by factors that differ not only from one culture to another but also within a single culture. Teaching ESL/EFL students to become successful writers, able to weigh and factor in all of these issues, is an especially complex task. But it can be a tremendously rewarding one as well.

This chapter has presented some of the general issues involved in establishing a writing curriculum and in teaching the writing class. But there are no "general" classes or "general" students. Each writing class must be shaped for a very specific population of English language learners. Since the ability to write well in a second language is no doubt even more difficult to achieve than the ability to read, speak, or understand the language, it is not surprising that many students take several years to achieve even a modicum of success. What must be emphasized to teachers in training is the importance of designing curricula and shaping classes with a clear understanding of how the acquisition of written skills can be fostered. Our real goal is to gradually wean our students away from us, providing them with strategies and tools for their continued growth as writers and for the successful fulfillment of future writing tasks they might face once they have completed their last writing course with us.

Just a few decades ago, as second language writing courses moved away from a "drill and skill" approach, curriculum planners and teachers modeled their methodology and practices on what was going on in NES writing courses and tended to assume that research insights in L1 composition applied to L2 composition as well. With increasing professionalization in the field of English language teaching in general, that is no longer the case. Second language writing has become a field with its own body of research and its own internal debates as to what constitutes the best transfer of research into practice. In fact, the interplay between research and practice in the field of second language writing is a two-way street. Research insights drive practice and concerns for practices that do not seem to be working drives additional research. This makes for a vibrant environment in which to teach ESL/EFL writing.

Earlier hopes of finding the best method "were based on the faulty assumptions that there was a best method and one just had to find it, that teaching writing was a matter of prescribing a logically ordered set of written tasks and exercises, and that good writing conformed to a predetermined and ideal model" (Zamel 1987, p. 697).

There can be no "best" method when students' learning styles are so different; our hope now is rather to find methodologies which empower students rather than restrict them, and to create courses which arise from principled reasons derived from thorough investigations.

DISCUSSION QUESTIONS

1. What are some of the specific ways in which the teaching of writing to English language learners has changed over the past 20, 30, or 40 years?
2. What would be the consequences of claiming that there is just a *single* composing process?
3. In what ways can a syllabus for a writing course reflect the underlying teaching philosophy of a particular teacher?
4. How should a teacher react if a student can't seem to do one or more of the techniques for getting started identified in the text?
5. Discuss some ways to establish guidelines that teachers should consider in preparing feedback for students.

SUGGESTED ACTIVITIES

1. Observe a single ESL/EFL writing class for three to four class meetings in a row (with the teacher's permission!). On the basis of your observations, design a set of criteria that could be used to evaluate the extent to which the students are making progress in their writing.
2. Collect several composition textbooks designed for use in an ESL or EFL writing course. Review each textbook to determine the view each author adopts as to what constitutes the best ways to have students become more proficient writers. To justify your conclusions, use such "data" as the author's introduction to the teacher, the nature of the readings presented in the text, the type of writing assignments included, and so on.
3. Conduct an interview with the director of the English language composition program on your campus to explore how the composition program addresses the needs of students whose first language is other than English.

Some of the questions you might ask are: Are ESL students folded into classes for NES students or enrolled in separate ESL courses? Are ESL courses considered lower level or parallel level to courses for NES? Do the current placement procedures work? To whose advantage does it work to provide separate or combined courses for L1 and L2 students?

4. Arrange to tutor for two to four sessions a single ELL enrolled in a writing course. Have the student bring samples of his or her writing for you to work on together. After reviewing several examples of the student's writing, be prepared to report on the strengths and weaknesses of your student writer and analyze the extent to which his or her present writing course seems to be addressing his or her needs.
5. Design a brief survey of six to eight questions aimed at identifying whether faculty outside of English departments have different expectations for written work produced by NES and ELL students. Distribute your survey to a few faculty members in three or four departments at your school that have heavy enrollment of ESL students and summarize the results.

FURTHER READING

Background Resources

Campbell, C. 1998. *Teaching Second Language Writing: Interacting with Text.* Pacific Grove, CA: Heinle & Heinle Publishers.
   A short and practical guide that peeks into the author's own ESL writing classrooms and those of several other experienced teachers, providing very practical ideas for a variety of teaching situations. Focused primarily on immigrant rather than foreign students.

Ferris, D., and J. S. Hedgcock. 1998. *Teaching ESL Composition. Purpose, Process and Practice.* Mahwah, NJ: Lawrence Erlbaum.
   An extremely thorough teacher-training text providing extensive coverage of classroom concerns, well grounded in current theoretical perspectives.

Harklau, L., K. M. Losey, and M. Siegel, eds. 1999. *Generation 1.5 Meets College Composition.* Mahwah, NJ: Lawrence Erlbaum.

An anthology of 12 articles addressing a variety of issues related to how best to meet the writing needs of English language learners who have graduated from U.S. high schools.

Leki, I. 1992. *Understanding ESL Writers: A Guide for Teachers.* Portsmouth, NH: Boynton/Cook Heinemann.

A brief and highly readable compendium of information identifying the special characteristics and problem areas of ESL students, framed within a discussion of the field of ESL writing as a profession and its connections to second language learning. Especially helpful for those with little background in applied linguistics.

Silva, T., and P. Matsuda, eds. 2001. *On Second Language Writing.* Mahwah, NJ: Lawrence Erlbaum.

An anthology of 15 articles exploring central issues in theory, research, and instruction. Authors are leading scholars in the field and provide a state-of-the-art analysis of their particular area of focus.

Resources Containing Classroom Ideas for EFL Writing Teachers

Brookes, A., and P. Grundy. 1998. *Beginning to Write: Writing Activities for Elementary and Intermediate Learners.* Cambridge: Cambridge University Press.

Grellet, F. 1996. *Writing for Advanced Learners of English.* Cambridge: Cambridge University Press.

Hedge, T. 1988. *Writing.* Oxford: Oxford University Press.

White, R. V., ed. 1995. *New Ways in Teaching Writing.* Alexandria, VA: TESOL.

 **WEBSITES**

Journal of Second Language On-line

Homepage for this specialized journal, published three times a year since 1992, providing solid scholarly articles. Website includes all tables of contents and helpful links.

http://icdweb.cc.purdue.edu/~silvat/jslw/

Purdue University Online Writing Lab

Provides extensive writing help in all areas connected to written composition for both native and non-native English speaking writers, with helpful links for teacher resources as well.

http://owl.english.purdue/edu/

Second Language Writing Research Network Forum

Facilitates the exchange of information by providing links to bibliographical information, a directory of specialists, a discussion bulletin board, and related websites.

http://icdweb.cc.purdue.edu/~silvat/forum/

ENDNOTES

1 While there are numerous distinctions to be drawn between writing classes for ESL students (in English-speaking countries) and writing classes for EFL students (studying in countries where English is not an official language), the discussion in this chapter addresses issues of concern in shaping writing courses for both populations. Rather than focusing on the differences between these groups, I have chosen to blur the boundaries for the purposes of this chapter. Where *ESL* is noted in the chapter, the claim is limited to courses offered in North America and/or reporting on a study conducted in this environment; where *ESL/EFL* is noted in the chapter, the discussion applies to either locale. *ELL* is used to designate an English language learner in any context. Further, Cumming (2000), in a study of both ESL and EFL writing classes in a number of countries around the world, found a certain core level of common approaches and practices.

2 In this procedure, the writer is asked to verbalize all of his or her thoughts while composing and to write down only those words and thoughts that form part of the task of text production. The event is either audiotaped or videotaped, and a transcript, referred to as a "protocol," is prepared for subsequent analysis, also known as "protocol analysis."

3 A heuristic device refers to a specific set of steps one can follow in order to work through personal discoveries as a way of finding a solution, answer, or path to adopt in a given circumstance. While there are guidelines for utilizing heuristic devices, the important thing to remember is that they will yield highly individual results, i.e. there are no "right" or "wrong" answers. In contrast, algorithmic devices are steps which are tightly controlled and invariable; they yield the same results for all those who follow a given algorithm, such as the process of addition. A full discussion of a wide variety of heuristic devices useful in ESL teaching is presented in Hughey et al. (1983), pp. 62–84 and in Ferris and Hedgcock (1998), pp. 101–113.

Grammar in Writing

JAN FRODESEN

"Grammar in Writing" emphasizes that a focus on form in composition can help writers develop rich linguistic resources needed to express ideas effectively in addition to providing assistance in error correction. Frodesen summarizes current controversies about the role of grammar in writing, discusses learner and situational variables, and describes activities for incorporating grammar into writing instruction.

INTRODUCTION

In a California elementary school one morning, the teacher of a class of bilingual fifth graders was preparing her students for a standardized English test which required them to demonstrate their knowledge of English grammar rules by choosing appropriate forms to fill blanks in a set of decontextualized sentences—a typical, discrete-item, multiple-choice test. Up to this point in the class, the students had been creating their own illustrated bilingual storybooks about fantastical beasts, writing their texts first in Spanish, their native language, and then in English. To help her students develop their awareness of the need to meet readers' expectations, the teacher had been serving as a careful reader of their stories, letting them know whenever she had a problem understanding their meaning and providing vocabulary and grammar explanation as needed.

As the students pored over example sentences to prepare for the required exam, a task both teacher and students found tedious (especially in comparison to their story-writing activity), they encountered one item in which they had to choose the correct pronoun for a subject slot. The choices were the nominative pronoun *she* and the object pronoun *her*. As the teacher was prompting the correct form for the blank, one of the students exclaimed, "But teacher, this is a bad sentence! We don't know who *she* is!"

This story, related years ago to me by Barbara Hawkins, has remained one of my favorite real-life examples of what "grammar in writing" and the teaching of it should mean: helping writers develop their knowledge of linguistic resources and grammatical systems to convey ideas meaningfully and appropriately to intended readers. It is also a wonderful example of how even young second language learners can discover and use discourse-level grammatical principles, in this case creating a cohesive text by making sure each pronoun has an identifiable referent.

Not only *can* students of all ages learn principles of grammar in context, but a focus on form appears to be necessary to some extent for optimal second language learning. Second language acquisition (SLA) researchers Doughty and Williams (1998) report that years of research on classroom immersion and naturalistic acquisition studies suggest that when instruction is meaning focused only, learners do not develop many linguistic features at targetlike levels.

In second language writing, the role of grammar in writing—both explicit explanations of grammatical principles and teacher correction of errors—has remained a topic of controversy since the 1980s for several reasons. One has been the influence of first language (L1) composition research and pedagogy on second language (L2) writing practices. Hillocks's (1986) synthesis of research on native English speaking writers indicated that formal grammar instruction has little or no effect on writing improvement. In the paradigm shifts within composition theory from a focus on writing products to writing processes, and, more recently, to a focus on writing as a social activity (see Kroll's chapter in this volume), explicit grammar instruction in L1 writing classrooms has typically been relegated to teachers' direct correction of errors, if dealt with at all.

Another and perhaps even more significant influence on the weakened role of grammar in L2 writing instruction has been the widespread adoption by many second language teachers of Krashen's (1982) stated beliefs that form-focused instruction is not only unnecessary but thwarts natural acquisition processes. In fact, early L1 composition theorists' arguments against explicit grammar instruction, one of the most notable being Hartwell (1985), drew on Krashen's work as support for the *noninterventionist position,* a term used by Long and Robinson (1998) to describe the stance that Krashen and others have taken in rejecting explicit focus on form.

The wholesale adoption of L1 composition theories and practices for L2 writing classes seems misguided in light of the many differences between first and second language writers, processes, and products (Silva 1993). While ESL/EFL writing teachers certainly need to be knowledgeable about L1 composition theory and practices, they also need to address the special needs of second language writers.

The neglect of form-focused instruction for second language writers seems to have been most prevalent in the United States due to the adoption of communicative models of language learning that considered comprehensible input sufficient for language acquisition. As Scarcella (1996) has discussed, the effects of this instruction have been especially unfortunate for students who need advanced level writing proficiency for academic work or careers. Scarcella echoes the views of SLA researchers such as Lightbown (1998), who earlier had adopted the noninterventionist position but who, after seeing the results of deemphasizing corrective feedback and limited form-focused instruction, now believe that students need input on structure.

In addition to the influence of L1 composition research and noninterventionist positions regarding second language learning, misconceptions about the meaning and scope of the term *grammar* have fostered negative attitudes about the role of grammar in ESL/EFL writing. There is a great difference between the teaching of linguistic forms apart from a meaningful context, on the one hand, and a focus on language form to develop learners' ability to communicate meaningfully and appropriately, on the other, as Hawkins's bilingual classroom so beautifully exemplified. In the latter view, grammar is an integral part of language use; it is a resource to be accessed for effective communication, not just an isolated body of knowledge. As Widdowson (1988) states, "Language learning is essentially grammar learning and it is a mistake to think otherwise" (p. 154). This orientation leads writers to conceive of grammar as an essential component of language, a system that they can discover and exploit for their communicative needs, rather than as a tedious and complicated set of rules to be memorized or as a template to be used solely for identifying and correcting their errors.

From the perspective of grammar as a resource in shaping accurate and effective communication, it seems clear, then, that focus on form should to some extent be an integral part of the instructional design for second language writing classrooms. This does not mean, however, that all kinds of grammar instruction are useful in the ESL/EFL writing classroom. Nor does it mean that students will automatically be able to transform input received through explicit grammar instruction into productive output. Such transfer from input to output, or *uptake,* as it is termed in the SLA literature, requires that teachers consider and reflect on many learner, situational, and linguistic variables relevant to their students and classroom contexts. Awareness of these variables can greatly assist teachers in deciding when and how to incorporate grammar into writing instruction, as well as in selecting those grammatical features most deserving of students' attention and practice for any given context.

GENERAL GUIDELINES FOR INTEGRATING GRAMMAR IN WRITING INSTRUCTION

Where should a teacher begin in deciding what kinds of grammar focus are appropriate and relevant for students' needs in the writing classroom? Long and Robinson (1998) state that deciding whether the starting point should be the *learner* or the *language to be taught* is one of the most critical choices in course design; they note that in many classrooms worldwide, course design starts with structures to be learned. In the United States, however, much ESL pedagogy emphasizes learner-centered course design. Echoing this focus on learners, Byrd and Reid (1998) contend that teachers should begin with students and not structures to make decisions about grammar in ESL writing. Here, too, is where our discussion of variables will begin.

Learner Variables

Celce-Murcia (1985) suggests that the following learner variables be considered in making choices about grammar instruction: age, proficiency level, and educational background. According to her schema, a focus on formal aspects of language is increasingly useful as writers become older, more advanced in English proficiency, and more highly educated/literate. Ferris and Hedgcock (1998) note that students in ESL composition classrooms are typically a very heterogeneous population, characterized by many differences in backgrounds and abilities, including linguistic, ethnic, and cultural backgrounds as well as cognitive and metacognitive strategy use. Reid (1998) adds to this list the importance of considering different learning styles, pointing out contrasts in styles such as concrete learners, who prefer practical, hands-on activities working with others versus abstract learners, who learn best alone through theory and planning. Reid demonstrates how different kinds of lessons speak to one or more of these different learning styles. All of these variables can in turn create differences in learners' motivation and attitudes toward language learning in general and the acquisition of academic skills in particular.

With the ever-growing population of non-native English-speaking immigrants in English-speaking countries, differences in students' educational backgrounds and English acquisition have become extremely important in developing second language curricula. In the United States, one of the most important distinctions in types of learners relevant to grammar instruction at higher education levels has been that between international students who have received their education in their native country prior to attending an English-medium school and permanent resident students who have received some, if not most, of their education in the United States. (In EFL contexts, of course, most students will have educational backgrounds similar to the international students in English-speaking countries.)

International (or EFL) students have typically learned most of their English in the classroom and generally have received considerable explicit grammar instruction; thus, they are often able to access and explain grammar rules when doing text analysis and writing activities. Their writing may exhibit more "non-nativelike" structures, such as unidiomatic phrasing, than the writing of permanent residents does, but it may also demonstrate better skill in producing the complex structures typical of formal academic English.

Permanent residents, in contrast to international students, often acquire English "by ear" from exposure to the language in oral contexts, including, of course, the classroom, but in many informal, conversational contexts as well. For this reason, and because explicit grammar instruction has not been a significant part of their English language education, the knowledge that permanent residents have about English grammar tends to be implicit, similar to that of native English language speakers. They may know that an ungrammatical form "doesn't sound right" but may not be able to explain why, just as most native speakers would not be able to explain why they use definite article *the* rather than *a* in many contexts. Drawing on this same implicit knowledge, immigrant ESL students may regard structures used in formal written English, but seldom occurring in conversational English, as incorrect or sounding "strange," just as many novice native English language writers do. Like developing native English language writers, ESL writers often inappropriately import informal oral expressions and syntactic structures into academic writing contexts (e.g., using *I mean* rather than *that is* before a clarifying statement, or using object pronouns as grammatical subjects, such as *Me and my family are . . .*). Because of their educational backgrounds, permanent resident students may be unfamiliar with most grammatical terminology, and they also may be less aware than international students tend to be of their errors in English morphology and syntax.

Since terminology can be useful in providing learners with teacher feedback on syntactic and morphological error patterns in their writing, an awareness of individual learners' knowledge of grammatical terms is important. The instructor could ask students to describe briefly their backgrounds in a questionnaire at the beginning of a course and/or could give students a list of grammatical terms (subject, verb, gerund, infinitive, etc.) and ask the students to give examples of the ones they know, to indicate the ones they have heard of but don't really understand, and to note the ones with which they are totally unfamiliar.

Of course, there will be some basic terms that the teacher will want all students to be familiar with in order to help them develop editing skills. Terminology in general should be kept as simple as possible. For example, progressive verbs, gerunds, and present participles in adjective/adverb phrases might be distinguished as *-ing* main verbs, *-ing* modifiers, and *-ing* nouns, respectively. Infinitives could be referred to as *to* + verb. Relative clauses could be referred to as *which/who/that* adjective clauses. Such designations link grammatical functions with actual morphemes or words that students will see in writing so there is less need to memorize terms.

One final student variable that deserves consideration is the degree to which learners take risks in expanding their productive abilities or, conversely, employ avoidance strategies to reduce chances of errors. Schachter and Celce-Murcia (1977) contributed to error analysis research by showing that some learners avoid errors by not attempting constructions they find difficult, such as relative clauses or passives. Schleppegrell (2000) describes two very different strategies adopted by three ESL university students writing science lab reports: two of them used a strategy of "saying little but trying to say it right," while the other writer drew upon complex sentence structures and phrasing to elaborate her points. The two who "said little" produced fewer errors but failed in many ways to meet the genre demands of the task; the writer who extended her language use beyond her mastery level produced considerably more surface errors but responded more fully and appropriately to the content demands. These and other studies remind us that we cannot evaluate learners' performance or develop lessons simply on the basis of error diagnosis and corrective feedback. Some students who write simply to avoid difficult structures may need grammar instruction that encourages them to expand their linguistic repertoire.

From this discussion of learner variables, it is clear that ESL writing teachers have much to consider in meeting learners' needs. However, as Ferris and Hedgcock (1998) advise, there are ways to group and work with these variables in planning syllabi and lessons.

Situational Variables

Situational, or instructional, variables must also be considered in developing writing activities that focus on form. Celce-Murcia (1985) points out that the more professional the use of language, the greater the need for focus on form. Supporting this view in discussing pedagogical grammar within a communicative paradigm, Little (1994) states that a high level of correctness is required for effective communication in formal written and spoken discourse, and that native as well as non-native English speakers often use explicit knowledge, either from memory or reference books, when they are planning, monitoring, and editing formal written discourse. While grammar also has a role in less formal writing, the structural focus and emphasis on correctness will vary, depending on the extent to which writers are expected to observe standard English conventions in settings such as academic or business communities. Expectations may also vary for various forms of Internet communication, such as e-mail.

The specific objectives of a writing class will influence greatly how grammar will be integrated with writing. In ESL/EFL programs that place students with diagnostic tests, some courses may focus particularly on error analysis and editing strategies. Courses for these students might include considerable work with their own writing as the core materials. Advanced courses might emphasize the grammatical choices writers make to achieve cohesion and coherence, with more extensive text analysis followed by production activities.

The kinds of writing in which students will be expected to develop and demonstrate proficiency are another consideration. In academic or preparatory settings, courses may cover a range of genres common to academic writing, such as essays, lab reports, problem-solution texts, persuasive writing, or short essay examinations. Alternately, the focus may be on particular academic genres such as research papers or historical narratives. In business writing contexts, requirements may include memos, proposals, and evaluative reports. Genre-based and corpus-based studies (e.g., Swales 1990; Biber 1988, Biber, Conrad, and Reppen 1998) have identified various grammatical features and clusters of features typically used in particular kinds of writing. Biber's (1988) analysis, for example, characterizes the grammar of non-narrative communication as using present tense verbs, past participle clauses, and longer and more elaborate noun phrases than occurs in narrative communication.

Whatever the instructional objectives, the goal of developing writing proficiency should be at the forefront in making decisions about explicit focus on grammar. In general, learners can benefit from activities that help them understand how grammatical choices contribute to shaping meaning and put these insights into practice. It bears repeating that too much focus on error not only promotes a limited perception of the role of grammar in communication but

may create—or reinforce—negative attitudes about this very important component of second language writing instruction.

ACTIVITIES FOR INCORPORATING GRAMMAR INTO WRITING INSTRUCTION

Text Analysis

In developing linguistic resources, ESL/EFL writers can benefit greatly from learning how various grammatical features and grammatical systems are used in authentic written texts. On the one hand, analysis of such texts can help learners who are already familiar with prescriptive grammar rules but who still have problems understanding and appropriately using grammatical oppositions such as definite and indefinite articles and present-perfect and past- or present-tense verb forms. On the other hand, text analysis can also benefit learners with mostly implicit knowledge of grammar rather than explicit rule-based knowledge: These writers often need to become more familiar with the ways in which various genres of written English differ structurally from oral English forms.

Considerations for Selecting Grammar Points and Materials for Text Analysis

In selecting grammar points from authentic texts, the writing teacher should consider the proficiency levels of students and course objectives. The level of difficulty of a grammatical feature should not be far beyond the learners' developmental stages; for example, students struggling to produce well-formed relative clauses with subject relative pronouns (e.g., *the teacher who called me . . .*) would have difficulty with a lesson on object pronoun relative clauses (*the teacher to whom I gave my address*). This is not to say that new structures should never be introduced, but rather that students' readiness to give attention to them should be evident. As for grammar points relating to writing course objectives, such focus is, of course, necessary if grammar is to be subordinated to communicative goals. Both of these issues—students' proficiency levels and course goals—are relevant to the distinction that Long and Robinson (1998) have made between *teachers* focusing on form and *students* focusing on form: If in the course of a grammar lesson the teacher has not successfully engaged the student in noticing a language feature, then only the teacher, and not the learner, has ultimately focused on form.

The sources of authentic texts will vary depending on the writing course syllabus. Like writing courses for native English speakers, many ESL/EFL writing courses now include a variety of readings on which writing assignments are based. Such courses may be content-based (see Snow's chapter in this volume) or may include a reader arranged by text types or themes. The teacher can examine these texts to see what kinds of grammatical structures, contrasts, or systems are dominant and which contain forms that students will be able to use in their own writing. In content- and theme-based courses, readings can be distinguished by whether they represent models of text types, such as the research paper or the argumentative essay, which students will be expected to produce during the course, or whether the readings are expository articles, short stories, poems, or plays serving as "springboards" for generating topics.

In English for Academic Purposes writing courses, assigned readings typically include examples of the kinds of writing expected of students. In these courses, the instructor will want to consider what grammatical features characterize these writings. This is true even for the academic writing required of younger learners. In Schleppegrell's (1998) study on the descriptive science writing of middle school students, she found that this kind of writing required features such as modifying phrases after nouns (e.g., a lizard *with a big head*), relative clauses, and possessive phrases, which the second language learners had difficulty producing. A focus on language forms for particular genres should not be equated with teaching "formulas" for writing or conveying a view of written texts as static sets of language rules. Such a focus simply acknowledges that certain patterns of rhetorical

strategies, such as definition, often occur in particular text types and that L2 writers, just like L1 writers, need control of the forms typically used to realize these functions.

As for readings that are springboards for writing rather than text models, Holten (1997) notes that assigned novels and short stories can offer wonderful opportunities for grammar-focused activities since students typically find them easier to read and are thus more willing to examine them closely. Poetry, while not always easy for students to comprehend, often provides excellent examples of parallel structures. Readings based on authentic or fictional oral English, such as interviews or plays, can be rich sources for discussion about differences between spoken and written English, such as the use of fragments in spoken English versus complete sentences in formal written English. Other kinds of variation deserving analysis depending on course goals are grammatical and syntactic differences in written texts, such as journalistic prose in contrast to certain forms of academic writing. In many cases, these differences involve considerable overlap between grammatical and lexical features.

Finally, a word should be said about brief supplementary texts that can be integrated with course readings for grammar focus. Instructors often encounter excellent examples of particular grammatical structures in daily newspaper or magazine reading, such as segments of news articles, advertisements, and even cartoons. These texts can provide variety, and students often find them engaging either because the topics are timely ones or, as in the case of cartoons and many advertisements, they present language in humorous and creative ways. Especially for less advanced students, advertisements can be excellent sources for illustrating grammatical features; they often incorporate grammatical repetition as a rhetorical device. Creating files with short texts that exemplify grammar structures commonly covered in a course, such as verb tenses or count/noncount nouns, can serve as a good source for brief lessons.

In summary, when selecting texts and grammatical points for analysis, the following considerations may serve as guidelines.

1. The grammatical features should be appropriate for students' developmental stages
2. The grammatical features should reflect students' writing needs for the course or for future writing
3. When possible, assigned course readings should be sources of text analysis so that grammar focus is integrated with other pre-writing activities
4. The lessons should generally be kept brief, especially for less advanced writers
5. The instructor may want to enhance the texts by underlining or bolding certain elements, especially those that are not very salient for some learners
6. Productive tasks should follow text analysis so that writers have opportunities to practice the explicit knowledge gained from noticing features in written texts and so that teachers are able to assess to some degree what students have learned from the analysis tasks.

Sample Text Analysis Lessons

The following are a few examples of lessons that focus on grammatical features in texts. For each, it is assumed that the structure is appropriate for the level of the students, that the text used has sufficient examples of the particular grammatical item(s), and that the structures can be used by students in their own writing.

1. ***That and zero-that* clauses** Even advanced students sometimes have difficulty understanding complex sentence structures without explicit markers of subordination such as relative pronouns or complementizers. To help writers identify clauses in which "that" is optionally deleted and the verbs these clauses may follow, find comic strips in which the speakers have deleted "that" before a complement clause. This feature is quite common in spoken English; on one newspaper comic page, for example, the following instances were found:

   "Margaret *thinks* she's smarter than we are just because she's smarter than we are."
   "I *know* I'm no longer young and pretty . . ."
   "But I *guarantee* it won't happen again."

"It makes me feel good to *know* I might help save someone."

Briefly review complement clauses with and without "that" using a few examples; then ask students to find the places where "that" could be inserted following a verb. (Either point out or delete any reduced relative "that" clauses that might confuse them.) Discuss why speakers might omit these forms. Then examine an academic prose passage for comparison. Discuss reasons why writers might omit "that" and when they might need to use this form for clarity.

2. **Tense and Time Frame Shifts** ESL writers are often confused about the motivations for verb tense shifts and believe that they should not change verb tenses (e.g., from present to present perfect) or time frames (e.g., from present to past). Review the reasons why writers shift verb tenses and time frames. (See Frodesen and Eyring 2000, p. 8.) Then give students a passage with tense and time frame shifts. Underline and number the verbs selected for focus. Ask them to identify the tense and time frame (e.g., past progressive tense, past time frame) for each underlined verb and to explain any verb tense shifts (e.g., to support a claim about the present with examples from the past). Ask them also to circle adverbs or adverb phrases that signal time frame shifts (e.g., "last year"). Have students look at something they have written recently to identify tense shifts and reasons for them.

3. **Demonstrative Reference** Find a text that has examples of both "this" used in pronoun reference and "this"+ noun used for reference. Number the lines before reproducing or putting the text on a transparency. Ask students to skim the text and, with two different colored highlighters, distinguish the two types of demonstrative reference. Give students a graphic organizer with two columns. Ask them to write the reference in one column (e.g., "this idea") and the referent (a word, phrase, clause, or sentence) in the column across from it. Discuss under what conditions the demonstrative

adjective + noun form rather than the demonstrative pronoun is used. Have students edit drafts for any unclear use of demonstrative pronouns.

As the examples above indicate, these types of activities are especially appropriate for advanced level ESL writers. However, for less advanced or younger students, instructors can enhance text through underlining and bolding as well as limiting the scope and number of examples for students to examine.

Guided Writing Activities

The notion of "guided" writing unfortunately retains negative connotations for some writing teachers, who may associate it with the mechanical and noncommunicative practices of the past. For them it may conjure up formulaic pattern practice or slot filling. However, like guided practice in other language skills such as pronunciation or listening, guided writing serves to focus students' attention on language features that are difficult for them. In addition, exercises eliciting the use of grammatical structures can encourage learners to expand their linguistic resources. In fact, writing instructors often find that their students are much more receptive to grammar-based guided writing that offers them new ways of expressing their ideas.

Many of the guided writing activities described below were used long before process-centered approaches to writing became widespread. In the past, however, these exercises were sometimes presented without context and only in the framework of a structural syllabus. Here they are suggested as components of prewriting, revising, or editing processes in communicative writing tasks. As always, decisions as to which types of exercises are most helpful should be based on consideration of learner variables and the learning context.

Text Conversion

In text conversion exercises, students rewrite passages and short texts, changing some feature of the grammatical structure, such as rewriting a text that is in a present time frame as a past time frame text or changing direct speech to indirect

speech. As Celce-Murcia and Hilles (1988) point out, most of these exercises do not involve actual composing but rather provide practice in making structure-discourse matches. Consequently, they should be made relevant to learners' actual writing challenges. For example, rather than simply giving students a text to change verb tenses mechanically without motivation for the task, an exercise might be explicitly presented to address difficulties students are having in consistently using past tense verbs in past narratives; editing of actual writing assignments would follow. The following are some of the most common writing contexts that could employ text conversion activities.

Revision and Editing Focused Exercises

Perhaps the most obvious purpose for guided writing with focus on a particular grammatical structure is to address learners' grammar problems. For example, if students have frequent subject-verb agreement errors, as a pre-editing exercise they could change all third person present plural forms in a text to singular and make necessary verb changes. The content of the passage should be related as closely as possible to whatever topics students are working on so that they can review core vocabulary or concepts. Similar exercises could involve other frequent morphological errors, such as regular plural nouns without -s. Students would then check their own drafts to correct similar errors.

One common use of text conversion for practice in using appropriate forms in English for science and technology is conversion of sentences in active voice to passive in contexts where focus should be on objects and outcomes, not agents. In this kind of exercise, the instructor could create a text or use a student text from the methodology section of a research paper. The following example is from a student draft about procedures for measuring the effects of rainfall runoff on soil erosion:

> *We tested velocity by placing a green trace dye on the surface of the plot, at a measured point. After each run we estimated the vegetation cover using a five-point pin frame. We placed the pin frame in 20 places on the plot, moving downward.*

(used by permission of Trisha Marden)

Rewritten:

> *Velocity was tested by placing a green trace dye on the surface of the plot, at a measured point. After each run, the vegetation cover was estimated using a five-point pin frame. The pin frame was placed on the plot, moving downward.*

In using actual texts, the teacher may find that not all parts of a text can be transformed. Methodology sections of science research papers, for example, do not usually have all passive sentences. To make texts as natural as possible, the instructor can simply underline or number the sentences in a text to be rewritten. Afterward, students should identify contextual factors that influence use of the passive.

Sentence Combining

Prior to the paradigm shift from product to process in composition pedagogy, sentence combining was a topic of much research and discussion in L1 composition (Mellon 1969). In its early stages, this technique for developing syntactic fluency often involved combining a set of kernel sentences such as the following:

> *The man was old.*
> *The man had gray hair.*
> *The man walked down the street.*
> *The man walked slowly.*

Combined:

> *The old, gray-haired man walked slowly down the street.*

Like many language-based activities predating process-oriented pedagogies, this one fell into disfavor partly because the early applications often started with sets of sentences that were a far cry from authentic texts. De Beaugrande (1985) advises that writing samples used for sentence combining should resemble naturally occurring language; otherwise, "the whole exercise will be treated as some gratuitous venture into a bizarre domain of communication where people regale each other with inane kernel sentences" (p. 72). Most teachers who have used sentence combining are aware that, unless carefully structured, this technique can result in confusing or even incomprehensible sentences.

With these caveats in minds, sentence combining can be extremely useful for guided practice in producing particular grammatical structures, such as relative clauses or prepositional phrases, and in helping writers develop their repertoire of linguistic strategies for highlighting key information, subordinating less important information, and improving syntactic fluency.

One of the most useful applications of sentence combining for advanced ESL writers involves draft revision. With assistance, students can identify passages in their writing in which sentence combining could achieve a better flow of information through clearer connections between ideas. As one example, when learning to reference sources by introducing authors and their work, developing writers often use separate sentences such as the following:

> *Oliver Sacks is a neurologist. He wrote the article "Brilliant Light: A Chemical Boyhood." In this article, he describes how his "Uncle Tungsten" influenced his love of science.*

A more experienced writer of academic prose would subordinate some of this information:

> *In "Brilliant Light: A Chemical Boyhood," neurologist Oliver Sacks describes how his "Uncle Tungsten" influenced his love of science.*

In this way, sentence combining exercises can focus on particular rhetorical moves, such as introducing sources, that students will need to use frequently in academic writing.

Guided Paraphrase

One of the most important skills that students must develop for academic writing is the ability to paraphrase source materials to support claims and develop ideas. ESL/EFL writers often lack the facility with vocabulary and syntax to rephrase ideas in their own words; most experienced teachers are familiar with the distorted paraphrases that result when novice writers "slot" synonyms from a thesaurus into the original sentence without adjusting the grammar.

In cued paraphrase exercises, writers transform sentences or parts of sentences from assigned readings, using cues as the first step. The cues, which may be words or phrases, are designed to require syntactic restructuring in the paraphrase. Here are a few examples based on a sociology text about bystander intervention (Darley and Latane 1973) with possible transformations resulting from cues:

Original: *People trying to interpret a situation often look at those around them to see how to react. (base reactions on)*

Rewrite: *People trying to interpret a situation often base their reactions on those around them.*

Original: *Even if a person defines an event as an emergency . . . (decides)*

Rewrite: *Even if a person decides that an event is an emergency . . .*

As students further transform the structure resulting from the guided paraphrase cues, changing vocabulary and structures more fully so that the final version is not too close to the original, this activity becomes a true composing task. Students should be able to transfer these strategies to future paraphrasing tasks.

Text Elicitation

In form-focused text elicitation, the instructor specifies a topic or writing objective (e.g., a rhetorical strategy such as defining or summarizing results) and a grammatical structure or structures to be used. Certain writing topics naturally elicit particular forms, such as hypothetical conditionals in assignments speculating about what students would do under certain conditions (Celce-Murcia and Hilles 1988).

Assigned reading responses can also incorporate practice of grammatical structures needed for writing tasks. The shaded example below modeled after one by Holten and Marasco (1998, p. 214) which asked students to use conditionals in discussing brief problem-solution texts.

Excellent sources for eliciting summaries include surveys, graphs, or charts on topics related to writing themes, or genres such as research articles. These graphic sources can elicit texts that use a range of structures such as comparison/contrast connectors, passive verbs, common irregular verb forms (e.g., *rise* and *fall*), frequency adverbs (e.g., *often, rarely*), quantifiers (e.g., *most, the majority, a minority*) and, depending on the time frame, verb tenses such as simple past or present perfect. Any of these grammatical features could be the focus of a summary task. For example, advanced ESL writers often have difficulty using sentence connectors and subordinators in appropriate syntactic contexts.

Even prewriting exercises such as brainstorming or outlining could involve lists that use parallel structures such as noun phrases or infinitives. For example, to begin a composition unit on education, students in a university writing class were asked to list all of the purposes of higher education, using infinitive of purpose phrases (e.g., *to prepare for a career*). The grammatical objective here is not so much to practice such infinitive phrases as it is to use parallelism as a systematic way of organizing information in prewriting.

Text	Conditional Sentences
In many U.S. towns, the opening of large retail chain stores known as superstores has made it difficult for the local small businesses to keep customers.	If customers shop at chain superstores instead of their local businesses, the local stores may have to close.
However, some of these local businesses are now successfully using the Web to increase sales and improve customer service.	Unless small businesses find new ways to attract customers, such as advertising on the Web, they may not be able to compete with superstores.

In summary, text elicitation can be used to focus on diagnosed structural problems, to develop syntactic complexity, to familiarize students with discourse-based grammar conventions (e.g., the use of passive in survey reports), and to provide strategies for organizing and displaying information.

Dictation

Dictation can be an effective way to familiarize students with the ways in which grammar and vocabulary interact in common collocations as well as to address errors in writing that may result in part from mismatches between learners' aural perception of English forms and standard English grammar and spelling.

In one dictation procedure, the instructor reads aloud a short text several times, usually one related to the topic or genre on which students are working. The text is first read at a normal pace, with the students just listening. For the second reading, the teacher pauses after each phrase to allow students to write. Care should be taken not to put undue emphasis on word endings or function words that are not normally stressed. The third reading, done at a normal pace, gives students the opportunity to read over the texts and make corrections. The teacher then shows students the passage so that they can check their versions with the original and edit their texts. If the activity's main objective is error detection/correction, the instructor could give more specific directions, such as to put a circle at the ends of all words with missed *-s* third person singular or *-ed* endings. If the goal is to familiarize writers with particular grammatical features, students could be asked to underline them; the class could then discuss meanings and/or functions of the target constructions.

Text Completion

Grammar-based exercises involving text completion are, of course, very familiar to ESL/EFL students. Two of the most common types of text completion are the cloze passage and the gapped text. Whereas in cloze passages each blank represents a single word to fill in, in gapped texts the blanks may require one or more words. A third type of text completion, which focuses attention on the flow of information across sentence boundaries, requires students to use the discourse context to select sentences that best achieve "flow" and create effective cohesion. The formats and purposes of each of these completion types will be briefly described in this section.

Cloze passages can be created either by random deletion of words (e.g., deleting every seventh word) or by deletion of a specific item (e.g., articles). The second type is more suitable for grammatical focus. The source could be a published text or student writing; if a student text, the passage should be free of serious grammatical problems that might distract or confuse students. The following, from a student essay, has been made into a cloze passage by deleting articles. (Blanks have also been put before nouns with no article.)

____1____ pollution may be defined as ____2____ deterioration of ____3____ everyday life's natural resources. ____4____ pollution is ____5____ global problem that has affected ____6____ quality of ____7____ water we drink, ____8____ air we breathe and ____9____ land we use. ____10____ scientific solutions to overcome ____11____ problem have increased ____12____ destruction.

The text above illustrates the advantage of presenting a passage rather than a group of unrelated sentences for practice in article usage. In the last sentence, the definite article "the" is needed before the last two nouns because of second mention; "problem" is a partial repetition of "global problem," and "destruction" may be interpreted as either a synonym for "deterioration" or as a superordinate term for the effects mentioned previously.

Students usually enjoy exercises based on their own writing; they could even create their own cloze passages from a paragraph they have written and exchange them with a classmate. Cloze passages based on student texts can serve as an error correction technique if the writer has produced errors in the grammatical item deleted. Whatever the source, this type of cloze passage can provide an excellent context for discussing syntactic, semantic, or pragmatic features across sentence boundaries, ones that may influence writers' selections of such grammatical items as articles and pronouns.

Since gapped text completion exercises do not specify the number of words required for each blank, they can be used to elicit deleted verbs that include forms with more than one word, such as passives, progressive aspect, and present perfect. Other grammatical items that could be deleted for gapped exercises are comparatives, superlatives, phrasal verbs, and multi-word/phrasal logical connectors.

The third type of text completion asks students to consider syntactic structures with essentially the same meaning and to choose the more appropriate rendering of the information based on the preceding discourse context. This exercise type focuses students' attention on how features such as pronouns, partial repetition, and passive voice interact to create information flow. The following is an example, modeled after one by Rutherford (1988, p. 240). The appropriate choices are indicated by check marks:

> *Climatologists have predicted that the continual warming of the earth's surface, commonly known as "the greenhouse effect," could have dramatic consequences.*

1. (a) The melting of the polar ice caps could be one result.
   ✔ (b) One result could be the melting of the polar ice caps.

2. ✔ (a) This melting would, in turn, cause a rise of the sea level.
   (b) A rise of the sea level would, in turn, be caused by this melting.

This activity emphasizes the importance of context in making grammatical choices and shows how cohesion and coherence result from presenting information that is familiar to the reader at the beginning of the sentence, followed by the new information the writer wants to convey.

ERROR DIAGNOSIS AND CORRECTION

The discussion of grammar in writing in this chapter has emphasized the multidimensional aspects of grammar and the importance of form-focused instruction that does not center solely on errors. Grammar issues related to errors will, however, arise in almost every ESL/EFL writing class and for ESL writers in mainstream classes as well.

Truscott (1996) generated much debate about the wisdom of dealing with errors in composition; in response, Ferris (1999) noted flaws in Truscott's definition of error correction and in the research he used to support his argument. Teachers' classroom experience as well as research has indicated that ESL writers expect and appreciate assistance in improving their language accuracy (Ferris and Hedgcock 1998).

Error Detection and Correction Exercises

Once the teacher has assessed students' language needs, text-based exercises can be assigned to help students identify and correct errors and develop editing strategies. Whenever possible, the students' own writing should be used for exercises; students who do not have a particular problem can contribute via peer correction. The teacher will usually need to adapt a student text (e.g., correcting errors that are not the focus of the practice).

The following are useful error detection and correction techniques:

1. In a text with different types of errors, students are told the total number of each kind of error to identify and correct.
   Example: The text below has the following errors: 1 preposition, 1 verb tense, 1 subject-verb agreement, 1 missing article.

   This paper report on survey about values. Our English class take the survey last week in UCLA.

2. To focus on just one error type, students are given a text with numbered lines. They are told all of the line numbers that have a certain type of error.

Example: Identify and correct all of the verb form errors in the following text. Use the guide below to find the errors.

1 The Olympics were hold in Sydney, Australia
2 in 2000. Athletes from all over the world partici-
3 pated. The Olympics have inspire many young
4 people to excel in athletics.

Guide: Errors—Lines 1, 3

3. Use sentences from students' drafts to focus on one error type. Though the exercise will not consist of short texts, sentences from papers concerned with the same topic will provide coherence of theme and, most likely, vocabulary. The teacher can identify the grammar feature for correction focus, such as articles, word forms, prepositions, verb tense, or noun number.

Editing Strategies and Techniques

The benefits of focused work on diagnosing errors and developing editing strategies will certainly vary for students, depending on many complex variables involving the learners, the teachers' knowledge and experience in pedagogical grammar, and the writing context.

Shih (1998) identified characteristics of effective editors among ESL students. The more accurate writers devoted much time to revising and editing, continually worked on becoming aware of their gaps in linguistic competence and error patterns, and made a habit of reviewing their work constantly and editing recursively. The less accurate writers often waited until the final draft to give attention to language concerns, at which point they were overwhelmed by errors. Thus, the common advice to delay attention to grammar and editing until the final draft did not serve these students well.

Most ESL writers need to devote considerable time and effort to becoming good editors. Otherwise, many will fail to benefit from classroom exercises and practice or even from individual conferencing. Students should be encouraged to explore different strategies to find ones that serve them effectively.

The following are editing techniques some students find work well for them:

1. **Read-Aloud Technique** Many students find that slowly reading their drafts aloud to listen for errors can help them in making corrections. For shorter papers, some students who are aware of their error patterns read through the paper several times, listening for different kinds of errors each time. Shih (1998) notes that multiple readings are not realistic for long papers.
2. **Pointing to Words** Some writers use a pencil, pen, or finger to point to words one by one.
3. **"Slow-Down" Techniques** This involves reading a draft in some way that is in contrast to the normal linear process, such as starting with the last sentence in each paragraph and reading in reverse. Such a technique may help writers detect certain kinds of morphological errors such as missing plural endings, but would not work well for others, such as reference words or subject-verb agreement.
4. **Word Processing Grammar Checkers** Grammar checkers in word processors can flag certain kinds of errors. As long as writers do not blindly follow the suggestions (since grammar checkers can often create errors rather than correct them if suggestions are taken indiscriminately), checkers can be helpful in getting writers to pay attention to potential errors. If students do not understand the suggested correction, they should not make the change.

Teacher Feedback on Errors

The preceding discussion has focused on classroom exercises for identifying and correcting errors and on strategies for student editing. Another significant issue related to language errors in writing is, of course, teacher feedback on student writing. Kroll's chapter in this volume discusses this topic, which includes many kinds of response other than error feedback.

The following are some general guidelines and suggestions for providing feedback on grammar.

1. Indirect feedback is generally more useful (and often more desired by students) than direct correction of errors. Indirect feedback could involve one or more of the following: putting a check in the margin of the lines where errors occur; underlining or highlighting selected errors; coding errors either in the margins or above selected errors with symbols such as *vt* for verb tense, *wf* for word form, *art* for article, etc. (see, for example, Lane and Lange 1999); attaching a sheet to the writer's draft with a list of several structural errors along with exercises or handouts to help the writer better understand the grammatical system or feature involved (Celce-Murcia and Hilles 1988).

2. Teachers should not provide feedback on all errors in any one piece of writing—this can be overwhelming to students—but should focus on several errors the teacher considers as most needing attention.

3. Deciding which errors most deserve attention requires consideration of many student variables (e.g., metalinguistic knowledge, proficiency level) and the instructional situation. Errors to be pointed out may be those representing an individual's frequent error patterns, errors that most seriously affect communication, or stigmatizing errors.

4. While the bulk of teacher feedback on errors should occur in later stages of the writing process, teachers can alert students to areas of concern in early drafts also, so that all the attention to language errors does not need to be given with the last draft, when many students find they do not have sufficient time to address them effectively.

If the teaching environment permits conferencing with students outside of class, conferences are excellent opportunities to provide individual help. Alternatively, the teacher can hold "miniconferences" with individuals or small groups in the classroom. In conferences, teachers can demonstrate directly the difficulties a reader might have as a result of the grammatical errors in the students' writing. This setting allows the teacher to act as a collaborator rather than as an error detector/corrector. He or she can help students identify errors that create reader confusion or misinterpretation, explore the strategies for editing that best fit the writers' learning styles, set goals for improvement, and assess progress in these goals. Students can also provide insight into the sources of error, ones that a teacher might not even have considered, such as interference from a third language or an inaccurately formulated "rule." When students are able to analyze their error sources, the teacher can more effectively suggest editing strategies.

CONCLUSION

Second language writing pedagogy has been greatly influenced by developments in L1 composition teaching which have promoted the teaching of writing as a process and as a social activity. This process and social activity is also about language, however. This chapter's discussion of grammar in writing has supported the view that second language writers need attention to form in developing writing proficiency and that attention to form is not just about error but about resources for communicative goals. As Ponsot and Deen (1982, p. 133) put it, "Grammar is clearly not remedial. Like baking powder, it can't be stirred into the cake after the batter has been poured into pans."

ESL/EFL writing classroom pedagogy will certainly continue to change as the result of new research in related areas such as second language acquisition, rhetoric and composition, linguistics, education, and psychology. And future sociopolitical and sociolinguistic developments will no doubt cause us to reconsider long-held views about language and language teaching. Increased globalization and the development of world Englishes are even now challenging notions of "Standard English(es)." The increasing non-native English-speaking immigrant populations in English-speaking countries, especially in institutions of higher education, raise questions about what the expectations should be of "linguistic correctness," even in formal written English. And, of course, rapidly developing computer technology offers resources for individual tutorials in form-focused language instruction that were undreamed of in decades past. All these raise issues that writing teachers will need to be aware of and reflect on in making decisions about grammar in the writing classroom. Nevertheless, it seems that, in some form, the role of grammar will remain as an essential component of effective written communication.

DISCUSSION QUESTIONS

1. In what ways has the role of grammar in writing instruction been characterized? How do the different attitudes about grammatical instruction in composition reflect different ways of defining what grammar means?
2. How can grammar instruction be considered compatible with approaches that focus on writing as a process or with writing as a social activity?
3. Why is it important for grammar exercises to be (a) text based rather than a series of unrelated sentences, (b) developed from authentic discourse, and (c) presented in a communicative context rather than only as practice in grammatical structures?
4. If one of your students expressed disappointment that you did not correct all of the errors in his or her final drafts, how would you respond?
5. What are some advantages of teacher-student conferences in helping students with grammatical problems in writing?

SUGGESTED ACTIVITIES

1. Evaluate one or more grammar-oriented exercises in an ESL composition textbook or workbook. Use the following criteria: (a) What appears to be the purpose of the exercises? Do you think it is pedagogically sound? (b) Is the exercise text based? If not, do you think it is still appropriate for its purpose? (c) Does the language seem authentic? (d) If the exercise is included in a content-based or rhetorical framework (e.g., as part of a unit on persuasive writing), is it clearly and appropriately related to the discourse of that context? (e) If the exercise is not part of a larger writing context, for what aspect of writing instruction do you think it would be appropriate? (f) Does the level of difficulty seem appropriate for the intended learners? (g) Based on the previous criteria and any others you think relevant, summarize the strengths and weaknesses of the exercise or exercises.
2. Select a text that you think illustrates well the use of a particular grammatical structure (e.g., noncount nouns, frequency adverbs, agentless passives, presentative "there" to introduce information). Develop an exercise to accompany the text that students could complete in small groups as a classroom task or individually as a homework assignment. Explain the objective of the exercise and the writing context in which it might be used.
3. Write a reflective essay or journal entry on your own experiences with grammar in writing as a second language learner. To what extent was grammar associated primarily with diagnosing and correcting errors in your own second language writing? To what extent were you aware of the ways in which expanding your grammatical knowledge helped you improve your linguistic resources to express your ideas?
4. Examine several ESL/EFL compositions that have frequent and varied grammatical errors. For each composition, identify two of the most frequent or serious errors. Describe sets of exercises or activities that would help the writer to address these grammatical problems.
5. Interview ESL writing teachers about the techniques, both oral and written, that they have used to provide feedback on grammatical errors in their students' writing. During what stages of composing processes do they address errors? Which error feedback and/or correction techniques have they found to be most effective? What student variables have affected the success of techniques used?

FURTHER READING

Byrd, P., and J. Reid. 1998. *Grammar in the Composition Classroom: Essays on Teaching ESL for College-bound Students.* Boston, MA: Heinle & Heinle.

A collection of essays offering theoretical discussion and practical information for incorporating grammar in writing classes. Emphasizes learner-based approaches and selection of grammatical features based on corpus text analysis for teaching academic writing.

Ferris, D. Forthcoming. *Treatment of Error in L2 Student Writing.* Ann Arbor, MI: University of Michigan Press.

Provides a comprehensive overview of research on error feedback and other forms of grammar instruction. Discusses how teachers can prepare themselves to treat student error, describes error correction options, and other error treatment options such as revision and peer editing. Includes numerous suggestions and ideas for activities and lessons.

Shih, M. 1998. ESL Writers' Grammar Editing Strategies. *College ESL,* 8(2):64–86.

Describes characteristics of university ESL writers who developed successful editing strategies and those who were less successful. Offers suggestions for helping writers develop effective strategies and practice in all stages of composing.

UNIT II E

Language Skills

Grammar and Vocabulary

Grammar and vocabulary have often been viewed as competing elements in language teaching. The Reading Approach, for example, gave great emphasis to receptive vocabulary learning but treated grammar only sporadically, with the result that language learners using this approach could read literature but could not produce coherent and accurate sentences (in speech or writing) even after several years of language study. The Audiolingual Approach did the reverse: It emphasized grammar but suppressed vocabulary. The result was learners who had generally poor comprehension of natural, unedited spoken or written material, even after a year or more of intensive language instruction. We now know that both grammar and vocabulary are important for communication and that both can be taught without sacrificing one for the other. In this section, Larsen-Freeman's chapter presents effective grammar instruction as a multidimensional process that requires selective focus on form, meaning, and use within a communicative approach. Fotos's chapter argues for a cognitive approach to second or foreign language grammar instruction, using an information processing model to design grammar lessons for use in both traditional and communicative classrooms. The chapter by DeCarrico deals with issues in vocabulary pedagogy, vocabulary learning strategies, and the role of collocations; she then turns to new directions in vocabulary instruction (e.g., corpus-based research, multiword phrasal units). Taken together, these three chapters give us good coverage of what the linguist Michael Halliday refers to as *lexicogrammar*, a term that represents vocabulary and grammar as complementary and overlapping language resources.

Teaching Grammar

DIANE LARSEN-FREEMAN

In "Teaching Grammar," Larsen-Freeman challenges conventional views of grammar. Instead of simply analyzing grammatical form, she includes grammatical meaning and use as well. Then, building on what is known about the way grammar is learned, she offers ways to teach grammar consistent with contemporary theory and the need to "focus on form" within a meaning-based or communicative approach.

INTRODUCTION

Over the centuries, second language educators have alternated between two types of approaches to language teaching: those that focus on analyzing the language and those that focus on using the language. The former have students learn the elements of language (e.g., sounds, structures, vocabulary), building toward students' being able to use the elements to communicate. The latter encourage students to use the language from the start, however falteringly, in order to acquire it. Early in the previous century, this distinctive pattern was observable in the shift from the more form-oriented grammar-translation approach to the use-oriented direct method (Celce-Murcia 1980). A more recent example of the shift is the loss of popularity of the cognitive-code approach, in which analyzing structures and applying rules are common practices, and the rise of more communicative approaches, which emphasize language use over rules of language usage (Widdowson 1978).

Even though such language use approaches as task-based and content-based are in favor these days, educators agree that speaking and writing accurately is part of communicative competence, just as is being able to get one's meaning across in an appropriate manner. Further, it has been observed that although some learners can "pick up" accurate linguistic form from exposure to the target language, few learners are capable of doing so efficiently, especially if they are postpubescent or if their exposure is limited to the classroom, as is the case when English is taught as a foreign language. In contrast, research has shown that teachers who focus students' attention on linguistic form during communicative interactions are more effective than those who never focus on form or who only do so in decontextualized grammar lessons (Spada and Lightbown 1993; Lightbown 1998). It follows, then, that most educators concur with the need to teach grammatical form. However, they advise doing so by "focusing on form" within a meaning-based or communicative approach in order to avoid a return to analytic approaches in which decontextualized language forms were the object of study.

Focusing on grammatical form during communicative interactions rather than forms in isolation (Long 1991) is one way to prevent the pendulum from swinging beyond its point of equilibrium. In this chapter, we will encourage a balance between grammar and communication. The first step is to come to a broader understanding of grammar than has usually been the case. Equating grammar with form and the teaching of grammar with the teaching of explicit linguistic rules concerning form are unduly limiting, representing what we have called myths (Larsen-Freeman 1995), which only serve to perpetuate the pendulum swing between language form and language use. Grammar *is* about form and one way to teach form is to give students rules; however, grammar is about much more than form, and its teaching is ill served if students are simply given rules.

Thus, in this chapter, we will entertain a more robust view of grammar. Then, we will briefly touch upon issues concerning its learning. Finally, we will discuss its teaching.

A Three-Dimensional Grammar Framework

Since our goal is to achieve a better fit between grammar and communication, it is not helpful to think of grammar as a discrete set of meaning-less, decontextualized, static structures. Nor is it helpful to think of grammar solely as prescriptive rules about linguistic form, such as injunctions against splitting infinitives or ending sentences with prepositions. Grammatical structures not only have (morphosyntactic) form, they are also used to express meaning (semantics) in context-appropriate use (pragmatics). In order to guide us in constructing an approach to teaching grammar that strives to meet this definition, it would be helpful to have a frame of reference.

Our framework takes the form of a pie chart. Its shape helps us to make salient that in dealing with the complexity of grammar, three dimensions must concern us: structure or form, semantics or meaning, and the pragmatic conditions governing use.[1] Moreover, as they are wedges of a single pie, we note further that the dimensions are not hierarchically arranged as many traditional characterizations of linguistic strata depict.[2] Finally, the arrows connecting one wedge of the pie with another illustrate the inter-connectedness of the three dimensions; thus a change in any one wedge will have repercussions for the other two.

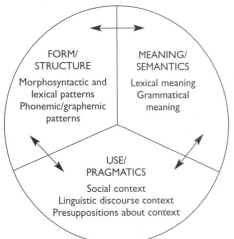

In the wedge of our pie having to do with structure, we have those overt lexical[3] and morphological forms that tell us how a particular grammar structure is constructed and how it is sequenced with other structures in a sentence or text. With certain structures, it is also important to note the phonemic/graphemic patterns (see the discussion of possessives and phrasal verbs below for examples). In the semantic wedge, we deal with what a grammar structure means. Note that the meaning can be lexical (a dictionary def-inition for a preposition like *down*, for instance) or it can be grammatical (e.g., the conditional states both a condition and outcome or result). It is very difficult to arrive at a definition of prag-matics distinct from semantics, and thus we are sympathetic to Levinson's (1983) suggestion that pragmatics deals with all aspects of meaning not dealt with by semantic theory!

Since this definition is too broad for our purposes here, however, we will limit pragmatics to mean "the study of those relations between language and context that are grammaticalized, or encoded in the structure of a language" (Levinson 1983, p. 9). We will leave the term *con-text* broad enough though, so that context can be social (i.e., a context created by interlocutors, their relationship to one another, the setting), or it can be a linguistic discourse context (i.e., the language that precedes or follows a particular structure in the discourse or how a particular genre or register of discourse affects the use of a structure), or context can even mean the pre-suppositions one has about the context.

The influence of pragmatics may be ascer-tained by asking two questions:

1. When or why does a speaker/writer choose a particular grammar structure over another that could express the same meaning or accomplish the same purpose? For example, what factors in the social context might explain a paradigmatic choice such as why a speaker chooses a yes-no question rather than an imperative to serve as a request for information (e.g., *Do you have the time?* versus *Please tell me the time*)?

2. When or why does a speaker/writer vary the form of a particular linguistic structure?

For instance, what linguistic discourse factors would result in a syntagmatic choice such as the indirect object being placed before the direct object to create *Jenny gave Hank a brand-new comb* versus *Jenny gave a brand-new comb to Hank?*

Despite the permeable boundaries between the dimensions, we have found it useful to view grammar from these three perspectives. We trust that the utility of this approach will become clearer as we proceed. A teacher of grammar might begin by asking the questions posed in the three wedges of our pie (for the sake of simplicity, labeled *form, meaning,* and *use*) for any given grammar point.

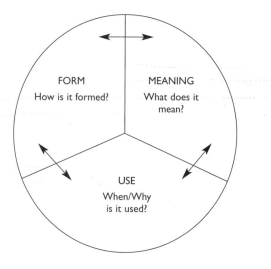

Let us consider an example. A common structure to be taught at a high-beginning level of English proficiency is the *'s* possessive form. If we analyze this possessive form as answers to our questions, we would fill in the wedges as below (analysis based on Celce-Murcia and Larsen-Freeman 1999).

Form of Possessive This way of forming possessives in English requires inflecting regular singular nouns and irregular plural nouns not ending in *s* with *'s* or by adding an apostrophe after the *s'* ending of regular plural nouns and singular nouns ending in the sound /s/. This form of the possessive has three allomorphs: /z/, /s/, and /əz/, which are phonetically conditioned: /z/ is used when it occurs after voiced consonants and vowels, /s/ following voiceless consonants, and /əz/ occurs after sibilants.

POSSESSIVES

Meaning of Possessive Besides possession, the possessive or genitive form can indicate description (*a debtor's prison*), amount (*a month's holiday*), relationship (*Jack's wife*), part/whole (*my brother's hand*), and origin/agent (*Shakespeare's tragedies*).

Also, although all languages have a way of signaling possession, they do not all regard the same items as possessable. For example, Spanish speakers refer to a body part using the definite article instead of a possessive form. ESL/EFL students will have to learn the semantic scope of the possessive form in English.

Use of Possessive Filling in this wedge requires that we ask when the *'s* is used to express possession as opposed to other structures that can be used to convey this same meaning. For example, possession in English can be expressed in other ways—with a possessive determiner (e.g., *his, her,* and *their*) or with the periphrastic *of the* form (e.g., *the legs of the table*). Possessive determiners are presumably used when the referent of the possessor is clear from the context. While ESL/EFL books will often say that the *of the* possessive is used with nonhuman head nouns and *'s* with human head nouns, we are aware of certain conditions where this rule does not apply. For example, native speakers often prefer to use the *'s* even with inanimate head nouns if the head nouns are performing some action (e.g., *the train's arrival was delayed*).[4] Finally, students will have to learn to distinguish contexts in which a noun compound (*table leg*) is more appropriate than either the *'s* form or the *of the* form.

Thus, by using our ternary scheme, we can classify the facts that affect the form, meaning, and use of the possessive structure. This is only a first step. Teachers would not necessarily present all these facts to students, recognizing that students can and do learn some of them on their own. And certainly no teacher would choose to present all these facts in a single lesson or on one occasion. Nevertheless, distributing the features of the target grammatical structure among the three wedges of the pie can give teachers an understanding of the scope and multidimensionality of the structure. In turn, this understanding will guide teachers in deciding which facts concerning the possessive will be taught and when and how to do so.

Before continuing to explore these decisions, however, it might be worthwhile to apply our approach to another grammar structure. Let us analyze phrasal verbs this time. By considering the three questions posed earlier, we can state the following about phrasal verbs (analysis based upon Celce-Murcia and Larsen-Freeman 1999):

PHRASAL VERBS

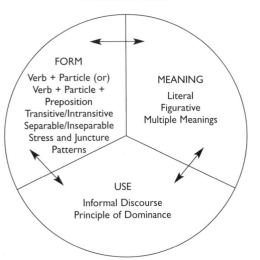

Form of Phrasal Verbs Phrasal verbs are two-part verbs comprising a verb and a particle (e.g., *to look up*). Sometimes, they can be constructed with three parts in that a preposition can follow the particle (e.g., *to keep up with*). As with all other verbs, phrasal verbs are either transitive or intransitive. A distinctive feature of phrasal verbs is that for many of them the particle can be separated from its verb by an intervening object (e.g., *Alicia*

looked the word up in the dictionary). Phrasal verbs also have distinctive stress and juncture patterns, which distinguish them from verb plus preposition combinations:

Alicia loòked úp#the word.

Alicia wálked#ŭp the street.

Meaning of Phrasal Verbs There are literal phrasal verbs, such as *to hang up*, where if one knows the meaning of the verb or the particle or both, it is not difficult to figure out the meaning of the verb-particle combination. Unfortunately, for the ESL/EFL student there are far more instances of figurative phrasal verbs (e.g., *to run into*, meaning "meet by chance") where a knowledge of the meaning of the verb and of the particle is of little help in discerning the meaning of the phrasal verb. Moreover, as with single-word verbs, phrasal verbs can have more than one meaning (e.g., *to come across*, meaning "to discover by chance" as in *I came across this old book in the library*, or when used intransitively, "to make an impression" as in *Richard came across well at the convention*.

Use of Phrasal Verbs When is a phrasal verb preferred to a single-word verb that conveys the same meaning (e.g., *put out a fire* versus *extinguish a fire*)? For the most part, phrasal verbs seem to be more common in informal spoken discourse as opposed to more formal written discourse. When is one form of a phrasal verb preferred to another; i.e., when should the particle be separated from its verb (e.g., *put out a fire* versus *put a fire out*)? Erteschik-Shir's (1979) principle of dominance seems to work well to define the circumstances favoring particle movement: If a noun phrase (NP) object is dominant (i.e., a long, elaborate NP representing new information), it is likely to occur after the particle; if the direct object is short, old information (e.g., a pronoun), it would naturally occur before the particle.

Identifying the Challenge Again, we would like to underscore the fact that it would not be reasonable for the ESL/EFL teacher to present all of this information to students at once. The framework does, however, help to organize the facts. Furthermore, by doing this, teachers can more easily identify where the learning challenge(s) will lie for their students. Identifying the challenging dimension(s) is a key step which should be taken prior to any pedagogical treatment.

All three dimensions will have to be mastered by the learner (although not necessarily consciously). For phrasal verbs, it is the meaning dimension which ESL/EFL students struggle with most. It is often the fact that there is no systematic way of learning to associate the verb and the particle. Adding to the students' woes, new phrasal verbs are constantly being coined. By recognizing where students will likely struggle, an important clue is given the teacher as to where to focus work on phrasal verbs. We will amplify this point later. For now, however, it is worth noting that although it is grammar structures which we are dealing with, it is not always the form of the structures which creates the most significant learning challenge.

"Grammaring" We should pause here to acknowledge that as important as it is to develop our understanding of the grammatical facts of the language we are teaching, it is not these facts that we wish our students to learn. We are not interested in filling our students' heads with grammatical paradigms and syntactic rules. If they knew all the rules that had ever been written about English but were not able to apply them, we would not be doing our jobs as teachers. Instead, what we do hope to do is to have students be able to use grammatical structures accurately, meaningfully, and appropriately. In other words, grammar teaching is not so much knowledge transmission as it is skill development. In fact, it is better to think of teaching "grammaring" (Larsen-Freeman 1997; 2001), rather than "grammar." By thinking of grammar as a skill to be mastered, rather than a set of rules to be memorized, we will be helping ESL/EFL students go a long way toward the goal of being able to accurately convey meaning in the manner they deem appropriate.

The Learning Process

However important and necessary it is for teachers to have a comprehensive knowledge of their subject matter, it is equally important for them to understand their students' learning process. This understanding can be partly informed by insights from second language acquisition (SLA) research concerning how students naturally develop their ability to interpret and produce grammatical utterances. Three insights are germane to our topic:

1. Learners do not learn structures one at a time. It is not a matter of accumulating structural entities (Rutherford 1987).[5] For example, it is not the case that learners master the definite article, and when that is mastered, move on to the simple past tense. From their first encounter with the definite article, learners might master one of its pragmatic functions—e.g., to signal the uniqueness of the following noun. But even if they are able to do this appropriately, it is not likely that they will always produce the definite article when needed because learners typically take a long time before they are able to do this consistently. Thus, learning is a gradual process involving the mapping of form, meaning, and use; structures do not spring forth in learners' interlanguage fully developed and error-free.

2. Even when learners appear to have mastered a particular structure, it is not uncommon to find backsliding occurring with the introduction of new forms to the learners' interlanguage. For example, the learner who has finally mastered the third person singular marker on present-tense verbs is likely to overgeneralize the rule and apply it to newly emerging modal verbs, thus producing errors such as *She cans speak Spanish.* Teachers should not despair, therefore, at regressive behavior on the part of their students. Well-formedness is usually restored once the new additions have been incorporated and the system self-organizes or restructures.

3. Second language learners rely on the knowledge and the experience they have. If they are beginners, they will rely on their L1 as a source of hypotheses about how the L2 works; when they are more advanced, they will rely increasingly on the L2. In understanding this, the teacher realizes that there is no need to

teach everything about a structure to a group of students; rather, the teacher can build upon what the students already know. It also follows that the challenging dimension for a given grammatical structure will shift from class to class depending on the students' L1 backgrounds and level of L2 proficiency. Successful teaching involves identifying the relevant challenge for a particular group of students.

To these three observations, we will add a fourth one that is not to our knowledge treated in the SLA research literature, but rather one based upon our observations and supported by learning theorists (e.g., Gagné and Medsker 1996).

4. Different learning processes are responsible for different aspects of language. Indeed, given that language is as complicated as it is, one would not expect the learning process to be any simpler. It is clearly an oversimplification to treat all grammar learning as resulting from habit formation or from rule formation. Being aware that different learning processes contribute to SLA suggests a need for the teaching process to respect the differences. How the nature of the language challenge and the learning process affect teaching decisions is the issue to which we turn next.

The Teaching Process

Consistent with the way we are conceiving grammar in this chapter, teaching grammar means enabling language students to use linguistic forms accurately, meaningfully, and appropriately. In this section we discuss various teaching strategies that can be employed to meet this goal.

In keeping with language form approaches, traditional grammar teaching has employed a structural syllabus and lessons composed of three phases: presentation, practice, and production (or communication), often referred to as "the PPP" approach. As we saw earlier, underlying this approach is the assumption that one systematically builds towards communication. However, as mentioned in the introduction to this chapter, these days, most teachers embrace a more

communicatively oriented approach, starting with a communicative activity such as task- or content-based material (see chapters by Savignon and Snow in this volume). The grammar that is taught is not scheduled in advance as it is with a structural syllabus/PPP approach, but rather supports students in their completion of the communicative task or their making sense of a particular content area. In addition, or alternately, teachers respond to grammar errors that students commit when engaged in communication. As such, it reverses the normal sequence (Skehan 1998b), putting communication first, rather than selecting and presenting a grammar structure in advance of its use in context.

Even if the grammar to be worked on is derivative rather than scheduled in advance, a teacher must still decide how to address it. A variety of options have been suggested (see Doughty and Williams 1998; R. Ellis 1998), although the research findings underpinning them are somewhat sparse and sometimes contradictory (see Mitchell 2000 for a recent review). One option is simply to bring to students' attention, or to promote their *noticing* of, some feature of a grammatical structure. For example, if a student makes an error and the teacher decides to respond to it, then the teacher might *recast* or *reformulate* what the student has said or written incorrectly in a more accurate, meaningful, or appropriate manner. For instance, if it is an error of form, the teacher would recast the student's production accurately.

STUDENT: This is Juan notebook.
TEACHER: Oh. That is Juan's notebook. (perceiving the error to be the form of the possessive)

If meaning is the problem, the teacher would recast what the student has said in a meaningful way.

STUDENT: I need to look at the word in the dictionary.
TEACHER: You need to look up the word in the dictionary. (perceiving the phrasal verb *look up* to be a better form for what the student means to say)

And if use is the problem, the teacher would recast what the student has said in a more appropriate manner:

STUDENT: I arise at six in the morning.
TEACHER: OK. You get up at six in the morning.
(perceiving that a phrasal verb would be more appropriate to convey the student's intended meaning)

A more proactive way to promote students' noticing a particular grammatical structure is to highlight it in a text in some fashion. *Enhancing the input* (Sharwood Smith 1993) might be an especially effective way to focus students' attention on grammar structures that operate at the discourse level of language, such as articles or verb tenses. By boldfacing all the normally insalient articles in a given passage, for instance, the students' attention could be drawn to them. Even simply choosing texts in which a particular structure or structural contrast is especially frequent would enhance its saliency and thus might promote noticing, a practice sometimes called *input flooding.*

Still another option is to use a *consciousness-raising task,* in which it is the students' job to induce a grammatical generalization from the data they have been given. For example, Fotos and Ellis (1991) ask students to work out the rule for indirect object alternation in English (e.g., *They gave a gold watch to him./They gave him a gold watch.*) by giving the students example sentences where indirect object alternation can and cannot be successfully applied. Indirect object alternation is difficult in English and therefore is an ideal candidate for this sort of explicit rule articulation. Indeed, Carroll and Swain (1993) suggest that when the rules are not that clear-cut, detailed instruction with explicit metalinguistic feedback may be the most helpful response to student errors.

Another option for promoting students' awareness is to use *the garden path* strategy (Tomasello and Herron 1988; 1989). As applied to grammar teaching, this means giving students information about structure without giving them the full picture, thus making it seem easier than it is, or in other words, "leading them down the garden path." If ESL/EFL students were told that the English past tense is formed with *-ed,* for example, this would be leading students down the garden path as there are many irregular verbs in English where this rule will not work to produce the past tense. The reason for giving students only a partial explanation is that they are more likely to learn the exceptions to the rule if they are corrected at the moment the overgeneralization error is made than if they are given a long list of "exceptions to the rule" to memorize in advance.

Another technique for directing students' attention to form is called *input processing* (Van Patten 1996). Rather than working on rule learning and rule application, input processing activities push learners to attend to properties of language during activities where the structure is being used meaningfully. For instance, if students are asked to carry out commands that teachers issue, they are working on matching the imperative form to its use in a meaningful way.

Of course, sometimes a communicative task itself requires that students attend to relevant features of the target language (Loschky and Bley-Vroman 1993), such as when using a particular grammatical structure is essential to completing the task. An example of this is when students have to use particular prepositions to accurately give each other directions using a map. The added value of using a communicative task to promote noticing is that students are encouraged to use the target structures, thereby generating "output" that attracts feedback from a teacher or another student.

Speaking of output, it might be surprising to experienced teachers to read descriptions of all these teaching options with very little mention of student production. But, of course, students' production plays a very important role in learning grammar. It is not enough to have awarenesses raised if students can't produce the language. *Output production* is, therefore, extremely important. For one thing, it pushes students to move beyond semantic processing to syntactic processing (Swain 1985). Then, too, when students attempt to produce structures, they get to test their hypotheses on how the structure is formed or what it means or when it is used. Following these attempts, as we have seen, they can receive feedback on their hypotheses and modify them as necessary.

Indeed, Donato (1994) has shown how students' participation in *collaborative dialogue,* through which learners can provide support for each other, has spurred development of learners' interlanguage. Other research (Swain and Lapkin 1998) corroborates the value of an interactive dialogue as both a cognitive tool and a means of communication which can promote grammatical development.

Beyond these reasons for giving students an opportunity to produce the target grammatical structures, we have already presented the idea that grammar teaching can better be thought of as developing "grammaring," i.e., helping students be able to use grammar skillfully, a goal that requires significant practice. To this point, Gatbonton and Segalowitz (1988) have argued that practice of grammatical patterns can lead to automatization of certain aspects of performance, which, in turn, frees up students' attentional resources to be allocated elsewhere.

It used to be that the practice phase of a lesson was devoted almost exclusively to grammar drills and exercises. Ever since the ineffectiveness of using drills which do not engage students' attention was acknowledged, there has been little by way of guidance offered on how to give students meaningful practice. What follows, therefore, is an attempt to fill this void. Practice activities will be addressed in terms of which dimension of language they relate to.

Form

From what we know of skill acquisition theory (e.g., Anderson and Fincham 1994), fluency or proceduralization of declarative knowledge (e.g., knowledge of a grammar rule or pattern) requires practice in which students use the target language point meaningfully while keeping the declarative knowledge in working memory (DeKeyser 1998).

It is important to emphasize *meaningful* practice of form for several reasons. First of all, meaningless mechanical drills, such as repetition drills, commonly associated with behaviorist approaches to learning, do not engage the learner in the target behavior of conveying meaning through language. Furthermore, because students are not engaged in target behavior, the inert knowledge problem (Whitehead 1929) is likely to materialize. Inert knowledge is knowledge that can be recalled when students are specifically asked to do so but is not available for spontaneous use, in, say, problem solving, even when the knowledge is relevant to the problem at hand. Knowledge remains inert when it is not available for transfer from the classroom context to the outside world. We know that when the psychological conditions of learning and application are matched what has been learned is more likely to be transferred (e.g., Blaxton 1989). Thus, rules and forms learned in isolated meaningless drills may be harder to retrieve in the context of communicative interaction (Segalowitz and Gatbonton 1994). Finally, student motivation is likely to be enhanced if students are able to interact in a way that is meaningful to them. Then, too, they are likely to be more attentive if they are saying something meaningful.

Identifying the type of learning involved helps us to think about the desirable characteristics of any practice activity. For instance, for declarative knowledge to be proceduralized a great deal of *meaningful* practice would be required. Further, students would have to receive feedback on the accuracy with which they produced the target form. They would have to be restricted to using just the particular target form; in other words, structural diversity would not be permitted.[6] Finally, for proceduralization to occur, it would seem important to concentrate on only one or two forms at a time, although, of course, the target form could be introduced in contrast to forms that the student already controls.

Let us take an example and see how these characteristics are applied. If our students show us that they are struggling with the inversion of the subject and operator in yes-no questions, it would be clear that their immediate learning challenge is linguistic form. We will need to design or select an activity that encourages *meaningful* practice of the pattern, not verbatim repetition. We want the students to concentrate on producing only yes-no questions. A game like Twenty Questions would appear to meet the criteria. Students get to ask 20 yes-no questions about an object or person in an attempt to guess the identity; hence, they receive abundant practice in forming the questions, and the questions they produce are meaningful. The teacher would work with each student to enable him or her to produce the pattern accurately, perhaps providing an explicit rule, perhaps not.

An example of a game that would work on the form of the English possessive comes from Kealey and Inness (1997). Students are given a family portrait in which the child's face is missing. They are also given clues as to what the child looks like, e.g., the child has the mother's eyebrows or the father's chin. A person from each small group into which the students are divided comes to the front of the room, takes a clue, memorizes it, and brings it back to his or her group so that the feature in the clue can be drawn. This continues until the child, a composite of his mother and father, is fully drawn.

In sum, certain games are good devices for practicing grammar points where the challenge resides in the formal dimension. While not an activity in and of itself, another useful device for working on the formal dimension is the use of cuisenaire rods. The rods are ideal for focusing student attention on some syntactic property under scrutiny. One example that comes to mind is an adaptation of Stevick's (1980) Islamabad technique. Practicing the form of OS[7] relative clauses, students might be asked to use the rods to construct a view of some spot in their hometown. The students would be encouraged to use OS relative clauses where appropriate (e.g., *There is a fountain that is located in the center of my town; Around the fountain there are many people who sell fruits, vegetables, and flowers,* etc.).

One final example of a type of useful activity for working on the formal dimension is a problem-solving activity. The problem to be solved could be most anything, but if we are dealing with the formal dimension, then we would want it to conform to the characteristics described above. An example might be an information-gap activity where the students are given a class information sheet with certain items missing (see bottom of this page).

Students could circulate asking one another *Wh*-questions (e.g., *What is Beatriz's major? How old is Werner?*) in order to complete the chart. Another example might be a sentence-unscrambling task. This is a useful problem-solving activity when the challenge is getting students to produce correct word order, such as when the objective is to have students use auxiliary verbs in the proper sequence.

It is important to take note that there is nothing inherent in the three examples we have provided (games, use of rods, problem-solving activities) which make them useful for addressing the formal dimension; i.e., we could easily use rods to work on some aspects of the meaning or use dimensions. What is significant to remember is that the activity should be structured in such a way that it is compatible with the characteristics presented earlier.

Meaning

If the teacher has decided that the challenge of a particular structure lies in the semantic dimension, then a different sort of practice activity should be planned. It would seem that meaning would call for some sort of associative learning (N. Ellis 1998), where students have opportunities

Name	Age	Country	Language	Major	Hobby
Beatriz	18	Bolivia	Spanish	Dentistry	_____
Mohammed	19	Algeria	_____	Accounting	Going to the movies
Jean Claude	_____	France	French	_____	Painting
_____	18	Brazil	_____	Education	Hiking
Werner	17	_____	Swiss German	Business	_____

to associate the form and the meaning of the particular target structure. It has been our experience that repetition is not needed to the same extent as it is when teaching some aspect of the formal dimension. Sometimes a single pairing of form and meaning suffices. Due to memory constraints, it seems prudent to restrict the number of new items being practiced at any one time to between two and six (Asher 1996). The students would receive feedback on their ability to demonstrate that they had acquired the form-meaning bond.

Celce-Murcia and Hilles (1988) mention that when dealing with the semantic dimension, realia and pictures are very useful. Thus, for example, if the teacher has decided to work on the semantics of comparative forms in English to support some communicative task or content, he or she might show students pairs of pictures and work with them to make comparisons using the form that reflects the relation depicted (e.g., *as _____ as, more _____ than, less _____ than*).

Actions, too, can make meaning salient. The initial challenge for ESL/EFL students grappling with prepositions is to associate the "core" meaning with each. Thus, prior to having students work on direction-giving tasks using maps (*Walk to the corner. Turn right at the corner. The cinema is near the corner, next to the bank.*), a good strategy might be to work with students on having them make an association between a preposition and its meaning in locating objects in space. One way of doing this is to conduct a Total Physical Response sequence where students act out a series of commands along with the teacher, involving the placement of objects in various parts of the room; e.g., *Put the book next to the desk, Put the pen on the book, Walk to the door, Stand near the door,* etc. Once students appear to have made the connection between form and meaning, the teacher can assess their ability to discriminate one form-meaning bond from another by having them carry out commands on their own and by issuing novel commands—e.g., *Put the pen on the desk*—and assessing their ability to comply.

We said earlier that a persistent challenge for students' learning phrasal verbs was the fact that the meaning is often not detectable from combining the meaning of the verb with the meaning of the particle. Sometimes teachers have had their students play Concentration, a version of the game in which the students have to associate a phrasal verb written on one card with its definition written on another card. Another example of an activity that would address this semantic challenge is an operation (Nelson and Winters 1993). In an operation, a series of separate actions are performed to accomplish some task. The teacher might issue commands, or mime the actions with the students as she or he describes them.

> *I want to call up my friend. First, I look up the phone number. Then I write it down. I pick up the receiver and punch in the number. The number is busy. I hang up and decide to call back later.*

By practicing this operation several times, the students can learn to associate the form and meaning of certain phrasal verbs (*call up, look up, pick up,* etc.). If students are given an operation with which to associate phrasal verbs, recall at a later time will likely be enhanced. To determine if students can distinguish among the various phrasal verbs, students might be given phrasal verbs out of sequence and asked to mime the appropriate action. Feedback on their ability to match form and meaning can be given.

Use

When use is the challenge, it is because students have shown that they are having a hard time selecting the right structure or form for a particular context. Working on use will involve students learning that there are options to be exercised and that they must select from among them the one which best suits a given context.

Thus, relevant practice activities will provide students with an opportunity to choose from two or more forms the one most suitable for the context and how they wish to position themselves (e.g., in a cooperative way, a polite way, an assertive way, etc.). Students would receive feedback on the appropriateness of their choice. In some cases, their choice might involve selecting between two options (e.g., when to use the passive versus the active voice). Other times, their choice would be from among an array of options (e.g., which modal verb to use when giving advice to a boss); hence, the number of forms being worked on at one time would be at least two, but could involve many more.

Role plays work well when dealing with use because the teacher can systematically manipulate social variables (e.g., increase or decrease the social distance between interlocutors) to have students practice how changes in the social variables affect the choice of form.

For example, if students have shown that they do not know how to use modals to give advice, they might be asked to role-play having a "dilemma." In this role play, one person has a problem; (e.g., the keys to the car have been lost. The car is locked and the person wants to get in.) Students are asked to use modal verbs to give advice to the person with the problem; e.g., *You might try breaking the window, You could try calling the police.* The teacher could next alter a salient feature of the context, thus creating a new social context in which a different modal verb would be more appropriate. For example, the teacher might ask, "What if it were a young child that had this dilemma?" A more appropriate form and content for the advice, then, might be *You had better wait for your mother to come!*

On another occasion, students might be asked to play the role of an advice columnist. They are to write a column and give advice to a classmate who is having a particular problem. Having students work with the same structure in writing and in speaking activities can highlight differences between written and oral grammars (Carter and McCarthy 1995).

Role plays are useful for highlighting other structural choices as well. Often we find that it is neither the form nor the meaning of the English tenses that presents the greatest long-term challenge to ESL/EFL students; rather it is when/why to use one tense and not the other. In other words, it is the pragmatic usage of the tenses that is the major obstacle to their mastery. Giving students practice with situations in which a contrast between two tenses is likely to arise may sensitize students to the usage differences. For instance, a notorious problem for ESL/EFL students is to know when to use the present perfect versus when to use the past tense. A situation where a

contrast between them would occur might be a job interview. In such a context, the perfect of experience is likely to be invoked (e.g., *Have you ever done any computer programming?*). An elaboration to an affirmative answer is likely to contain the past tense (e.g., *Yes, I have. I once worked on . . .* or simply, *Yes. When I worked at . . .*). Students can take turns role-playing the interviewer and interviewee.

As was mentioned earlier, it is not only the social context that will be involved in the choice of which forms to use, but also it is often the linguistic discourse context that will make a difference. Thus, it is very important to consider teaching discourse grammar (Celce-Murcia 1991a; Hughes and McCarthy 1998). Such is the case with the passive voice. Its use is not particularly sensitive to social factors; i.e., whether one is using the active or passive voice does not necessarily depend upon with whom one is conversing. What usually does cause students considerable difficulty with the passive voice, however, is determining when to use it. The fact that the agent of an action is defocused motivates the use of the passive. Furthermore, if the agent has already been established in the linguistic discourse, it would likely not even be mentioned in subsequent discourse. Thus, most passive sentences are agentless.

Challenges of this nature call for text-generation or text-manipulation-type exercises. As the passive is used more often in written than in spoken English, teachers might give their students a text-completion exercise in which the first few lines of the text are provided. For example, from the first few lines in the following text, it should be clear to the students that the theme of discourse is on the "issues," not the agents (i.e., participants), at the town meeting.

> Town meetings were held throughout New England yesterday. Many issues were discussed, although the big one for most citizens was the issue of growth. Many changes have been made recently. For example, . . .

Students then are asked to complete the text using the appropriate voice. As not all the sentences should be in the passive voice, students will be making choices, in keeping with a characteristic of practice activities designed to work on the use dimension. The teacher will give feedback to the students on the appropriateness of their choices.

Before leaving our discussion of the passive voice, it would be useful to illustrate why we feel that identifying the challenging dimension is a worthwhile step to take before teaching any grammar structure. When we are clear where the challenge lies, the challenge can shape our lessons. For instance, as we stated earlier, it has been our experience that the greatest long-term challenge for students working on the passive voice is for them to figure out when to use the passive. Keeping this in mind will help us avoid a common practice of ESL/EFL teachers, which is to introduce the passive as a transformed version of the active (e.g., "Switch the subject with the direct object . . ."). Presenting the passive in this way is misleading because it gives the impression that the passive is simply a variant of the active. Moreover, it suggests that most passive sentences contain agents. What we know in fact to be the case is that one voice is not a variant of the other, but rather the two are in complementary distribution, with their foci completely different. We also know that relatively few passive sentences contain explicit agents. Thus, from the first, the passive should be taught as a distinct structure which occurs in a different context from the active. (See Celce-Murcia and Larsen-Freeman 1999, for several examples of how to do this.)

It should be noted that the pie chart, the observations about learning, and the characteristics of practice activities enumerated here may not significantly alter the way grammar is taught today. Indeed, many of the activities recommended here are currently being used. What these tools do offer, how-ever, is a principled means for dealing with grammar. They should help teachers to make clear decisions they teach grammar. They should help teachers to design effective activities or to choose from among those in a textbook without assuming that just because a textbook activity deals with the target structure, it necessarily addresses the particular learning challenge that their students are experiencing.

This brings us to the close of our discussion on how to design practice activities for grammar points.

Providing Feedback

Providing learners with feedback, negative evidence which they can use to correct their misapprehensions about some aspect of the target language, is an essential function of language teaching. Even such indirect feedback as asking a learner for clarification of something he or she has said may be helpful (Schachter 1986). It has always been a controversial function, however (Larsen-Freeman 1991). There are, for instance, those who would proscribe it, believing that a teacher's intervention will inhibit students from freely expressing themselves or that there is little evidence demonstrating that learners make use of the feedback they have been given—there is little immediate "uptake" of the correct form. While there are clearly times that such intervention can be intrusive and therefore unwarranted (e.g., in the middle of a small-group communicative activity), at other times focused feedback is highly desirable. Further, immediate uptake cannot be the sole criterion of its usefulness. Negative evidence gives students the feedback they need to reject or modify their hypotheses about how the target language is formed or functions. Students understand this, which explains why they often deliberately seek feedback.

The same pie chart that we used when identifying the learning challenge and creating practice activities can also be a useful aid in diagnosing errors. When an error is committed by a student, a teacher can mentally hold it up to the pie chart to determine if it is an error in form, meaning, or use. Of course, sometimes the cause of an error is ambiguous. Still, the pie chart does provide a frame of reference, and if the diagnosis is accurate, the remedy may be more effective. More than once we have observed a teacher give an explanation of linguistic form to a student, when consulting the pie chart would have suggested that the student's confusion lay with the area of use instead.

As for how the feedback is to be provided, we have already mentioned several useful options— recasting, for instance. Getting students to self-correct is another (see Lyster and Ranta 1997). Giving students an explicit rule is a third. Some teachers like to collect their students' errors, identify the prototypical ones, and then deal with them collectively in class in an anonymous fashion. Which of these options is exercised will depend on the teacher's style, the proficiency of the students, the nature of the error, and in which part of the lesson the error has been committed.

None of these have to be used exclusively, of course. For instance, Aljaafreh and Lantolf (1994) offer a graduated 12-point scale ranging from implicit to explicit strategies, beginning with student identification of errors in their own writing, moving to where the teacher isolates the error area and inquires if there is anything wrong in a particular sentence, to where the teacher provides examples of the correct pattern when other forms of help fail to lead to a self-correction on the part of the student.

RELATED PEDAGOGICAL ISSUES

Sequencing

Earlier we noted that grammar structures are not acquired one at a time through a process of "agglutination" (Rutherford 1987). Rather, different aspects of form, meaning, and use of a given structure may be acquired at different stages of L2 development. This observation confirms the need for recycling—i.e., working on one dimension of a form and then returning to the form from time to time as the need arises. To some extent this will occur naturally, as the same structures are likely to be encountered in different communicative tasks and content areas. However, it is also the case that not all linguistic structures that students need to learn will be available in the language that occurs in the classroom.

Therefore, it will be necessary for the teacher to "fill in the gaps," i.e., to introduce structures that don't naturally arise in classroom discourse (Spada and Lightbown 1993). For this reason, teachers might think in terms of a *grammar checklist*, rather than a grammatical sequence. By this, I mean that it would be a teacher's responsibility to see that students learn certain grammatical items by the end of a given course or

period of time, but not by following a prescribed sequence. Many structures would arise naturally in the course of working on tasks and content and would be dealt with then. Other structures might be introduced as the teacher determined that the students were ready to learn them. Rather than adhering to a linear progression, the choice of sequence would be left up to the teacher and would depend on the teacher's assessment of the students' developmental readiness to learn.

Many teachers, of course, have little control over the content or sequence of what they work on. They must adhere to prescribed syllabi or textbooks, although even in such a situation, it may be possible for teachers not to follow a sequence rigidly. But for those teachers who have more flexibility, research on acquisition orders is germane. Some SLA research has shown that learners progress through a series of predictable stages in their acquisition of particular linguistic forms. One explanation for the order rests on the complexity of the speech-processing strategies required. Thus, all structures processable by a particular strategy or cluster of strategies should be acquired at roughly the same developmental stage. This approach has been shown to account for certain acquisition orders in ESL (Pienemann and Johnston 1987).

Despite these findings and their potential implications for grammatical structure sequencing, there has been no definitive acquisition order established, and thus teachers are still left to their own resources for judgments on how to proceed. We should also note that even if an acquisition order were to be fully specified for English, there might be justification for preempting the acquisition order when students' communicative needs were not being met and when, therefore, certain structures would need to be taught, at least formulaically. Furthermore, Lightbown (1998) has suggested that even if students are asked to work on structures before they are ready to acquire them, such effort may not be in vain because such instruction might prime subsequent noticing on the part of the students, thereby accelerating acquisition when they are indeed ready.

Inductive Versus Deductive Presentation

An additional choice teachers face is whether to work inductively or deductively. An inductive activity is one in which students infer the rule or generalization from a set of examples. In a deductive activity, on the other hand, the students are given the rule and they apply it to examples. For instance, when practicing an inductive approach to the mass/count noun distinction in English, students could be presented with a language sample, such as a grocery advertising circular. They then would be encouraged to make their own observations about the form of mass and count nouns. The teacher might listen to their observations and then might summarize by generalizing about the two categories of nouns. If practicing a deductive approach, the teacher would present the generalization and then ask students to apply it to the language sample.

As we see, if a teacher has chosen an inductive approach in a given lesson, a further option exists—whether or not to give or have students articulate an explicit rule. Earlier, we stated that equating the teaching of grammar with the provision of explicit rules was an unduly limited view of what it means to teach grammar. We said this because what we are trying to bring about in the learner is linguistic behavior that conforms to the rules, not knowledge of the rules themselves. Having said this, we see no reason to avoid giving explicit rules as a means to this end, except perhaps if one is working with young children. Usually students request rules and report that they find them helpful. Moreover, stating a rule explicitly can often bring about linguistic insights in a more efficacious manner, as long as the rule is not oversimplified or so metalinguistically obtuse that students must struggle harder to understand the rule than to apply it implicitly (Robinson 1996).

Returning now to the inductive versus deductive question, we again find that the choice is not one resolvable with an either/or approach. There are many times when an inductive approach such as using a consciousness-raising task is desirable because by using such an approach one is nurturing within the students a way of thinking, through which they can arrive at their own generalizations. In addition, an inductive approach allows teachers to assess what the students already know about a particular structure and to make any necessary adjustments in their lesson plan. Clearly, a teacher's anticipation of where the challenge lies is not always borne out when he or she assesses students' actual behavior.

Other times, when students have a particular cognitive style that is not well suited for language analysis or when a particular linguistic rule is rather convoluted, it may make more sense to present a grammar structure deductively.

Indeed, Corder's sensible observations offer comfort:

> What little we know about . . . second language learning . . . suggests that a combination of induction and deduction produces the best result. . . . The old controversy about whether one should provide the rule first and then the examples, or vice versa, is now seen to be merely a matter of tactics to which no categorical answer can be given (Corder 1973 in Rutherford and Sharwood Smith 1988, p. 133).

Patterns and Reasons, Not Rules

Before concluding, we should make two final observations about grammar teaching. With the increased access to large corpora of language data that computers afford, it has become clear that grammatical structures and lexical items occur in a large number of regularly occurring patterns (Sinclair and Fox 1990; Biber, Conrad, and Reppen 1998). Not all lexical items can be freely substituted into a particular pattern. Once one lexical item is selected, the likelihood of a particular item or phrase following is increased. For example, if the verb *insist* is chosen, either *on* or *that* is very likely to follow. An implication of corpus-based research is that teachers of grammar should pay more attention to conventionalized lexicogrammatical units, and not simply focus on teaching grammatical rules (Pawley and Syder 1983; Nattinger and DeCarrico 1992;

Lewis 1997). Indeed, connectionist modeling has demonstrated that morphology (Ellis and Schmidt 1997) and syntax (MacWhinney 1997) acquisition may be accounted for by simple associative learning principles (N. Ellis 1998), rather than as a product of rule application.

Another challenge to equating the teaching of rules with the teaching of grammar comes from Larsen-Freeman's (2000a) suggestion that teachers concentrate on teaching "reasons, not rules." Larsen-Freeman points out that although rules don't allow for change, language is changing all the time. A consequence is that most rules have "exceptions." Furthermore, many rules appear arbitrary because they are form based, ignoring the meaning and use dimensions. For instance, rather than telling students they must use an indefinite noun phrase after the verb in a sentence beginning with existential *there*,

> *There is a snowstorm coming.*

help them understand the reason: *there* introduces new information in the noun following the verb, and in English, new information is marked with indefinite determiners. This reason is broad based and explains a number of English word-order phenomena. While rules provide some security for learners, reasons give them a deeper understanding of the logic of English and help them make it their own. Besides, reasons are meaning based and use based and are in keeping with the more robust view of grammar we have been promoting in this chapter.

PROFESSIONAL DEVELOPMENT

Finally, the form, meaning, and framework can be used by teachers to assess where there are gaps in their own knowledge of English grammar. When they can't fill in all the wedges in the pie chart for a given structure, they can consult reference grammars. Of course, there are many gaps in what is known about the three dimensions. In particular, there is much to learn about the pragmatic conditions governing the use of particular structures. For this reason, the pie chart can also be used to generate items for a research agenda. By exploring the three dimen-

sions of grammar and how to teach them, teachers will continue to develop their professional knowledge base, which will, in turn, benefit their students as they strive to enhance their grammatical proficiency.

DISCUSSION QUESTIONS

1. Think of all the language teaching approaches with which you are familiar. Can you categorize them according to whether they favor language form or language use?
2. In explaining the pragmatics of phrasal verbs, the principle of dominance was invoked. Explain why the principle of dominance falls in the pragmatic dimension.
3. The effect of the native language on second language learning has traditionally been seen to be one of *interference*. How does observation 3 on the learning process (pp. 255–256) differ in its perception of L1 influence?
4. Why was it stressed that the repetition in a practice activity for working on form should be meaningful?
5. Why is it important to identify the challenge in a particular grammar structure for a particular group of students, even if the aspect of structure you are planning to teach lies in a different wedge of the pie from where the challenge lies?

SUGGESTED ACTIVITIES

1. Think of a language teaching approach which tends to favor language use over language form. How could the approach incorporate more language form? Now think of an approach that favors language form over language use. How could a focus on language use be integrated?
2. Analyze restrictive relative clauses in terms of the three dimensions of the pie chart. What has been the most challenging dimension for the students with whom you have worked?
3. Design practice activities for dealing with the pragmatics of the following:

a. falling versus rising intonation in tag questions

b. indirect object alternation

c. presence or absence of existential *there*

 FURTHER READING

Bygate, M., A. Tonkyn, and E. Williams, eds. 1994. *Grammar and the Language Teacher.* Hemel Hempstead. UK: Prentice Hall International.
Offers ways that grammar in language teaching can be reaffirmed and maintained in order to avoid the pendulum swing.

Celce-Murcia, M., and S. Hilles. 1988. *Techniques and Resources in Teaching Grammar.* New York: Oxford University Press.
Discusses issues germane to teaching grammar and provides abundant examples of techniques and materials applied to teaching English structures.

Celce-Murcia, M., and D. Larsen-Freeman. 1999. *The Grammar Book: An ESL/EFL Teacher's Course.* 2d ed. Boston, MA: Heinle & Heinle.
Seeks to guide teachers to an understanding of the grammar of those structures they will have to teach (their form, meaning, and use in context) and offers relevant teaching suggestions for those same structures.

Doughty, C., and J. Williams, eds. 1998. *Focus on Form in Classroom Second Language Acquisition.* Cambridge: Cambridge University Press.
Provides an overview of second language acquisition research that has investigated "focus on form."

Larsen-Freeman, D. 2001. *Teaching Language: From Grammar to Grammaring.* Boston, MA: Heinle & Heinle.
Argues for a reconceptualization of grammar and the way it is taught, featuring grammar as a complex, nonlinear, dynamic system.

Rutherford, W. 1987. *Second Language Grammar: Learning and Teaching.* London: Longman.
Treats grammar in an interesting and provocative way that challenges the view that learning grammar is an "accumulation of entities."

Ur, P. 1988. *Grammar Practice Activities: A Practical Guide for Teachers.* Cambridge: Cambridge University Press.
Discusses pedagogical issues followed by a number of grammar teaching activities grouped according to the grammar structure for which they work best.

ENDNOTES

1 Some time after I had begun view grammar in this way, the work of Charles Morris (1939) was brought to my attention. Although he uses the terms in a somewhat different manner, Morris applies the ternary scheme of syntactics, semantics, and pragmatics in portraying the field of semiotics or the study of signs. The ternary scheme we are adopting here may also sound reminiscent of Kenneth Pike's "particle, wave and field" (1959). Although there is some overlap, there is no isomorphism between the models.

2 For example, the model of language that descriptive linguists prefer is one in which various areas of language are depicted as strata in a linguistic hierarchy, beginning with the sounds of language as the lowest level from which all else is composed and following in turn with morphemes, lexicon, syntax, and discourse.

3 We include lexis here, acknowledging that grammar and lexis are just two poles on a continuum and that there are many patterned multiword phrases that are basic intermediate units between lexis and grammar. Following Halliday (1994), then, it is probably more accurate to think in terms of "lexicogrammar."

4 For more exceptions to this rule, consult Celce-Murcia and Larsen-Freeman (1999, pp. 314–316).

5 For this reason, Rutherford has suggested that an optimal approach to dealing with the nonlinearity of grammatical acquisition might be one where teachers help students achieve an understanding of general principles of grammar, e.g., how to modify basic word order, rather than concentrating on teaching structure-specific rules.

6 Such a restriction might seem uncharacteristically autocratic in today's climate, where one of the features of the Communicative Approach is that students be given a choice of how they wish to express themselves. It is our contention, however, that students have a true choice only if they have a variety of linguistic forms at their disposal which they can produce accurately. Without being restricted to using a particular target form during a form-focused activity, students will often avoid producing the structure and, hence, never have an opportunity to truly learn it.

7 An OS relative clause is one in which the subject of the embedded sentence is replaced by a relative pronoun because the subject is identical to an object or objectlike noun in the predicate of the preceding main clause. (For example: I like the book that he wrote.)
o   s

Cognitive Approaches to Grammar Instruction

SANDRA FOTOS

Fotos's chapter presents a cognitive approach to second/foreign language teaching. An information-processing model is used to design a grammar lesson that develops formal grammatical knowledge of the target grammar structure and promotes its acquisition through meaning-focused use of the form in communicative activities. This approach can be used in both traditional and communicative classrooms.

INTRODUCTION

This chapter presents a cognitive approach to teaching English grammar in the ESL or EFL context. We will consider different perspectives on the relationship of language to thought to see where a cognitive approach fits in, examine the components of a cognitive model from the perspective of language teaching, and then develop a cognitive approach to grammar instruction for both communicative and traditional classrooms. This approach is designed to help learners develop both fluency and accuracy.

What Is a Cognitive Approach?

Cognitive science is a relatively new field emerging in the mid-1950s with the work of cognitive psychologists, linguists such as Chomsky (1957), and the establishment of artificial intelligence as a research area. It is cross-disciplinary, with contributions from psychology, philosophy, psycholinguistics, neuroscience, artificial intelligence, and cognitive anthropology, but the shared focus of research is the working of the mind. Within psycholinguistics and applied linguistics are a number of cognitive approaches which, unfortunately, cannot all be addressed in this short chapter. We will therefore treat language learning and grammar instruction from the information-processing perspective, the dominant cognitive paradigm, and the reader is referred to cognitive scientists such as Eysenck and Keane (1995) or Harley (1995) for a discussion of other approaches.

In a review article on cognitive approaches to second language acquisition (SLA), one major researcher (N. Ellis 1999) notes that the study of cognition in language learning deals with "mental representations and information processing" (p. 22) and seeks to develop "functional and neurobiological descriptions of the learning processes which, through exposure to representative experience, result in change, development and the emergence of knowledge" (p. 23). In this definition, both first and second language learning are seen to use the same general information-processing mechanisms that are responsible for all forms of knowledge and skills development. Language learning is thus placed within the context of cognitive development in general. This approach differs from views which hold that language development takes place within a special module in the brain, a point which will be discussed in more detail later.

The Need for a Cognitive Approach

The usefulness of a cognitive approach to grammar instruction in ESL/EFL becomes clear when we consider the problems with purely communicative approaches. These tend to be based on theories which distinguish between language *acquisition*—an unconscious process similar to the way children learn their first language—and language *learning,* or formal instruction on rules, forms, and vocabulary. These theories claim that the best way to learn a language, either inside or outside a classroom, is not by treating it as an object for study but by experiencing it meaningfully, as a tool for communication—perhaps with target grammar structures physically highlighted or embedded within communicative activities as recommended by current "focus-on-form" approaches to grammar instruction (see Doughty and Williams 1998).

This view may be acceptable for many ESL classrooms, although considerable research shows that when students receive only communicative lessons, with no instruction on grammar points, their level of accuracy suffers (see R. Ellis 1997 and Mitchell 2000 for reviews). However, such an approach is not useful by itself in EFL contexts because adequate access to communicative use of English is usually not available, and students need to develop accurate English grammar, vocabulary, and translation skills to pass high school and university entrance examinations. Thus, in the EFL setting, formal grammar instruction is usually the norm, even though many teachers would like students to develop communicative skills as well.

It is therefore not surprising that many ESL/EFL teachers look for a compromise between the two extremes of a structure-based curriculum, with its teacher-led classrooms and formal instruction on a series of isolated language forms, versus a purely communicative classroom, with its emphasis on group work and no focus on linguistic forms whatsoever. Many teachers now prefer an eclectic approach, administering some type of grammar instruction within a communicative framework, and this is reflected in the mixture of activities in the newer multidimensional textbooks for ESL/EFL students.

There is considerable research support for this position, and it is common to distinguish between two types of classroom activities: *meaning-focused,* referring to purely communicative practices where the goal is to process meaning, and *form-focused,* referring to practices that draw attention to the way language forms are used in discourse. This distinction is very important in current pedagogy, and both meaning-focused and form-focused activities are thought to be necessary for successful development of both fluency and accuracy in second/foreign language learning (DeKeyser 1998; R. Ellis 1997; also see Rutherford and Sharwood Smith 1988).

The value of meaning-focused communicative activities that provide learners with comprehensible input (also called "positive evidence") and opportunities to improve and correct their own output through interaction with others has been demonstrated repeatedly. However, form-focused activities emphasizing the features of particular grammar points are also necessary in order for learners to develop accuracy. Such activities range from indirect approaches to grammar instruction, such as the focus-on-form activities mentioned above, to traditional formal instruction where students are presented with grammar rules, examples, and practice exercises. Such form-focused approaches have been found to be effective in developing the learner's ability to use grammar forms communicatively if instruction is then followed by opportunities to encounter the instructed grammar point frequently in communicative usage, a consideration which will be discussed in detail later.

Below we will consider different views of the relationship of language to thought as a way of understanding why a cognitive approach to communicative grammar instruction is recommended.

THE RELATIONSHIP BETWEEN LANGUAGE AND THOUGHT

Fossil evidence indicates that Broca's area, the part of the human brain associated with language, existed in hominids more than two million years ago, and many scientists believe that the capacity for symbol construction and language use developed from this time as the brain increased in size and complexity. The origin of language has been linked to the development of consciousness, and it is suggested that the ability to use language has been determined by the process of Darwinian natural selection[1] (Pinker 1994). It is no wonder that the nature of the relationship between language and thought has been debated for the past two thousand years. Theories of grammar instruction must therefore be informed by this debate.

A major controversy has been the initial state of the mind. Is it blank at birth, a *tabula rasa* waiting for experience to determine the structure of thought and language, as empiricists such as the philosophers Locke and Hume have argued, or are there preexisting mental modules, inborn templates which organize language and thought in the developing child, as suggested by rationalists (including Chomsky) ever since Plato? The empiricist-rationalist debate continues to the present, and in our field of second language teaching/learning these two general positions continue to influence grammar instruction.

Currently there are four main views of the relationship between language and thought (for a fuller discussion, see the overviews in Bialystok and Hakuta 1994 and in Harley 1995). One view derives from the attempts of structural linguists in the early part of the twentieth century to characterize cultures by the features and complexity of their languages. This is represented by the Sapir-Whorf hypothesis (see Carroll 1956), which suggests that both thought and language are determined by culture. For example, culturally determined phenomena such as the time of events or the color or shape of objects might become especially important for grammar learning in a given language, and, by extension, in thinking as well. Known as linguistic determinism, this position refers to the idea that people's thought processes are culturally determined by the features of the language they speak.

However, research indicates that the strong version of the Sapir-Whorf hypothesis, that language determines thought, is unsupported whereas the weak version has significant implications for intercultural communication. If a concept exists in one language but cannot be expressed easily in another, this difference may have an impact on cognitive style and the ease of cross-cultural communication involving the concept. For example, it has been suggested that Chinese or Japanese ESL/EFL learners might avoid using articles since their languages lack this grammar form. Likewise, teachers must be aware of learners' culturally determined rhetorical pattern preferences when teaching academic writing in ESL/EFL classes.

The second view of the relationship between language and thought is held by researchers such as the child psychologist Piaget (1967), and suggests that cognitive development in the infant occurs in clearly defined stages and precedes language. Thus, before infants can learn language forms such as nouns, they must possess certain cognitive prerequisites such as an understanding that objects have a permanent existence. However, research does not support a strong version of this view either and it is not currently a central focus of investigation.

A third theory derives from the rationalist concept of innate mental structures and views language and cognition as separate. This approach is represented by the work of Chomsky (1957) and, more recently, by Pinker (1994) who argue that language is an innate, human-specific ability which is not dependent on other cognitive processes. Children are genetically equipped to acquire language in infancy, when they are not capable of complex thought, and therefore instinctively do so without extensive exposure to a variety of language forms (an argument called the "poverty of stimulus"). Thus some type of language template must already exist in the mind—an autonomous module of "universal grammar," awaiting minimum input for activation and "setting" according to the rules of the specific language. Language is considered to be syntax and morphology—and, more recently, also grammatical features encoded in the lexicon. Syntax and morphology are the grammatical rules that determine how morphemes are combined into grammatical units to produce meaning. Features common to all languages, termed language universals, include nouns, verbs, and certain word order rules which link syntactic categories to functional roles such as "agent."

Although the existence of innate principles has received some empirical support, it has also been suggested that social interaction is of major importance in developing language capacity. This fourth view comes from interactionists such as Vygotsky ([1934] 1962), who hold that thought and language are initially separate but become interdependent during acts of communication since meaning is created through interaction. Empirical support for the sociocultural position is not yet abundant; however, current research on the formation of "communities of practice" in second/foreign language classrooms (see, for example, Donato and McCormick 1994), this defined as "a social area in which learning is constructed as gradually increasing participation in the values, beliefs and behaviors takes place" (Donato and McCormick 1994, p. 454), suggests that such collaborate construction of meaning promotes proficiency gains.

A related social interaction theory comes from investigation of infant grammatical development in Western Samoa and Papua New Guinea by Ochs and Schieffelin (1995). These researchers recommend a language socialization approach to grammar acquisition, where sociocultural contexts, rather than innate structure or grammatical frequency, are suggested to guide grammar development. For example, very common grammar structures may not be used by children if these structures are not socially or culturally appropriate, whereas grammar structures seldom used in general may be used often by children if such use is expected and appropriate.

An additional contribution in this area is the cross-discipline field of Cognitive-Functional Linguistics, as represented by the work of Tomasello (1998) and others. These researchers view grammar as a functional response to communicative needs shaped by the social contexts in which these needs arise.

A Cognitive Perspective

As the noted cognitive psychologist Trevor Harley (1995) observes, support exists for the weak version of all four positions and the relationship between thought and language is most likely quite complex. Thus it reasonable to suggest that all these positions have a part in the language development sequence. Language capacity appears to be innate, but its development is mediated by prior cognitive development, social interaction, and culture-specific concepts expressed through structures and vocabulary. Whereas the immature brain appears to be "wired" for unconscious and rapid language acquisition, successful activation of this capability appears to change with time so that the cognitive functions of attention and effort become increasingly necessary for older children and adults to learn a second language, just as for learning any skill. Today's cog-

nitive perspectives treat language learning within the context of general skills development, "not as an autonomous 'mental organ' but rather . . . [as] a complex mosaic of cognitive and social communicative activities closely integrated with the rest of human psychology" (Tomasello 1998, p. ix). As a consequence, Bialystok and Hakuta observe (1994), there are no barriers to second language acquisition and there is no single correct method for language teaching. These researchers recommend that

> [A]n integrated view that assembles components from various disparate sources in both theory and practice . . . then attempts to piece them together in a complex pattern, is precisely what practitioners need in order to allow them the freedom to interpret these patterns for their own purposes and from their own point of view (1994, p. 218).

THREE COMPONENTS OF A COGNITIVE MODEL OF SECOND/FOREIGN LANGUAGE LEARNING

Researchers using cognitive models to study second/foreign language learning (e.g., McLaughlin 1987; Ellis 1999; Skehan 1998; Tomasello 1998) note that psycholinguistic perspectives have been underrepresented due to influences from structural linguistics and Chomskian theories of an innate language acquisition module. As mentioned, although granting that innate processes appear to guide first language acquisition in small children, many researchers suggest that after a certain age (called the "critical period," suggested to be at puberty, when myelination of neuron connections occurs [Pulvermüller and Schumann 1994]) second/foreign language learning can be explained cognitively using the three components of an information processing model: (1) input, (2) central processing, and (3) output. These three components will be discussed on the following pages.

Input

In a cognitive approach to second/foreign language learning, access to target language input is seen as perhaps the most critical requirement for language development. In fact, one influential researcher asserts that "second language acquisition is shaped by the input one receives" (Gass 1997, p. 161). Input provides essential positive evidence, the language data that allows acquisition to occur. Although a direct relationship between language learning and input has yet to be determined, there has been considerable work on manipulating input to make it easier for students to understand (see R. Ellis 1997 and Gass 1997 for reviews). For example, teachers have simplified the grammar and vocabulary of written or audio material, decreased sentence length, decreased the speed of audio material, provided clarifying interaction during the input process, and physically highlighted important grammar points and vocabulary, or repeated them many times during communicative activities. These operations make it more likely that the learners will be able to selectively perceive or *notice* the input—a necessary step since people cannot take up and process all of the input they constantly receive, but rather can select only certain input for attention, uptake, and processing. Since the brain's input processing capacity is limited, researchers such as Skehan (1998a) and Tomasello (1998) emphasize that many ESL/EFL students, especially those at lower levels of proficiency, cannot process target language input for both meaning and form at the same time. Therefore, it is suggested that students have to be able to selectively perceive or notice target forms in input before processing can take place. This is a cognitive explanation for the research finding that a purely communicative approach to language instruction for all but the youngest learners will usually not develop high levels of accuracy. The students process input for meaning only and do not attend to specific forms. Thus, the forms are not taken up and processed and are consequently not acquired.

The stages for processing selected/noticed input are: (1) the encoding stage, where existing knowledge located in long-term memory is activated and used to interpret the new input and construct meaning from it; (2) a transformation stage, where the input is transformed to meaning, this taking place in short-term or working memory, and (3) a storage stage, in which the meaning is rehearsed and then transferred for storage in long-term memory.

Information Processing

Information processing refers to the many complex mental transformations which occur between input and output. Two basic psychological concepts are used to understand the mind's construction of meaning from language input: *bottom-up* and *top-down* processing. The first refers to the process of decoding specific bits of information from input. For example, a reader recognizes the individual letters that make up words and the syntactic rules which organize the words into sentences, or a listener recognizes the individual sounds which make up words and the words which make up sentences. In contrast, top-down processing refers to the use of world knowledge, past experience, expectations, predictions, and intuitions stored in the individual's mind in order to make sense of input. Top-down processing is necessary to understand the implications, context, and pragmatic meaning of input. In an information processing approach, top-down and bottom-up processing are suggested to operate simultaneously to interpret incoming information. Here the individual combines the new information from input with existing information stored in long-term memory—new knowledge being developed from the interaction of input with prior knowledge.

From the language teaching perspective, it is clear that ESL/EFL students can use top-down processing to understand the general meaning of communicative input without needing to understand all of the grammar forms or vocabulary. This is another reason that purely communicative approaches often fail to develop accuracy in producing the target language, even though students appear to comprehend it reasonably well.

Short-Term and Long-Term Memory Cognitive scientists make a distinction between short-term, or working memory, and long-term, or secondary memory. Short-term memory receives input but is limited in storage capacity. Research suggests that generally only seven items can be stored for about a minute in short-term memory, whereas long-term memory is limitless. Transfer from working memory to storage in long-term memory is therefore very important, and has been suggested to be facilitated by *noticing* an item in input, a process that recently has become very important in second/foreign language pedagogy. Two types of long-term memory are distinguished—semantic memory, which is the organized knowledge an individual possesses, considered to exist in hierarchies or *schemata*, and episodic memory, the global memory of a particular event. However, both types of memory, short- and long-term, are important in the development of knowledge about a language.

Two Forms of Knowledge   Knowledge has been divided into two general types: (1) declarative or explicit knowledge and (2) procedural or implicit knowledge.[2] Declarative/explicit knowledge is knowledge *about* something. It is factual information which is conscious, and is thought to consist of propositions (language-based representations) and images (perception-based representations). For example, when students are able to remember grammar rules, they are drawing on their explicit knowledge.

In contrast, procedural/implicit knowledge is knowing *how* to do something and is usually unconscious. Like any other skill, such as driving a car, singing a song, or playing the piano, the ability to speak a second/foreign language fluently is a skill that is dependent on procedural knowledge used automatically. When discussing the difference between the two forms of knowledge, one language researcher suggests that

> declarative knowledge is factual knowledge, for example . . . knowing that most English verbs take "s" in the third person. Procedural knowledge encodes behaviour. It consists of condition-action pairs that state what has to be done under certain circumstances or with certain data . . . Fully automatized procedural knowledge

means, for instance, that one uses the 3rd person "s" . . . without having to think about it (DeKeyser 1998, pp. 48–49).

These two types of knowledge are suggested to exist in long-term memory as different systems. For example, a student may have formal knowledge of the grammar rules for English indirect object placement but be unable to use indirect objects correctly in conversation. This is because formal grammar lessons develop only explicit/declarative knowledge, or the ability to talk about grammar rules, whereas the ability to use the form correctly depends on the operation of implicit/procedural knowledge.

In the past, many advocates of communicative language teaching argued that these two knowledge systems lacked any interface, so to teach students the grammar rules of a second/foreign language only gave them explicit knowledge and did not develop their ability to use the grammar points in real communication. However, recent research (see N. Ellis 1999; DeKeyser 1998; Skehan 1998; and Schmidt 1990) suggests that the two language knowledge systems are, in fact, connected by noticing or awareness, a connection which has been referred to as the "Noticing Hypothesis" (Schmidt 1990).

Noticing and Awareness   Noticing works as follows. Once a student becomes aware of a particular grammar point or language feature in input—whether through formal instruction, some type of focus-on-form activity, or repeated exposure to communicative use of the structure—he or she often continues to notice the structure in subsequent input, particularly if the structure is used frequently (Fotos 1993; Schmidt 1990). Repeated noticing and continued awareness of the language feature is important because it appears to raise the student's consciousness of the structure and to facilitate restructuring of the learner's unconscious system of linguistic knowledge. Thus, when a student pays attention when receiving a grammar lesson and doing practice exercises, he or she becomes aware of the grammar feature. When that feature is subsequently encountered in communicative input, the student often tends to notice it, recalling that he or she learned about it previously. When this happens frequently, his or her unconscious language system begins to develop new hypotheses about language structure, altering his or her existing language system or *interlanguage*. The student tests the new hypotheses—again unconsciously—by noticing language input and by getting feedback on the accuracy of his or her own output when using the form. In this way, explicit knowledge developed by formal instruction about a language feature has led to the acquisition of that feature although indirectly and over time.

Schmidt's Noticing Hypothesis has stimulated the development of teaching methods which are "consciousness raising" (see discussions of the term in Fotos 1993 and Rutherford and Sharwood Smith 1988) in that they promote noticing and continued awareness of the target language form. A good example of this approach to teaching is the "focus on form" approach, a term defined in the words of its originator, as "Overtly drawing students' attention to linguistic elements as they arise incidentally in lessons whose overriding focus is on meaning or communication" (Long 1991, pp. 45–46). As mentioned earlier, focus-on-form activities (Doughty and Williams 1998) usually constitute implicit grammar instruction only, and include "flooding" communicative material with target forms, physically highlighting them within purely communicative activities in such a way that students' attention is drawn to them, and structuring communicative activities so that students must use the forms for successful performance/completion.

Serial and Parallel Processing A final point concerns the distinction between serial and parallel processing of information. *Serial processing* is linear or sequential and takes place one step at a time, whereas *parallel processing* is a special model of cognition based on the idea that many processes occur simultaneously and are interconnected, forming neural networks of various levels of activation depending on what is being processed. Initial processing steps are usually done serially; input is received and selectively taken into short-term memory with the aid of attention and various strategies. However, the encoding or organization of input is complex since some items are encoded consciously, with effort, attention, and other strategies, whereas other items are encoded unconsciously, and it is even possible for a particular item to be encoded both consciously and unconsciously at the same time. Thus, a parallel processing model of language input better represents the nature of this complex co-occurring process (see the Appendix in Harley 1995 for a discussion of connectionism and parallel processing).

Output

Output is the final part of an information processing model. In second/foreign language learning theory it has been suggested that giving learners the opportunity for output is just as important as giving them input (Swain 1985) because output serves critical functions in the learning process. When language learners experience difficulties as they attempt to use the target language to communicate, they often become aware of what they need to know to express themselves effectively. They may ask their fellow students or their teacher for help, or use their textbook or dictionary to locate the required phrases or forms. Such effort tends to focus attention on the difficult language form and promotes noticing of it. Comprehension alone does not produce this favorable result since, as mentioned, it is possible for students to understand the general meaning of what is being said by using top-down processing—guessing, predicting and world knowledge—without fully understanding all the grammar or vocabulary.

Furthermore, according to the Interactionist view of the relationship of language to thought, when students produce the target language or ask/answer questions about grammar points or vocabulary, they are focusing on form, which assists them in extending their knowledge of the target language. This is particularly true when learners are forced to deal with their own problematic utterances and modify or elaborate them so that listener understanding is facilitated, a process called "negotiation of meaning" (see R. Ellis 1997 for a fuller discussion).

Negative Evidence

When learners produce utterances with errors, if they receive corrective feedback from teachers/peers explaining the correct use of the form, or if the teacher/peer "recasts" or repeats the utterance so that the correct form is used, such error correction can provide "negative evidence," thereby facilitating learners' noticing of the correct form. In addition, error correction can encourage students to build form-meaning relationships and, through self-correction, to "push" their output further in the direction of improved accuracy (Swain 1985). In fact, the learner's production of output—particularly when the output has been successfully corrected as the result of feedback from others—can then serve as new input.

Practice in a Skills-Based Approach

Another pathway for converting explicit to implicit knowledge is suggested by skill acquisition theory, a branch of cognitive science studying how people develop skills (see Anderson 1995). In this theory, knowledge is first seen to be declarative (although not all knowledge starts off as conscious knowledge); then, through practice and the application of learning strategies, declarative knowledge becomes proceduralized so that it becomes automatic. Automatic processes are quick and do not require attention or conscious awareness. For example, many second/foreign language learners memorize and practice vocabulary items or "chunks" of language such as greetings or collocations (words which are always used together). Frequent practice in using these forms helps the language items to become automatic in the sense that the learner can use them quickly and unconsciously.

Automatization can take place with both implicit and explicit knowledge. An example of nonautomatic explicit knowledge is monitoring, paying conscious attention to the use of correct forms during language production, whereas nonautomatic processing of implicit knowledge can be seen in the use of hesitation phenomena during the English speech produced by an ESL/EFL learner as he or she unconsciously searches his or her long-term memory for the correct form. From the automatization perspective, practice drills and repetitions of instructed grammar points—methods now very much out of favor in communicative ESL pedagogy because they remind people of the behaviorist Audiolingual Approach of the 1950s and early 1960s—are useful in that they facilitate both automatization of the practiced form and noticing (DeKeyser 1998), so that the form can make its way into the implicit knowledge system.

The Teachability Hypothesis

An important consideration at this point relates to the Chomskian concept of a natural or pre-determined "universal" order for language acquisition. Is there a set order for language development in the brain, in which case formal instruction may be ineffective if the student is not at the appropriate stage? This question has been investigated since the 1960s (see Corder 1967), and has received new attention recently as a Teachability Hypothesis (Pienemann 1989), proposing that second/foreign language learners will not acquire a new structure until they are developmentally ready to do so. If there were no connection between the development of explicit knowledge about a grammar point and the eventual restructuring of the unconscious linguistic system to accommodate the point in the learner's internal interlanguage, then, indeed, grammar instruction would not be of much use. However, it has been suggested that there *is* a connection, so grammar instruction is ultimately useful. Further, as the previous section emphasizes, practice of language points can lead to automatization, thus bypassing natural order/teachability considerations.

A COMMUNICATIVE ESL/EFL GRAMMAR LESSON

Shortly we will present a cognitive model for second/foreign language learning showing the relationship between explicit knowledge, gained through instruction, and implicit knowledge, developed through both restructuring of the internal target language system and through practice. This model also emphasizes the facilitating role of production and strategy use. Let us work through the model, using as an example a communicative ESL/EFL grammar lesson combining explicit formal instruction with performance of a structure-based communicative task (for more discussion of this task type, see Fotos 2001), followed by practice and production exercises and subsequent communicative exposure to the grammar point. From the students' perspective, the important features of this grammar lesson are that students

1. become aware that a particular grammar point is difficult for them;
2. become aware—either through teacher instruction (a deductive method) or by their own discovery learning (an inductive method)—of grammar rules which determine the correct forms of the grammar point and the variety of meanings it can convey in communicative language;
3. are provided with examples of the structure in communicative input so that they can notice the various form-meaning relationships;
4. are provided with opportunities to produce the grammar point.

Pedagogical Grammar

Combining the terms *communicative* with *grammar teaching* might seem to be a contradiction to many teachers, but let us recall that research strongly supports administering some type of grammar instruction within otherwise communicative language lessons (see the review in Mitchell 2000). Thus, the concept of *pedagogical grammars*, or the way a grammar point is instructed, is important here because of its emphasis on the various communicative roles a particular grammar point can serve within natural language use.

Pedagogical grammars have been defined as "the types of grammatical analysis and instruction designed for the needs of second language students" (Odlin 1994, p. 1) and are a concept of

grammar which differs from "linguistic grammars," which are complex linguistic analyses of language forms and functions. For pedagogical grammar, teachers select grammar points on the basis of their students' communicative needs, considering the language functions they will encounter. Such a functional approach to grammar is not new, but recently there has been a strong emphasis on the use of *authentic materials* (e.g., materials used by native English speakers to communicate with other native speakers, in contrast to simplified material written especially for use with ESL/EFL students) to provide examples of the various discourse functions that grammar points can serve in communication (see Odlin 1994 for more discussion). It is therefore essential to teach students that meaning can be expressed in a variety of ways, using various grammar forms, and that often there is no single "correct way" to express a particular meaning.

An overview article on grammar instruction in applied linguistics (Mitchell 2000) notes that grammar teaching/learning research has not yet determined (1) which model of language acquisition best informs pedagogic grammar; (2) how grammar forms should be chosen and sequenced; (3) how necessary it is for students to know general rules about grammar; and (4) what types of corrective feedback are best. Nonetheless, the same author presents a useful set of research-based general principles which can guide the teaching of grammar in second/foreign language classrooms:

1. grammar teaching should be planned and systematic, driven by a strategic vision of eventual desired outcomes;
2. grammar teaching should nevertheless be "rough tuned," offering learners at slightly different stages a range of opportunities to add increments to their grammar understanding;
3. grammar teaching may involve acceptance of classroom code switching and mother tongue use, at least with beginners;
4. grammar teaching should be "little and often," with much redundancy and revisiting of issues;
5. text-based, problem-solving grammar activities may be needed to develop learners' active, articulated knowledge about grammar;

6. active corrective feedback and elicitation will promote learners' active control of grammar;

7. grammar teaching needs to be supported and embedded in meaning-oriented activities and tasks, which give immediate opportunities for practice and use (Mitchell 2000, p. 297).

Guided by these considerations and the cognitive principles of language learning explored earlier, the next section introduces a model grammar lesson.

An Example of a Communicative Grammar Lesson Using Explicit Instruction

In this grammar lesson, the medium of instruction is English, the target language. Use of English rather than the students' native language (L1)—often the default choice in EFL situations—promotes the development of implicit knowledge since the students are focused on the meaning of what is being said, even though what is being discussed is English grammar. However, when the students do not understand, the teacher uses the students' L1 to facilitate comprehension.

The lesson consists of the following five parts: (1) a general orientation to the lesson followed by explicit instruction on the target grammar structure; (2) performance of a communicative task in which the task content is a problem involving the grammar structure; (3) review of the grammar structure as it is used in the task material; (4) multiple postlesson exposures to communicative material containing the grammar structure; (5) systematic review of the structure after each communicative activity.

Part 1: Using an Advance Organizer, a learning concept developed by the cognitive psychologist Ausubel (1968) which has been popular in general education since the 1960s, the teacher begins by giving the students a general orientation to the activities to come. To assist comprehension, this introduction may be given in the students' L1. First the teacher tells the students about the purpose and procedures of the task

activity, then he or she explains the target grammar structure. Use of an Advance Organizer is believed to activate the students' previously developed knowledge for top-down processing, and assist them in linking the new information to what they already know. In this case, the students are told that they will study a problematic grammar structure—indirect object placement. The teacher explains that English indirect object placement is often confusing because there are different rules for different verbs. The teacher then presents three patterns for indirect object placement in English verbs, writing examples on the board.

The first pattern allows placement of the indirect object either after the verb or as a prepositional phrase at the end of the sentence (e.g., He gave *me* the book. He gave the book to *me.*); the second allows placement only as a clause-final preposition phrase, which is generally the case for Latinate verbs (e.g., She translated the letter for *him.*); and the third, applicable to a limited set of verbs such as "cost," places the indirect object immediately after the verb. (e.g., The book cost *me* twenty dollars).

This lesson takes a *deductive* approach to instruction in that the teacher presents the grammar rules. Alternately, the teacher might take an *inductive* approach, allowing the students to infer the placement rules themselves from consideration of specific examples.

Reference is made to previously studied patterns of English verb usage to assist the students in organizing the new information in relation to what they have learned before, and the teacher writes additional examples of indirect objects on the board, eliciting them from the students as a way to promote noticing of the form. Such grammar instruction assists the student in becoming familiar with the structure they will use in the communicative activity, thereby lessening any diversion of their attention away from processing meaningful input during subsequent task performance, and perhaps facilitating the processing of both meaning and form at the same time.

Part 2: After the grammar lesson, students work in pairs or groups to perform a structure-based communicative task which contains multiple uses of the target structure. Furthermore, in the lesson described here, the task content is actually study of the structure itself. The task goal is to determine which English verbs fall under the different placement pattern types; thus, there is an explicit focus on grammar. Each student has a task card with three or four sentences using different verbs and indirect objects, and he or she must read the sentences to his or her partner/group members. The listeners must write down the sentences and note the position of the indirect object. As a task solution, each pair/group makes a list of the verbs in the sentences and assigns each verb to one of the three patterns of indirect object placement presented at the beginning of the lesson. To further focus attention on the target structure, the indirect objects on the task cards are written in italics.

Regarding use of a task with explicit grammar content instead of a purely communicative task, it must be noted that most proponents of task-based curricula recommend use of communicative tasks only, although the target structure may be embedded in the task or its use may be required to reach the task solution (see Loschky and Bley-Vroman 1993 and Skehan 1998a). Real-life communicative situations are strongly recommended as task content, especially for ESL learners who have to master survival English skills such as going to the post office, shopping, asking directions, filling out forms, and so forth. However, without denying the usefulness of purely communicative tasks, especially in the ESL context, insisting that they are the only appropriate subject matter for interactive task content assumes that ESL/EFL students do not want to talk about the language they are studying and that there is no point in their doing so. These assumptions do not take into account the fact that many ESL/EFL students come to the language classroom with years of study of English grammar behind them, and therefore may actually enjoy discussing grammar. This is especially true in the EFL context, where the students' overwhelming "real-life" need is to develop target language accuracy to pass examinations. Moreover, research, even in ESL situations, suggests (e.g., Willing 1988) that some students prefer explicit grammar teaching to communicative activities with no grammatical component. Thus, it is up to the teacher to judge which task type best meets his or her students' needs and learning style preferences (for a review of learning styles, see Cohen 1998).

Part 3: After task performance, the teacher reviews all the sentences, listing the verbs under the correct pattern type and asking for more examples.

Part 4: After discussing the task solution, the teacher provides the students with practice exercises. In a traditional classroom, this might involve moving from highly structured, fill-in-the-blank exercises to open-ended exercises, where students use supplied verbs and indirect objects to make sentences, to communicative exercises, where they develop their own sentences containing indirect objects. After this activity, the students read their sentences to their partners/group members and receive corrective feedback. The Interactionist view of cognition regards such feedback as critical for creating meaning and promoting noticing of communicative functions served by the grammar structure.

In a predominantly communicative classroom, practice might include activities such as reading/listening material containing many uses of the target grammar structure and having the students ask and answer questions which require production of the structure (e.g., *What did Ann tell you? Who did Ray translate that paragraph for? What did you give your friend?*).

For several classes after the grammar lesson on indirect object placement, the students are given communicative material to read or listen to. This material contains many instances of the target structures, which may be highlighted or placed in italics to promote noticing. Following each presentation of the communicative material, the teacher again reviews the rules for indirect object placement and points out the communicative function served by the structure. This step facilitates activation of the new material which has been linked and subsumed within a framework of previously learned material. Such *spiral review,* or the systematic review of recently instructed material within increasingly broader contexts, has been found to be an important

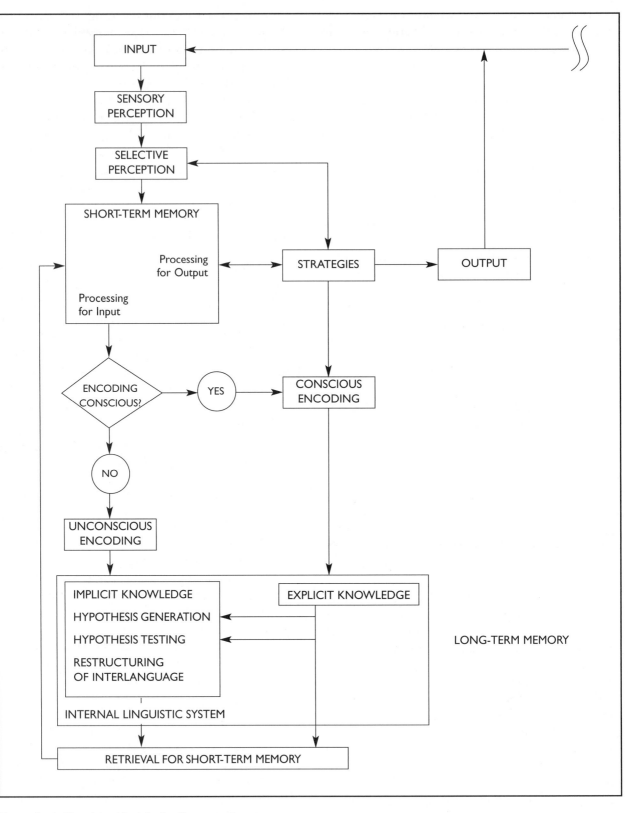

Figure I. A Cognitive Model of a Grammar Lesson

memory strategy for the successful development of explicit knowledge and an awareness of form-meaning relationships (see Cohen 1998).

Applying a Cognitive Model to the Communicative Grammar Lesson

Figure 1 is a model of the cognitive steps involved in processing the lesson described above. It is based on the assumption that there is an interface between implicit and explicit knowledge. However, these two forms of knowledge are not fixed but dynamic, with constant reorganization taking place as a result of unconscious linguistic hypothesis generation and testing done against new input. Implicit linguistic knowledge, explicit linguistic knowledge, and hypothesis testing are seen to be dynamically related, as connectionist models suggest. As mentioned earlier, connectionism views cognition as associative patterns in neural networks operating in parallel, for a parallel processing perspective.

Let us now consider what cognitive processes occur during performance of the above task on indirect object placement.

Step 1: Sensory Reception   Auditory and visual input is received.

Step 2: Selective Perception   The student is already paying attention and consciously focuses on the location of the indirect object. Does it come directly after the verb or is it a clause-final prepositional phrase? Are both positions possible? At this point, the location of the indirect object is selectively perceived in input.

Step 3: Short-Term Memory   Correct placement of the indirect object with different verbs enters short-term memory through conscious effort gained by directed attention and other cognitive strategies such as practicing, analyzing, and reasoning, and by creating structure for the new input, often through written means (Oxford 1990). These strategies are also used for the next step.

Step 4: Encoding into Long-Term Memory   Many educators believe that encoding or entering information into long-term memory is the most significant event of the learning process. The model presented here shows two encoding processes. The first is a conscious process involving effort, attention, and strategy use. The second encoding process is unconscious—the first stage in language acquisition whereby those forms which successfully convey meaning to the learner are somehow flagged for entry into long-term memory.

Step 5: Storage in Long-Term Memory   Although the model shows implicit knowledge and explicit knowledge existing separately, we have to ask whether they differ in location or in representation (the form in which the knowledge is stored). In the grammar lesson and communicative task performance, explicit knowledge involved learning rules for indirect object placement. Therefore both syntactic and semantic forms may be stored because students can often recall exact sentences as well as give paraphrases of grammatical rules.

Step 6: Hypothesis Generation and Testing; Restructuring of Implicit Knowledge   Cognitive theorists have suggested that the language learner unconsciously goes through the following three steps when processing language:

1.   The learner notices linguistic features in processed input.
2.   The learner makes a comparison between his or her existing linguistic knowledge, or interlanguage, and the newly processed input.
3.   The learner then constructs new linguistic hypotheses on the basis of the new information and his or her existing system.

Step 7: Retrieval from Long-Term Memory   Connectionist models of parallel processing suggest that there are "prompts" which either excite or inhibit elements in long-term memory, resulting in a pattern of activity among sets of interrelated elements. Experience is seen as strengthening the connections which exist among the elements, thus allowing easier retrieval.

Step 8: Production Strategies and Output In the interactive task for indirect object placement, the students do not have to produce the correct form, only recognize it, so there is no need for simplification or correction of output during task performance. However, subsequent practice activities will require output, and the use of planning and correcting strategies will be helpful at this time (McLaughlin 1987; Oxford 1990). It is important to recognize that since improvement of performance is related to the amount of automaticity, the restructuring process often results in discontinuities which delay successful production. Therefore, even though students can recognize which pattern of indirect object placement various verbs take, they cannot be expected to immediately produce the grammar forms correctly in communicative utterances. However, student output during task performance—reading sentences from task cards and discussing which pattern of indirect object placement the various verbs take—becomes new input that then provides feedback to the learners' implicit knowledge system.

Step 9: Feedback Feedback on the correctness of language is essential for hypothesis testing and the development of implicit linguistic knowledge. The learner tests hypotheses in two main ways: receptively, by comparing input to existing interlanguage, and productively, by producing utterances in the target language and assessing their correctness from the feedback received. In the grammar lesson and task described earlier, the students receive feedback from the teacher on the correctness of the indirect object placement patterns.

Strategy Use

Strategies can be defined as conscious techniques for achieving a goal and have been shown to mediate cognitive change (Oxford 1990); they have also been defined as "learning processes which are consciously selected by the learner" (Cohen 1998, p. 4). Both definitions emphasize the learner's conscious decision to use strategies. In fact, extensive research in general education indicates that students who report active use of strategies are likely to be more successful in learning new skills than are students who do not use strategies. When students have clearly defined goals, high motivation, and control of their learning through strategy use, favorable learning outcomes result. Therefore, no cognitive model of second/foreign language grammar learning would be complete without considering strategies.

Although there are many researchers investigating strategies for language learning (e.g., see the literature review and strategy taxonomy in Cohen 1998), Oxford's approach (1990) is useful because she uses a simple taxonomy, dividing strategies into direct and indirect types, and then recommends specific pedagogical applications. Direct strategies consist of memory strategies, cognitive strategies, and compensation strategies, all of which involve conscious manipulation of the target language structure. The first type, memory strategies, facilitates storage and retrieval of new information through grouping, associating, and contextualizing new information. Cognitive strategies include practicing new language items, analyzing new material such as grammar rules, and organizing structure for new material. The last step is often written practice and may involve summarization. Indirect strategies enable the student to control learning, and include (1) metacognitive strategies, such as using Advance Organizers to approach new material at a higher level of generality, and goal setting; (2) affective strategies for managing emotion and developing motivation; and (3) social strategies for interaction and the collaborative creation of meaning. Many educators have suggested that students should receive special training on the active use of strategies to control and enhance their language learning process (see Oxford's chapter in this volume and Cohen 1998).

Summary

This cognitive model of language processing illustrates how a grammar lesson given in the target language and containing both formal instruction and communicative activities can be expected to promote language acquisition through development of both implicit and explicit knowledge. Even though the nature of the relationship between these two forms of knowledge is still undetermined, the critical process in language acquisition—and all learning—is the modification of the learner's existing knowledge system on the basis of comparisons between it and newly processed input. An important pedagogical implication of the model is that there will necessarily be a lag between the presentation of the grammar lesson and the learner's ability to use the target form successfully in communication. However, practice will help the process by allowing the proceduralization of explicit knowledge, and communicative activities containing the grammar form will facilitate the development of implicit knowledge.

PEDAGOGICAL IMPLICATIONS

The preceding sections have identified and discussed the following features of a cognitive approach to grammar teaching:

1. It is useful if students receive an orientation in advance of the grammar lesson to activate their previous knowledge and to promote the integration of the new material into their existing knowledge hierarchies.
2. Some type of grammar instruction is necessary for students to attain high levels of accuracy in the target language. This instruction may be explicit or may be implicit (involving only communicative use of the target structures), and rule presentation may be inductive or deductive. Communicative activities used alone are not considered to be sufficient for development of learner accuracy in the use of grammar points.
3. Extensive communicative exposure to the instructed grammar point is essential for students to notice, then process, the instructed form, linking it to previously developed linguistic knowledge.
4. Production activities are essential to provide practice in the use of the form, to raise awareness of the form, and to give students the chance to receive feedback on the correctness of their language. Production activities also provide new input.
5. Group work and task performance are recommended since they give students the chance to receive communicative input and produce output; such interaction allows the collaborative construction of meaning to occur.
6. Postlesson activities include further communicative exposure to the grammar point as well as a systematic review of the instructed form that points out its use in a variety of communicative contexts.

A Cognitive Approach to Traditional Grammar Teaching

Traditional grammar instruction has generally consisted of a presentation of grammar rules followed by practice drills, sentence production, and translation. This approach is still prominent in many parts of the world although a communicative component has often been added. The following is a generalized version of an English lesson currently used in many EFL settings.

1. The new grammar point is explained;
2. new words and phrases are explained and there may be a pronunciation lesson as well;
3. a tape of a dialogue containing the new grammar structure and vocabulary is played;
4. students practice the dialogue in chorus or in pairs;
5. students translate the dialogue into their native language;
6. as a final activity, listening exercises and practice drills are presented.

From a cognitive perspective emphasizing skills development, the problem with this lesson is that the grammar point is not presented in a way that facilitates its processing and proceduralization; nor have form-meaning correlations been made through the presentation of communicative activities designed to promote noticing of the form's variety of meanings in discourse. Transforming the traditional lesson, therefore, means adding communicative activities using the form in various ways. These activities are structured to require both interaction and output using the form, as well as corrective feedback from group members or the teacher. The lesson is reinforced by subsequent communicative activities which use the form to perform a variety of discourse functions, and also by teacher review. Repeated communicative practice of instructed forms can lead to their eventual automatization.

A Cognitive Approach to Communicative Teaching

Researchers now agree that it is essential to integrate some form of grammar instruction within a communicative framework if students are to attain high levels of target language accuracy, particularly in the EFL context, where opportunities to encounter communicative use of the target language are rare. As an alternative to delivery of a formal grammar lesson, task work has been recommended to supply students with communicative use of target grammar points, as well as to promote interaction, production, and opportunities for corrective feedback (Skehan 1998a). The use of purely communicative tasks which nonetheless require comprehension and production of target grammar points has been recommended (Loschy and Bley-Vroman 1993). In addition, grammar problem-solving tasks in which students discuss the structure as task content, such as the previous example requiring students to assign verbs to patterns of indirect object placement, are also useful since they combine communicative task performance with explicit instruction on grammar points. Such tasks have even been suggested to be equivalent to traditional grammar lessons in the development of explicit knowledge (Fotos 1993; 2001), yet do not compromise the essentially meaning-focused nature of communicative pedagogy. Furthermore, when students discuss the language they produce during task performance, it is suggested that this "metatalk" helps them develop awareness of the relationship of form to meaning (Swain 1985). It should also be acknowledged that such structure-based interactive tasks, with their obvious grammatical content, provide an acceptably serious type of communicative activity within the framework of a traditional approach to grammar instruction.

CONCLUSION

This chapter has presented a cognitive approach to language learning and grammar instruction. A cognitive model has been used to design a grammar lesson which develops both explicit and implicit knowledge of a grammar point, supplies opportunities for information exchange through task performance, and then provides purely communicative input containing the target structures so that students can notice form-meaning relationships. The approach described is useful for traditional instructional settings as well as primarily meaning-focused classrooms.

DISCUSSION QUESTIONS

1. What are the general features of a cognitive approach to grammar teaching/learning?
2. What is the Noticing Hypothesis and why is it considered important for grammar teaching/ learning? Discuss this hypothesis in relation to explicit and implicit approaches to grammar instruction.
3. Many theories of second language acquisition maintain that practice is not necessary for learning to take place. However, a cognitive approach to grammar instruction suggests that it may be useful. Do you agree or disagree? Why?
4. What type of language learner would find a cognitive approach to grammar teaching/ learning most effective and why? Would a cognitive approach work for you? Why or why not?

SUGGESTED ACTIVITIES

1. Select a grammar point with easily explained rules and develop the outline of a lesson using the cognitive approach suggested for teaching indirect object placement.

Unit II E Language Skills/Grammar and Vocabulary

2. Using the same grammar point, design a focus-on-form activity featuring only communicative use of the grammar structure. The communicative material should be designed so that the students will notice it and have to use the target structure to complete the activity.

3. Develop an interactive structure-based task requiring students to read each other sentences containing the structure, to write the sentences down, and then to develop grammar rules for the structure's use. (Possible structures with easily explainable rules include adverb placement; the modals *would, could,* and *should;* order of adjectives; cause and result with *so, such, very,* and *too; Wh* + noun questions; comparisons.)

4. Design three follow-up communicative activities for the task in Activity 3. The communicative activities should promote noticing of the structure in a variety of functional contexts.

 **FURTHER READING**

Bialystok, E., and K. Hakuta. 1994. *In Other Words: The Science and Psychology of Second-Language Acquisition.* New York: Basic Books.
An easy-to-read survey presenting theories of second language acquisition illustrated by real-world examples. The book pays special attention to issues of bilingualism and the impact of culture on language learning.

Ellis, R. 1997. *Second Language Research and Language Teaching.* Oxford: Oxford University Press.
An essential reference for ESL/EFL teachers, this book accessibly summarizes the extensive body of research on language learning and links the findings to classroom practice and opportunities for action research.

Eysenck, M., and M. Keane. 1995. *Cognitive Psychology: A Student's Handbook.* East Sussex, UK: Psychology Press.
A psychology textbook useful as a general reference because of its clear explanations of the workings of memory, knowledge creation, attention and awareness, and language comprehension and production.

Hinkel, E., and S. Fotos, eds. 2001. *New Perspectives on Grammar Teaching in Second Language Classrooms.* Mahwah, NJ: Lawrence Erlbaum Associates.
A useful collection of articles presenting a range of grammar teaching approaches and activities for ESL/EFL classrooms.

Skehan, P. 1998a. *A Cognitive Approach to Language Processing.* Hong Kong: Oxford University Press.
A key book for understanding the cognitive aspects of language acquisition and the role of individual differences, such as learning style, in promoting favorable learning outcomes. The book also presents a strong rationale for task-based instruction.

Tomasello, M., ed. 1998. *The New Psychology of Language: Cognitive and Functional Approaches to Language Structure.* Mahwah, NJ: Lawrence Erlbaum Associates.
This edited volume presents papers by authors working in the area of Cognitive-Functional Linguistics, an approach to grammar development based on consideration of the communicative function of a form and the cultural context for expressing that function. Tomasello's introduction is especially useful.

ENDNOTES

1 Givón (1998) suggests that the use of grammar appeared relatively late in human cognitive evolution, commenting that hominoids appear to possess both noun and verb concepts as well as the necessary brain neurology for semantic and episodic memory. He therefore considers grammar to consist of the following components: (1) morphology; (2) intonation, including clause-level intonation contours and word stress; (3) rhythmics, including length and pauses; and (4) sequential order of words and/or morphemes (pp. 48–49).

2 In this chapter, declarative knowledge is considered to be the same as explicit knowledge and procedural knowledge is considered to be the same as implicit knowledge. However, some researchers distinguish among each type. For a fuller discussion, see Skehan 1998a.

Vocabulary Learning and Teaching

JEANETTE S. DECARRICO

"Vocabulary Learning and Teaching" focuses initially on current issues in teaching, i.e., deciding which items to teach and how to teach them; on explicit and implicit learning and vocabulary learning strategies; and on the role of collocations. The other focus is recent corpus studies and their implications for analysis of multiword phrasal units and for new directions in vocabulary instruction.

INTRODUCTION

Vocabulary learning is central to language acquisition, whether the language is first, second, or foreign. Although vocabulary has not always been recognized as a priority in language teaching, interest in its role in second language (L2) learning has grown rapidly in recent years and specialists now emphasize the need for a systematic and principled approach to vocabulary by both the teacher and the learner. The increased interest in this topic is evidenced by a rapidly expanding body of experimental studies and pedagogical material, most of which addresses several key questions of particular interest for language teachers. For example, what does it mean to know a word? Which words do learners need to know? How will they learn them? These questions reflect the current focus on the needs of learners in acquiring lexical competence and on the role of the teacher in guiding them toward this goal.

HISTORICAL OVERVIEW

There is now general agreement among vocabulary specialists that lexical competence is at the very heart of communicative competence, the ability to communicate successfully and appropriately (Coady and Huckin 1997). Given the current focus on vocabulary study, many nonspecialists might be surprised to learn that, in past years, this area of teaching was often neglected because it was thought that vocabulary could simply be left to take care of itself. Although by the late 1970s and early 1980s more and more voices began to challenge this view (Judd 1978; Meara 1981; McCarthy 1984; Laufer 1986), in 1988, Carter and McCarthy were still taking note of the relative neglect of vocabulary in previous years. By then its reputation as the poor relation in language teaching was rapidly coming to an end.

The low status of vocabulary study and vocabulary teaching was in large part due to language teaching approaches based on American linguistic theories that had been dominant throughout the 1940s, 1950s, and 1960s. Most influential in the early years was Charles Fries's *Teaching and Learning English as a Foreign Language* (1945), based on American structural linguistics, which emphasized grammatical and phonological structure. Fries believed that grammar should be the starting point of language learning, and he also adopted the view, borrowed from behaviorist psychology, that learning was a matter of habit formation. His audiolingual method incorporated these ideas by paying systematic attention to intensive drills of basic sentence patterns and their pronunciation. Because the emphasis was on teaching grammatical and phonological structures, the vocabulary needed to be relatively simple, with new words introduced only as they were needed to make the drills possible (Larsen-Freeman 2000b; Zimmerman 1997). The assumption was that once students learned the structural frames, lexical items to fill the grammatical slots in the frames could be learned later, as needed.

Although the shift to generative (transformational) linguistics in the 1960s brought about revolutionary changes in linguistic theory, triggered by Chomsky (1957), it did little to challenge the idea that the role of lexis was secondary to that of grammar. Chomsky rejected the behaviorist notion of habit formation and supplanted it with a rationalist framework, the central assumption being that language is represented as a speaker's mental grammar, a set of abstract rules for generating grammatical sentences. The rules generate the syntactic structure, and lexical items from appropriate grammatical categories (noun, verb, adjective, etc.,) are selected to fill in the corresponding slots in the syntactic frame. The interests of generative linguists centered mainly on rule-governed behavior and on the grammatical structure of sentences and did not include concerns for the appropriate use of language. Language learning approaches based on this theory viewed learning as rule acquisition, not habit formation, and emphasized grammatical rules. Vocabulary was afforded somewhat more importance, but the focus on rules of grammar still served to reinforce the idea that lexis was somewhat secondary (Carter and McCarthy 1988).

Hymes (1972), while not rejecting Chomsky's model, extended it and gave greater emphasis to the sociolinguistic and pragmatic factors governing effective use of language. Hymes was especially concerned with the concept of *communicative competence,* which emphasized using language for meaningful communication, including the appropriate use of language in particular social contexts (for example, informal conversation at the dinner table versus formal conversation at the bank, etc.). The teaching approach that evolved from these notions (see also Halliday 1973), referred to as communicative language teaching, promoted fluency over accuracy and consequently shifted the focus from sentence-level forms to discourse-level functions (e.g., requests, greetings, apologies, and so on). Once again, though, vocabulary was given secondary status, taught mainly as support for functional language use. As in previous approaches, it was generally assumed that vocabulary would take care of itself (Schmitt 2000).

This picture has changed dramatically within the last two decades. The challenge to the status quo began in the late 1970s and early 1980s, and by the late 1980s and early 1990s, vocabulary studies were developing exponentially and vocabulary teaching was coming into its own. One reason for the resurgence of interest on the part of researchers was that computer-aided research was providing vast amounts of information that had not previously been available for analysis, such as information about how words behave in actual language use, larger units that function in discourse as single lexical items, and differences between written and spoken communication. Further, psycholinguistic studies were providing insights concerning mental processes involved in vocabulary learning, such as memory, storage, and retrieval. Interest in these issues led in turn to related studies concerned with developing more effective vocabulary teaching and learning strategies.

CURRENT ISSUES

A central debate emerging from these studies deals with whether effective vocabulary learning should focus on explicit or implicit learning. In the 1970s and 1980s, the communicative approach led naturally to a focus on implicit, incidental learning. Teachers encouraged students to recognize clues to word meanings in context and to use monolingual dictionaries rather than bilingual dictionaries, and textbooks emphasized inferring word meaning from context. Currently, however, while acknowledging that exposure to words in various contexts is extremely important to a deeper understanding of a word's meaning, most researchers recognize that providing incidental encounters with words is only one method of facilitating vocabulary acquisition, and that a well-structured vocabulary program needs a balanced approach that includes explicit teaching together with activities providing appropriate contexts for incidental learning.

Explicit Learning

In explicit vocabulary learning students engage in activities that focus attention on vocabulary. Sökmen (1997) highlights several key principles of explicit learning that can help guide teachers in deciding basic questions of what to teach and how to teach. These principles include the goal of building a large recognition vocabulary, integrating new words with old, providing a number of encounters with a word, promoting a deep level of processing, facilitating imaging, using a variety of techniques, and encouraging independent learning strategies.

What to Teach

How do we decide how many words to teach and which ones to teach? Many researchers now advocate that learners should initially be taught a large productive vocabulary of at least two thousand high frequency words. Meara (1995), for example, argues against earlier "vocabulary control" approaches in which students were taught only a basic vocabulary of several hundred words, and read restricted sorts of texts such as language textbooks and graded readers. He maintains that students should learn very large vocabularies when they first start to acquire a language. In fact, this base of two thousand words now seems to be the most commonly cited initial goal for second language learners.

The justification for this view is that, first, any given language has a small number of words that occur many times in material we see most often and a large number of words that occur only once or twice. The actual figures for English suggest that a basic vocabulary of about two thousand words accounts for approximately 80 percent of what we regularly see or hear. For almost any common context, a learner restricted to five hundred words or so would encounter a very large number of unfamiliar words and the really important meanings would be carried by the words that the learner is not likely to know. Meara concludes that a vocabulary of five hundred words is relatively useless, while a vocabulary of two thousand words goes a long way towards achieving a realistic level of lexical competence. A second reason why it would be sensible to teach beginners a very large vocabulary very quickly is that most learners expect to have to learn vocabulary, and it would be a mistake not to capitalize on these expectations.

The most famous list of high-frequency words is the *General Service List of English Words*

(West 1953). It contains about two thousand words with semantic and frequency information drawn from a very large corpus of several million words and, though quite old, has still not been replaced. It is often cited as the most useful list available because it lists the different parts of speech and the different meaning senses and, in terms of frequency, gives the frequency of the main headword plus the relative frequency of its meanings (Nation 1990; Sökmen 1997; Schmitt 2000). It has been very influential, perhaps because "it is claimed that knowing these words gives access to about 80 percent of the words in any written text and thus stimulates motivation since the words acquired can be seen by learners to have a demonstrably quick return" (Carter 1998, p. 207). However, it is based on very old word counts and is currently being revised.

Some researchers also emphasize that, for certain groups of students, a base of two thousand words will be inadequate. Learners with special goals, such as university study, need to acquire a further one thousand high-frequency words beyond the initial two thousand base, plus the strategies to deal with the low-frequency words they meet. A list to consider for academic English is the *Academic Word List,* in an appendix in Nation (1990), updated in Coxhead (2000).

Another very important consideration is that we can maximize vocabulary considerably by teaching word families instead of individual word forms. A word family is a set of words that includes a base word plus its inflections and/or derivations. For purposes of teaching, especially, it makes more sense to view sets such as *talk, talked, talking,* and *talks* as members of a closely related "family," not as four single words, and to help students recognize them as such. Presenting word families, with many words built around a particular root, gathers words together so that associations among them can be seen. The psychological literature also supports this view, providing evidence that the mind groups members of a word family together. An important implication is that when we think of teaching a productive vocabulary of two to three thousand "words," we should actually be thinking in terms of word families as the unit for counting and teaching (Schmitt 2000).

Meaning associations attached to words are also important. Words appear to be organized into semantically related sets in the mind, and thus the associations attached to a word will affect the way that it is stored in the brain. Psychologists investigate these associations by presenting subjects with a word and asking them to suggest other words that it brings to mind. For example, they present the word *table* and ask what other words first come to mind. For *table*, the most common association is *chair*; for *boy* it is *girl*, and so on.

Teaching Techniques and Activities

New words should not be presented in isolation and should not be learned by simple rote memorization. It is important that new vocabulary items be presented in contexts rich enough to provide clues to meaning and that students be given multiple exposure to items they should learn. Exercises and activities include learning words in word association lists, focusing on highlighted words in texts, and playing vocabulary games. More recently, computer programs that include the sounds of the words as well as illustrative pictures provide opportunity for practice with a variety of contexts, both written and spoken.

Especially at beginning levels, the teaching of word lists through word association techniques has proven to be a successful way to learn a large number of words in a short period and retain them over time. Nation (1990) notes, for instance, that knowing *meaning* and *hopeful* can make the learning of *meaningful* easier. This result should not be surprising, given that words are associated in various ways and that these associations reflect underlying relationships in the mind. That is, as noted previously, the meaning of a word depends in part on its relationship to similar words, and words in a word family are related to each other through having a common base.

Semantic mapping is an activity that helps bring into consciousness relationships among words in a text and helps deepen understanding by creating associative networks for words (see especially Stahl and Vancil 1986). A text is chosen based on the words to be learned and students are asked to draw a diagram of the relationships between particular words found in the text. A variation on this technique, a "vocabulary network," could be designed to help even beginning students learn to make semantic associations within particular superordinate headings. As a somewhat simplified example, consider a text describing a scene with a red house, a blue sky, and a yard with green grass and puppies and kittens playing on it. The teacher could first discuss the chosen words, provide superordinate category headings such as *animal* and *color* in circles on the chalkboard, and then help students learn to illustrate the relationships among the words by having them first identify the related words in the text, then draw circles below each category heading connected by associative lines, and finally write the appropriate related words in the circles connected to the headings (e.g., *animal* connected with *puppy* and *kitten* in associated circles; color connected with *red, blue,* and *green* in associated circles).

Word association activities can also be constructed with lists of words that are to be learned. For example, students could be given word-match lists such as the following and asked to draw lines from words in the left column to those that seem most closely related in the right column.

cough	blue
grass	pepper
red	tea
salt	kitten
puppy	sneeze
coffee	green

The pairs to be matched should have a clear associative link, such as those given in the list, but closely related synonyms or antonyms should probably be avoided. Research shows that similarities between words can make learning more difficult because of interference, or "cross-associations." In particular, care should be taken with pairs whose meanings are very similar. Learners can easily confuse pairs such as *left* and *right*, for example, because they have the same semantic features except for "lateral direction." Research indicates that 25 percent of similar words taught together are typically cross-associated. Antonyms are a particular problem because they tend to come in pairs such as *deep/shallow* and *rich/poor.* Synonyms and other closely related semantic groupings (food, clothing, body parts) are also problematic. The way to avoid cross-associations in closely related semantic groups is to integrate new words with old by teaching the most frequent or useful (i.e., "unmarked") word first (e.g., *deep*), and only after it is well established introduce its less frequent ("marked") antonym partner (e.g., *shallow*) (Nation 1990; Schmitt 2000).

For presenting word families, one way is simply to introduce such a family along with the definitions for each word, as for example, the derivational set *act, action, active, actively, activate, actor.* Another way to isolate the word families that occur in a particular text is by highlighting them so that students can see the relationships. Highlighting passages in texts has the advantage of providing a more natural context in which students can trace words through the discourse and observe how the forms change according to discourse function. Texts may be authentic materials or, for initial learning, may be simple but natural texts constructed by the teacher. For example:

> A *conductor* of an orchestra must spend years studying music and must also learn how to *conduct* other musicians so they can play together. The proper *conduct* of each musician will contribute to the success of the performance.

Another consideration in teaching vocabulary is promoting a deep level of processing. The reason is that learning may involve either *short-term memory* or *long-term memory.* Short-term memory has a small storage capacity and simply holds information temporarily while it is being processed, usually for only a matter of seconds. The importance of promoting a deep level of processing is to transfer information from short-term memory to long-term memory, which has almost unlimited storage capacity. The more students manipulate and think about a word, the more likely it is that the word will be transferred into long-term memory. Research indicates that efficient learning of vocabulary is an incremental process, one that requires meaningful recurring encounters with a word over time. With respect to classroom activities, for instance, a semantic

mapping or other semantic network activity could be followed later with pair matching activities, along the lines illustrated earlier. For suggestions on how to use word set grids and other gamelike tasks for more advanced learners, see Carter (1998).

Teachers can add variety to the techniques employed in the classroom by alternating other activities with language games that recycle vocabulary, e.g., Scrabble, Word Bingo, Concentration, Password, Jeopardy. Language games have the added advantage of being fun, competitive, and consequently, memorable. These games are also activities that students can be encouraged to do on their own.

Implicit Learning

Incidental vocabulary learning is learning that occurs when the mind is focused elsewhere, such as on understanding a text or using language for communicative purposes. A common view in vocabulary studies is that we have not been explicitly taught the majority of words that we know, and that beyond a certain level of proficiency in a second language, vocabulary learning is more likely to be mainly implicit (incidental). Various researchers have concluded that learners should be given explicit instruction and practice in the first two to three thousand high-frequency words (i.e., word families), while beyond this level, most low-frequency words will be learned incidentally while reading or listening. The reason that explicit learning is thought to be necessary in the initial stages is that, unless a high percentage of words on a page are known, it is very difficult to guess the meaning of new words from context. A two to three thousand word base is considered a minimum "threshold" that enables incidental learning to take place when reading authentic texts.

Just as having multiple exposures to a word is important in explicit learning, so it is important for incidental learning. Lack of exposure is a common problem facing language learners; a good way to combat this problem is to expose students to extensive reading, sometimes referred to as a "book flood" approach, in which reading is done consistently over a period of time. For beginning students, graded readers will probably give the best access to a large amount of input. For intermediate students just on the threshold of reading authentic texts, it may be appropriate to read numerous authentic texts, but all on the same topic (narrow reading) so that the texts will provide multiple exposure as topic-specific vocabulary is repeated throughout. Advanced students, on the other hand, should be encouraged to read a wide variety of authentic texts (wide reading). This type of exposure is important because meeting a word in different contexts expands what is known about it, thus improving quality of knowledge, with additional exposures helping to consolidate it in memory. Given an incremental view of vocabulary acquisition, both elaboration and consolidation are crucial (Schmitt 2000).

VOCABULARY LEARNING STRATEGIES

Incidental learning from exposure to texts will be greatly facilitated if learners use vocabulary learning strategies. These strategies will undoubtedly be required initially, in any case, as students are encouraged to make the transition to independent learning by determining meanings of the less frequent words they read or hear. Strategies should aid both in discovering the meaning of a new word and in consolidating a word once it has been encountered. Thus, learners should approach independent learning of vocabulary by using a combination of extensive reading and self-study strategies.

Guessing Meaning from Context

One of the strategies most often discussed in the literature is guessing word meaning from context. Making the transition to independent learning can be easier and more efficient if teachers help students learn to recognize clues to guessing word meaning from context. This strategy is a key vocabulary learning skill for dealing with low-frequency vocabulary, particularly in reading authentic texts.

Factors that affect the likelihood of success in inferencing include a context rich enough to provide adequate clues to guess a word's meaning. Because many contexts are not rich enough, a single context is often not sufficient to allow students to guess the full word meaning. This fact underscores the need for repeated encounters with a word in diverse contexts. It is clear, of course, that background knowledge about the topic and the culture greatly aid inferencing and retention by providing a framework ("schema") for incorporating the new word with information already known, but even without such a background learners can become skilled in guessing. The key is to learn what clues to look for and where to find them.

Clarke and Nation (1980) propose a guessing strategy based on such clues (also in Nation 1990). A beginning step is to get the learner to look closely at the unknown word, next to look at its immediate context, and then to take a much broader view of how the clause containing the word relates to other clauses, sentences, or paragraphs. Clarke and Nation also include a system for learners to check that the guess they made was the best one possible.

The basic steps in this system include first deciding the part of speech of the unknown word (e.g., noun, verb, adjective, adverb), and then examining the context of the clause or sentence containing the word. For instance, if the unknown word is a noun, what adjectives describe it? What verb is it near? If the new word is a verb, what nouns does it go with? Is it modified by an adverb? If the new word is an adjective, what noun does it go with? The next step is looking at the relationship between this clause or sentence and other sentences or paragraphs. Signals to look for might be a coordinating or subordinating conjunction such as *but, because, if, when* or an adverbial such as *however,* or *as a result*.

Even if there is no explicit signal, it is helpful to be aware of the possible types of rhetorical relationship, which include cause and effect, contrast, inclusion, time, exemplification, and summary. Punctuation may also be helpful as a clue, since semicolons often signal a list or an inclusion relationship, and dashes may signal restatement or clarification. Reference words such as *this, that,* and *such* also provide useful information if the antecedent can be identified.

Final steps include using knowledge gained from such clues to guess the meaning of the word, and then checking in the following ways to see if the guess is correct: See if the part of speech of the unknown word is the same as that of the guess; if so, replace the unknown word with the guessed word; if the sentence makes sense, the guessed word is probably a good paraphrase for the unknown word. As a final check, break the unknown word into its prefix, root, and suffix, if possible, to see if the meanings of the prefix, root, and suffix correspond to the guessed word; if not, check the guessed word again but do not make changes if it still seems to be the correct choice.

The steps in this strategy focus mainly on context rather than looking at word parts, a step that is delayed until last. The reason is that, in the experience of Clarke and Nation, using affixes and roots alone is not a very reliable aid to guessing, whereas using the context is more likely to lead to correct guesses.

An important assumption of this procedure is that, once the strategy is mastered, learners can begin to skip some of the steps and the other steps will become more automatic. A second assumption is that guessing word meanings in context also leads to dictionary work, but only as a final way of checking since learners will often be unable to choose the most suitable meaning from those given unless they already have some idea of what the word might mean.

Mnemonic Devices

Among various other strategies often discussed in the literature, one that requires a considerable amount of manipulation and deep processing is the *Keyword Method,* an aid to memory, or a "mnemonic device," which helps to link a word form and its meaning and to consolidate this linkage in memory. There are three stages. First, the learner chooses an L1 or L2 word, preferably a concrete entity, based on a phonological or orthographic similarity with the L2 target word. Then a strong association between the target word and the keyword must be constructed so that, when seeing or hearing the target word, the learner is reminded immediately of the keyword.

Finally, a visual image is constructed to combine the referents of the keyword and the target word, preferably an odd or bizarre image that will help make it more memorable (Hulstijn 1997).

The important point to remember is that the student must learn to concentrate on remembering the image of the interaction between the keyword and the foreign word. An example cited by Kasper (1993) illustrates this point. The target word is the Spanish word *payaso* ("clown"), and the keyword is the English *pie.* The association between the target word and the keyword is to think of the image of a clown throwing a pie at a friend. Students can also be encouraged to draw simple pictures with stick figures to illustrate the image and thus further aid memory—in this case, stick figures representing the clown and the friend, with the pie in midair between them.

Vocabulary Notebooks

A further suggestion for a memory aid in independent learning is setting up vocabulary notebooks. Schmitt and Schmitt (1995) recommend arranging the notebook in a loose-leaf binder or index card file, in which, for instance, students write word pairs and semantic maps which help them visualize the associative network of relationships existing between new and familiar words. Other activities related to the notebooks include keeping a tally of every time they hear or see a new word within a certain period and noting its frequency, learning roots and derivatives in the word's family by studying what affixes are used to change its part of speech, making notes on stylistic aspects of the word, or writing a sentence illustrating its use.

Other Learner Strategies

Various other learner strategies can help in discovering word meaning and in consolidating it in memory. Teachers can encourage students to check for an L1 cognate, study and practice in peer groups, connect a word to personal experience or previous learning, say a new word aloud when studying, use verbal and written repetition, and engage in extended rehearsal (review new material soon after initial learning and then at gradually increasing intervals).

It is, of course, neither possible nor desirable for learners to try to use all strategies all the time, but they may find it useful to vary strategies that seem more appropriate to a given situation, for example, depending on whether the context is explicit classroom learning activities or independent learning such as reading or speaking. Often, individual preferences will determine strategy use.

COLLOCATIONS

So far we have considered vocabulary only in terms of single words and word families. However, vocabulary knowledge involves considerably more than just knowing the meaning of a given word in isolation; it also involves knowing the words that tend to co-occur with it. These patterns, or *collocations*, consist of pairs or groups of words that co-occur with very high frequency and are important in vocabulary learning because, as Nattinger notes, "the meaning of a word has a great deal to do with the words with which it commonly associates" (1988, p. 69). These associations assist the learner in committing these words to memory and also aid in defining the semantic area of a word.

If collocational associations are not learned as part of L2 vocabulary knowledge, the resulting irregularities will immediately mark the learner's speech or writing as deviant or odd in some way and as decidedly non-native. Native speakers of English, for example, refer to "spoiled" butter as rancid butter and "spoiled" milk as sour milk, but not as *sour butter* or *rancid milk*. A few examples of wrong word combinations that have occurred in non-native speech are *feeble tea, *laugh broadly, *hold a burial, and *healthy advice (Bahns 1993).

It is also important for learners to recognize that collocational relationships are not equally powerful in both directions, so that *rancid* strongly suggests the collocate *butter,* for instance, but *butter* only weakly suggests *rancid,* if at all. Thus *rancid* does not readily co-occur with other nouns, but *butter* can co-occur quite freely with any number of other adjectives, such as *sweet butter, soft butter, dairy butter, unsalted butter, creamy butter, tasty butter, artificial butter,* and so on. The word in the combination that is restricted in

this way, such as *rancid* or *sour,* is known as the "key" word of the collocation. The key word does not always occur as the first word in the collocation, as for example, the key word *fire* in *set/start a fire,* but not *begin/commence/initiate a fire.*

Very commonly, collocations are associated pairs such as adjective-noun or verb-noun, but it is misleading to think of them in terms of pairs only. One reason is that they often occur as multiword linear sequences three to five words long, e.g., *a short-term strategy, to pay attention to something/someone.* Another reason is that a collocate member may co-occur with a cluster or range of words, rather than being limited to one word with which it pairs. Thus even a highly restricted pair member such as *rancid* co-occurs with several other nouns, mainly *rancid lard, rancid oil, rancid dressing* (as in salad dressing). Likewise, *sour* co-occurs with other nouns, as in *sour cherries, sour apples* (i.e., describing the taste of nonsweet fruit, or a similar non-sweet fruit taste in certain candy), or even metaphorically, as in *sour note, sour disposition.* However, the range of restricted collocates for words like *rancid* and *sour* is quite limited. We do not normally say, for instance, *rancid cheese, rancid jam, rancid syrup* or *sour meat, sour beets, sour fish.*

These restrictions may at first glance seem to present additional learning problems to overcome, but in fact they may be incorporated into vocabulary study as useful aids in learning. This is what Nattinger has in mind when he maintains that collocational associations assist the learner in committing these words to memory and help in defining the semantic area of a word. Concerning collocational associations as memory aids, researchers have noted that vocabulary is best learned in context and that words that are naturally associated in a text are more easily learned than those having no such associations.

Semantic Associations

With respect to their usefulness in helping to define the semantic area of a word, note that in the examples discussed earlier the words in each collocational range are clustered according to certain semantic features they have in common. For instance, *rancid* co-occurs with *butter, lard, oil, salad dressing*, all of which have in common the semantic feature of "oily" as part of their base, thus disallowing *rancid cream, rancid milk, rancid cheese, rancid jam, rancid syrup*. Similarly, *sour* co-occurs with *milk* or *fruit*, having in common the semantic feature "type of bad taste" or "tart taste," both of which are associated with causing the lips to pucker, thus disallowing *sour butter, sour lard, sour meat, sour beets, sour fish, sour tomatoes*.

Teachers can exploit these characteristics of restricted collocational clusters by presenting them in contexts in which they naturally occur and by pointing out the semantic links among them. Notice also that the words in these clusters, while having semantic features in common, are not so similar as to be a likely cause of confusion. Recall the cautionary note mentioned earlier concerning the problem of cross-association when teaching closely related semantic pairs or groups such as synonyms and antonyms. Cross-association difficulties are not likely to be caused by these clusters because, although the collocational members have associated semantic links, their meanings are not nearly as closely associated as are synonyms or antonyms, which either have very similar meanings or have only one opposing feature.

Syntactic Collocation Types

Collocations fall into two main syntactic groups. They may be either *grammatical collocations* or *lexical collocations*. Grammatical collocations are those in which a noun, verb, or adjective frequently co-occurs with a grammatical item, usually a preposition. Examples are *reason for, account for, rely on, afraid of, leery of, by accident, in retrospect*. Lexical collocations differ in that they do not contain grammatical words, but consist of combinations of full lexical items, i.e., nouns, verbs, adjectives, and adverbs. They include combinations such as verb + noun (*spend money, inflict a wound*), adjective + noun (*rancid butter, dense fog*), verb + adverb (*laugh loudly*), and adjective + adverb (*deeply absorbed*).

Bahns (1993), in a contrastive study of collocations, reports that learners seem to rely on a "hypothesis of transferability," whereby the majority of collocational errors found in learner English can be traced to L1 influence. Examples are **drive a bookshop* instead of *run a bookshop*,

based on influence from a Polish equivalent; **make attention at* instead of *pay attention to*, from a French equivalent; and **finish a conflict* instead of *resolve a conflict*, from a German equivalent. Bahns recommends that, whenever possible, it would be helpful to identify those collocations (of the set to be learned) that a learner with a particular L1 background "knows already" because of an equivalent in the L1 and in English. Teachers could then help students focus on identifying the differences for a chosen group of semantically equivalent L1/L2 pairs.

Teaching Activities

As we have seen in the previous discussion, collocations play an important role in vocabulary learning. "Knowing a word" includes not only knowing the meaning of a word, its part of speech, and its word family and other associations, but it also means knowing if its occurrence is restricted by certain collocations. And if so, it also means knowing the range of these collocational patterns (for a more detailed discussion of various collocational sets, ranges, and restrictions, see Carter 1998, Chapter 3). For more advanced learners, knowing a word should include at least some knowledge of collocations to the extent possible.

Classroom activities can be designed for this purpose. For example, following presentations in which collocations have been illustrated in context, perhaps by highlighting them in passages from texts, word-match activities can help in consolidating the patterns. As an illustration, a noun such as *intellect* can be given with lists of adjectives with which it does and does not co-occur, with directions to circle the appropriate collocates and then check answers against a key given on a separate sheet.

He has a { keen / sharp / high / superior / exceptional / strong / healthy } intellect.

key: keen, sharp, superior, exceptional

A similar matching exercise can be constructed for verbs (*introduce* collocates with *a person, a bill, a motion, an amendment,* but not *an idea, an object, a conclusion*), for adjectives (*likely* collocates with *choice, prospect, story, tale,* but not *article, memoir, belief*), and so on.

Gap-filling activities provide another type of practice. Students are asked to choose all possible words from a thematically related list, some of which will be needed more than once, and some of which will not be needed at all. For example:

| job | work | labor | occupation |
| position | task | employment | |

  a. That job requires hard physical _____.

  b. In today's _____ market, computer skills are important.

  c. I'll meet you for dinner after _____ today.

  d. You need to concentrate on the _____ at hand.

  e. What line of _____ are you in?

  f. Her chosen _____ is carpentry.

  g. He was promoted to a supervisory _____.

Finally, with respect to *when* collocations should be introduced, a word of caution is in order. For vocabulary instruction in the earliest stages, some researchers recommend that collocations not be included at all. They represent a more advanced type of word knowledge that should be left to higher-level students who are enhancing and consolidating vocabulary already partially learned. Beginners should focus instead on developing a large basic vocabulary and learning the typical contexts in which the words occur.

Idioms

In the previous section, collocations were discussed in terms of restricted pairs or sets of multiword combinations. Restrictions on patterns are described in terms of key words and the range or set of associated words that can co-occur with them. Not all collocational patterns are entirely equal, however, as some are relatively more "fixed" than others.

Idioms are multiword units that are completely fixed. They are further distinguished as having a unitary meaning that cannot be derived from the meanings of the component parts. That is, the combination of words in *blow one's mind* have the unitary meaning *astonish;* those in *be under the weather* have the unitary meaning *feel ill.* This unitary meaning is the main characteristic that sets idioms apart from ordinary collocations, in which the meanings do reflect the meaning of each constituent part.

It is the unitary meaning of idioms that makes them particularly troublesome for second language learners since the meaning cannot normally be guessed by the meaning of the words that make them up. Learners are likely to be mystified by idioms such as *to let the cat out of the bag* (to reveal a secret), *to shoot the breeze* (to engage in casual conversation), *to shed crocodile tears* (to be insincere), or *to bite the dust* (to die). On the other hand, they are likely to be entirely misled by what appears to be a transparent literal meaning of other idioms such as *to have cold feet* (to lack courage), *to have second thoughts* (to have doubt), *to tighten one's belt* (to be more economical), or *to have a good heart* (to be a kind person).

Idioms are a commonly occurring type of multiword unit in English, especially in informal conversational settings, and should not be ignored in vocabulary studies. Activities for the classroom could include presentation in authentic texts, such as daily newspaper cartoons/comic strips and dialogues from modern drama, and exercises that match idioms and their meanings, similar to the matching activities suggested earlier for other types of collocational units.

RECENT DEVELOPMENTS

Corpus Studies

Recent developments in corpus studies have led to major changes in language description and have greatly expanded our knowledge of collocations, idioms, and other multiword units (see especially Sinclair 1991). One problem in teaching collocations, for example, is deciding which ones ought to be included. Researchers have pointed out that, given the huge number of possible collocations for even a limited number of words, there needs to be some principled way to limit the total to a manageable number. Data from corpus studies have provided new possibilities for finding solutions to such problems.

Computers have made possible the collection of huge databases of language ranging in length from short phrases or sentences up to entire books. These corpus studies allow access to a variety of samples from language as it is actually used in real-world settings in a wide range of genres, both written and spoken. One of the most often cited studies is the COBUILD project (The Collins-Birmingham University International Language Database), with a corpus of many millions of words. This project has also produced several dictionaries and grammars, including a dictionary of collocations.

One insight from corpus studies is that many words collocate with other words from a definable semantic set. This insight gives teachers guidance by providing another criterion for choosing which collocational sets to include in vocabulary lessons. Stubbs (1995), for instance, shows that *cause* typically collocates with unpleasant things such as *problems, difficulties, trouble, damage, death, pain, anguish,* and *disease.* Conversely, *provide* collocates mainly with positive things such as *insights, information, services, aid, assistance, support,* and *money.* This difference can be highlighted with the word *work.* To *provide work* is considered a good thing, but to *cause work* is not.

The results of corpus studies has been incorporated into recent dictionaries such as the *Collins COBUILD English Dictionary* (1995) or the *Dictionary of Selected Collocations* (Hill and Lewis 1997). Advanced learners can be encouraged to use these dictionaries themselves to look up collocations for particular words they may encounter incidentally in reading or elsewhere. Also, teachers can refer to such dictionaries to select collocational sets for words chosen from frequency lists for explicit vocabulary studies.

Another innovation from corpus research concerns Sinclair's observations of patterns that extend beyond the collocational units themselves. In particular, there are cases in which a word that is chosen guides and constrains the lexical choices several words away. Schmitt (2000) discusses this discourse patterning in relation to the word *sorry.* He describes various contexts and patterns for this word and notes that, for example, one of its collocates is *so*, creating the sequence *so sorry.* If the concordance data from the corpus are examined more carefully, however, it turns out that the patterning is much more restricted.

The main occurrences of *so sorry* are in two patterns, one with *so sorry to* and one with *so sorry for.* The former is usually followed by some inconvenience the speaker regrets having caused, such as being late or troubling someone. An example is *I'm so sorry to have to ask you these personal questions.* The latter, on the other hand, is normally followed by a reference to people who have experienced some type of unfortunate situation such as injury or loss of a loved one, and it tends to cluster with some form of the verb *feel,* as in *I feel so sorry for that dead boy's family.* Schmitt notes that, from this perspective, we see that words are not chosen in isolation, but rather, can have ramifications some distance away from their actual placement in the discourse.

While it is difficult to see how this sort of patterning could be taught explicitly, it does seem worthwhile to at least point it out in vocabulary lessons. If learners are made aware of such patterns as part of the context in which collocations occur, they can then be encouraged to pay attention to similar patterns in the context of new words they encounter.

Lexical Phrases

Lexical phrases represent another common type of multiword unit. Nattinger and DeCarrico (1992) define lexical phrases as "chunks" of language of varying length, conventionalized form/function composites that occur more frequently and have more idiomatically determined meaning than language that is put together from scratch. Some are completely fixed expressions such as *by the way, how do you do?, give me a break.* Others are relatively fixed phrases that have a basic frame with slots for various fillers. They include shorter phrases such as *a ___ ago,* or longer phrases or clauses such as *the ___er X, the ___er Y; If I X, then I'll Y.* Examples with the slots filled are *a year ago; a month ago; the higher the mountain, the harder the climb; the longer you wait, the sleepier you get; if I hear that one more time, I'll scream.*

Lexical phrases are types of collocations and they are more or less idiomatic (e.g., more so in *by the way, how do you?,* but less so in *the higher the mountain, the harder the climb*). However, they differ from idioms and other ordinary collocations in that each is associated with a particular discourse function, such as expressing time, greetings, relationships among ideas, or condition. The evidence from various studies, especially computer analyses of texts, indicates that lexical phrases and other prefabricated units are pervasive in language.

Types of Lexical Phrases

In order to make lexical phrases more pedagogically useful, they have been classified according to function and grouped into three broad categories. A few representative examples are the following (for more detailed lists of types and functions, see Nattinger and DeCarrico 1992):

Social Interactions

greetings/ closings:	*hi; how are you?; what's up?/ gotta run now; see you later*
politeness/ routines:	*thanks so/very much; if you don't mind; if you please*
requesting:	Modal + Pronoun + Verb phrase (i.e., *would/could you [mind] X?*)
complying:	*of course, sure thing; I'd by happy to; no problem (at all)*
etc.	

Necessary Topics

language:	*do you speak X?; how do you say/spell X?; I speak X (a little)*
time:	*when is X?; to X for a long time; a X ago; since X; it's X o'clock*
location:	*where is X?; across from X; next to X; how far is X?*

shopping:	*how much is X?; I want to buy/see X; it (doesn't) fit(s)*
etc.	

Discourse Devices

logical connectors:	*as a result (of X); nevertheless; because (of) X; in spite of X*
temporal connectors:	*the day/week/month/year/before/ after X; and then*
qualifiers:	*it depends on X; the catch here is X; it's only in X that Y*
relators:	*on the other hand; but look at X; in addition; not only in X but Y*
exemplifiers:	*in other words; for example; to give you an example*
etc.	

In general, social interactions and discourse devices provide lexical phrases for the *framework* of the discourse, whereas necessary topics provide them for the *subject* at hand. These phrases are the primary markers which signal the direction of discourse, whether spoken or written. When they serve as discourse devices, their function is to signal, for instance, whether the information to follow is in contrast to, in addition to, or an example of information that has preceded. Those such as *on the other hand, but look at X* signal contrast; *in addition, moreover* signal addition; *it depends on X, the catch here is X* signal qualification of previous comments, and so on. When lexical phrases serve as social interactional markers, on the other hand, their primary function is to describe social relations and, in general, to help structure discourse in ways appropriate to maintaining social relations.

Why Teach Lexical Phrases

Lexical phrases offer various advantages for teaching conversation and other types of discourse. For example, because they are stored and retrieved as whole chunks, they allow for expressions that learners may as yet be unable to construct creatively. Thus even for lower level learners, they can help ease frustration and promote motivation and a sense of fluency. These phrases also ought to prove highly memorable, since they are embedded in socially appropriate situations. More importantly, they provide learners with an efficient means of interacting with others about self-selected topics.

Another advantage in teaching lexical phrases is that they can first be learned as unsegmented wholes, together with their discourse functions, and in later encounters can be analyzed and learned as individual words, thus providing additional vocabulary.

Teaching Activities

One way of teaching lexical phrases is to start with a few basic fixed routines, which learners then analyze as increasingly variable patterns as they are exposed to more varied phrases. Thus, practice with a few phrases in appropriate contexts can be followed by pattern drills as a way of promoting fluency with certain basic fixed routines. The challenge for the teacher is to use such drills to allow confidence and fluency, yet not overdo them to the point that they become mindless exercises, as was often the unfortunate result in strict audiolingualism.

The next step is controlled variation in using these basic phrases with the help of simple substitution drills to demonstrate that the chunks learned previously are not invariable routines, but instead patterns with open slots. For example, in teaching formulas for sympathy, the phrase *I'm (really/so) (very) sorry to hear (that/about) X* can be introduced first as, *I'm sorry to hear that you can't come to the party,* followed later by substitution drills with more expanded patterns, such as *I'm very sorry to hear that you had the flu,* and then later on, *I'm really very sorry to hear that there was a death in your family.* To highlight the appropriate variation for given contexts, the first version should be practiced in the context of minor inconvenience (missing a party), the second, a more serious misfortune (having an illness), and the third, a very unfortunate situation (a death or other personal tragedy). Nattinger and DeCarrico (1992) also provide suggestions for incorporating lexical phrase activities into listening or reading classes (see especially Chapter 6).

Lexical Approaches

Whereas Nattinger and DeCarrico emphasize that current texts and teaching approaches can be adapted to include lexical phrases, some applied linguists have recently promoted approaches that take lexis itself as the basis for organizing the syllabus or the overall teaching approach (Sinclair and Renouf 1988; Willis 1990; Lewis 1993; 1997). The basic organizing principle of these approaches is the frequency and usefulness of words and word combinations.

Lewis (1993), for instance, concentrates on lexical chunks themselves as the foundation of teaching. For Lewis, "language consists of grammaticalised lexis, not lexicalised grammar," and language teaching needs to develop awareness of and ability to "chunk" language successfully (p. vi). Common words are common precisely because they occur in so many expressions.

Lewis stresses the importance of learning chunks of language made up of lexico-grammatical patterns, a large number of which are pre-patterned and can be used by learners in formulaic, rehearsed ways. These chunks include lexical phrases, but also include other types of collocations, such as nouns learned in appropriate chunks with adjectival and verbal collocations, verbs learned with probable adverbial collocates, common metaphors and metaphor sets, and so on.

CONCLUSION

Lexical competence is a central part of communicative competence, and teaching vocabulary a central part of teaching language. While some questions remain concerning how to teach and what to teach, considerable progress has been made concerning the issues of explicit versus implicit learning, which strategies to teach, and which and how many lexical items to include in initial instruction. Recently, corpus studies have yielded important insights concerning the nature of lexis. As these studies continue to expand investigations into patterns of lexis in discourse, they hold great promise for exciting new directions in vocabulary learning and teaching.

DISCUSSION QUESTIONS

1. In the past century, vocabulary was a neglected area of study in the ESL/EFL classroom. Discuss several reasons for this period of neglect as well as the major influences that resulted in the current emphasis on vocabulary study.

2. Should more emphasis be given to explicit or implicit vocabulary learning at the beginning level? At more advanced levels? Why do you think so?

3. From your own experience, either as a teacher or as a learner of an L2, which vocabulary learning strategies or combination of strategies do you feel would be the most effective for incidental learning? Which do you feel might be more helpful in motivating students to learn vocabulary at a faster rate while at the same time helping them to consolidate words in long term memory?

4. Do you agree that collocations, idioms, and lexical phrases should be included in vocabulary study? Why or why not? If they are to be included, what are some of the difficulties that need to be considered? What are some possible solutions?

5. Explain some of the ways in which insights from corpus studies provide guidance for incorporating collocations and other patterned phrases into vocabulary teaching and learning.

SUGGESTED ACTIVITIES

1. Select ten words and compare their entries in three or four dictionaries. What differences do you find in the definitions? Does it seem to you that some entries would be more useful than others for second language learners? Why?

2. Select and evaluate a vocabulary text according to the following criteria:

a. Do the words seem to you to be frequent and useful ones?

b. Are at least some words presented in sets of word families, either inflectional or derivational?

c. Does the text involve explicit learning only?

d. Does it include suggested strategies for implicit learning?

3. Select one beginning reading text and one advanced reading text. From one chapter in each, identify ten lexical items that you think might present problems for learners. Discuss how you would approach teaching these lexical items, first for the beginning level learners and then for the more advanced learners.

4. Explain how you would use the following dialogue to teach more advanced learners various lexical phrases as appropriate to particular types of contexts.

Situation: The two speakers are acquaintances who work for the same company and live in the same apartment building, but are not close friends. [Mary knocks on John's apartment door.]

J: Well, hello, Mary. What a surprise.

M: Hello, John. (1) *I'm sorry I didn't call before coming over* (apology), but my phone is out of order.

J: Oh well, (2) *that's OK* (acceptance of apology). (3) *Come on in* (invitation).

M: Look John, the real reason I came over is that I need a favor. I have to catch a plane to Chicago and I just discovered my car has a flat tire. (4) *I wonder if you would mind terribly driving me to the airport right away* (request).

J: (5) *Sure thing* (compliance), Mary. I know you'd do the same for me.

M: (6) *Thanks so much.* (7) *You saved my life!* (6 and 7: expressing gratitude)

FURTHER READING

Learning Strategies

Nation, I. S. P. 1990. *Teaching and Learning Vocabulary.* Boston, MA: Heinle & Heinle. (Also good for classroom activities and exercises.)

Schmitt, N. 1997. Vocabulary learning strategies. In *Vocabulary: Description, Acquisition, and Pedagogy,* edited by N. Schmitt and M. McCarthy. Cambridge: Cambridge University Press.

———— 2000. *Vocabulary in Language Teaching.* Cambridge: Cambridge University Press.

Classroom Activities and Exercises

Allen, V. F. 1983. *Techniques in Teaching Vocabulary.* New York: Oxford University Press.

Gairns, R., and S. Redman. 1986. *Working with Words: A Guide to Teaching and Learning Vocabulary.* Cambridge: Cambridge University Press.

Redman, S., and R. Ellis. 1989. *A Way with Words. Book 1.* Cambridge: Cambridge University Press.

UNIT III

Integrated Approaches

Since the 1980s, we have witnessed a gradual movement away from rather narrow language teaching methods toward broader integrated approaches in language teaching, approaches that encourage the teaching of all four skills within the general framework of using language for learning as well as for communication. The first such approach presented in this section is content-based language teaching, which is discussed in Snow's chapter. This approach assumes that language is best learned when it is used as a medium of instruction for learning something else, such as academic content. McKay's chapter advocates a literature-based approach by showing the teacher how to use well-selected pieces of literature in the target language as content for a variety of activities that enhance language learning. Eyring's chapter shows how the learner's life experiences (those he or she has already had and those the class initiates) can form the basis for meaningful language development and use. Finally, McGroarty's chapter surveys the various models used in bilingual education, noting that the more effective maintenance and two-way models offer learners an opportunity for quality content education along with a mastery of at least two languages. All four of these multiskills approaches promote effective language development; they indicate both the cutting edge and future directions for the profession.

Content-Based and Immersion Models for Second and Foreign Language Teaching

MARGUERITE ANN SNOW

In "Content-Based and Immersion Models," Snow provides a rationale for integrated language and content instruction as well as detailed descriptions of program models in both second and foreign language teaching. She also provides examples of instructional strategies that can be used by language and content instructors and discusses current and future trends in content-based teaching.

INTRODUCTION

Throughout the history of second/foreign language teaching, the word *content* has had many different interpretations. Historically, in methods such as grammar-translation, content was defined as the grammatical structures of the target language. In the audiolingual method, content consisted of grammatical structures, vocabulary, or sound patterns presented in dialogue form. More recently, communicative approaches define content in an altogether different way. Content in these approaches generally is defined as the communicative purposes for which speakers use the second/foreign language. Thus, in a class following a notional/functional orientation, the content of a unit might be invitations, and individual lessons might cover question types, polite versus informal invitation forms, and ways to accept or decline invitations. Similarly, the content of a Natural Approach lesson might be a game in which students must locate the person who matches a certain description by asking each other questions, thereby using language for problem solving.

More recently, another definition of content has emerged in an approach that is the focus of this chapter. Content, in this interpretation, is the use of subject matter for second/foreign language teaching purposes. Subject matter may consist of topics or themes based on student interest or need in an adult EFL setting, or it may be very specific, such as the subjects that students are currently studying in their elementary school classes. This approach is in keeping with the English for Specific Purposes (ESP) tradition, where the vocational or occupational needs of the learner are identified and used as the basis for curriculum and materials development (see the chapter by Johns and Price-Machado in this volume). Content-based second language instruction generally has a strong English for Academic Purposes (EAP) orientation, in which the main instructional goal is to prepare second language students for the types of academic tasks they will encounter in school, college, or university.

Content-based models can be found in both the foreign and second language settings. They can be implemented to teach foreign languages to English-speaking children at the elementary school level in immersion programs or applied to secondary and postsecondary settings. Models of content-based instruction differ in implementation due to such factors as educational setting, program objectives, and target population. All share, however, a common point of departure—the integration of language teaching aims with subject matter instruction. This chapter begins with a rationale for content-based instruction followed by descriptions of well-established models and more recent variations. Later, sample activities for integrating language and content are presented. The chapter concludes with a discussion of current and future trends in integrated language and content instruction.

CONTENT-BASED INSTRUCTION: A RATIONALE

The theoretical foundations for content-based instruction can be drawn from a variety of sources, including second language acquisition research and work in educational and cognitive psychology. Content-based instruction fulfills a number of conditions which have been posited as necessary for successful second/foreign language acquisition. According to Krashen (1984), second language acquisition occurs when the learner receives comprehensible input, not when the learner is memorizing vocabulary or completing grammar exercises. Therefore, methods that provide students with more comprehensible input will be more successful. He states that "comprehensible subject-matter teaching *is* language teaching" (p. 62) since learners acquire language when they understand messages in that language. In content-based instruction, the focus is on the subject matter and not on the form or, as Krashen says, on "*what* is being said rather than *how*" (p. 62).

Based on many large-scale studies of Canadian immersion programs, Swain (1985, 1993) suggests that in order to develop communicative competence, learners must have extended opportunities to use the second/foreign language productively. Thus, in addition to receiving comprehensible input, they must produce comprehensible output; in other words, explicit attention must be paid to the productive language skills of speaking and writing. She maintains that learners need to be "pushed toward the delivery of a message that is . . . conveyed precisely, coherently, and appropriately" (1985, p. 249). Content-based instruction can provide this push since students learn to produce language which is appropriate in terms of both content and language.

More recently, sociocultural approaches which draw theoretical support from the work of Vygotsky have been used to promote first language (L1) literacy development in multicultural elementary school settings (see Tharp and Gallimore 1988) and offer promise for enhancing our understanding of second language (L2) learning (Lantolf and Appel 1994; Schinke-Llano 1993). Vygotsky's notions of (1) the zone of proximal development (in which learners are assisted by teachers or "more capable peers" in their development) and (2) inner speech (internally directed speech as strategies for problem solving and rehearsing) can be effectively realized in content-based settings where students have opportunities to negotiate not just language, but content as well, in increasingly complex ways.

Grabe and Stoller's (1997) review of the research foundations of content-based instruction looks outside the second language acquisition literature to research in educational and cognitive psychology for some of the most persuasive support. Research in learning theory (Anderson 1993) has been used to support the Cognitive Academic Language Learning Approach (CALLA) (Chamot and O'Malley 1994). Anderson's theory reinforces teaching approaches which combine the development of language and content knowledge, practice in using this knowledge, and strategy training to promote independent learning. Another area of cognitive investigation, depth-of-processing research, reveals that when learners are exposed to coherent and meaningful information and have opportunities to elaborate the information their linkages are more complex and recall is better (Anderson 1990). Content-based approaches promote extended practice with coherent content coupled with relevant language learning activities such as teaching how knowledge structures can be realized through language and content (see Mohan 1986; Tang 1992, 1997).

Research on the nature of expertise also provides support for content-based approaches. Bereiter and Scardamalia (1993) argue that expertise is a process in which learners reinvest their knowledge in a sequence of progressively more complex problem-solving tasks. As learners are exposed to increasing complexity in learning activities, their learning improves and they develop intrinsic motivation. They seek connections between sets of information, acquire the relevant skills to accomplish tasks, and become increasingly more adept at problem solving. Grabe and Stoller (1997) note that effective content-based instructional approaches "combine coherent and interesting informational resources to create increasing, but manageable, task complexity" (p. 14).

MODELS OF CONTENT-BASED INSTRUCTION

Models of content-based instruction can be distinguished from each other by several different means. One is by setting; some models are typically implemented in the foreign language setting while others are more common in the second language context. Another way to distinguish content-based models is by instructional level. There are many well-developed examples reported in the literature of integrated language and content teaching at the elementary school level; other models have typically been implemented successfully at the secondary or postsecondary levels with adolescents or adults. A third way to capture underlying differences in content-based models is to look at the degree of emphasis on language and content which underlies a particular program (Met 1998). In Figure 1, Met (1999, p. 7), envisioning a continuum, places "content-driven" models at one end while "language-driven" models appear at the other end.

In the sections that follow, five models of content-based instruction are described. The first two are well-developed examples of models designed to teach foreign languages to English-speaking children at the elementary school level. The last three models have been implemented in secondary and postsecondary second language

settings. Some can be classified as more "language-driven," others as more "content-driven," depending upon the objectives of the program, its target student population, and the demands of the instructional setting.

Immersion Education

The immersion model of foreign language education is perhaps the prototypical content-based approach. First established in 1965 in a suburb of Montreal, Canada, immersion programs can now be found across Canada and the United States, providing education in such foreign languages as French, Spanish, German, Chinese, and Japanese.[1] In the total immersion model, English-speaking elementary school students receive the majority of their schooling through the medium of their second language. Immersion students, in Culver City, California, for instance, learn to read, to do mathematics problems, and to conduct science experiments in Spanish; in fact, they go about the business of school like all other children, albeit in their second language. The immersion model is one of the most carefully researched language programs (see Genesee 1987; Johnson and Swain 1997). Immersion children consistently perform at or above grade level scholastically, are on par with their monolingual peers in English language development, and by the end of the elementary school, become functional bilinguals.

The Culver City Spanish Immersion program is an example of early total immersion; in early immersion the foreign language is generally used for most or all academic instruction beginning in kindergarten or grade 1. Other variations

Content-Driven					Language-Driven
Total Immersion	Partial Immersion	Sheltered Courses	Adjunct Model	Theme-Based Courses	Language Classes with Frequent Use of Content for Language Practice

Figure 1. Content-Based Language Teaching: A Continuum of Content and Language Integration

have developed over the years which differ with respect to the amount of time the foreign language is used for instruction and the grade in which the program begins. In middle or delayed immersion, onset of instruction in the foreign language begins in the middle elementary grades, usually in the fourth grade. Late immersion programs do not typically begin until the end of elementary school or the beginning of secondary school. In early partial immersion programs, there is usually a 50/50 time allocation of English and the foreign language to teach academic content.[2] While the bulk of immersion programs exist in Canada and the United States, the model has also been implemented in international settings such as Hungary, Spain, and Finland (Johnson and Swain 1997). According to Cloud, Genesee, and Hamayan (2000), despite differences in program design and delivery, most immersion programs share the following four objectives:

1. grade-appropriate levels of primary language (L1) development,
2. grade-appropriate levels of academic achievement,
3. functional proficiency in the second/foreign language,
4. an understanding of and appreciation for the culture of the target language group (p. 5).

Content-Enriched Foreign Language in the Elementary School

During the 1950s and 1960s, Foreign Language in the Elementary School (FLES) programs were widespread across the United States. In this model, "traveling" language teachers met with elementary school children for approximately 20 to 30 minutes, several times per week, for instruction in the foreign language. These classes tended to focus on formal study of the foreign language and were often criticized for their failure to produce functional users of the foreign language. "Content-enriched" FLES offers an updated approach to traditional FLES, in which subjects from the standard school curriculum are selected for introduction or reinforcement in

the FLES class (Curtain and Pesola 1994). In this content-based approach to the teaching of foreign language, teachers find points of coincidence with the standard school curriculum which can be paired with the objectives of the foreign language curriculum. So, for example, terms and structures for describing weather are coordinated with a science unit on meteorology, rather than being presented in isolation.

There are a number of advantages that the content-enriched approach has over traditional FLES. First, students in content-enriched FLES have a more relevant, meaningful context for language learning. They use the foreign language to talk about the content of the unit instead of completing grammar exercises, which was more typical of traditional FLES. Second, since students have already been exposed in English to the content under study, there is a richer context for use of the foreign language for meaningful communication, which is especially important given the learners' limited exposure to the foreign language. The foreign language class thus takes on the new role of providing reinforcement of content. Finally, the foreign language teacher does not have to search for material for the language class because the school curriculum provides a wealth of ideas which can be incorporated into instruction.

There are at least three distinct models of content-based instruction that have been developed in the second language instructional setting (Brinton, Snow, and Wesche 1989). These tend to be found in elementary, secondary, and postsecondary school settings.

Theme-Based Model

Thematic curricula have been widely implemented in U.S. elementary schools serving native English-speaking populations (see, for example, Walmsley 1994; Kovalik with Olsen 1997), special education students (Falvey 1995), and second language learners (Gianelli 1997). The theme-based model is a type of content-based instruction in which selected topics or themes provide the content from which teachers extract language learning activities.

The model has also been widely implemented in language institutes at the college or university level, where classes are often composed of students of diverse language backgrounds or interests whose common goal is to attend college or university in an English-speaking country. The teacher's goal is to select topics suitable for a heterogeneous class of international students who need to improve their academic English (EAP) skills. Thus, a unit on advertising might engage the students in a variety of EAP activities such as designing and administering a marketing survey, plotting a graph of the survey results, and comparing and contrasting consumer attitudes.

To gauge the extent of implementation of theme-based instruction in intensive English programs, Hafernik, Messerschmidt, and Vandrick (1996) analyzed the results of a survey of 32 programs to see how they defined and incorporated content-based instruction in their curricula. While the majority of the programs surveyed described their curriculum as still predominantly skills-based (60%), the results indicated that skills instruction integrated with thematic content was increasing. The programs reported that content was incorporated through a variety of means. One approach was the adoption of content-based, commercial ESL textbooks. Other programs incorporated content through instructor-designed thematic materials. Still another avenue for incorporating content was the development of thematic courses such as Computer English, or English for Special Purposes (ESP)-type courses such as Business English.

Stoller and Grabe (1997) offer the first systematic framework for theme-based instruction. Their *Six T's Approach* is a principled approach to the organization of content resources and the selection of appropriate language learning activities.[3] The first *T* is *theme*. Themes are the central ideas that organize major curricular units selected for their appropriateness to student needs and interests, institutional expectations, program resources, and teacher abilities and interests. Insects might constitute an elementary school theme while demography might be chosen for a postsecondary ESL program. The second *T*, *topics*, is the subunits of content which explore more specific aspects of the theme. A theme unit on Native Americans might include as topics the Navajo, the Hopi, and the Apache. *Texts*, the third *T*, are defined in a broad sense as the content resources which drive the basic planning of theme units. Texts could include readings from various genres, videos, audiotapes, maps, software, lectures, graphic representations, guest speakers, or field trips. *Threads*, the fourth *T*, are linkages across units that create greater curricular coherence. They are relatively abstract concepts (e.g., responsibility, ethics) that provide a natural means of linking themes. The thread *responsibility*, for example, might be used to link the units developed around the themes of civil rights, pollution, or Native Americans. The fifth *T*, *tasks*, is the day-to-day instructional activities utilized to teach content, language, and strategy instruction. Tasks in a typical EAP curriculum include listening to lectures and taking notes, participating in small group discussions, performing reading and writing activities across various genres, and practicing test-taking strategies. Finally, *transitions*, the sixth *T*, are explicitly planned actions which provide coherence across the topics in a thematic unit and across tasks within topics. An example of a topical transition in a theme unit on demography would be shifting the emphasis from trends in global population to trends in developing countries, to developed countries, and, finally, to students' home countries.

Sheltered Model

Sheltered courses currently exist in a variety of secondary and postsecondary settings. The term *sheltered* derives from the model's deliberate separation of second/foreign language students from native speakers of the target language for the purpose of content instruction. The original sheltered program was implemented in the postsecondary setting at the University of Ottawa in 1982 as an alternative to the traditional university foreign language class (Edwards et al. 1984). At the University of Ottawa, students could opt to take a content course such as Introduction to Psychology conducted in their second language in lieu of taking a traditional second language class. All instruction in the sheltered class was given in the second language by content faculty members who gauged their instruction to an audience made up of second language students.[4] French sections were offered for native English speakers and English sections for native French-speaking students. At the beginning of each content lecture, the ESL/FSL instructors held short sessions of about 15 minutes in which they would go over key terms or provide students with useful expressions, such as polite ways to interrupt the professor to request clarification; however, there was no separate language class per se.

Comparisons of sheltered psychology students with students attending more traditional ESL and FSL classes have found no significant differences in the gains of the two groups in second language proficiency despite the fact that the sheltered students did not "study" the second language. In addition to their gains in second language proficiency, the sheltered students demonstrated mastery of the content course material at the same levels as did comparison students enrolled in regular native-speaker sections of psychology. Furthermore, the sheltered students reported greater self-confidence in their abilities to use their second language as a result of participation in the sheltered class. Since the first sheltered courses were developed in the early 1980s, several formats for discipline-based instruction have been tried, including adjunct classes which require fewer financial resources (see Burger, Wesche, and Migneron 1997 for an updated discussion of "late, late" immersion at the University of Ottawa).

In elementary and secondary school settings in the United States, ESL students are often placed in sheltered content courses such as "ESL Math" or "ESL Social Studies." These courses are frequently an alternative to content courses taught in the students' native languages in settings where trained bilingual teachers are not available or the student population is so heterogeneous as to preclude primary language instruction. Sheltered courses offer language minority students an alternative to traditional ESL classes, which are often taught in isolation from the rest of the school curriculum, giving them access to school subjects from which they might otherwise be barred on the basis of their limited English proficiency. Students in sheltered classes follow the regular curriculum; however, instruction is geared to their developing levels of second language proficiency through the use of various instructional strategies and materials (see Rosen and Sasser 1997; Echevarria and Graves, 1998; see also Strategies for Content-Based Instruction in this chapter). When properly conducted, sheltered courses can offer an effective approach to integrating language and content instruction for intermediate ESL students whose language skills may not yet be developed enough for them to be mainstreamed with native English speakers in demanding content courses.

Adjunct Model

The adjunct model is a content-based approach in which students are concurrently enrolled in a language class and a content course. This model is typically implemented in postsecondary settings where such linking or "adjuncting" between language and content departments is feasible. However, it has also been successfully implemented in paired biology/ESL or history/ESL classes in a California high school (Wegrzecka-Kowalewski 1997). A key feature of the adjunct model is the coordination of objectives and assignments between language and content instructors. The language class becomes content based in the sense that the students' needs in the content class dictate the activities of the language class.

In the Freshman Summer Program (FSP) at the University of California, Los Angeles, for example, native and non-native English speakers concurrently enroll in one of six undergraduate survey courses and an English or ESL composition class. The material of the content courses become a springboard for activities and assignments in the English/ESL classes, as students have their immediate academic needs treated as well as being exposed to more general academic skills that could be transferred to other content courses. Comparison of the ESL students who have participated in FSP with students who have followed a more typical EAP curriculum revealed that, despite having significantly lower ESL placement scores, the FSP students performed as well as the higher proficiency students on a task requiring them to use lecture and reading material in the composition of an essay (Snow and Brinton 1988).[5] In the EFL setting, a modified adjunct model was implemented in the People's Republic of China at the Social Science English Language Center (SSELC) in Beijing. In the SSELC program, Chinese students attended English-language lectures in selected social science topics given by visiting American professors. The EFL classes focused on general academic skills development before the professor's arrival and then coordinated with the content course once it was under way.[6]

Another example of an adjunct model can be found in Project LEAP: Learning English for Academic Purposes, a project at California State University, Los Angeles (Snow 1997; Snow and Kamhi-Stein in press). In this model, language minority students were concurrently enrolled in two linked courses: an undergraduate general education course (e.g., Introduction to Cultural Anthropology, Humans and their Biological Environment) and a study group team taught by a peer study group leader and a language specialist. Participating content faculty modified their syllabi and teaching methods to integrate language and content instruction with the aim of improving the academic literacy skills of the students enrolled in the adjunct courses. Evaluation of the project revealed that, overall, the performance of students in the adjunct courses approximated or exceeded that of the students who had not been enrolled in the study group courses in which content-based activities were introduced and practiced (Snow and Kamhi-Stein 1997).

Expansion of Content-Based Models

The five content-based models described in the preceding section present well-documented prototypes of content-based instruction. In recent years, the models have evolved into new formats and different features have been borrowed, blurring many of the key distinctions. Brinton, Snow, and Wesche (1989) anticipated this trend: "The key point to be made is that depending on the setting, the configuration of the model may differ significantly, and the features of the three models [theme-based, sheltered, and adjunct] may tend to blend together" (p. 23).

Numerous examples exist in recent literature of the application of a model designed for one population to a different target population or of a program traditionally implemented at a particular educational level being used in another. One such example took place at UCLA in the ESL Service Courses; the curriculum of the multiskill courses has evolved from theme-based units used in the 1970s and 1980s to the "simulated" adjunct model currently in use (Brinton and Jensen in press). In this hybrid model, videotapes of actual lectures by UCLA content faculty and assigned course readings provide the content base for the ESL courses. Another case is the theme-based model's growing popularity in the EFL context. Murphey (1997) reports on the challenges of implementing "workshop" courses (e.g., "Rock 'n' Roll History," "Health and Fitness Awareness") in a traditional university EFL setting in Japan.

Another area of significant expansion for content-based instruction is foreign language teaching at the postsecondary level. Ryan and Krueger (1993) present an interesting set of case studies of "discipline-based" programs developed by foreign language and discipline faculty, reflecting a variety of configurations and ways to combine language and content. For example, the Foreign Languages across the Curriculum (FLAC) program at the University of Minnesota links the major European languages with social science disciplines. Students enroll in weekly seminars conducted in the target language and devoted to comparison of news coverage in the American press and a major daily newspaper published in Spanish, French, or German. In another variation, an anthropology professor, an East Asian studies department professor, and an anthropology graduate student at Brown University designed "Japanese Culture and Society," an existing course to which a content-based component in Japanese was added.

Two of the most dramatic examples of the changing configurations of models can be seen in the United States. Starting in the mid-1980s, *two-way* immersion programs began to appear. Also called *bilingual immersion* or *dual language,* they are a blending of immersion and developmental bilingual programs. Language minority (limited English speaking) and language majority students (native English speaking) are grouped in the same classroom with the goal of academic excellence and bilingual proficiency for both student groups. By 1995, after approximately a decade of implementation, more than 182 two-way programs have been established in the United States (Christian et al. 1997).

The second example, also an application of the immersion model, is the use of "structured immersion" (also called English immersion) in states such as California to teach limited English proficient students (Kuhlman and Murray 2000). Of English immersion, Cloud, Genesee, and Hamayan (2000) state:

> There is no generally accepted definition or set of criteria to define English immersion programs. They are recommended by some educators and policymakers as programs for English language learners in the U.S. It can refer to regular programs for native English speaking students where English is the only language of instruction. They may or may not include special provisions for English language learners such as ESL instruction. They aim for proficiency in oral and written English and full academic achievement; they do not aim to maintain or develop language minority students' primary language or culture (p. 205).

According to Ovando and Collier (1998), structured immersion is a "misnamed program model that was promoted by English-only proponents with a political agenda in the 1980s" (p. 56). There are strong feelings in many quarters that structured immersion represents a misapplication of the original Canadian immersion model designed to teach French to English-speaking students.

Strategies for Content-Based Instruction

This section is divided into two parts. The first provides instructional strategies for use by language teachers to exploit content material. The second part is directed to content teachers to provide ideas for making content more accessible to second/foreign language learners while simultaneously teaching language skills. Sample lessons are provided for both settings to illustrate the strategies in use.

Strategies for Language Teachers Content-based instruction provides a rich context for teaching the traditional four skills—listening, speaking, reading, and writing—in the ESL/EFL class. In addition, since the focus of many content-based ESL/EFL courses is on academic language learning, teaching strategic competence is essential. To be successful academically, all students must, for example, be able to take good lecture notes. They must develop strategies for condensing large amounts of reading material into reading notes or preparing study guides. Clearly, students need to learn to manage their time wisely and to develop effective test-taking strategies. These and other study skills are perhaps even more critical for the ESL/EFL students who may need more time to read and master content material and who may lack familiarity with the educational system and/or lack experience with common Western modes of critical thinking and writing.

Strategies to teach the four skills, discussed individually in other chapters of this volume, can be used effectively in content-based instruction. The purpose of this section is to illustrate how the four skills, plus study skills, can be integrated in content-based instruction. Three sample units are presented (see pp. 311–312) that integrate the teaching of the five skills within an instructional unit. The units were developed for use in the adjunct program at UCLA for a high intermediate ESL course paired with Introductory Psychology.[7] The units reflect a "receptive to productive" teaching cycle. Each unit begins with a recognition or exposure activity. Students are presented with models which illustrate the teaching point of the unit. These models may be in the form of a passage taken from the content textbook and used for a dictation, as in Unit 1; alternatively, the model may take the form of an example text to introduce the notion of coherence, which is the focus of Unit 2. The second activity of each unit engages the students in a directed exercise with the teaching point. So, for example, in Unit 1, students underline the logical connectors of classification or, in Unit 3, they complete a cloze passage constructed from the ESL instructor's model lecture notes in which key terms or information has been deleted. Subsequent activities provide extended practice; for instance, in Unit 2, students reconstruct a paragraph (i.e., dictocomp) after listening to the instructor read it aloud. The culminating activity of each unit requires the students to put their newly acquired knowledge to work in the production of a text, such as a composition or a summary. In some cases, there are immediate follow-up activities such as analysis of common error patterns found in the compositions as in Unit 1. In other cases, persistent problems such as essay organization, source material documentation, or punctuation become the focus of peer-editing groups or are recycled into other types of practice activities throughout the term.

Unit 1: Focus—Classification

SKILL:	ACTIVITY 1:
Listening	Dictation—Model paragraph of classification on the topic "Personality"
SKILL:	ACTIVITY 2:
Prewriting	Using their dictations, students underline the nouns describing categories (e.g., types, kinds, stages) and the logical connectors of classification; discussion of the rhetorical organization of classification
SKILL:	ACTIVITY 3:
Prewriting	Using a list of characteristics of individuals, students classify the information into the appropriate categories and label them (e.g., shyness, assertiveness, aggressiveness)
SKILL:	ACTIVITY 4:
Reading	Students reread their content text to check their categories and the accuracy of their classifications
SKILL:	ACTIVITY 5:
Speaking	In groups, students compare/defend their categories and classifications
SKILL:	ACTIVITY 6:
Writing	Students are given the following prompt: "Grace Ursini, a junior high school student, has an IQ of 140. She does well in school, especially in English, Spanish, and music." They are also given several explanations such as "Grace's mother is president of the local Parent-Teacher Association" to use as supporting data for their claims. Using this situation, students take the example of Grace Ursini and compose a classification essay on the topic "Environment vs. Heredity"
SKILL:	ACTIVITY 7:
Grammar	Group work—Students examine sentences taken from their compositions, determine the error patterns, and make the appropriate corrections; review of passive voice based on error analysis of compositions

Unit 2: Focus—Text Coherence

SKILL:
Reading/
Speaking

ACTIVITY 1:
Instructor introduces notion of text coherence; students read passage from content text on "The Development of Language" and underline elements of cohesion (e.g., pronouns, logical connectors, lexical chains, etc); discussion of different ways in which ideas can be joined (includes a review of articles/pronouns and a review of synonyms/word forms)

SKILL:
Listening/
Prewriting

ACTIVITY 2:
Dictocomp—Teacher reads a short passage on "Piaget's Stages of Cognitive Development" two times; the students listen the first time, take notes during the second reading, then recreate the passage in their own words; students compare their reformulations with the original passage from the content text, noting the different types of cohesive devices used

SKILL:
Writing

ACTIVITY 3:
Students compose an essay comparing Bruner's and Piaget's theories of child development

SKILL:
Speaking/
Writing

ACTIVITY 4:
Students critique each other's essays in peer editing groups and discuss ways to improve their papers; students revise their papers based on the feedback

Unit 3: Focus—Understanding Lectures

SKILL:
Listening

ACTIVITY 1:
Lecture on "Altered States of Consciousness" (simulated by the ESL instructor or presented on video); students take notes

SKILL:
Study skills

ACTIVITY 2:
Students complete a cloze passage constructed from instructor's model lecture notes

SKILL:
Speaking

ACTIVITY 3:
Group work—Students compare their notes with the model notes and discuss ways to determine relevant/extraneous material, use of abbreviations, organization of notes

SKILL:
Writing

ACTIVITY 4:
Students prepare one-page summaries of the main points contained in their lecture notes

Strategies for Content Instructors The first part of this section presented techniques which the ESL/EFL instructor can use to teach language skills through content. In this case, the instructor is using the content as a vehicle to present and practice language in the ESL/EFL class; the primary objective is the teaching of language skills, although the content is clearly reinforced in the process. In content classes, on the other hand, the instructor is primarily concerned with delivering subject matter instruction. Immersion and sheltered model instructors, for example, are responsible for presenting cognitively demanding subject matter in a manner that is comprehensible to second/foreign language students. The same is true for regular classroom teachers who have ESL students in their classes. The challenge to content teachers lies in "unpacking"—to use a new term—difficult content in ways appropriate to the learner's developing language system. To do this, teachers must utilize a variety of techniques and strategies for making content instruction comprehensible. These instructional techniques fall into four general categories:

1. Modifying Input Recalling that second language learners have difficulty with the cognitively demanding language of academic texts, it is critical that content teachers adapt the delivery of instruction to the second language learners' level of proficiency. The following techniques are useful ways to modify input:

a. slower (yet natural) rate of speech;
b. clear enunciation;
c. controlled vocabulary/limited initial use of idioms.

2. Using Contextual Cues Content teachers must provide second language learners with multiple cues to meaning so that they do not have to rely solely on the spoken or written word to understand difficult material. These contextual cues include

a. gestures;
b. dramatization of meaning through facial expressions, pantomime, role play;
c. visuals, including pictures, photographs, slides, maps, graphs, diagrams;

d. realia (i.e., actual physical objects);
e. bulletin boards;
f. word banks (e.g., charts which associate math vocabulary with their corresponding symbols);
g. building predictability into instructional routines such as opening and closing activities, directions, and homework assignments so that students can figure out what to do from the context even if they do not completely understand the spoken instructions;
h. building redundancy into lessons through repetition, restatement, and exemplification.

3. Checking for Understanding There are a variety of techniques which can be used to insure that students understand both the language used in instruction and the concepts being imparted. Among these checks of comprehension are

a. asking students to decide if information is true or false;
b. asking students to provide examples;
c. having students paraphrase important terms in their own words;
d. having students summarize key information;
e. asking students both factual questions (e.g., *Who?*, *What?*) and referential questions (*Why?* and *What would you do if . . . ?*);
f. having students ask each other questions.

4. Designing Appropriate Lessons All effective instruction requires adequate pacing, attention to students' developmental levels, specification of appropriate objectives, a variety of activity types, and ongoing, formative evaluation. In addition to these basic considerations, content teachers working with second language learners must take extra measures in lesson planning in the following areas:

a. **Vocabulary instruction** Systematic activities for vocabulary instruction must be devised since second language learners often lack the basic and specialized vocabulary that characterizes academic texts.
b. **Prioritizing objectives** The content teacher must decide what key concepts should receive the most attention since covering all of the material may not always be possible.
c. **Providing schema-building activities** Techniques such as reviewing previously covered

materials, relating ideas to the students' own experiences, and using brainstorming or clustering activities help students develop a frame of reference for cognitively demanding content material. Advance organizers such as outlines, charts, and study guides also help students see the inherent structure of academic material.

d. **Learner grouping strategies** A variety of grouping arrangements should be employed. Students can work in pairs, in small groups, and in structured cooperative learning groups to maximize different sources of input and output and to increase interaction.

CURRENT AND FUTURE TRENDS IN CONTENT-BASED INSTRUCTION

One of the more noticeable current trends is the innovative ways in which teachers have incorporated communicative teaching practices into content-based instruction. The recent literature is rich in examples. Stoller (1997), for instance, describes how she integrated project work into content-based instruction and Short (1997) reports on the use of graphic organizers to teach social studies; similarly, Brinton and Holten (1997) apply "into, through, and beyond" techniques into a content-based lesson planning framework. Teachers are also integrating technology into content-based instruction, increasingly looking to the Internet as a rich resource for language and content activities. The need to teach information competence in ESL classes to prepare students for content-area classes has also been underscored (Mitoma and Son 1999). A rich collection of teaching techniques for integrating language and content can be found in Brinton and Masters (1997).

Expansion and innovation in content-based instruction will undoubtedly be boosted by the trend toward standards-based instruction and assessment. In the United States, educational reform has led to federal legislation supporting the development of standards for the public

Making Lectures Comprehensible[8]

Objective: To make lectures more comprehensible by defining, simplifying, and recycling content-specific and noncontent vocabulary.

Rationale: Defining, embedding, and restating terminology helps students learn new content-specific terms (e.g., *communalist, democratic, centralism*) and noncontent terms in new contexts (e.g., *the left, a watershed event*).

Procedures:
1. It is very important to expose ESL students to sophisticated academic vocabulary during lectures.
2. *Before the lecture*, review lecture notes to anticipate difficult or unfamiliar content-specific and general academic vocabulary items. *During the lecture*, monitor what you are saying to help yourself become aware of your use of difficult terminology. Use the strategies below to help students understand new terms and expand their academic vocabulary.
   - Define and explain new terms—whether or not they are content specific.
   - Embed and restate new terms. For example, "The impetus for reform, that is, *the driving force or stimulus for reform,* was the Watergate scandal."
   - Break down terms for the students so that they can understand the meanings. For example, *bicameral*: bi=two, *camera*=chamber.
   - Explain the meaning of colloquialisms or slang expressions. For example, take care to describe what a phrase like *to beat a dead horse* means and clarify its relevance to the conceptual point.

schools in arts, civics and government, economics, foreign languages, English, history, geography, mathematics, and science (Gomez 2000). Reform has also influenced second/foreign language teaching. The standards of the American Council on the Teaching of Foreign Languages were published in 1996 (ACTFL 1996; also, see ACTFL's website), and the *ESL Standards for Pre-K–12 Students* in 1997 (TESOL 1997; also, see TESOL's website). Both documents promote an expanded role for integrated language and content learning. For example, in Goal 2 of the ESL Standards, students are "to use the second language to achieve academically in all content areas." Standards 3.1 and 3.2 of the ACTFL Standards call for students to "connect with other disciplines and acquire information." With the development of national standards (and state/local standards in some locales) for foreign language and ESL, teachers have useful guidelines around which to design curricula and instruction. It should also be pointed out that the standards movement is a broadly based reform. Work on bandscales in Australia (National Languages and Literacy Institute of Australia 1993) and learner outcomes in Canada (Alberta Education 1997) indicates the international scope; moreover, TESOL has begun to explore the feasibility of international standards for English language institutions (Fujimoto 2000).

Perhaps one of the greatest challenges in the ongoing expansion and innovation of content-based instruction is the search for the right balance of language and content teaching. Swain prophetically stated in 1988 that "not all content teaching is necessarily good language teaching" (p. 68). Echevarria, Vogt, and Short (2000), Brinton (2000), Crandall (1998), Lorenz and Met (1988), and Peterson (1997), among others, have pursued this issue from the point of view of teacher preparation. What are the requisite skills needed in order to be an effective teacher of content-based instruction? Others have approached the issue with a call for more systematic planning of instruction. There seems to be an interesting reversal, with "language-driven" models seeking a stronger emphasis on content (see Stoller and Grabe's Six T's Approach) and the "content-driven" models promoting a stronger language focus (see Kinsella 1997).

To this end, Snow, Met, and Genesee (1989) developed a framework in which language and content teachers work collaboratively to define two types of language teaching objectives. The first type of objective is content-obligatory language. Content-obligatory language is the language (e.g., vocabulary, functions, structures) which is required for students to master concepts or material in any given content class. Without content-obligatory language, students will not be able to handle the demands of academic tasks which are cognitively demanding and context-reduced. The second objective is content-compatible language. This includes specification of the types of language which pair naturally with content material. Content-compatible language instruction allows teachers to provide students with extended practice with a troublesome grammar point, such as irregular past-tense forms, for example, through contextualized academic tasks.

A final trend is a growing concern with empowerment and equity within content-based instruction methodology. Kinsella (1997) argues that "the pedagogical emphasis on comprehensibility and contextualization of instructional delivery in much of CBI [content-based instruction] has been somewhat too 'teacher driven' and 'curriculum centered,' with less careful consideration given to the development of effective, self-directed learners" (p. 50). She takes aim at sheltered instruction, in particular, noting that this approach does not "necessarily contribute to the ESL students' ability to confidently and competently embark on independent learning endeavors. . . . students instead [are] frequently assigned a relatively passive role . . . " (p. 51).

The faculty development component in Project LEAP described earlier in this chapter is another way to address the equity and empowerment issue. In a significant departure from the traditional adjunct model, in which ESL instructors typically have had limited input in the instructional decisions of content faculty, participating content faculty in this project were required to revamp their syllabi, assignments, and instructional styles to make their courses more accessible to language minority students. Snow and Kamhi-Stein (in press) present a case study of the successes and challenges of requiring content faculty to assume greater responsibility for meeting the needs of second language learners.

Still others in content-based instruction have looked to critical pedagogy, with its roots in Freire's approach (1970, 1998), in discussions of learner empowerment. Benesch (1993) notes that EAP has developed an "accommodationist ideology instead of an ideology of opposition and change" (p. 714), and calls for teachers to "negotiate academic curricula responsive to social, economic, and political issues, rather than serving one that is so narrowly focused on career preparation" (p. 714). An example of an ideology of change can be found in Benesch (1996), where she, as the EAP teacher in an adjunct ESL/psychology course, conducted a "critical needs analysis" which revealed contradictory demands on her students from the academic hierarchy (university, college, English, and psychology departments) and developed a set of activities to help students manage these demands and create possibilities for change. One such activity was having the students generate questions for the professor to answer in the psychology class; another was to invite the professor to the ESL class to engage in more informal interaction with the students. Another example of student empowerment comes from Hones (1999), who created a content-based course on the U.S. justice system, with particular focus on the provocative case of death row inmate Mumia Abu-Jamal. The course was designed to challenge international students to improve their English language skills while developing their awareness of issues of social justice.

CONCLUSION

Content-based instruction differs from more traditional second language teaching methods in a number of ways. First, the roles of the language teacher and the content teacher are necessarily expanded. Since the content dictates the selection and sequence of teaching points, the language teacher must learn to exploit the content material for its language teaching potential. This means that the language teacher must select content material judiciously, or in the case

where the materials are already selected (such as in adjunct classes), seek out material which is most suitable for language teaching aims. It also means that the language teacher must become familiar enough with the content material to put it to meaningful use. This is one of the most difficult, yet indispensable, requirements of content-based teaching. By the same token, the content teacher in content-based approaches needs to become sensitized to the language needs of second/foreign language students. For the immersion teacher who wears two hats, both language and content considerations must stay indelibly at the forefront. No matter the model, content-based teaching entails systematic planning of integrated instruction using a rich repertoire of strategies and techniques.

Content-based instructors must also develop appropriate curricula and materials which reflect the assumptions of the approach. Thus, while commercial language texts may be appropriate for some activities and are certainly useful references, content-based instruction necessarily requires extensive development of curricula and materials which integrate the teaching of language skills with content, and hence, may be very labor intensive. The sample lessons presented previously in this chapter reflect many hours of preparation and planning.

Content-based instruction is a student-centered approach. Choice of content should revolve around considerations of students' current proficiency levels, academic or vocational objectives, interests, and needs. When selecting a content-based instructional model, these considerations must be taken into account. Assessment, therefore, plays an important role on a number of levels. First, the needs of the learner must be determined. These may be very general in the case of students who are enrolled in college preparatory programs in intensive language institutes, or very specific, as in the case of ESL students in the public schools who will be mainstreamed quickly into regular content classes. The needs of foreign language students must be considered as well, guided by the standards developed for this particular teaching context. Second, the students' language proficiency levels must be carefully assessed in determining the type of content which will be most appropriate to select for instruction. Finally, once a content-based approach is implemented, assessment must be carefully planned to take into consideration both language development and content mastery (see Cohen's chapter in this volume).

The teaching of language through content is not so much a method as a reorientation to what is meant by *content* in language teaching. The literature offers strong theoretical support for content-based approaches and abundant examples of successful programs in both the foreign and second language settings which effectively teach language through content. As we have seen, content-based instruction crosses over age groups and settings and is very much in keeping with the communicative approach to second language teaching.

DISCUSSION QUESTIONS

1. If you were studying challenging content in your second language, which of the techniques and strategies listed in the chapter do you think would be particularly helpful in making the subject matter more comprehensible?
2. The author states that the immersion model might be considered the prototypical content-based program. Upon completion of elementary school, immersion students have acquired nativelike reading and listening skills, but typically are not nativelike in the productive skills of speaking and writing. How might these findings be explained in terms of the notions of comprehensible input and comprehensible output?
3. Recall Kinsella's concern with "teacher-driven" and "curriculum-centered" methods. She suggests that students in content-based classes be taught strategy usage or "learning to learn" strategies. What do you think she means by this? Give examples of "learning to learn" strategies.
4. Several points were raised at the end of the chapter about ways in which content-based instruction differs from more traditional methods. Can you think of any other differences?

SUGGESTED ACTIVITIES

1. Imagine that you are a fourth grade teacher who has limited English proficient students in your class. You are planning a unit on explorers of the New World. What content-obligatory language skills should you anticipate? What content-compatible language could you reinforce in your lesson?
2. The author describes five different models currently in use which integrate language and content instruction. Compare and contrast them in terms of
   a. the degree to which they are "language-driven" or "content-driven";
   b. the degree of explicit language teaching;
   c. the types of curricula and materials used;
   d. the role of the language and/or content teacher;
   e. the purpose of assessment.
3. Ellis (1985) states: "Different features may aid development at different times. For instance, in [his study] teacher self-repetitions were more frequent at an early stage of development, and teacher expansions at a later stage. . . . Both the learner and the native speaker adjust their behavior in the light of the continuous feedback about the success of the discourse with which they provide each other" (p. 82). Consider these findings in terms of the list of techniques and strategies for content instruction. Consider the four categories (modifying input, using contextual cues, checking for understanding, and designing appropriate lessons) and decide which techniques might be most appropriate for
   a. beginning students;
   b. advanced students;
   c. teaching mathematics;
   d. teaching history;
   e. immigrant students;
   f. international students.
4. Using the receptive to productive cycle illustrated in the sample ESL/psychology units, design an integrated content-based unit for teaching:
   a. comparison/contrast
   b. conditionals
   c. guessing the meaning of words from context

FURTHER READING

Cloud, N., Genesee, F., and E. Hamayan. 2000. *Dual Language Instruction: A Handbook for Enriched Education.* Boston, MA: Heinle & Heinle Publishers.

A handbook for K–12 teachers, educational professionals, and policy makers who teach students in two languages.

Genesee, F. 1987. *Learning Through Two Languages.* New York: Newbury House.

A thorough discussion of the history of the immersion model and research findings in Canada and the United States.

Johnson, R. K., and M. Swain, eds. 1997. *Immersion Education: International Perspectives.* Cambridge: Cambridge University Press.

Descriptions of both U.S. and Canadian immersion programs and those in other international settings such as Spain, Finland, and Hungary.

Kasper, L. F., ed. 2000. *Content-Based College Instruction.* Mahwah, NJ: Lawrence Erlbaum.

A collection of articles by experienced content-based professionals dealing with issues such as the role of technology, grammar, and materials development.

Snow, M. A. 1998. Trends and issues in content-based instruction. *Annual Review of Applied Linguistics,* 18: 243–267.

A review of recent research in content-based second/foreign language instruction.

Snow, M. A., and D. M. Brinton, eds. 1997. *The Content-Based Classroom: Perspectives on Integrating Language and Content.* New York: Longman.

A comprehensive anthology covering theoretical underpinnings, K–12 and postsecondary instruction, teacher preparation, assessment, alternative models, and practical issues.

WEBSITES

American Council on the Teaching of Foreign Languages (ACTFL):
  www.actfl.org
Center for Applied Linguistics:
  www.cal.org

Project LEAP:
  http://curriculum.calstatela.edu/faculty/asnow/ProjectLEAP/
Teaching English to Speakers of Other Languages (TESOL):
  www/tesol.org

ENDNOTES

1 A list of existing U.S. immersion programs and key programmatic information for each program can be found on the website of the Center for Applied Linguistics. To locate the list, look under the heading "Databases and Directories."

2 For a more detailed discussion of the features of immersion programs, see Genesee (1987).

3 For a more detailed description of the Six T's Approach, see Stoller and Grabe (1997).

4 For an interesting discussion of the strategies used by a French-speaking professor and an English-speaking professor lecturing in psychology, see Wesche and Ready (1985).

5 For a more detailed discussion of the Freshman Summer Program, see Brinton, Snow, and Wesche (1989).

6 For more information on SSELC, see Brinton, Snow, and Wesche (1989).

7 These units were jointly developed by the author and Donna Brinton.

8 This activity was devised by Project LEAP participants and political science professor Dr. Nadine Koch for use in "Introduction to American Politics and Society" at California State University, Los Angeles. This activity and others designed to teach academic literacy skills can be found on the Project LEAP website.

Literature as Content for ESL/EFL

SANDRA LEE MCKAY

In "Literature as Content for ESL/EFL," McKay argues that using literature as content provides three major benefits for learners: (1) it demonstrates the importance of authors' choice of form to achieve specific communicative goals, (2) it is an ideal resource for integrating the four skills, and (3) it raises cross-cultural awareness. Example classroom activities are developed based on two short stories.

INTRODUCTION

Why use literature in ESL/EFL classes? There are those who maintain that due to the special nature of literary texts, literature can contribute little to language learning (see McKay [1982] for a summary of these arguments). However, in this chapter I argue that using literature as content in ESL/EFL classes provides three major benefits. First, because literary texts depend on how the language is used to create a particular effect, literature demonstrates for learners the importance of form in achieving specific communicative goals. Second, using literature as content in the L2 classrooms provides an ideal basis for integrating the four skills. And third, in an era when English is used in a great variety of cross-cultural encounters, literary texts are valuable in raising students' and teachers' cross-cultural awareness. (See also Hinkel's chapter on cross-cultural communication in this volume.) This chapter opens with an examination of what is meant by literary texts. Then each advantage listed above for using literature is examined in detail. Throughout the chapter, examples of classroom activities are provided to show how such activities can be designed.

DEFINING LITERARY TEXTS

The *How* of Literary Texts

Typically, language is used to convey a message by relaying information. Although literary texts exemplify other features of normal communication, they generally lack this purpose. Rather, their aim is to convey "an individual awareness of reality" (Widdowson 1975, p. 70). What makes literary texts unique is that in literature the what and how of the text are inseparable. As Widdowson puts it,

> An understanding of what literature communicates necessarily involves an understanding of how it communicates: what and how are not distinct. It is for this reason that literary works cannot be satisfactorily paraphrased or explained by any single interpretation: to do so is to recast their essential ambiguity into the definite shape of conventional statement. The basic problem in the teaching of literature is to develop in the student an awareness of the what/how of literary communication and this can only be done by relating it to, without translating it into, normal uses of language (1975, p. 70).

The fact that in works of literature the "what and how are not distinct" makes literature valuable for extending learners' awareness that how they say something is important in two ways. First, how something is said often contributes to speakers' achieving their purpose in communication; and second, in deciding how something is said, speakers often communicate something about themselves—they establish their voice.

Kramsch (1993) offers a simple illustration of the importance of form in conveying information. At a conference workshop she attended, the linguist A. L. Becker asked the participants to describe in one sentence what he was about to do. He then walked up the steps to the podium and laid a book on the desk. Following this, he asked a variety of participants to read their descriptions. After several people read their sentences, it was clear that even in describing such a simple act, each text provided a unique perspective on what had been observed. Whereas some participants referred to Becker as "a linguist," others referred to him as "the man," "you," or "he." Whereas some stated that Becker "put" the book on the podium, others stated that he "slapped" or "placed" the book on the podium. Whereas some described the action in the simple past ("you stepped onto the stage"), others described it in the past continuous ("he was walking up the steps") (p. 107).

For Kramsch, this exercise is significant because it demonstrates that every writer has available a variety of choices for conveying a message. For example, the fact that the participants wrote rather than spoke affected the shape of their text. The choice of grammatical form enabled them to relate the act to a particular time and place and to define what was new and old information. Perhaps most significantly, the participants had a choice of what to say and what not to say. For Kramsch, the particularity of literary texts rests on an author's use of six aspects of text development. Specifically, in creating a literary text, authors shape the medium of written texts, make grammatical and lexical choices that enable them to define spatial and temporal frames of reference, negotiate interpersonal relationships with their readers, look through language to a believed world, evoke prior language, and leave many things unsaid. It is these dimensions of literary texts that contribute to the "what/how of literary communication," making them difficult to paraphrase.

Carter (1996) makes a case for extending the notion of literary texts to include such things as advertisements, newspaper headlines, jokes, and puns since they all provide examples of verbal play. As he points out, "the language used in such texts does not refer to activities, entities and events in the external world; it displays and creatively patterns its discourse in such a way as to

invite readers to interpret how it represents that world" (pp. 7–8). He supports this by providing several instances of the literary qualities present in everyday examples of language, such as an advertisement from a British airline on its wider and more comfortable seating, which states "Relief from aches on planes," or an advertisement for the Swiss chocolate bar Toblerone, which reads "The one and Tobleronly." Such examples offer a convincing argument for introducing learners to the playfulness of literary language by drawing on selected instances of everyday language use.

Literary Texts and the Reader

Whereas Widdowson, Kramsch, and Carter define literary texts by their unique form, Rosenblatt (1978) defines literary texts primarily in terms of how readers interact with them. She maintains that the common way of distinguishing literary works of art from other types of texts has been to examine the text itself. For Rosenblatt, a text is merely an object of paper and ink until a reader interacts with it. Hence the question of defining literary texts does not depend on examining how literary and nonliterary texts differ, but rather depends on considering what a reader does in these different kinds of reading.

According to Rosenblatt, readers perform very different activities during aesthetic and non-aesthetic reading. To illustrate these differences, she relates the example of a mother whose child has just swallowed a poisonous liquid and is frantically reading the label to discover what course of action to follow. The mother's main concern is to get the essential information in the text. Rosenblatt describes the type of reading in which the main purpose of the reader is to decipher what message can be carried away from the text as *efferent*, from the Latin, *efferre* "to carry away." In efferent reading, the reader focuses on the message of the text. In contrast, in aesthetic reading, "the reader's primary concern is with what happens *during* the reading process" (p. 24).

The distinction between efferent and aesthetic reading rests on the stance a reader adopts in relation to a particular text. Rosenblatt maintains that the same text can be read either efferently or aesthetically. Hence, a reader could read a literary text aesthetically so that his or her "attention is centered directly on what he [or she] is living through during his relationship with that particular text" (p. 25) or he or she could read it efferently by gathering specific information. For Rosenblatt, too often literature classrooms focus on the latter type of reading in that they analyze the form of the text and thus reduce learners' engagement with literature. This concern with conscious attention to form in a literature class reflects an ongoing debate among teachers of literature.

There are many who argue that stylistics, or literary text analysis, can be of great value to language learners (e.g., Widdowson 1975; Carter 1996). Carter, for example, summarizes the advantages of using stylistics in language classrooms in the following way:

> (i) stylistics provides students with a method of scrutinizing texts, a "way in" to a text, opening up starting points for fuller interpretation. . . .
> (ii) basing interpretation on systematic verbal analysis reaffirms the centrality of language as the aesthetic medium of literature.
> (iii) non-native students possess the kind of conscious, systematic knowledge about the language which provides the best basis for stylistic analysis. In many respects, therefore, non-native students are often better at stylistic analysis than native speakers (1996, pp. 5–6).

Others, however, argue that a focus on stylistics undermines the reading of a literary text for enjoyment, for an aesthetic experience. Gower (1986), for example, poses the following question: "Can we, then in any sense, say that 'stylistic analysis' helps the EFL student, when its declared aim is to illuminate the 'mechanism' of a 'text' under the microscope . . . ? This, as I have said, is a very different thing from reading: the students operate on the 'text' rather than let a poem or novel speak to them" (pp. 129–130). Gower, like Rosenblatt, believes that literary texts should be read and enjoyed and that literary analysis necessarily undermines this possibility.

The question of whether or not to use stylistics or language analysis in L2 classrooms depends on what is meant by stylistics. Clearly, if stylistics entails mere analysis of literature to support one central meaning of a text, usually one arrived at by so-called literary scholars, then there is little possibility that this will engage language learners or contribute to their enjoyment of reading a literary text. If, on the other hand, stylistics provides learners with the tools to justify their own opinions of a text, then the analysis of the text can be related to the student's own aesthetic reading of it. Widdowson (1992) terms this approach one of practical stylistics in which the goal is "to stimulate an engagement with primary texts, to encourage individual interpretation while requiring that this should be referred back to features of the text" (p. xiv). Carter (1996) makes a distinction between what is traditionally thought of as stylistics and what he terms a *language-based approach* to literature. For Carter, a language-based approach is student centered, activity based, and process oriented in that classroom tasks help students support their interpretation of a text by engaging them in the process of meaning-making.

How then can language analysis be productively used in L2 classrooms to enhance students' enjoyment in reading literature and develop their awareness of language?

USING LITERARY TEXTS TO DEVELOP LANGUAGE

Comparing Two Short Stories

In order to illustrate how literary texts might be approached in L2 classrooms, let us compare how two short stories that recount the experience of young adolescents in their school environment might be used ("Eleven" by Sandra Cisneros [an excerpt from her novel entitled *Woman Hollering Creek*] and "Out of Order" by William Saroyan). "Eleven" tells the story of Rachel on her eleventh birthday. The story takes place at school where the teacher, Mrs. Price, asks who in the class owns a red sweater that has been "sitting in the coatroom for a month." No one in the class says it belongs to them until suddenly one of the students, Sylvia Saldivar, says, "I think it belongs to Rachel." Although Rachel states that it is not hers, the teacher answers, "Of course it's yours. . . . I remember you wearing it once." When Rachel shoves the sweater to the edge of her desk, Mrs. Price tells her, "You put that sweater on right now and no more nonsense." The incident ends right before the bell rings for lunch when Phyllis Lopez, another student in the class, remembers that the sweater is hers Rachel takes it off and gives it to her.

"Out of Order" tells the story of William Saroyan's first day in seventh grade at Longfellow Junior High School. The story begins with the ancient history teacher, Miss Shenstone, telling the students to turn to page 192 in their books. William comments that "it would seem more in order to turn to page one for the first lesson." The teacher responds by telling William to be quiet and let her do the teaching. Then she points to a photograph in the textbook of two stones that she says are 20,000 years old. William questions how she knows this. This leads Miss Shenstone to "fling" herself at William, resulting in his leaving the room. He returns five minutes later, and again Miss Shenstone "flings" herself at William. This results in William going to see Mr. Monsoon, the principal of the school, to tell him why he left the class. Mr. Monsoon meanwhile wants to know William's name and who he is, specifically what nationality he is. When William tells him that he is Armenian, the principal replies, "Nobody but an Armenian would have asked a question like that." William's meeting with the principal ends with the principal saying that he "must give him a thrashing." At this point, William goes home and tells his Uncle Alecksander what occurred. He then returns to the school accompanied by his uncle, who talks to the principal alone. After a short time, William is asked to come into the office to talk with the principal, Miss Shenstone, and his uncle and is told by his uncle that Miss Shenstone has agreed to look into the matter of how the age of the stones was determined. He is also told that it was with "admiration" that Mr. Monsoon commented that only an Armenian would ask a question like that. In the end William has to spend the rest of the day away from school and then return to his classes the

next day as though "nothing had happened." When he returns to school, William apologizes to both the principal and Miss Shenstone. However, after four days, Miss Shenstone leaves the school. Meanwhile, Mr. Monsoon talks about manners at several student body meetings, but after a month he leaves, too.

In order to promote aesthetic reading, it is important to begin by having students read and enjoy the stories. Obviously students will enjoy reading literature only if the text is accessible to them. Hence, it is important in selecting literary texts to ensure that the theme of the text is engaging for the students and that the text itself is not too difficult on either a linguistic or conceptual level. To encourage aesthetic reading, the initial discussion of the stories should focus on having students discuss what they enjoyed or didn't enjoy about the story, what it means to them, how it relates to their own personal experiences, and so on. It is this very kind of discussion that can lead to what Widdowson (1992) terms *practical stylistics*, in which students are encouraged to express individual interpretations and must refer these interpretations back to the text. To illustrate how this might occur in L2 classrooms, let us consider how students' individual interpretation of the characters in the two stories described above could be the basis for a literary task.

Characterization

Readers assess characters in a story based on what the character says and does, what others in the story say about the character, and how the author describes the character. To encourage students' own responses to the stories, a teacher might begin by having students describe both Rachel and William. This could involve students' listing the adjectives they believe best describe each character, describing each in a short paragraph, gathering pictures that depict their image of Rachel and William, or comparing each character with someone they know.

The next part of the literary task should encourage students to return to the text to justify their interpretations. One activity might be to have students complete a character web, such as the one suggested by McCloskey and Stack (1993, pp. 154–155) for each character. Students would complete the following type of chart, citing specific details from the story.

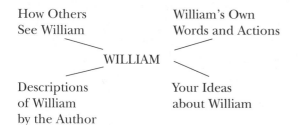

How Others See William

William's Own Words and Actions

WILLIAM

Descriptions of William by the Author

Your Ideas about William

The list of what William says would include the following passages from Saroyan's story.

"How do you know?"

"She said the rocks were twenty thousand years old . . . All I said was, 'How do you know?' I didn't mean they *weren't* that old. I meant that maybe they were older, maybe thirty thousand years old. How old is the earth? Several million years old, isn't it? If the book can say the rocks are twenty thousand years old, somebody ought to be able to say how the book got that figure. This isn't Emerson School, it's Longfellow Junior High. I came here to learn. I don't expect to be punished because I want to learn."

The list of what Rachel says, on the other hand, would include the following:

"That's not, I don't, you're not . . . Not mine."

"But that's not."

Once students complete their individual webs, teachers can then encourage them to examine the language of the text. The contrast in length of both characters' responses illustrates aspects of their personality. However, more subtle features such as the false starts in Rachel's speech and the use of questions in William's speech also suggest differences in their characters.

Because both stories are told from the first person point of view, students' interpretation of William and Rachel will undoubtedly be affected by what they learn about the characters from their thoughts. Hence, with these stories, the teacher may want to draw attention to the concept of first person point of view. In using literature in the classroom, exactly what tasks are developed should depend on what features of the text are salient in the story and on what elements of the text are relevant to students' interpretation of it. Let us then consider how teachers might address the element of point of view in relation to these two stories.

Point of View

Fowler (1986) distinguishes three types of point of view: (1) *spatio-temporal,* (2) *ideological,* and (3) *psychological.* The spatio-temporal point of view refers both to the sense of time that the author conveys by using such techniques as flashbacks or the interweaving of stories (the temporal dimension), and to the manner in which an author depicts items such as objects, buildings, and landscapes in relation to one another (the spatial dimension). The ideological point of view, on the other hand, refers to the "set of values, or belief system, communicated by the language of the text" (p. 130).

The psychological point of view is the one most frequently referred to in literary analysis and involves the question of "who is presented as the observer of the events of a narrative, whether the author or a participating character" (p. 134). Fowler delineates two types of psychological points of view: internal and external. In the internal psychological point of view, either the story is told from first person point of view by a character who shares his or her feelings about the events and characters of the story or it is told by someone who is not a participating character but who has knowledge of the feelings of the characters, the so-called omniscient author. In the external psychological point of view, the narrator describes the events and characters from a position outside of the main character with no access to the characters' feelings and opinions.

Psychological Point of View

"Eleven" and "Out of Order" are both told from the first person point of view by Rachel and William, who share their feelings about the events. In both stories, the authors let the reader into the thoughts of the junior high student. The opening of each story illustrates this first person point of view.

"Eleven" begins with the following:

What they don't understand about birthdays and what they never tell you is that when you're eleven, you're also ten, and nine, and eight, and seven, and six, and five, and four, and three, and two, and one. And when you wake up on your eleventh birthday you expect to feel eleven, but you don't. You open your eyes and everything's just like yesterday, only it's today. And you don't feel eleven at all. You feel like you're still ten. And you are—underneath the year that makes you eleven.

"Out of Order," on the other hand, begins in the following way.

Longfellow High was not strictly speaking a high school at all. It was the seventh and eighth grades of grammar school, and its full name was Longfellow Junior High School. The Longfellow in question was of course *the* Mr. Longfellow, or Henry Wadsworth, although nothing much was ever made of that.

It was in ancient history class that I first astonished my class into an awareness that here was a truly original mind. It happened that this was the first class of the very first day.

In order to help students recognize how the difference in tone between the two openings is achieved, a teacher might pose a series of questions for students to consider, such as the following.

1. Who does *they* refer to? Why do you think the author chose to use *they* rather than a specific reference? Who do you think *you* refers to? Why do you think the author chose to use *you*?
2. What effect does the author achieve by having Rachel list all of the years of her life rather than just saying "When you're eleven, you're also all the other years of your life"?

"OUT OF ORDER"

1. William is in seventh grade yet points out the first and middle names of Longfellow. Why do you think William Saroyan (the adult author of the story) has William, the seventh grader, point this out?
2. What kinds of things *astonish* you? Why do you think Saroyan chose to describe himself as a seventh grader using that word? Why do you think Saroyan described himself as a *truly original mind*?

The aim of such questions is to help students recognize the way in which their assessment of the two characters has been influenced by how the authors have used first person point of view to develop a childlike voice for Rachel and a self-confident and arrogant voice for William. In the case of "Out of Order," the relationship of the author and narrator is even more complex since Saroyan, the author, is writing about his own youth.

Another activity that could be used to highlight the manner in which the authors depict the characters is to have students list all of the sentences in "Eleven" that sound childlike. This list might include such sentences as the following:

1. "Like some days you might say something stupid, and that's the part of you that's still ten."
2. "Or maybe some days you might need to sit on your mama's lap because you're scared, and that's the part of you that's five."

Students might also make a list of comments William makes that demonstrate his outspoken self-confidence. This might include comments like the following:

1. "I remarked that it would seem more in order to turn to page one for the first lesson."
2. "I was asked my name, whereupon, I was only too glad to say honestly, 'William Saroyan.'"

The main point of such activities is requiring students to return to the text to examine *how* the story is told and in what ways this has influenced their judgment of the characters.

Spatio-Temporal Point of View

Cisneros chose to use the present tense to recount her story while Saroyan uses the past tense. To explore the difference that verb tense has on telling a story, teachers might refer to passages such as the following and ask students which of the two accounts they felt they were actually witnessing.

"Eleven"

> "Whose is this?" Mrs. Price says, and she holds the red sweater up in the air for all the class to see. "Whose? It's been sitting in the coatroom for a month."

"Out of Order"

> Miss Shenstone flung herself at me with such speed that I was scarcely able to get away. For half a moment she clung to my homeknit sweater, and damaged it before I got away.

Such comparisons are useful in helping students recognize that the use of the present tense in storytelling suggests the immediacy of events, inviting the reader to witness them.

The temporal point of view also involves the order in which the events of a story are told. In some instances the story time and real time are identical, whereas in others the author uses flashbacks so that the story time and real time differ. In dealing with such stories, teachers might have students complete a chart such as the one at the bottom of this page in which students use clues from the text to guess at the actual time of the event. This type of chart is particularly useful in situations where the story line is quite complex temporally.

Another way of addressing the temporal point of view is to ask students to visualize key events in a story by completing a collage. In the case of "Out of Order," students could be asked to identify what they consider to be central events of the story, such as Miss Shenstone's chasing William, the principal's questioning William, and Uncle Alecksander's coming to the principal's office. Then individually or in small groups, students create a collage of these events using photographs, objects, line drawings, and texts.

As mentioned earlier, what Fowler calls the spatial point of view addresses how objects, buildings, and landscapes are described. For example, in "Eleven" the red sweater is introduced in the story when Mrs. Price "holds the sweater up in the air for all the class to see." Later she takes the "ugly sweater with red plastic buttons and a collar and sleeves all stretched out like you could use it for a jump rope" and puts it on Rachel's desk. This leads Rachel to "move the red sweater to the corner of my desk" until eventually she shoves "the red sweater to the tippy-tip corner" of her desk and "it's hanging all over the edge like a waterfall." To address the spatial dimension, teachers might begin by asking students why they think Rachel felt so humiliated by having the teacher insist that the sweater was hers. This undoubtedly would lead to a discussion of what the sweater was like. At this point, students might be asked to list all of the descriptions of the sweater in the story. The goal of such an activity is to help students recognize that their opinion of the sweater has been influenced by how the author chose to describe it.

Ideological Point of View

Examining stories' ideological point of view is closely related to what has been termed *critical literacy* or *critical reading*. Kress (1985) maintains that readers should approach all texts with three questions in mind; namely, why is the topic being written about, how is the topic being written about, and what other ways could the topic have been written about? In critical reading, readers are encouraged to examine the values and belief

Line Number	Historical Time	Location	Characters	Events

systems that underlie a text or what Fowler (1986) refers to as the ideological point of view of a story. According to Fowler, the narrator or characters in literary texts frequently rely on modal structures to convey their beliefs and attitudes. These structures include such things as modal auxiliaries (e.g., *may, might, should*), modal adverbs or sentence adverbs (e.g., *surely, perhaps, It is certain that . . .*), evaluative adjectives and adverbs (e.g., *lucky, fortunate, regrettably*), and verbs of knowledge, prediction, and evaluation (e.g., *seem, believe, foresee, dislike*).

One suggested way of encouraging students to see the ideological point of view in "Out of Order" is for the teacher to begin by asking students why they think the story was entitled "Out of Order." As a follow-up to this question, a teacher could have students underline all the references to the "old school" (i.e., when teachers do the questioning) and the "new school" (i.e., when students do the questioning) and have them use these references to determine whether or not they think the author is sympathetic to the old or the new school, citing sentences from the text to support their view. Such an approach would lead students to consider such passages as the following one, which occurs after William questions how Miss Shenstone knows the age of the stones at Stonehenge. William comments that "the truth of the matter is that neither Miss Shenstone . . . nor Mr. Monsoon himself, the principal, had anything like a satisfactory answer to any legitimate question of this sort, for they (and all the other teachers) had always accepted what they had found in the textbooks." The goal of this type of an examination of a literary text is to help students see that authors often have a particular set of values that inform how they choose to tell a story.

In concluding this comparison of these two short stories, it is important to emphasize several points regarding the use of literary texts to develop students' language awareness. First, in order to promote students' enjoyment of reading literary texts, classroom activities should always begin with having students individually or in small groups share their personal reactions to a literary text. Second, as a way of developing students' awareness of how their interpretation of the text has been influenced by how the story is told, classroom tasks should encourage students to go back to the text to support their interpretations. Finally, exactly what type of classroom tasks are used will depend on what features of the story are most salient (e.g., temporal or spatial description, point of view, or characterization).

USING LITERARY TEXTS TO INTEGRATE SKILLS

Reading

Using literature as content provides an ideal way to integrate the development of the four skills. As the previous discussion has made clear, encouraging students to carefully examine a literary text to support their interpretations promotes students' close reading of texts, a skill which will benefit their reading of other material. Literature, of course, is also ideal as content for extensive reading programs in L2 classrooms. Becoming engaged with a piece of literature will certainly increase students' interest in reading often and widely in English. (For a good source of literature for language learners, see Day and Bamford [1998], which includes six hundred titles divided by levels of difficulty as well as by age group, genre, and region of the world.)

Listening

When read aloud, literature also offers an excellent context for developing global listening skills. The many books available on audiotape can be used as a basis for an extensive listening library. One clear advantage of encouraging students to listen to literature read by professionals is that such material exposes students to a variety of dialects and voice qualities.

Another type of listening task that can be used in L2 classrooms involves storytelling. Morgan and Rinvolucri (1983) in their book, *Once Upon a Time*, argue convincingly that the quality of listening that occurs when someone is telling a story "is radically different from that during listening comprehension from a tape. The latter is always third-person listening, a kind of eavesdropping that is strangely uncompelling. To be told a story by a live storyteller, on the contrary, involves one in 'I-thou' listening, where the listeners can directly influence the telling" (pp.1–2). Their book contains a variety of strategies for using storytelling to develop listening skills.

Speaking

Perhaps the greatest benefit of using literature in the language classroom lies in its potential for developing students' speaking skills, particularly their sociolinguistic and pragmatic competence. Unlike dialogues written for traditional language learning texts, story dialogues typically offer a detailed account of the speakers' backgrounds and role relationships. Hence, such dialogues provide students with a basis for judging the appropriateness of language use. For example, in "Out of Order," William apologizes to the principal and his teacher, saying to Mr. Monsoon, "I've come to apologize. I don't want any special privileges," and to Miss Shenstone, "I'm sorry about the trouble I made. I won't do it again." Because the story itself has provided the background on why William is apologizing and to whom he is apologizing, students have a context for evaluating the appropriateness of particular linguistic forms. Students also have a full context for determining when discourse is not appropriate as, for example, when Miss Shenstone tells William, "I might say, *Mister* William Saroyan, just shut up and let me do the teaching of the ancient history class."

Teachers can also use literary texts as a basis for having students write their own dialogues. For example, in "Out of Order," Saroyan leaves untold what William's uncle actually says to the principal regarding William's behavior and the principal's questioning of William's nationality. However, Saroyan does recount what agreement the uncle and principal reach at the conclusion of their meeting, giving learners several clues as to what might have been said. In addition, learners have a sense of both the uncle's and Mr. Monsoon's personalities, based on what has

previously occurred. Students thus have a great deal of relevant information to draw on to write a dialogue.

Plays provide a rich context for developing students' sociolinguistic and pragmatic awareness (see McKay [in press]). It is important, however, to recognize that plays differ in significant ways from natural conversation. As Simpson (1997) points out, drama and naturally occurring discourse are not identical types of communication.

> The most obvious difference between the two is that characters in plays are not real people in the way that interlocutors in conversation are. Another difference is that whereas naturally occurring conversation is straightforwardly "face to face," in drama dialogue the channel of communication is more complex. This is because there are two communicative layers at work in drama discourse. . . . On the one hand, there is interaction within a play: this is the character-to-character dialogue which is displayed on stage or in the text. On the other, there is communication between the dramatist and audience or reader (p. 164).

Nevertheless, plays can be used to examine such things as the sequencing of turns in conversation, stated and implied meanings, ellipsis, and so on. Fish (1989) suggests one strategy for increasing students' awareness of the nature of conversation. He recommends giving students a list of the cast of characters in a play, which includes some background information on the characters (e.g., a journalist, a coach, a black athlete, a sponsor). With this information and the title and setting of the play, students are asked to make hypotheses about the play in terms of the plot, theme, and so on. Then Fish suggests giving students a section of the play with the lines but with the characters' names deleted. Students first try to guess who is speaking from the list of characters. Finally, students are asked to sequence the lines of the play. In doing so, students can develop sensitivity to the fact that "conversations are complicated, but orderly and rule-governed events" (Burton 1982, p. 86).

Writing

Literature can be used to develop students' writing abilities by having students react in personal journals and formal essays to the literary texts they read. Using writing in this way offers two benefits. First, it provides students with a way to express their personal interpretation of a story, thus promoting the type of aesthetic response to reading literary texts referred to earlier. Second, to the extent that students are asked to refer to the text to justify their conclusions about the literary selection, they learn to support their opinions with relevant information, an important skill for various types of academic writing.

Using literary texts in writing classes is also valuable for helping students become aware of voice and point of view in written texts. For example, with "Out of Order" and "Eleven," one strategy for developing point of view would be to have students rewrite these stories from the point of view of the teacher. Another possibility would be to have students rewrite "Eleven" as if told and experienced by William. In this case, students would need to consider how William, given what they know of him from "Out of Order," would react to being wrongly accused of owning an old red sweater, and then assume William's voice in recounting the story.

One excellent genre for develop fluency in writing, particularly for less proficient language learners, is poetry. Because poetry is less restricted by the grammatical and lexical constraints of other types of discourse, poems can provide learners with a medium for exploring and playing with language. Maley and Duff (1989) present a variety of strategies for encouraging students to create their own poems. One strategy, for example, involves having students draw several familiar shapes, such as a ladder or staircase. Next, students list words that they associate with this shape. Then they use some of these words to write a poem in the shape of the object itself. To increase students' awareness of the importance of word choice, Maley and Duff suggest giving students poems in which descriptive words have been deleted and having students fill in the blanks. Students then compare their choices and discuss the differences in effect that arise from making specific word choices.

Widdowson (1992) makes a convincing argument for using poetry in the language classroom. He argues that, although the content of poems can often be reduced to ordinary observations (e.g., time passes, life is lonely), "the essentials of poetry lie in the way language is used to elaborate on such simple propositions so that they aµre reformulated in unfamiliar terms which somehow capture the underlying mystery of the commonplace" (p. 9). The simple themes of poetry and the unconventional method of expressing these themes thus provide an avenue for language learners to use the English they have to express sophisticated ideas, unrestricted by the typical constraints of conventional discourse.

USING LITERARY TEXTS TO DEVELOP CULTURAL AWARENESS

A third benefit of using literary texts in the language classroom rests in their potential for developing cross-cultural awareness. This is especially important in an era when learners communicate in English, not only with native speakers of English in Western countries, but also with other non-native speakers around the globe. In order to discuss the benefits of using literary texts to develop cultural awareness, it useful to distinguish various dimensions of culture. Adaskou, Britten, and Fahsi (1989) distinguish four dimensions of culture: *the aesthetic sense* in which a language is associated with the literature, film, and music of a particular country; *the sociological sense* in which language is linked to the customs and institutions of a country; *the semantic sense* in which a culture's conceptual system is embodied in the language; and the *pragmatic sense* in which cultural norms influence what language is appropriate for what context.

A literary text frequently exemplifies several dimensions of culture. For example, when considering "Out of Order" and "Eleven," the aesthetic sense of culture is evident in the mention of Henry Wadsworth Longfellow and Stonehenge. The sociological sense of culture is demonstrated in various ways—in the assumption in "Eleven" about the importance of clothes in American schools and in the accepted role of the teacher to question and command students. The semantic sense of culture is clear in word choice when, for example, William reports that the teacher "flung herself" at him rather than saying she chased him or ran after him, and it is evident in the metaphorical use of language in "Eleven" when Rachel, for example, states, "The way you grow old is kind of like an onion or like the rings inside a tree trunk or like my little wooden dolls that fit one inside the other, each year inside the next one." Finally, the pragmatic sense of culture is exemplified in the dialogue passages in "Out of Order" when, for example, the formal contractual sense of Uncle Alecksander and Mr. Monsoon's agreement regarding William is sealed with the exchange of the uncle saying, "I shall be interested in his progress," and Mr. Monsoon responding, "We all shall."

There are those who argue that a language cannot be taught without culture. Kramsch (1993), for example, maintains that if language "is seen as social practice, culture becomes the very core of language teaching. Cultural awareness must then be viewed both as enabling language proficiency and as being the outcome of reflection on language proficiency" (p. 8). She argues, however, that knowing about a culture (i.e., gaining cultural competence) does not mean that one has an obligation to behave in accordance with the conventions of that culture. Thus the ultimate goal of cultural learning is not to convey information about a culture nor to promote the acquisition of culturally influenced ways of behaving, but rather to help learners see their culture in relation to others so as to promote cross-cultural understanding.

If one accepts this view of cultural learning, it is clear that literary texts provide an ideal context for exploring cultural differences. However, approaching literature to develop cross-cultural understanding requires that teachers first carefully examine the cultural assumptions present in a particular literary work and then structure activities that help students gain an understanding of those assumptions. Teachers and students need to explore how their cultural assumptions differ,

both from each other's and from those portrayed in the literary text. As a way of clarifying this approach, let us consider how a specific text might be used in a second language classroom to promote cross-cultural understanding.

In general, immigrant literature offers a rich context for exploring cultural differences since the stories frequently deal with individuals who have literally and figuratively crossed borders and, hence, have experienced many cultural differences in their lives. A short story by Hisaye Yamamoto entitled "Seventeen Syllables" exemplifies this type of cultural border crossing. It recounts the experience of a Japanese immigrant family working as tomato pickers in California. The Hayashi family is composed of Rosie, a young teenager, and her parents. Rosie is involved in many aspects of American culture and has acculturated to the extent of preferring to use English instead of Japanese. In the course of the story she falls in love with Jesus, another young immigrant worker, who is Hispanic. The story revolves around Rosie's mother, Tome, who assumes a pen name for writing haiku to submit to a contest sponsored by the *Mainichi Shimbu* newspaper. Mrs. Hayashi's talent in writing haiku results in her receiving an award from the editor of the newspaper, one of his favorite Hiroshiges prints depicting four sampans on a pale blue sea. However, Rosie's father, upset by the disturbances that the haiku writing has caused the family, destroys the Hiroshige his wife receives. The story ends with Mrs. Hayashi admitting to her daughter that she came to the United States as part of an arranged marriage after having given birth out of wedlock to a stillborn son. After the birth, Tome had written to her favorite sister in the United States, threatening to kill herself if her sister did not send for her. Her sister then had arranged a marriage for her in the United States with a young man who had recently arrived from Japan. The story concludes when Rosie's mother kneels on the floor and takes Rosie by the wrists: "'Rosie,' she said urgently, 'Promise me you will never marry!'"

This story contains several cultural schemas—the schema of the Japanese immigrant family in which various Japanese traditions such as arranged marriages and particular gender roles are still upheld; the schema of American popular culture, with references to movie stars like Shirley Temple and songs like "Red Sails in the Sunset"; and finally, the schema of farm workers with expectations about tomato picking and poor housing conditions. Which schemas are familiar to teachers and students depends upon their cultural background. In teaching the story, however, the first step the teacher needs to undertake is to examine what cultural schemas the story portrays. This might be accomplished by simply clustering all of the examples in the text that relate to a particular cultural schema.

Next, teachers need to design ways to make these differences accessible to students. One strategy for doing this is to merely present some of the assumed cultural information. In this case, a teacher might show pictures of farm workers, read some examples of haiku, or familiarize students with relevant aspects of United States' popular culture. This level of cultural awareness is not difficult to exemplify. The significant cultural differences in the story, however, rest in such factors as the assumed gender roles of the Japanese father and mother, the acceptance of arranged marriages, and Tome's thoughts of suicide as a result of a significant loss of face. With these kinds of cultural assumptions, the goal should not be to evaluate these assumptions but rather to help students understand why the characters acted as they did. Ultimately, this should lead students to clarify their own understanding of such culturally bound phenomenon as gender roles, loss of face, and marriage.

How these aspects of culture are approached in the classroom depends largely on the background of the teacher and the students. If, for example, the story is taught in Japan with Japanese students and a Japanese teacher, then the classroom participants most likely share many cultural assumptions evident in the behavior of Mr. and Mrs. Hayashi. What might seem unusual to this class is the fact that Rosie has not kept up her Japanese and is willing to meet secretly with Jesus. On the other hand, if the story is taught in the United States with an American teacher and some Japanese students, the teacher, while familiar with many references to American

culture and with an understanding of the farm worker community, may not understand the many references to Japanese culture nor be willing to accept Mrs. Hayahsi's willingness at the end of the story to give up her writing of haiku. In short, to the extent that English language classrooms represent individuals from various cultural backgrounds, the cultural information in particular literary texts may be known to and accepted by some of the classroom participants, yet unfamiliar to others.

Ultimately, what the literary text provides is a medium for sharing and illuminating the cross-cultural differences it exemplifies. The value of selecting texts that portray aspects of the culture of some of the classroom members is that those students who come from this culture can explain many of the cultural elements that may not be understood by members of other cultures. Ideally, the cultural discussion that occurs will illuminate why particular characters from a specific cultural background acted as they did. Such an approach hopefully will avoid the cultural stereotyping that can occur when discussing cross-cultural differences, since these discussions will be grounded in specific behavior portrayed in a particular literary context. This is one of the major cross-cultural benefits that literary texts can bring to L2 classrooms.

CONCLUSION

Using literature as content in ESL/EFL classes has a variety of benefits. While reading literature should be primarily an enjoyable aesthetic experience, using literature in L2 classrooms can also develop students' language awareness. Because literary texts are unique in their ability to illustrate that *what* is communicated cannot be separated from how it is communicated, they provide an ideal context for demonstrating the importance of form in language learning and language use. Exactly how they are used in a particular classroom depends on a wide variety of factors—students' language learning goals, proficiency level in English, and personal interests, as well as the teachers' knowledge of and interest in literature, the teacher's teaching philosophy, and his or her classroom objectives. Perhaps the greatest benefit of using literature as content in an era of increasing globalization is that literary texts provide an ideal context for examining cross-cultural differences and exploring them in a manner that particularizes rather than stereotypes these differences.

DISCUSSION QUESTIONS

1. Drawing on the ideas presented in this chapter, discuss what you believe are the essential differences between literary and nonliterary texts.
2. Discuss what you believe are the major advantages and disadvantages of using literary texts with second language students.
3. Do you think explicit attention should be given to examining the form of literary texts in L2 classrooms? What reasons do you have for your opinion? Do you believe this attention to form detracts from students' aesthetic experience with a text? Why?
4. This chapter has argued that even though there are differences between dialogues in literary texts and natural conversation, such material is valuable in developing students' pragmatic competence? Do you agree or disagree? Why?
5. Discuss ways in which you would find information about unfamiliar cultural schemas in literary texts.

SUGGESTED ACTIVITIES

1. Select a short story that you believe would be engaging for a group of language learners you are familiar with. Then design one of the following:
   a. an activity that encourages students to draw on the text to support their opinion of a particular character in the story
   b. an activity that encourages students to explore how the text would be different if told from another point of view
   c. a series of activities that involve the development of all four skills—reading, writing, speaking, and listening
2. Select a piece of literature that involves several cultural schemas. Begin by analyzing the cultural schemas that exist in the text, listing specific details that contribute to each schema. Then describe how you would make those schemas accessible to a particular group of language learners.
3. Select a second language textbook that uses literary texts as content. Review the follow-up activities that are included in the text and discuss whether you believe the activities contribute primarily to students' aesthetic reading of the text, their efferent reading of the text, or both.
4. Observe an ESL or EFL class that uses literary texts. Describe the activities in the class that contribute to students' awareness of the language in the text and the activities that develop students' awareness of the cultural schemas in the text.

 **FURTHER READING**

Carter, R., and J. McRae. 1996. *Language, Literature and the Learner.* London: Addison Wesley Longman.
This collection of essays is derived from three international seminars on the teaching of literature in second and foreign language classrooms, held at the University of Nottingham. The editors note that the papers in the volume share a commitment to practical, classroom-based activities, particularly those that are language based and student centered.

Collie, J., and S. Slater. 1987. *Literature in the Language Classroom: A Resource Book of Ideas and Activities.* Cambridge: Cambridge University Press.
The opening chapter of this book examines why literature should be included in second language classrooms, how texts should be selected, and how they should be used. The other chapters are devoted to illustrating specific classroom activities to use with literary texts in the prereading, while-reading, and postreading process.

Kramsch, C. 1993. *Context and Culture in Language Teaching*. Oxford: Oxford University Press.

The text contains two excellent chapters that are particularly relevant to using literature as content. The first, "Stories and Discourse," elaborates on the dimensions of a text that contribute to its uniqueness. The second, "Teaching the Literary Text," describes various strategies for dealing with literary texts in the classroom.

Lazar, G. 1993. *Literature and Language Teaching*. Cambridge: Cambridge University Press.

This is addressed to language teachers who want to explore how they can use literature in their classrooms. The book consists of a series of tasks and activities that teachers can do on their own or with other teachers to develop their skill in lesson planning using literary texts.

McCloskey, M. L., and L. Stack. 1993, 1995, 1996, 2000. *Voices in Literature*. Boston, MA: Heinle & Heinle Publishers.

This three-level series of literature-based second language texts is organized by theme. Each book in the series includes a variety of literary genres. All of the literary texts have a series of prereading and postreading activities that deal with students' personal response to the texts while at the same time promoting their language awareness. The texts are beautifully illustrated with photographs and line drawings.

Experiential and Negotiated Language Learning

JANET L. EYRING

Eyring's chapter derives the Western "Experiential and Negotiated Language Learning" movement from the humanistic classroom of the 1960s and 1970s and the community-based learning and project work of the 1970s and 1980s. Because it provides rich opportunities for negotiation and attends to individual and collaborative learning, teachers of all cultures may find this approach relevant well into the 2000s.

INTRODUCTION

Experiential learning, a concept as old as Socrates, Confucius, and the Garden of Eden, made a comeback in schools in the late 1960s and early 1970s, when educational and social institutions were under attack in the United States and in other industrialized nations around the world. An example of this was the "open classroom" of the 1960s, in which traditional seating arrangements and classroom levels were dissolved and students of different ages were allowed to freely interact on tasks or larger projects without separation of walls.

Experiential *language* learning, borrowing from these experiential learning roots, is rightfully placed within the context of the Communicative Language Teaching (CLT) movement which began in the mid 1970s and continues until today (see Savignon's chapter in this volume). Legutke and Thomas (1991) label it a "strong version of CLT" and a solution to the negative classroom cultures of so-called "communicative classrooms," which they have observed as being characterized by (1) dead bodies and talking heads; (2) deferred gratification and the loss of adventure; (3) lack of creativity; (4) lack of opportunities for communication; (5) lack of autonomy; and (6) lack of cultural awareness (pp. 7–10). They emphasize that experiential language learning is not a new method but an "educational framework" around which to organize learning tasks. The roots of this promising framework in humanistic and democratically organized classrooms and its reliance on "negotiation" in the learning and teaching of communication will be discussed in this chapter. Guidelines for organizing an experience-oriented curriculum using project work will also be discussed.

EXPERIENTIAL ACTIVITIES IN A HUMANISTIC CLASSROOM

To understand experiential learning in the Western world, it is important to review the sociocultural climate of American society in the mid 1960s. During this period, awareness of the need for warm, human experience was raised to new levels as large numbers of individuals railed against the bureaucracy and depersonalization of modern society. Legutke and Thomas (1991) provide a concise discussion of this period:

> This was a crisis whose main characteristics were the deadening of human communication within technocratic and bureaucratic institutions, the progressive destruction of livable space in the cities, the aggravation of spiritual impoverishment and poverty in spite of a rapid growth of affluence, the obvious chauvinism of the so-called civilized world and its democracies towards

the countries of the Third World and the exploitative relationship with nature which led to a progressive reduction of the quality of life in the name of progress (p. 41).

Some psychologists argued that the solution to this alienation and lack of awareness was to raise personal consciousness and self-recognition. Rogers's work in client-centered psychotherapy (1961), Maslow's psychology of self-actualization (1962), and Perls' Gestalt Therapy (Perls, Hefferline, and Goodman 1951) were widely discussed in psychological and psychotherapeutic circles.

Subsequently, these ideas infused into the field of education. Legutke and Thomas (1991) state that "Confluent Education" (Galyean 1977) borrowed greatly from psychotherapeutic principles and promoted certain awareness-raising principles such as sensitivity training, perception and activation of emotions, body training (relaxation, breathing, movement), psychodramatic expression of feelings (drama), empathy training, training in communication skills, and the stimulation of imagination, projection, and creativity (p. 47).

Not surprisingly, confluent education made an impact on language teaching methods as well. Counseling-Learning (Curran 1960) adopted the client-counselor relationship, Total Physical Response (Asher 1977) adopted body movement for language training reinforcement, and Suggestopedia (Lozanov 1982) adopted relaxation training. Moskowitz's (1978) then innovative book *Caring and Sharing in the Foreign Language Class* offered many suggestions for introducing trust building and empathy into the language classroom.

Today, the aspect of experiential language learning which acknowledges the socioaffective component of the learning process and the importance of the learner in instruction (learner-centeredness) is well established (Nunan 1995). Teachers wishing to humanize the classroom experience treat students as individuals, patiently encourage self-expression, seriously listen to learner response, provide opportunities for learning by doing, and make learning meaningful to students in the here and now.

EXPERIENCE FOR DEMOCRATIC LEARNING

Incorporating experiences that address the affective needs of learners has been an important theme in the educational literature. Providing learning experiences as a backdrop to learning about cooperative principles has also been an important emphasis in western education. Dewey (1916) believed that the classroom should reflect society outside the classroom. He argued for democratized classrooms in which students were not simply funneled information but where they participated with the teacher and with each other in Socratic dialogue about subjects near to their own life experiences. Schmuck (1985) summarizes Dewey's philosophy:

> Dewey argues that if humans are to learn to live cooperatively, they must experience the living process of cooperation in schools. Life in the classroom should represent the democratic process in microcosm, and the heart of democratic living is cooperation in groups. Moreover, Dewey argues that classroom life should embody democracy, not only in how students learn to make choices and carry out academic projects together, but also in how they learn to relate to one another. This approach could involve being taught to empathize with others, to respect the rights of others, and to work together on rational problem solving (p. 2).

In an egalitarian learning community such as this, all have the opportunity to voice opinions. Consensus is favored in decision making but majority rules. What gets done or does not get done is dependent upon individual initiative and group cooperation. Logical reasoning and discussion are essential in group problem solving.

Kilpatrick (1918) further explicated Dewey's ideas and proposed that classrooms should "provide a place for the adequate utilization of the laws of learning" but no less "for the essential elements of the ethical quality of conduct" (p. 3). He also introduced *The Project Method*. Kolb (1984) has extended Dewey's and Kilpatrick's ideas by emphasizing that observation of experience is insufficient for learning but must be followed by abstract conceptualization, reflective observation, and active experimentation.

Dewey introduced projects as an ideal experiential method to develop citizens for a democratic society. The adoption of the project method, sometimes called Project Work or community-based learning, within the Communicative Language Teaching approach, has again reinforced the importance of groups working toward mutually beneficial goals. Students learning collaboratively have been shown to use higher level learning strategies (Johnson and Johnson 1985), are more motivated to learn (Dörnyei 1997), and are able to learn through cooperative problem solving (Swain and Lapkin 1998). They also produce more significant projects than they could have as individuals. Some of these include conducting large-scale surveys, cataloging large amounts of information, writing multiarticle magazines, and producing feature films. In addition, these projects often have social benefits (e.g., to orient handicapped individuals to accessible sites in a city or to teach elementary school students about international cultures), which hearken back to the original political and ethical goals of the project work method.

LEARNING AS A NEGOTIATION PROCESS

The "experiential" classroom of the twenty-first century combines features of the two aforementioned philosophies—experiences that address the needs of the individual in the learner-centered classroom and experiences that reinforce the goals of a group in a democratic classroom in which the teacher is an active coparticipant in the learning process.

The potential conflict in this arrangement, between the needs and interests of the individual, the group, and the teacher, is resolved through sometimes difficult negotiation. Breen (1985) claims that all classrooms are jointly constructed by teachers and learners; this is even more apparent in the experiential classroom with its restructuring of power, in which learners are elevated to assume more responsibility for decisions and teachers suppress their dominant roles to become facilitators and colearners. This partnership approach to language learning sometimes involves conflict resolution as teachers train themselves to stand back and support while learners are trained to initiate, cooperate, and explore (Eyring 1989; Foster 1998).

Besides the social negotiation of roles and goals, experiential learning provides opportunities for the negotiation of meaning between learners in pair work and group work activities. Much research has confirmed the importance of such interaction for second language acquisition (Krashen 1978; Swain 1985). This sociocultural explanation for learning has also been confirmed in studies of learner development based on Vygotsky's (1978) zone of proximal development, in which learning is conceptualized as a mediated process between experts and novices (teachers and students), peers and peers, self (through private speech), and other sources such as computers and the community through which people learn various subject matters with the assistance of others (Lantolf 2000).

Experiential classrooms in which learners negotiate with their classmates and the teacher throughout a course what they want to learn, how they want to learn, and how they want to be assessed acquire "process competence" (Legutke and Thomas 1991). Negotiating information inside and outside the classroom with sometimes unsympathetic interlocutors and natural, unsimplified texts creates an extremely rich language learning environment for the development of "communicative competence," which includes not only linguistic competence, but sociolinguistic, strategic, and discourse competence as well (Canale 1983).

THE NEGOTIATION OF CURRICULUM

Nunan (1995, 1999) claims that students can be moved more or less easily along the continuum of a "negotiation curriculum" as they learn how to learn. His first three steps relate to course content and the last six to course learning processes.

1. *Make instructional goals clear to learners.* Learners must understand what they are doing and why. Teachers should ensure the topic and focus of learning activities are appropriate for learners and should explicitly identify and explain to them what the goals are. Students also benefit from a simple review of goals accomplished after a lesson.

2. *Allow learners to create their own goals.* Some learners may be comfortable with teacher-selected goals. However, learners should increasingly be given opportunities to create their own goals, or at the very least, choose from among a set of provided goals. These self-selected goals are sometimes more powerful if they are written up in the form of learning contracts or have been negotiated by consensus with other members of the class.

3. *Encourage learners to use their second language outside the classroom.* When purposes are real and authentic, learners will be more motivated to obtain language input from authentic sources and real people outside the classroom (Strevens 1987). Teachers need to prepare students for the language demands and unpredictability of natural discourse settings. Functional language use and negotiation strategies should be emphasized.

4. *Raise awareness of learning processes.* Students taking greater responsibility for their own learning in a cooperative classroom need to be made aware of possible learning strategies (Wenden and Rubin 1987; Oxford 1990), such as memory, cognitive, compensation, metacognitive, affective, and social strategies, and be given opportunities to overtly verbalize while using them during learning tasks (Swain 2000). Greater awareness of strategies as well as rehearsal in the classroom can lead to future transfer of learning to independent learning situations.

5. *Help learners identify their own preferred styles and strategies.* Inventories for identifying one's learning style and strategies are now available (see Oxford 1988 for an example). Knowledge of these preferred styles and strategies, which sometimes differ according to cultural background of the students (Oxford and Anderson 1995), makes it possible for the teacher to include learning activities which address these preferences. Learners also become more proficient at choosing approaches that reinforce their particular ways of learning.

6. *Encourage learner choice.* Learners should be presented with opportunities to make choices of various types—from whom they want to work with, to which task they want to do first, to what task they want to eliminate altogether.

7. *Allow learners to generate their own tasks.* Students who have determined their own goals are now ready to create some of their own learning tasks, such as bringing in their own texts, writing quizzes to test their classmates, or determining pretasks leading to a final target task.

8. *Encourage learners to become teachers.* A learner who is able to logically plan tasks is also able to plan learning environments for others. In the learner-centered classroom, students can serve as tutors and teachers for each other, sharing their expertise or presenting information that they have mastered.

9. *Encourage learners to become researchers.* In a true experiential course, learners will become researchers of information they want to know. They may state hypotheses, verify them through data collection, and analyze and report their results to other members of the class or to other audiences.

PROJECT WORK: THE QUINTESSENTIAL EXPERIENTIAL LANGUAGE LEARNING APPROACH

Legutke and Thomas (1991) note that it was not until the mid 1970s that language teachers realized the rich potential of projects for promoting meaningful interaction and seriously began implementing this approach in the language classroom. Project work epitomizes every dimension of Kohonnen's (1992) experiential education model in terms of its view of learning, power relations, teacher and learner roles, view of knowledge, view of curriculum, learning experiences, control of process, motivation, and evaluation. It also provides the ideal context to move learners along a negotiated curriculum, as described by Nunan (1999).

Successful projects have been implemented in kindergartens, elementary schools, secondary schools, intensive language programs, community colleges, adult schools, and university settings from the beginning to advanced levels. They have also been implemented in ESL and EFL settings, although some argue with far greater ease in English-speaking contexts and with westernized populations (Eyring 1989; Legutke and Thomas 1991; Nunan 1995; Beckett 1999). The greater integration of multimedia, computers, and the Internet in language projects throughout the world, however, has made the advantages of living in the target culture less important for authentic communication and discourse-oriented learning today (Syed 1997; Warschauer 1997; Adair-Hauck, Willingham-McLain, and Youngs 1999).

Because of the difficulty of training students to work on extended projects, some researchers have advised doing projects alongside other regular classroom activities in order to provide traditionally-oriented students with familiar classwork (Eyring 1989; Haines 1989). Other researchers have suggested "preparatory projects" (Henry 1994) to prepare students for project work by giving them practice working in groups on structured mini-projects before the actual project begins. At the very least, most have highlighted the need for lead-in activities (Haines 1989) or pretasks (Legutke and Thomas 1991) along the way. This allows for rehearsal and modeled problem solving of various positive group work routines and research structures necessary for project completion.

ORGANIZING A PROJECT

Various authors have provided guidelines for organizing projects (see Fried-Booth 1982, 1986; Haines 1989; Henry 1994 for examples). The use of different skills (listening, speaking, reading, and writing) and combinations of skills are more important at some stages than others. Stoller's (1997) ten-step model applied to English for Academic Purposes content-based classes is a straightforward way to design meaningful projects at any level of ESL/EFL instruction:

1. Agree on a theme
2. Determine the final outcome
3. Structure the project
4. Prepare students for the language demands of Step 5
5. Gather information
6. Prepare students for the language demands of Step 7
7. Compile and analyze information
8. Prepare students for the language demands of Step 9
9. Present final product
10. Evaluate the project

Steps 1 and 2 represent the stages in which the teacher and students are negotiating the nature of the course project. First, learners consider several topics the teacher has provided or brainstorm some of their own from scratch. Once students have reached a consensus about the topic, they consider a final outcome they would like to produce, such as a booklet, a play, a demonstration, or a debate. When students have determined the final outcome, they work backward with the help of the teacher to organize how they will accomplish their final goal. In Step 3, they may specify an outline, flow diagram, learning contract, or project proposal for what needs to be done and when.

At Step 4, the teacher in consultation with the students plans language intervention lessons/activities which they will require for gathering information from text materials, native-language informants, media broadcasts, or other sources. These activities may include reviewing appropriate citation procedures in academic research, examining question formation for interviews, or listening for transition cues in spoken discourse. During Step 5, students actually gather information inside and outside the classroom. Again, in Step 6, the teacher discusses with students techniques for compiling and analyzing the large amounts of written or spoken data they have accumulated, always with the final project outcome in mind. This step may involve guiding students to categorize information in grids or charts.

In Step 7, which is often considered the most difficult step in terms of time and effort, students think about what they have collected, how one part relates to another, and begin summarizing and extrapolating from their data. In Step 8, students again receive input from the teacher on possible language demands in the final activity. If students are involved in creating a poster, organizing a debate, or writing a booklet, language conventions and audience expectations must be discussed. In this way, by Step 9 students will be ready to present their research and findings to fellow classmates or to another audience. Step 10, which is in many ways the most important, is a time for reflection on and evaluation of the entire project—what worked, what didn't, why it didn't, how it could be improved if redone, and what might be the next logical step.

Legutke and Thomas (1991) also present a similar process for organizing projects. Their seven phases are opening, topic orientation, research and data collection, preparation of data presentation, presentation and sharing, evaluation, and follow-up. Appendix 1 elaborates on these phases and includes detailed information about input options and examples of stimulus questions, activities, and learner texts. Important to note is the inclusion of awareness raising, trust building, and values clarification activities in the first three phases of the project, anticipating the challenge of negotiating meanings between teacher and learners in this power-reconstructed classroom.

In both Stoller's and Legutke and Thomas's frameworks, assessment occurs not only at the end but throughout a project. It is normally collaborative in the sense that both the teacher and individual students provide input in the evaluation process. Types of common progress assessment measures include checklists, questionnaires, weekly reviews, draft evaluations, freewriting, notetaking, class discussions, reflective journals, observation tasks, and oral presentations. Grading scales and rubrics are often tailored to the needs of a particular project task. Sometimes an unbiased evaluator or an invited audience may participate in the evaluation process.

PROJECT TYPES

Many types of projects have been reported in the literature. Table 1 presents four general types with their accompanying final products. Some have been completed in ESL settings; others in EFL or foreign language classroom settings (in which case this is noted). *Collection projects* require students to collect materials or physical objects in order to meaningfully categorize or interrelate them. *Informational projects,* probably the most typical, require extensive amounts of interpersonal contact (through interviews or surveys) or extensive amounts of reading or library research to obtain information about a wide range of topics. *Orientation projects* also require extensive amounts of research, but their main purpose is to orient people to a new place. Social welfare projects, the most altruistic of the projects, are designed to serve the needs of audiences other than the students themselves. They can be considered the most experiential of the projects because they truly reflect the humanistic, social, and democratic principles of this framework.

"Process" has generally been considered what is most important in the project work experience. However, final "products" such as the ones listed in Table 1. highlight the importance of group-selected goals and the negotiated curriculum to motivate students to participate and stay engaged for long periods of time.

CONCLUSION

This chapter has reviewed the benefits of an experiential learning environment for language acquisition opportunities. This environment provides for the emotional and social needs of learners as they negotiate meaning inside and outside the classroom. Projects, which have been exceptional environments for promoting language learning in the Western world, exemplify the best of the humanistic approaches in facilitating negotiation of meaning.

Table 1. Projects and Their Products

Collection Projects

a. Scavenger hunt to collect items from a list (a twig, something red, something brittle, etc. (Jerald and Clark 1983)

b. Map display showing the origin of various collected bottles, food labels, wrappings on cartons, tins, packets from around the world (Fried-Booth 1986)

c. Cookbook with favorite collected recipes from around the world (Gaer 1995)

d. Creation of a rock and fossil museum for real audience after collecting and borrowing various rock and fossil specimens (Diffily 1996)

e. Classification guide for authentic English language materials (newspapers, tourist brochures, letters, etc.) for a library for future project work use (EFL setting) (Haines 1989)

f. Report on how English-speaking cultures have influenced the way of life in the students' native country after collecting photographs, realia, videos, etc. (EFL setting) (Haines 1989)

g. Report on potential English language institutes or schools for students wishing to study English outside their native country after collecting language school prospectuses, maps, and tourist information (EFL setting). (Haines 1989)

Informational Projects

a. Report on recorded interviews between students and English-speaking travelers in airport (EFL setting) (Legutke 1984/1985)

b. Article for local newspaper based on a news event (EFL setting) (Fried-Booth 1986)

c. Café-Theater Evening/Day which informs guests of food, music, and entertainment of target culture (foreign language/EFL settings) (Semke 1980; Haines 1989; Fried-Booth 1986)

d. Buffet luncheon for invited second language guests hosted by students preparing for an overseas assignment (foreign language setting) (Kaplan 1997)

e. Report on interviews with performers (members of a circus and of the Theater Royale) about their crafts (Victoria Markee 1988, personal communication)

f. Report on training and education needed for jobs after researching employment information (Wrigley 1998)

g. Correspondence project report after students write letters and get information from school wastebasket or junk mail or from a week's post delivery from another school (EFL setting) (Legutke and Thomas 1991)

h. Survey report after interviewing townspeople about their knowledge of English (EFL setting) (Haines 1989)

i. Simulated political debate related to American elections after reading newspapers and magazines, writing letters to political parties, locating relevant organizations (Stoller 1997)

j. Videotape and dossier on a contemporary topic incorporating sketches, interviews, discussions, music, etc. (foreign language setting) (Coleman 1992)

Orientation Projects

a. City guide for Los Angeles after investigating beaches, parks, amusement parks, restaurants, and night spots (Eyring 1989)

b. Slide show and oral presentation to Rotary Club and elderly residents on cultural and recreational opportunities in one city (Candlin et al. 1988)

c. Magazine to assist international students adjusting to American life (Gertzman 1988)

d. Leaflets and advertisements for university self-access center to orient other students to available computer software, satellite channel access, magazines, etc. (Aston 1993)

e. Orientation handbook for women after researching no-cost activities in the city (Cray 1988)

f. Videotape documentary on a field trip to places in a city (Padgett 1994)

Social Welfare Projects

a. Report on the homeless situation after interviewing homeless people on the street (Victoria Markee 1988, personal communication)

b. Jumble (rummage) sale after collecting items to sell for charity (Legutke and Thomas 1991)

c. "Animals in Danger" article and poster about threatened species (Hutchinson 1991)

d. Oral histories created for elderly interviewees (Jerald and Clark 1983)

e. Wheelchair guide for handicapped visitors, which was shared with city tourist offices and the media (Fried-Booth 1986)

f. Third World display and shanty house based on research of people living in developing countries (Fried-Booth 1986).

g. Videotape of spastic unit in a hospital which was shown to prospective patients' parents (Fried-Booth 1986)

h. Storytelling performance of native Laotian folktales to middle school children (Gaer 1998)

i. Teaching four-day unit to elementary school students following extensive preparation in the subject matter (Carter and Thomas 1986)

Looking ahead, we need to know more about the best conditions for achieving negotiation of meaning between learners and their teachers as well as between learners and their environment in order for this approach to be implemented on a wider scale. The effects of age, language proficiency, and educational context on student learning mediated by teacher experts, peers, texts, and computers demand further investigation. More also needs to be known about how to train teachers to implement this approach. Time will tell if experiential learning, cultivated largely in Western civilizations and democracies in the twentieth century, will be adopted by learners and teachers around the world in this new information age. If the translated and familiar words of Confucius in 451 B.C. are a reflection of what was and is to come in Eastern populations around the globe, it is very likely that project-based learning will take root and be adapted to cultures far different politically and culturally than the ones in which it originated. Confucius says, "What I hear, I forget; what I see, I remember; What I do, I understand."

DISCUSSION QUESTIONS

1. Is experiential language learning a viable approach for fostering second language acquisition? Why or why not?
2. What are the similarities and differences between Stoller's and Legutke and Thomas's steps for organizing project work? Which framework do you prefer and why?
3. What relationship does "power" have to negotiating a curriculum in an experiential language learning classroom?
4. What are some of the challenges and benefits of incorporating computer-assisted language learning into the project work classroom?
5. Based on student backgrounds, ages, interests, learning styles, etc. of English learners in your community, how well do the goals of experiential language learning correspond to the goals for your schools?

SUGGESTED ACTIVITIES

1. Review Table 1 summarizing class projects and products and then brainstorm various topics for large-scale relevant projects which could be conducted in your community. Choose one of these topics and outline how library research, observation, interviews, questionnaires, and field trips could be incorporated into the learning process.
2. Read the pivotal work on experiential learning by John Dewey (*Experience and Education.* New York: MacMillan, 1938). Then, join the Dewey discussion group linked to the website for the Center for Dewey Studies at Southern Illinois University at Carbondale. Provide comments about how Dewey's original ideas can be applied to experiential language learning today and summarize for your classmates the on-line responses you receive.
   http://www.siu.edu/~deweyctr/
3. Negotiation is a key element of project work instruction. With a group of three or four other teacher trainees, spend one hour negotiating a topic and a plan for a ten-week social welfare project in your community. Write a short report on (1) the roles that group members assumed (e.g., secretary, leader, passive observer) during the discussion and (2) the problems or surprises which occurred during the negotiation process.

FURTHER READING

Haines, S. 1989. *Projects for the EFL Classroom.* Edinburgh: Thomas Nelson and Sons.
   A practical handbook with case studies of past projects in EFL settings, resource material, and step-by-step instructions for additional projects to be implemented in international contexts.
Legutke, M., and H. Thomas. 1991. *Process and Experience in the Language Classroom.* Harlow, UK: Longman.
   A comprehensive book about the theoretical roots of experiential language learning and key components of the framework.
Nunan, D. 1995. Closing the gap between learning and instruction. *TESOL Quarterly* 29 (1): 133–158.
   An article that proposes that giving learners a key role in selecting experiential content, learning processes, and language content will lessen the gap between teaching and learning.

WEBSITES

This on-line version of *Focus on Basics,* a publication of the National Center for the Study of Adult Learning and Literacy, focuses on project-based learning. It includes the Gaer and Wrigley articles mentioned in this chapter.
   http://gseweb.harvard.edu/~ncsall/fob/1998/fobv2id.htm
FORUM, a traditional paper-based as well as on-line journal, published by the United States Information Agency, focuses on the teaching of English abroad. This particular issue presents a useful framework by Stoller for organizing projects.
   http://e.usia.gov/forum/vols/vol35/no4/p2.htm
The National Society for Experiential Education is a national organization committed to all forms of experiential learning in the classroom, workplace, or community. It sponsors conferences and publications for anyone wishing to extend their knowledge in this area.
   http://www.nsee.org

The National Service Learning Clearinghouse, maintained by the University of Minnesota, is a consortium of various organizations committed to service learning/project work opportunities from kindergarten to university levels. Consult the Frequently Asked Questions page, which has special links to English and foreign language projects. **www.nicsl.coled.umn.edu**

APPENDIX I

General Structure for Project Work

Inputs (teacher/learner)	Process Phases (examples)	Stimulus Questions (examples)	Activities (examples)	Learner Texts
– process materials – information materials	**(1) OPENING** • introducing learners to a communicative approach • developing group dynamics • introducing use of media for text retrieval and production • introducing texts as data for research PROJECT IDEA	• what did I/we feel doing the task? • what was the purpose for me/us of the task? • how did I communicate with others? • how did we organize ourselves? • what communication difficulties did we have?	• awareness and trust building • information sharing • problem solving • process evaluation • imagination gap	– posters – profiles – stories – drawings/ photographs and captions – diary entries – collages
– open-ended stimuli (pictures, words, sentences, titles) – short texts – slogans – preceding learner texts and information materials	**(2) TOPIC ORIENTATION** • sensitizing towards the theme • mobilizing existing knowledge • arousing curiosity • exchanging personal experiences • creating awareness of the research area • appreciation of difficulties • formulation of hypotheses after evaluating prior knowledge and experience	• what do we know about the problems, the theme as shown in pictures or texts? • how do I react to the picture? • what do we associate it with? • what makes us stop and think? • what does not seem interesting at first glance? • which of the items attract me most or least?	• imagination-gap projection • awareness activities • communicative tasks • values clarification • plus/minus interesting evaluation • brain/heart-storming	– word-roses (word clusters) – associograms – slogans – collages – posters OHP-hypotheses poster-hypotheses

Inputs (teacher/learner)	Process Phases (examples)	Stimulus Questions (examples)	Activities (examples)	Learner Texts
– teacher lecture – language input – information materials – process materials – preceding learner texts	(3) RESEARCH AND DATA COLLECTION • focusing on the theme • articulating interest • defining project tasks • weighing up time factors • determining areas of deficit in terms of skills and competence • carrying out the target tasks of the project	• which of the items, topics would I like to work on? • who would I cooperate with? • how much time is needed to accomplish the task? • does the group have sufficient knowledge to go about working on the tasks? • how can I collect more information on the topic?	• communicative tasks (interpersonality and interaction: values clarification) • language exercises • skills training • determined by the group themselves • interim plenary process evaluation	– list of themes – project plan – work contracts
– information materials – process materials – preceding learner texts	(4) PREPARING DATA PRESENTATION • selecting results for presentation • deciding on the form of the presentation • practicing the presentation • allocating areas of responsibility • creating the presentation texts	• which parts of our results would be interesting for the whole class? • how can we put our results across to the class? • what should we tell the others in spoken text, in writing, pictures? • what could be difficult to communicate? • what kind of help do our classmates need to understand our presentation? • do we have to produce extra worksheets? • do we want to use media for our presentation (OHP, blackboard, tape, film)?	• determined by the group – information handout	many types of texts: – poster/collage – minutes/essays – commentary – summary – listening text – film text – drama script – song texts – mime instructions – programme of events
– preceding learner texts	(5) PRESENTATION AND SHARING • giving a lead-in to a video film • giving a short lecture • acting in a drama/sketch/mime • giving a show-and-tell session • presenting a tape/slide show • singing a "song"		• determined by groups: many forms of communicative task possible (learners as leaders and participants)	

Inputs (teacher/learner)	Process Phases (examples)	Stimulus Questions (examples)	Activities (examples)	Learner Texts
– teacher lecture – teacher feedback – group feedback (evaluation sheets)	(6) EVALUATION • evaluating process and product • extending ability to make judgements • raising cognitive sensitivity • evaluating input materials • evaluating the roles of the experts • evaluating the group dynamic processes, etc.	• how did the project tasks, the demonstration work out? • which activities/presentations were particularly effective, ineffective? • what could or should be improved? • were there any language problems? • what could or should be done about them? • how did the group cooperate with the teacher? could the group make use of his/her competence? • was the textbook/workbook/ resource package a satisfactory help? • etc.	• process-evaluation activities	– theme list for follow-up
– preceding learner texts	(7) FOLLOW-UP • further work on areas of language weakness • work on gaps in knowledge of content • agreeing on follow-up projects • changing to related/non-related themes as basis for new project idea EXTENSION PROJECTS			

(*Source:* Legutke and Thomas 1991, pp. 182–186. Used by permission.)

Bilingual Approaches to Language Learning

MARY MCGROARTY

"Bilingual Approaches to Language Learning" describes the various bilingual models found at different levels (elementary, secondary, post-secondary, and adult education), identifying key instructional features and emphasizing the drive for quality instruction. The chapter makes reference to consideration of the political contexts as well as pedagogical factors affecting the choices and outcomes related to bilingual instruction.

INTRODUCTION

In many parts of the world, the attainment of proficiency in two or more languages is viewed as a highly desirable goal. Sometimes the development of bilingual skills takes place outside the bounds of formal education, impelled by individual factors in the sociocultural context. This chapter is not concerned with persons who become bilingual outside the bounds of formal instruction. (Readers interested in learning more about the many ways people may become bilingual should consult any of the several good general introductions to bilingualism and language learning, such as Bialystok and Hakuta 1994; Hoffman 1991; Hakuta 1986; and Grosjean 1982, among others.) Rather, the emphasis here is on understanding how two (or more) languages are used within an educational system to promote the goal of bilingual proficiency for enrolled students.

Some definitions are in order, because both the terms *bilingual* and *bilingual education* are used to refer to a great variety of phenomena (indeed, lack of uniformity regarding the term *bilingual education* is one of the many reasons why it is difficult to compare program data; see Hakuta 1986 and Hornberger et al. 1999). In this chapter, *bilingual,* when used to refer to an individual, means a person who has age-appropriate language skills in two languages, though the nature and extent of skill in each language will vary according to many individual and situational

influences.[1] A person with bilingual oral skills in two languages may or may not be *biliterate,* that is, able to read and write in two languages (Hornberger and Skilton-Sylvester 2000). A *bilingual education* approach is one in which two languages are used as media of classroom instruction for the same group of students, so that students receive some of their instruction in one language and some in the other, with the nature and proportion of each language varying according to program type, instructional goals, and various contextual influences.[2] Bilingual programs may or may not be aimed at producing students with biliterate skills; this is one of the features on which they differ, as will be discussed presently.

Before proceeding to describe bilingual approaches, a crucial clarification is in order: There is no necessary opposition between use of bilingual instruction and English as a second language (ESL) instruction. Indeed, in the United States and wherever the language of the dominant society is English, it is generally expected that ESL should be a part of any good bilingual program because a principal goal of any instructional program is the development of high-level academic language skills in the language(s) used as the medium of instruction. Such development does not come about automatically through simple exposure to a language; it requires instruction that is well planned and carefully sequenced. For this reason, it is important that any bilingual program include systematic attention to the development of students' first as well as second language skills, necessitating a sound, comprehensive curricula to support increased proficiency in each language. Hence, ESL should be a part of any bilingual program in an English-speaking context.

This chapter first discusses the audience for bilingual approaches, then presents the most common program types found under the broad banner of bilingual education; next, it discusses the pedagogical features that help to determine the level of quality in any bilingual instructional program; and, last, it notes some current educational concerns that bear on provision of bilingual education.[3]

WHO CAN BENEFIT FROM BILINGUAL APPROACHES?

Any student has the potential to benefit from a bilingual approach to instruction as long as the particular approach chosen suits the student's linguistic situation and provides good quality instruction. Bilingual education is not only for recent immigrants; there are particular approaches aimed at monolingual students who speak only the majority language and wish to develop strong proficiency in another language (TESOL 1992). It is potentially appropriate for linguistic majority students—students whose native language is that spoken in the larger national community, e.g., native speakers of English in the United States or in Anglophone Canada—as well as linguistic minority students—students whose native language is not the same as that used in larger national community, e.g., native speakers of Spanish, Chinese, or Navajo in the United States. Furthermore, some of the approaches used in bilingual education may also prove useful for bidialectal students (that is, students who regularly use a dialect different from the standard, such as speakers of African-American Vernacular English in U.S. schools, for whom Adger, Christian, and Taylor [1999] suggest some particularly pertinent issues). While the linguistic and sociocultural circumstances of bilingual and bidialectal students are not comparable

in many respects (Baugh 2000; Dillard 1978), there are reasons to explore the utility of bidialectal approaches, particularly in the area of initial literacy acquisition (Rickford and Rickford 1995; Siegel 1999) and expansion of linguistic range in a home language (Valdés 1995). Hence, bilingual approaches are potentially useful for any student at any educational level. However, their appropriateness and feasibility for particular instructional levels and settings varies and depends in part on school-related factors and in part on matters of the social context surrounding the school. The following review of typical bilingual program types provides some sense of the wide range of bilingual approaches now found in various parts of North America.

BILINGUAL APPROACHES: PROGRAM TYPES

The following discussion of bilingual programs is meant to illustrate the considerable variety observed in programs designated *bilingual*. It is not exhaustive and is based on program types most common in North America, drawing on the descriptions in Crawford 1999; Genesee 1999; Hornberger et al. 1999; and Kuhlman and Murray 2000. It should again be noted, though, that the degree to which any educational program in North America or elsewhere can reasonably be called bilingual can only be established by direct observation of the language use patterns—oral and literate—observed in the classrooms concerned. Programs are labeled bilingual for a variety of reasons, only some of which reflect the actual language of instruction, the criterial feature emphasized here. Each of the program models summarized here has different implications for program length, type of curriculum, materials needed, teacher qualifications expected, and nature of assessments used to determine success. Most bilingual program types combine considerations of the language of instruction with the age of the students involved. Hence, it is common to see somewhat different types at elementary, secondary, and postsecondary levels.

Elementary-Level Program Models

Bilingual programs found at the elementary school level are generally one of three types: early-exit (or transitional) bilingual instruction; late-exit (or maintenance) bilingual instruction; or immersion/dual-language immersion (see also Snow's chapter in this volume for more information on the immersion approach to language education). Each of these is explained below.

Early-exit, or transitional, bilingual education programs are usually developed to serve young students who are recent immigrants to a new country (and thus are language-minority students). These programs aim to use two languages for classroom instruction up until the point at which children have developed sufficient oral and literacy skills to receive all classroom instruction in their second language. (Thus the label *transitional;* two languages, the children's native language and the dominant societal language, are used in classroom instruction only until the children can make the transition to receiving all instruction in the dominant language.) Early-exit programs always include oral use of the children's native language in the classroom; they may or may not include the active teaching of literacy skills in the children's native language. To the degree they do, they may aim to develop biliteracy, but only the degree of biliteracy needed to make a transition to literacy in the dominant language. Program length varies, usually from one to three years. Most such programs begin in kindergarten or first grade. The goals of transitional bilingual programs are to ensure mastery of grade-appropriate academic content and facilitate the speedy acquisition of the dominant language so that children can move into mainstream classrooms within three years of program entry (Genesee 1999, p. 14). Transitional programs require a sufficient number of certified bilingual teachers able to teach at the corresponding grade level; access to sufficient academic materials in the students' native language; specialized instruction in the second language (English, in most cases in the United States) so that students are prepared to move into classrooms using only that language, and specialized linguistic support for students during and after the transition;

appropriate and regular assessment of student progress; and support for and from students' family and community members. One such program, beginning at kindergarten level and described by Genesee and his collaborators (1999, pp. 17–19), is found at a school they call Kinney Elementary, located in a Spanish-speaking community. Experienced bilingual teachers and the bilingual program coordinator work with students entering the school in grades K and 1 to assist them in developing literacy skills and conversation skills in Spanish and English. Teachers in grades 3 and 4, with years of experience in helping students in the process of transition, use many sheltered English techniques (see Snow's chapter in this volume) to support students' academic progress during the transition to mainstream English-medium instruction.

Late-exit, or maintenance (or *developmental bilingual,* in some sources), models also aim to serve young students who are either immigrants to a country or who are members of relatively large groups within a country and who speak a native language different from the dominant one. Thus such programs, too, have been established to serve language-minority students. The goals of such programs typically include development of literacy skills in both the native language and the second language, and development of academic literacy skills in both languages theoretically continues for the duration of the program. Thus such programs explicitly aim to develop biliteracy. (The designation of *maintenance* refers to the program goal of maintaining the use of the children's native language all the way through the program. This goal does not in any way exclude the learning of academic literacy skills in the second language. On the contrary, maintenance bilingual programs are meant to use and develop two languages to the point of age-appropriate academic literacy skills.) Because such programs aim to maintain and develop skills in two languages, there is no theoretical limit on the number of years they might extend. In practice, however, such programs are usually found at the elementary level, and extend from grades K through 6, depending somewhat on how the particular school system organizes levels of instruction.

What kinds of resources are required to implement and sustain such programs? Like transitional bilingual programs, maintenance bilingual programs require a sufficient number of certified bilingual teachers to teach all the grade levels included in the program; access to sufficient academic materials in the students' native language and in the second language (English, in the United States); specialized second language instruction; appropriate assessment; and parental and community support. Because the programs extend longer than transitional programs, they require a greater number of certified bilingual teachers and native language academic materials that cover a wider range of grade levels. In maintenance bilingual education, teachers are encouraged to keep the languages separate, and the entire school staff and community is expected to create an atmosphere of equal status for both languages involved. Maintenance bilingual programs depend to some degree on the interest of a particular language community in supporting the academic use of its language, along with the second language, and insisting on high academic standards in both languages. Genesee and collaborators (1999, pp. 21–24) describe a K–5 maintenance bilingual program at Mariposa Elementary School, which grew out of a previously implemented transitional bilingual program. Cahnmann (1998) shows how the delivery of bilingual instruction at one Philadelphia school shifted over time from transitional to maintenance to transitional, in part as a result of changes in funding sources and leadership.

Immersion programs, pioneered in Canada to serve language majority students, in this case, native speakers of English desirous of developing high levels of skill French (see also Genesee 1987, and Snow's chapter in this volume), aim to immerse students in a language different from their native language. The ultimate goal is to build strong academic literacy skills in that language and to give students access to subject matter taught entirely through the second language. In the classic immersion model, students receive instruction completely or almost completely through the medium of the second language for the first few years of their educational experience, with literacy instruction in their native language added once they have established a base of literacy in the second language. By the latter years of the program, they usually receive instruction in each language about half the time. This progression of time allocation is thus referred to as starting with 90/10 (most instruction initially takes place in the second language, with little or no use of the students' native language) and moves to 50/50. Immersion models may extend all the way through elementary and even secondary education. For examples of immersion approaches used in various international contexts, see Genesee 1987 and Johnson and Swain 1997.

In the United States, there is a great deal of interest in dual-language immersion (also called two-way immersion), a variant of the immersion model, designed to serve both language-minority and language-majority children who wish to learn through the medium of two languages and develop literacy skills in both languages (see Christian 1996 and Christian et al. 1997). Such programs typically begin in kindergarten or grades 1 or 2 and extend all the way through elementary school. Instructional allocation of languages follows one of several patterns: It may be based on subject matter (i.e., math taught in one language, social studies in the other); on particular days of the week (e.g., two days per week are "English" days, three days are "Spanish" days, then the allocation is changed the following week); on parts of the day (e.g., morning in Spanish, afternoon in English); or on weekly assignment (a week in Spanish, then a week in English, etc.). Whatever pattern is chosen, the teaching staff and students know and follow it. Initially, children entering such programs are proficient in only one of the two languages but, because the enrolled students are native speakers of each of the languages used, children teach each other in addition to learning from the adult models around them. Because there are native-speaker or highly proficient models of both languages among both teaching staff and student participants, the likelihood that students will in fact develop high levels of proficiency in both languages is increased. Freeman (1998) provides a comprehensive description of the history and function of a Spanish-English dual language program at the

Oyster School in northwest Washington, D.C. Her account offers many insights into the confluence of parental and community interest, presence of qualified and dedicated teachers and administrators, and other issues to be considered in implementing such programs.

Secondary Bilingual Approaches

At the secondary level, issues of program model and choice of instructional language are affected by the departmentalized nature of instruction found in most secondary schools. Moreover, the greater cognitive demands of secondary school instruction also create pressures for both students and teachers to cover more, and more challenging, content material in a limited period of time. Hence, bilingual programs found at the secondary level are usually some variant of early-exit or transitional bilingual programs in which the students' native language is used just long enough to help them make a transition to the socially and politically dominant language, which they are then expected to use through the rest of secondary school.

Because of the specialized nature of instruction at the secondary school level, it is rare to find an entire program that is completely bilingual. Some secondary schools serving students who come largely from a single language background have been successful in establishing bilingual instruction that continues through school; for an example of one such program serving Navajo students, see McLaughlin 1992. Nonetheless, there is growing interest in devising adaptations of the two-way immersion approach for secondary schools (Montone and Loeb 2000). Although the number of two-way immersion (TWI) programs in middle schools and secondary schools is still quite small, many districts around the United States, especially those in which elementary level dual immersion programs have become better established, are exploring the possibility of adapting this model to suit older students. Time and subject allocations vary considerably, according to student population and teacher expertise. For example, at Bowen High School in Chicago, a 50/50 Spanish-English two-way immersion program, students spend most of the day together; content courses such as algebra, biology, and world history are taught in both languages, with languages alternating by unit of instruction within any given subject. The program-within-a-school model is also followed at Casey Middle School in Boulder, Colorado, where TWI students are instructed together for two one-hour blocks, one in science and social studies and the other in language arts. For all other classes, TWI students are mixed with other students. Other secondary-level TWI programs have been established in Arlington, Virginia; Brooklyn, New York; and Santa Monica/Malibu and Valley Center, California (all program information cited is from Montone and Loeb 2000).

Additionally, in some localities, notably large cities where there are newcomer schools (or newcomer programs within schools)[4] that serve large numbers of immigrant students from the same language background, there may well be bilingual content-area classes, numbers of students and availability of qualified teachers permitting. For example, core secondary school classes such as social studies and science have been offered in Spanish, Chinese, and Bengali, according to the prevalent language groups enrolled, at Newcomers High in Queens, New York (Schnailberg 1996, p. 36). While some particular classes may be offered predominantly in languages other than those used in the mainstream, there is still programwide emphasis on assisting students to develop the English language skills needed to make a speedy transition to English language instruction. Hence, while such programs are not called transitional bilingual programs, certain classes within them (and the overall goal of transition to English) make them somewhat comparable to such programs. Educators and others have some concerns about separating newcomer students from others for too long a period, but this approach has been used successfully in parts of California and in some other large cities across the country with large numbers of secondary level students from the same language groups (Adger and Peyton 1999; Chang 1990). Hence it should figure among the options to be considered as teachers and administrators seek alternatives to provide a variety of paths to success for secondary level students (Lucas 1997).

Postsecondary Bilingual Approaches

Postsecondary institutions serve students beyond the age of compulsory attendance. In the US, postsecondary students are an extremely diverse lot of traditional- and nontraditional- age students whose goals range from very specific occupational training to more general aims such as acquiring a liberal education to highly specialized preparation for further professional study. The role and extent of bilingual approaches observed for each such student group varies considerably. Because no national body or organization is charged with collecting related data, it is quite difficult to determine when and where bilingual approaches are used.

Some bilingual programs for adults in the United States have been developed to provide short-term, highly focused vocational training for special populations such as refugees who qualify for special government support. Where there are large numbers of English learners who share a native language background, native language instruction may be included as a part of relatively short (less than six months) programs aimed at helping participants find employment as soon as possible.[5] Bilingual programs that include native language literacy instruction for adults tend to be found in the geographic areas representing the largest proportional settlement of recent immigrants: New York, California, Texas, and Illinois (Gillespie 1994).

Postsecondary students enrolled in degree programs may have access to language instruction designed to accommodate various professional and personal goals. Some universities offer immersion programs that are best viewed as a variant of foreign language immersion programs (again, see Snow's chapter in this volume). University immersion programs may combine intensive language instruction (that is, instruction from four to six hours per day for a semester or summer term) with a period of residence in another country where the language is spoken, with the goal of rapidly building profi-

ciency. (In such cases, the instruction is mainly in the second language, so these programs would not necessarily qualify as bilingual programs, although they are aimed at producing students who become bilingual to some degree as a result of participation.) Many colleges and universities in the United States offer special language courses ("heritage language") that may be taught either bilingually or entirely in Spanish for native speakers of Spanish; often, though not always, the goal of such courses is language maintenance and development of formal literacy skills in Spanish for students who have received all or most of their formal education in schools in the United States and thus have not had the opportunity to build advanced literacy skills in Spanish (Valdés 1995). Finally, some postsecondary institutions in the United States offer courses that combine language instruction with occupationally relevant material in courses designed for particular majors such as education or business. Courses emphasizing Spanish for teachers or businesspeople may or may not be taught bilingually, depending on the level of proficiency shown by the students and the instructor's language capabilities. In Canada, some universities offer highly proficient students the option of taking special content area courses completely through the medium of their second language, either English or French; such courses, a kind of tertiary "sheltered" approach, offer graduates of secondary level immersion programs a way to maintain and develop proficiency while learning new subject matter (see Snow's chapter in this volume).

FROM PROGRAM MODELS TO QUALITY INDICATORS

From the 1960s until about 1990, most discussion of bilingual education centered on the possible program models. Thus, many methods texts emphasized taxonomies, often elaborate, of types of bilingual education and descriptions of various bilingual approaches (e.g., Mackey 1978). Increasingly, though, researchers, policy makers, and practicing educators have realized there are, in fact, very few "pure" bilingual program models in existence, and that, in practice, most bilingual programs combine elements found in various models. Consequently, it makes little sense to discuss educational models without reference to the social, political, and economic contexts in which they are implemented (Brisk 2000, 1998). Contemporary discussions of bilingual education (August and Hakuta 1997; Brisk 1998, 2000; Dentler and Hafner 1997; Genesee 1999) emphasize the match between the characteristics of an educational program, the sociocultural context of the students it serves, and the resources (both tangible and intangible) available to support educational efforts. All these affect the nature of related teacher expertise, choice of instructional approach, and outcomes to be expected in any instructional program, including bilingual approaches. We now turn to those quality indicators most closely related to language teaching.

Availability of Qualified Teachers and Other School Staff

It is impossible to implement any sort of bilingual program without qualified bilingual teachers. For this reason, availability of qualified staff members is the cornerstone of successful bilingual programs (Dentler and Hafner 1997, pp. 40–49). Teachers must be both highly proficient in at least one of the languages of the program and appropriately certified to teach the grade level or subject area for which they will be responsible. Moreover, program effectiveness is enhanced if teachers share the linguistic and cultural backgrounds of the students they teach. Although teachers are vital, they are not the only relevant personnel; the presence of school administrators committed to bilingual instruction (Soto 1997) and other instructional personnel such as classroom aides increase the likelihood of effective and consistent instruction.

Sound Curriculum and Instructional Organization

Qualified staff members must establish and follow high quality age-appropriate curricula. Too often, bilingual education programs are viewed as remedial rather than enriching. The use of students' first or native language for instruction is part of any bilingual program, but is not by itself sufficient to guarantee program quality (Cummins 1999), which is influenced by additional factors. Effective bilingual approaches exemplify the same characteristics as other effective programs, including access to the core curriculum; close articulation of grade and subject levels; flexible groupings; team teaching; use of meaningful tasks and pedagogy that actively involve the students in instruction; teaching materials appropriate in quantity and quality to subjects taught; peer and cross-age tutoring; and collaborative staff planning (Dentler and Hafner 1997, p. 40; Brisk 1998). Such curricular matters require careful planning and monitoring, and must be implemented sensibly, keeping in mind local conditions such as average class size, budget for materials and teacher training, and other resources, tangible and intangible, available to support and maintain bilingual instruction.

To this must be added, specifically for bilingual approaches, the selection and consistent implementation of a school- and programwide plan for language allocation throughout the school day and across the length of the school program (Baker 1996, pp. 232–241). Appropriate decisions about language allocation depend greatly on the particular school, neighborhood, and community context (Freeman 1998; Pérez and Torres-Guzmán 1992); thus, it is impossible to make blanket recommendations, except to observe that, if both languages are to be developed appropriately, both must be accorded the status of medium of instruction for a variety of curricular activities and, depending on student age and program type, both may also be school subjects. (For further considerations related to sound pedagogical techniques for second language development and subject matter mastery in classrooms, see chapters by Ediger and Hawkins in this volume.)

Appropriate Regular Assessment

Good bilingual programs demonstrate a regular and systematic approach to assessment of student progress in all curricular subjects in the relevant language. In assessment of overall program quality, these two aspects of evaluation are related but distinct. Each requires attention, though the nature and types of assessments used to gather relevant data varies considerably according to local and national assessment traditions and practices. In the United States for the last several decades, public (and most private) schools have depended on large-scale, norm-referenced standardized tests given in English as indicators of student progress. In some states, standardized tests in Spanish may also be used, particularly where elementary level bilingual programs have existed for some time.[6] Tests that rely on reading and writing certainly have a place in all educational programs, but researchers caution that, particularly for second language learners, any test that uses a second language reflects, in part, language proficiency as well as whatever other constructs or concepts are being tested (AERA 2000). Considerable tension surrounds the use of such tests in all school programs, and bilingual programs are no exception.[7] On the one hand, many politicians and state legislators are committed to the idea that institution of large-scale testing programs will improve education; on the other, practicing educators, researchers, and professionals in assessment express concerns about the inordinate importance accorded to standardized testing (Heubert and Hauser 1999). In the United States at present, scholars in education generally (Shepard 2000) and those concerned specifically with second language (Gottlieb 2000; Katz 2000) and bilingual assessment (Miramontes, Nadeau, and Commins 1997), call for a more diverse, curriculum-specific, and engaging philosophy of the assessment of student progress. Within the realm of informed second language practice, then, there is growing consensus about the need for alternative methods of student assessment, including portfolio systems, learning logs, checklists of student learning, etc. (see also Cohen's chapter in this volume). Because many nontraditional approaches to assessment are so labor intensive to develop and score, they require some investment of time and resources beyond conventional, published multiple-choice tests. Their use thus demands increased teacher training and administrative and public support.

Multiple Channels of Parent/Community Outreach

Besides having the leadership needed to recruit and retain qualified teaching staff and plan and implement a sound curriculum, bilingual programs of all sorts must determine the most effective ways to establish and maintain links between school-level efforts and the activities of students' families and communities (McGroarty 1998). (Optimally, all educational programs should do this, but the need for community linkages is particularly crucial when one of the languages in a bilingual program represents a language regularly used by the students' families.) Individual teachers can take many steps within their own classrooms to draw on parents' interests in their children's education (see McCaleb 1994 for many relevant suggestions), but effective community linkages also require schoolwide leadership and support. Explicit efforts to create such links are particularly crucial when teachers do not share the linguistic and cultural characteristics of their students. The challenge is greater still when students represent not one single linguistic and cultural background but many different ones, as is often the case in large urban and suburban school districts. Community outreach is an area in which very few teachers or other school personnel receive any systematic training, but it is one that shows up repeatedly as a characteristic of effective school programs for second language learners and bilingual students (Dentler and Hafner 1997; Miramontes, Nadeau, and Commins 1997).

Ongoing Concerns

The implementation of good bilingual education programs requires concerted efforts on the parts of teachers, school leaders, students, and families. To establish good programs, schools must define program goals and instructional designs that focus on the development of proficiency in two languages while at the same time promoting access to the full range of curricular subjects appropriate to students' ages and developmental levels. Instituting a program that meets any definition of bilingual instruction is not always an easy task, but it is certainly feasible given trained personnel, leadership, and support. Moreover, successful bilingual programs have been established in many places in North America and internationally.

There is no single best model for bilingual instruction; a range of possibilities exists, each with particular requirements. At the same time, results of bilingual programs are in part a function of the community contexts surrounding schools. As Crawford (1998) notes, it is ironic (and unfortunate) that, even as the foundation of research results and informed practice surrounding bilingual education in the United States has become better established since the 1960s, public opposition, based partially on misunderstanding, has grown. It is often believed that bilingual instruction means instruction in one non-English language only, when, as emphasized in this discussion, the bilingual approaches most commonly used in the United States always involve the use of *two* languages, one of which is English. Associations of linguists (e.g., AAAL 1996, 1997; LSA 1996) and language educators (NCTE 1982; TESOL 1992) have, for some years, endorsed the usefulness and potential complementarity of both bilingual or bidialectal approaches and specific second language techniques in education and have opposed any sort of official language designation that would restrict access to bilingual instruction. As teachers-in-training and practicing language instructors, readers of this chapter can be instrumental in clarifying some of the misunderstandings related to bilingual instruction while at the same time working to provide good quality language education programs. Depending on context and resources, many such programs might well include some of the bilingual approaches to language proficiency and academic progress described here.

DISCUSSION QUESTIONS

1. In your country or state, what is meant by the term *bilingual*? Which languages does this term usually refer to, and which of these are found in the educational system?

2. In your teaching context, why are teachers, students, and families interested in bilingual approaches to language learning? What kinds of goals do they hope to achieve?

3. In your locality, are there any other institutions, community groups, or broadcast media where use of a language other than the dominant one is usual? Identify any settings where use of another language is a regular occurrence; comment on whether and how the use of language in such a setting might promote an interest in bilingual instruction in that language.

4. In your view, is comprehensive academic literacy in two languages a reasonable goal for students enrolled in the bilingual programs you know about? Why or why not? What conditions are conducive to the development and maintenance of literacy in two languages?

5. Has your city or state ever considered any kind of language legislation? What was the proposal, and what kinds of public discussion surrounded it? Did the discussion of this language measure reveal anything about attitudes toward language and/or education?

SUGGESTED ACTIVITIES

1. Call your local school district to find out whether they have any classrooms that follow some sort of bilingual model. If they do, try to visit a classroom for an hour or two to observe some typical classroom activities and see how the teachers and students negotiate the use of two languages.

2. If there are any bilingual programs located at schools (public or private) near you, arrange to talk with one of the teachers in the program. Ask the teacher how the curricular design and materials are employed to develop proficiency in two languages. Examine the materials used for literacy instruction in each language to get some idea of the language models used to help students become biliterate.

3. Gather some information on student assessment from one or two schools or school districts. What kinds of student assessments are

regularly administered, and in what language? If the district includes non-native speakers of English, are testing and assessment requirements modified or altered in any way to accommodate them? If so, how?

4. Ask staff members from schools serving different levels of students (elementary/middle school/secondary) how they address issues of family contact and community outreach. Gather samples of any communications sent to students' homes. See which languages are used to communicate with families; find out how often and why families are asked to come to the school. Do you think such modes of outreach are likely to engage students' families? Why or why not?

5. Contact the legislative analyst's office for your state to see whether any legislation affecting language use or study has been proposed within the last two years. See if you can identify the sponsors and the intent of this legislation. If it has passed, ask some bilingual and ESL teachers if it has affected their work in any way.

 FURTHER READING

These sources will help those interested in understanding more about the development and implementation of bilingual approaches to language learning.

Baker, C., ed. 1996. *Foundations of Bilingual Education and Bilingualism.* 2d ed. Clevedon, UK: Multilingual Matters.
A comprehensive, interdisciplinary presentation of the theoretical and practical issues central to provision of bilingual education.

Brisk, M. E. 1998. *Bilingual Education: From Compensatory to Quality Schooling.* Mahwah, NJ.: Lawrence Erlbaum.
A thorough presentation of issues related to provision of good quality bilingual education programs defined in light of present-day interest in overall efforts directed at school improvement in the United States.

Crawford, J. W. 1999. *Bilingual Education: History, Politics, Theory, and Practice.* 4th ed. Los Angeles: Bilingual Educational Services.
A clear and readable account of the development and program varieties observed in contemporary bilingual education programs in the United States, with discussion of the political impetus as well as pedagogical questions related to its establishment.

García, O., and C. Baker, eds. 1995. *Policy and Practice in Bilingual Education: Extending the Foundations.* Clevedon, UK: Multilingual Matters.
A fine collection of many of the seminal articles that have shaped current approaches to bilingual education research and practice.

Genesee, F., ed. 1999. *Program Alternatives for Linguistically Diverse Students.* (Educational Practice Report No. 1.) Washington, DC: Center for Research on Education, Diversity, and Excellence/Center for Applied Linguistics.
A concise and practical discussion of the principal areas to be addressed when considering the choice and design of bilingual and English as a second language programs for schools in the United States, with descriptions of several program types.

 **WEBSITES**

Center for Applied Linguistics (CAL)
CAL is a nonprofit organization devoted to providing resources in language education to researchers, educators, parents, and students.
http://www.cal.org

National Association for Bilingual Education (NABE)
NABE is a professional and advocacy association dedicated to "addressing the educational needs of language minority students in the United States and advancing the language competencies and multicultural understanding of all Americans." It sponsors an annual conference to enable practitioners and supporters of bilingual education to share their experiences, provides advocacy on behalf of bilingual education and bilingual students, and publishes a newsletter.
http://www.nabe.org

National Clearinghouse for Bilingual Education (NCBE)
NCBE is a federally funded clearinghouse for information related to bilingual education whose charge is to "collect, analyze, and disseminate information relating to the effective education of linguistically and culturally diverse learners in the United States." It offers many

free and low-cost materials related to bilingual education theory, methodology, and assessment.
http://www.ncbe.gwu.edu

University of California Linguistic Minority Research Institute (UC LMRI)

The UC LMRI, funded by the University of California system, is a multicampus research effort devoted to identifying effective educational practices for language minority students in California. It sponsors research projects, disseminates information through research reports, and publishes a newsletter.
http://lmrinet.ucsb.edu

ENDNOTES

1 Zentella (1997) provides a particularly telling account of the way that use of two languages also changes with the life experiences of a group of young Puerto Rican women in New York City.

2 Hence, this chapter is only concerned with bilingual programs in which the use of two languages takes place with the same group of students during the same academic time frame. It is not concerned with educational programs where, for example, a single language may be used in preschool through grade 3, with students and teachers doing a full scale switch to another language (usually a language of wider communication or national visibility) in grades 4 and onwards (see Mackey 1978 for additional possible configurations of bilingual education). In such an arrangement, one could justifiably argue that the entire educational system is bilingual because of the use of one language and then the switch to another, although a student's experience at any point in time would, in theory, be monolingual. This model of "successive bilingual education" raises some issues in addition to those noted here for the more commonly discussed "simultaneous bilingual "approaches.

3 This chapter concentrates on pedagogical aspects of bilingual approaches to education and does not explore the political contexts of bilingual instruction in depth. However, given the trends toward nativism in language instruction in the United States (McKay 2000) and the many efforts by organized pressure groups in the United States to ban bilingual instruction (see, among other sources, Crawford 1992, Krashen 1999, and McGroarty in press), it is crucial to note that discussion of pedagogical issues in bilingual education is often entirely overshadowed by political concerns, some expressed overtly and some not, that have little or nothing to do with the daily choices facing teachers and administrators as they determine how to best educate the students they serve. While pedagogical and political questions are certainly related, teachers need to be able to distinguish between them in order to focus their efforts according to the student and community contexts in which they work.

4 Like many terms in education for linguistically diverse students, *newcomer programs* have a range of meanings in actual practice. They sometimes refer specifically to programs where newly arrived immigrant students are separated from other students for a period of time, usually six months to a full academic year, in order to receive specially designed linguistic and cultural services aimed at helping them make a transition to the mainstream classes which they must attend once the allotted time period is over (see Schnailberg 1996 for description of one such program). In other situations, *newcomer programs* refer generically to all programs, including bilingual and ESL instruction provided as part of an education that otherwise takes place in regular classrooms enrolling non-newcomer students (a meaning used in some of the programs described in Chang 1990; and Dentler and Hafner 1997). As with the term *bilingual education,* readers are advised to use specific information about a program (whether or not the focal students are separated from other students of the same age; how long the program lasts; what the curricular allocation is of any special language services such as native language instruction, ESL instruction, or tutoring; how student progress is assessed; what kinds of additional services to facilitate social and cultural adjustment might be provided, etc.) to determine what such programs provide in a given set of circumstances. The label itself suggests a range of possible school structures and services that vary greatly in their realization across school districts in the United States (Adger and Peyton 1999).

5 In the United States, both bilingual education and considerations of programs designed for refugees and immigrants are often marked by considerable misunderstanding, controversy, and disagreement in the public's mind about the nature and extent of services provided. Hence, instructors in some programs that offer native language instruction and support for adult students may be reluctant to admit to doing so, if there is a sense that influential persons within funding agencies or the community at large disapprove (even where program

regulations require or permit native language use). This perspective was brought home to me at a TESOL conference presentation in the 1990s on vocational training for refugees, when a presenter stated that his program in California's central valley used native languages to communicate with Hmong and Lao adult students but did not emphasize this in discussions with other authorities, establishing a kind of "don't ask/don't tell" policy regarding native language instruction. The political sensitivity of the topic is an additional reason why data on bilingual instruction for adults is hard to locate and verify.

6 It might first appear that testing Spanish-speaking students in Spanish solves problems of equity in assessment, but changing the language of a test does not necessarily make a particular test suitable for a group of students who use that language.

Other considerations such as level and nature of students' prior schooling, type and extent of literacy instruction, match between instructional content and test content, and the possibility that a test includes culturally irrelevant or misleading items must also be addressed (see Valdés and Figueroa 1994).

7 Space does not permit a consideration of a related problem of public perception, namely, that in former decades students in the United States, including immigrants, achieved at higher levels than is presently the case. This belief, pervasive in much public discourse, has represented an influential current in public discussion in the United States since at least the 1920s, even though research conducted through a variety of methods shows no support for such claims based on results of any type of test (for further discussion, see Rothstein 1998).

UNIT IV

Focus on the Learner

Many of the preceding chapters have focused on what the ESL/EFL teacher should know or what the teacher can do to facilitate student practice (and, one hopes, learning and improvement) in a language skill (or in all four skills). However, unless teachers tutor individuals, they must deal with a class—a group of individuals with different needs and ways of learning, often with diverse linguistic and cultural backgrounds. The chapter in this section by Oxford discusses learning styles and learning strategies, which are factors that can influence any student's ability to learn in a particular instructional context. Thus, the teacher needs to be aware and informed of these variables. Hawkins's chapter describes appropriate learning environments and materials for teaching both academic content and English language to ESL children, suggesting that the instructional context is a more important factor in success than the distinction many teachers make between basic interpersonal communication skills and cognitive academic language proficiency. Hilles and Sutton's chapter offers an insightful overview of the characteristics of adult ESL learners with many practical tips to help teachers meet these special learners' needs.

Language Learning Styles and Strategies

REBECCA L. OXFORD

In "Language Learning Styles and Strategies," Oxford synthesizes research from various parts of the world on two key variables affecting language learning; *styles*, i.e., one's general approach to learning a language; and *strategies*, the specific behaviors or thoughts learners use to enhance their language learning. These factors influence the student's ability in a particular instructional framework.

INTRODUCTION

Language learning styles and strategies are among the main factors that help determine how—and how well—our students learn a second or foreign language. A second language is a language studied in a setting where that language is the main vehicle of everyday communication and where abundant input exists in that language. A foreign language is a language studied in an environment where it is not the primary vehicle for daily interaction and where input in that language is restricted. Following the tradition in our field, the term *L2* is used in this chapter to refer to either a second or a foreign language.

The readers of this book will be primarily in the field of English as a second or foreign language (ESL or EFL), and most of the studies in this chapter were conducted in ESL/EFL settings. However, some of the studies here focused on native English speakers learning French, German, Japanese, or other languages foreign to them.

Learning styles are the general approaches—for example, global or analytic, auditory or visual—that students use in acquiring a new language or in learning any other subject. These styles are "the overall patterns that give general direction to learning behavior" (Cornett 1983, p. 9). Of greatest relevance to this methodology book is this statement: "Learning style is the biologically and developmentally imposed set of characteristics that make the same teaching method wonderful for some and terrible for others" (Dunn and Griggs 1988, p. 3). This chapter explores the following aspects of learning style:

sensory preferences, personality types, desired degree of generality, and biological differences.

Learning strategies are defined as "specific actions, behaviors, steps, or techniques—such as seeking out conversation partners, or giving oneself encouragement to tackle a difficult language task—used by students to enhance their own learning" (Scarcella and Oxford 1992, p. 63). When the learner consciously chooses strategies that fit his or her learning style and the L2 task at hand, these strategies become a useful toolkit for active, conscious, and purposeful self-regulation of learning. Learning strategies can be classified into six types: cognitive, metacognitive, memory-related, compensatory, affective, and social. We will discuss each of these later.

Because this chapter contributes to an instructional methodology book, it is important to emphasize that individual students' learning styles and strategies can work together with—or conflict with—a given instructional methodology. If there is harmony between (a) the student (in terms of style and strategy preferences) and (b) the instructional methodology and materials, then the student is likely to perform well, feel confident, and experience low anxiety. If clashes occur between (a) and (b), the student often performs poorly, lacks confidence, and experiences significant anxiety. Sometimes such clashes lead to serious breakdowns in teacher-student interaction. These conflicts may also lead to the dispirited student's outright rejection of the teaching methodology, the teacher, or the subject matter. Now we move to the detailed discussion of learning styles.

LEARNING STYLES

Ehrman and Oxford (1990) cited nine major style dimensions relevant to L2 learning, although many more style aspects might also prove to be influential. This chapter discusses four dimensions of learning style that are likely to be among those most strongly associated with L2 learning: sensory preferences, personality types, desired degree of generality, and biological differences.

Learning styles are not dichotomous (black or white, present or absent), but generally operate on a continuum or on multiple, intersecting continua. For example, a person might be more extroverted than introverted, or more closure-oriented than open, or equally visual and auditory but less kinesthetic and tactile. Few if any people could be classified as having all or nothing in any of these categories (Ehrman 1996).

Sensory Preferences

Sensory preferences can be broken down into four main areas: visual, auditory, kinesthetic (movement-oriented), and tactile (touch-oriented). Sensory preferences refer to the physical, perceptual learning channels with which the student is the most comfortable. Visual students like to read and obtain a great deal from visual stimulation. For them, lectures, conversations, and oral instructions without any visual backup can be very confusing. In contrast, auditory students are comfortable without visual input and therefore enjoy and profit from unembellished lectures, conversations, and oral instructions. They are excited by classroom interactions in role plays and similar activities. They sometimes, however, have difficulty with written work. Kinesthetic and tactile students like lots of movement and enjoy working with tangible objects, collages, and flashcards. Sitting at a desk for very long is not for them; they prefer to have frequent breaks and move around the room. Reid (1987) demonstrated that ESL students varied significantly in their sensory preferences, with people from certain cultures differentially favoring the four different ways of learning. Students from Asian cultures, for instance, were often highly visual, with Koreans being the most visual. Many studies, including Reid's, found that Hispanic learners were frequently auditory. Reid discovered that Japanese were very nonauditory. ESL students from a variety of cultures were tactile and kinesthetic in their sensory preferences. See also Reid (1995) and Oxford and Anderson (1995).

Personality Types

Another style aspect that is important for L2 education is personality type, which consists of four strands: extroverted versus introverted; intuitive-random versus sensing-sequential; thinking versus feeling; and closure-oriented/judging versus open/perceiving. Personality type (often called psychological type) is a construct based on the work of psychologist Carl Jung. Ehrman and Oxford (1989, 1990) found significant relationships between personality type and L2 proficiency in native-English-speaking learners of foreign languages. For more on personality type in language learning, see Ehrman (1996) and Oxford (1996b).

Extroverted versus Introverted By definition, extroverts gain their greatest energy from the external world. They want interaction with people and have many friendships, some deep and some not. In contrast, introverts derive their energy from the internal world, seeking solitude and tending to have just a few friendships, which are often very deep. Extroverts and introverts can learn to work together with the help of the teacher. Enforcing time limits in the L2 classroom can keep extroverts' enthusiasm to a manageable level. Rotating the person in charge of leading L2 discussions gives introverts an opportunity to participate equally with extroverts.

Intuitive-Random versus Sensing-Sequential Intuitive-random students think in abstract, futuristic, large-scale, and nonsequential ways. They like to create theories and new possibilities, often have sudden insights, and prefer to guide their own learning. In contrast, sensing-sequential learners are grounded in the here and now. They like facts rather than theories, want guidance and specific instruction from the teacher, and look for consistency. The key to teaching both intuitive-random and sensing-sequential learners is to offer variety and choice: sometimes a highly organized structure for sensing-sequential learners, and at other times multiple options and enrichment activities for intuitive-random students.

Thinking versus Feeling Thinking learners are oriented toward the stark truth, even if it hurts some people's feelings. They want to be viewed as competent and do not tend to offer praise easily—even though they might secretly desire to be praised themselves. Sometimes they seem detached. In comparison, feeling learners value other people in very personal ways. They show empathy and compassion through words, not just behaviors, and say whatever is needed to smooth over difficult situations. Though they often wear their hearts on their sleeves, they want to be respected for personal contributions and hard work. L2 teachers can help thinking learners show greater overt compassion to their feeling classmates and can suggest that feeling learners might tone down their emotional expression while working with thinking learners.

Closure-oriented/Judging versus Open/Perceiving Closure-oriented students want to reach judgments or completion quickly and want clarity as soon as possible. These students are serious, hardworking learners who like to be given written information and enjoy specific tasks with deadlines. Sometimes their desire for closure hampers the development of fluency (Ehrman and Oxford 1989). In contrast, open learners want to stay available for continuously new perceptions and are therefore sometimes called "perceiving." They take L2 learning less seriously, treating it like a game to be enjoyed rather than a set of tasks to be completed. Open learners dislike deadlines; they want to have a good time and seem to soak up L2 information by osmosis rather than hard effort. Open learners sometimes do better than closure-oriented learners in developing fluency (Ehrman and Oxford 1989), but they are at a disadvantage in a traditional classroom setting. Closure-oriented and open learners provide a good balance for each other in the L2 classroom. The former are task-driven learners, and the latter know how to have fun. Skilled L2 teachers sometimes consciously create cooperative groups that include both types of learners, since they can benefit from collaboration with each other.

Desired Degree of Generality

This strand contrasts the learner who focuses on the main idea or big picture with the learner who concentrates on details. *Global* or *holistic* students like socially interactive, communicative events in which they can emphasize the main idea and avoid analysis of grammatical minutiae. They are comfortable even when not having all the information, and they feel free to guess from the context. *Analytic* students tend to concentrate on grammatical details and often avoid more free-flowing communicative activities. Because of their concern for precision, analytic learners typically do not take the risks necessary for guessing from the context unless they are fairly sure of the accuracy of their guesses. The global student and the analytic student have much to learn from each other. A balance between generality and specificity is very useful for L2 learning.

Biological Differences

Differences in L2 learning style can also be related to biological factors, such as biorhythms, sustenance, and location. *Biorhythms* reveal the times of day when students feel good and perform their best. Some L2 learners are morning people, while others do not want to start learning until the afternoon, and still others are creatures of the evening, happily "pulling an all-nighter" when necessary. *Sustenance* refers to the need for food or drink while learning. Quite a number of L2 learners feel very comfortable learning with a candy bar, a cup of coffee, or a soda in hand, but others are distracted from study by food and drink. *Location* involves the nature of the environment: temperature, lighting, sound, and even the firmness of the chairs. L2 students differ widely with regard to these environmental factors. The biological aspects of L2 learning style are often forgotten, but vigilant teachers can often make accommodations and compromises when needed.

Beyond the Stylistic Comfort Zone

L2 learners clearly need to make the most of their style preferences. However, occasionally they must also extend themselves beyond these preferences. By providing a wide range of classroom activities that cater to different learning styles, teachers can help L2 students develop beyond the comfort zone dictated by their natural style preferences. The key is systematically offering a great variety of activities within a learner-centered, communicative approach.

Assessing L2 Learning Style

By far the most common type of assessment tool for L2 learning styles is the written survey in which students answer questions that reveal their particular style preferences. Style surveys vary in reliability and validity, but in the last few decades they have provided data from which teachers and students have begun to understand L2 styles. See Reid (1995) for examples of such surveys.

We have touched upon a number of important dimensions of L2 learning style. Now we are ready to turn to learning strategies, which are related to learning styles but are far more specific.

LEARNING STRATEGIES

As seen earlier, L2 learning strategies are specific behaviors or thought processes that students use to enhance their own L2 learning. The word *strategy* comes from the ancient Greek word *strategia,* which means "steps or actions generals take for the purpose of winning a war." The warlike meaning of *strategia* has fortunately fallen away, but the control and goal-directedness remain in the modern version of the word (Oxford 1990).

A given strategy is neither good nor bad; it is neutral until the context of its use is thoroughly considered. What makes a strategy positive and helpful for a given learner? A strategy is useful if the following conditions are present: (a) the strategy relates well to the L2 task at hand; (b) the strategy fits the particular student's learning style preferences to one degree or another; and (c) the student employs the strategy effectively and links it with other relevant strategies. Strategies that fulfill these conditions "make learning easier, faster, more enjoyable, more self-directed, more effective, and more transferable to new situations" (Oxford 1990, p. 8). Learning strategies can also enable students to become more independent, autonomous, lifelong learners (Allwright 1990; Little 1991).

Yet students are not always aware of the power of consciously using L2 learning strategies to make learning quicker and more effective (Nyikos and Oxford 1993). Skilled teachers help their students develop an awareness of learning strategies and enable them to use a wider range of appropriate strategies.

Strategy Use Often Relates to Style Preferences

When left to their own devices, and if not encouraged by the teacher or forced by the lesson to use a certain set of strategies, students use learning strategies that reflect their basic learning styles (Ehrman and Oxford 1989; Oxford 1996a, 1996b). However, teachers can actively help students "stretch" their learning styles by trying some strategies that are outside of their primary style preferences. This assistance can happen through strategy instruction, as discussed later in this chapter.

Conscious Movement Toward Goals

Learning strategies are intentionally used and consciously controlled by the learner (Pressley with McCormick 1995). In our field, virtually all definitions of strategies imply conscious movement toward a language goal (Bialystok 1990; Oxford 1990, 1996a). Let us consider Divna, whose goal is to conduct research in chemistry with the help of articles written in the L2. She is a busy professional with no extra time for reading journals, but she needs the information they contain. To meet the need, she plans a manageable task: finding and reading one L2 article per week on chemistry until she develops a rapid reading rate and is able to identify and understand published research findings. Strategies to help Divna accomplish this task might include scheduling time each week to search for an article in the library or on the Internet, or preparing herself by looking at articles on related topics in her own language. In addition, she could use strategies such as skimming for the main points, reading carefully for supporting details, keeping a notebook for L2 scientific vocabulary, using the dictionary to look up difficult words, guessing the meaning of words from the context, and making a written outline or summary if needed. The well-orchestrated set of strategies Divna uses might be called a *strategy chain*—a set of interlocking, related, and mutually supportive strategies.

Positive Outcomes from Strategy Use

In subject areas outside of L2 learning, the use of learning strategies is demonstrably related to student achievement and proficiency (Pressley and Associates 1990). Research has repeatedly shown this relationship in content fields ranging from physics to reading and from social studies to science. In light of this remarkable association between learning strategy use and positive learning outcomes, it is not surprising that students who frequently employ learning strategies enjoy a high level of self-efficacy, i.e., a perception of being effective as learners (Zimmerman and Pons 1986).

In the L2 arena, early studies of so-called "good language learners" (Naiman et al. 1975; Rubin 1975) determined that such learners consistently used certain types of learning strategies, such as guessing from context. However, later studies found that there was no single set of strategies always used by "good language learners." These studies found that less able learners used strategies in a random, unconnected, and uncontrolled manner (Abraham and Vann 1987; Chamot et al. 1996), while more effective learners showed careful orchestration of strategies, targeted in a relevant, systematic way at specific L2 tasks. In an investigation by Nunan (1991), more effective learners differed from less effective learners in their greater ability to reflect on and articulate their own language learning processes. In a study of learners of English in Puerto Rico, more successful students used strategies for active involvement more frequently than did less successful learners according to Green and Oxford (1995). The same researchers also commented that the number and type of learning strategies differed according to whether the learner was in a foreign language environment or a second language setting. In their review of the research literature, Green and Oxford discovered that second language learners generally employed more strategies with higher frequency than did foreign language learners.

Strategy Instruction Research

To increase L2 proficiency, some researchers and teachers have provided instruction to help students learn how to use more relevant and more powerful learning strategies. In ESL/EFL studies, positive effects of strategy instruction emerged for proficiency in speaking (Dadour and Robbins 1996; O'Malley et al. 1985) and reading (Park-Oh 1994), although results for listening were not significant (O'Malley et al. 1985). Chamot et al. (1996), Cohen et al. (1995), and Cohen and Weaver (1998) investigated the effects of strategy instruction among native-English-speaking learners of foreign languages and found some positive results mixed with neutral findings. In other studies, strategy instruction led to increased EFL learning motivation (Nunan 1997) and, among native-English-speaking learners of foreign languages, greater strategy use and self-efficacy (Chamot et al. 1996).

The most effective strategy instruction appears to include demonstrating when a given strategy might be useful, as well as how to use and evaluate it, and how to transfer it to other related tasks and situations. So far, research has shown the most beneficial strategy instruction to be woven into regular, everyday L2 teaching, although other ways of strategy instruction are possible (Oxford and Leaver 1996).

Six Main Categories of L2 Learning Strategies

Six major groups of L2 learning strategies have been identified by Oxford (1990). Alternative taxonomies have been offered by O'Malley and Chamot (1990) and others.

Cognitive strategies enable the learner to manipulate the language material in direct ways, e.g., through reasoning, analysis, notetaking, summarizing, synthesizing, outlining, reorganizing information to develop stronger schemas (knowledge structures), practicing in naturalistic settings, and practicing structures and sounds formally. Cognitive strategies were significantly related to L2 proficiency in studies by Kato (1996), Ku (1995), Oxford and Ehrman (1995), Oxford, Judd, and Giesen (1998), and Park (1994), among others. Of these studies, three were specifically in EFL settings: Ku (Taiwan), Oxford, Judd, and Giesen (Turkey), and Park (Korea). The other two studies involved the learning of Kanji by native English speakers (Kato 1996) and the learning of various foreign languages by native English speakers (Oxford and Ehrman 1995).

Metacognitive strategies (e.g., identifying one's own learning style preferences and needs, planning for an L2 task, gathering and organizing materials, arranging a study space and a schedule, monitoring mistakes, evaluating task success, and evaluating the success of any type of learning strategy) are employed for managing the learning process overall. Among native English speakers learning foreign languages, Purpura (1999) found that metacognitive strategies had "a significant, positive, direct effect on cognitive strategy use, providing clear evidence that metacognitive strategy use has an executive function over cognitive strategy use in task completion" (p. 61). Studies of EFL learners in various countries (e.g., South Africa [Dreyer and Oxford 1996] and Turkey [Oxford, Judd, and Giesen 1998]) uncovered evidence that metacognitive strategies are often strong predictors of L2 proficiency.

Memory-related strategies help learners link one L2 item or concept with another, but do not necessarily involve deep understanding. Various memory-related strategies enable learners to learn and retrieve information in an orderly string (e.g., acronyms), while other techniques create learning and retrieval via sounds (e.g., rhyming), images (e.g., a mental picture of the word itself or the meaning of the word), a combination of sounds and images (e.g., the keyword method), body movement (e.g., Total Physical Response), mechanical means (e.g., flashcards), or location (e.g., on a page or blackboard) (see Oxford 1990 for details and multiple examples). Memory-related strategies have been shown to relate to L2 proficiency in a course devoted to memorizing large numbers of Kanji characters (Kato 1996) and in L2 courses designed for native-English-speaking learners of foreign languages (Oxford and Ehrman 1995). However, memory-related strategies do not always positively relate to L2 proficiency. In fact, the use of memory strategies in a test-taking situation had a significant *negative*

relationship to learners' test performance in grammar and vocabulary (Purpura 1997). The probable reason for this is that while memory strategies are often used for memorizing vocabulary and structures in initial stages of language learning, learners need such strategies much less when their arsenal of vocabulary and structures has become larger and automatic responses are expected.

Compensatory strategies (e.g., guessing from context in listening and reading, using synonyms and "talking around" the missing word to aid speaking and writing, and—strictly for speaking—using gestures or pause words) help the learner make up for missing knowledge. Cohen (1998) asserts that compensatory strategies that are used for speaking and writing (often known as one form of *communication strategies*) are intended only for language use and must not be considered to be language learning strategies. However, Little (personal communication, January, 1999) and Oxford (1990, 1999a) have contended that compensation strategies of any kind, even though they might be used for language use, nevertheless aid in language learning as well. After all, each instance of L2 use is an opportunity for more L2 learning. Oxford and Ehrman (1995) demonstrated that compensatory strategies are significantly related to L2 proficiency in their study of native-English-speaking learners of foreign languages.

Affective strategies, such as identifying one's mood and anxiety level, talking about feelings, rewarding oneself for good performance, and using deep breathing or positive self-talk, have been shown to be significantly related to L2 proficiency in research by Dreyer and Oxford (1996) among South African ESL learners and by Oxford and Ehrman (1995) among native English speakers learning foreign languages. However, in other studies, such as that of Mullins (1992) with EFL learners in Thailand, affective strategies showed a negative link with some measures of L2 proficiency. One reason might be that as some students progress toward proficiency, they have less need for affective strategies. Perhaps because learners' use of cognitive, metacognitive, and social strategies is related to greater L2 proficiency and self-efficacy, over time there might be less need for affective strategies as learners progress to higher proficiency.

Social strategies (e.g., asking questions to get verification, asking for clarification of a confusing point, asking for help in doing a language task, talking with a native-speaking conversation partner, and exploring cultural and social norms) help the learner work with others and understand the target culture as well as the language. Social strategies were significantly associated with L2 proficiency in studies by South African ESL study by Dreyer and Oxford (1996) and the investigation of native-English-speaking foreign language learners by Oxford and Ehrman (1995).

Assessing Learners' Use of Strategies

Many assessment tools exist for uncovering the strategies used by L2 learners. Self-report surveys, observations, interviews, learner journals, dialogue journals, think-aloud techniques, and other measures have been used. Each one of these has advantages and disadvantages, as analyzed by Oxford (1990) and Cohen and Scott (1996). The most widely used survey, the *Strategy Inventory for Language Learning* (an appendix in Oxford 1990), has been translated into more than 20 languages and used in dozens of published studies around the world.

Various learning strategy instruments have disclosed research results beyond those that have been already mentioned. These additional findings include the following: L2 learning strategy use is significantly related to L2 learning motivation, gender, age, culture, brain hemisphere dominance, career orientation, academic major, beliefs, and the nature of the L2 task. A number of these findings have been summarized in Oxford (1999a, 1999b).

IMPLICATIONS FOR L2 TEACHING

The research synthesized in this chapter has four implications for classroom practice: assessing styles and strategies in the L2 classroom, attuning L2 instruction and strategy instruction to learners' style preferences, remembering that no single L2 instructional methodology fits all students, and preparing for and conducting strategy instruction.

Assessing Styles and Strategies in the L2 Classroom

L2 teachers could benefit by assessing the learning styles and the strategy use of their students, because such assessment leads to greater understanding of styles and strategies. Teachers also need to assess their own styles and strategies, so that they will be aware of their preferences and of possible biases. Useful means exist to make these assessments, as mentioned earlier. Teachers can learn about assessment options by reading books or journals, attending professional conferences, or taking relevant courses or workshops.

Attuning L2 Instruction and Strategy Instruction to Learners' Style Needs

The more that teachers know about their students' style preferences, the more effectively they can orient their L2 instruction, as well as the strategy instruction that can be interwoven into language instruction, matched to those style preferences. Some learners might need instruction presented more visually, while others might require more auditory, kinesthetic, or tactile types of instruction. Without adequate knowledge about their individual students' style preferences, teachers cannot systematically provide the needed instructional variety.

Remembering That No Single L2 Instructional Methodology Fits All Students

Styles and strategies help determine a particular learner's ability and willingness to work within the framework of various instructional methodologies. It is foolhardy to think that a single L2 methodology could possibly fit an entire class filled with students who have a range of stylistic and strategic preferences. Instead of choosing a specific instructional methodology, L2 teachers would do better to employ a broad instructional approach, notably the best version of the communicative approach that contains a combined focus on form and fluency. Such an approach allows for deliberate, creative variety to meet the needs of all students in the class.

Preparing for and Conducting Strategy Instruction

L2 teachers should consider various ways to prepare to conduct strategy instruction in their classes. Helpful preparatory steps include taking teacher development courses, finding relevant information in print or on the Internet, and making contacts with specialists.

Although we do not yet know all we wish to about optimal strategy instruction, there is growing evidence that L2 teachers can and should conduct strategy instruction in their classrooms. For some teachers it might be better to start with small strategy interventions, such as helping L2 readers learn to analyze words and guess meanings from context, rather than with full-scale strategies-based instruction involving a vast array of learning strategies and the four language skills (reading, writing, speaking, and listening). (See Oxford 1990 for a table of L2 strategies based on the six categories cross-indexed by the four language skills.)

Other teachers might want to move rapidly into strategies-based instruction. Strategies-based instruction is not so much a separate "instructional method" as it is sound strategy instruction interwoven with the general communicative language teaching approach noted above. Chamot and O'Malley (1996) describe the CALLA model, a form of strategy-based instruction for ESL learners that includes explicit strategy instruction, content area instruction, and academic language development. Cohen (1998) presents a different but somewhat related version of strategies-based instruction for native English speakers learning foreign languages. In evaluating the success of any strategy instruction, teachers should look for students' progress toward L2 proficiency and for signs of increased self-efficacy or motivation.

DISCUSSION QUESTIONS

1. What is the difference between learning styles and learning strategies?
2. How are learning styles and strategies related?
3. Why are learning styles and strategies important for L2 teachers to understand?
4. What do we know about "optimal" strategy instruction?
5. Notetaking is sometimes thought of as an academic survival skill. What criteria would need to be present to make notetaking an actual learning strategy?

SUGGESTED ACTIVITIES

1. Find a published learning style instrument and administer it to yourself. Score it. What kind of learner are you?
2. Write down ways that your learning style affects your teaching. Compare your findings with those of a colleague or friend. Consider in what ways you can build flexibility into your instruction to meet the needs of your students.
3. Take a strategy survey, responding according to the most recent L2 you have learned (or to which you have been exposed). What are your patterns of strategy use? Which categories of strategies do you use the most, and which do you use the least? Consider why this is so.
4. Administer a style instrument and a strategy instrument to your L2 students. Score these two instruments and compare the group's results on both. What linkages do you see between the students' styles and their strategies? What differences exist?
5. Start weaving strategy instruction into your L2 teaching. What effects do you see? What might you do next to strengthen strategy instruction?

FURTHER READING

Cohen, A. D. 1998. *Strategies in Learning and Using a Second Language.* Essex, UK: Longman.

Ehrman, M. 1996. *Second Language Learning Difficulties: Looking Beneath the Surface.* Thousand Oaks, CA: Sage.

O'Malley, J. M., and A. U. Chamot. 1990. *Learning Strategies in Second Language Acquisition.* Cambridge: Cambridge University Press.

Oxford, R. L. 1990. *Language Learning Strategies: What Every Teacher Should Know.* Boston, MA: Heinle & Heinle Publishers.

Oxford, R. L. 1996. *Language Learning Strategies Around the World: Cross-cultural Perspectives.* Manoa: University of Hawaii Press.

Reid, J. 1995. *Learning Styles in the ESL/EFL Classroom.* Boston, MA: Heinle & Heinle Publishers.

Supporting Second Language Children's Content Learning and Language Development in K–5

BARBARA HAWKINS

Hawkins's chapter examines teaching academic content to children in their L2, basing it on teaching and learning academic content in the primary language. She proposes that teaching academic content in the L2 is not helped by the Basic Interpersonal Communication Skills and Cognitive Academic Language Proficiency distinction, and suggests that it is more useful to concentrate on the context required to teach academic content successfully.

INTRODUCTION

This chapter presents what I believe to be two principal layers involved in content area instruction for second language (L2) students in elementary school (K–5): (1) effective core content instruction in elementary school, independent of L2 issues, and (2) the interaction of L2 issues with the above when teaching in the elementary grades. The first layer provides the groundwork for examining the second layer by telling us the "business" of elementary school instruction; without it, the second layer makes little sense. If we are to provide equal educational access to L2 students, then we must be very clear about the academic goals that exist for native speakers (NSs). Each layer uncovers elementary school children's learning needs, revealing corresponding knowledge and pedagogical requirements for effective planning and delivery of instruction.[1]

The first layer describes what we try to teach in terms of discipline-specific content in elementary school. What is the teaching charge as it applies to content-area education? This layer also considers the language of the classroom as a vehicle through which teachers carry out their charge to teach discipline-specific content to their students. Discussing the second layer, I will examine what it means to teach discipline-specific content to L2 children. Can we provide equity of core content instruction to non-native speakers (NNSs) of English in grades K–5 when we compare it to what we try to provide their NS peers?

LAYER I—TEACHING DISCIPLINE-SPECIFIC CONTENT TO CHILDREN

As elementary school teachers, we are called upon to provide the most fundamental understandings of the core disciplines to our students. These fundamental understandings underlie our students' future ability to broaden and deepen their knowledge of these disciplines. Therefore, it is essential that we ourselves have both a profound understanding of the fundamentals of these core subjects as well as a clear, working knowledge of the pedagogical principles involved in teaching them. Teachers must be in the position of "knowing"; i.e., understanding the desired concept or information *and* the process through which one must go in order to arrive at such an understanding.

What it means to teach discipline-specific content to children in grades K–5 is a vast topic. To narrow it down, we will first discuss general approaches that might be taken in presenting such content instruction. We argue that movement toward an experiential approach, based on the knowledge and practices of adults proficient in the disciplines is essential to deep learning. Second, we will talk about the special role of language in the delivery of content-area instruction. Language plays a major role in initially gaining entry to the disciplines, as well as in sustaining and building future understandings within them.

Some General Ideas on the Presentation of Content-Area Instruction in Elementary School

What is content-area education in elementary school? Although we may easily identify the major or core content areas as social studies, science, and mathematics (in addition to reading/language arts), this identification is not the same as identifying the specific content elements we wish to stress in elementary school. In general, is it learning *about* science, mathematics, and social studies, or is it learning to *do* science, mathematics, and social studies? What is the difference? What is the role of factual knowledge within the disciplines, and what is the role of process knowledge?

Within education, there has been a push to have students understand the disciplines from the "inside out" (American Association for the Advancement of Science 1993; Becker and Shimada 1997; Lemke 1993; Parker 1993). One way to interpret this is to consider learning to think about the content areas as those proficient in them think. By this we mean to consider science education as learning to think and do as scientists, mathematics education as learning to think and do as mathematicians, and social sciences education as learning to think and do as social scientists. Dewey calls for this emphasis when he speaks of "the psychology of occupation": "By occupation I mean a mode of activity on the part of the child which reproduces, or runs parallel to, some form of work carried on in social life." (1990 [1956], p. 132).

Learning to "do" a discipline means, among other things, that one gradually moves toward membership in the community of experts represented by that discipline. This movement toward fellowship with scientists, mathematicians, and social scientists involves the learner in a gradual educational process, a *situated* process involving language as one of its main resources for constructing knowledge over time. One does not only learn facts about and/or from the disciplines; rather, the goal is to immerse the learner in the creative processes that direct the discipline, the belief being that students will gradually become knowledgeable about and control the integral, critical factual information related to content as they learn and adopt the ways of the discipline. In addition to this factual base of knowledge, they will also have constructed a sense of the discipline—its major questions, its approaches to answering those questions, what it counts as research and knowledge, and its limits and crossovers in relation to other disciplines. It is in building this sense of the discipline that learners will gain factual information about it; i.e., by learning to "do" the discipline, they also learn "about" the discipline.

For clarification, let us present contrasting examples. Suppose that culinary arts was included in our curriculum. Suppose further that, as part of the curriculum for our grade level in culinary arts, we needed to teach the students to prepare a certain recipe. Our goals are that our students learn to cook this dish in such a way that they can identify what makes it taste good and what the effects of various ingredients and cooking strategies are on its taste. They should be able to troubleshoot the recipe if they get less than desired results, use appropriate ingredient substitutions for various cooking situations, and make variations based on taste, number of servings desired, and dietary preferences.

The first type of class is concerned with students learning "about" culinary arts. Here, we set up our instruction as a compilation of important facts *about* the dish and its preparation, using a chapter of the textbook to guide us. It describes the dish, lists the ingredients and the amounts needed for it, and discusses the preparation of the ingredients, the procedures involved in mixing and cooking the ingredients, the time required to prepare the dish, the calories and the fat, salt, sugar, and carbohydrate grams per serving, and the expected number of servings. In order to provide context, the chapter may include historical information on the dish's development, times of year for which the dish is most appropriate, and the beverages that might complement it. In order to ensure students learn the information presented, the text includes advanced organizers, vocabulary lists, bolded vocabulary accompanied by margin annotation, pictures of the ingredients and processes, an outline, and discussion questions at the end of the chapter. Additionally, it includes language skill practice activities to ensure student engagement in reading and writing across the curriculum.

The teacher's edition lists the applicable standards that will be addressed in the chapter, distinguishing between those to cover thoroughly and those to receive exposure, but not mastery. It also includes guided reading questions with possible student answers and suggested class and homework activities, some of which are "hands on." Also found are titles from children's literature that could be integrated into instruction, suggestions for integration with mathematics, science, and social studies, and a description of how activities can be introduced to encourage students to develop and use higher order thinking skills. An assessment packet offers multiple-choice, matching, fill-in-the-blank, short definition, and essay assessments. All qualitative assessments are accompanied by clearly delineated, well operationalized rubrics. Finally, we note that the textbook authors have taken special care to ask "real chefs" to give their stamp of approval to the content by making sure that all of the factual information contained in the chapter is correct.

While covering the chapter in class, we would do reading circles with the students in order to support their reading of the text, have them attack the chapter questions in cooperative groups, and have them draw and write about each step involved in the preparation of the dish. We would give the students the various assessments provided, some as self-measures of their understanding, and some as more formal measures. We would have each student prepare a portfolio of his or her work, and eventually we would be able to give the students a grade in the category on the report card labeled "Culinary Arts."

Toward the end of the year is the standardized test required by the state to hold both the students and the teacher accountable for meeting the culinary arts standards. Even though the teacher could only cover the sections on doubling and halving the recipe and alternative seasonings in the last three days before the exam, he or she hopes that at least some of the students will be able to recognize those items on the test and to answer the questions correctly.

Let us next give a contrasting example of the same task, this time where emphasis is on learning to "do" the discipline of culinary arts. We now need to look to the *experiences* of the children with regard to the dish we want them to be able to understand and create. "It is a cardinal precept of the newer school of education that the beginning of instruction shall be made with the experience learners already have; that this experience and the capacities that have been developed during its course provide the starting point for all further learning" (Dewey 1948, p. 88). We might begin by having the students taste samples of the dish as prepared by various chefs. We clearly assume that they have tasted food, but we may also assume they have probably not yet learned what creates the taste sensations they have experienced. If we begin by letting them taste the samples, we can then present them with an open-ended problem[2] that will direct them to greater appreciation of taste while incorporating their common experience of the sample tasting. The goal is to have the students learn more about taste as they try to formalize their experience of it. "It is also essential that the new objects and events be related intellectually to those of earlier experiences, and this means that there be some advances made in conscious articulation of facts and ideas" (Dewey 1948, p. 90).

We will pose our problem in the form of a series of questions: How can you explain/describe how all of these versions of the dish taste? Do all of them taste the same? Different? Are there any similarities? How do you know?

As students try to capture their taste experience, the teacher might help them classify it by having them first list the ingredients that they taste and then to describe the similarities and differences they taste among the samples.

The students might spend several classes trying to characterize and then refine their characterizations of what it is that they taste. As they do so, they are engaged in one of a chef's most basic activities. At the same time, they will be learning at least the most elementary "taste vocabulary" used by chefs. Their cheflike attempts to classify their experience will most likely result in more questions. Among these might be whether everyone's perception of the food is the same when the dish is the same, whether what they taste is the same as what the chef tastes, whether all of the samples have the exact same amounts of ingredients, whether the samples have been cooked differently (e.g., baked as opposed to grilled), etc. These questions more closely resemble those of the chef than any which might arise from the textbook-driven unit described above, and they can provide the class with a continual source of new problems around which to organize its ongoing investigation. As this unit develops over time, the students will have the opportunity to experiment in a truly *experiential* way with the ingredients, cooking methods, portion control, etc. Their first trial-and-error attempts will be further catalogued into a growing body of knowledge about cooking. At the same time, students will be developing a "culinary arts script," learning to attach new and meaningful language to their understandings.

We will also take advantage of some techniques used by the first class. The students will work cooperatively, in pairs or small groups. They will develop portfolios, which will contain among other items an ongoing diary of their experiences accompanied by a notebook showing how they codified those experiences into descriptions, definitions, directions, classifications, etc. There will be smaller assessments along the way which will ask students to identify and select ingredients, clearly state why they chose one ingredient over another, identify ingredients by taste both separate from and within the dish they are preparing, and critique their own and other classmates' various cooking attempts. This critiquing will help students to develop a rubric that clearly identifies essential elements surrounding the preparation of the dish. The final assessment will be the actual preparation of the dish, with individualized,

specific requirements as to amounts and variations for diet and taste. While this second class clearly incorporates "skills"—for example, reading and writing across the curriculum, higher order thinking skills—the driving force is always learning to understand the dish as a chef would, taking notes and talking about the dish as a chef would, learning to taste and rate the tastes of food as a chef would, and preparing the dish as a chef would.

The unit of instruction surrounding this one dish may take three months to complete, but the students will have delved deeply into the content area, the discipline of the culinary arts. How will they do on the standardized test that comes at the end of the year? In fact, they should do just fine. If we teach well, the test scores will follow. The greatest loss at this point is that the standardized test will not begin to capture the depth of the students' knowledge.[3]

What are we to make of these two contrasting examples? Are both methods successful? It depends, of course, on how one chooses to define success. Let us return to our original statement about what it was that we had hoped to accomplish regarding the preparation of our special dish:

> Our goals are that our students learn to cook this dish in such a way that they can identify what makes it taste good and what the effects of various ingredients and cooking strategies are on its taste. They should be able to troubleshoot the recipe if they get less than desired results, use appropriate ingredient substitutions for various cooking situations, and make variations based on taste, number of servings desired, and dietary preferences.

On paper (i.e., the standardized test) both groups appear to have been successful, with the first group being perhaps a little more successful. The more serious question, however, is what if success were defined as *actually* being able to meet our objectives as listed above? Just because students can read and write about cooking the dish is no guarantee that they will be able to recognize what they have studied about in any variation of the dish. The first group has learned to cook, taste, and modify the dish in theory only. The second group has an experiential, real-world knowledge of the dish and can parlay this experience into new knowledge as new experiences present themselves. They now have at least the beginnings of a profound, fundamental notion of taste, one which can be built upon as they proceed further into the world of culinary arts. The first group will probably have to review and relearn the four tastes whenever the next teacher decides to take up the theme, following a "reteach section" in the teacher's guide.

However, since "culinary arts" is not a core content area, how do our imaginary examples play out in the elementary school classroom? We can gain some insight if we re-examine the second approach to teaching the students how to prepare a dish, analyzing this approach to distill some basic principles for planning instruction. First, we need to start where the children are, providing them with an experience that is easily understandable, but that will connect them directly to the fundamental issues we wish to teach. Of course, the students are not yet aware of these connections, and we must carefully organize the lesson or unit such that they eventually become clear to the students. The choice of the initial experience is important, since it will mark the students' entry into the instructional unit; if they cannot relate to it, they will be left on the outside from the very start. Notice that the experience of tasting the various versions of the dish is easily accessible to the students. At the same time, it is an experience that can be used to move the students into a deeper discussion and understanding of what it means to taste.

Once we have provided the experience, we need to present an open-ended problem that will engage students in an analysis of the experience, drawing them headlong into the heart of what we wish to teach. At this point, the children truly begin their emulation of the community of adults who are proficient within the discipline, for it is here that they begin their *initial* (i.e., to be broadened and deepened as they go through school) investigation of a concept both central and fundamental to the discipline. Once one understands how vital the open-ended problem

is for guiding the rest of the lesson or unit, one also realizes the enormous importance of this step in planning. In fact, this issue of a "good problem" is easily overlooked as teachers often become absorbed in other, less important tasks, e.g., organizing cooperative groups, planning activities and the materials needed for them, etc. Finding or creating a problem that will act as the vehicle for moving the children from their personal experiences to new, profound understandings is actually one of the most difficult, even vexing, aspects of planning instruction (Sawada 1997).[4] However, this is also one of its most creative aspects. The problem in the culinary arts example was put in the form of a series of questions that required the students to try to describe and/or explain what they tasted and to discriminate among tastes. An earnest struggle to do this engages students immediately in an essential activity, pivotal in their ability to continue to develop in culinary arts.

Once the problem is established and students understand it accurately, the teacher must now call upon his or her own deep understanding of the fundamentals of the discipline to guide the students with their observations, findings, and questions, such that "the new objects and events be related intellectually to those of earlier experiences," thus promoting "advances made in conscious articulation of facts and ideas" (Dewey 1948, p. 90). This is where teachers really need to "know their stuff" in terms of the content, because if they themselves do not have control of fundamental understandings of the disciplines, it will be impossible to lead children along this path of gradually constructing these understandings. We do not mean that teachers have to be something they are not— i.e., scientists, mathematicians, or social scientists—but it is essential that they have a profound understanding of the *fundamentals* of each field, regardless of the grade level taught. As Ma (1999) has termed it when speaking about teachers' preparation for teaching elementary school mathematics, teachers need "PUFM"— a "*P*rofound *U*nderstanding of *F*undamental *M*athematics" (p. 124)— or to paraphrase Ma, a profound understanding of the fundamentals of the discipline.

Thus far, we have outlined three lesson or unit preparation steps from our sample culinary arts unit: (1) know what the students' current understandings are from their life experiences, (2) set up an experience that can serve as a bridge to move the students from their current life experiences to a deeper understanding, and (3) present an open-ended problem that will engage the students in the very heart of the core conceptual understandings that you wish them to acquire. What happens after these three steps are in place? There are many helpful techniques that teachers can use to move students to the kind of analyses that are required to construct new, important understandings. For example, cooperative grouping can be used very effectively, as can various "hands on" activities. A major facet of instruction, however, necessarily focuses on the classroom discourse that results from teacher guidance. This is not easily converted into a list of steps, but it nevertheless requires our full attention.

On the Role of Language in the Delivery of Content-Area Instruction

At the same time that teachers must know content, they also must know pedagogy. We now turn to one of the major tools of pedagogy, language. The language of a discipline needs to be situated in the educational process, insofar as the language of the classroom both defines and is defined by the discipline. It is through classroom discourse that most instruction gets accomplished. This is to say, through watching, listening, asking, recording, and examining, learners fashion "meaning out of events and phenomena through prolonged, complex processes of social interaction" (Schwandt 1994, p. 118). As they work to interpret experiential data, learners construct a reality of meanings, including both the processes of meaning construction (i.e., how meaning is "made" in this field or discipline), as well as what and how many meanings are involved in the instruction (i.e., what is to be learned in this field, the content of the discipline). How might this be played out in the elementary school classroom?

If the social interaction in the classroom promotes learning *about* content, then that is most likely the meaning that learners will construct over time. On the other hand, if the social interaction encourages learners to *do* the discipline, "to conjecture, invent, probe, search for relationships, value diversity [of explanations], communicate and represent their ideas and findings as they work both collaboratively and independently to resolve complex problems" (Parker 1993, p. 16), then *that* is most likely the meaning of the discipline that will be constructed by them over time.[5]

A constructivist approach to instruction relies on the integration of cognitive, social, and linguistic features to achieve the classroom discourse that promotes learning to *do* content. (See Schwandt 1994). To understand or know something, one must use cognitive powers of elucidation to construct meaning; this only happens when language and social knowledge are closely integrated with cognition. Even when we work independently, we are involved in this integrated triad of cognition, language, and social knowledge. To separate out any one of the three is to undermine the process of constructing meaning.

Lemke, in his work on discourse in science classrooms (grades 9–12), argues that science is a social process. "When we talk science we are helping to create, or re-create, a community of people who share certain beliefs and values" (1993, p. x). He also argues that language is a major factor in establishing and maintaining the community of scientists—language is "not just vocabulary and grammar: Language is a system of resources for making meanings" (p. ix). He is perhaps clearest when he states:

> "Talking Science" does not simply mean talking about science. It means doing science through the medium of language. "Talking science" means observing, describing, comparing, classifying, analyzing, discussing, hypothesizing, theorizing, questioning, challenging, arguing, designing experiments, following procedures, judging, evaluating, deciding, concluding, generalizing,

reporting, writing, lecturing, and teaching in and through the language of science (p. xi).

Finally, Lemke argues that the role of the science teacher is clear if we view science teaching as a social process. Teachers are "bridge people" in that they already belong to the community of people that speak the language of science; their charge is to bring their students, who do not yet understand this language, into the community. It is through their teachers that students will be able to enter the discourse community of scientists.

Lemke's arguments about science are also true for other disciplines. That is, there is a community of people who speak the languages of mathematics, of social science, of literature. These are the proficient adults in the communities of the various disciplines. Vitally important to recognize is that this language is socially situated within these communities; not to be identified with specific vocabulary or grammatical constructions. To do so is to simplify its power and to miss it "as a system of resources for making meaning" (p. ix).

In fact, the language of each of these disciplines has much in common when one compares them purely at the level of vocabulary and grammatical constructions. Short (1994) reports on her group's research of classroom discourse used in middle school social studies classes. The researchers analyzed their data in hopes of identifying the academic language competencies L2 students would need in order to be successful. They defined the academic language of social studies to include semantic and syntactic features, "such as vocabulary items, sentence structure, transition markers, and cohesive ties" and "language functions and tasks that are part of social studies class routines" (p. 595). Contrary to what they expected, they found that the academic language used in "American history classes was commensurate with much of the academic language in other humanities courses, and in fact, similar to the non-technical language used in math and science classrooms. . . ." (p. 595). As Lemke asserts:

> The content of every scientific and technical subject can be expressed in language (and in specialized offshoots of language, such as mathematics). In

fact, the same scientific ideas can be expressed in many different ways, because the semantics of a language always allows us to use grammar and vocabulary in different ways to express the same meaning. The wording of a scientific argument may change from one book to the next, one teacher to the next, even one day to the next in the same classroom. But the semantic pattern, the pattern of relationships of meanings, always stays the same: That pattern *is* the scientific content of what we say or write (1993, p. x).

If this is the case, then what is a teacher to do in terms of guiding classroom discourse in the content areas? How does this socialized learning work? There are many points Vygotsky (1978) makes. The first has to do with how children learn to use language to accomplish goals. He gives an example of an infant learning to point as a meaningful gesture (Vygotsky 1978, p. 56). Initially, the pointing gesture is just an unsuccessful attempt by the child to grasp something out of reach. The child does not realize that he or she has any power over the environment other than what he or she can do physically to alter it. As his or her hands stretch out towards the object, the mother comes to the child's assistance and gives him or her the object. At this point, "the situation changes fundamentally," in that the child's unsuccessful attempt to retrieve the object has brought about a reaction, not from the object, but from another person; at this point, the child's grasping action becomes pointing, a gesture for others, even though the child may not yet know it. Eventually, the child will link this action with the situation as a whole, and he or she will understand the movement as pointing. "At this juncture, there occurs a change in that movement's function: from an object-oriented movement it becomes a movement aimed at another person, a means of establishing relations . . . . Its meaning and functions are created at first by an objective situation and then by people who surround the child" (p. 56).

There are several important points that Vygotsky makes here. The first is that "an operation that initially represents an external activity is reconstructed and begins to occur internally." This is to say, via the experience that the child has in learning the pointing gesture, there is a transformation of "grasping" into "pointing," and that means a transformation into a "sign-using" activity. The child has learned the mediating power of the gesture. Second, "an interpersonal process is transformed into an intrapersonal one" (p. 57). This is to say that the reconstruction process begins as an actual relation between the child and another person. The child was not born with the pointing gesture, and did not understand it when he or she first used it, coming to understand it by his or her mother's (or others people's) repeated reactions to it. Thus, Vygotsky says that "every function in the child's cultural life appears twice: first on the social level and then on the individual level; first *between* people (interpsychological) and then *inside* of the child (intrapsychological)" (p. 57). Finally, Vygotsky sees in the development of the pointing gesture that "the transformation of an interpersonal process into an intrapersonal one is the result of a long series of developmental events" (p. 57). Since the internalization process is accomplished on the basis of external signs, and the signs themselves also undergo change, the transformation from interpersonal to intrapersonal is gradual.

Vygotsky's ideas about how language development is situated in a social context are very powerful, and very helpful in terms of our discussion of content area education in elementary school. His work provides us with a very credible scenario for how experiences external to the learner become internalized. We need to have a way of understanding how what we don't originally know or understand becomes a part of our working knowledge, of how what is external to us gets internalized. According to Vygotsky, this development is a mediated social process, always situated within a specific context. Within any given context, there are a number of unexamined experiences present to the learner. Some of these experiences will be more familiar than others, and some may be so unfamiliar that they may go unnoticed.

Let us return to the class tasting experience presented as the opening activity to the "learning to *do*" group. External to the learners are the various sample dishes that they will all taste. Some of the students may only be able to judge the dishes as *good* or *bad* tasting, while others may be able to judge them as *salty* or *spicy*. At the very moment that the discussion begins—i.e., when language among the social actors about the experience begins—students are confronted with new possibilities for learning about taste. Perhaps the teacher mentions that one of the samples tastes "more garlicky" than the others. One student may have no idea of what that means, while another may agree completely. The one who has no idea might ask to taste the dishes again, trying to figure out what "more garlicky" means. The teacher may bring the student a piece of fresh garlic to smell, then ask him or her to compare that with the sample dish, and next to compare that sample with the others that seem to have less garlic. Within this community of learners, a community of tasters is gradually being built. It may take several instances in several different settings before the child who had no idea of "more garlicky" comes to a full realization of what that means. The students have the opportunity to internalize new information based on highly contextualized interaction surrounding a common experience. It is via this kind of interaction that knowledge very gradually gets built.

If we think about the hypothesized taste discussion presented above we can see that the teacher had a very special role of being able to *scaffold* new information for the students. Wood, Bruner, and Ross define scaffolding as "the means whereby an adult or 'expert' helps somebody who is less adult or less expert" (1976, p. 89). Integral to the notion of scaffolding is the idea that learners are in the position of solving a problem that is initially beyond their level of competence. At the same time, the person who is helping them can do so precisely because he or she knows both the content and how one arrives at the understanding of such content. The teacher in the above example knows about taste and has presented the students with an open-ended problem that is initially beyond their level of competence to solve independently; they are not yet capable of describing on their own the nuances of taste that they need to describe in order to solve the problem. Through the medium of language in the classroom setting, the teacher interacts with the students, introducing new ideas about taste. This is the teacher's most important classroom work: to provide for the social interaction within the community of learners such that the learners may move from what they know to what they don't yet know, from their own experiences to new understandings of the disciplines represented by the content they are studying.

Summary of Layer 1

As indicated earlier, knowing one's students, then using that knowledge to offer them experiences of which they have partial understanding, and then confronting them with a problem that calls on them to re-examine those experiences to learn new information satisfies the first three requirements for teaching discipline-specific content to elementary school children. Each of these requirements does its part to situate the learning context such that all members of the community can have access to the learning opportunity. The next major requirement for teachers is to scaffold further learning opportunities by guiding classroom interaction surrounding the shared experiences and their open-ended problems. This involves going from "talking the discipline" (to paraphrase Lemke 1993), to *doing* the discipline. It is this very highly situated talking about common experiences within the environment that will lead students, very gradually, to the community of proficient adult members of the discipline.

LAYER 2—TEACHING ELEMENTARY SCHOOL CHILDREN CONTENT IN THEIR SECOND LANGUAGE

Now that we have presented and discussed what we see as the demands placed on the elementary school teacher for presenting effective content-area education in general, we speak to the issues surrounding content-area education for L2 elementary school students. The first point to recognize is that the instruction we refer to in this section is "sheltered," also referred to as "Specially Designed Academic Instruction in English" (SDAIE). (See Snow's chapter in this volume for a discussion of sheltered instruction techniques.) This means that the first goal of instruction is to teach the content, not to see the content as a vehicle for the acquisition of the second language. As it turns out, this is extremely important to keep in mind, as it influences the entire discussion. The teacher will absolutely need to support the L2 needs of the children as he or she provides content-area instruction, and as the instruction progresses, the children will definitely progress in their acquisition of the L2. However, the driving force behind the instruction is to provide high quality content-area instruction in the sense we have been describing it thus far.

We will first consider the relation between NNS children's L2 proficiency and their ability to learn effectively in the various content areas that are included in the elementary school curriculum. A common idea is that it is impossible to teach children in content areas until they first speak English. On the other hand, another often expressed and rather widespread idea is that children can "pick up" languages "naturally," often more easily and quickly than adults can. Beyond these ideas is the fact that L2 children are enrolled in the K–5 classroom, and that we cannot wait the 3 or 7 years, or however many years it will take for them to learn English to a sufficient degree to begin the serious study of discipline-specific content. What, then, do we do about this issue?

This second layer of our discussion will be divided into three parts. The first part will consider some of the theory that has helped shape what many believe about the nature of content-area education for L2 speakers. It will present a brief summary of the ideas that come from a language distinction proposed by Cummins (1976, 1979, 1981), Basic Interpersonal Communication Skills (BICS) and Cognitive Academic Language Proficiency (CALP). The second part suggests that we abandon the BICS/CALP distinction, and presents a rationale for doing so. Adopting this suggestion from part two, the third part discusses the implications for content-area instruction in the elementary grades for L2 children. An effort will be made throughout to link all this to our discussion of layer one above.

A Brief Summary of Second Language Theory That Has Helped Shape Our Beliefs About Content-Area Education

Cummins's work on bilingual and second language acquisition (SLA) has had an enormous influence upon L2 instructional practices in the elementary school setting. Many program administrators, materials developers, and teachers have relied upon his distinctions to organize, describe, and implement their programs. In this section, I would like to revisit the work of Cummins in which he delineates the BICS/CALP distinction (1976, 1979, 1981), since practitioners seem to rely upon it almost universally, and since it relates directly to the issue of core content instructional practices for L2 elementary school children.

Cummins outlines his ideas about Basic Interpersonal Communication Skills (BICS) and Cognitive Academic Language Proficiency (CALP) in several articles. In general, "this work has profoundly influenced methodology for all teachers of Limited English proficient students by distinguishing between language used for social and academic purposes" (Sasser and Winningham 1991, p. 33). In summarizing the distinction between BICS and CALP, Chamot and O'Malley note that BICS is characterized by social communication skills which are context embedded and cognitively undemanding (1994, pp. 7, 24, and 40). BICS has often been described as "the language students use among themselves on the school playground"; i.e., the language of BICS takes place in situations which offer many contextual clues and can become easily routinized since the interaction typically surrounds everyday transactions. (Sasser and Winningham 1991, p. 33). This social language "typically deals with fairly uncomplicated topics that are familiar to the speaker" (Chamot and O'Malley 1994; p. 40). Proficiency in BICS,

which can usually be attained "in about two years" (*ibid.*, p. 7), can "fool" the uninitiated into thinking that learners have a higher level of language proficiency than they actually do, simply because they appear to be very fluent. BICS, however, is not considered as critical to success in the classroom as is CALP, the context-reduced and cognitively demanding language of the content classroom.

CALP requires a "different type of language skills" (*ibid.*, pp. 7 and 40), i.e., those needed for successful participation in content classrooms. According to this theory, content classrooms present instruction using language that is "context reduced" and "cognitively demanding." "The cognitive demands for which academic language is used, and the fact that academic language is frequently not supported by the rich array of nonverbal and contextual clues that characterizes face-to-face interaction, make academic language more difficult to learn" (*ibid.*, p. 7). Academic language "may be less interactive and may provide limited context clues to assist comprehension" (*ibid.*, p. 40). CALP is believed to develop much more slowly than BICS, and takes about 5–7 years to acquire. During the time when students' competency lies largely in the area of BICS, they may not have the cognitive academic language proficiency to perform well in school (Cummins 1981).

Both BICS and CALP are constructs that align closely with the threshold hypothesis (Cummins 1976; Toukomaa and Skutnabb-Kangas 1976) which:

> assumes that those aspects of bilingualism that might positively influence cognitive growth are unlikely to come into effect until children have attained a certain minimum or threshold level of proficiency in the second language. Similarly, if bilingual children attain only *a very low level of proficiency in one or both of their languages,* their interaction with the environment through these languages both in terms of input and output is likely to be impoverished (Cummins 1981, p. 38; emphasis added).

The hypothesis goes on to state that there are two thresholds, a lower one and a higher one. "The attainment of a lower level of bilingual proficiency would be sufficient to avoid any negative effects; but the attainment of a second, higher level of bilingual proficiency might be necessary to lead to accelerated cognitive growth" (*ibid.,* pp. 38–39). Important for this discussion is the idea that cognitive academic language and basic social language are separated out from their respective settings by means of the levels of cognitive demand and contextualization they involve. Cognitive demand can be made only when a certain level of linguistic proficiency has been attained; if made earlier, there can be negative effects. These assertions assume a dependency model between language acquisition and cognition, with a threshold level of language proficiency being a prerequisite for cognitive development. A causal relationship seems to be implied between context and the attainment of the threshold level of language proficiency, since cognitive demand is minimal (can it be nonexistent?) during this period of initial acquisition, and is therefore generally unavailable for the acquisition process. Once the threshold proficiency has been reached, however, context takes an increasingly smaller role and cognitive forces begin to take an increasingly larger role.

The distinction Cummins makes between BICS and CALP seems to preclude serious content instruction for beginning or lower-level L2 proficient children. If L2 students receive core content instruction (i.e., in areas that are less apt to be contextualized and more apt to be cognitively demanding) too early, before they have had a chance to reach a threshold level of L2 proficiency, are we not pushing them exactly into the situation in which "negative cognitive effects" may accrue, or where development in both their L1 and L2 will be "impoverished"? More specifically, if we accept the dichotomy between BICS and CALP, then the kind of cognitively demanding social interaction and language required to construct meaning within the first layer of content areas are simply not available to L2 learners before they reach the threshold of minimal language proficiency. Practically speaking, in elementary schools this has meant an attempt to control content and linguistic forms for students not meeting a threshold level of L2 proficiency.[6]

On the other hand, there have been studies whose results call into question the BICS/CALP distinction, as well as the threshold hypothesis. Flashner (1987) "went on a search" for decontextualized language in a fourth grade class, examining the daily oral and written classroom language use of teachers, L1 students, and L2 students in all subject areas over a period of two months. She found that the BICS/CALP distinction did not obtain in her classroom data. Rather, she discovered a full array of language in the classroom, its uses governed by the context in which it occurred. Flashner concludes, "I suggest that there is no such thing as decontextualized language. There are, rather, varieties of language that have more of one feature than another when purpose, audience, mode, and planning are altered" (p. 165).

Hawkins (1988) reports a study in which she looked at scaffolded classroom interaction as it relates to SLA. Her data, collected daily over a two-month period, was also from a fourth grade classroom where the children were both NS and NNS. When she examined the data for instances of scaffolded interaction, she found that it occurred most often when the classroom discourse was both interactively and cognitively demanding. This indicates the very opposite of what Cummins (1981) and Toukomaa and Skutnabb-Kangas (1976) argue in the threshold hypothesis. That is, rather than cognitively demanding material being a possible detriment to cognitive and linguistic development, when combined with high interactive demand it is actually supportive of both, in terms of the learner receiving scaffolding. As we have seen earlier, scaffolding is a most important way for the learner to move from a position of not knowing to one of knowing.

An Alternative to the BICS/CALP Distinction

What would happen if we were to consider the BICS/CALP distinction as representing a false dichotomy? Instead of viewing BICS as relatively free of cognitive demand, we could recognize that it "appears" to be relatively free of cognitive demand precisely because the context is so well defined. It is the clarity of the context which allows the "seemingly rapid" acquisition to proceed, but this does not mean that the work a learner does in becoming proficient is cognitively undemanding. Hawkins describes her efforts to understand "playground language," language normally thought to be a prototypic example of BICS:

> I have been amazed continually at the cognitively demanding level of interaction that occurs as students, both L1 and L2, *explain* and *describe* subtle nuances of the games they play; they *justify;* they *prove, debate* and *persuade* others when conflict about procedures, "unfair" behavior or results arise, and *compare, classify* and *evaluate* each others' actions in relation to the rules of the games, etc. When this becomes most apparent to the teacher is when students bring a complaint or problem to her. If the teacher decides to truly deal with the issues involved, it can become a cognitive nightmare in trying to sort out actual events as students *inform* the teacher about what has happened . . . . Most times it is because the students have such a complex understanding of the details of the game that have been "constructed" over time, and of how these details fit into the whole picture, that a teacher's rudimentary understandings of the games—e.g., soccer or kickball—are simply not enough to understand the issues involved. The teacher needs instruction, and the students become the teachers (1996, p. 43).

The teacher's difficulty in understanding the children is not because the language is decontextualized, since in fact, it is firmly rooted in the social context of the games the children play. Rather, it is because the teacher does not completely understand the context of the children's language that makes its interpretation so difficult. It is cognitively demanding for the teacher to try to understand the students' language, even though one would classify it as BICS.

Turning to the other half of the coin, what would abandoning the BICS/CALP distinction mean about the way we view CALP? Lemke's claim is most helpful in this regard: "Talking science does not simply mean talking about science. It means doing science through the medium of language" (1993, p. ix). This statement clearly implies that science is situated social knowledge, whose meaning is clearly communicated among those who are proficient members of the science community. As such, the problem for Lemke is not that science instruction is too cognitively demanding; rather, it is that students do not yet belong to the community of scientists, and, therefore, do not yet understand what they are talking about. For Lemke, it is the teachers' role to "learn to see science teaching as a social process, and to bring students, at least partially, into this community of people who talk science" (p. x).

An understanding of content areas as representing highly situated social knowledge turns the idea of CALP on end. Instead of being decontextualized language, the language of discipline-specific content is so very contextualized that it may appear decontextualized to the outsider, to the novice, in much the same way that playground "BICS" may appear cognitively undemanding to the person who fully understands the context. Instead of thinking of academic content instruction as *de*contextualized, if teachers thought of it as *highly contextualized,* they would realize that what they need to bring to their students in terms of content education is the context enjoyed by insiders. And instead of thinking of social language as being cognitively undemanding and generally outside the realm of academic content instruction, they would realize that it takes a great deal of cognitive effort to master the various contexts in which the disciplines operate, to become *socialized* to the disciplines.

Short's finding that the academic language used in "American history classes was commensurate with much of the academic language in other humanities courses, and in fact, similar to the nontechnical language used in math and science classrooms . . . " (1994, p. 595), suggests that the decontextualized language of CALP is far more elusive than would be expected. That is, if we view academic language as decontextualized, then we should be able to isolate linguistic markers particular to a given content area ahead of time, and then use these features first to predict difficulty, and ultimately to improve our delivery of instruction. Yet, that view may not be the case. If we take the perspective that there is no such thing as decontextualized language associated with the content areas, it diminishes the surprise that the predicted linguistic differences were not found. Perhaps it was because the linguistic features were taken out of the context of the content area that they did not prove to be significant. That is, by separating out vocabulary and other structures that we think would mark the decontextualized nature of a discipline, we have removed them from their social situation, at which point they lose meaning. Once again, we are left with the question of how content knowledge gets constructed by learners. If we do not separate out two entities—BICS and CALP—will it affect the way we teach core content to elementary school students?

Content-Area Instruction in the Elementary Grades for L2 Children

Fortunately, the ideas presented about abandoning the BICS/CALP distinction are congruent with our earlier view of content education as a situated process whose eventual goal is the membership of students in the community of adults proficient in the discipline. If we wish to provide quality education for our L2 elementary school students, we need to do at least what is asked of elementary school teachers for their L1 students. That is, we need to come from a position of knowing the fundamentals of the disciplines we teach. Additionally, we need to realize what it means to "talk a discipline" in the sense that Lemke (1993) describes it; i.e., we need to realize that our role as teachers is to guide our students in the social construction of content knowledge such that the norms of the discipline eventually become available to them. In doing so, we need to be able to use language to scaffold new knowledge structures for our students as we interact with them. We need to be able to build

on their language to help move them beyond where their thoughts currently take them. We need to know our students well, and be able to provide them with experiences they can readily enter into, through which we can provoke new learnings. When our students do not seem to understand what we are doing, we need to ask several questions:

1. Can they relate to the experience I have provided?
2. Do they have the words to describe what it is that they are experiencing?
3. Do they understand the open-ended problem that I have presented to them?
4. Are they developmentally ready for the concepts I am trying to teach them?
5. Do they have enough situational support to understand the classroom discourse?

What is special for elementary school teachers when they teach L2 children in the content areas? The above questions seem appropriate for both L1 and L2 students. Because our L2 students come from cultures different from the "mainstream" culture, we need to be particularly sensitive in terms of the experiences we provide them at the start of our lessons or units. Since it is pivotal for learners to be able to relate to the experience in order to proceed, the teacher must carefully consider whether something he or she has chosen is too specific to mainstream culture. If learners have trouble when we ask them to describe the experience we give them, we need to think about why this might be. Is it because the experience is too different for them? Is it because they don't have the words to describe the experience? Is it because there is too much (or too little) information in the setting, so they cannot use the context provided to help them out? For example, if the teacher wants a child to distinguish between two attributes, the setting needs to provide at least one clear example of each of the two attributes (less than this would be too little information) such that the child does not confuse them with several other possibilities (too much information).

If a student has trouble with any one of these areas, it most often means backing up and changing something in the lesson. Returning to the culinary arts lesson, upon tasting the different dishes in the initial experience, a student may stumble in trying to describe what he or she tastes because he or she does not know how to say *salty* in English. What will the teacher do? It means backing up and providing an experience of, for example, salty, sour, sweet, and bitter so that students will be able to attach that language to their next experience.

In the case of L2 students, precisely because they are "further away" from the context of the content, one of the biggest differences will be that teachers will need to take more time to cover the same amount of material. The backing up that a teacher does when there are problems always takes time, and for the L2 students there may be more instances of backing up because the children may not have the language and/or cultural references to move as quickly.

The most important attributes that a teacher can have are those of being able to listen and reflect upon what the students tell him or her. In the case of elementary school, students are not always able to tell the teacher directly what is going on in their minds, and this is much more true of L2 students. Teachers must learn to listen and observe in new ways, bringing everything they know about pedagogy, development, and language (L1 and L2) to bear on the situation. Without having this vital information, teaching and learning become trivialized; i.e., the teacher sets up his or her lesson plans, and covering the material becomes the paramount goal, making everything else subservient to it. In such a scenario, if students don't understand the material, in some way or other it reverts back to them; i.e., it becomes *their* fault.

In conclusion, we seek a great deal of competence from our elementary school teachers, in several arenas. They need to know the fundamentals of their subject matter; they need to know pedagogy; they need to know the interplay between language and content education; they need to know the cultures and experiences of their students; and they need to know how to talk and listen to children. Teachers can never know too much to teach, and in the case of elementary school teachers working with second language learners this is especially true.

DISCUSSION QUESTIONS

1. A charge often given to K–5 teachers is that they must provide content education to L2 learners that does not "water down" the standard curriculum. Is this an unreasonable charge? Are L1 and L2 students necessarily going to receive different coverage of the curriculum? Will both groups cover the same amount of curriculum? In what ways can the presentation of the curriculum be considered equally rigorous, of equal depth?

2. Suppose you are going to teach a social studies unit to a group of fifth graders who are all L2 students. You want to introduce the concept of the connections between culture, geography, and history as they relate to Native Americans. How will you begin your plans? Do the plans change for a mixed group of L1 and L2 students? Why? Why not?

3. You have a mixed group of L1 and L2 students in your second grade class. You have been teaching the algorithm for subtraction requiring regrouping (often referred to as "borrowing" in the USA) for two to three weeks. The majority of your students are not able to demonstrate that they control the algorithm with any degree of regularity. How will you troubleshoot what is going on in the class? Will there be problems that exist for the L2 learners that do not exist for the L1 learners? If so, what are they? What might be problems that both groups of students are having?

4. How can you incorporate fourth grade L2 children into a lesson that calls for them to explain in writing something they cannot clearly see? For example, how can they investigate and then write an explanation of the force of gravity? What is a context that can be provided that will help with instruction and the ultimate explanation?

5. Children often find it hard to believe that the earth is spinning. They may say that the world is spinning, because they have been told that it is, but they do not really understand what that means. A typical and very good question that often arises in third grade classrooms is, "Why aren't we blown off the world if it is spinning so fast?" Other than the obvious,

why is this a good question? What can it tell the teacher about his or her students? Do you think this question could come from a L2 student who is learning the subject matter in his or her second language?

SUGGESTED ACTIVITIES

1. Spend an hour or two observing children at play during recess, focusing especially on their language. Observe them playing a game or sport with which you are very familiar (e.g., soccer, kickball, jump rope, etc.). Have they developed their own set of context-specific rules to augment those that traditionally accompany the game/sport? How long does it take you to understand them? If the children use higher order thinking skills, describe them.

2. "When a new material is made by combining two or more materials, it has properties that are different from the original materials. For that reason, a lot of different materials can be made from a small number of basic kinds of materials" (*Benchmarks for science literacy: Project 206*, p. 76).Given the above benchmark on the structure of matter for the end of fifth grade, design an open-ended question/problem that will introduce a unit to a fifth grade class, one which will require that students learn the information included in the benchmark in order to arrive at a solution. The class for whom you are designing the question/problem has equal numbers of L1 and L2 students.

3. Using the question/problem you designed in number 2 above, plan how you will make sure that all of your students understand it clearly, keeping in mind that if students do not have a thorough understanding of the problem/question, they will be left out of the ensuing activities.

4. One way to help teachers ensure that they move the class at the pace of the students rather than at their pace (or the book's pace) is to stop and think about how the children will receive and respond to the information

and tasks with which you present them. Using your plans from numbers 2 and 3 above, write three short dialogues for each of the following groups: a) high-achieving L1 and L2 students, b) medium-achieving L1 and L2 students, and c) low-achieving L1 and L2 students. In order for these dialogues to be successful, they must *scaffold* information for the students, and not merely tell them information or pronounce their solutions as correct or incorrect.

 **FURTHER READING**

Vygotsky, L. 1978. *Mind in Society: The Development of Higher Psychological Processes*. Cambridge: Harvard University Press.

This book presents many of Vygotsky's basic ideas in a very interesting and readable way. It is especially important for understanding Vygotsky's notions about the mediating nature of language, whereby knowledge begins first *inter*personally and then *intra*personally. He also presents and discusses at length his idea of the "zone of proximal development," which is supportive of later ideas about scaffolded interaction.

Cummins, J. 1979. Cognitive/academic language proficiency, linguistic interdependence, the optimum age question and some other matters. *Working papers on bilingualism 19*: 121–129.

———— 1981. The role of primary language development in promoting success for language minority students. In *Schooling and Language Minority Students: A Theoretical Framework* (pp. 3–49). Office of Bilingual Bicultural Education, California State Department of Education, Sacramento. Los Angeles: Evaluation, Dissemination and Assessment Center, California State University.

Both of these seminal works are important to read in order to understand the theory behind many current educational practices in both bilingual and second language settings. The theory presented also forms the backdrop for more recent attempts to define and develop L2 curriculum sensitive to CALP requirements.

Lemke, J. L. 1993. *Talking Science: Language, Learning, and Values*. Norwood, NJ: Ablex.

Although this book focuses on high school (rather than K–5) science classroom discourse as the context for studying the language of science, it is quite helpful in several ways. It provides a framework for examining classroom language as it connects to the language of experts in a given content area. It also provides useful ways of looking at teacher language as a bridge between the students and the language of those who are experts in a content area. Finally, it helps define what it means to talk the language of science, with definite applications for other content areas.

Ma, L. 1999. *Knowing and Teaching Elementary Mathematics: Teachers' Understanding of Fundamental Mathematics in China and the United States.* Mahwah, NJ: Lawrence Erlbaum.

The author asked four questions surrounding four seemingly simple arithmetic problems of a group of Chinese school teachers and a group of American school teachers. The book presents the outcomes of her interviews with both groups of teachers, and results in a dramatic picture of the need for teachers to have a profound understanding of fundamental mathematics if they are going to be effective teachers. Although the book's focus is mathematics, it is very helpful towards establishing definitions of "profound understanding," and "fundamental."

Becker, J. P., and S. Shimada, eds. 1997. *The Open-ended Approach: A New Proposal for Teaching Mathematics.* Reston, VA: National Council of Teachers of Mathematics.

This book presents very helpful ways of approaching open-ended problems for mathematics, as well as several very clear examples. Much of what is contained in the book is very applicable to other content areas.

Schwandt, T. 1994. Constructivist, interpretivist approaches to human inquiry. In N. K. Denzin and Y. S. Lincoln, eds., *Handbook of Qualitative Research.* Thousand Oaks, CA: Sage.

This is a rather dense but very informative view of constructivism, both as a theory of knowledge, and as a research method. It summarizes the history of constructivism, and presents some of its current iterations.

ENDNOTES

1   Although space does not permit a discussion of the developmental needs of elementary school students, it is a very important element. There are many developmental understandings about children that teachers need to keep in mind when they engage their students in core content instruction.

2   We are using Becker and Shimada's (1997) definition of open-ended problems as those "problems that are formulated to have multiple correct answers" (p. 1).

3   See Carroll (1997) for the longitudinal comparison of student achievement on standardized tests for students taught via a "reform" mathematics curriculum as compared to those taught within a "traditional" framework. He also assesses the problem solving abilities of the two groups in ways not specifically assessed in the standardized test format. In general, Carroll found that the students in the "reform" group matched or outperformed the students in the "traditional" group on the standardized tests after spending minimally two years in the program. He also discovered that the students in the "reform" group far outperformed the students in the "traditional" group on the separate problem solving assessment.

Finally, an anecdote comes from Sally Grogg (1994 personal communication), an experienced and extremely competent third grade teacher. Ms. Grogg had spent a good two to three months on an experientially driven social studies unit on three Native American tribes. At the end of the unit, she gave the students the unit test from the textbook. Although the students did all right on the test, Ms. Grogg was disappointed because she had thought they would do better. The next day, she told the students to simply write whatever they knew about Native Americans. The children wrote on and on, their knowledge seemingly inexhaustible. The unit test had not been able to capture the true, deep understanding the children had acquired. From the official assessment point of view, the children were "adequate" in meeting the content standards for that unit, whereas in fact they were superior in their understanding.

4   Sawada (1997, pp. 24–33) provides information on classifying, constructing, judging the appropriateness of, and developing teaching based on problems in mathematics. He also includes criteria for judging students' solutions to problems.

5 See Parker (1993, pp. 4–11) for a comparison of learning "about" mathematics with learning to "do" mathematics.

6 However, because of the large numbers of L2 children enrolled in our schools coupled with the inability of many school districts to offer bilingual education, teachers have found themselves in the position of presenting content to L2 children, whether those children have achieved a set threshold proficiency in the L2 or not. Sheppard and his colleagues as reported in Snow found that "in sharp contrast to the widespread belief that students need intermediate proficiency to benefit from content-based instruction, 79 percent of the programs surveyed reported no English proficiency requirement for participation" (Snow 1998, pp. 244–245).

Teaching Adults[1]

SHARON HILLES • ANDRÉ SUTTON

In "Teaching Adults," Hilles and Sutton define adult education and briefly review its history. They give an overview of adults as second language learners and consider one program in depth to construct an adult-school teacher, student, and program profile. They conclude with practical suggestions for working with this population and a review of recent research directions.

INTRODUCTION

In the United States and Canada, the term *adult education* commonly refers to public education for adults that does not fall within the mainstream credit/degree objective programs offered by universities or colleges. This type of education is funded primarily by state, local, and (sometimes) federal (national) governments, and is delivered by adult schools, community colleges, and sometimes university extension divisions or other units. Adult education has several purposes. First, it allows students who, for whatever reasons, were unable to complete their elementary or secondary educations to get their diplomas. Second, it provides a resource for those who desire to pursue vocational training or continue their education after graduating from secondary school or university, but do not opt to do this in the setting of a college or graduate school. Third, some adult programs allow concurrent enrollment, i.e., allow students enrolled in secondary schools to take adult classes after school or on weekends, which can count towards graduation or simply provide extra instruction and practice in specific subjects. Finally, in recent years, the major burden of adult education has been teaching English as a Second Language (ESL) to an ever-increasing immigrant population in North America. For this reason, adult education has, to a great degree, become synonymous with ESL. In this chapter we shall concern ourselves primarily with teaching adults in this setting.

Adult and continuing education have had a long tradition in the United States, even though they have waxed and waned in popularity and status over the years. (For an excellent review of the literature, see Cotton 1968; McIntire 1988.) It has been suggested that perhaps the earliest example of adult education in the United States was Benjamin Franklin's Junta groups in 1727 (Knowles and Klevins 1975, p. 12; McIntire 1988, p. 20), which provided weekly discussions of intellectual subjects for adults. Josiah Holbrook's Lyceum Movement, begun in 1826, made the lecture popular as a format for disseminating information, and attracted lectures by such luminaries as Emerson and Lincoln.[2] According to P. Johnson (1999), the movement targeted "young, unmarried men—bank clerks, salesmen, bookkeepers, and so forth—who then made up an astonishingly high proportion of the population of the new towns" and aimed "to keep them off the streets and out of the saloons, and to promote simultaneously their commercial careers and their moral welfare" (p. 407). The movement rapidly spread throughout the union and "by the end of the 1830s almost every considerable town had one" (p. 407). Various other programs grew up following the Civil War, including an abundance of correspondence courses, which were very popular and widely accepted by the public. According to Knowles and Klevins (1975), the main thrust of early adult education was remedial. This began to change in 1919 when adult education was recognized as "a permanent national necessity, an inseparable aspect of citizenship" (p. 13).

Between World War I and World War II, adult education passed through stages, from highly idealistic notions characterizing it as "a means of bringing about social reform, reconstruction and progress" to the more conservative stance that "the country could be better served if the ideals were modified to that which could be judged realistic" (p. 13). After World War II, government and philanthropic groups began to participate in adult and continuing education, and in 1965 the Bureau of Adult and Vocational Education was formed as a part of the U.S. Office of Education.

According to McIntire (1988, p. 48), adult education currently serves a diverse population, including the following:

1. Students who did not have an opportunity to attend school during the traditional elementary and/or secondary range.
2. Students who dropped out of school.
3. Immigrants who are learning English as a second language, acquiring basic skills in English, preparing for citizenship, or obtaining a high school diploma in English.
4. Students acquiring vocational training skills.

Moreover, adult learners participate in a variety of programs. For example, the breakdown of students enrolled in Belmont Community Adult School, the largest adult school in California in terms of absolute population, is as follows:[3]

1.	Elementary basic skills	1,756
2.	Secondary basic skills	1,993
3.	ESL	14,608
4.	Handicapped/Exceptional Adults	178
5.	Vocational Education	361
6.	Parenting	227
7.	Program for Older Adults	590
8.	Citizenship	977
9.	Health Education	361

Non-native speakers of English are present in all of the above categories, though classes in ESL are often a steppingstone to other adult classes. In the United States, ESL classes are typically offered by either visa programs or resident programs. The former are restricted mainly to foreign students who are in the United States on student visas. Students participating in these programs must be present in a classroom a specified number of hours per week and must be making reasonable progress toward a degree objective in order to retain their visas. They are allowed up to two years to master English before beginning their higher education. Most visa students plan to return to their respective countries after finishing their higher education in the United States. In California, visa programs are offered by colleges, universities, and numerous private language schools. On the other hand, the ESL programs we find in adult schools do not—indeed, may not—enroll foreign students who hold student visas; in fact, many of the students in resident programs are not in the United States on any type of visa at all. This category includes a number of both "economic" and/or political refugees, and their presence in adult school classrooms is invariably a reflection (and often a precursor) of global events.

ADULT LEARNERS

Whether they are ESL students or native speakers, in the United States or in another country, adults differ from "typical" or "traditional" K–12 students in that they bring a great deal of life experience and cognitive maturity to the classroom. In many cases, they have borne and reared children, earned a living, seen life and death, and, all too often, survived extreme political and economic hardship. Adult students have a maturity and an understanding of priorities that many younger students do not. According to Knowles (1976), "a prime characteristic of adultness is the need and capacity to be self-directing" (p. 181). In other words, adults will, to some extent, "direct" their own learning agendas. If the learning environment does not to some degree match cultural expectations and perceived needs, the self-direction may take the form of challenging the teacher or syllabus in class, of filtering out what they perceive as nonessential, of simply leaving the class and seeking some other way of learning, or of abandoning the enterprise altogether. This difference between adult and child learners is so crucial that

Knowles and Klevins (1975) maintain that the term *pedagogy* should not apply to adults because the word "taken literally from its roots means the leading of children, the implication thereof being that the learner is guided within a rather rigid system. A basic problem with pedagogy is that most teachers have known only how to teach adults as if they were children" (p. 14). Knowles and Klevins argue that "a more explicit and realistic term which may be applied to adult education is *andragogy*. From its root, it denotes the leading of man; or the art or science of helping adults learn" (p. 14). Though their proposed term has never really caught on in the literature, their point is well taken. Without question there are numerous differences between adults and children; much too frequently, however, an inexperienced adult ESL teacher may interact with his or her students as if they were children, perhaps because of their limited English proficiency. The results are often a disastrous paternalistic attitude, one symptom of which can be baby talk. At the very least, this presents an unnatural, not to mention insulting, model of spoken English when addressed to adults.

In addition to being mature and self-directed, adult learners are often, of necessity, more focused. McIntire (1988) points out that "because time is such a valuable commodity, participating in educational programs is often a personal sacrifice. Typically, adults can devote only limited time to their educational endeavors, which often translates into their being dedicated students who take learning seriously" (p. 47). According to McIntire's survey, approximately three-quarters of adult ESL students work at a job 40 hours or more per week—a dedicated and focused group, indeed.

Adult learners are also psychologically vulnerable, perhaps in a way that children are not, precisely because they are adults and have already formed a strong sense of who they are. They have a great deal invested in their identities as proficient speakers of their first language. In her ethnographic study of adults learning Welsh as a second language, Trosset (1986) found that these learners often experienced anomie, which Lambert et al. defined as "the feelings of social uncertainty or dissatisfaction which characterize not only the socially unattached person but also, it appears, the bilingual or even the serious student of a second language and culture" (1963, pp. 38–39 cited in Trosset, p. 183). In her study Trosset also found that "the process of learning a new language temporarily takes away people's ability to talk, and the resultant sense of inadequacy leads them to experience shame" (p. 184). She points out that Stengel had already observed some 40 years earlier that "speech is an accomplishment of the ego . . . Acquiring a new language in adult life is an anachronism and many people cannot easily tolerate the infantile situation" (Stengel 1930, p. 475–476, cited in Trosset, p.184). Trosset further notes that many of the adult learners she observed experienced not only a sense of inadequacy, but also fear of failure as well as fear of success, all of which seemed to be intimately associated with feelings of shame. In connection with Trosset's observations, it is particularly interesting to note that Schumann (1997) reports that "there is research that shows that shame experiences generate cortisol in the body, which interferes with cognition" (p.155).

Another characteristic that seems to set apart adults learners is the enormous variability that they display in their goals and reasons for tackling a second language. One class with which we are familiar comprised almost entirely Korean grandparents who didn't particularly want to speak English, but wanted very much to understand their grandchildren. We have known other learners who wanted some sort of communicative system but were not particularly concerned with grammatical accuracy. Still others felt that language without grammatical correctness was no language at all. Another group of adult EFL students we met were interested in studying English because at the time studying English was a fashionable hobby, but they were not at all interested in speaking, reading, writing, or understanding English. Bley-Vroman (1988) points out that "some develop just the subpart of foreign language competence necessary to wait on tables or to lecture in philosophy; others may become skilled at cocktail party story telling. Some have good pronunciation but primitive grammar. Some lay great importance on vocabulary size. Some work at passing for a native speaker; others seem proud of their foreignness ('The Charles Boyer phenomenon')" (p. 21). Adults have numerous reasons for studying a second or foreign language (L2), and this variety of reasons presents its own challenges to the teacher.

Variability also characterizes the outcome of adult foreign language learning endeavors, though native-like proficiency in the L2 is probably unlikely.[4] As Bley-Vroman (1988) points out, "[a]mong adults, there is substantial variation in degree of success, even when age, exposure, instruction, and so forth are held constant. Adults not only generally do not succeed, they also fail to different degrees" (p. 20). This somewhat bleak prognosis is not meant to discourage the adult ESL/EFL teacher or to be construed as suggesting that adult school teachers ought not aim for target-like proficiency in their students; rather, it is meant to temper expectations so that they are realistic and so that teachers do not demand from their students as a whole the unreasonable goal of native-like proficiency. We hasten to add that in discussions such as this we feel it is important to remember that social science statistics can predict the behavior of a group, but certainly not the behavior of any one particular individual within that group. Every student deserves our best efforts and each new class we teach may very well be the one that houses an individual who will learn English to near native speaker proficiency.

Finally, adult learners are most often voluntary learners. Unlike their younger counterparts, who are required by law or by their parents to be in school until a particular age, adult learners are in school because they want to be, a desire which is almost always inconvenient and often interrupted by family and job responsibilities and commitments. As a result, adult learners tend to have little patience with classes which they perceive are not furthering their own educational agendas.

A TYPICAL ADULT SCHOOL SETTING

Part of the challenge of teaching adult school ESL is the diversity. Iwataki (1981) describes the typical adult ESL classroom as follows:

Picture a classroom of some 30 or more students, ranging in age from 18–80. The learners come from heterogeneous language and experiential backgrounds . . . this is a voluntary, not a captive audience, found in churches, recreation centers, vacant elementary or secondary school bungalows, or classrooms unoccupied at night (p. 24).

Adult school classes haven't changed much since Iwataki's original description. Heterogeneous classes populated by nontraditional students in nontraditional venues are certainly characteristic of the adult school classroom, and part of its unique challenge. This notwithstanding, we can speak of at least a statistically typical adult ESL student and classroom in each neighborhood. Let us consider Belmont Community Adult School once again as a case in point. The typical Belmont student is a single, male Hispanic, between the ages of 21 and 29, who is employed full time and has between a sixth-grade and a secondary school education. At one time, this student would have been enrolled in a large class (often over 50 students) because large classes were once characteristic of many adult schools. Today, however, given the current budget, he is studying English in a class of between 30 and 35 students. Our typical ESL student feels that his teachers are "excellent," and that there is adequate opportunity for him to get individual help from them.

Even though classes are currently of a more manageable size than they have traditionally been, many seasoned teachers and administrators fear that class size will increase dramatically if budget cuts are implemented. In the Los Angeles Unified School District, an adult school class must be closed when it ceases to be cost-effective, regardless of whether it starts out with 30 students or 55. Attrition is a natural phenomenon in adult school; therefore, maintaining class numbers is important. Organized and prepared teachers have little trouble. Less experienced teachers, however, sometimes find this particularly challenging. It has been our experience that new ESL teachers often begin their adult school assignment with the reasonable expectation that students come to school to learn; soon they notice, however, that students enjoy the social aspect of adult education as well. For many students, adult school is not only a place to learn, but also a place to get together with friends, catch up on the latest gossip, establish new relationships, and even form and nurture romances. Unfortunately, new teachers sometimes find the social aspect of school more salient than the educational, and they mistakenly assume that students are more highly motivated by social than by educational goals. As a result, some teachers do not take their adult education teaching responsibilities seriously, but rather try to provide an entertaining social atmosphere in order to maintain class numbers. Perhaps a word of caution based on years of experience might help in maintaining class size: We have found that students attend night school as long as they perceive that they are learning. Students expect teachers to be professional, knowledgeable, and prepared. No matter how entertaining or charming the teacher may be, and no matter how much students may like a teacher, they can always have more fun at home. When the teacher is seen as incompetent or unprepared, and when perceived learning ceases, so does attendance.

Adult school is also important in another sense. In his book on "America's underprepared," Rose (1989) recounts how his adult ESL students wanted to talk to their children's teachers, "but felt funny about seeing the teacher for their English was so bad and . . . well . . . who were they to presume to talk to the teacher about what she does?" (p. 130). The teaching supervisor pointed out to Rose and his colleagues that their ESL classes were bringing parents "comfortably into the schools, breaking down some of the intimidating barriers that traditionally keep them away, distant from the places where their kids were learning how to read and write" and that "there's more to look for here than just an increase in vocabulary" (p. 131). All too often we forget that many of our students are parents, or will be parents in the near future. Perhaps school was inaccessible to them in their native lands, but it will be a central and not necessarily an altogether pleasant experience for their children. It is vital for all concerned that immigrant parents be brought "comfortably into the schools" and adult ESL classes can help accomplish this important social goal.

Students in a particular community adult school will usually reflect the (changing) ethnicity of the neighborhood. As immigrant populations tend to concentrate in particular areas and adult schools draw from the surrounding community, it is not unusual to see different groups reflected in different schools. Belmont Community Adult School is no exception. Its main campus student body (90 percent Hispanic, 4 percent American Indian or Alaska native, 3 percent Asian or Pacific Islander, 3 percent Black, not of Hispanic origin) is a microcosm of the surrounding neighborhood. At the branch locations, these numbers go up or down slightly, reflecting the immediate community. Belmont has an active student body of approximately 8,500 at any one given time, with an enrollment of about 27,500 over the course of an academic year; about 70 percent of its students are enrolled in ESL classes.

ADULT SCHOOL TEACHERS

Because Belmont Community Adult School is so large, it offers 167 day and night classes in a variety of locations, including the main campus, three major branches, retirement homes, recreation centers, churches and synagogues, convalescent hospitals, community centers, centers for the handicapped, businesses, and missions and homeless centers. These classes are staffed by 109 teachers, 78 percent of whom are part timers, working 10 hours or less each week. In fact, the majority of adult teachers in the Los Angeles Unified School District fall into the part-time category. This makes them ineligible for benefits through their adult school assignment. The typical adult ESL teacher is female and has a bachelor's degree. Her adult school assignment is 6–12 hours per week. Although she teaches ESL at night, she usually has day employment outside of the adult ESL educational field. She participates in district-sponsored workshops and in-service training and belongs to at least one professional organization, though not necessarily one related to ESL teaching. According to Hurst (1985), ESL teachers in general have good rapport with their students, and are remarkably attuned to what they perceive to be their students' needs and aspirations. They do not, however, typically read professional journals or recent publications on second language acquisition, ESL pedagogy, or methodology or have specialized training (such as a master's degree or a certificate in teaching ESL).

Iwataki (1981) warns that "those who teach ESL to adults need to be made of sturdy stock. They need special qualities of understanding, cultural sensitivity, adaptability, stamina and resourcefulness to help them cope with the realities of the adult ESL classroom. Furthermore, they need to possess full command and knowledge of the subject area—the English language" (p. 24). Due to the current credentialing procedures in California, Iwataki's last point (full command and knowledge of the English language) is probably the typical adult ESL teacher's weakest area. The state requires simply a baccalaureate with 20 semester units in English for the Adult Designated Subjects Credential in ESL. Individual districts are then allowed to set up their own specific standards for ESL teaching. Virtually any teacher with a K–12 credential, regardless of area, is "credentially" qualified to teach ESL. The Los Angeles Unified School District requires only a minimum of 8 semester units in English and 12 units in any foreign language, linguistics, or speech to obtain a temporary credential to teach ESL. No formal training in teaching ESL is required, which may be why most adult ESL teachers do not have this type of preparation. This profile, of course, is changing as more and more universities produce ESL teaching professionals who enter the ranks of adult education.

Hurst's comment regarding the unusual sensitivity of ESL teachers should come as no surprise. According to Bley-Vroman (1988), "[s]ince the early seventies, beginning with the work of Gardner and Lambert (1972), numerous empirical studies have shown significant correlations between affective factors and [language] proficiency" (p. 24). Common wisdom has always been that affective factors are more important in adult second language learning than in any other type of learning. However, Schumann (1997) in his study of the neurobiology of affect[5] in sustained deep learning, concluded that affect and cognition are inseparable and that positive affective assessment is essential in order for learning to take place. Such an assessment causes biochemicals to be released in the brain that facilitate cognition. Negative assessment has just the opposite effect; it blocks learning. In other words, positive assessment of the stimuli associated with any sustained deep learning (including learning a second language) is vital. On the other hand, the kinds of factors that will be appraised as positive are highly individual, though there may be shared tendencies among members of the same cultural group. Schumann's suggestion, that members of a particular cultural group may tend to appraise a classroom in similar ways (which may be different from the appraisal tendencies of individuals from another culture) seems to resonate with our experience in the classroom. In general, we have found that some students are more comfortable with peer interaction and a noise level which might not be acceptable to other ESL learners. We have also found that for some learners it appears that peer interaction is the preferred method of constructing meaning, while for others the preferred method is taking meaning directly from a printed source. Some students prefer verbal input. This variety in stimulus appraisal suggests to us that accommodating as many individual and cultural preferences as possible is a logical way to offer the greatest number of students the best chance at a positive affective appraisal of the stimuli. This accommodation could be realized through the teacher providing bimodal input, both written and spoken, or allowing students some latitude to negotiate meaning among themselves, especially when a cultural or individual preference for doing so is clear. Certainly learning strategies and preferences (see Oxford's chapter in this volume) should be taken into account whenever possible. However, we hasten to add that stimulus appraisal is exceedingly complex and that it is impossible for any teacher to conduct a classroom in such a way that every student will appraise it positively every time. Even twins have sufficiently different life experiences to appraise stimuli differently. Because cognition and affect are so intertwined, Schumann has concluded that that we are all on individual affective/cognitive trajectories as second language learners. This could account for the great variability in second language learning so well documented in the literature. A logical pedagogical conclusion of Schumann's work resonates with what many professionals in the field have argued for decades: We need to vary our approach in order to meet the needs of as many students as possible. In any case, warmth, compassion, empathy, and kindness seem to be constant personal qualities in good ESL teachers, along with a keen ability to observe and respond.

UNDERESTIMATING ESL STUDENTS

Because we often assume that emotional and intellectual satisfactions are incompatible (and the emotional satisfaction in teaching adult school is legendary among ESL professionals), and perhaps because our students frequently have a limited formal education, we often tend to underestimate the ESL students who populate our adult school classrooms. It is widely assumed that adult school students have little interest in or aptitude for "more academic" approaches to ESL, and should be taught "the way children learn"—by speaking, with little emphasis at first on reading and writing. Instruction in grammar should be avoided in favor of more practical "survival English"—learning how to ride a bus or fill out a job application. To our knowledge there is no evidence supporting the assertion either that adult school students do not have the interest or ability to master ESL through a more sophisticated approach or that adults learn a second language the way that children do. Moreover, students routinely complain about teachers who do not have an easily identifiable direction in their program or syllabus. Our experience has been that it is essential for adult students to feel that they are making progress; often this progress translates into moving from one grammatical concept to another that logically seems to follow. Moreover, many students expect formal grammar instruction to be a part of language learning, regardless of whether or not they have a particular aptitude for grammar study, and they suspect incompetence of any teacher who cannot provide at least minimal grammatical explanations.

Most students who enroll in an adult school already possess a vast storehouse of knowledge. They frequently arrive in this country with an extensive network of family and friends who have come before them. They are quickly tutored in how to take a bus, use the laundromat, make a call from a pay phone, and buy a money order. According to McIntire (1988), most adult school students have jobs; moreover, they get those jobs through friends, or through sheer luck, rather than through reading newspaper ads or using other more conventional job-seeking avenues. Most of them are "surviving," and doing it quite well.

One colleague pointed out the irony of teaching "survival" English only (and the key word here is *only*). When she made a factual mistake in her lesson on taking the bus in Los Angeles, several of her students promptly corrected her. At that point she realized that she had been teaching something about which she had no practical, first-hand knowledge. She had never been on a bus in Los Angeles. On the other hand, most of her students had not only come to school by bus that night, they also knew, from experience, how to use the bus to get to work, to the park, to the house of a friend, or to a specialty shop in the San Fernando Valley. The students accepted the superfluous lesson with grace. As teachers we would all do well to accept a lesson from them with equal grace: don't underestimate adult school students. The point here is not that survival English has no place in the ESL classroom, for of course it does; it is part of the adult ESL teacher's responsibility to teach skills that will help students "access the system." These kinds of skills are essential. That which has no place in the ESL classroom is the paternalistic assumption that students are capable of nothing else. We have found that basic science, math, and social science concepts make excellent vehicles for grammar, conversation, pronunciation, reading, and writing lessons. We can reasonably predict that most students will appraise "learning more" more positively than "learning less." For some excellent suggestions on how to put content back in the ESL classroom, see Snow's chapter in this volume and Snow and Brinton (1997). Following Freire (1970a, 1970b), in spirit if not in letter, and Eyring's and Weinstein's chapters in this volume, many ESL professionals have found that their students themselves and their concerns provide valid, relevant, and perhaps even essential content for lessons. For example, the temporary statewide state-funded Community Based English Training Program (CBET) teaches parents at Belmont the skills and content necessary to help their children with homework. We think this might be a wonderful base for a series of ESL lessons if our students have school-aged children. The Secretary of Labor's Commission on Achieving Necessary Skills (SCANS) 1991, a report on skills and competencies required in the workplace by all workers, from top management down, is also an excellent source of elements around which to organize lessons; it can also serve as a vehicle for many parts of a classroom lesson (see Grognet 1997 and sources cited therein). SCANS objectives have become so popular that many ESL texts are now incorporating the SCANS skills and competencies into their scope and sequence. The SCANS document is probably another one of those essential references for the adult ESL teacher in that its skills and competencies can (and perhaps should) be incorporated into virtually any lesson.

As for the second assumption mentioned above regarding the nature of adult second language learning, there is no empirical evidence that adults learn a second language the way children learn a first. Indeed, there is compelling anecdotal, logical, and empirical evidence that this is not the case.[6] Virtually all research on child first language learning tells us that overt instruction and error correction is of no value in learning a first language, but is beneficial to both adults and children in learning a second language (Long 1983), which is good news for those of us who have chosen teaching ESL as our profession.

ADULT SCHOOL PROGRAMS VERSUS TRADITIONAL PROGRAMS

Because of the nature of adult learners outlined earlier, adult schools have traditionally been more responsive to students' needs than other educational programs have been, and the courses they offer reflect the changing concerns and needs of the community (McIntire 1988). Adult classes usually meet at night, and often on Saturdays. Extraordinary measures may also be taken. During the 1986-87 academic year, over 30,000 students were turned away from ESL classes in the Los Angeles area because there were no funds for teachers, classrooms, etc. However, "[i]n response to a request from the Board of Education to provide ESL instruction to persons who could not be accommodated in overcrowded classrooms," the Los Angeles Unified School District's adult education division produced an 80-lesson ESL series for television (Figueroa et al. 1988). In the 1988-89 academic year, in order to meet the requirements of amnesty students, a number of classes in the Los Angeles Unified School District were conducted literally around the clock at Evans Community Adult School. The last class of the day met from 9:00 P.M. to midnight. The first class was from midnight to 2:00 A.M., and so on throughout the day and night. Both scenarios are unusual, but they illustrate how responsive adult schools can be to urgent and unanticipated student needs.

Another way in which adult schools differ from traditional schools in reflecting community needs is open enrollment, a procedure that has grown out of the reality of the constant change and flux characteristic of immigrant communities in the Southwest. Open enrollment or entry allows students to enroll in and then leave a class at any time during the term, up to the last week of class. This is necessary because there are always new arrivals and sudden departures in any immigrant community. Job schedules also change, making it necessary for students to switch from night to day classes, or vice versa. The attrition rate is high, yet it is interesting to note that students surveyed by McIntire identified changing job or family responsibilities rather than educational dissatisfaction as the reason for their having left school (McIntire, personal communication). As a result of these and other factors, the composition of any one ESL class constantly changes. The challenge, of course, is to maintain class standards and retain students while accommodating a constant stream of new students, some of whom have never been in school before. In response to open enrollment, some schools have a multilevel "holding" class which accepts all newcomers, tests them, and teaches basic skills until an opening is available at the appropriate level. Most ESL teachers find constant newcomers part of the adult school challenge; regular and consistent review, in greater depth than might be expected in a class without open enrollment, is one solution. Contrary to what one might expect, such review is always welcomed by the veteran students and goes a long way toward orienting new ones. Some teachers also assign student "hosts" or "buddies" to help the newcomers find their way around the school and to explain classroom procedures, school rules, and schedules. Surprisingly enough, according to many adult ESL teachers, open enrollment is more of a problem in principle than in fact, and once accepted by the teacher as a variable which he or she has to factor into classroom operations, it is of little consequence. This notwithstanding, Kit Bell, Coordinator of the Adult ESL and Citizenship programs for the Los Angeles Unified School District, has commented, "Open enrollment is now being challenged in some districts throughout the state. It is not mandated by the state and experimental 'managed enrollment' programs are experiencing great success" (personal communication, 7/24/00).

Multilevel Classes

Multilevel classes are also a challenge in adult ESL, especially at branch locations. A *branch* is a site which is responsible to and administered by a central school, but which typically has only one or two classes, though of course it can have many more. Branches are often located in makeshift schoolrooms in churches, community centers, libraries, or sometimes even in hospitals or businesses throughout the community, to make classes accessible and convenient, particularly for those who might live some distance from the main school or who might find it difficult or even impossible to attend classes at the main school for any number of reasons. There are frequently not enough students at a branch location to support an entire class at any one level. Therefore, a teacher may have a single class in which there are very advanced students as well as some beginners who are unable to write their own names. In many ways, branch locations are much like the old one-room schoolhouse, which was once typical of the rural United States. The task of teaching such a diverse group to speak English might seem impossible, but the teachers we have talked to, all experienced in teaching multilevel classes, say they would never give up their assignments for more traditional ones. They all agree that timing and planning are the most important factors in handling a multilevel class. The first step is to divide students into more or less homogeneous groups. Two or three groups are usual. The second task is to structure activities so that the teacher can spend equal time with each group. For example, if the class can be divided into three groups—beginning, intermediate, and advanced—the classroom management plan might look something like the one in Figure 1 on the next page.

Notice that the opening activity has the whole class together. The activity might include learning vocabulary items, pronunciation practice, or learning a popular song or a folk song. These are all activities in which students with a wide range of proficiencies can participate on a more or less equal footing. An opening activity that is an old standby of ESL teachers is bringing in a shoe box containing several items from around the house. Sometimes the teacher brings items from a particular room, such as the kitchen (e.g., a knife, fork, can opener, spatula, saucer, saucepan, and wooden spoon). The teacher carries the box around the room and various students are allowed to remove an item without looking, which makes the activity fun and holds the interest of the students. Once all

	Beginners	Intermediate	Advanced
9:00–9:15	Teacher-directed	Teacher-directed	Teacher-directed
9:15–9:45	Teacher-directed	Desk work	Group work
9:45–10:00	Break	Break	Break
10:00–10:15	Desk work	Group work	Teacher-directed
10:15–10:45	Group work	Teacher-directed	Desk work
10:45–11:25	Teacher-directed	Teacher-directed	Teacher-directed

Figure 1. Classroom Management Plan for a Multilevel Class

of the items are distributed, each student holding an item is asked to stand and tell the class what he or she has. If the student can't answer, the teacher elicits help from the entire class. If no one in the class knows, the teacher provides the lexical item. After the proper term has been elicited, it is written on the board, and the teacher models the pronunciation several times. He or she then allows students to repeat by asking for the name of the item being held by their classmate. As the list of items progresses and becomes longer, the teacher reviews them frequently and randomly, asking the student holding the item to stand up as the item is called. The task becomes more and more lively as the teacher calls off items more quickly and students stand up and sit down, often at the encouragement of their classmates. For variety, a student may volunteer to come to the front of the room and pronounce and identify each of the objects. It is suggested that items be reviewed frequently, and after items from the house are exhausted, including cleaning supplies, teachers may substitute items from business, children's small toy animals, or anything else relevant to the students.

After the opening activity, students divide into groups according to level. It is essential that students know exactly what to do at this point. They need to know where in the room to go and exactly what activity to begin with. Early training is the key to success at this point because teachers have found that time spent directing students to their proper groups during the first few days of class is time well invested and results in smooth transitions later. A schedule of class activities for each group should be posted in each group area. Adhere stringently to the schedule for the first few weeks, and it will become automatic for the students. It is not unusual for a teacher to take a kitchen timer to class and set it for each activity. Some have watches with alarm clocks, and some bring in bedside alarm clocks. Once the routine has been established, students move from one station to the next with surprising efficiency, and veteran students can help new students get used to the routine. Accustoming students to transitioning between activities is crucial if this model is to work, but it can be very challenging. Depending on their cultural sense of time, some students may find punctuating their experiences in this way to be bizarre and deeply arbitrary.

Pedagogically, the idea behind such a timetable is that all students spend opening and closing time with the teacher, and one-third or one-half of the remaining time (depending on the number of groups) in teacher-directed activities. Each teacher-directed lesson leads to individual desk work, which can then move naturally into communicative group work. Advanced students may be able to work from written instructions, but most students will need verbal instructions supplied during the teacher-directed lesson, which can be reinforced by the posted schedule. Sometimes advanced students can also help beginning students, under teacher supervision. Teachers agree that multilevel classrooms are challenging but definitely manageable, as long as the students are properly grouped and sufficient time is devoted to learning the class routine.

Testing

Managing a multilevel class requires a valid and reliable placement instrument (see Cohen's chapter in this volume). Frequently textbooks have placement exams in the teacher's guide that reflect the scope and sequence of the text. It is also very likely that the school will have some sort of placement instrument. In schools in which multilevel grouping is not dictated by necessity, it is probably most efficacious to place students with others of like proficiency.

At Belmont, for example, all entering students take a placement test. In the upper levels, they are tracked according to their language strengths and deficiencies. They are offered classes in grammar, reading, listening, speaking, writing, and computer-based instruction. Students take two classes per night. Those who are weak in grammar but strong in reading might take two grammar classes, or a reading class at one level and a grammar class at a lower level. Over the course of several years, this system changed the structure of the school's ESL program from a pyramid configuration, with the majority of students at the lower levels, to a columnar configuration. In other words, the attrition rate decreased as more and more students moved on to the upper levels and fewer students dropped out. The school also developed exit tests for each level so that students with like proficiency tended to remain grouped. It is often felt (erroneously, we think) that actual testing is so stressful that it will cause students to abandon classes. The Belmont experience seems to indicate otherwise. Observation suggests that students expect and respect formal testing and are challenged rather than overwhelmed by the process. In fact, it is not unusual for attendance to be particularly high on nights during which testing is scheduled, or for some students to insist on remaining in a level, regardless of test results, until they meet their own criteria for passing the course. The fact that students appreciate honest and valid testing should come as no surprise and is very much in keeping with the adult learner profile outlined earlier. Of course, it is certainly questionable, on the face of it, whether a paper-and-pencil test is a valid measure of language at all. Surely a communicative test (Wesche 1987) would be closer to the ideal. Unfortunately, sheer numbers discourage a direct, communicative test in most schools. (See Stoynoff 1996 for a helpful review of three good testing books.)

Currently, all California adult schools have moved over to competency-based programs, which in theory should require competency-based exams. McIntire (1988, p. 15) defines competency-based education as "[c]urriculum based on predetermined competencies identified as necessary for adults to function successfully. Students must demonstrate mastery of these competencies successfully to complete a class or a program." The idea, then, is that a student might be required to be able to enroll his or her child in school, write a letter of excuse to the teacher, report the child's health and immunization history, and similar details in order to pass a unit. According to McIntire, "An underlying philosophical tenet of competency based education is the belief that a student must achieve skills rather than 'earn credits.' Thus adults may attend a class for a short or for an extended period of time in order to satisfactorily demonstrate the attainment of competencies . . . Success is measured in the mastery of specific competencies rather than through hours of attendance, commonly referred to as 'seat time'" (p. 37).

The state of California has specified the proficiencies and outcomes for each level of ESL (frequently called the *model standards*) in the *English-as-a-Second Language Model Standards for Adult Education Programs* (1992). This document (or the appropriate equivalent) is vital for teachers who are teaching in a school with mandated model standards. Programs, assessment, placement, funding, and accreditation in such a system will all most likely be tied to the relevant document and to demonstrable compliance with it. At first blush it may seem that this takes away from the autonomy and creativity of the individual teacher; based on our experience, however, we argue that teachers can still be autonomous and creative, and that model standards simply help to focus where the teacher's autonomy and creativity can be exercised. The model standards assure continuity for the students as well as provide continuity and direction for new teachers. For experienced teachers, the model standards make "levels of proficiency" competencies and outcomes sufficiently explicit that teachers can more accurately select from or expand their repertoire of pedagogical materials and strategies. At the same time, the language in the document is sufficiently generic to allow teachers to exercise as much or as little independence and creativity as they are comfortable with, while assuring direction and benchmarks of progress for the student. In California, the model standards are based on the input of literally thousands of practicing teachers and administrators. As a result, the outcomes and competencies are realistic and grounded in practice. Thus far, they have been well received and appear to benefit both students and teachers.

The Value of Adult Education

The workplace is vitally important for our students, and often the adult ESL class has to take a back seat to our students' working overtime or training for a new job. As Iwataki (1981) points out, adult ESL students have as their frame of reference "not the school but their families, jobs, their outside responsibilities" (p. 24). Adult ESL teachers need to be aware of the importance of family and economic factors in the lives of their students. For many adult students, economic upward mobility will be achieved, if not by them, by future generations. If they learn enough English to survive, their children and grandchildren will most likely be able to take advantage of the upward mobility that education can bring. Even though not all of our students will become rich as a result of their adult ESL classes, there are by-products of education which most of our students routinely do experience that need to be considered. In addition to bringing students "comfortably into the classroom," adult schools, in many cases, are the first positive contact immigrants have with American social institutions. Increased self-esteem, cultural awareness, tolerance, and a positive affective stance toward American schools and teachers are important epiphenomena of adult ESL classes, and

their significance cannot be overstated. Both the immigrant community and the community at large benefit greatly from such effects, even if the students do not immediately achieve great wealth and native-like mastery of English.

Future Trends

Without question, state-mandated standards and accountability (evidence through student performance that competencies and outcomes have been demonstrated) seem to be the direction in which adult education as a field is headed. Many states require them, and it seems likely that other states will follow. There are also other factors in the field of second language acquisition that we think will have an impact on adult education.

Recent sociocultural/sociohistorical/language socialization studies have demonstrated that the demands and consequences of our profession are considerably more complex than we might previously have thought. A number of researchers[7] have argued quite compellingly for a shift in second language research. They have found evidence that learning and teaching a second language is considerably more complex, layered, and profound than we had ever imagined, and that our current pedagogy does not begin to reflect or take into account "the complex social and cultural worlds into which a second language learner must enter" (Rymes 1997, p. 143). Only a sea change in our research paradigm will illuminate these worlds and ultimately lead to more effective classrooms. Virtually all of the researchers working from this perspective

place language learning within the more comprehensive domain of socialization, the lifelong process through which individuals are initiated into cultural meaning and learn to perform the skills, tasks, roles and identities expected by whatever society or societies they may live in . . . The language socialization perspective implies that language is learned through social interaction. It also implies that language is a primary vehicle of socialization: When we learn a second language, we are learning more than a structure for communication; we are also learning (for example) social and cultural norms, procedures for interpretation, and forms of reasoning (Watson-Gegeo 1988, p. 582).

Preliminary findings from this type of research suggest that using one's first language can be an act of resistance, as opposed to an unwillingness to cooperate with the teacher or to practice English, and that what appears to be an opportunity for language practice can actually discourage second language use (Rymes 1996). Rymes and Pash (2000) found that students can be so involved in "looking like they're learning" that it can interfere with learning. In another study of high school students in Los Angeles, Rymes (1996) found that collaboration among students is vital for second language learning, though such collaboration may be beset by difficulty in "integrating students' own perspectives and experiences with what collaboration is and how it works" (p. 409). Hall (1995) found that learning a language is inseparable from issues of (shifting) power and that specific social forces rather than "language proficiency" constrain the type and amount of linguistic participation afforded a second language learner. In fact, the social aspects of learning a second language may be more basic than the intellectual ones. Finally, learning a second language changes one's identity (Trosset 1986). Add to this Schumann's suggestion (1997) that cognition and affect are in practice inseparable and that everyone is on an individual affective/cognitive trajectory in language learning. Clearly these are not trivial matters and very likely this research direction will affect the form and content of the adult classroom in the twenty-first century.

CONCLUSION

Adult ESL teachers are routinely effusive when describing their adult ESL experience, as are the students. Teachers who come to work "exhausted" speak about renewed energy and of taking several hours to "wind down" after teaching an adult ESL class because the experience is so exciting and intense. The bond between ESL student and teacher is nothing short of remarkable, and the satisfaction teachers experience is truly profound. It has been said that in the United States, the last bastion of genuine respect for teachers and, indeed, for education in general is the adult ESL classroom. Perhaps Dale McIntire[8] said it best: Adult ESL is what you thought education was going to be when you first decided to become a teacher.

DISCUSSION QUESTIONS

1. What are some characteristics of adult learners which set them apart from younger language learners or from university students? In what way(s) do you think those differences should or do affect your approach to adult school students?

2. Investigate the adult education program in the area in which you intend to teach. How is it different from and how is it similar to the program described in this chapter? You might want to consider the major points covered, such as the history of the program, its funding, the target population, classes available, placement, etc.

3. The state of California currently mandates that schools that receive public funds provide quantitative and qualitative evidence that students are making progress. This mandate is tied to funding (among other things), so it is taken very seriously. However, we occasionally find learners who simply fail to make progress or who insist on repeating a class with a single teacher over and over again. What kind of tension might this situation create? How might that tension be resolved or at least lived with?

SUGGESTED ACTIVITIES

1. If you have access to the internet, go to the website for the National Clearinghouse for ESL Literacy Education (**http://www.cal.org.ncle**) and look at the ten areas in

which there are concise overviews of research and best practices. Select three that you find particularly helpful and share them with your group.

2. Find out if the state, province, or country in which you plan to teach has mandated standards. If so, get a copy of the document and read it carefully. (You might begin online with the State/Provincial/National Department of Education.) Based on the document, plan a lesson to teach the following to adult ESL students:

   a. use of present tense
   b. pronunciation of final /d/ in English
   c. writing an absence excuse to a child's teacher
   d. writing a note of explanation to a supervisor or coworker

3. Part of a grammar lesson might include asking students to practice using a structure in a communicative context. This would occur after the presentation and the focused practice phases of the lesson. Imagine that you are teaching the present perfect to an intermediate adult ESL class and are now ready to begin the communicative phase of the lesson. If you have access to the Internet, search under *SCANS Report* or go to one of the following websites:

   http://www.coe.tany.edu/~epsy/cded/jennyl.htm

   or

   http://www.academicinnovations.com/report.html.

   Work out several communicative exercises that would incorporate SCANS into your grammar lesson.

4. Plan in detail a two-and-a-half hour lesson for a multilevel ESL class. Decide the proficiency of each level. What will your opening exercise(s) be? Why will this exercise be a good one for students at different levels? How will you time the rest of the lesson? How will you move students from one activity to another? How will you assure that when the teacher is with one group, he or she will not be needed by another?

FURTHER READING

For understanding and teaching English grammar

Celce-Murcia, M., and D. Larsen-Freeman. 1999. *The Grammar Book: An ESL/EFL Teacher's Course*, 2d ed. Boston, MA: Heinle & Heinle Publishers.

Celce-Murcia, M., and S. Hilles. (1988). *Techniques and Resources in Teaching Grammar*. New York: Oxford University Press.

For understanding adult education and relevant pedagogy

Ilyin, D., and T. Tragardh, eds. 1978. *Classroom Practices in Adult ESL*. Washington, DC: TESOL.

Rose, M. 1989. *Lives on the Boundary*. New York: Free Press.

Other useful resources

Brown, H. Douglas. 1994. *Teaching by Principles: An Interactive Approach to Language Pedagogy*. Englewood Cliffs, NJ: Prentice Hall.

U.S. Department of Labor. 1991. *The Secretary's Commission on Achieving Necessary Skills*. Washington, DC: Department of Labor.

Your state, provincial, or national standards document.

WEBSITES

NCLE/ERIC Digests and Q&A.
   http://www.cal.org/ncle/DIGESTS/

Both the U.S. National Literacy Act of 1991 and the U.S. Adult Education Act of 1991, along with related policy resources, are available on-line at:

   www.nifl.gov/lincs/collections/policy/resource.html

ENDNOTES

1 We are indebted to Dale McIntire, Marianne Celce-Murcia, and to the late Sadae Iwataki for their very helpful comments, suggestions, and discussions regarding earlier versions of this chapter. We would also like to thank Marianne Celce-Murcia and Kit

Bell for their invaluable input. The responsibility for any errors, omissions, or problems in interpretation is ours, of course.

2 For the complete text of Lincoln's eloquent 1838 address to the Young Men's Lyceum of Springfield, see *Current* 1967, pp. 11–21.

3 All the statistical data regarding Belmont Community Adult School are taken from the 1995 Application for Accreditation and current school demographics. Although many of our illustrations will be drawn from this one particular adult school, our observations will be informed by programs in other schools, as well as conversations and consultations with colleagues, teachers, administrators, and students throughout the United States and in other countries.

4 Work by Bley-Vroman 1988; Celce-Murcia and Hilles 1988; Higgs and Clifford 1982; McIntire 1988; Selinker 1972 and sources cited therein discuss this issue.

5 *Affect* is a term from psychology, which the *American Heritage Dictionary, Second College Edition* (1991) defines as "a feeling or emotion as distinguished from cognition, thought, or action" (p. 84).

6 Studies by Bley-Vroman 1988; Hilles 1991; Johnson and Newport 1989; Krashen, Scarcella, and Long 1982; Long 1990; Richards 1985; Schumann 1997 (among others) address this issue. For a different perspective, see Bialystok and Hakuta 1994.

7 For example, see Hall 1995; Markee 1994; Rymes 1997; Trosset 1986; and Watson-Gegeo 1988.

8 Dale McIntyre, personal communication.

UNIT V

Skills for Teachers

We end with a section on the needs of ESL/EFL teachers. What do teachers need to know to perform their jobs effectively and professionally? What are the skills and competencies all too frequently left undiscussed? Jensen's chapter shows how lesson plans can be structured and prepared in the context of an entire course. Byrd's chapter then discusses textbooks: how to evaluate them for initial selection and how to analyze them to ensure effective implementation. Medgyes raises issues important for those ESL/EFL teachers who are non-native speakers of English. Since these teachers now constitute the majority of English language teachers worldwide, all ESL/EFL teachers—native and non-native—should be informed of and sensitive to the issues. Hinkel's chapter treats culture, a related matter; since all ESL/EFL learners have a non-English-speaking cultural background, their teachers must be aware of the cultural differences between their learners and native speakers of English. Hinkel gives suggestions on how to foster cross-cultural communication. Next, Brinton shows teachers the genuine usefulness of instructional media along with demonstrating how both technical and non-technical resources can be used in lessons to enhance teaching. Sokolik then gives an introduction to the use of computers, the most technical of media, in language teaching, stressing that sound pedagogy will be the most important factor in deciding the usefulness and success of this technology. Bailey defines and distinguishes action research, teacher research, and classroom research, showing their potential usefulness to language teachers. Then Murphy's chapter on reflective teaching, presents several options teachers can explore for their long-term professional growth. Cohen's language assessment chapter covers many issues (test types, test items, test administration, reliability, validity); every language teacher should have a general understanding of this area for every teacher is involved in assessment. Finally, Crandall reminds ESL/EFL teachers of all the resources they can exploit to keep up to date. The field is growing rapidly, and a major part of any teacher's responsibility is to keep abreast of new developments.

Planning Lessons

LINDA JENSEN

Jensen's "Lesson Planning" chapter serves as a guide for novice teachers who need to create formalized lesson plans. The chapter covers why, when, and how teachers plan lessons, as well as basic lesson plan principles and a lesson plan template. A sample lesson plan is provided in the context of a weekly overview, module overview, and course overview.

INTRODUCTION: DEFINITION OF A LESSON PLAN

All good teachers have some type of plan when they walk into their classrooms. It can be as simple as a mental checklist or as complex as a detailed two-page typed lesson plan that follows a pre-scribed format. Usually, lesson plans are written just for the teacher's own eyes and tend to be rather informal. But there may be times when the plan has to be written as a class assignment or given to an observer or supervisor, and therefore will be a more formal and detailed document. This chapter will serve as a guide for creating these more formalized lesson plans.

A lesson plan is an extremely useful tool that serves as a combination guide, resource, and historical document reflecting our teaching philosophy, student population, textbooks, and most importantly, our goals for our students. It can be described with many metaphors such as road map, blueprint, or game plan (see Ur 1996); but regardless of the analogy, a lesson plan is essential for novice teachers and convenient for experienced teachers.

Why We Plan

Deciding what to teach, in what order, and for how much time are the basic components of planning. The lesson plan serves as a map or checklist that guides us in knowing what we want to do next; these sequences of activities remind us of the goals and objectives of our lessons for

our students. As previously mentioned, a lesson plan is also a record of what we did in class; this record serves as a valuable resource when planning assessment measures such as quizzes, midterms, and final exams. A record of previously taught lessons is also useful when we teach the same course again, so that we have an account of what we did the term or year before to avoid reinventing the wheel. When we have to miss class, a lesson plan is a necessity for the substitute teacher, who is expected to step in and teach what had been planned for the day. In addition, just as teachers expect their students to come to class prepared to learn, students come to class expecting their teachers to be prepared to teach. A lesson plan is part of that preparation.

Yet in spite of the importance of planning, a lesson plan is mutable, not written in stone; it is not meant to keep a teacher from changing the duration of an activity or forgoing an activity altogether if the situation warrants. A good lesson plan guides but does not dictate what and how we teach. It benefits many stakeholders: teachers, administrators, observers, substitutes, and of course, students.

When and How We Plan

To be perfectly honest, a certain amount of lesson planning takes place the night before a class is taught. This planning, taking place just hours before entering the classroom, should be the fine or micro tuning of the lesson, not the big picture or macro planning that is based on a

403

programmatic philosophy or syllabus design. A good lesson plan is the result of both macro planning and micro planning. On the macro level, a lesson plan is a reflection of a philosophy of learning and teaching which is reflected in the methodology, the syllabus, the texts, and the other course materials and finally results in a specific lesson. In brief, an actual lesson plan is the end point of many other stages of planning that culminate in a daily lesson.

Before a teacher steps into the second language classroom, he or she should have developed his or her own understanding of second language learning and teaching. This background includes knowledge of theories of second language acquisition and learner characteristics (see Oxford's chapter in this text) as well as familiarity with both historical and current trends in second language pedagogy (see chapters by Celce-Murcia and Savignon in this text). This background knowledge will create a personal philosophy that is realized whenever the teacher is preparing lessons, teaching classes, or grading assignments or tests. A good teacher cannot help but bring his or her own sense of good learning and teaching into the classroom. Ideally, this philosophy will be consistent with the teaching methodology employed by the institution since the methodology will then help implement the syllabus and influence the choice of textbooks for most programs.

Once the syllabus and texts have been decided, planning for the year or term takes place. For many teachers, especially newly hired ones, these decisions have already been made and the macro planning has been taken care of by colleagues or supervisors. In some cases, however, the new teacher may be responsible for the macro planning as well as the micro planning. Consulting or planning with fellow teachers about syllabus design and textbook selection can be very helpful in this type of situation (see chapters by Nunan and Byrd in this text). In rare cases, nothing may be in place so it may be entirely up to the instructor to design the course syllabus, choose the teaching materials, and plan the daily lessons. Generally the opposite is true for the novice teacher, however, who will have very little input at first in terms of macro and even micro planning. (See Appendices B, C, and D for examples of macro planning: a course overview, a module overview, and a weekly overview.)

What a Lesson Plan Looks Like

Although there are a variety of formats to use when creating a lesson plan, most templates share certain characteristics. When creating a lesson, a teacher must consider the background of the students, the objectives of the lesson, the skills to be taught, the activities, the materials and texts, the time constraints, and the connections to previous and future lessons. Like most activities, a lesson plan has stages: a beginning, a middle, and an end. As mentioned previously, the amount of detail actually written down will vary with individual preferences and experience. Some instructors like to keep notebooks of lessons plans for each class; others may use note cards or loose sheets of paper that can be shuffled around. Many instructors now use computers to write up lesson plans; the advantages of this are that the lessons are neatly typed, easy to save, and can readily be copied and modified as needed. Keeping at least one paper copy filed away in case of a technological breakdown is also a good idea.

Most plans begin with a brief description of the class and students; for example, the name of the course and the level, and the background of the students are useful to note. It is also important to add the date as well as the week and day of the course. Given the trend of adhering to competency requirements and published standards, a lesson plan may also need to include the competencies and standards that the lesson addresses. Some teachers list the grammatical structures and key vocabulary terms that will be introduced as well.

Teachers also find it wise to note what has been covered during the previous class or what students already need to know for the particular lesson, especially if it will begin with a review of previous material. The day's goals and objectives should be included as should a list of texts, materials, and equipment such as audiovisual aids. Some instructors find it helpful to list the day's materials and audiovisual aids in a box at the top of the page to serve as a reminder of what they need to bring to class. If more elaborate material preparation is necessary before class, teachers may also list the steps necessary to prepare these materials. Noting any homework or assignments to be returned or collected that day is also useful information to have at the beginning of the lesson plan.

The middle component of a lesson plan is the lesson's content; this includes procedures or activities along with transition notes, as well as time management and class management notes such as the students' seating arrangements for different activities. Novice teachers should also try to anticipate what may go wrong or prove to be problematic so that contingency plans are prepared in advance and written into the lesson plan.

Lessons usually begin with warm-up and/or review activities. Teachers need to decide how they will connect the day's lesson to the previous class meeting and how they want to interest and motivate their students for the day's activities. Once warmed up, the class is then ready for the presentation and practice stages of the lesson. These stages have been referred to with a variety of labels such as *into, through, beyond* (Brinton, Goodwin, and Ranks 1994); *engage, study, activate* (Harmer 1998); *lead-in, elicitation, explanation, accurate reproduction,* and *immediate creativity* (Harmer 1991); and *verbalization, automatization,* and *autonomy* (Ur 1996). All of these labels describe stages in which first, the language form or content is introduced and presented; second, comprehension is checked before a form of guided practice is implemented; and third, some type of less structured, communicative activity takes place so that students can practice what they have just learned in a less controlled, more natural situation. The communicative stage also provides an opportunity for students to integrate the new knowledge presented in the lesson with previous knowledge. Finally, teachers and students should evaluate how well the new material has been learned in order to determine the shape of future lessons.

Some teachers find it useful to write brief comments on a lesson plan that help with the transition from one activity to another, so that the lesson flows well and the various activities have a sense of connection. For example, when transitioning from a listening activity to a reading activity a teacher can discuss how certain listening strategies can be adapted as reading strategies. Creating smooth transitions and links can be challenging for novice teachers, so planning these moves and noting them in a lesson plan is worthwhile and valuable for both instructors and students.

Time management can also be challenging for beginning teachers and even experienced teachers cannot always accurately predict how long a certain activity will take or when a discussion will become so engaging that it should be allowed to continue longer than planned. Nonetheless, it is important to note the number of minutes allotted for each activity in the margin of the lesson plan; this also means that the teacher should wear a watch or be able to see a clock in the classroom in order to be aware of the time. More often than not, an activity is underestimated in terms of length, so teachers should decide ahead of time what part of a lesson could be skipped or shortened or saved for the next class. This does not mean that teachers should not overplan. There are times when an activity will take less time than anticipated or suddenly seems too easy or difficult, so the teacher will decide to sacrifice it; good teachers err on the side of overplanning and/or have some useful five to ten minute supplementary activities available in their repertoire of teaching tricks. It can be a very frightening experience for the novice teacher to look up at the clock and see that she has ten minutes left until the end of class and no idea of what to do. Initially, it is useful for inexperienced teachers to plan their lessons so that each minute of class is accounted for before they step into the classroom.

Seating arrangements for various activities should also be noted in the lesson plan. Pre-planning pair and group work seating arrangements is more efficient than standing in front of the class and moving students around randomly.

There are times when random pairs or small groups may make sense but there are many other times when a rationale is needed in deciding who works with whom. Often we want groups to contain a mixture of talkative and quiet students; we probably want to mix language groups or separate best friends who talk only to each other. Planning these seating arrangements beforehand helps the class run smoothly and saves time. Most teachers also find it useful to give instructions for group or pair work to the class as a whole before breaking the class up; once students start moving around, they may become so active that getting their attention can take up valuable class time.

Teachers also need to anticipate where a lesson may break down. Especially when trying out a new activity or teaching a grammar point for the first time, novice teachers need to think about what may go wrong. What part of the lesson may be difficult for the students? What kinds of questions can the instructor expect? Will there be problems with student-student interactions? This type of forethought is especially important for lessons that rely on technology or equipment that may fail or not be available as planned. Anticipating problems and thinking of solutions beforehand makes both novice and experienced teachers feel more comfortable and confident when they walk into the classroom.

The final section of a lesson plan should include comments that end the lesson such as a review or summary of the lesson and that indicate homework or other assignments. Although homework may be noted at the end of a lesson plan, it is probably not a good idea to wait until the end of class to assign it to the students. Find a place on the board where homework can be consistently posted so students always know where to check for it. Post it there at the beginning of class or during the break so that everyone has a chance to write it down before those final hectic minutes of class when students are packing up their belongings and running out the door.

Some teachers like to leave a space on their lesson plans to comment on what needs to be covered during the next class session based on

what went on during the day's lesson. Perhaps an activity had to be placed on hold or a teaching point needs to be covered again. Some teachers also like to note students' unanswered questions in order to research their responses before the next class meeting.

It is also a good idea to include space for lesson evaluation by the teacher after the class is over. The evaluation component of lesson planning provides an opportunity for honest reflection about what activities worked or did not work and why, as well as how the lesson could be improved or modified the next time around. Teachers also find it useful to add comments concerning student reactions to the lesson. It is these evaluative comments that can make a lesson plan a truly useful resource for future course and lesson planning. (See Appendices A and E for a lesson plan template and a sample lesson plan.)

Basic Principles of Lesson Planning

As with any skill, lesson planning becomes easier over time. As teachers gain experience in the classroom, they learn certain principles about planning. When seasoned teachers are asked to list some basic principles of lesson planning that novice teachers should be aware of, the ones that are frequently mentioned are actually basic principles of good teaching: coherence, variety, and flexibility. These principles have proven useful for all teachers, not just the second/foreign language teacher.

1. A good lesson has a sense of coherence and flow. This means that the lesson hangs together and is not just a sequence of discrete activities. On a macro level, links or threads should connect the various lessons over the days and weeks of a course. On a micro level, students need to understand the rationale for each activity; also, they learn best when there are transitions from one activity to the next.

2. A good lesson exhibits variety. This variety needs to be present at both the macro and micro levels. While for most students, a

certain degree of predictability in terms of the teacher, the texts, classmates, and certain administrative procedures is comforting; however, to avoid boredom and fatigue, lesson plans should not follow the same pattern day after day. On a macro level, there should be variety in terms of topics (content), language, and skills over the length of the course. On a micro level, each daily lesson should have a certain amount of variety in terms of the pace of the class, such as time spent on various activities, depending on the difficulty or ease of the material being covered. The percentages of teacher-fronted time and student-centered activities should vary from lesson to lesson; there are days when we want our students to participate and be active, but there are other days when we want them a bit calmer in order to be receptive to new material or practice a listening or reading strategy. Some teacher-trainers have referred to this as the ability to "stir" or "settle" our students depending on the need. Each lesson should also have some variety in terms of classroom organization such as whole-class, small-group, pair, and individual activities. The mood of different lessons will vary as well; mood shifts can reflect the teacher's disposition on a certain day, the chemistry of the mix of students, the weather, current events, or something unexplainable.

3. A good lesson is flexible. Lesson plans are *not* meant to be tools that bind teachers to some preordained plan. Good teachers think on their feet and know when it is time to change an activity, regardless of what the lesson plan says. An interesting student question can take the class in an unanticipated direction that creates one of those wonderful "teaching moments," not to be missed. A brilliant idea can come as the teacher is writing on the board; sometimes pursuing these ideas is well worth a risk of failure. Even failure can be a valuable lesson for both the novice and experienced teacher.

CONCLUSION

Knowing how to go about planning a second/foreign language lesson is the result of many other stages of preparation. The teacher must be familiar with the principles of second language learning and teaching, as well as the needs of the institution and the student population. He or she must first see the big picture of the course and be aware of the goals and objectives for the entire term before planning weekly and daily lessons. If the big picture is kept in mind, the individual lessons will connect to form a learning experience that benefits both the teacher and the students.

DISCUSSION QUESTIONS

1. How will your knowledge of second language acquisition theories inform your decisions in lesson planning? Give some concrete examples.
2. List what you consider to be the characteristics of good students and good teachers. How will this affect your lesson planning?
3. How much detail do you feel is necessary in writing your own lessons plans? Would this change if a supervisor wanted copies of your lesson plans?
4. As a novice teacher, what aspects of lesson planning are the most daunting? How will you go about getting assistance in planning your lessons?
5. How much autonomy are you comfortable with in terms of lesson planning? Would you prefer a teaching situation in which lesson plans are given to you and you are expected to closely follow them, or would you prefer being handed a textbook and told to write your own daily lesson plans? What are the advantages and disadvantages of each situation?

SUGGESTED ACTIVITIES

1. Observe several ESL/EFL classes and ask each instructor for a copy of the day's lesson plan. How closely did the instructor follow the plan? How is the plan similar or different from the actual lesson?

2. Interview one or two experienced teachers about their own lesson planning strategies. Ask if you can look at some of their lesson plans. Ask if over the years they have changed the way they plan lessons.

3. Examine an ESL/EFL text that you may have the opportunity to teach in the future. Create three sample lesson plans with a variety of skill or language foci. How would you avoid marching through the text page by page? How would you incorporate supplementary material?

4. Create a lesson plan for an ESL/EFL class in a computer lab (see chapter by Sokolik, this volume). What lesson plan considerations need to be made for teaching in this situation?

5. List a variety of opening and closing activities. Compare your list with the lists of others in your class. How do these activities reflect individual teachers' personalities?

 FURTHER READING

Harmer, J. 1998. *How to Teach English.* (Chapter 12: How to plan lessons). Harlow, UK: Longman.
Excellent discussion of lesson planning for the inexperienced or novice teacher. Includes a "Task File" with a sample lesson plan on teaching the comparative degree to a low-level class as well as useful activities.

Harmer, J. 1991. *The Practice of English Language Teaching* (New Edition). (Chapter 12: Planning). Harlow, UK: Longman.
A more detailed chapter on lesson planning than *How to Teach English* with a focus on the teacher's background knowledge. Also includes a "specimen plan" for an intermediate adult class.

Nunan, D. 1999. *Second Language Teaching and Learning.* Boston, MA: Heinle & Heinle Publishers.
A very humanistic and personal account of second language learning and teaching. Enjoyable to read, especially for novice teachers.

Ur, P. 1996. *A Course in Language Teaching: Practice and Theory.* (Module 15: Lesson Planning). Cambridge: Cambridge University Press.
A reflective approach to lesson planning that is especially useful for experienced teachers.

Woodward, T., and S. Lindstromberg. 1995. *Planning from Lesson to Lesson: A Way of Making Lesson Planning Easier.* Harlow, UK: Longman.
Lots of lesson planning ideas based on the metaphor of using threads to create continuity.

APPENDIX A

Lesson Plan Template for a 50-minute Class

	Background Information:	**To do before class:**
	course/level	
	description of students (if necessary)	
	aims/objectives	
	skills focus/grammar/vocabulary	**Bring to class:**
	texts/materials	
	previous class work	
	work to be collected or returned	
Time Frame (in minutes)	**Procedures:**	**Notes:**
3–5	warm-up	transitions
4-5	review	seating plans
10	introduction	potential trouble spots
10	presentation activities	
15–20	communicative activities	contingencies
3–5	questions/homework	
	extra activities (if necessary)	
	Comments/Evaluation:	

APPENDIX B

Course Overview (10 Weeks) ESL 33C/UCLA Service Courses

LISTENING:
lectures:
History 160 and Anthropology 9

SPEAKING:
group work
discussions/presentations

READING:
Academic Publishing Services (APS)
Farewell to Manzanar (FM)
weekly paced and timed readings
Insights I

WRITING:
in-class essays
out-of-class essays
3–5 pp. research paper
weekly journals
St. Martin's Handbook (SM)

WEEK	READING	WRITING	SPEAKING	LISTENING
	Module I—The Immigrant in America (History 160)			
1	diag. essay previewing skimming/ scanning	diag. essay	diag. intros	diag. dict.
2	FM 1-5	brief def. relative clause paraphrasing	group work	hist. lect. 1 notetaking
3	FM 6–11 eye mov. 1	extended def.	group work	hist. lect. 2 notetaking/ summary
4	FM 12–15	IN-CLASS WRITING comp./cont. cause/effect essay exams SM ch.6/46	group work	hist. lect. 3 notetaking/ summary
5	FM 16–22	IN-CLASS WRITING articles	group work	
	Module II–Kinship and Marriage (Anthropology 9)			
6	APS	library tour verb tenses	group work conferencing	anthro. lect. 1 notetaking/ summary
7	APS	argumentation SM ch.5	group work	anthro. lect. 2 notetaking/
8	SM 39–40	passive voice research	group work	summary anthro. lect. 3
9	SM 41-42 SM 44	draft 1–paper IN-CLASS ESSAY	peer response debate	
10	Final Reading	draft 2–paper final draft due	peer response conferencing	final exam notes/summary

APPENDIX C
Module Overview (5 Weeks) ESL 33C/UCLA Service Courses

I.   Topic = HISTORY 160–The Immigrant in America

II. Rhetorical Modes: Definitions

                                        Comparison and Contrast

                                        Cause and Effect

III. Multiskill Components

    A. Listening: Videotaped Lecture—Prof. John Laslett
   1. Notetaking
   2. Outlining
   3. Mapping
   4. Summaries

    B. Speaking
   1. Group work
   2. Presentations

    C. Reading: Core Readings
   1. Previewing/Skimming
   2. Scanning for Details
   3. Vocabulary Development
   4. Comprehension Questions
   5. Rate Development

    D. Writing/Structure
   1. Paraphrasing
   2. Summaries
   3. Brief and Extended Definitions
   4. Relative Clauses
   5. Comparison and Contrast Essay Questions
   6. Cause and Effect Essay Questions

    E. Assignments
   1. Journals
   2. Video Notetaking: Outlining/Summaries
   3. Reading: Outlining/Summaries
   4. Skimming and Scanning Exercises
   5. Reading Comprehension Exercises
   6. Brief and Extended Definition/In-class Writing
   7. In-class Essay
   8. Conferencing/Rewrite

APPENDIX D

Weekly Overview (Week 3) ESL 33C/UCLA Service Courses

READING

Insights 1: Assimilation and Amalgamation
Farewell to Manzanar (ch. 3–11)

WRITING

using relative clauses in definitions
brief and extended definitions
Journal #3—*I*/p.124, Task 23

STUDY SKILLS

summary
paraphrasing
predicting exam content

LISTENING

video seg. 2 "Variables of Assimilation"
video seg. 3 "The Melting Pot Model"

SPEAKING

group work
class discussions

LESSON SEQUENCING

Hour One: *Insights* p. 116—video seg. 2 "Variables of Assimilation"

Insights pp.117–120 (brief definitions/relative clauses)

Hour Two: *FM* 3–8, *APS* p. 54 (discussion questions)

hw: *APS* pp. 28–30, 34–37(extended definitions)

I. pp. 120-124 / *FM* ch. 9–11(by Fri)

Hour Three: paraphrasing *APS* pp. 28–30 / *SM* pp. 596–600, 617–618

extended definitions in *APS* pp. 34–37, *SM* p. 136

Hour Four: summary / *I.* 123–124

I. pp. 120–123—video seg. 3 "The Melting Pot Model"
(Amalgamation)

group work: begin extended definition—amalgamation

hw: finish extended definitions/journal #3 (*I.* p. 124/task 23)

Hour Five: go over hw: extended definitions

brainstorm terms for definitions for in-class writing

FM 9–11

hw—*FM* ch. 12–15/prepare for in-class writing

APPENDIX E

Sample Lesson Plan (Wk. 3/Hr. 5) ESL 33C/UCLA Service Courses

	Background Information: ESL 33C (advanced multi-skills)/ content-based course studying models of assimilation UCLA undergrads/mostly Asian **Objectives:** to be prepared for in-class writing next class **Skills focus:** writing extended definitions/ predicting content of a midterm **Texts/materials:** *Insights 1, St. Martin's Handbook,* *Farewell to Manzanar* **Previous class work:** group work writing an extended definition of amalgamation **Work to be collected and returned:** return Journal #2/collect Journal #3	**To do before class:** print in-class writing prompts **Bring to class:** *Insights 1* *FM* *SM* *APS*
Time Frame (in minutes)	**Procedures:**	**Notes:**
5	Warm-up: greetings/questions about weekend plans/check roll	whole class
10	Share extended definitions of amalgamation finished for hw/pick one to put on ovrhd. proj.	5 small groups at tables
15	Group presentations of amalgamation definitions on a transparency in front of class	give feedback on relative clauses
10	Remind class of in-class writing (extended definitions) on Monday / Brainstorm possible terms to define	list on board
10	Class discussion of *FM* ch. 9–11 (discussion questions in *APS*, p. 53) hw: *FM*: ch. 12–15 for next Friday/review for in-class writing	large circle
	Comments/Evaluation: *Good idea to focus feedback on relative clauses* *only with their extended definitions of* *amalgamation; otherwise the activity takes too* *much time.* *Students did a great job of predicting the terms* *that they will be asked to define.*	

Textbooks: Evaluation for Selection and Analysis for Implementation

PATRICIA BYRD

In "Textbooks: Evaluation for Selection and Analysis for Implementation," Byrd argues that the decisions made in selecting textbooks are different from the decisions made for implementing textbooks. After showing how the processes differ and the confusion that results from using the same approach for both, she provides guidelines for selecting as well as implementing textbooks.

INTRODUCTION

In addition to our students and ourselves, another constant in the lives of most teachers is our textbook. Few teachers enter class without a textbook—often a required textbook—that provides content and teaching/learning activities that shape much of what happens in that classroom. For teachers, use of a textbook involves first the selection of a book and then the steps taken to implement the book in class.

While having rational and effective selection procedures is surely important for educational systems, programs, schools, teachers, and students, the selection process is one that is not open to many ESL/EFL teachers working in settings where textbooks have been selected through an administrative process—at the ministerial level or by the school board or by the program director or by a committee of teachers that selects texts for the whole program, or by the teacher who taught the course the previous semester but who is teaching something else this term. As a result, although information about evaluation for selection is important for teachers to understand, most teachers have different encounters with textbooks as they make decisions about how to implement and supplement materials for the most effective classes possible for their students and for themselves. To reflect on the two different ways in which textbooks are scrutinized by teachers, I will separate "evaluation for selection" from "analysis for implementation" in the following discussion.

EVALUATION FOR SELECTION

Evaluation and selection of textbooks is a complex process that is carried out in many different ways. In a few settings, teachers decide on the books that they want to use in their classes. For example, in university settings in the United States and elsewhere, ESL teachers can often make individual decisions about the textbooks that they will use. With information from publishers and colleagues, they select a text or texts, have the books ordered through the campus bookstore, and then use them in their classes. In many other settings, such text selections are made by administrators or by committees of teachers. Another scenario, centralized decision-making by the government, can be seen in Egypt, where decisions about the English language curriculum and the textbooks used to teach it are made by the Ministry of Education in Cairo. In this system, a unified series of textbooks is created for use throughout the country, rather than selecting textbooks from a generic collection created by commercial publishing companies. A much smaller centralized approach is seen in boards of education in various U.S. states that have systems through which textbooks are analyzed and lists of recommended books developed. Because of the decentralized nature of U.S. education, no national requirements exist, and individual schools often have considerable flexibility in implementing state curricular requirements. Textbooks and supplemental materials are, however, frequently selected through a system that involves input from supervisors and colleagues, and does not emphasize the individual teacher making a personal decision. Even in schools that are not part of centralized ministerial or board systems, textbook selection is often the work of a faculty committee or of a program administrator. An intensive English program might have a textbook committee to evaluate textbooks and to make selections as a way of ensuring some unity across multiple sections of the same course. Overall, few ESL/EFL teachers use textbooks that they have themselves selected through a process that has focused simply on their interests and the needs of the students in their individual section of a course.

However, teachers can sometimes influence the decision-making process and thus need to be aware of how it works in their own situation. That is, teachers have to be aware not just of their lives inside their classrooms, but they must also be knowledgeable about the larger system in which they work and about possible ways that the system might allow for teacher participation in its administrative processes. Influencing the selection process in these situations is not just a matter of pedagogical knowledge but also of political skill.

Systematic Evaluation

Systems for evaluation of textbooks (and other instructional materials) generally provide checklists built around numerous aspects of teaching and student-teacher interactions (Bader 2000; Daoud and Celce-Murcia 1979; Gomes de Matos 2000; Skierso 1991). In reviewing such lists, I am reminded of the time many years ago when a colleague and I sat down to make a list of things for our students to check as they revised their compositions. Our first list had over 100 items on it. Clearly, it wasn't going to be very useful for many students. We quickly revised it to a more reasonable number that we and our students could handle. But we also realized that our checklist was useful only for a particular kind of writing; it worked reasonably well for the personal essays being written for our course but would not have worked nearly so well if the students had been

writing lab reports or reviews of books for history courses. Similarly, making a comprehensive yet reasonable checklist for evaluation of textbooks is an enormous challenge that requires different lists for different types of courses in different settings. Published checklists like those referenced above are offered as models that present important categories that should be considered in the selection process. Like other suggestions from colleagues, these models need to be considered carefully and adapted to fit the particular situation in which they will be used. In the body of this chapter, I will provide a general rationale for the considerations that seem fundamental to such a selection-guiding checklist, delaying until the "Suggested Activities" creation of detailed checklists designed to fit the situations of the teachers using this book. The issues that must be addressed in a textbook evaluation system are the fit between the materials and (1) the curriculum, (2) the students, and (3) the teachers.

The Fit Between Curriculum and Texts

Generally, the first area included in textbook analysis is the fit between the materials and the curriculum. For large educational systems, publishers create materials based on published curriculum statements. For example, in Egypt, the Ministry of Education arranges for publication of its own textbooks. Because the books are created for use only in Egypt, the Ministry can be sure that the materials are appropriate and carry out its particular curricular goals. In the United States, some public school systems publish their curriculum guidelines and invite publishers to submit materials that fit those guidelines. For states with large ESL populations, such as Texas, Florida, New York, and California, publishers compete fiercely to provide materials that meet the stated curricular guidelines. For these educational systems with their considerable purchasing power and various methods for control of content, the fit between the textbook and the curriculum is assumed to be a reasonable and achievable goal.

For smaller programs and individual teachers, the fit between curriculum and textbooks can be harder to achieve for two reasons. First, all too many programs do not have clearly articulated curriculum statements; teachers have groups of students who want to learn English but the program lacks a general statement of purposes and methods. Second, when there is a curriculum statement for a smaller program or an individual class, it may have features that are unique to that particular program; however, the program is not large enough for publishers to provide textbooks based on its individual curriculum statement. In the first situation, the textbook must be selected based on features other than curriculum—and therefore the text itself becomes the curriculum. In the second situation, textbooks are unlikely to be found that are completely congruent with the pedagogical goals of the program, and the purpose of the selection process must be to find books that have as good a fit as possible—with the expectation that the textbooks will need to be adapted and supplemented with additional materials to support the curriculum.

The Fit Between Students and Texts

Textbooks are for students. To meet their needs, the textbook must have not just the English language or communication skill content demanded by the curriculum, but it must also fit the needs of students as learners of English. Textbooks are made up of three major elements: content (and explanations), examples, and exercises or tasks. In support of these three elements, textbooks also employ a variety of graphical elements, including print size and style and white space as well as illustrations. In the evaluation-for-selection process, the person or group making the selection needs to know enough about the students to be able to answer questions such as the following.

1. **Content/Explanations:** Is the content likely to be of interest or use to the students? Is there any chance that the content could be offensive or inappropriate for its intended audience? Do the explanations work for these learners—do they help learners understand what they need in order to learn?

2. **Examples:** Are the examples appropriate to the lives and interests of the students? Do the examples fit closely with the concepts they are supposed to be explaining?

3. **Exercises/Tasks:** Do the exercises or tasks provide enough variety to meet the needs of different kinds of learners in the class(es)? Will they be of interest to these students?

4. **Presentation/Format:** Does the book look right for these students? Are the illustrations and other graphical and design elements appropriate for their age and educational level? Is the printed text easy to read and appropriate for their reading level? Is the mix between print and white space balanced so that readability is enhanced and appropriate? Does the book have an index, appendices, or other sections that are usable by students? Is the book well constructed—will it last a term of hard use by students?

The Fit Between Teachers and Texts

Textbooks are also for teachers. As with students, teachers seek three things from textbooks: content/explanations, examples, and exercises or tasks. The evaluation-for-selection process needs to find out if the textbook can be used effectively by the teachers to whom it will be assigned. The basic questions will always be *Can our teachers handle this material?* and *Will our teachers find that the textbook meets their needs and preferences for teaching materials?*

Questions such as the following should be included in the analysis of the fit between a potential textbook and the teachers who will use it.

1. **Content/Explanations:** In all settings, evaluators need to consider if the textbook provides content that teachers will find useful to carry out the goals of the course and the program— is this a teacher-friendly textbook? In some settings, it is important to ask if teachers will have adequate English to be able to understand the content and to be able to explain it to their students. A question of special importance in English for Specific Purposes texts but of importance in all textbook analysis is, is there a reasonable fit between the content

and the knowledge-base of the teacher? Other questions include, Is there an instructor's manual that helps the teacher better understand the content and ways of using the content with the students? Does the textbook supply or require ancillaries such as audiotapes or workbooks? If so, is the content of these ancillaries appropriate to and usable by the teachers in this program?

2. **Examples:** Are the examples usable for the teacher—can they be expanded on or recast to be useful in the lessons?

3. **Exercises/Tasks:** Does the text provide enough things for the teacher to give his or her students to do for the period of time to be covered by the course? Are the exercises or tasks doable in this setting? Do they provide for a variety of learning styles? Is there an instructor's manual and does it make suggestions for implementation of the exercises? Does it provide an answer key for any exercises that have discrete answers, such as grammar drills or vocabulary activities?

4. **Presentation/Format:** Does the illustrative material provide the teacher with teaching opportunities? Is there a close connection between the content and the illustrations?

ANALYSIS FOR IMPLEMENTATION

Although the evaluation-for-selection systems are created to make the selection process as rational as possible, our encounters with textbooks in the selection process always involve a series of value judgments: this is good or this is bad or this fits well or this doesn't fit at all. Evaluation is about making a judgment call— yes or no, in or out, buy it or don't buy it, thumbs up or thumbs down. Because the types of analysis and decision-making when using a textbook in the classroom are radically different from those in the selection process, the experiences of classroom teachers with the textbook involve an evaluation that uses different criteria. In the evaluation-for-selection process, the basic question is *Does this book have the features that we*

want it to have so that we can adopt it? After adoption, the basic question changes to, *How do I as a teacher working with particular students in a particular class in a particular program make this book work to ensure effective and interesting lessons?*

To avoid confusion over the type of "evaluation" required at this stage in the life of a textbook in a course or program, I would like talk about *textbook analysis in the implementation process.* The categories that a teacher can use are the same as in the selection process: the textbook provides content/explanations, examples, and exercises or tasks. The text might also provide illustrative or graphic materials that can be used for teaching purposes. Additionally, the publisher of the textbook might provide an instructor's manual that should help in the implementation of the materials. While the categories are the same, the purpose is much different and often much more urgent, since teachers can find themselves analyzing a textbook only hours before going into a class to teach a lesson that will be built around the materials in the text.

Getting an Overview of the Resources in the Textbook

Prior to implementing a textbook, a teacher needs to read the whole book—from start to finish, including any appendices. In working with inexperienced teachers, I've found that one of their mistakes in working with a textbook is not seeing it as a whole and not finding out about the text in detail before the first day of class. I have repeatedly had the experience of having a new teacher tell me near the end of a term that he or she has just discovered some useful feature of the textbook—something that was in a late section of the book or in an appendix. A basic rule of textbook implementation: You can only implement materials if you know they are there.

Teaching usually involves an overlapping cycle of presentation, practice, and evaluation. *Presentation* can involve introduction of new materials or information or a re-introduction for a review session; it can be direct or indirect; it is whatever the teacher does to get students started on a unit of study. *Practice* can be any type of activity, from a drill to writing an essay, from the least communicative form of repetition to an unscripted discussion; it is whatever the teacher sets up to help the students learn to do whatever it is they are studying in that unit. *Evaluation* is whatever the teacher does to find out what the students have learned. This teaching cycle is bounded by the academic calendar of the school system in which the class is taught; a class is always limited in time to the number of hours a week it will be taught and to any additional time that might be added for homework, if homework is appropriate in the setting.

Initial Reading of a Textbook

Before undertaking a detailed analysis of the textbook to be used in a course, a teacher can benefit from doing a general overview reading of the book. A reasonable series of questions that a teacher should ask during an initial reading should include the following.

1. **Presentation/Format:** What kinds of units does the book have? How is each organized? What kinds of illustrations or other graphic elements are used? How many of these graphic elements are there? How are they connected to the rest of the materials in the unit? What additional features does the book have beyond the basic units—appendices, index, glossary? Are there any ancillary materials such as workbooks or audiotapes?
2. **Content/Information:** What does each unit give me to present? What is each unit about?
3. **Practice:** What does each unit give me to use with my students for practice? Where are the exercises or tasks placed and how do they relate to the presentation of content? What connections are made between the activities provided in the various units?
4. **Evaluation:** What does each unit give me to use for evaluation of student learning? When will assessment occur during the term? How long will each activity take?
5. **Support for the teacher:** Is there an instructor's manual? Is there an introduction for the instructor that has information on using the book? Are the instructions for the activities clear enough for me to know exactly what the students and I are supposed to do?

This initial reading of the textbook should give the teacher an overview of the features of the book and of the ways that the textbook organizes its combination of content and activities. After gaining that overview, the teacher needs to analyze the text in more detail while making plans for using the materials over the time allowed for the course.

Analysis of the Content of the Textbook

Language textbooks differ considerably from those in other disciplinary areas. A biology textbook, for example, is dominated by presentation of information about biology—theory, examples, and definitions of terminology. The purpose of the book is for students to learn a certain segment of the body of knowledge that makes up the disciplinary area of "biology." Discussions of problems with public school textbooks for other disciplines often concentrate on two related areas: (1) inaccurate or incomplete content (see for example, Suidan et al. 1995) and (2) poor readability for the student audience because content experts do not necessarily understand how to present complex content for new, young learners (see for example, Britton, Woodward, and Binkely 1993). These problems should be of concern to ESL/EFL programs that use authentic materials as the basis for ESL/EFL study, especially those that use content-area textbooks as resources for ESL/EFL materials. Kearsey and Turner (1999) used genre analysis techniques to evaluate textbook materials written in Great Britain for secondary science courses; they reveal a text that is made up of very simple examples written for the audience (although probably not accessible to newcomers to that society), interspersed with hard nuggets of scientific writing to provide the content that is the real focus of the curriculum.

In contrast, ESL/EFL textbooks tend to be made up of two strands of content: (1) the linguistic content (grammar, vocabulary, skill area) and (2) the thematic content ("school," "gender issues," "Native Americans," and the topical content used to present and practice the linguistic content). The teacher can expect the topics in content-based materials to be emphasized and clearly visible. In most other materials, however, the teacher will need to look past the linguistic content to find out what themes have been included in the textbook. If, for example, the teacher notices in his or her initial analysis that a grammar textbook includes numerous examples and passages based on biographies of famous people, then he or she can plan to supplement the text with other materials and activities (visits to local museums, readings about people famous in the cultures of the students, and so on). The analysis-for-implementation angle on content involves both the linguistic and the thematic content of the textbook, as shown in Table 1.

Analysis of Exercises/Tasks in the Textbook for Implementation in Classes

While planning the ways in which the textbook will be used for the whole academic term, a teacher needs to be making concrete if tentative decisions about how different activities will be used during the academic term, asking questions such as those in Table 2.

Seeking Help in Implementation of the Textbook

Teachers have both formal and informal sources of information and support as they analyze textbooks for implementation. Formal resources include the instructor's manual as well as other written materials available in the school or program. These other materials can include a curriculum statement, course syllabi used in previous terms, and copies of handouts used by previous teachers. Additionally, many schools provide teachers with formal help through structured interactions with senior teachers and supervisors.

Informal support is generally available if teachers seek it. When teaching a course for the first time or for the first time with a particular textbook, teachers can sometimes get help with implementation of materials in a course by talking with colleagues who are teaching the same course or who have taught it before.

Table 1. Analysis of Content for Implementation in Teaching

Linguistic Content	What language is being taught? In what chunks and what sequence? What adjustments must be made to fit the program's curriculum? Are there any adjustments that I would like to make in content and sequencing to better fit my course and my students?
Thematic Content	What topics are used in each unit? What topics recur throughout the whole book? What connections can I make between these topics and the backgrounds/interests of my students? How can I make enriched use of these themes?

Table 2. Analysis of Teaching Activities for Implementation in Teaching

Which of the activities provided in this text-book will I do in class?	The teacher is looking for a variety of activities that can be used to meet the needs of different learners and to achieve the pedagogical goals of the course. Initial decisions can be made about using individual, pair, or small-group configurations for the activities. Experienced teachers also look for change-of-pace activities—a high-energy task, requiring a lot of moving around, balanced by something more contemplative.
Which activities in the textbook will I assign as homework?	This decision needs to be made on the basis of the purpose that homework has in this particular class. Generally, teachers use homework for follow-up practice and for activities that may have students engaging in "outside of class" use of English. Some teachers use homework to prepare students for new work, not just to review and practice things already presented.
Which activities in the textbook will I hold back to use for testing?	If no tests are provided by the text (or the instructor's manual), some activities might be reserved to use for testing.
Which activities in the textbook can be used for review later in the term?	Some activities might be reserved for review, or a variation on an activity might be used for review later in the term.
Which activities in the textbook require longer periods of time to accomplish—special projects?	The initial reading of the textbook is especially important for identifying tasks that would be useful for students to do but that require long-term planning by the teacher.
Which activities in the textbook might require special equipment that has to be ordered ahead of time?	In most settings, specific equipment requires extra effort and planning ahead.
Where are connections being made between various units of the book, connections that might require review?	By reading the whole book prior to the beginning of the term, the teacher can become aware of topics and themes that recur in the book. Connections can be made that give more coherence to the class.
Which activities in the textbook do I not want to do at all?	Because the fit between any textbook and the curriculum of a program will seldom be perfect, some parts of the text might not be appropriate for a particular course. Additionally, some content and activities might not fit a particular group of students. Equally important, there are things that may not fit our personalities as teachers and that we may not be comfortable doing. (For example, although I have colleagues who make wonderful use of music in their classes, I do not sing in class and would never attempt an activity that required it.)

CONCLUSION

These are the fundamental questions asked by teachers: What am I going to do in class (to achieve the goals of the program and of the students)? What are my students going to do in class (to achieve the goals of the program as well as their personal goals)? What are they going to do for homework (and how does that connect to what we do in class))? In the evaluation-for-selection process, those with the responsibility for choosing textbooks need to consider not just the fit between the curriculum and the textbook but also the practical issues of usability by teachers and by students. Once a textbook has been selected, teachers need to analyze the resources in the textbook to create a plan for daily lessons and for the whole course that helps them both implement and supplement what is already given in the most efficient and effective way (see Jensen's chapter on lesson planning in this volume).

In discussions written by some teacher educators, a common demand is that teachers be free agents—creating their own materials for their own students. Such discussions are built on a vision of the teacher as an individual, in his or her own classroom, making unique decisions for that unique group of students. In this vision, the commercially published textbook is a restraint forced upon teachers that limits their creativity (Ur 1996, Nunan 1988b). At the other extreme, and probably the source of some of the negative emotions that teacher educators express about textbooks, is the administrative desire for a "teacher-proof text" that can be taught by even the most untrained and unqualified of individuals; this magic textbook guarantees that the whole system or school has complete uniformity in the delivery of administratively selected content.

Of course, reality for most teachers lies somewhere between these two extremes. We are generally part of a larger system that does have legitimate concerns about being sure that all students receive instruction that leads to a more or less uniform result. At the same time, each of us is different in our background knowledge and personalities—as are our students. Having a textbook with appropriate content and a variety of possible teaching activities can serve both needs, giving some uniformity to the information and activities in class while expecting that different teachers will adapt, implement, and supplement the materials based on the needs of a particular class in a particular academic term.

DISCUSSION QUESTIONS

1. How are textbooks selected in the K–12 school system where you live? Discuss with a partner in your class.

2. If you are teaching in an intensive English program or some other type of college or university ESL program, how are textbooks selected for that program? How was the textbook chosen that you are using now? How do teachers have input into the selection process? Discuss your answers with classmates.

3. Publishers at TESOL conventions have noticed what is sometimes referred to as the "30-second evaluation." In those 30 seconds, a teacher picks up a textbook, flips through, and then puts it down to pick up another book for a brief study. Sometimes the short analysis leads to a purchase or to a request for an inspection copy. Discuss what information can be gained in conference exhibits. What kinds of things do you look for when you have only a minute or so to look at books before going on to the next conference event? Discuss your categories with classmates.

4. The appendices to this chapter provide two different checklists for evaluation of textbooks. Discuss the categories used in the two checklists and the approaches to textbook evaluation that appear to lie behind each system.

5. Reviews of textbooks in professional journals can be valuable sources of information in the evaluation-for-selection process. Textbook reviews can be found in publications such as the *TESOL Journal,* the *TESOL Quarterly,* and in the newsletters or journals of regional affiliates of TESOL. Such reviews generally provide brief summaries of the content and organization of a text along with some evaluation of any of a variety of textbook features. Because they present a colleague's considered opinion and understanding of the features of the textbook, they can provide the person or

group evaluating textbooks with additional information. From recent editions of one or more professional publications, select reviews of three textbooks that might be used for a course that you are now teaching or that you might teach. What criteria do the reviewers use as the basis for their evaluations of the textbooks? What additional information would you have wanted the reviewers to include? Discuss the reviews with your classmates.

SUGGESTED ACTIVITIES

1. Interview a teacher who works in the K–12 system where you live to find out (a) how teachers have input into the selection process for the textbooks they use, (b) any flexibility that teachers have in selecting books (perhaps choosing from a list of required books), and (c) any flexibility that teachers have in supplementing the text with additional materials. In class, compare the information that you obtain from several different teachers.

2. Based on a course that you have taught recently, that you are now teaching, or that you might teach in the future, modify the evaluation checklist in Appendix B to make it focus as closely as possible on that particular course. Discuss the changes that you have made with your classmates.

3. Based on reviews in recent issues of professional publications, select a textbook that seems potentially appropriate for a course that you are teaching or might teach in the future. Using as the evaluation tool one of the checklists in the appendices to this chapter or a version that you modify to fit the particular course, evaluate the textbook. Then, compare your evaluation with that of the published review. Report to your class on any insights that you gained from the review and any areas of disagreement between your evaluation and that of the reviewer.

4. Select a textbook that is used in a program where you are now teaching, have recently taught, or might teach in the future. (Select a textbook that you have not used before.) Approach the textbook as if you were going to be using it to teach a class—and the class begins soon! Read the textbook to gain an overview of its content and organization. Consider the (a) presentation/format, (b) content/information, (c) practice activities, (d) evaluation activities/instruments, and (e) support provided for the teacher. Prepare a short report to share the information that you have about the general purpose and design of the textbook. Include ideas about the general pattern that you would use to implement the text in an academic term.

5. With a partner, select one unit of the textbook that you analyzed in Activity 4 above. Using Table 2 on page 421, analyze the activities in that unit. Compare your analysis of how you would use the activities to your partner's analysis. Discuss similarities and differences in your plans for using the activities.

6. After completing Activities 4 and 5, decide on content or activities that you would like to add to complement or supplement the textbook. What is missing from the book that is required by your curriculum or by your students? Or by your teaching style?

FURTHER READING

Britton, B. K., S. Gulgoz, and S. Glynn. "Impact of good and poor writing on learners: Research and theory." In B. K. Briton, A. Woodward, and M. Binkley, eds. *Learning from Textbooks: Theory and Practice* (pp. 1–46). Hillsdale, NJ: Lawrence Erlbaum.

This useful discussion shows why simplified readings can make comprehension of content more difficult for learners. The authors also demonstrate a method for enhancing the readability of expert writing by adding connections and making relationships between ideas more explicit.

Chambers, F. 1997. "Seeking consensus in coursebook evaluation." *ELT Journal* 51(1): 29–35.

The author discusses the application of strategies from business for group decision making in the textbook evaluation and selection process. He makes a strong case for the importance of involvement of all teachers in a consensus-based model for shared decision making.

Ciborowski, J. 1995. "Using textbooks with students who cannot read them." *Remedial & Special Education* 16(2):90–102.

The overt audience for this article is teachers working with public school students in the United States who have had trouble learning to read—and therefore trouble learning from the textbooks used in their classes. However, the author's thoughtful analysis of the ways in which students are required to use textbooks in learning new content and skills can stimulate thinking about ways in which ESL/EFL students are expected to learn from their ESL/EFL textbooks. This article and others on student learning from textbooks suggest that ESL/EFL teachers should think about what it is that students are expected to do with their textbooks in their ESL/EFL classes and what students are supposed to learn from studying the textbooks.

Nelson, G. with J. Burns. 2000. "Managing information for writing university exams in American history." In Marcia Pally, ed. *Sustained Content Teaching in Academic ESL/EFL* (pp. 132–157). Boston, MA: Houghton Mifflin.

What content to use in textbooks is a particular challenge in ESL/EFL materials. We can't teach "pure grammar" or "writing in the abstract." The struggle to define the most appropriate content has led to both the content-based and the task-based approaches. This chapter—along with the rest of the book—argues for the use of the same content across an entire ESL course rather than following the tradition of having many different topics used in a single unit of a textbook or having each unit with a single topic. It also demonstrates how sustained content can be used to teach academic writing.

Tomlinson, B., ed. 1998. *Materials Development in Language Teaching*. Cambridge: Cambridge University Press.

This collection includes chapters on (1) data collection and materials development, (2) the process of materials writing, (3) the process of materials evaluation, and (4) ideas for materials development. In a chapter titled "What Do Teachers Really Want from Coursebooks?" H. Masuhara discusses the importance for materials development of needs analysis that provides information not just about the needs of learners but also about the needs and preferences of teachers.

Ur, P. 1996. *A Course in Language Teaching: Practice and Theory*. Cambridge: Cambridge University Press.

This methods book includes a textbook evaluation checklist (see page 186) along with helpful instructions for ways to analyze the criteria that will be used in a particular evaluation process. The section on "Using a Coursebook" exemplifies a common problem in methods books. The entire focus of this section is on probable limits and failings of a textbook and ways to overcome them with supplementary materials. That is, no distinction or transition is made from evaluation for selection to analysis for implementation.

 **WEBSITES**

Byrd, P. 2000. Issues in textbook selection and use: Resources from a variety of disciplinary areas.

Developed as part of the process of writing this chapter, this list includes resources that show the common concerns about textbooks across a variety of disciplines. The list will be updated on a regular basis. Suggestions for additions to the list can be e-mailed to the authors through a link provided on the site.

http://www.gsu.edu/~eslhpb/material/textbooks.htm

APPENDIX A

Sample Checklist for Textbook Evaluation

Source: Daoud, A.-M., and Celce-Murcia, M. 1979. Selecting and evaluating a textbook. In M. Celce-Murcia and L. McIntosh, eds. *Teaching English as a Second or Foreign Language* (pp. 302–307). New York: Newbury House.

The Checklist

The Textbook

	Excellent	Good	Adequate	Weak	Totally lacking
	4	3	2	1	0

a. Subject matter
   1. Does the subject matter cover a variety of topics appropriate to the interests of the learners for whom the textbook is intended (urban or rural environment; child or adult learners; male and/or female students)?
   2. Is the ordering of materials done by topics or themes that are arranged in a logical fashion?
   3. Is the content graded according to the needs of the students or the requirements of the existing syllabus (if there is one)?
   4. Is the material accurate and up-to-date?

b. Vocabulary and structures
   1. Does the vocabulary load (i.e., the number of new words introduced every lesson) seem to be reasonable for the students of that level?
   2. Are the vocabulary items controlled to ensure systematic gradation from simple to complex items?
   3. Is the new vocabulary repeated in subsequent lessons for reinforcement?
   4. Does the sentence length seem reasonable for the students of that level?
   5. Is the number of grammatical points as well as their sequence appropriate?
   6. Do the structures gradually increase in complexity to suit the growing reading ability of the students?
   7. Does the writer use current everyday language, and sentence structures that follow normal word order?
   8. Do the sentences and paragraphs follow one another in a logical sequence?
   9. Are linguistic items introduced in meaningful situations to facilitate understanding and ensure assimilation and consolidation?

c. Exercises
   1. Do the exercises develop comprehension and test knowledge of main ideas, details, and sequence of ideas?
   2. Do the exercises involve vocabulary and structures which build up the learner's repertoire?
   3. Do the exercises provide practice in different types of written work (sentence completion, spelling and dictation, guided composition)?
   4. Does the book provide a pattern of review within lessons and cumulatively test new material?
   5. Do the exercises promote meaningful communication by referring to realistic activities and situations?

d. Illustrations
   1. Do illustrations create a favorable atmosphere for practice in reading and spelling by depicting realism and action?
   2. Are the illustrations clear, simple, and free of unnecessary details that may confuse the learner?
   3. Are the illustrations printed close enough to the text and directly related to the content to help the learner understand the printed text?

Textbooks: Evaluation for Selection and Analysis for Implementation

	4	3	2	1	0

e. Physical make-up
 1. Is the cover of the book durable enough to withstand wear?
 2. Is the text attractive (i.e., cover, page appearance, binding)?
 3. Does the size of the book seem convenient for the students to handle?
 4. Is the type size appropriate for the intended learners?

The Teacher's Manual

a. General features
 1. Does the manual help the teacher understand the rationale of the Textbook (objectives, methodology)?
 2. Does the manual guide the teacher to any set syllabus for that level?
 3. Does the index of the manual guide the teacher to the vocabulary, structures, and topics found in the Textbook?
 4. Are correct or suggested answers provided for all of the exercises in the textbook?
 5. Is the rationale for the given sequence of grammar points clearly stated?

b. Type and amount of supplementary exercises for each language skill
 1. Does the Manual provide material for training the students in listening and understanding the spoken language?
 2. Does the Manual provide material for training the students in oral expression?
 3. Does the Manual suggests adequate and varied oral exercises for reinforcing points of grammar presented in the textbook?
 4. Does the Manual provide drills and exercises that enable the teacher to help the students build up their vocabulary?
 5. Does the Manual provide questions to help the teacher test the students' reading comprehension?
 6. Does the Manual provide adequate graded material for additional writing practice?

c. Methodological/pedagogical guidance
 1. Does the Manual help the teacher with each new type of lesson introduced?
 2. Does the Manual provide suggestions to help the teacher review old lessons and introduce new lessons?
 3. Does the Manual provide practical suggestions for teaching pronunciation and intonation?
 4. Does the manual provide suggestions to help the teacher introduce new reading passages?
 5. Does the Manual provide guidance to the teacher for introducing various types of written work?
 6. Does the Manual provide guidance to the teacher for evaluating written work and identifying the students' most serious mistakes?
 7. Does the Manual advise the teacher on the use of audiovisual aids?

d. Linguistic background information
 1. Does the Manual provide contrastive information for the teacher on likely pronunciation problems?
 2. Are English vocabulary items and English structures well explained?
 3. Are lists of cognate words (true and false cognates) provided for the teacher?
 4. Does the Manual provide information on grammar to help the teacher explain grammatical patterns presented in the lessons and anticipate likely problems (i.e., data from contrastive analysis and error analysis)?

APPENDIX B

Textbook Evaluation Checklist

Source: Patricia Byrd and Marianne Celce-Murcia

Evaluation of the fit	Yes (a good fit)	Perhaps (an adequate fit)	Probably not (a poor fit)	Absolutely not (wrong for curriculum, students, and/or teachers)
Fit between the textbook and the curriculum				
* fits curriculum/goals				
* has appropriate linguistic content				
* has appropriate thematic content				
* fits the pedagogical and SLA philosophy of the program/course				
Fit between the textbook and the students				
* explanations understandable and usable for students				
* examples understandable and usable for students				
* activities appropriate for students				
* thematic content understandable and culturally appropriate for students				
Fit between the textbook and the teachers				
* fits the language skills of our teachers				
* fits the knowledge-base of our teachers				
* provides explanations that can be used by our teachers				
* provides examples that can be used and expanded by our teachers				
* fits the needs and preferences of our teachers				
* provides in-book or instructor's manual support for teachers				
Overall evaluation of the fit of the book for this course in this program				
Should the text be selected?				

When the Teacher Is a Non-native Speaker

PÉTER MEDGYES

In "When the Teacher Is a Non-native Speaker," Medgyes examines the differences in teaching behavior between native and non-native teachers of English, and then specifies the causes of those differences. The aim of the discussion is to raise the awareness of both groups of teachers to their respective strengths and weaknesses, and thus help them become better teachers.

INTRODUCTION

It is commonplace to state today that English is the unrivaled lingua franca of the world, and that it is rolling ahead like a juggernaut. In our age of globalization, Fishman's remark that "the sun never sets on the English language" (1982, p. 18) rings truer than ever, and although there is no guarantee of eternal hegemony, the chances are that English will reign supreme for several more decades. The fact that the number of second and foreign language speakers of English far exceeds the number of first language speakers of English (Graddol 1997) implies that the English language is no longer the privilege of native speakers; the suggestion that Standard British English and American English should be superseded by English as an International Language can be heard with increasing frequency. Nevertheless, people who speak English as their native language continue to have a distinct advantage over those for whom it is a foreign tongue. Put differently, non-native speakers of English find it hard to compete with native speakers on equal terms, and this linguistic handicap applies to non-native teachers of English as well.

Native speakers and non-native speakers used to be considered two different and clearly distinguishable categories. In recent years, however, this view has come under heavy attack, as a growing number of researchers have discovered the ambiguities with which this dichotomy is loaded. New terms, alleged to better reflect the complex nature of linguistic heritage and profi-ciency, have been recommended to project new concepts and identities. Although there are persuasive arguments against the native/non-native dichotomy, most of them legitimate on any ground—linguistic, educational, ideological, or pragmatic—none of the alternative phrases have come into common use.

The controversy over native versus non-native distinction has also been brought to bear on language pedagogy and ELT methodology. The "native English-speaking teacher" (NEST) and its opposite, the "non-native English-speaking teacher" (non-NEST), have been deemed politically incorrect phrases, and those who still use them can expect to be accused of employing discriminatory language. Nevertheless, the superordinate terms "native speaker" and "non-native speaker" seem to persist in the language use of researchers and teachers alike. The reason for the perseverance of these terms may be that most teachers, as well as their students, *do* come from either English-speaking or non-English-speaking countries; most of them *are* either native or non-native speakers of English. But even a bilingual or polyglot whose identity may be equivocal seems to display dominant features of belonging. Therefore, it is suggested that the dichotomy, for all its shortcomings, should not be rejected, overlooked, or blurred, but rather subjected to close scrutiny.

This chapter attempts to do just that: it strives to examine differences in teaching behavior between NESTs and non-NESTs, and then specify the causes of those differences. By drawing on both empirical evidence and on experience, it argues that most of the archetypal deviations between the two groups of teachers are ultimately attributable to their divergent language backgrounds. This is not the same as suggesting that a high degree of English-language proficiency alone is a guarantee for successful teaching. Indeed, despite their linguistic impediment, non-NESTs have an equal chance of becoming successful teachers, and it is the advantages that they have over NESTs with which this chapter is chiefly concerned. Although pride of place is granted to the teacher's language proficiency throughout the discussion, there is no denying the importance of other attributes, most notably teaching qualifications, professional skills, and experience. (The role these attributes play in the teaching/learning process is examined in detail in other chapters of this volume.)

WHO IS THE NATIVE SPEAKER?

The Linguistic Perspective

Who *is* a native speaker? A native speaker of English is traditionally defined as someone who speaks English as his or her native language, also called mother tongue, first language, or L1. The next question that springs to mind is: What qualifies someone as a native speaker? Among the criteria for "native speakerhood," the most oft-cited and, at first glance, most straightforward one is birth (Davies 1991). That is to say, a native speaker of English is an individual who was born in an English-speaking country. The trouble with this is that birth does not always determine language identity. What about Christine, for example, who was born in the United States, but moved to Austria at the age of one, after she had been adopted by Austrian parents? Since she never learned to speak English, it would be odd to define her as a native speaker of English. Or take Kevin, born in the United States, who went to live in Togo with his family when he was four, and subsequently attended a French school. Is he a native speaker of English or French—or both, or neither? If not birth, is it childhood that underpins native speakerhood? But what is the range of childhood? Where does it begin and where does it end?

The situation becomes further complicated if we consider offspring from mixed marriages. There is eight-year-old Pablo, for example, whose father is Colombian and whose mother is Finnish. Provided both parents speak to him in their respective native language, Pablo becomes bilingual. However, if the family lives permanently in Australia, the boy becomes a trilingual speaker. Does this include the possibility that Pablo is a native speaker of English?

Another problem has to do with the fuzziness of geographical entities. Which countries qualify as English-speaking countries? The United States, the United Kingdom, Australia, and a few more. But how about such countries as India, Nigeria, or Singapore, where English, though widely spoken, is not the native language for the majority of the population and its use is limited to particular spheres of life? On the other hand, these countries also differ from countries like Poland, Peru, or Japan, where very few children encounter English at any great lengths before they have formal school instruction.

Recognizing the difficulty of setting up a division line between English- and non-English-speaking countries, Kachru (1985) arranged countries into three concentric circles. The *Inner Circle* includes nations where English is the primary language. The countries in the *Outer Circle* have been historically affected by the spread of English, often as colonies; in these multilingual settings English is the second language, generally the major *intranational* means of communication. The *Expanding Circle* involves nations which have accepted English as the most important international language of communication and teach it as a foreign language. However, in Kachru's visual representation the differences are not watertight and countries in each circle exhibit a great deal of variation and internal mobility.

The Educational Perspective

The native speaker model is not only the concern of linguists and sociolinguists, but is an issue which has fueled debate among language educators as well. The controversy became particularly acrimonious in the 1980s and early 1990s. There were a number of researchers who claimed that there is no such creature as the native or non-native speaker, an opinion well rendered by the title of a seminal book, *The Native Speaker Is Dead!* (Paikeday 1985). Ferguson formulated this radical approach as follows: "The whole mystique of the native speaker and the mother tongue should probably be quietly dropped from the linguist's set of professional myths about language" (1982, p. vii).

Considered to be useless, the native/non-native dichotomy was to be replaced by new concepts and new terms, including *more* or *less accomplished* and *proficient* users of English, *expert* versus *novice speakers,* and *bilingual speakers* to include both natives fluent in another language and non-natives fluent in English. In similar fashion, Kachru (1992) spoke of *English-using speech fellowships* to stress "we-ness" instead of the rigid "us and them" division.

In spite of the cogent arguments against the native/non-native separation, the polemic seems to have abated these days, and the weathered terms "native speakers" and "non-native speakers" are as widely used in the professional jargon today as ever. But why is this distinction so impervious to change? There are at least two possible answers. The more down-to-earth answer is that the majority of people are not borderline: they clearly belong to either the group of native speakers or to that of the non-native speakers of English. The more paradoxical answer is that the native/non-native epithet is useful, to quote Halliday, "precisely because it isn't too closely defined" (cited in Paikeday 1985, p. 64). In a similar vein, Davies remarked that "the native speaker is a fine myth: we need it as a model, a goal, almost an inspiration. But it is useless as a measure; it will not help us define our goals" (1996, p. 157).

Speaking of goals, what are the goals of language learning? For most learners, the ultimate aim is an effective use of the target language. People seldom aspire to more than what they find professionally and personally necessary. It is a case of quid pro quo. Remember that the attainment of native proficiency in English not only demands strenuous efforts, but it may also lead to a loss of native identity in one's L1—a price many would find far too great to pay.

Nevertheless, can any learner hope to achieve full mastery of a second language, with all its linguistic subtleties and cultural allusions? Most researchers agree that this is an impossible task for the overwhelming majority after puberty, but exceptions do exist. This induces further questions: What are the criteria for native proficiency? What is the cut-off point between native proficiency and various levels of non-native proficiency? Researchers are rather skeptical about the feasibility of designing adequate measuring instruments to separate the two groups. This being the case, Davies (1991) points out, membership to one or the other category is not so much a privilege of birth, education, or language proficiency as a matter of self-ascription. In other words, anyone who claims to be a native speaker is one—with the proviso, Kramsch observes, that they are in fact accepted "by the group that created the distinction between native and non-native speakers" (1997, p. 363). However, just as non-native outsiders typically do not want to turn into natives, native insiders are not always eager to admit non-natives. In short, mobility between the two groups is possible but rare.

The Ownership of English

Granted that the majority of non-native speakers do not metamorphose into natives, can they still claim ownership of English? Or does English remain the property of natives by virtue of their better language proficiency and stronger cultural affiliation?

In this regard, Widdowson forcefully sums up the view of many other ELT professionals. He argues that English is an international language, which implies that "it is not a possession which [native speakers] lease out to others, while still retaining the freehold. Other people actually own it" (1994, p. 385). In a similar way, Norton contends that English "belongs to all the people who speak it, whether native and non-native, whether ESL or EFL, whether standard or nonstandard"

(1997, p. 427). The validity of these statements can be proven most spectacularly by the example of such eminent twentieth-century novelists as Conrad, Nabokov, or Soyinka, all of them being non-native speakers of English, writing in English. Far more generally, however, it is claimed that any non-native speaker who engages in genuine communication can use the second language creatively, molding it until it becomes an adequate tool of self-expression. In short, the ideal of the multilingual, multicultural speaker to replace that of the monolingual, monocultural speaker is gaining ground in the professional literature (Kramsch 1997).

This brings us to the subject of English as an International Language (EIL). While EIL as a linguistic construct is accepted by most researchers, it is more controversial whether EIL is a *special* kind of Standard English with norms distinct from those of other standard Englishes, or *any* kind of Standard English used in international settings. It has also been observed that, short of a proper description of its grammar, EIL is no more than an idealization, an amalgam of beliefs and assumptions about rules and norms to which people adhere with varying degrees of success (Medgyes 1999a). Paradoxically, it is teachers and learners from monolingual EFL settings who typically are doubtful that deviation from standard norms is acceptable (Jenkins 1998), while the staunchest advocates of EIL as a self-contained entity are most commonly found among applied linguists and teachers who speak English as their native language.

Hiring Policies

Let us now turn to the teaching profession within the framework of the native/non-native dichotomy. While non-native speakers of English are generally contented with their non-native status, non-native teachers of English often feel disadvantaged and discriminated against. Their complaint is mainly leveled at unequal job opportunities: teaching applications from even highly qualified and experienced non-NESTs often get turned down in favor of NESTs with no such credentials. For example, here is a letter of rejection sent to a non-NEST applicant by the principal of a language school in London: "I am afraid we have to insist that all our teachers are native speakers of English. Our students do not travel halfway round the world only to be taught by a non-native speaker (however good that person's English may be)" (Illés 1991, p. 87).

Language schools which advertise themselves as employing only native English speakers often do so with the excuse that NESTs are better for public relations and improve business. Another explanation is their clients' alleged needs. With reference to newly arrived immigrants in the United States, an American teacher argued that "a teacher's lack of native instincts about American English usage and cultural expectations could be detrimental to [the immigrants'] chances in job interviews" (Safadi 1992).

In spite of these arguments, hiring practices in the two ELT strongholds, the United States and the United Kingdom, are in a state of transition. While in the past, major organizations involved in ELT often shut their eyes to discrimination against non-NESTs, albeit never officially endorsing it, today the same institutions are in the habit of making clear and progressive policy statements. Incidentally, the most important resolution was the one passed by the Executive Board of TESOL in 1991, which not only expressed its disapproval of discriminatory hiring policies, but also decided to take steps to abolish all forms of restriction based on the applicant's native language.

It must be admitted, though, that discrimination in hiring policies is not a priority issue in most parts of the world, mainly because the percentage of non-NESTs in search of a teaching job in English-speaking countries is negligible. Perhaps to a lesser extent today than in the past, non-NESTs typically work in EFL and NESTs in ESL environments. While brain drain does not seriously affect the language teaching profession, other forms of discrimination are far more acute.

The Center and the Periphery

The Center/Periphery dichotomy was imported into ELT by Phillipson (1992). To the Center belong powerful Western countries where

English is the native language, whereas the Periphery is constituted of underdeveloped countries where English is a second or foreign language. ELT today is a huge enterprise and, as Phillipson argues, organizations as well as individuals from the Center have high stakes in maintaining its operation. Research projects, aid programs, and training courses are run by and/or in the Center, quite often under the auspices of powerful government agencies such as the United States Information Service and the British Council. Standard ELT methodologies are often based on the needs and background of the NEST who teaches in an ESL rather than an EFL environment (Holliday 1994). Recommendations submitted by native speaker experts are often taken at face value and acted upon by local authorities.

In ordinary classrooms in the Periphery, Phillipson states, NESTs are invariably granted jobs with a salary far exceeding that paid to local teachers. In certain countries and historical circumstances, even backpackers with no teaching qualifications or teaching experience are extended a warm welcome. The ELT business is backed by a book trade which serves the interests of the Center and disseminates its prevailing ideologies and methodologies. Communicative language teaching often is imposed on Periphery classrooms while tried and tested methods are condemned, despite their popularity among teachers and learners (Liu 1999). Most textbooks imported from the Center not only destroy national ELT publishing, but also are ill-suited for local needs, projecting a "to-whom-it-may-concern" aura. As a consequence, Periphery experts become more and more dependent on the Center-based ELT establishment (Canagarajah 1999), and the attainment of sustainability remains but wishful thinking as a rule.

The needs and attributes of local teachers had been all but ignored until the 1990s, when an interest in the non-NEST gained momentum. This recognition was long overdue considering that there are far more non-NESTs in the world than NESTs, and that their numbers are rapidly growing. In addition to numerous articles and a collection of essays written on the subject (Braine 1999), a full-length book is wholly devoted to an analysis of the distinguishing features of non-NESTs (Medgyes 1994). Most of the ideas presented below have been borrowed from this book.

NESTS AND NON-NESTS: PROS AND CONS

As mentioned above, native speakerhood is an intricate concept, which includes birth, education, the environment in which the individual is exposed to English, the sequence in which languages are learned, levels of proficiency, self-confidence, cultural affiliation, self-identification, and political allegiance. There are two ways out of this maze. One is to shortcut it by abandoning the neatly defined categories of native versus non-native, offering instead the image of a line, along which non-natives move towards the native end. The other route leads through the retention of the native/non-native construct for all its apparent weaknesses. From a theoretical stance, the first option appears more promising. From a practical point of view, however, the second one is more straightforward, if only because the larger part of the world's teaching pool falls into two fairly clear-cut categories: NESTs and non-NESTs. Hence the decision to choose the second route for the purposes of this chapter.

Most commonly, a non-NEST may be defined as a teacher:

- for whom English is a second or foreign language;
- who works in an EFL environment;
- whose students are monolingual groups of learners;
- who speaks the same native language as his or her students.

This definition only partially applies to a much smaller group, that of non-native teachers who work in ESL environments, often with students from heterogeneous linguistic backgrounds. By extension, the NEST may be defined as the opposite of the non-NEST, most characteristically as a teacher who speaks English as a native language.

The basic assumption, then, is that NESTs and non-NESTs are two different species, and teachers belong to either this or that category. Given this, four assumptions follow (Medgyes 1994):

1. NESTs and non-NESTs differ in terms of their language proficiency
2. They differ in terms of their teaching behavior
3. The discrepancy in language proficiency accounts for most of the differences found in their teaching behavior
4. They can be equally good teachers on their own terms

In order to validate his assumptions, Medgyes carried out a survey which included 325 teachers from 11 countries; 86 percent of the participants were non-natives and 14 percent natives. Although the sample was fairly large, the author suggested caution in interpreting the results, largely because the project was based on questionnaire-elicited self-reports, which reflect a teacher's *stated* behavior rather than his or her *actual* behavior; there may be a wide gap between the two. In any case, the results reported here have been obtained from this survey; for detailed statistical analyses, see Reves and Medgyes 1994.

The Linguistic Handicap

Not surprisingly, the primary advantage attributed to NESTs lies in their superior English-language competence. Their superiority was found particularly spectacular in their ability to use the language spontaneously and in the most diverse communicative situations. Non-NESTs, on the whole, are well aware of their linguistic deficiencies and of the all-pervasive nature of their handicap. In no area of English-language proficiency can they emulate NESTs: survey participants viewed themselves as poorer listeners, speakers, readers, and writers. True enough, long stays in English-speaking countries, hard work, and dedication might help narrow the gap, but very few non-NESTs are ever able to catch up with their native colleagues. When asked

to identify the major source of difficulty, most non-NEST participants mentioned vocabulary, together with idiomatic and appropriate use of English. This was followed by problems in speaking and fluency, pronunciation, and listening. Grammar featured to a far lesser extent and so did writing skills, whereas reading skills and cultural knowledge were not even mentioned.

Many non-NESTs participating in the survey commented about their inferiority complex caused by the defects in their English-language proficiency and about some kind of cognitive dissonance due to the double role they played as both teachers and learners of the same subject. All these problems together constitute the dark side of being a non-NEST. In view of these results, the first assumption, namely that NESTs and non-NESTs differ in terms of their language proficiency, may be regarded as confirmed.

Differences in Teaching Behavior

When asked whether they perceived any differences in teaching behavior between NESTs and non-NESTs, 82 percent of the participants gave a positive answer. Furthermore, they stressed that the discrepancy in language proficiency accounted for most of the differences found in their teaching behavior. Thus both the second and third assumptions above seem to have been borne out by the survey findings. The collated results are supplied under comprehensive headings in Table 1.

In explaining the differences, many participants pointed out that non-NESTs are usually preoccupied with accuracy, the formal features of English, the nuts and bolts of grammar, the printed word, and formal registers. Many lack fluency, have a limited insight into the intricacies of meaning, are often in doubt about appropriate language use, have poor listening and speaking skills, and are not familiar with colloquial English. It is only logical to assume that non-NESTs place an emphasis on those aspects of the language that they have a better grasp of. If they have a restricted knowledge of context, they tend to teach unfamiliar language elements

Table 1. Perceived Differences in Teaching Behavior Between NESTs and Non-NESTs

NESTs	Non-NESTs
own use of English	
speak better English	speak poorer English
use real language	use "bookish" language
use English more confidently	use English less confidently
general attitude	
adopt a more flexible approach	adopt a more guided approach
are more innovative	are more cautious
are less empathetic	are more empathetic
attend to perceived needs	attend to real needs
have far-fetched expectations	have realistic expectations
are more casual	are stricter
are less committed	are more committed
attitude to teaching the language	
are less insightful	are more insightful
focus on:	focus on:
fluency	accuracy
meaning	form
language in use	grammar rules
oral skills	printed word
colloquial registers	formal registers
teach items in context	teach items in isolation
prefer free activities	prefer controlled activities
favor group work/pair work	favor frontal work
use a variety of materials	use a single textbook
tolerate errors	correct/punish for errors
set fewer tests	set more tests
use no/less L1	use more L1
resort to no/less translation	resort to more translation
assign less homework	assign more homework
attitude to teaching culture	
supply more cultural information	supply less cultural information

in a context-poor environment or in isolation. Preoccupied with their own language difficulties, they are reluctant to loosen their grip over the class. As group work and pair work often create unpredictable situations full of linguistic traps, non-NESTs favor more secure forms of classwork, such as lock-step activities. Similar reasons were claimed to account for the non-NEST's preference for standard coursebooks, which by their very nature provide security. For the same reason, non-NESTs are inclined to adopt a more controlled and cautious pedagogic approach. Incidentally, these results tie in nicely with more recent data reported by Samimy and Brutt-Griffler (1999). (Further divergences displayed in Table 1 are dealt with in the following sections.)

Before providing arguments to prove the fourth assumption, let us turn to a discussion of certain advantages attributed to non-NESTs over NESTs.

The Bright Side of Being a Non-NEST

One item in the questionnaire inquired whether the participants thought the NEST or the non-NEST was a better teacher. While an approximately equal number of votes went for either option (27 percent for NESTs and 29 percent for non-NESTs), 44 percent inserted "both," an alternative which had not even been supplied in the questionnaire. The proportion of participants who chose non-NESTs as their favorites is high, especially given their linguistic inferiority. It follows from this that non-NESTs should be in possession of certain unique features that NESTs lack. But what are they? What gives non-NESTs their competitive edge? What assets enable them to make up for their linguistic handicap?

Partly inspired by the teachers participating in the survey, Medgyes advanced a second set of assumptions. Namely, compared to NESTs, non-NESTs can:

1. provide a better learner model;
2. teach language-learning strategies more effectively;
3. supply more information about the English language;
4. better anticipate and prevent language difficulties;
5. be more sensitive to their students;
6. benefit from their ability to use the students' mother tongue.

Below, we elaborate on these six assumptions.

1. Non-NESTs Provide a Better Learner Model

Any language teacher can set two kinds of models before the students: a language model and a learner model. Medgyes's basic claim is that, while NESTs make better *language* models, non-NESTs can provide better *learner* models. In terms of a language model, non-NESTs are relatively hindered, since they are learners of English just like their students, albeit at a higher level. Although a more proficient non-NEST is likely to provide a better language model than a less proficient one, non-NESTs cannot rival NESTs. In compensation, as it were, only non-NESTs can be set as proper learner models, since they *learned* English after they acquired their native language, unlike NESTs who *acquired* English as their native language—two completely different processes (Krashen 1981).

Another area of investigation concerns a comparison of learning success and teaching efficacy. In this regard, two questions may be asked. The first one is, Do you have to be a successful learner in order to become a successful teacher? Medgyes's answer is a tentative yes, arguing that a successful teacher by definition is a successful learner of English: poor language learners do not make good language teachers. This is not to deny that there are unsuccessful learners equipped with outstanding teaching qualities which help them offset their language deficiencies. However, such teachers are few and far between, and hence only those non-NESTs should be set as models who are successful learners themselves—anything less is a compromise.

The second question is, Does every successful learner become a successful teacher? The answer to this question is a definite no. If a perfect command were a sufficient prerequisite for successful teaching, Medgyes contends, NESTs would by definition be better teachers—which they are not! With respect to non-NESTs, too, it is common experience that successful learners turn out to be lousy teachers. This may be explained by several factors, most evidently by inadequate professional training. It appears, then, that success in learning English is a necessary but not a sufficient condition for success in teaching it.

2. Non-NESTs Teach Language-learning Strategies More Effectively

It is a truism that some people pick up languages more quickly and effectively than others. Success depends on several things, such as background, motivation, age, intelligence, aptitude, level of education, and quality of instruction, as well as knowledge of other foreign languages. An additional factor with a bearing on success is the use of *language learning strategies*. What are they? Language learning strategies, according to Wenden and Rubin (1987), are specific actions employed to facilitate the learning and recall of one or several components of proficiency. Facilitation implies not only making the process easier, but also making it "faster, more enjoyable, more self-directed, more effective, and more transferrable to new situations" (Oxford 1990, p. 8).

All learners employ language learning strategies. Success with learning largely depends upon the ability to select the most appropriate strategy for dealing with a specific learning task. Good learners are capable of gleaning a repertoire of strategies which suits their personality as well as their particular learning environment. However, the majority of language learners grope in the dark unless they are fortunate enough to receive tailor-made support from knowledgeable teachers. Although researchers have long been intrigued by the question of the teachability of strategies, hardly any tangible results have been produced thus far. After having interviewed seven extremely successful language learners, Stevick concludes that there is no common pattern emerging: everyone seems to learn in his or her own way. What works for some learners utterly fails for others: "Hardly a clear model for an aspiring language student who wants to profit from their example!" (1989, p. 138).

As successful learners of English, non-NESTs are supposed to be conscious strategy users, able to tell which strategies have worked for them and which have not. Thus they stand a better chance of sensitizing their students to the employment of strategies than their native-speaking colleagues do. Their ability consists in imparting their own learning experiences as well as providing assistance for students to discover other strategies that should work specifically for them. To be fair, NESTs have also pursued strategies in their contact with foreign languages. However short-lived or distant their learning experience may have been, they may harness it in their job as teachers of English.

3. Non-NESTs Supply More Information About the English Language

Any language teacher's expertise consists of three components: (a) language proficiency, (b) language awareness, and (c) pedagogic skills. While language proficiency implies skills *in* the target language, language awareness involves explicit knowledge *about* the language, which does not necessarily assume near-native language proficiency. In his or her role as an instructor, the teacher obviously exhibits varying degrees of pedagogic skills as well.

Returning to a comparison of teaching behavior between NESTs and non-NESTs shown in Table 1, non-NESTs were found to be more insightful than NESTs. This follows from the differences in the process of mastering the English language. Their acquisition being largely unconscious, NESTs were perceived as largely unaware of the internal mechanisms directing language use and, therefore, less able to give their students relevant information about the target language. On the other hand, non-NESTs have amassed a wealth of knowledge about the English language during their own learning process. Their antennae can intercept as a possible source of problems even the minutest item which NESTs may take no notice of. Put differently, whereas NESTs have better intuitions about what is right and wrong in language use, non-NESTs have deeper insights into what is easy and difficult in the learning process.

Naturally, NESTs are also capable of refining their language awareness. They can improve, provided that they avail themselves of the opportunities offered by teacher education, foreign language learning, and, above all, experience. Those NESTs who have spent an extended period of time in a host country and have taken pains to learn the students' mother tongue should be incomparably more knowledgeable than those who have not.

4. Non-NESTs Better Anticipate and Prevent Language Difficulties

Having jumped off the same springboard as their students, non-NESTs are intrinsically more perceptive about language difficulties than

NESTs. For them to discover trouble spots requires little time and energy; messages can be exchanged merely by winking an eye. Most non-NESTs have developed a "sixth sense," and those who have been on the job long enough are able to predict, with a fair degree of accuracy, what is likely to go wrong before the student opens his or her mouth. In possession of this anticipatory device, non-NESTs stand a good chance of preventing linguistic problems which materialize in the form of deviant usage or, for want of a better word, errors.

As Table 1 shows, NESTs and non-NESTs behave differently with regard to error correction. Since native speakers generally view language as a means of achieving some communicative goal, they tend not to make a fuss about errors unless they hinder communication. In contrast, non-NESTs are notorious for penalizing errors, grammatical errors in particular, probably because they regard English primarily as a school subject to be mastered and only secondarily as a medium of genuine communication. Another reason for their heavy-handed attitude may lie in their deficient knowledge of English. In any case, teacher education should perhaps place more emphasis on strategies for error *prevention* than on techniques of error *correction*.

As far as NESTs are concerned, those expatriates who stay put in one country manage to gather far more experience about their students' specific language problems than those who drift from place to place, year after year. Since language is a major carrier of, and in fact is inseparable from, a people's culture, familiarity with the local language can bring NESTs closer to their students' cultural roots and shed light on the students' inability to comprehend a specific language element.

Speaking of culture, Table 1 indicates that NESTs and non-NESTs also differ in terms of their attitude toward teaching culture. By virtue of coming from an English-speaking country, NESTs are able to provide more information about their native culture. However, the more the English language spreads and diversifies in the world, the less it remains the privilege of NESTs, which harks back to the issue of English as an International Language addressed earlier.

To be sure, the non-NEST teaching in a monolingual class has far more background information about his or her students than even the most well-informed NEST can. Indirectly, this knowledge is instrumental in enhancing the teacher's capacity to anticipate and prevent cross-cultural difficulties.

5. Non-NESTs Are More Sensitive to Their Students

As Table 1 demonstrates, non-NESTs are potentially more sensitive on several counts. First, they can be more responsive to the students' real needs. In contrast, NESTs, working either with linguistically heterogeneous groups in an English-speaking country or with monolingual groups overseas, probably have but a vague picture of their students' needs and aspirations, including their linguistic, cultural, and personal backgrounds.

Second, thanks to thorough familiarity with the teaching/learning context, non-NESTs are in a position to set realistic aims for students. For example, they are more cognizant of the constraints of the national curriculum, the teaching materials available, and the examinations to be taken. They are also better able to gauge the level of motivation that students studying in a particular type of school are supposed to have.

Third, due to their deeper understanding of the prevalent circumstances, non-NESTs are usually stricter than their native-speaking colleagues. If they are aware of an imminent language examination, for instance, they will adapt their teaching methods to the stringent exam requirements; this may involve having to assign more tests and more homework. Living in a kind of symbiosis with the students, non-NESTs cannot afford to be as casual as NESTs.

It must be added, however, that a higher degree of sensitivity is merely a potential: just as there are non-NESTs who exhibit precious little empathy, some NESTs are amazingly understanding. It must be repeated here that, in addition to teacher education, the best sensitivity training for NESTs is to learn the language of the host country.

6. Non-NESTs Benefit from Their Ability to Use the Students' Mother Tongue

As native speakers of the local language, non-NESTs can obviously take advantage of this shared competence, provided they are allowed to harness it.

To use or not to use the mother tongue? This was one of the thorniest problems in language teaching methodology throughout the twentieth century as the pendulum swung from one extreme to the other. Until recently, the monolingual principle predominated, mostly advocated by NESTs, if only because they themselves felt disabled by their lack of competence in the students' first language (L1). As a consequence, non-NESTs were made to feel either defensive or guilty at their inability or unwillingness to conduct a class entirely in English. In the 1990s, however, the judicious use of the learners' native language was once again legitimized. Among the reasons for its comeback is the recognition of the L1 as the most genuine vehicle of communication between non-NESTs and their students in the monolingual classroom. Another major reason is that the native language proves to be a powerful teaching/learning tool in countless situations. Suffice it to say, today non-NESTs may switch into the L1 at their discretion, and so may NESTs—to the extent they can.

WHO IS MORE VALUABLE, THE NEST OR THE NON-NEST?

One item in the survey questionnaire inquired about the ideal proportion of NESTs or non-NESTs to be employed in schools. Whereas 52 percent of the participants said that they would prefer an equal number of NESTs and non-NESTs, 17 percent favored more NESTs and 31 percent more non-NESTs. A further breakdown of the data reveals that both native and non-native participants would rather have a majority of their own language group in the staff; as there were more non-NEST than NEST participants in the sample, the balance of choice tilted towards non-NESTs.

Be that as it may, the idea of a mixed staff is wishful thinking for most schools in most parts of the world. Short of NESTs, schools use the few around as efficiently as possible. On grounds of their native proficiency in English, in many places NESTs are assigned advanced level groups and conversation classes. Elsewhere, in order to make their contribution accessible to everybody, they are torn into as many small bits as there are groups in the school. Needless to say, NESTs are not always pleased with this task allocation—a recurrent complaint is that they are regarded as rare animals in a zoo (Árva and Medgyes 2000).

These results correlate strongly with the results of another item in the questionnaire which asked: Who is the better teacher, the NEST or the non-NEST? As mentioned previously, a similar percentage favored either NESTs or non-NESTs, whereas nearly half the respondents said that the two groups had an equal chance of success. When asked to justify their choice, participants typically referred to the differences summarized in Table 1. The same attribute was often judged as a positive feature by some and a negative feature by others.

Apart from a few extremists, survey participants expressed moderate views. They agreed that since each group had its own strengths and weaknesses, they would complement each other well in any school. A proportionate number of natives and non-natives would give the further advantage of offering a variety of ideas and teaching methods. Some respondents referred to the desirability of native/non-native interaction and cooperation; "There is a lot we can learn from each other!" one person remarked.

Organized collaboration and its most intensive form, team teaching, have become fairly well researched areas in recent years (Nunan 1992). Team teaching is a system whereby a group of teachers jointly undertake a program of work with a group of students. In the context of NEST/non-NEST collaboration, the largest and best documented team teaching initiative has been developed in Japan, called the Japan Exchange and Teaching Program, also known as the JET program (Tajino and Tajino 2000). The program's primary aim is to recruit young native speakers from English-speaking countries to teach under the guidance of, and together with, qualified Japanese teachers of English.

Let us reiterate: NESTs and non-NESTs teach differently in several respects. Non-NESTs are (more or less) handicapped in terms of their command of English. Paradoxically, this shortcoming is their most valuable asset, as it helps them develop capacities that NESTs must struggle to acquire. NESTs and non-NESTs are potentially equally effective teachers, because in the final analysis their respective strengths and weaknesses balance each other out. *Different does not imply better or worse!* Thus the question, Who's worth more, the native or the non-native? is pointless, conducive to drawing wrong conclusions from the differences discovered in teaching behavior. It is suggested, therefore, that language teachers should be hired solely on the basis of their professional virtues, regardless of their language background. The data and the arguments supplied thus far seem to be powerful enough to validate the fourth assumption put forward on page 434, namely that NESTs and non-NESTs can be equally good teachers on their own terms.

CONCLUSION: THE IDEAL TEACHER

In recent literature, the concept of the ideal teacher has gained some notoriety, especially in relation to the native/non-native dichotomy. It appears that the glory once attached to the NEST has faded, and an increasing number of ELT experts assert that the "ideal teacher" is no longer a category reserved for NESTs. It is becoming a generally accepted view that outstanding teachers cannot be squeezed into any pigeonhole: all outstanding teachers are ideal in their own ways, and as such are different from each other. The concept of the ideal teacher resists clear-cut definitions, because there are too many variables to consider.

In order to get a better grasp of the ideal teacher, however, let us suppose that all the variables are kept constant momentarily, except for the language proficiency component. In relation to non-NESTs, the question arises: Does

somebody with a better command of English stand a better chance of becoming an ideal teacher? In other words: Is a more proficient speaker a more efficient teacher as well? All other things being equal, the answer is yes: *the ideal non-NEST* is someone who has achieved near-native proficiency in English. The importance of this attribute is seldom questioned in the literature. Britten (1985) claims that an excellent command of English is a major selection criterion and a good predictor of a non-NEST's professional success. Lange (1990) rates language proficiency as the most essential characteristic of a good language teacher, and Murdoch (1994) calls it the bedrock of the non-NEST's professional confidence. Liu's (1999) study conducted among non-native TESOL students at a university in the United States confirms that English-language proficiency is generally recognized as a make-or-break requirement in ESL environments as well. Therefore, it must be a valid claim that the most important professional duty that non-NESTs have to perform is to make linguistic improvements in their English.

In contrast, the success of NESTs hinges on the extent to which they can acquire the distinguishing features of non-NESTs. In view of this, *the ideal NEST* is someone who has achieved a fair degree of proficiency in the students' native language. Cook (1999) must be right in saying that the multicompetent, multilingual teacher is qualitatively different and incomparably more capable than the monolingual teacher.

The trouble is that "all other things" are never equal in the classroom, so the phrase "the more proficient, the more efficient" is only partially valid. In this regard, Samimy (1997) mentions certain factors which are as important as language proficiency, particularly relevant teaching qualifications and extent of one's teaching experience. Seidlhofer reiterates this point: "There has often been the danger of an automatic extrapolation from *competent speaker* to *competent teacher* based on linguistic grounds alone, without taking into consideration the criteria of cultural, social and pedagogic appropriacy" (1996, p. 69). Indeed, an issue waiting to be addressed is the complex relationship between the different aspects of teachers' classroom practice. The study of the non-NEST remains overall a largely unexplored area in language education.

In conclusion, within the framework of the native/non-native division, the ideal NEST and the ideal non-NEST arrive from different directions but eventually stand quite close to each other. Both groups of teachers serve equally useful purposes in their own ways. In an ideal school, therefore, there should be a good balance of NESTs and non-NESTs, who complement each other in their strengths and weaknesses. Given a favorable mix, various forms of collaboration are possible, and learners can only gain from such cross-fertilization.

DISCUSSION QUESTIONS

1. What is your native language? Are there any "complicating factors" concerning your linguistic and cultural identity?
2. Do you agree or disagree with the native speaker/non-native speaker distinction? What are your arguments for or against?
3. **a.** If you are a native speaker of English, do you think that the English language is your property, or are you willing to share the "copyright" with non-native speakers?
   b. If you are a non-native speaker, do you believe you have the right to "tinker" with the norms and rules of English to the same extent as native speakers have?
4. Take a close look at Table 1 in this chapter. Which are the points your own experience supports and which are the ones it challenges?
5. In addition to the six advantages assigned to non-NESTs, can you think of any more? In addition to their linguistic superiority, can you list any further assets for NESTs?

SUGGESTED ACTIVITIES

1. In a replication study, Davies (1996) measured differences between native and non-native speakers of English in terms of grammaticality judgments. His sample consisted of applied linguists with experience as English teachers. All the non-native participants (18 persons)

were highly proficient speakers of English; the native speakers (16 persons) were mostly speakers of British English. Davies included 12 sentences in his survey, and the participants were required to rate the sentences on a 4-point scale as follows:

1 The sentence sounds perfect. You would use it without hesitation.
2 The sentence is less than perfect—something in it just doesn't feel comfortable. Maybe lots of people could say it, but you never feel quite comfortable with it.
3 Worse than (2), but not completely impossible. Maybe somebody might use the sentence, but certainly not you. The sentence is almost beyond hope.
4 The sentence is absolutely out. Impossible to understand, nobody would say it. Un-English.

Here are the 12 sentences to be rated on the scale:

1 Under no circumstances would I accept that offer.
2 Nobody who I get along with is here who I want to talk to.
3 We don't believe the claim that Jimson ever had any money.
4 The fact he wasn't in the store shouldn't be forgotten.
5 What will the grandfather clock stand between the bed and.
6 I urge that anything he touch be burned.
7 All the further we got was to Sudbury
8 That is a frequently talked about proposal.
9 Nobody is here who I get along with who I want to talk to.
10 The doctor is sure that there will be no problems.
11 The idea he wasn't in the store is preposterous.
12 Such formulas should be writable down.

Grade these sentences on the 4-point scale. Remember to give 1 point for a perfect sentence and 4 points for a totally unacceptable sentence.

Here are the results of Davies's study:

Sentence	Mean Natives (N=16)	Non-natives (N=18)
1	1.1	1.1
2	2.7	3.0
3	1.6	1.8
4	1.7	1.6
5	2.7	3.5
6	1.7	2.5
7	3.3	3.0
8	1.2	2.2
9	2.3	2.5
10	1.0	1.0
11	1.7	1.5
12	3.0	3.3

Note that the aggregate mean for all 12 sentences for natives and non-natives is 1.99 and 2.23, respectively. This suggests that natives are more tolerant of uncertainty with regard to grammaticality. Compute your own score and compare it with the mean of natives and non-natives in Davies's sample. Are you more or less tolerant than either group?

2. Give an honest answer to this question: Suppose you were the principal of a commercial language school in your country. Who would you prefer to employ?
a. I would employ only native speakers even if they were not qualified teachers.
b. I would prefer to employ NESTs, but if needed I would choose a qualified non-NEST rather than a native without ELT qualifications.
c. The native/non-native issue would not be a selection criterion (provided the non-NEST was a highly proficient speaker of English).

Ask three or four colleagues about their choices. If there are discrepancies between your views, justify your preference. Has anyone hedged their bets by saying "It depends"? Ask them to explain their ambiguous stance.

3. If you were asked the above question in the context of an ordinary state school, would your choice be different? How about your colleagues' choices?

4. In groups, collect as many features of the successful language teacher as you can. Suppose that the "ideal teacher" is someone who has a maximum score of 25 points. Individually, allocate as many points as you wish for each feature within the maximum 25 points. Then, in groups again, compare your scores and argue for your allocation.

5. Interview ten non-native speakers of English to find out what traits they value most in language teachers. Do they specify any features which are more characteristic of non-NESTs than NESTs?

 **FURTHER READING**

Braine, G., ed. 1999. *Non-native Educators in English Language Teaching*. Mahwah, NJ: Lawrence Erlbaum.
A collection of essays that articulates the concerns, struggles, and triumphs of non-native teachers, mostly those living and working in the United States.

Davies, A. 1991. *The Native Speaker in Applied Linguistics*. Edinburgh: Edinburgh University Press.
A thorough discussion of the native/non-native dichotomy from an applied linguistic perspective, going beyond the immediate concerns of the language teacher.

Graddol, D. 1997. *The Future of English?* London: The British Council.
A thought-provoking book about the current position and the future of English as the lingua franca of the world. It examines the possible effect of globalization on the status and spread of English.

Medgyes, P. 1999. *The Non-native Teacher*. Revised second edition. Ismaning, Germany: Hueber Verlag.
A provocative book analyzing the differences in teaching attitudes between NESTs and non-NESTs, with language improvement exercises for the non-native teacher.

Phillipson, R. 1992. *Linguistic Imperialism*. Oxford: Oxford University Press.
A passionate and much-cited analysis of the causes and impact of the dominance of English worldwide. The book criticizes several ruling dogmas in ELT.

Building Awareness and Practical Skills to Facilitate Cross-Cultural Communication

ELI HINKEL

Hinkel's chapter points out the importance of developing cultural competence when teaching and learning a second language, noting that cultural assumptions affect practically all aspects of language use, even though they may not be obvious to native speakers or L2 learners. It offers examples of cultural impact on language use and provides guidelines for teaching culture.

INTRODUCTION

In language teaching and research on language, the term *culture* includes many different definitions and considerations that deal with forms of speech acts, rhetorical structure of texts, sociocultural behaviors, and ways in which knowledge is transmitted and obtained. Culture may find its manifestations in body language, gestures, concepts of time, hospitality customs, and even expressions of friendliness. While all these certainly reflect the cultural norms accepted in a particular society, the influence of culture on language use and on the concepts of how language can be taught and learned is both broader and deeper. To a great extent, the culture into which one is socialized defines how an individual sees his or her place in society.

Although attaining linguistic proficiency is essential for learners to be considered communicatively competent, particularly in the case of ESL learners, this is not sufficient. On the whole, to become proficient and effective communicators, learners need to attain second language (L2) sociocultural competence. Knowing how to say *thank you*, for example, does not automatically confer the knowledge of when to say thank you, how often to say thank you, and whether any additional action is called for. Quite reasonably, learners first apply the standards that exist in the first language (L1) communities where they were socialized. People who

interact with ESL students have commented that some learners seem to express gratitude excessively for small considerations, even to the point of embarrassing the person they are speaking to. Other learners may seem downright rude because they do not say thank you when expected to. If a receptionist at an office spends a lot of time trying to help someone but fails to provide concrete help, it may not be obvious to an ESL student that a *thank you* is warranted. After all, the receptionist did not provide any real assistance, and isn't it his or her job to help? However, if no thanks is given, the receptionist may not be likely to even attempt to help in the future. Not understanding sociocultural expectations could impact non-native speakers' (NNSs') ability to function in a L2 community.

Expressing thanks is just a small example. Teachers of L2 writing often encounter student essays that contain large excerpts of text copied verbatim from books, Internet sites, or other published sources. However, in the eyes of learners from some cultures, copying from a published source does not necessarily represent an unethical act (*"published" means for the public to use, right?*). In fact, learners from some cultures may view copying from a source as a means of expressing respect for the author's ideas and displaying their familiarity with the material. However, the negative outcome of copying the text in their papers could be severe in an English-language college or university where such copying constitutes plagiarism, which may be punished by the student's dismissal from the institution.

Hymes (1996) emphasizes that the learning of culture is an integral part of language learning and education because it crucially influences the values of the community, everyday interaction, the norms of speaking and behaving, and the sociocultural expectations of an individual's roles. He further notes that those who do not follow the norms of appropriateness accepted in a community are often placed in a position that exacerbates social disparities and inequality.

Today, when the numbers of ESL/EFL students have grown dramatically worldwide, it is becoming increasingly clear that the learning of a second culture does not take care of itself. Thus, L2 learners cannot always make the best of their educational, professional, and vocational opportunities until they become familiar with fundamental L2 cultural concepts and constructs. Most importantly, an ability to recognize and employ culturally appropriate ways of communicating in speech or writing allows learners to make choices with regard to linguistic, pragmatic, and other behaviors.

Although traditionally courses and texts for language teachers concentrate on teaching L2 linguistic skills, it may be difficult to separate the teaching and learning of English from the culture of its speakers. For example, what represents polite ways of speaking and the appropriate ways of writing an essay may depend on culturally dependent concepts that are closely bound up with the linguistic skills needed to speak or write well in the L2.

THE VISIBLE AND THE INVISIBLE CULTURE

In L2 teaching, the term *culture* has been employed to refer to distinctly different domains of people's lives. It can be used to refer to the literature, the arts, the architecture, and the history of a particular people. When asked about their native culture, many L2 learners and ESL/EFL teachers alike would undertake to describe the history or geography of their country because these represent a popular understanding of the term *culture*. In addition, some definitions of culture can include style of dress, cuisine, customs, festivals, and other traditions. These aspects can be considered the visible culture, as they are readily apparent to anyone and can be discussed and explained relatively easily.

Yet another far more complex meaning of culture refers to sociocultural norms, worldviews, beliefs, assumptions, and value systems that find their way into practically all facets of language use, including the classroom, and language teaching and learning. The term *invisible culture* applies to sociocultural beliefs and assumptions that most people are not even aware of and thus cannot examine intellectually. Scollon and Scollon (1995) state that the culturally determined concepts of what is acceptable, appropriate, and expected in one's behavior is acquired during the process of socialization and, hence, becomes inseparable from an individual's identity. For example, in the classroom, the roles of the student and the teacher are defined by the sociocultural values of the larger community and the society. If students believe that the teacher is responsible for explaining the material and that speaking up in class is considered rude, presumptuous, and selfish, the fact that the teacher simply instructs students to participate in discussion may do little to change learners' notions of what is appropriate and how they may be viewed by others if they actually speak in class. Most teachers, even those with minimal classroom experience or exposure, know how difficult it can be to convince some students to speak in front of their classmates, whereas other students may appear to have trouble allowing classmates an opportunity to have their turn.

Why Second Culture Learning Does Not Take Care of Itself

The complexity of teaching culture lies in the fact that, unlike speaking or writing, culture does not represent a separate domain of L2 instruction; instead, the learning of the L2 culture makes learners better communicators. In language learning and teaching, the crucial sociocultural principles that determine the norms of appropriate and polite behavior and language use within the frameworks of the society represent the invisible culture. As Stewart (1972, p. 16) comments, "[T]he typical person has a strong sense of what the world is really like, so that it is with surprise that he discovers that 'reality' is built up out of certain assumptions commonly shared among members of the same culture. Cultural assumptions may be defined as abstract, organized, and general concepts which pervade a person's outlook and behavior." To members of a particular community and culture, these assumptions appear to be self-evident and axiomatic. On the other hand, they are not always shared by members of other cultures whose values are similarly based on unquestioned and unquestionable fundamental assumptions and concepts. It is also important to note that ways of using language (e.g., speaking, listening, reading, and writing) and sociocultural frameworks in different communities may conflict to varying extents (Hinkel 1999).

Learners' awareness of sociocultural frameworks and the concepts they acquire as a part of their socialization into beliefs, assumptions, and behaviors remain predominantly first-culture bound, even for advanced and proficient learners (Hinkel 1999). As Byram and Morgan (1994, p. 43) point out, "[l]earners cannot simply shake off their own culture and step into another . . . their culture is a part of themselves and created them as social beings . . . ."

SECOND OR FOREIGN LANGUAGE: IDENTIFYING LEARNERS' NEEDS AND GOALS

There is little doubt that learners who live and/or study in English-speaking communities have a much greater need for developing their cultural competencies than do those who study EFL as a part of their foreign language requirements. The learners' actual goals in attaining English proficiency may serve as guides for determining their needs in learning culture. For example, if learners intend to enter English-medium colleges or universities, their need for L2 cultural competencies may be different from learners simply enrolled in weekend conversation classes. In many settings, however, instruction highlighting the influence of culture on second language use can be made effective and productive when working on particular L2 tasks or activities.

Those learners who live, study, or work in English-speaking communities have a particularly acute need to become aware of how the use of English they are exposed to reflects the sociocultural norms of the L2 community. For these individuals, a lack of language skill that prevents them from speaking and writing according to the norms accepted in the community can be particularly costly and even damaging in terms of lost opportunities for better grades, jobs, professional and economic advancement, or even social relationships. In the case of teenagers, university students, and educated adults, the pragmatic and sociocultural norms of L2 use in speaking and writing can and should be taught, and these learners are most likely to benefit from both explicit and implicit instruction in the L2 culture. In general terms, the purpose of teaching culture together with other language skills is to increase learners' interactional as well as linguistic competencies.

TEACHING CROSS-CULTURAL AWARENESS IN THE LANGUAGE CLASSROOM

Because the culture of any community has many facets and manifestations, it would be practically impossible to deal with all of them in the classroom and prepare students for the many situations that they may encounter in the course of their functioning in ESL/EFL environments. However, many important aspects of teaching the second culture can be brought forth and addressed via classroom instruction, and some of these are discussed below. The most important long-term benefits of teaching culture may be to provide learners with the awareness and the tools that will allow them to achieve their academic, professional, social, and personal goals and become successful in their daily functioning in L2 (or EFL) environments.

Recent studies, as well as teachers' experiences, have shown that NNS students in colleges and universities in the United States, Canada, and other English-speaking countries do not always follow the norms of politeness and appropriateness commonly accepted in their L2 communities despite having lived in those countries for several years (Hinkel 1996, Hymes 1996). Similarly, in their academic studies, L2 learners may experience difficulties because they do not always understand what is expected of them and do not have access to the necessary sociocultural concepts that are ubiquitously manifested in the academy (Johns 1997). For example, when they are assigned to read material at home, many professors expect that university students will actually "master" the content and be prepared to discuss and apply it. NNS students are often seen as coming to class unprepared because they may not always understand that a relatively high degree of familiarity with the material is implicit when academic reading is assigned. To compound the problem, the learners may have difficulty understanding the text or they may be unwilling to participate in class discussions. In any of these situations, the instructor (and even the native speaker [NS] classmates) may form somewhat negative impressions of the NNSs' academic skills and preparation.

Causes and Outcomes of Sociocultural Values

Because the sociocultural norms for politeness, appropriateness, and propriety are acquired during socialization, learners, in their daily interactions with NSs, are exposed only to the *outcomes* of linguistic and other types of behaviors and *not their causes*. For example, when their classmates are reluctant to share lecture or textbook notes, many learners simply conclude that their NS classmates may not like them and are unwilling to help them. However, the reluctance to share notes may stem from several sociocultural constructs that are fundamental in many English-speaking communities: the value of intellectual property, self-reliance, and the right of an individual to refuse a request with which he or she is not comfortable. In addition, in many U.S. colleges and universities, students believe that they are expected to do their own work and are given credit based on their individual effort and achievement. However, in the situation above where the learner wants to borrow class notes, neither the ESL learner nor the NS classmate who has the notes may even question why the request was made and refused. In general terms, the "behavioral prescriptions," the term coined by Stewart (1972), are assumed to be known to most (if not all) socially competent adults and, hence, are rarely overtly discussed: a need for such a discussion would imply one's lack of basic and essential social competence.

The Importance of Noticing

In learning about the impact of sociocultural norms on language use, the first step is noticing that these norms exist in all languages, including learners' L1s. To become prepared for a practically infinite number of L2 interactions, learners need to become astute and consistent people-watchers. Building on their observations of their L1 sociocultural norms and behaviors, the next task in culture learning is to separate individual behaviors from those that are culturally determined. For example, repeated politeness routines, behaviors, and body language (e.g., eye contact) probably signal that these speech acts and behaviors are socioculturally acceptable (and/or expected) in a particular community. Once learners note a particular routine or behavior on several occasions from several different individuals, they can investigate its sociocultural purposes and causes. An ability to identify the sociocultural purposes of L2 linguistic behaviors in a community allows learners to identify cultural patterns in situations, to understand how they are realized in other situations, and to anticipate their manifestations in the future.

The fundamental factors to consider in all interactions include: the gender of the speaker or the hearer, their respective ages, similarities or disparities in their social statuses (e.g., even if a professor wears blue jeans to class, he or she still has a higher status than a student does), the social distance between the speaker and the hearer (e.g., class friends, acquaintances, or strangers), the purposes of the speech events, the time available for the interaction, and its physical setting/location. In their investigations, learners should pay careful attention to politeness routines, expressions, and phrases that are employed by speakers or hearers, and then identify the reasons for the use of these language devices. For example, they could observe how a student asks the teacher to take a look at his or her paper (*Could you look at my paper and see if I'm on the right track?*). Were the participants in the interaction of the same age, gender, and social status? What politeness expressions did the speaker use? How did the hearer respond? Why did the hearer give this particular response? What politeness devices were used in the response and why?

Practice, Practice, Practice

The tasks associated with training learners to be careful and sharp people-watchers and observers of culturally appropriate and common interactional routines and expressions can serve as a basis for very productive and effective activities that are interesting and enjoyable for learners. For intermediate ESL learners, a teacher could make a basic checklist of linguistic and social features of speech events and interactions to encourage students to carry out their "field research" in cafeterias, restaurants, stores, and libraries. In EFL settings, a similar field study could take place in the students' L1, since the primary goal of this activity and people-watching is to make learners aware of the linguistic and social factors that play a crucial role in interactions in any language or culture. In teaching EFL, the next step would be to compare the politeness and conversational routines in the learners' L1 to those found in English-language materials (e.g., movie clips, recorded audio and

video interviews, taped dialogues that accompany many student texts, or perhaps even materials for standardized test preparation).

When working with high-intermediate or advanced ESL learners, teachers can make similar checklists for expanded and more sophisticated linguistic, social, and behavioral features of interactions, such as the location where the interaction takes place (an office, a hallway, a street), the availability of time (a scheduled appointment, a lunch hour, a break between classes), and/or the complexity of the task entailed in the speech act. In addition, students can be assigned to investigate various types of speech acts such as making appointments, seeking clarifications, or responding to requests, and even longer conversational exchanges such as making small talk or negotiating the time and the place of meetings. On the other hand, advanced EFL students can participate in role plays, short skits, or mini-plays, for which they write scripts to center on linguistic features of particular speech acts or types of conversational exchanges in their L2.

In addition to learning to note the linguistic and situational variables in interaction, it is important that learners focus on the sociocultural features of speaking and behaving. In general, however, it would not be very comfortable or appropriate for interactants to become involved in discussing the reasons that a particular linguistic structure is used or a specific interactional behavior is displayed. To return to an earlier example, if the request for notes is refused, this may not be a good opportunity to ask why. However, at a later time, another individual, such as a different classmate, a roommate, or better yet, a teacher, can be asked to explain the sociocultural causes for a particular behavior. Although many native speakers of English may not be aware of the reasons for their own behaviors, they are usually aware of "behavioral prescriptions" in abstract terms. That is, most native speakers would be able to tell the difference between rudeness and what is considered to be polite or even acceptable in a particular situation and, if asked, some may even be able to say why some expression, phrase, or behavior would be perceived as more polite than another.

TEACHING CULTURE AND THE WAYS OF SPEAKING

Much research carried out in pragmatics and sociolinguistics over the past three decades has focused on the sociocultural norms of politeness and appropriateness in performing various types of speech acts, such as requests, apologies, compliments, and complaints. The linguistic and social features of such specific speech acts can be taught in the classroom with a focus on repeated and frequently routinized uses of language, along with the differences according to the social status of the speaker and the hearer, and other situational factors. Similarly, appropriate body language and gestures can also become a part of the explicit instruction in speaking and listening classes. However, most importantly, the key to productive culture teaching is to provide learners with the tools to enable them to become aware of the sociolinguistic norms reflected in the ways of speaking in the community. Thomas (1983) explains that violations of cultural norms of appropriateness in interactions between NSs and NNSs often lead to sociopragmatic failure, uncomfortable breakdowns in communication, and the stereotyping of NNSs. She points out that when many NNSs display inappropriate language behaviors, they are often not even aware that they do. The teaching of ways of speaking in the L2 has to include developing learners' heightened awareness of the sociocultural features of interaction so as to provide them appropriate choices.

The Pragmatic Function and a Linguistic Form

In the teaching of L2 speaking and pragmatics, two overarching goals lie at the focus of instruction. The *pragmatic function* (i.e., the sociocultural purpose/goal) of speech acts, such as requests, apologies, compliments, and complaints, can be found in practically every curriculum for teaching speaking. The *linguistic form* of speech acts and conversational routines is one of the most easily accessible and ubiquitous areas of teaching L2 speaking, e.g., *Give me a penny* vs. *Could you/would you give me a penny*. The pragmatic function of these expressions is the same (request), but the speaker's choice of form may cause different responses from the hearer. For example, in order to increase learners' linguistic repertoire, the majority of ESL/EFL textbooks for speaking devote a great deal of attention to the forms of polite and casual expressions, idioms, and short dialogues, and even their appropriate pronunciation and intonation. One reason for this is that transfer of intonation from L1 to L2 can have very subtle negative consequences for interaction.

Sociocultural Variables in Interaction

What makes a particular expression or speech act situationally appropriate is not so much the linguistic form or the range of the speaker's linguistic repertoire, but the *sociocultural variables*, which are rarely addressed in explicit instruction. Partly for this reason, it is not uncommon to hear ESL learners say *How is it going, What's up*, or *Later* to peers, professors, and even university deans.

Such socioculturally inappropriate greetings and conversational closures, as well as other speech acts, are likely to raise an eyebrow or two, but as has been mentioned, their impropriety has little chance of being overtly discussed, and thus, the learning value of the experience may be lost. The sociocultural variables that can make a perfectly acceptable expression unacceptable in different interactions or settings reflect the invisible aspects of L1 or L2 culture that do not easily lend themselves to textbook exercises or listings of expressions. Nonetheless, it is the sociocultural features, such as gender, age, and the social status of the participants in the interaction that can create pragmatic failure (Thomas 1983).

For example, a lesson on conversation openers is very common and can be found in many ESL/EFL textbooks. Usually, most lessons (or textbook chapters) start with a few models: *Good morning/afternoon. How are you (today/this evening)?, How is it/ everything going?, What's up?, How are you doing?, How do you like this weather/Isn't this weather wonderful/terrible?, How do you like this city?*. Few of these resources, however, distinguish between those utterances that are appropriate in peer-level interactions and those that should be used in conversational exchanges with hearers who have a different sociocultural status. In such examples, furthermore, the situational variables are rarely taken into account: while it is very appropriate to open a conversation with a brief mention of the weather with an acquaintance in the cafeteria, it may not be a good opener when asking a bank teller to cash a check or a bus driver for route details. Similarly, *What's up?* and *How's it going?* are used almost exclusively in short and casual encounters with friends, but are not the best options when talking in a business or professional context to a waiter, a store clerk, an office receptionist, or a doctor.

Variability of Politeness

One activity for developing learners' awareness of the *variability* of politeness and appropriateness in interactions with different types of hearers and situations in which various conversational openers are used is to conduct field observations and experiments. In an experiment to determine the sociocultural and situational appropriateness of a speech act, ESL learners can ask their NS friends or roommates to evaluate the degree of politeness entailed in each of the conversational openers and explain the factors that make one expression "softer" or more appropriate than another. For example, which expression seems more polite: *I want to make an appointment for 3 o'clock, I would like to make an appointment for 3 o'clock,* or *May/Could I make an appointment for 3 o'clock?* What are the specific words and/or constructions that make one expression more polite than the other? Why is the question form used in one of these? Are there situations in which the least polite expression can be used? Who are the people (the speaker and the hearer) in these situations, and do they have an equal social position?

The results of such experiments can be discussed in pairs or small groups so that with the teacher's guidance students are able to identify the linguistic, pragmatic, and situational features of language that come into play in conversational

exchanges. In follow-up activities and role plays, students can put to use what they have learned as an outcome of their observations and experiments. They can be assigned to visit local shops, libraries, university offices, or other places in the community where they can practice their speaking skills in real-life situations.

A Pragmatic Force and the Linguistic Form

Another important characteristic of real-life interactions is determining the *pragmatic force* (i.e., interactional/conversational purpose) of expressions used in daily interactions. For example, *How are you (today/this morning)?* or *How is it going?* are not intended to be real questions or conversation openers. Rather, their pragmatic force is to be a greeting to signal to hearers that they are recognized and acknowledged. As an outcome, these formulaic expressions do not require a response, beyond the formulaic (*Fine, Great, Good, OK*). On the other hand, these expressions contrast with *How have you been?* or *How is everything/this term/your class going?*. Because the linguistic form of *How have you been (lately)?* and formulaic expressions, such as *How are you?* is similar, many learners interpret their pragmatic force to be equivalent. The field research or experiments carried out by pairs or small groups of students to investigate the varying pragmatic force of such expressions can be very beneficial in making them aware of the divergences between the form and the conversational intent of pragmatic routines in English. Other such investigations can include a great number of formulaic conversational expressions and exchanges, in which the pragmatic force may be difficult for learners to determine since it is not always apparent from the linguistic form and content. Examples include *Call me some time* vs. *Call me on Tuesday; Let's get together/have lunch sometime* vs. *Let's get together/have lunch on Friday; Call me if you have any questions* vs. *Call me any time; Do you have any questions?* (it is now time to ask questions, if you have them) vs. *I'll be happy to answer all your questions during my office hours* (please do not ask me any questions now but come to my office at the designated time); *Your paper needs a little work* (this expression does not mean necessarily that the paper needs only a little bit of work to be improved) vs. *Maybe you need to spend more time on your homework* (this does not mean that spending more time without greater effort will result in better grades).

Many conversational routines are closely tied to the sociocultural variables that affect the interactional effect of an expression or routine, and these variables can be taught to learners at practically all levels of proficiency, from beginning to highly advanced. For example, when and to whom to say *thank you* can be taught at the beginning level. In EFL settings, to raise learners' awareness of the important sociocultural dimensions of conversations, students can be asked to gather similar information in their native language. In pairs or small group discussions, learners can determine what characteristics of language (e.g., the linguistic form, stress, or tone) make one expression more polite than another. Then learners can be taught to identify parallel (but not necessarily similar) L2 features that can make a difference in the appropriateness of L2 conversational expressions and routines.

CULTURE IN THE TEACHING OF WRITING

In English, what is appropriate and inappropriate in academic written discourse is highly conventionalized (Swales 1990). In practically all U.S. and Canadian ESL programs in colleges and universities, a great deal of attention, time, and resources are devoted to the teaching of academic writing. L2 writing instruction focuses on such fundamental features of written academic discourse as the organization (e.g, introduction, body, conclusion, and other discourse moves), the presence and the placement of the thesis statement, the structure of the paragraph (e.g., the topic sentence), the rhetorical support for the thesis included in every paragraph, and an avoidance of needless digressions, repetition, and redundancy, among many other factors. The reason that these features of academic writing need to be explicitly and persistently taught to ESL/EFL students is that they represent

conventionalized (and prescribed) characteristics of academic genres that are not necessarily found in written discourse in rhetorical traditions other than the Anglo-American one. For example, educated L2 learners who were socialized in other rhetorical traditions are rarely aware that a clear thesis statement should be placed close to the beginning of one's essay. Similarly, as mentioned previously in terms of plagiarism versus copying, various sociocultural concepts and prescriptive behaviors play an important role in determining what can or cannot be included in academic discourse. There are even sociocultural differences regarding what can or cannot be discussed in an academic essay.

The Sociocultural Construction of Writing and Literacy

In writing instruction, learners are typically presented with models and examples of paragraphs and essays to demonstrate the discourse paradigms commonly accepted in Anglo-American writing. However, as many teachers know from experience, learning to write in accordance with the rhetorical formats and norms expected in English-language academic discourse can be a difficult and tedious process. L1 socialization regarding written discourse paradigms usually has so much influence on learning to write in the L2 that often, even with explicit instruction, learners are not able to recognize the rhetorical features of the L2 discourse, much less produce these features (Hinkel 1994). As in most L2 interactions and communications, in the course of writing instruction, learners are faced with the outcomes, and not the causes, of the L2 sociocultural norms and conventions, making it harder for them to understand and apply what they are instructed to do. (*Why should the thesis be placed at the beginning of an essay if I know that it should be in the conclusion? Why does the teacher say that this example is not clear when I think that it is very clear?*)

Stewart (1972, p. 3) explains that when faced with cross-cultural contradictions and uncertainties, "people tend to impose their own perspectives in an effort to dispel the ambiguity" created by the norms of appropriateness found in a second culture and to "assume unconsciously that their own ways are normal, natural, and right." Another outcome of the need to resolve contradictions is that the ways of the other culture are therefore seen as "abnormal, unnatural, and wrong." Stewart further notes that presumptions of the superiority of one's own culture and its ways of being and doing are characteristic of "most peoples of the world." Because literacy represents one of the most highly valued and prized domains of socialization in many societies, it stands to reason that many L2 learners of writing may reject discourse frameworks that are at odds with those specific to their own L1 socialization to literacy and the value associated with the appropriateness of writing in a particular way.

When teaching paragraph and essay structure, most ESL/EFL teachers know that the topic sentence and the thesis statement are usually placed near the beginning of a piece of writing in the Anglo-American tradition. The reason that the main idea is stated at the outset is very similar to the organization of spoken information in various languages; the teacher can work with the sociocultural factors that affect discourse organization in speech and writing at the same time.

For example, in English, speakers are expected to present their points in a manner that is more direct than is common among speakers of many other languages (Scollon and Scollon 1995). In contrast, it is considered almost requisite in Japanese and Chinese cultures to engage in social conversations to establish a relationship before making one's purpose known. That is, in these cultures the main point of a conversation comes closer to the end of the discourse. Similarly, in writing, in the Chinese and Japanese rhetorical tradition, the main point of the piece of writing does not come until the end because the writer needs to lead the reader gently to the conclusion, which is expected to be clear and obvious by the time it is stated at the end (or sometimes, not even stated at all). If in speaking, vague and indirect hints are considered to be more socially acceptable, then in writing, stating one's point directly and early may be viewed as presumptuous and excessively forward. Similarly, in the Anglo-American rhetorical tradition, it is important that the main idea or the purpose for writing is stated

at the outset, and writers undertake to support their thesis with additional information, intended to validate their main points.

Writing within Sociocultural Contexts of Language Use

Teaching combined, parallel sociocultural features when working with various L2 skills not only helps learners to understand the influence of sociocultural factors on how language is used, but also establishes a context for explaining why members of a particular culture do things in a particular way. Furthermore, learners can thus see a larger picture of the culture in which the language is used.

In the teaching of L2 writing, teachers may draw on many examples from speaking and establish parallels to help learners develop cultural awareness in language use. One of the thorniest problems in the teaching of writing in English is that learners often do not provide a sufficient amount of support and detail in their writing to make their points meaningful and convincing. In many cultures other than Anglo-American, the right to speak is considered to be the prerogative of those who have the authority to speak. Similarly, in writing, learners often believe that detailed support is excessive and unnecessary because readers are not really concerned with "trivial" descriptions. They may also think that they have little of value to say and that providing too much detail implies a lack of humility. To help learners take a different view of the necessary detailed support expected in L2 writing, teachers may need to provide explicit instruction on L2 reader expectations, the value of explicit explanations in the Anglo-American rhetorical tradition, and their uses in writing.

THE TRICKY NATURE OF SECOND OR FOREIGN LANGUAGE READING

By and large, two main types of materials are employed in teaching reading: highly controlled and often simplified readings from ESL/EFL textbooks, on the one hand; and authentic materials that vary in their level of difficulty, on the other. Textbook materials are most often used to develop learners' reading tactics and strategies and to improve their vocabulary base. In contrast, authentic texts can include a great variety of genres, such as introductory and advanced textbooks, scholarly articles, print media publications on hobbies, health, politics, and sports, how-to books, and literature for readers of all ages. Although most books on teaching reading distinguish between reading for pleasure and reading for information, visual media (TV, videos, and the Internet), realistically speaking, have reduced the numbers of those who read for pleasure. As a result, a majority of readers, especially when they are reading in their L2, read for information.

Culture in Reading Textbooks

Because ESL/EFL textbooks present a limited and controlled range of ideas, vocabulary items, and culturally-dependent concepts, they may not be the best means of explaining how the second culture affects language use. However, even within the limited thematic and lexical scope of textbook readings, learners may encounter comprehension difficulties that have to do with culture, since cultural inferences often need to be made to understand text (and context). For example:

> Treatments that are unconventional, or out of the ordinary, have gained so much prestige and attention that the U.S. government has created an Office of Alternative Medicine . . . . Many people have lost faith in modern medicine because researchers have been unable to find cures for a variety of problems, from cancer to the common cold (Broukal 1994, pp. 58–59).

In this textbook excerpt, learners often do not see the connection between the implied low prestige of unconventional treatments and the creation of a government office. In fact, some of them believe that the sentence is constructed backwards and that the author of the textbook has obviously made a mistake—the first sentence in this excerpt should have stated that because the U.S. government created an Office of Alternative Medicine, unconventional treatments gained much prestige. In other words, the government approval surely brings about the prestige. Reading may turn out to be problematic if learners are often expected to rely on their own experience to provide textual inferences and construct the context. In the second sentence in the above example, a reference to "modern" medicine and the disappointing results of medical research may be so dramatically misinterpreted that some learners misunderstand the text completely. Specifically, alternative medicine is modern because the interest in it has arisen only recently, and why should the people be disappointed when the government is doing its best?

This demonstrates the complexity of the invisible culture that can confound learners even in an intermediate level textbook, specifically designed for ESL/EFL reading instruction. As we can see, a considerable amount of background teaching and explanation may be necessary for learners to interpret the text appropriately and to identify its main points. Understanding the text can be an even more daunting task when reading involves authentic materials.

The Cultural Load of Authentic Texts

Culture teaching in L2 reading goes far beyond instruction in vocabulary, idioms, and collocations, all of which are essential for understanding the meaning of the text. Context- and culture-specific connotations and implications of word and phrase meanings also need to be addressed. More urgently, however, sociocultural meanings and values greatly affect a learner's ability to comprehend text and the context in which it is employed. In authentic texts, such as those excerpted from advanced print media (i.e., news magazines and literature), culture-specific references, allusions, metaphors, and symbolism play a prominent role. However, instructing learners to rely on their background knowledge and experience is not always productive or helpful.

In teaching ESL, it is relatively easy to obtain diverse types of reading materials and to gradually increase their cultural and linguistic complexity. Most importantly, however, the teaching of culture and its impact on text comprehension needs to be addressed at all levels of proficiency in order to build learners' awareness of cultural implications and references, without which few texts can be understood. For advanced learners, materials on popular hobbies, science, and even introductory college textbooks can provide a relatively smooth transition to more complex readings such as authentic literature.

For ESL/EFL purposes, literature should be chosen carefully to allow learners an opportunity to comprehend the text and enjoy it. However, the amount of work expended on pre-reading and preparing learners for reading literature may be sufficiently great for teachers to weigh its benefits relative to the cost (Carrell and Eisterhold 1988). In EFL environments, in addition to textbooks, materials from many Internet sites, English-language newspapers, or free brochures for tourism and travel can provide access to texts that contain fewer culture-bound and advanced metaphors and allusions because they are oriented for readers in various geographic locations and of varied language skills. Such materials allow the teacher to concentrate on the culture-specific references and sociocultural values invariably present in most texts, but they may not be so numerous and complex that learners are unable to comprehend the reading material. For example:

> Instead of counting sheep, the next time you have trouble sleeping, try putting socks on your feet. A researcher says people with chronically cold feet might drift off faster if they warm their feet with socks or a hot water bottle . . . . She and her colleagues didn't directly test whether socks or water bottles promote sleep. But they did analyze data from 18 healthy young men who participated in studies . . . . The report appears in today's issue of the journal *Nature* (*Seattle Times*, September 2, 1999, Health and Science Section, p. 3).

This passage provides a few cultural references that the teacher can discuss and explain, such as *counting sheep, a hot water bottle, testing data directly*, and the fact that reports *appear* in journals (instead of, for example, *are printed*). While *counting sheep* and *a hot water bottle* may be easy to explain, *testing data directly* refers to a cultural concept associated with research and analysis that many ESL/EFL learners find culturally bound. That is, events can be observed, but in academic reports and presentations they are analyzed and tested to obtain proof and validation (Stewart 1972). This concept is also helpful in writing instruction when working with the thesis statement and topic sentences and the need for detailed support and valid arguments. The use of the present tense in *a researcher says* deals with the convention in English tense use whereby the present tense can refer to past time events that have present time relevance and are true regardless of when the actual event takes place.

In general terms, readings selected for culture and L2 teaching combined can be examined for discourse and text organization, cultural concepts, vocabulary, grammar, and the conventions of writing in English. The readings can be selected relatively easily to be appropriate for various levels of reading proficiency and the range of attendant L2 skills. It is important, however, not to miss an opportunity to engage learners in a discussion of how culture impacts language use.

DEVELOPING EFFECTIVENESS IN THE CLASSROOM

Because most individuals are socialized into their first culture, they are usually unaware of the influence of culture on language. To become effective, classroom teachers are often faced with the need to develop their professional knowledge of the fundamental sociocultural variables essential for L2 teaching. A great deal of literature was published in the 1980s and 1990s on the impact of cultural awareness and knowledge on learners' overall language proficiency. In addition, it has become apparent that cultural concepts affect how learners learn and teachers teach. Teaching adult learners to be or speak "like a native"

(Saville-Troike 1989, p. 26) is not likely to result in success because sociocultural norms of language use are acquired during the L1 socialization process. Thus, classroom teachers need to advance their own knowledge of how learners' first cultures work and how it impacts their ability to learn. For example, why is it that some students rarely speak in class, why do some learners memorize whole chapters instead of trying to "understand" the material, or why do some people never ask questions even if they need more explanation from the teacher?

Teacher, Teach Yourself

To develop effectiveness and a sufficient knowledge base *about* learners' cultures does not mean that a teacher needs to become an expert ethnographer on the fifteen different cultures represented in his or her classroom. For instance, the teacher does not need to be concerned with roles and responsibilities of children and parents, religious rituals, or ways to celebrate holidays and life events such as weddings and funerals. The ESL/EFL teacher is primarily concerned with cultural considerations that have a direct impact on his or her students' ability to learn and do their best in a second language and in a second culture environment. If students from a particular culture (or several cultures) do not participate in a speaking activity, it would be interesting to find out why this is so. On the other hand, if members of another culture seem to dominate most classroom interactions, it may be necessary to learn why they behave in this way, if the teacher is seeking to make the classroom a productive learning place for all students.

Thus, teachers' first priority is to identify their own needs in culture learning, in addition to those of their students. Another consideration is to investigate how teachers' own socioculturally determined beliefs, assumptions, and expectations affect their views on student learning and behaviors. For example, if a student does not want to speak up, the teacher may respectfully allow the student to maintain silence for the duration of the class or take appropriate steps to make it more comfortable for all students to volunteer opinions in paired or small-group activities or other settings that are less threatening than speaking in front of the entire class. If the student maintains polite silence and the teacher accommodates the student's choice of behaviors, the student is unlikely to improve his or her speaking proficiency and fluency.

Making Choices

As with teaching most ESL/EFL skills, teachers often need to develop their own approach to teaching a second culture. One of the central objectives in developing effectiveness in culture instruction is to address the *causal knowledge about culture* (Buttjes and Byram 1991) and the *sociocultural reasoning* that underlies practically all culturally determined behavior. Examining the causes that lead members of a particular culture to do something in a particular way helps learners make choices in speaking, writing, and behaving. For example, in many English-speaking communities, students are expected to arrive to class on time. On the other hand, such an expectation may not be common in certain other cultures. The reason that students need to be punctual is that in English-speaking cultures, the value of time is very high, and it is considered to be a scarce and important commodity, similar to money. In fact, time is often referred to in ways similar to money (e.g., *spend time, waste time, to be short on time, time is money*). Therefore when students arrive late, they disrupt the class, *take* other people's *time*, and display a certain level of disrespect for the teacher and other students. Students make a choice whether to come on time or to take the liberty of coming late. To help learners make appropriate choices (or to make them aware that they are indeed making choices with consequences), teachers need to develop cultural knowledge and classroom effectiveness.

RESEARCH ON CULTURE AND SPECIFIC CULTURES

Two parallel types of research have been carried out to identify the role of culture in society and its influence on human behavior. The research on culture as it applies to social norms, beliefs, assumptions, and value systems that affect many (if not most) human activities is carried out in the domains of ethnography, anthropology, sociology, and intercultural communication. In these disciplines, culture is examined in terms that apply to most human societies and organizations, and research on culture seeks to determine the similarities and differences that exist in human constructions of reality. Applied linguistics (more specifically, sociolinguistics) is concerned with the inextricable connection between language and sociocultural norms and frameworks and seeks to identify patterns that can lead to an understanding of how members of particular cultures use their language to refer to, describe, or function within social organizations. For example, politeness is considered to be a universal feature of language use in social organizations, but its pragmatic, linguistic, social, intentional, and conceptual realizations vary substantially among different languages and/or cultures (even speakers of the same language or different dialects may belong to different sub-cultures and thus have different concepts of what it means to be polite and how politeness should be realized in speech and behavior).

In addition, research in ethnography, anthropology, and applied linguistics also includes studies of specific cultures, such as American, Chinese, Japanese, or Mexican. These studies identify and describe ways of doing, speaking, and behaving in specific cultural communities, without necessarily attempting to determine commonalities and differences among various cultures. Both research into culture in general and into specific cultures can be useful for L2 teachers who wish to allow learners to become more aware of the connection between the culture of the community and the language of its speakers.

CREATING MATERIALS TO BUILD CROSS-CULTURAL AWARENESS

Because manifestations of the influence of culture on language use are very common, materials for teaching cultural concepts and implications

can be easy to create. The following ideas for teaching L2 sociocultural concepts and their outcomes are merely suggestions. All these have been used for years with many different groups of ESL or EFL learners. Extensive culture-teaching projects and activities presented below certainly do not need to be used as they are described, and teachers can choose to use only portions of them, which include isolatable steps.

(1) In teaching ESL, one of the most effective activities that can be used for investigating a second culture are interviews of NSs or experienced L2 learners because they provide testimonials and evidence that comes from real people (instead of a classroom or textbooks). The greatest advantages of conducting interviews are that it allows learners to practice a variety of L2 skills, and that several productive assignments can be derived from this activity.

The first step is for learners to develop appropriate and focused questions. These can provide a fruitful avenue for working on various forms of polite speech acts and the notions of appropriateness (e.g., what represents personal information, what topics can be discussed, and how to approach them), as well as linguistic forms of questions and requests. Because interviews allow learners access to the invisible aspects of L2 culture, the questions should focus on the causal information that deals with L2 cultural concepts and sociocultural norms and behaviors that cannot be observed. Examples of questions can include:

- Why do people ask you *How are you* and then do not listen to the answer?
- Why do teachers say that students have to come on time if, when students come late, the missed material is their own loss?
- Why do Americans smile so much?
- Why is it okay to call professors by their first names?
- Why do strangers say *hello* to me on the street?
- Why is it necessary to explain everything in so much detail in writing?
- If my essay explains everything (!), would readers think that I view them as a little slow?

It is strongly recommended that the instructor approve the questions before the actual interviewing takes place.

In addition, learners can work at eliciting the polite and appropriate requests for appointments/meetings, "softening" devices, appropriate telephone or e-mail skills, negotiating the times and places for meeting, and seeking clarification. The interviews can be conducted in pairs, but it is preferable not to include more than two students in an interviewing team.

Following the interview, the information can be used for a presentation to other small groups of students or to an entire class. In a writing class, the outcomes can be turned into a short or long paper, depending on the learners' level of L2 proficiency. In any case, the presentations or written assignment should not turn into mere descriptions of responses or behaviors but should set out to determine their causes. When working on the presentation or on writing assignments, the cultural conventions of L2 public speaking (e.g., eye contact, organization of content, and demeanor) or L2 written discourse (e.g., thesis statement, topic sentences, and their detailed support) can be addressed in conjunction with the work on the assignment content. In general, such a project can take approximately two to three weeks, depending on circumstances.

(2) In EFL settings, learners can work on short questionnaires that similarly have the goals of identifying the manifestations of culture in language use and heightening learners' awareness of politeness norms, sociocultural variables, pragmatic functions, and linguistic forms of speech acts (such as the types of "softening" devices and their variability). The questionnaires can be administered in the learners' L1 to gather information that can be later used in L2 presentations or written assignments. The tasks can be simplified for intermediate level learners or be made more complex for advanced L2 speakers.

(3) In either ESL or EFL, home videos, movie clips, and videotaped excerpts from newscasts and TV programs (sitcoms, juvenile shows for younger learners, or interviews) can provide a practically inexhaustible resource for examining the influence of culture on language (e.g., routinized expressions, "softening" devices, questions, requests, etc.), interactional practices, body language, turn-taking, and the length of a pause signalling the end of a turn. The information on sociocultural and politeness norms of the community obtained from such materials can be used in subsequent role plays, skits, or short plays that learners can script and present, as well as formal presentations and written assignments. In this case, written assignments can include the aspects of L2 speech acts and behaviors that learners found surprising, the descriptions of polite and routinized expressions that they noted, and culturally determined conventions displayed in the video excerpts. These projects can be worked on from one to two weeks, depending on the amount of the material used in the video lesson.

CONCLUSION

It is important for both teachers and students to be aware of the manifestations and outcomes of L2 sociocultural values, concepts, and norms on people's speech and behavior. To this end, learners need to be taught to notice polite (and often routinized) expressions and behaviors common in the L2 community because without becoming astute people-watchers, they may find it difficult, if not impossible, to become interactionally competent in the L2. Being aware of the sociocultural frameworks does not mean that learners have to become "native-like," but an awareness of the L2 cultural norms can allow learners to make their own informed choices of what to say and how to say it. The teacher's task is to provide learners with the tools they need to recognize that they are indeed making choices.

Although ESL/EFL teachers devote a great deal of work, time, and attention to the teaching of L2 linguistic skills, being linguistically competent is not enough for many learners to attain their educational, professional, and social goals. Because language use reflects the culture of its speakers, the teaching of L2 culture can be closely intertwined with the teaching of most L2 linguistic skills. Teaching L2 culture together with speaking, listening (and noticing), reading, and writing more adequately represents the connections between language and culture than teaching L2 linguistic skills—or culture—in isolation.

Acknowledgments: My appreciation to Bethany Plett and Mary Geary, both of Seattle University, for their helpful comments and suggestions.

DISCUSSION QUESTIONS

1. The article mentions that culture teaching does not represent a separate domain of L2 teaching. If this is so, would it be useful for learners to develop lessons to deal with folk dances, festivals, facts, and foods (the 4-F approach to teaching culture)?

2. The distinction between the visible and the invisible culture is described as one of the most important aspects of teaching the influence of culture on L2 use. What are the key features of the invisible culture and what impact do they have on L2 learning and use?

3. Why does the teaching of L2 culture seem to be more directly relevant to ESL rather than EFL learners? Why is contrasting culturally determined ways of speaking and writing useful for teaching second culture to EFL learners?

4. In many ways, cultural references are closely intertwined with reading, discourse, and text. What is the role of linguistic proficiency and cultural proficiency in ESL/EFL reading and/or writing? What importance can L1 literacy have in learning to read and write in ESL/EFL?

5. Why is it that many teacher-training programs stay away from preparing teachers to work with a second culture? If you were in charge of an ESL/EFL program, would you choose to include teaching culture as a component of teacher-training? Why or why not?

SUGGESTED ACTIVITIES

1. Create lists of common linguistic expressions or behaviors, each associated with two or three types of speech acts (agreeing, disagreeing, inviting someone to do something or visit, and/or accepting or declining invitations) and arrange them from the least polite to the most polite expressions. What are the characteristics of the least polite or the most polite speech acts? What are the sociocultural variables that would make each of them acceptable or unacceptable in real-life interactions?

2. Various types of writing genres require the uses of different conventions. Gather samples of different texts and include, for example, a personal letter, a popular magazine article, an excerpt from an introductory textbook, or a formal essay/academic paper. Identify the features of these texts that make them different in important ways. What are the culturally prescribed conventions common in personal, expressive, or formal academic writing? What do these genres share? What do the shared and different conventions say about the culture of each discourse community?

3. Observe a group of people who are simultaneously engaged in an activity (e.g., standing in line, waiting for the teacher to arrive in class, or making small purchases in a drugstore). What verbal and nonverbal behaviors do these individuals have in common? How do they, for instance, maintain eye contact or hold their hands? What do most of them say and what do only some individuals say? How can culturally determined ways of behaving and speaking in a community be identified and isolated from those that are based on individual choices?

4. To find out what represents a popular understanding of culture in the community, find five or six individuals in a similar age group and with similar social status who are native speakers of the same language and ask them to tell you about their culture. For example, ask several American or Japanese students to tell you about their culture. What do their responses include? How do these individuals identify the visible and the invisible aspects of their culture?

 **FURTHER READING**

Mey, J. 1993. *Pragmatics: An Introduction.* Oxford: Blackwell.

Presents pragmatics as the study of language use in real-life interaction and describes the effects of various language forms on communication. Focuses on everyday conversation and the sociocultural variables that determine choices of language features made by interacting participants.

Saville-Troike, M. 1989. *The Ethnography of Communication*. Oxford: Blackwell.

Describes how and why language is used in particular ways that vary in different cultures. Illustrates essential concepts in sociolinguistics and cites examples from many languages to outline frameworks of communication and cultural competence.

Scollon, R., and S. W. Scollon. 1995. *Intercultural Communication*. Oxford: Blackwell.

A practical guide to the main concepts and problems of intercultural communication. Centers on principles of interactive sociolinguistics, the discourse of members of divergent cultures, pragmatics, and ethnography. Underscores the importance of language use in cross-cultural discourse and cultural norms of interaction.

Singer, M. 1998. *Perception and Identity in Intercultural Communication*. Revised edition. Yarmouth, ME: Intercultural Press.

Analyzes cultural and group identities and the communication process to determine how perceptions of self and others affect language and behavior. Delves into the significance of culture-based perceptual identity and the role of identity in intercultural communication.

Stewart, E., and M. Bennett. 1991. *American Cultural Patterns: A Cross-cultural Perspective*. Revised edition. Yarmouth, ME: Intercultural Press.

Discusses fundamental concepts of American culture in terms of similar or different characteristics of other cultures. Also focuses on the impact of culture on communication and implications for cross-cultural interactions.

The Use of Media in Language Teaching[1]

DONNA M. BRINTON

In "The Use of Media in Language Teaching," Brinton presents a rationale for and an overview of media materials and equipment traditionally used in the second/foreign language classroom. To better guide teachers in their use of media, she provides a five-part framework for structuring media-based language lessons, accompanied by a variety of sample lessons that illustrate this framework.

INTRODUCTION

As a tool for language learning/teaching, media have undoubtedly always facilitated the task of language learning for both instructed and noninstructed learners. Just as children learning a first or second language grasp the meaning of words from the objects that surround them, non-native speakers (both inside and outside the classroom) make use of the here and now or objects in the immediate environment (see Hudelson 1984; Pica, Young, and Doughty 1987; Wesche and Ready 1985; Lynch 1996) to process incoming speech.

In the second language classroom, the extent to which media are used has varied widely, depending on the methodology selected. In some methods, media have figured prominently as a force that drives the curriculum. In the St. Cloud (or audiovisual) method, which was developed primarily for the teaching of French as a foreign language (Bowen, Madsen, and Hilferty 1985; Stevick 1976), all language items were introduced to learners via contextualized, audiovisual presentations (usually filmstrips or slide shows with an accompanying soundtrack. The underlying approach assumed that language is an acoustic-visual whole that cannot be separated from its constituent elements. Similarly, in the Silent Way (Gattegno 1972; Larsen-Freeman 1986; Stevick 1998), the sound-color charts and rods form a central visual component of the method, allowing the teacher to present and elicit language while at the same time providing the students with tools for the creative construction of language.

In other methods, media are relegated more to the design or procedure level.[2] In Communicative Language teaching (Larsen-Freeman 1986, Littlewood 1981; see also Savignon's chapter in this volume), for example, much emphasis is placed on the need for real-life objects or texts (e.g., maps, railroad timetables, application forms) to lend authenticity to the communicative situation, while in the Natural Approach (Krashen and Terrell 1983), magazine pictures are used as an elicitation device in the listening comprehension and early production stages, and charts, maps, and props are used to motivate and enhance communicative interchange in later stages of acquisition. Finally, in experiential approaches to language learning (see Eyring's chapter in this volume), language teaching media are often taken out of the hands of the teacher and placed in the hands of the students, such that students involved in project work might be expected to produce a scripted slide show or a voice-over video documentary as their final class product.

Whatever the approach, language teachers seem to agree that media *can* and *do* enhance language teaching, and thus in the daily practice of language teaching we find the entire range of media—from nonmechanical aids such as household objects, flashcards, and magazine pictures all the way up to sophisticated mechanical

459

aids such as video cameras and computers (see Sokolik's chapter in this volume)—assisting teachers in their jobs, bringing the outside world into the classroom, and, in short, making the task of language learning a more meaningful and exciting one. Keeping this fact in mind, let us examine the types of instructional media used in the language classroom.

MEDIA: A DEFINITION

Just as we often differentiate the teaching of "large *C* culture"—i.e., the great literature, art, and other contributions of a society—from that of "small *c* culture"—i.e., the customs and habits of a people—(Chastain 1988), it is germane here to differentiate between "large *M* media" and "small *m* media." Certainly, as with culture, media means many different things to different people. The most immediate connotation of the term "media," at least as related to language teaching, is that of the "large *M* media"—of technological innovations in language teaching, of mechanical paraphernalia, and of glossy, polished audiovisual aids—with all the media anxiety that these can conjure up in teachers. However, there is little evidence that such glossy audiovisual aids are any more effective than teacher-made, nonmechanical aids (e.g., paper plate hand puppets, butcher paper verb charts, and the like) or props from daily life (e.g., cereal boxes, campaign buttons, travel pamphlets, bumper stickers) that have been adapted for classroom teaching purposes. I would therefore like to suggest that all these aids, mechanical and nonmechanical, glossy and non-glossy, commercially available and teacher-made, should be part of our definition of language teaching media.

A RATIONALE FOR THE USE OF MEDIA IN LANGUAGE TEACHING

I often assume that the reasons why we should use media when teaching second or foreign languages are self-evident to experienced classroom teachers. All too frequently, however, I overhear snatches of conversation in classroom hallways or at professional gatherings that disabuse me of this notion. These comments, made by colleagues regarding their inability or unwillingness to use audiovisual aids in their classrooms, fall roughly into the following "categories":

Statement 1: I'm all thumbs. I can't use media.
Statement 2: My school district has no budget for media.
Statement 3: I have no time to prepare media materials of my own.
Statement 4: The syllabus I teach from is too tightly structured to allow for media materials to be brought into the classroom.
Statement 5: I teach advanced levels (alternatively, a given skill area such as composition or reading) and therefore don't need to use media.

Before proceeding with a rationale for using media in the language classroom, let us first examine the underlying fallacies of the above statements.

The first two statements, I believe, can be dealt with summarily by realizing that those who have made such statements are subscribing to the aforementioned "large *M*" definition of media. That is, these individuals are assuming that classroom media materials are by definition (1) mechanical (and therefore unavailable, unwieldy, and/or anxiety-provoking) and (2) commercial (and therefore costly and inaccessible). In fact, as I have already pointed out, classroom media need be none of the above—they can be nonmechanical, unthreatening to both teachers and students, teacher-produced rather than commercial, easily available (especially in the case of the realia of everyday life), and reasonably priced (or often even free).

The fallacies that underlie statements 3 through 5 are somewhat more difficult to refute. On the surface, statement 3 (the time factor), presents a somewhat viable argument against using media. Certainly, if one disregards the many attractive commercially available media materials that teachers can select from (see Appendix B for a partial list of these) and assumes that statement 2 also holds true in a given case, the preparation of teacher-made media materials *does* demand an investment of time and energy above and beyond that of normal lesson planning. However, this statement overlooks the reality that *any* lesson preparation is time-consuming, and that many media materials (such as the preparation of vocabulary flashcards or the selection of magazine pictures to elicit and practice a given language point) do not require exhaustive amounts of time. Additionally, and perhaps more importantly, the statement ignores the "payoff" that can result from the hours spent preparing or assembling simple classroom media materials (e.g., a set of prespecified role assignments prepared on index cards to set up a role-play situation, or a collection of menus from local restaurants for a lesson on food items). In fact, this payoff, which is realized in terms of the teacher's continuously recycling these same materials with different student audiences (and even for different teaching purposes), is often far greater than the amount of time invested in more traditional classroom lesson planning (see Jensen's chapter in this volume).[3]

Statement 4, I believe, is based on a commonly held misunderstanding of media as "extraneous" to normal lesson activities. In other words, proponents of this view fail to recognize that media can form a viable point of departure for achieving lesson objectives. In fact, rather than taking up additional class hours, the use of media designed with a particular student population and teaching objective in mind can often help to *economize* the teaching task. This is achieved in the sense that the media appeal to students' senses and help them process information (Hartnett 1985), thus reinforcing the teaching point and saving the teacher unnecessary explanation.

Finally, those who hold the view expressed in statement 5 are neglecting the fact, grounded in the very definition of language, that language skills are not isolated entities, and that as language teachers we need to build bridges between skills. We can do so by creating a unified context in which the teaching of various skills is effectively integrated around media. For example, we can structure multiskill thematic units[4] requiring students to process information from a variety of sources (e.g., a political cartoon, a video documentary, and letters to the editor, all concerning the same controversial topic) followed by an interview assignment in which students poll native speakers for their opinions on this topic and, as a culminating activity, write a paper summarizing the opposing points of view on the topic.

In short, media help us to motivate students by bringing a slice of real life into the classroom and by presenting language in its more complete communicative context. Media can also provide a density of information and richness of cultural input not otherwise possible in the classroom, they can help students process information and free the teacher from excessive explanation, and they can provide contextualization and a solid point of departure for classroom activities. The following statements summarize the rationale for using media in the language classroom:

- Given the role media play in the world outside the classroom, students expect to find media inside the classroom as well. Media thus serve as an important motivator in the language teaching process.
- Audiovisual materials provide students with content, meaning, and guidance. They thus create a contextualized situation within which language items are presented and practiced.
- Media materials can lend authenticity to the classroom situation, reinforcing for students the direct relation between the language classroom and the outside world.
- Since the learning styles of students differ (Oxford 1990; Reid 1987; Skehan 1989; Wenden and Rubin 1987; see also Oxford's chapter in this volume), media provide us with a way of addressing the needs of both visual and auditory learners.
- The role that input plays in language learning is virtually uncontested (Krashen 1987). By bringing media into the classroom, teachers can expose their students to multiple input sources. Thus, while decreasing the risk of the students' becoming dependent on their teacher's dialect or idiolect, they can also enrich their language learning experiences.

- With reference to schema theory (Schank and Abelson 1977), which proposes that we approach new information by scanning our memory banks for related knowledge, media can help students call up existing schemata and therefore maximize their use of prior background knowledge in the language learning process.
- Finally, research suggests that media provide teachers with a means of presenting material in a time-efficient and compact manner, and of stimulating students' senses, thereby helping them to process information more readily (Mollica 1979).

CLASSROOM MEDIA: AN OVERVIEW

At the height of the audiolingual era, if we had asked the average second or foreign language teacher to designate those media that they felt were appropriate for the teaching of languages, we would no doubt have received a fairly large range of responses, with the blackboard and other simple classroom aids along with the audiotape medium (and the ubiquitous language laboratory) dominating the responses. Today, needless to say, that range of responses would be even larger, as the ever-expanding horizons of technology present us with exciting new advances such as computer-assisted instruction, satellite transmission, and interactive video.

Despite these expanding horizons, we find today that rather than abandoning the more traditional, or small *m*, media and shifting allegiance to the newer, more technological innovations, language teachers are simply incorporating new technology into their repertoire of teaching aids, with many using sophisticated video and computer technologies (see Sokolik's chapter in this volume) alongside the less sophisticated (but tried and true) magnetboard or overhead projector. In attempting to provide an overview of the range of media available to classroom teachers today, it is perhaps best to use the traditional classification of "nontechnical" and "technical" media, as listed below.[5]

Nontechnical Media

This category presents obvious advantages in settings where electricity is unreliable, technical resources are scarce, or funding is limited. Other advantages of the forms of media included in this category are their low cost, their availability, their accessibility, and their user-friendliness. Items that belong in this category typically include:

blackboards/ whiteboards	cartoons/ line drawings
magnetboards/ flannelboards/ pegboards	objects/realia pamphlets/ brochures/
flashcards/index cards	flyers/menus
wall charts, posters, maps, scrolls	equipment operation manuals
board games	puppets
mounted pictures/ photos	newspapers/ magazines

Technical Media

Although these forms of media are costlier and less user-friendly than the nontechnical media, they carry with them a larger degree of "psychological reality" in that they can bring the outside world in all its complexities into the classroom. In fact, since students in today's language classes tend to surround themselves with technology in their daily lives, they may grow to expect it in the language classroom as well. Items that belong in this category typically include:

record player	filmstrip/ film projector
audiotape player/ recorder	opaque projector
CD player/recorder	slide projector
radio	computer
television	language lab
video player/ recorder	computer lab multimedia lab
telephone/ teletrainer	self-access center
overhead projector	

In considering this group, it is important to make a few further distinctions—namely, whether the media constitute software (consumable media items) or hardware (equipment), whether the materials are commercially produced or teacher-produced, and whether they are authentic or not.[6] We must also consider whether they are being used alone or together with other media in a multimedia environment. Finally, we must also consider the purposes for which these media are being used—i.e., to aid in presentation, to provide practice or stimulate communicative interaction, or to provide feedback (as in the case of audio/videotaping student oral products for subsequent discussion and evaluation).

To include a description of the possible uses of all the above forms of media is beyond the scope of this chapter. However, to take but one example, the blackboard, we can see how even this simple medium can function effectively at the various stages of a lesson. In the presentation stage, for example, the blackboard can be used for verb paradigms, time lines, or other graphic or visual cues to elucidate a teaching point, while matrices or grids written on the blackboard can serve as elicitation tools. In the practice stage, maps, stick figures, and other line drawings can function as contextualizers for a given activity. Finally, in the communication stage, the blackboard can be used to storyboard student ideas in a group-produced narrative or to cluster and map student concepts as they are being developed.

Suffice it to say, then, that each form of media presents unique advantages—be it the availability and immediacy of feedback that the black/whiteboard can supply, the economy of time that pre-prepared overhead transparencies or a Powerpoint presentation can provide the teacher, or the richness of authentic input that film or the Internet can offer. Ultimately, each medium leaves its own imprint on the teaching/learning process, and it is up to the teacher to decide which one to select in order to teach a given point.

GUIDELINES FOR USING MEDIA IN THE CLASSROOM

Given the range of classroom media (both hardware and software) discussed above, it is not surprising that language teachers are overwhelmed by the choices available to them. As Penfield (1987, p. 1) rightfully notes, "too often [media] are neglected because teachers are not always certain how to adapt these rich and complex learning materials to students' needs and language competencies." Clearly, guidelines for use are in order.

In fact, guidelines for the selection, adaptation, development, and implementation of media-based materials do not differ radically from the kinds of guidelines we find mentioned more universally regarding lesson planning and textbook evaluation (see, e.g., Jensen's and Byrd's chapters in this volume). Thus, such issues as the appropriateness of the materials for the target audience, their technical and pedagogical quality, their teaching objective(s), and the pre-/post-procedures to be used all play as important a role in the selection and use of *audiovisual* media in the classroom as they do in those of conventional *print* media. Further, and this point cannot be stressed enough, media-based materials should not be viewed simply as extraneous to the lesson, or as contingency plans. Rather, they should be planned as carefully as the lesson itself and should form a central (if not *the* central) component of the lesson—one that is interwoven with the other lesson components, such as the reading text, the writing assignment, or the speaking task.

A FRAMEWORK FOR STRUCTURING MEDIA LESSONS

The framework presented below[7] is intended to put the application of media to language teaching into a unified perspective and to assist teachers in better structuring media lessons. In constructing this framework, I've divided up the typical "lesson" into five stages: (1) the *information and motivation stage*, where the topic and relevant background information are presented; (2) the *input stage*, where the teacher ensures comprehension of the item or items presented; (3) the *focus stage*, where the students practice the tasks and are provided with guided opportunities to manipulate items until they feel comfortable and confident;

(4) the more communicatively oriented *transfer stage,* in which students are given opportunities to offer personal comments or share experiences relating to the given context; and (5) an *optional feedback stage* in which audio or video recordings of students are used to guide the assessment of the students' performance (e.g., a student speech, an interview, a class discussion, a role play, a group problem solving activity).[8] Figure 1 presents the framework.

In applying this framework, teachers need to be aware that the above points in the framework outline *options* available to teachers in designing and implementing media lessons and are not intended to represent procedures that must be followed lockstep. Note also that media can play a role at *any* or *all* of the five stages of the lesson, and that a variety of media might be used in the various stages to complement each other and to achieve the designated teaching objective.

I. Information and motivation stage

II. Input stage
  1. Teacher presents/elicits vocabulary
  2. Teacher presents/elicits structures
  3. Teacher presents/elicits functions
  4. Teacher presents/elicits concepts
  5. Teacher presents/elicits content

III. Focus stage
  1. Teacher models language items/procedures/tasks
  2. Students practice items/tasks in context
    a. Drill
    b. Elicitation
  3. Students manipulate language/content/tasks
    a. Notetaking
    b. Information transfer
    c. Pair work/small-group work

IV. Transfer stage
  1. Class discussion
  2. Students interact, using context set by media materials as a point of departure
    a. Role play/sociodrama
    b. Problem solving activity
    c. Information gap activity
    d. Game
  3. Task-based assignment
  4. Follow-up writing assignment
  5. Sharing of personal experience
  6. Field trip

V. Feedback stage
  1. Teacher tapes the activity.
  2. Students listen to/view the tape.
  3. Students perform a self-assessment of their performance.
  4. Students provide peer feedback to others.
  5. Teacher provides feedback to students.

Figure 1. A Framework for Structuring Media Lessons

SAMPLE MEDIA LESSONS

The following sample lessons, selected to illustrate a range of available media, demonstrate how the framework in Figure 1 can be applied in making decisions about media use for language teaching purposes.[9] Note that numbers in brackets indicate the relevant parts of the framework that have been applied in designing each lesson.

Sample Lesson 1: The "Ugly Lamp" (magazine picture)

Audience: Beginning-level adult students enrolled in an intensive language/visa program; intermediate level EFL students.

Teaching Objective: To provide students with the language needed to express pleasure/displeasure; request an exchange for an unwanted item.

Media: Mounted magazine picture of woman holding an ugly lamp (see Figure 2).

Skills: Speaking, vocabulary, writing.

Time: 2 class periods (1 hour each) plus follow-up (15 minutes).

Procedures:

1. Teacher introduces the concept of gift giving and receiving. If appropriate (e.g., holiday time), students may want to share information about what they are giving to friends or wish to receive [I].

2. Teacher introduces the magazine picture of the ugly lamp (see Figure 2), eliciting explicit vocabulary (e.g., lampshade, bow, frown) [II.1.] and structures (present progressive, descriptive adjectives) [II.2.].

3. The students and teacher examine the picture more closely, and the teacher asks questions which elicit more implicit vocabulary [II. 1.] and structures [II.2.]. For example: "Who do you think gave the woman this gift?" (sister-in-law, elderly relative); "Where do you think Aunt Harriet *might* have bought the lamp?" (She *might* have bought it from a thrift shop/garage sale/etc.).

4. Teacher presents language functions relevant to giving and receiving gifts [II.3] and provides students with guided practice [III.2.a.]. In pairs (gift giver and receiver), students practice the sequence of giving the gift, opening it, and expressing thanks [III.3.c.].

5. For homework, as follow-up writing practice, students write a letter to the giver of the gift thanking him or her [IV.4.].

6. On a subsequent day, the context is recycled, and the language necessary for returning unwanted items to a store and requesting cash/an exchange is presented [II.4.] and practiced [III.2.a.].

7. Students are videotaped [V.1.] role-playing the situation [IV.2.a.]. They then watch the video footage [V.2.] and receive peer [V.4.] and teacher [V.5.] feedback.

8. As a culminating activity, students bring in unwanted items they have received and share their reactions to receiving these gifts with their classmates [IV.5.].

Figure 2. The Ugly Lamp

Sample Lesson 2: Computer Hardware/Software Ads
(mounted advertisements from magazines and journals)[10]

Audience: Advanced ESL/EFL students enrolled in EAP courses at the university; students enrolled in university-bound programs (e.g., advanced students in intensive language institutes).

Teaching Objective: To introduce, practice, and reinforce the task of writing formal definitions for academic purposes; secondary objectives include reading practice involving skimming and scanning, speaking in small groups, in-class writing, and follow-up writing error detection.

Media: Mounted advertisements of computer hardware and software products with accompanying text from magazines and journals.

Skills: Writing, grammar (sentences of definition), reading, and speaking.

Time: 90 minutes plus additional follow-up as desired.

Procedures:

1. Students are led in a brief discussion of where we are apt to find academic definitions of items—e.g., in textbooks, product manuals, journals, and magazines [I.].

2. Teacher reviews previously covered material—i.e., the structure of sentences of definition [II.2.].

3. Teacher distributes photocopies of a computer hardware or software advertisement. Together, the class members identify the item being advertised and locate any information relevant to writing a concise sentence definition of the product [III.2.b.]. [*Note:* This advertisement and the subsequent advertisements should be carefully selected so that there is no overt sentence definition of the product. The ad should, however, contain the necessary information for students to draw from in writing their definition.]

4. Together, students construct a complete sentence definition of the product. The teacher writes this definition on the blackboard [III.1.], stressing the previously studied formula for definitions, as in the following example:

A(n) [X] is a(n)
[Y] that [Z]

[X]	[Y]	[Z]
SPECIFIC TERM	GENERAL CLASS	CHARACTERISTICS
Software Bridge	is a software program	that converts documents from one word-processing program to another without losing formatting specifications.

5. Students are next divided into small groups of three or four students, with each group receiving one advertisement for a computer software or hardware item. Using the pattern provided, each group of students works for roughly four or five minutes to construct a sentence definition of the product [III.3.c.]. At the end of this time period, the groups pass their ads to another group, with each group receiving a new ad. This process continues until all groups have seen all ads and students in each group have had a chance to write appropriate sentences with definitions for each product.

6. With the help of the teacher, students now pool their answers. They decide for themselves the most useful information to include [IV.1.]; the teacher then writes the agreed-upon definition on the board under the headings indicated above. Errors in spelling, sentence structure, etc., can be dealt with at this stage by eliciting peer correction.

7. On a subsequent day, the teacher can recycle the material in a more game-like atmosphere [IV.2.d.], either by giving students names of fictional products and having them compete to write the "best" definition of the product or by having students play a "sort and unscramble" game in which they are given mixed-up items from categories X, Y, and Z on separate strips of paper and asked to put the items together to form sentence definitions.

Sample Lesson 3: Over-the-counter Drugs[11]

Audience: Beginning- or intermediate-level adult/community education students.

Teaching Objective: To develop an awareness of the availability, use, and potential misuse of over-the-counter preparations; to increase reading for specific information skills; to expand topic-related vocabulary.

Media: Packages/containers of over-the-counter drug preparations (e.g., headache remedies, cold medications); information grid (see Figure 3).

Skills: Reading, vocabulary, and speaking.

Time: 2 class periods (1 hour each).

Procedures:

1. Teacher introduces concept of over-the-counter (OTC) drugs; elicits from students information on the types of OTC products they typically use [I].
2. Common complaints (e.g., headache, allergy, cold sores, constipation) are reviewed [II.1.].
3. Teacher introduces information grid and demonstrates the procedure students are to follow via the example (Sudafed) [III.1.]. Terms in the grid are explained [I.1.].
4. Students are divided into small groups of four or five and OTC products are distributed to each group.
5. Students work in groups to transfer information into the grid [III.3.b.].
6. Once all student groups have completed the task, they share their results with the class at large.
7. Students discuss previous experiences they have had with OTC drugs (side effects experienced, etc.) [IV.5.]
8. As a follow-up, each student is assigned a symptom (e.g., warts, fever blisters, heartburn) and told to go to the drug store and find three products intended to remedy this condition. They are to compare these products using the grid format and report back on their findings to the class on the following day [IV.3.].

Product Name	Symptoms	Form	Dosage	Frequency	Age	Time Limit	Restrictions	Side Effects
1. Sudafed	cold hayfever allergy	tablet	12yrs-adult 2 tablets 6-12yrs, 1 tablet	every 4-6 hrs	Adults; children 6-12	7 days	Not for children under 2 yrs; for children 2-6 use Sudafed syrup	nervousness dizziness sleeplessness
2.								
3.								
4.								
5.								
6.								

Figure 3. Over-the-counter Drugs Chart

Sample Lesson 4: Postcard Description Activity
(photographic postcards from various countries)[12]

Audience: Recently arrived international students living in the ESL context (any level).

Teaching Objective: To increase awareness of cultural stereotyping; to serve as a discussion stimulus for impressions formed of the United States, its people, and its culture.

Media: Picture postcards depicting stereotypical images of countries (one for each pair of students); a barrier (e.g., a notebook, manila folder) to separate students.

Skills: Speaking, cultural awareness, writing.

Time: 1 class period (1 hour) plus follow-up (10–15 minutes).

Procedures:

1. Teacher introduces the activity by discussing postcards in general and the kinds of postcards that people send to their friends when they are on vacation [I.]. A model postcard (e.g., one depicting a Dutch girl wearing wooden shoes with a windmill and tulips in the background) may be shown to promote discussion.

2. Students are asked what kinds of postcards they have sent home since arriving in the United States, who they have sent these to, and what kinds of messages they have written on them [II.4].

3. Teacher explains/models the paired activity: Students are to form pairs, with Student A receiving a postcard from a given country. They erect a barrier between them so Student B cannot see Student A's postcard. It is Student A's task to describe this postcard to Student B, without mentioning the name of the country [III.1.]. Student B then attempts to discover the identity of the country [IV.2.c.].

4. Once all students have completed the task, students share their postcards and the cultural stereotype depicted with the rest of the class.

5. Follow-up discussion ensues on the general topic of cultural stereotyping, with the teacher eliciting a definition of cultural stereotyping from the students [IV.1].

6. Teacher elicits cultural stereotypes of Americans and organizes these on the blackboard under the headings "Positive" and "Negative" [II.4.]. Students discuss the possible harm of cultural stereotyping and share some stereotypes held about their own cultures [IV.1.].

7. As a follow-up assignment, students are asked to bring in postcards from their country (alternately: postcards from the United States) and share further information [IV.5.]. Depending on class level and focus, they may be asked as well to write a brief paragraph defining cultural stereotypes [IV.4].

8. Teacher videotapes the student activity [V.1.] for subsequent playback. He or she has students view the tape [V.2.]; in groups, they discuss the performances and give each other feedback [V.4.].

Sample Lesson 5: Radio Psychiatrist
(phone-in broadcast taped off-air)[13]

Audience: High-intermediate to advanced international students enrolled in an intensive language institute or other visa program; advanced EFL students in the secondary or postsecondary context.

Teaching Objective: To expose students to authentic English; to help them gain insights into issues which concern Americans; to provide them with a forum for problem solving activities.

Media: Advice column (Dear Abby, Ann Landers) on topic of audiotape (mounted on index cards); pre-prepared audiotape of phone-in radio psychiatrist show (possibly slightly edited).[14]

Skills: Reading, listening, speaking.

Time: 2–3 class periods (1 hour each).

Procedures:

1. Teacher introduces the lesson by asking students how people who are experiencing personal problems can get advice [I.4]. What forums are available (e.g., advice columns, counselors, psychologists/psychiatrists)? Students are asked to name specific situations in which people might seek the advice of a psychiatrist.

2. The first half of the advice column is distributed to students, and topical vocabulary is discussed [II. 1.].

3. In groups, students discuss the problem [III.3.c.] and write their "answer" to the person requesting advice [IV.4.]. They then share this with the class and compare it with the actual answer written by the advice columnist [IV.1.].

4. In the subsequent class period, the teacher introduces the topic of radio talk shows and asks students what kinds of talk shows they are familiar with [I.4.].

5. After a brief introduction to the topic of the taped phone-in call, students listen to the first half of the call—i.e., the caller's explanation of the problem. As necessary, difficult vocabulary is discussed [II.1.]. Depending on class level, the students may listen to this segment of the tape more than once and may also work on answering prepared questions in groups [III.3.c.].

6. As in step 3 above, students are then asked to formulate their own answer to the predicament and to predict the answer that the expert will give [IV.2.b.].

7. Students listen to the expert's advice (again, more than once if necessary) and subsequently discuss whether they feel this advice will be of assistance to the caller. They compare their own advice with that of the expert [IV.1.].

8. Optionally, on a third day, students can participate in a problem solving [IV.2.b.] or role-play [IV.2. 1.] activity, with situations prepared by the teacher. For each role play, one student plays the role of the advice seeker, and one or more students can play the role of the advice giver.

Sample Lesson 6: "People's Court"
(off-air videotape)[15]

Audience: High-intermediate or advanced young adult or adult ESL students.

Teaching Objective: To increase listening comprehension in authentic situations and to introduce specialized vocabulary items; to provide a format for problem solving; to familiarize students with one aspect of the American judicial system.

Media: Videotape of "People's Court," a broadcast of actual small claims court proceedings, recorded off-air.

Skills: Listening, speaking, vocabulary, culture.

Time: 2 class periods (1 hour each).

Procedures:

1. The lesson is introduced by the teacher, who gives a brief introduction to the U.S. judicial system [I.] and explains the role of small claims court within this system [II.5.].

2. The program "People's Court" is explained, and relevant vocabulary (e.g., judge, plaintiff, defendant) is presented [II. 1.]. Students are asked if they have ever watched this program; those who have share their impressions of it [IV.5.].

3. Students view a selected case (broadcasts of "People's Court" typically consist of two cases) up to the point where the judge retires to make a decision. Class members consider the basic points of the case, judge the arguments of the plaintiff and defendant, and predict what the judge will decide [IV.2.b.].

4. Students then view the remainder of the tape and compare their decisions with that of the judge. They may wish at this point to suggest how the litigants could have improved their arguments, or discuss the testimony of the witnesses [IV.1.].

5. On a subsequent day, the teacher may present students with various situations which might be heard in small claims court (e.g., a dry cleaner who damaged someone's expensive dress, or a florist who delivered the wrong flowers to a wedding) and prepare the students for a role-play situation in which students take various roles (witnesses, plaintiff, defendant, bailiff, judge). Students are given time to practice the role play prior to performing it [IV.2.a.].

6. Students perform the role play, which is videotaped by the teacher [V.1.] and then placed in a viewing facility so that students can review their performances [V.3.] outside of class.

7. A follow-up to the video role play can include an actual site visit [IV.6.] to a small claims court. (These visits should be scheduled in advance by the teacher; the courts are usually glad to accommodate.)

8. Following the field visit, a debriefing session is held, and students share their impressions [IV.1.].

CONCLUSION

As outlined above, instructional media come in an almost infinite variety of forms and can play equally varied roles. The following are factors that should be considered when incorporating instructional media into our language teaching goals:

- Type of skill/concept to be presented
- Student preference: the age, interests, experiences, and learning styles of the students concerned
- Teacher preference: facility with equipment, familiarity/adroitness with the given medium, teaching style
- Availability of software and hardware
- Physical circumstances of the classroom/lab

However, as Wright (1976, p. 65) notes, we should also keep in mind that "language teaching is a collective title for a variety of activities undertaken by different people in very different circumstances. There is consequently no single medium 'ideal for language teaching' as is so often claimed." Ultimately, availability and teacher creativity/adaptability will play major roles in determining to what extent media will be used and which media will be selected.

In closing, I encourage you to think creatively about ways to incorporate media into your language teaching and I reiterate the following useful guidelines: Use media materials when variety is called for, when they help you to reinforce the points you wish to make or serve as contextualization, when they expedite your teaching task and serve as a source of input, and/or when they help you to individualize instruction and appeal to the variety of cognitive styles in your classroom. But above all, use media to involve students more integrally in the learning process and to facilitate language learning by making it a more authentic, meaningful process.

DISCUSSION QUESTIONS

1. Elsewhere in this volume, a number of language teaching methods and approaches (both traditional and innovative) have been discussed. At home, review these sections of the text and come prepared to discuss the role that media play in these methods. In which methods/approaches do you feel that media play a central role (i.e., are part of the underlying philosophy)? In which methods/approaches do media play a more peripheral role?

2. Examine the rationale given in this chapter for the use of media in language teaching. Which reasons do you feel are most convincing? Can you think of any others?

3. Select three items from the list of technical media and three items from those listed under non-technical media that you are likely to use in the language classroom. Draw up a list of the advantages and disadvantages of each. Can you think of specific teaching applications for these forms of media?

4. Is there a feasibility factor involved in the use of audiovisual media? In other words, are certain teachers or teaching situations limited to the types of media they can select? Why or why not?

SUGGESTED ACTIVITIES

1. Collect packaged food items that you have around your household and design a survival level grid activity similar to the one described in this article for over-the-counter medication. Keep in mind that the purpose of the grid is to provide students with guidance in selecting food items and to train them in reading package labels for specific information.

2. Select a picture or series of pictures from a magazine and apply the framework for designing media lessons discussed in this chapter. Bring this material to class and share with others your ideas on how you would use it. Be prepared as well to discuss your selection criteria.

3. Observe an ESL class. What was the objective of the lesson? What aids did the teacher use? Think of additional aids that would have improved the lesson.

4. Drawing on the suggestions given in Byrd's chapter in this volume, develop a list of criteria for selecting and evaluating media materials.

FURTHER READING

The following sources contain a wealth of information for classroom teachers on the use of instructional media for language teaching purposes:

Larimer, R. E., and L. Schleicher, eds. 1999. *New Ways in Using Authentic Materials in the Classroom.* Alexandria, VA: TESOL.

Murphey, T. 1992. *Music and Song.* Oxford: Oxford University Press.

Penfield, J. 1987. *The Media: Catalysts for Communicative Language Learning.* Reading, MA: Addison-Wesley.

Stempleski, S., and B. Tomalin. 1990. *Video in Action: Recipes for Using Video in Language Teaching.* New York: Prentice Hall.

Ur, P. 1984. *Teaching Listening Comprehension.* Cambridge: Cambridge University Press.

Wright, A. 1989. *Pictures for Language Learning.* Cambridge: Cambridge University Press.

ENDNOTES

1 This chapter is a revision of the one that I wrote for the 2nd edition of this text (Celce-Murcia , ed., 1991, pp. 454–472). That chapter replaced two in the 1st edition—"An Audiovisual Method for ESL" by James Heaton and "Language Teaching Aids" by Marianne Celce-Murcia (Celce-Murcia, M., and L. McIntosh, ed., 1979, pp. 38–48; 307–315). I am grateful to both authors for their ideas, from which I have borrowed liberally. I am also grateful to Marianne Celce-Murcia for her suggestions concerning revisions to this chapter, and to Christine Holten, Janet Goodwin, Linawati Sidarto, Mike Silverman, and Susan Ryan for their additional input.

2 I refer here to the distinction made by Richards and Rodgers (1987) in their use of the terms *approach, design,* and *procedure,* in which *approach* designates the underlying theories of language learning in a given methodology, *design* refers to the form and function of the materials and activities used in the classroom, and *procedure* refers to the specific techniques employed.

3 I strongly suggest that teachers share such materials, institute a materials library, and even collaborate in audiovisual materials preparation, since this can further ease the materials development burden and further increase the above-mentioned payoff.

4 See Edelhoff (1981) Brinton, Snow, and Wesche (1989), Pally (2000), and Murphy and Stoller (forthcoming) for a discussion of such multiskills thematic units. For samples of thematic units that successfully integrate media in a thematic context, see Brinton et al. (1997a) and Brinton et al. (1997b).

5 Far from exhaustive, this list is simply intended to give an idea of the range of media that are typically encountered in the second language classroom.

6 I use the term *authentic* here in its broad sense, to refer to materials that were *not* produced for language teaching purposes per se. Both types of materials (i.e., authentic and pedagogical) have their legitimate use in the language classroom.

7 This framework is loosely adapted from a framework for using magazine pictures in the language classroom developed by McAlpin (1980).

8 These stages are adapted from Edelhoff (1981).

9 I have chosen to highlight teacher-produced media lessons rather than commercial materials since the latter are usually accompanied with teacher guidelines.

10 This idea was provided by Doug Beckwith and is used with his permission.

11 This idea and the accompanying grid were provided by Jean Turner and are used with her permission.

12 This idea was provided by Karen O'Neal and is used with her permission.

13 This idea was provided by Wendy Saul and Atsuko Kato and is used with their permission.

14 According to the guidelines established for off-air recording by nonprofit educational institutions, a broadcast program may be recorded off-air and retained by the educational institution for a period of up to 45 calendar days after the date of recording. Upon conclusion of this period, the off-air recording must be erased or destroyed (Penfield 1987).

15 Used with the permission of Paula Van Gelder.

APPENDIX A

The materials listed below are useful teacher reference texts that contain additional suggestions for using instructional media to teach second languages.

Allan, M. 1985. *Teaching English with Video*. London: Longman.

Anderson, A., and T. Lynch. 1988. *Listening*. Oxford: Oxford University Press.

Bassano, S., and M. A. Christison. 1987. *Drawing Out*. Hayward, CA: Alemany Press.

Cooper, R., M. Lavery, and M. Rinvolucri. 1991. *Video*. Oxford: Oxford University Press.

Cranmer, D., and C. Laroy. 1992. *Musical Openings: Using Music in the Language Classroom*. Essex, UK: Addison Wesley Longman.

Duncan, J. 1987. *Technology Assisted Teaching Techniques*. Brattleboro, VT: Pro Lingua Associates.

Ely, P. 1984. *Bring the Lab Back to Life*. Oxford: Pergamon Press.

Geddes, M., and G. Sturtridge, series eds. *Practical Language Teaching*. Volumes 1–8. London: George Allen and Unwin/Heinemann.

1. *Planning and Using the Blackboard*. 1980. Mugglestone, P.
2. *Using the Magnetboard*. 1980. Byrne, D.
3. The Magazine Picture Library. 1980. McAlpin, J.
4. *Using Blackboard Drawing*. 1980. Shaw, P., and T. de Vet.
5. *Photographic Slides in Language Teaching*. 1981. Ayton, A., and M. Morgan.
6. *Video in the Language Classroom*. 1982. Geddes, M., and G. Sturtridge.
7. *Using the Overhead Projector*. 1982. Jones, J. R. H.

Gerngross, G., and H. Puchta. 1992. *Pictures in Action*. New York: Prentice Hall.

Griffee, D. T. 1992. *Songs in Action*. New York: Prentice Hall.

Grundy, P. 1993. *Newspapers*. Oxford: Oxford University Press.

Hill, D. A. 1990. *Visual Impact: Creative Language Learning Through Pictures*. Harlow, UK: Longman.

Lonergan, J. 1984. *Video in Language Teaching*. Cambridge: Cambridge University Press.

Mejia, E., M. Kennedy Xiao, and J. Kennedy. 1994. 102 *Very Teachable Films*. Englewood Cliffs, NJ: Prentice Hall.

Shapiro, N., and C. Genser. 1993. *Chalk Talks*. Berkeley, CA: Command Performance Language Institute.

Steinberg, J. 1992. *Whatcha Gonna Learn From the Comics? How to Use Comics to Teach Languages*. Markham, Ontario: Pippin.

Wright, A. 1974. *1000 Pictures for Teachers to Copy*. Reading, MA: Addison-Wesley.

———— 1976. *Visual Materials for the Language Teacher*. London: Longman.

APPENDIX B

The materials listed below are useful audiovisual packages that are commercially available for the teaching of English as a Second Language. This list is not intended to be an exhaustive one, but rather to give an idea of the range of materials available.

Ashkenas, J. 1985. *Comics and Conversation: Using Humor to Elicit Conversation and Develop Vocabulary*. Studio City, CA: Jag Publications.

———— 1991. *More Comics and Conversation: Using Humor to Elicit Conversation and Develop Vocabulary*. Studio City, CA: Jag Publications.

————, ed. 2000. *New Comics and Conversation: Using Humor to Elicit Conversation and Develop Vocabulary*. Studio City, CA: Jag Publications.

Ballard, M. 1985. *The Magnetic Way into Language*. Amherst, NY: Creative Edge.

Clark, R. C., ed. 1982. *Index Card Games for ESL*. Brattleboro, VT: Pro Lingua Associates.

————, ed. 1993. *More Index Card Games and Activities for English*. Brattleboro, VT: Pro Lingua Associates.

Educational Solutions. *Silent Way Materials* (Cuisenaire rods, sound-color charts, fidels, pictures, etc.). New York: Educational Solutions.

Frauman-Prickel, M. 1985. *Action English Pictures*. Hayward, CA: Alemany Press.

Fuchs, M. S., J. Critchley, and T. Pyle. 1986. *Families: 10 Card Games for Language Learners*. Brattleboro, VT: Pro Lingua Associates.

Hadfield, J. 1984. *Harrap's Communication Games: A Collection of Games and Activities for Elementary Students of English.* Walton-on-Thames, UK: Nelson Harrap.

——— 1990. *Intermediate Communication Games: A Collection of Games and Activities for Low to Mid-Intermediate Students of English.* Walton-on-Thames, UK: Nelson Harrap.

Hancock, M. 1995. *Pronunciation Games.* New York: Cambridge University Press.

Henry, L. 1999). *Pronunciation Card Games.* Brattleboro, VT: Pro Lingua Associates.

Jacot, Y. 1981. *See It—Say It.* Reading, MA: Addison-Wesley.

Ligon, F., and E. Tannenbaum. 1990. *Picture Stories: Language and Literacy Activities for Beginners.* White Plains, NY: Longman.

Ligon, F., E. Tannenbaum, and C. R. Rodgers. 1992. *More Picture Stories: Language and Problem-Posing Activities for Beginners.* White Plains, NY: Longman.

Maley, A., and A. Duff. 1975. *Sounds Interesting.* Cambridge: Cambridge University Press.

——— 1979. *Sounds Intriguing.* Cambridge: Cambridge University Press.

Maley, A., A. Duff, and F. Grellet. 1980. *The Mind's Eye.* Cambridge: Cambridge University Press.

Markstein, L., and D. Grunbaum. 1981. *What's the Story: Sequential Photographs for Language Practice.* Volumes I–IV. New York: Longman.

Moran, P. R. 1984. *Lexicarry: An Illustrated Vocabulary Builder for Second Language.* Brattleboro, VT: Pro Lingua Associates.

Nelson, G., and T. Winters. 1993. *Operations in English: 55 Natural and Logical Sequences for Language Acquisition.* Brattleboro, VT: Pro Lingua Associates.

Silverson, S. K., M. Landa, and J. Smith. 1983. *Speak Easy: English Through Video Mime Sketches.* London: Longman.

Yedlin, J. 1981. *Double Action Picture Cards.* Reading, MA: Addison-Wesley.

Computers in Language Teaching

MAGGIE SOKOLIK

In "Computers in Language Teaching," Sokolik examines the forms and functions of computer technology in second language learning. These forms and functions, she contends, are separate from any particular state of technology. She concludes that good teaching methodology depends more on sound pedagogy than on access to any particular form of computer technology.

INTRODUCTION

The Shakers, a religious sect that formed in the 1700s, did not generally believe in writing that was "scriptural." They felt the act of writing made the malleable less flexible, the fluid artificially static. In spite of this belief, the Shakers wrote tomes about their theology.

This contradiction is also true for writing about educational technology in the early twenty-first century. Anyone writing for the print medium about technology fully realizes that the technology will be outmoded by the time that the book or article is published. Yet we keep writing tomes. For that reason, this chapter will focus less on the artifacts of technology—hardware and software, which will be different by the time this book is published—and more on the teaching approaches and techniques related to technology, which should still exist regardless of whatever the hardware and software of the day might be.

PRELIMINARY TO CLEAR VISION OF THE FUTURE: HISTORICAL OVERVIEW

With the development of new technologies, there has been an attendant interest in applying these technologies in the educational arena, and in making predictions of how they would affect the educational future of our classrooms and students. Although most people associate the birth of educational technology with the 1970s and 1980s, the history of educational computing actually goes back to the 1940s. Writers such as Bush foresaw a future in which communication and science would be enhanced with hyperlinked systems of information:

> Consider a future device for individual use, which is a sort of mechanized private file and library. It needs a name, and to coin one at random, "memex" will do. A memex is a device in which an individual stores all his books, records, and communications, and which is mechanized so that it may be consulted with exceeding speed and flexibility. It is an enlarged intimate supplement to his memory (Bush 1945, p. 106).

Of course, in the 1940s, the physical technology tied these ideas to microfilm, phonographic recordings, and punch card-style computing machines. In the 1950s and 1960s, the most powerful computers occupied entire rooms, not corners of desktops or small briefcases. However, the development of the microchip and miniaturization of components enabled educational technology to move forward rapidly in the 1970s and 1980s.

Many of the technological restrictions of the 1940s have melted away, and financial barriers instead hamper our visions of educational technology. Just as short a time ago as 1988, the vision of the technological future was the following:

What will happen is that in the university of the year 2000, students will be given a computer on their first day. Over the years that they spend at the university, a fixed cost will be assessed each term. This cost will pay for the computer, tuition, access to a myriad of database services, and online textbooks (Young et al. 1988, p. 259).

While the technology certainly exists to realize this vision, the financial support and bureaucratic structures do not. Some institutions have implemented programs such as the above, but they are rare.

In forecasting the technological future, it is important to consider what the capabilities of educational computing are, and what can be done in the language classroom that will remain current, even if the technology does not.

WHAT COMPUTERS CAN'T DO

The image of the fully automated, teacherless classroom has disappeared from the landscape, if it indeed ever was there. Although computers are useful adjuncts in second language learning, there are still many things they cannot accomplish. We look below at five major areas into which computers and technology have not yet made significant inroads.

1. Machine Translation

The hope of pushing a button to translate from one language to another has, for the most part, gone unrealized. Although there are dozens, if not hundreds, of new tools for machine translation, most fail at creating a text that a native speaker would consider idiomatic, or even grammatical. Although simple language with high-frequency vocabulary and little idiomatic usage can be translated fairly accurately, any deviations from that formula still cause serious breakdowns in the comprehensibility of machine-translated text.

An example of a machine translation, completed July 21, 2000, is presented on the next page. The text is a small portion of the opening of the play *Cyrano de Bergerac*, written in French by Edmond Rostand (1897). The first column is the original text, the second, a translation done by a human translator, and the third, an example of machine translation.

It is clear that the machine translation fails in several areas. First, it does not have a vocabulary database that allows for an understanding of a nineteenth century idiom. But even more basic issues are at stake: the misinterpretation of the preposition à as "with" rather than "at" ("A Representation with the Hotel of Burgundy") and an inability to appropriately detect plural forms ("Riders, middle-class man, lackey, pages") or imperative word order ("Exert we with the foil"). These mistranslations show that this software is not sensitive enough to contexts that distinguish important semantic, syntactic, or morphological features.

Students or instructors who seek translation assistance from computers will receive a text that may be somewhat comprehensible; however, knowledge of the basics of the language being translated, the context in which words might be used, and an understanding of idiomatic as well as archaic usages are important for a fuller understanding. This last issue is particularly problematic, even ironic; for someone needing translation assistance, idiomatic use is the element of language least likely to be known by the learner.

2. Providing Appropriate Feedback to Learners

Instructors in language education know that feedback, in whatever form, is a critical part of learning and communication. In face-to-face interaction, the teacher's feedback adapts to any number of factors, including but not limited to what the instructor feels the student can understand, the instructor's knowledge of the student's affective state, what is appropriate for the class or subject matter, and so on. Mechanized systems do not have the capability to customize feedback with the same sensitivity that a human instructor does. In fact, the best feedback systems give a simple explanation of the right or wrong answer, and many merely emit a noise, either pleasant or

ORIGINAL[1]	HUMAN TRANSLATION INTO ENGLISH	MACHINE TRANSLATION INTO ENGLISH
Acte I. Une Representation à l'Hotel de Bourgogne. *Scene 1.I.* Le public, qui arrive peu à peu. Cavaliers, bourgeois, laquais, pages, tire-laine, le portier, etc., puis les marquis, Cuigy, Brissaille, la distributrice, les violons, etc. (On entend dérrière la porte un tumulte de voix, puis un cavalier entre brusquement.) LE PORTIER (le poursuivant): Hola! vos quinze sols! LE CAVALIER: J'entre gratis! LE PORTIER: Pourquoi? LE CAVALIER: Je suis chevau-leger de la maison du Roi! LE PORTIER (à un autre cavalier qui vient d'entrer): Vous? DEUXIEME CAVALIER: Je ne paye pas! LE PORTIER: Mais. . . DEUXIEME CAVALIER: Je suis mousquetaire. PREMIER CAVALIER (au deuxième): On ne commence qu' à deux heures. Le parterre est vide. Exerçons-nous au fleuret.	Act I. A Representation at the Hotel de Bourgogne. *Scene 1.I.* The public, arriving by degrees. Troopers, burghers, lackeys, pages, a pickpocket, the doorkeeper, etc., followed by the marquises; Cuigy, Brissaille, the buffet-girl, the violinists, etc. (A confusion of loud voices is heard outside the door. A trooper enters hastily.) THE DOORKEEPER (following him): Hollo! You there! Your money! THE TROOPER I enter gratis. THE DOORKEEPER: Why? THE TROOPER: Why? I am of the King's Household Cavalry, 'faith! THE DOORKEEPER (to another trooper who enters): And you? SECOND TROOPER: I pay nothing. THE DOORKEEPER: How so? SECOND TROOPER: I am a musketeer. FIRST TROOPER (to the second): The play will not begin till two. The pit is empty. Come, a bout with the foils to pass the time.	Act I. A Representation with the Hotel of Burgundy. *Scene 1.i.* The public, which arrives little by little. Riders, middle-class man, lackey, pages, footpad, the gate keeper, etc., then marquis, Cuigy, Brissaille, the saddle jib crane, violins, etc. (One hears dérrière the gate a tumult of voice, then a rider enters abruptly.) The GATEKEEPER (the prosecutor): Hola! your fifteen grounds! THE RIDER: I enter gratis! THE GATEKEEPER: Why? THE RIDER: I am chevau-light house of the King! The GATEKEEPER (with another rider who has just entered): You? SECOND RIDER: I do not pay! THE GATEKEEPER: But. SECOND RIDER: I am a musketeer. FIRST RIDER (with the second): One starts only at two hours. The floor is empty. Exert we with the foil.

unpleasant, indicating whether the user has provided the correct answer. More complete feedback may be indirectly available in the form of links to other areas of a text or website to read or review.

Figure 1 shows a common feedback mechanism—the use of an ✗ (usually red) to show an incorrect answer and an arrowhead or similar icon to show a correct answer. In this example, there is no explanation of either the right or wrong answer. Figure 2 shows somewhat more elaborate feedback. In this case, it restates the prompt in different words, and emphasizes the vocabulary items that are key to understanding the correct answer.

I'm not familiar _____ California.

➤ with

   of

✗ to

Figure 1. Sample Minimal Computer Feedback
Adapted from an item from Dave Sperling's ESL Café (http://www.eslcafe.com) Quizzes. The ✗ shows the user's answer; the arrowhead shows the correct answer.

One of my best _____ already married with 4 kids!

○   A. friend is
○   B. friends are
○   C. friends is
○   D. friend are

"C" is correct—I have many friends, and one of them is married.)

Figure 2. Sample of More Complete Feedback
Adapted from Jim Duber's Grammar Web Quiz #1 (http://www.sirius.com/~dub/CALL/grammar1.html)

Although the second example has more complete feedback, it is clear that it cannot provide a user with customized feedback addressing an issue that the exercise designer might not have anticipated. Perhaps the user understands the structure "one of ✗" perfectly well, but does not understand the concept of "best friend." For the feedback to be rich, the designer of the item would have to anticipate all possible questions, from the use of an idiom, to the history of a word, to the cultural context of the item.

3. Voice Recognition

Voice recognition refers to the capability of a computer or software program to accept and interpret spoken dictation, or to understand and carry out voice commands. Voice recognition is used to dictate text into the computer or to give commands to the computer (such as opening programs and menus, saving files, and so on). The Bell Labs began a project for voice recognition in the 1960s (Gilbert and Mallows 1984). Although many modern home and office computer systems are equipped with some type of voice recognition software, these programs are still inefficient in accurately dividing up a natural speech stream into discrete words. It should be noted, however, that speech *production* programs, that is, programs that read text aloud, have been successful for several years. These programs have been especially beneficial for sight-impaired computer users.

4. Grammar Checking

Modern word-processing software usually comes equipped with grammar-checking routines. Unfortunately, as most users will attest, this software falls short of the grammatical editing that is required in a language classroom. The software is not sensitive to context or conventions of use, such as the difference between academic English written for the humanities versus that written for the sciences. Consider the following sentence, written by a second language learner in an English writing class:

> "In Typical American, the Changs become Americanized in order to succeed."

Since the current grammar-checking routines are sensitive to passive constructions, Microsoft Word 97 makes the following suggestion: Passive voice (consider revising)

Unfortunately, two issues potentially confuse the learner here. First, there has to be a full understanding of how to revise in order to eliminate passive voice. This introduces the same sort of irony that we find in machine translation: the student must already understand English grammar to make full use of the suggestions offered by the grammar-checking software. But more troubling in this case is the fact that this sentence is not easily rewritten in an active voice. Thus, the suggestion to revise may introduce additional difficulty for an ESL/EFL student who may trust the software more than she or he trusts her or his own judgment about English grammar.

5. Essay Marking

Although there is software that allows instructors to insert their comments neatly in students' word-processed text, there is no software that can "read" a text and write relevant comments on it. The Educational Testing Service (ETS) has developed software for the marking of GMAT (Graduate Management Admission Test) examinations, called the e-rater. This software marks essays based on the same six-point scale used by human graders. Authors from ETS and Hunter College, describing the software, explain the source of "misses" or disagreements with human raters: "[T]he greatest source of e-rater misses may be in the topical analysis components" (Burstein et al. 1998, p. 11). That is, although the software can be trained to look for structures that show certain rhetorical moves, it does not assess whether the writer has in fact addressed the essay topic.

WHAT COMPUTERS *CAN DO*

Although the above are areas in which computer tools are not proficient, there are many arenas in which computers equal, or surpass, human performance. As computers can store and process enormous amounts of information, they excel in areas where human memory may be deficient, or where human patience may be easily exhausted. We will look at five of these areas in this section.

1. Drills

Much of language learning is facilitated by repetition, whether it is the repetition of individual sounds, intonation patterns, conversational gam-

bits, or other types of words and phrases. Computers are useful in delivering drills for practice, whether in grammar, vocabulary, pronunciation, or listening, as they are tireless in their delivery. Unlike human interlocutors who may grow weary of repeating a word for a learner, a computer will repeat a word a hundred times if the user wishes.

According to McCarthy (1994), the computer has some specific advantages: organization of materials, including volume of material and random presentation, scoring and record-keeping, graphics and animation, including allowing student control, audio-cuing, and recording and storage of student responses. McCarthy also sees the computer's "literal approach" to checking answers and its ability to focus learner attention on a specific area of the screen as advantages in grammar drilling in particular.

2. Adaptive Testing

If we accept the premise that the most effective language learning happens when the learner's target is just slightly above his or her current level of understanding (sometimes called the I +1 theory[2] [see Krashen 1982]), then it becomes clear that computer adaptive testing (CAT) can be very useful in the language classroom.

As test takers respond to test items in CAT, the test adapts itself to each user by choosing subsequent test items based on the test taker's performance on preceding items. For example, if a learner performs well on a set of beginning-level items, the computer program will next present a set of questions at the intermediate level. If the learner performs poorly on the intermediate-level questions, the computer presents lower-level items (e.g., high beginner) in the next question set. Therefore, the CAT continually attempts to ascertain the appropriate level for the learner's performance and ceases testing once performance at a particular level is demonstrated to be the best possible performance for that individual. In other words, it can establish more quickly than a standard pencil-and-paper test what the learner's proficiency is.

3. Corpora and Concordancing

Computers are expert at storing large amounts of information and categorizing or sorting it by user-determined categories. Concordancing programs and linguistic corpora are types of tools and data that are increasingly being used in the language classroom. A concordance is a type of index that searches for occurrences of a word or combinations of words, parts of words, punctuation, affixes, phrases, or structures within a corpus, and can show the immediate context. The output from a concordance search can be used in the preparation of such teaching materials, such as grammar and vocabulary activities. Teachers can gather examples of language and usage for creating exercises.

Count	%	Word
97	0.4611%	all
92	0.4373%	shakespeare
69	0.3280%	years
57	0.2709%	other
54	0.2567%	about
51	0.2424%	time
50	0.2377%	stratford
49	0.2329%	out
47	0.2234%	law
47	0.2234%	legal
46	0.2187%	their

Figure 3. Results from concordancing of "Is Shakespeare Dead?" by Mark Twain, using MonoConc software. Numbers in the left column represent occurrences of words in the right column. "Non-content" words (such as *the, is, of, that,* and so forth) were removed from the search algorithm.

In an article about concordances, Stevens states,

> with concordance software and a corpus of natural English, language learners can short-cut the process of acquiring competence in the target language, because the computer is able to help students organize huge amounts of language data so that patterns are more easily discerned (1993, p. 11).

Another way in which concordances can be used is to create lists of collocations, or words that are commonly found together. Figure 4 lists the twenty most popular words found to collocate with the word *chocolate*. Again, the practical application can be seen for developing classroom activities. However, as the collocations given by the program do not indicate word order, teacher direction is needed in order to convert these lists into meaningful activities or information. For example, in the figure below, the symbol ◆ has been placed to show where the word *chocolate* would come in the phrase. (In some instances, it can go before or after the listed word.)

1.	◆ milk ◆	11.	◆ coffee
2.	◆ cake	12.	plain ◆
3.	hot ◆	13.	◆ fudge
4.	white ◆	14.	◆ egg
5.	◆ cream	15.	rich ◆
6.	◆ bar	16.	box (of) ◆
7.	dark ◆	17.	eat ◆
8.	◆ mousse	18.	◆ biscuits
9.	◆ bars	19.	◆ ice
10.	melted ◆	20.	◆ cocoa

Figure 4. From CobuildDirect Collocation, words collocated with "chocolate" (edited from top 100).

Finally, concordances can be used to look at the context in which a given word or phrase occurs in a database. The example in Figure 5 shows how the word "paradise" appears in a variety of texts taken from the Collins-Birmingham University International Language Database (also known as COBUILD), which contains thousands of exemplars. As seen in the example, learners can, following Stevens' observation, discern patterns in the use of a word, such as the frequent occurrence of a human noun with a possessive inflection preceding *paradise*.

Concordancing techniques and corpus linguistics are growing fields in second language acquisition and teaching. Only because of larger and faster computers have databases of the current size become practically available for use by second language learners, teachers, and researchers.

is also a sign of trouble in	**paradise.**	9. Maintaining love isn't
p] Grand Cayman is another diver's	**paradise,**	almost completely surrounded by
Socialist Republics—the worker's	**paradise**	as it was once called earlier in
s garden, on the other hand, was a	**paradise**	at this time of year. Flowering
dormitory. It was a bachelor's	**paradise.**	Attractive, intelligent women
venerable past. Squaw is a skier's	**paradise**	because of the sheer variety and
South America, that he'd discovered	**paradise.**	Columbus also happened to think
Garden of Eden, but that image of	**paradise**	doesn't quite hold up in the 85
of Martha's Vineyard is known as a	**paradise**	for artists and photographers.
fee required to enjoy our shopper's	**paradise,**	home to world-famous Mrs. Knott's
intends to erect his gambler's	**paradise.**	I am not now, and nor have I ever
Paradise" is a cliché, but	**paradise**	it is. [p] Bitter End has 81
come over. I'm like—it was like	**paradise.**	It was just like, you know,
afforded; yet had we been even in	**paradise**	itself with these governors, it
into what they regard as the fool's	**paradise**	of interdisciplinary work. If the
The Apostles are a vacationer's	**paradise**	of sunshine, clear water, and deep
boutiques — a shopper's	**paradise**	that may even distract you from
war intruded even on this island	**paradise.**	The Coast Guard patrolled many of
stroll about this little slice of	**paradise,**	the animals seem to blend in with
techniques, this is a vision of a	**paradise**	to preserve, made in the USA in

Figure 5. Output from the CobuildDirect Corpus Sampler (edited for length), searching for the term "paradise."

4. Computer Mediated Communication (CMC)

The most common use of networked computers is as a tool of communication between users. This makes it a natural choice as a tool for language learning. Many researchers have argued that CMC presents an opportunity for authentic language use, making it an excellent tool in the language classroom. There are several forms of CMC, which are either asynchronous or synchronous in form.

E-MAIL

E-mail has become the communication tool of choice for a lot of people. Much has been written about its use in the language classroom: for asynchronous communication between students, between students and teachers, and between students and others outside of the classroom.

Many instructors and researchers have designed e-mail tasks to focus its use on language learning (Kern 1998). International culture exchanges such as "key-pal"[3] programs help students to communicate authentically. Table 1 (p. 484) provides a brief summary of the types of activities that have been designed for use with e-mail, given the different possible arrangements of interlocutors.

Chat

Chat is real-time, or synchronous, communication. It has the informal feel of conversation, yet is mediated through writing. Chat can be used to facilitate class discussions, for immediate feedback between students and teachers outside of class time, or for communication between students outside of class.

Chat logs, or written records of a chat session, can be kept in most chat programs and used as data for research or future classroom work. Chat can be used in many of the same ways as e-mail, but has the added feature of immediate response rather than the time lag involved with e-mail.

MUDS AND MOOS

Multi-user domains, MUDs, or multi-user domains object-oriented, MOOs, are both synchronous and asynchronous in form. They are typically

Table 1. E-mail Activities (Adapted from Warschauer 1995)

Teacher↔Teacher	Teacher↔Student	Student↔Student
Use e-mail discussion lists for peer support	Submit assignments by e-mail rather than on paper	Discuss current events among groups of geographically dispersed students
E-mail mentoring with master and pre-service teachers	Class announcements	Peer collaboration on assignments
Receive resources such as syllabi and class materials from other instructors	Question and answer sessions outside of class time	Group work conducted electronically

text-based virtual spaces that rely on the ability of the user to (1) describe environments (asynchronously or synchronously), and (2) interact within those environments (synchronously).

The following are two brief descriptions of areas within a virtual space called "Storytelling Central" (part of Café MOOlano, the University of California, Berkeley's MOO) written by students in the Fall of 1999. The first is by a native Spanish speaker:

The Garage

You have entered a large, plain, and cold room. Three of the walls are made of solid cement, as well as the floor. The fourth wall is a large wooden door. A pole hangs above the wooden door. The pole has a dusty red cloth hanging from it that drops all the way to the floor. In the center of the room there lies an old rug, weathered by time. There is an old chest in the right corner, sealed shut by a rusty lock. You also see an artificial Christmas tree in the left-hand corner with a few ornaments on it. The room has makes you feel like something happened here long, long, ago . . .

You see mouse and Old Chest here.

Obvious exits: [south] to Home Sweet Home, [north] to The Barn, [west] to Top of the Hill

The following was written by a native Spanish speaker who was also learning Arabic:

The Sultan's Room

Ahlan wa Shahlan, you have entered The Sultan's Room. There is a rectangular Persian rug from the 14th century on the floor. To your right there is a big bookshelf with The One Thousand and One Books collection. One of the books contains a secret code that will enable you to open the Nightingale's Eye Bottle located on the very top of the bookshelf. The bottle is seal with a beautiful Syrian silk scarf, soft as the touch of a rose's petal.

MUD and MOO users create stories by inventing rich environments filled with objects that other users can manipulate and investigate. By navigating through space, students create stories in an impromptu fashion. They hold dialogues, open boxes, find secret messages and secret passages, and move through "space."

This type of interaction is more than mere game-playing. Aside from provoking learners to use language in both planned ways (i.e., writing) and unplanned ways (i.e., interacting in the virtual space), it is also satisfies the neurobiological correlate of "foraging" for information, critical in the learning process (Schumann 1994).

5. Multimedia Production

Currently, there are two widely used media (or sets of media) for multimedia production:

- Digital video in which digital multimedia tools are used to construct, edit, and produce a linear story
- Hypertext/Web-based stories in which digital multimedia tools are used to build and deliver stories (via the Web or local storage media) that allow user interaction through hyperlinks

Digital Video

Digital video requires that learners bring a story to life with voice, images, a soundtrack or sound effects, and a sense of movement, through cuts and transitions. The most complex of the CALL options, learners often find it the most satisfying. This format allows learners to relate a story of importance in the target language, with attention not only to language, but also to image and sound and their interconnection.

Multimedia productions are becoming increasingly common, and are now part of the standard hardware and software that comes with many home computers. Table 2 below summarizes the hardware and software needed for digital video production.

Hypertext/Web-Based Stories

Hypertext, or interactive stories, create a medium on the Web through which learners can explore issues of nonlinearity. More accessible than digital video, the Web is an environment in which learners can imagine and produce stories.

The media for and process of making web pages is well documented elsewhere (see, for example, O'Haver 1995). However, an important part of this process is the creation of story—in particular, a discussion of the nonlinearity of writing in this environment. Students' pages can be written as storyboards in which they indicate links, sketch out media use, and create and edit text in a collaborative environment.

CREATING AND EVALUATING COMPUTER-BASED ACTIVITIES

Whether an instructor decides to create his or her own materials, or use materials found on the Internet or on commercially available software, it is important that several features be evaluated and addressed. The following list will help an instructor in either evaluating or in creating computer-delivered instructional materials.

Appearance

Good instructional material should be attractive, but good design goes beyond being merely "eye-catching." Several issues regarding the appearance of an application should be attended to.

- Colors should be chosen carefully. Red/green colorblindness is common, so avoid colors that are likely to cause problems for users with this. Low-glare hues are preferable for reading; grays, soft whites, blues, and browns are better choices than bright yellows, reds, and greens.
- Fonts should be simple and without serifs (This font has no serifs; this font has serifs).

Table 2. Hardware and Software Needed for Digital Video Production

Software	Hardware
Photo or image editing software	Computer capable of running software named in first column
Digital video editing software	Sound card
Audio editing software for voice recording, capturing, and editing	Video capture and output card (Necessary only if capturing from or outputting to traditional linear video)

- The viewable screen should not extend to the right of the viewing space on an average computer monitor.
- Graphics should be kept small for faster loading over slow Internet connections.
- Limit the amount of text on one page. Keep downward scrolling to a minimum.

Navigation

- Navigating through an activity should be easy. Arrows or other navigational links should be clear to the user.
- Avoid "click here" for linking. Use content words for text links.
- Provide navigation that takes the user backward as well as forward when practical.
- Always provide a way to quit the activity.
- Navigation for important actions should appear on the first screen of a page. That is, the navigation should not be outside the normally visible area on an average computer monitor.
- Navigation should be "shallow." That is, learners should not have to click through screen after screen in order to reach a particular piece of information.

Interactivity and Feedback

If an activity is intended as self-study, feedback is extremely important. Every learner action should provide an opportunity for learning.

- Feedback should anticipate the learner's possible wrong responses and give full explanations.
- Correct answers should also be explained, in the event that the user chose randomly.
- The answers must reflect the full range of possible answers. Ambiguity should not be inherent in the activities unless there is planned teacher interaction.
- Links to review material should be provided when available.
- The activity should take advantage of interactivity. Unless formatted for printing, pages should be presented on the computer using interactivity, and not merely presented as potential printouts to be completed with a pencil.

Value

- The computer activity should be something that is done better with a computer than without. That is, does the activity require interactivity, large databases, or other things the computer does well, or could it be done as easily (or more easily) with paper and pencil?
- The activity should address a specific need in the planned curriculum.

Other Considerations

- Instructions should be minimal. Good planning should obviate the need for elaborate and complex instructions.
- Require special hardware or software only if you're certain your users will have easy access to it.
- Check computer-delivered activities on different types of computers, if possible. Good activities should be independent of computer type.

CONCLUSION

The hope that computers would be a panacea for those trying to learn second languages has not been realized. However, it is clear that computers are providing instructors and students alike with a new battery of tools with which language can be learned more effectively.

The advent of the Internet has changed the way we look at Computer Assisted Language Learning (CALL). Machines are now used as tools for communication rather than simply as ways of delivering automated drills or exercises. Vast amounts of reading on any topic and in many languages are now available on the Web, and the chance to participate in discussions with people from all walks of life is motivating for many learners.

In addition, the speed and size of computers now allow large databases to be manipulated, offering insights into language that we did not have access to previously. Corpus linguistics and concordancing can help provide the data and tools that students and instructors need to make sense out of usage.

There is nothing certain about the future of technology, except that it will no doubt become more ubiquitous an powerful. It is no longer possible in language education to ignore this force, which is changing global cultures. Fortunately, the same principles that instructors and policymakers use to evaluate print materials can be brought to bear on technological materials as well. In either case, it obliges us to ask and answer this question: How can this tool be used to augment the language learning process?

DISCUSSION QUESTIONS

1. In your opinion, what is the most useful application of computer technology to language learning? What is the least useful?
2. Some instructors worry that too much class time is spent "teaching technology" at the expense of teaching language. Do you agree with this observation? Why or why not?
3. Policy makers and others are concerned about the "digital divide"—the economic differences that give greater access to technology to those institutions and people with more money. Do you think there is a digital divide? If so, how does it affect the population(s) of learners that concern you?
4. Review the section of the reading subtitled "What Computers Can't Do." Do you agree with its analysis? Could computers do some of these things, given different or better technology?
5. How have you used computers in your own education? How could you teach ESL/EFL students to use computers to their advantage?

SUGGESTED ACTIVITIES

1. Choose a website or a software package that focuses on English language learning. Based on your understanding of good educational practices, list at least five things that you would improve the website or package.
2. Create a syllabus for a beginning English grammar course for ESL/EFL learners in which you integrate at least three different types of computer use (for example, drills, e-mail, and so forth). Discuss how your use of technology will enhance the grammar learning experience.
3. Look at Table 1 (p. 484). What activities could you add to this table? Try to think of one new activity for each column.
4. Locate a website intended for ESL/EFL teachers. Provide a summary and review of what this site offers, and how it is useful to ESL/EFL instructors.

 FURTHER READING

Boswood, T., ed. 1997. *New Ways of Using Computers in Language Teaching.* Alexandria, VA: TESOL.
Part of TESOL's "New Ways" series, this volume focuses on pedagogy rather than technology. It presents an array of activities including word processing and desktop publishing, e-mail and MOOs, the Web, multimedia, concordancing, and other applications.

Egbert, J., and E. Hanson-Smith, eds. 1999. *CALL Environments: Research, Practice, and Critical Issues.* Alexandria, VA: TESOL.
This collection of articles focuses on research issues that offer a theoretical framework based on ESL and second language research, and describes theory-based practice for different technological environments and learners.

Sperling, D. 1998. *Dave Sperling's Internet Guide.* Englewood Cliffs, NJ: Prentice Hall Regents.
A practical guide for teachers using the Internet with ESL/EFL students. A good companion for the Dave's ESL Café website (http://www.eslcafe.com).

Swaffar, J., S. Romano, P. Markley, and K. Arens, eds. 1998. *Language Learning Online: Theory and Practice in the ESL and L2 Computer Classroom*. Austin, TX: Labyrinth Publications.

This research-based book looks at how students use technology, particularly in writing.

Warschauer, M. 1995. *E-Mail for English Teaching*. Alexandria, VA: TESOL.

This text focuses solely on e-mail communication, and explains very completely both the technology and what can be done with it. Good for teachers who are just starting to use technology in their classrooms.

ENDNOTES

1. The original excerpt comes from Project Gutenberg's (http://promo.net/pg/) archives. The human translation also comes from Project Gutenberg. The machine translation was done with Babel Fish software, available at altavista.com.

2. According to Krashen's hypothesis, the learner acquires a second language when he or she receives second language input ("i") that is one step beyond his or her current stage of linguistic competence (+1).

3. This is the modernization of "pen pal" now that users work on computer keyboards and send mail electronically.

Action Research, Teacher Research, and Classroom Research in Language Teaching

KATHLEEN M. BAILEY

Bailey's chapter compares and contrasts three terms that are often confused: action research, teacher research, and classroom research. While action research is an actual research method, teacher research is defined by who conducts it, and classroom research is defined by the setting in which the data are collected.

INTRODUCTION

The purpose of this chapter is to introduce language teachers to the research being done in language classrooms. I have structured the chapter around a series of questions. It begins with a comparison of classroom research, teacher research, and action research. It includes a summary of some recent studies directly related to the work of language teachers, and ends with some activities readers can do to enhance their understanding of the concepts presented here. Although space constraints do not permit a comprehensive review of the available literature, I hope the studies cited here will encourage teachers to learn more about classroom research.

DEFINITIONS OF KEY TERMS

In recent years there has been a marked increase in the frequency with which studies of *classroom research, teacher research,* and *action research* have been published in the field of language teaching. These themes occur regularly in the program abstracts at language teachers' conferences. But what do the three terms mean? They are sometimes used interchangeably, but are they in fact synonymous? We will begin by comparing and contrasting these three terms in order to get a better understanding of what sorts of research projects are being done in language classrooms.

WHAT IS LANGUAGE CLASSROOM RESEARCH?

Of these three concepts, the one with the longest tradition in language teaching is *classroom research* (or *classroom-centered research,* as it used to be called). As early as 1980, Long defined classroom research as "research on second language learning and teaching, *all or part of whose data are derived from the observation or measurement of the classroom performance of teachers and students*" (Long 1980, p. 3). In other words, a study about language learning in formal instructional settings for which students had filled out a questionnaire about their participation in language lessons, while interesting and potentially useful, would not fit this definition of classroom research. If, however, the researchers added a classroom observation component to the study, visiting classrooms to see if those learners actually exhibited the same behaviors they had reported in their questionnaire responses, we would then have an example of classroom research, according to Long's definition.

Classroom research, however, isn't just research where the data are collected within the confines of a physical classroom. Consider, for example, Allwright's statement:

> Classroom-centered research is just that—research *centered* on the classroom, as distinct from, for example,

research that concentrates on the *inputs to* the classroom (the syllabus, the teaching materials) or on the *outputs from* the classroom (learner achievement scores). It does not ignore in any way or try to devalue the importance of such inputs and outputs. It simply tries to investigate what happens inside the classroom when learners and teachers come together. At its most narrow, classroom-centered research is in fact research that treats the language classroom not just as the *setting for* investigation but, more importantly, as the *object of* investigation. Classroom processes become the central focus (1983, p. 191).

Classroom research, then, can be conducted by anyone using any approach to data collection and analysis, so long as it meets the definitions above. It is not the province of one school of thought, one group of researchers, or one methodological tradition.

WHAT IS TEACHER RESEARCH?

Teacher research, in contrast, is research conducted by classroom teachers. Although the idea of teachers doing research was not common when the experimental approach was dominant, it has gained momentum in the past two decades, particularly in first language education (see, e.g., Kincheloe 1991). Teacher research is often connected with the concept of teacher development and empowerment (Brindley 1991)—the idea being that by investigating teaching and learning processes in classrooms, we ourselves learn more about the craft and the science of teaching so that we may improve our work as teachers. The *Teachers Develop Teachers Research* series (e.g., Edge and Richards 1993) reports on language teaching projects that take this stance.

Teacher research usually does take place in classrooms, and it typically focuses on some element(s) of classroom interaction, but it doesn't necessarily have to. For example, a teacher could study the written negotiation for meaning between him or her and his or her intermediate ESL students through the students' dialogue journals and his or her responses to them. While such a study would not be considered classroom research, it would be teacher research, because it was designed and carried out by a teacher. In this case, then, the agent conducting the research is the defining feature. In our field you can find discussions of teacher research written by Burns (1995), Freeman (1998), Johnson (1998, 1999), and Nunan (1997b), among others.

WHAT IS ACTION RESEARCH?

Finally, the term *action research* does indeed imply a particular methodological approach. The concept is sometimes confused with teacher research and classroom research because in our field, action research is often conducted by teachers in language classrooms. In addition, it focuses on particular features of classroom interaction. But action research is more than simply research conducted by teachers in classrooms.

The term *action research* is an approach to collecting and interpreting data that involves a clear, repeated cycle of procedures. The researcher begins by planning an action to address a problem, issue, or question in his or her own context. This action (which is also called a "small-scale intervention") is then carried out. (This is the source of the label *action research.*) The next step is the systematic observation of the outcomes of the action. The observation is done through a variety of procedures for collecting data. These include audio or video recordings, teachers' diary entries, observers' notes, etc. (Christison and Bassano [1995] provide clear examples of several data collection procedures teachers can use in action research to gather information from students.) After observing the apparent results of the action, the researcher reflects on the outcome and plans a subsequent action, after which the cycle begins again (Kemmis and McTaggart 1982; Nunan 1993; van Lier 1994).

The broad goals of action research are to seek local understanding and to bring about improvement in the context under study (Bailey 1998a). Kemmis and McTaggart describe action research as "a form of 'self-reflective enquiry' undertaken by participants in social situations in order to improve the rationality and justice of their own social or educational practices, as well as their understanding of these practices and the situations in which these practices are carried out" (1989, p. 2).

Action research was begun in the United States by Lewin (1946) in the 1940s as a means of addressing social problems. Although this approach was overshadowed in the United States for many years by psychometric research in the experimental tradition, it has been widely used for some time in England, Australia, and Hong Kong. A number of action research anthologies and a great deal of the methodological guidance available has been published in general education (see, e.g., Carr and Kemmis 1986; Kemmis and McTaggart 1982; McLean 1995; and Oja and Smulyan 1989). In recent years, however, more and more books and articles have been published about the use of action research in second or foreign language education contexts. (See, for instance, Burns 1998; Nunan 1990; and Wallace 1998 for methodological guidance about how to conduct action research).

HOW DO THESE CONCEPTS FIT TOGETHER?

To summarize, then, the term *classroom research* refers to the location and the focus of the study. *Teacher research* refers to the agents who conduct the study. *Action research* denotes a particular approach, a codified but flexible set of reiterated procedures, for participants to conduct research in their own settings. Action research might or might not be conducted in classrooms, and it might or might not be done by teachers. Figure 1 depicts the overlapping relationship of classroom research, teacher research, and action research.

McPherson (1997) provides a good example of an action research project by a language teacher in her own classroom. She teaches adult ESL classes for recent immigrants to Australia. One year her students had a very wide range of abilities because many had had to wait a long time for a place in the course after the initial assess-

1 = Classroom research conducted by teachers using approaches other than action research
2 = Research conducted by teachers outside of classrooms using approaches other than action research
3 = Action research conducted by teachers outside of classrooms
4 = Classroom research conducted by teachers using the action research approach

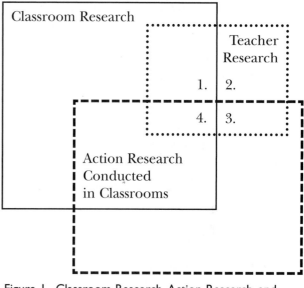

Figure 1. Classroom Research, Action Research, and Teacher Research

ment of their English skills. McPherson and 25 other ESL teachers in 4 states of Australia undertook action research projects, all in their own contexts but each focusing on some aspect of teaching diverse learners. McPherson's article describes the three cycles of her action research study. It is an example of teacher research, using the action research model, situated in the wider approach of language classroom research.

In the first cycle, McPherson reviewed the literature on teaching mixed-ability classes, talked to other teachers, and tried various ways of grouping her students based on their proficiency levels. She found that the students appeared to have goals different from her own and sometimes resisted the group and pair work she had organized.

In the second cycle, McPherson elicited the students' input about the activities. They were surprised that she saw mixed levels as a problem and said they were happy to work in mixed-ability classes. As a result of these discussions, McPherson gave the students more responsibility to select their own materials and activities. She was then able to observe them making their own learning choices, which she carefully documented. She found that the students had reasons quite different from her own for their choices. For instance, many students experienced intra-group tensions (e.g., in choosing partners for group work) related to their own ethnicity as well as to the political problems of their home countries. The students had developed strategies for maintaining civil relations in class, but the teacher's grouping efforts had inadvertently undermined the delicate balance. Of their reticence, McPherson writes, "They had tried in subtle ways to make me aware of the sensitive and precarious nature of the classroom dynamics by declining to carry out the activities which they believed could upset the equilibrium" (1997, p. 58). Allowing the students more choice was the first step toward resolving this issue.

The third cycle of the action research project occurred near the end of the course. Although the rest of the class had begun to work well together, there were still two students who seemed to be marginalized by the ethnic group that was dominant in the class. McPherson implemented a strategy of deliberately calling on these two students and validating their contributions to class discussions. As the term ended, even these two students had begun to get more involved.

WHAT DEVELOPMENTS HAVE OCCURRED IN LANGUAGE CLASSROOM RESEARCH?

In Bailey (1985), I published a review of the classroom research literature that identified four major research themes up to that point. These were (1) students' patterns of participation in language classrooms, (2) investigations of language teachers' classroom behavior, (3) teachers' treatment of learners' (oral) errors, and (4) individual student (or teacher) variables.

An extensive literature review by Chaudron in 1988 also identified four main areas of research: (1) teacher talk in second language classrooms, (2) learner behavior in second language classrooms, (3) teacher and student interactions in second language classrooms, and (4) learning outcomes. Chaudron's book-length treatment covered a much greater range of the available classroom research literature than did the chapter by Bailey (1985).

These topics have continued to be important areas of classroom research. For example, Kasper (1985) and Tomasello and Herron (1989) have investigated error treatment in language classes—one of the earliest foci of classroom research. But in some instances the focus of a topic has changed to keep up with developments in language teaching. For example, while many of the early studies looked at patterns of student participation in teacher fronted classes, more recent investigations—influenced by the emergence of communicative language teaching as the preferred approach—have compared small group or dyadic interactions with large group interactions (see, e.g., Long and Porter 1985; Pica and Doughty 1985; Rulon and McCreary 1986).

Another area where an early topical focus has broadened considerably is that of individual learner variables and second language learners' behaviors. One way these topics have been investigated is through language learners' diary entries about their learning experiences. In the early days of language classroom research, most of the language learning diaries were kept by linguists who studied a language but concurrently studied the process of learning that language. This procedure has been criticized (e.g., by Seliger 1983) because it is unlikely that trained linguists represent the majority of language learners—the processes they undergo in learning a language may not be the same as those of the more typical students in language classrooms. More recently, however, diaries have been kept by actual learners but analyzed by researchers. These studies include Ellis's (1989) study of two adult learners of German; Hilleson's (1996) investigation of reticence and anxiety among secondary school students in Singapore; Brown's (1985a) research comparing older and younger adult learners of Spanish; and Matsumoto's (1989) analysis of a young Japanese woman's diary of her ESL learning.

Some classroom studies have used multiple data collection procedures to investigate learner variables. For example, Schmidt and Frota (1986) analyzed a diary kept by Schmidt as he learned Portuguese in Brazil. Frota—a native speaker of Portuguese—also conducted periodic error analyses of Schmidt's speech. In Spain, Block (1996) compared students' tape-recorded oral journal entries with his observations and the teacher's journal entries to compare the various viewpoints expressed on the classroom events. Shaw (1996) used language learners' diary entries, his fieldnotes, and interviews with teachers to investigate content-based language instruction at the graduate level in the United States. Katz (1996) used classroom observations, tape recordings and teacher interviews to document four different teaching styles used by four teachers who were working at the same level in the same program and using the same curriculum.

It is interesting to me, both as a language teacher and as a researcher and reader of others' research, how much development has occurred in language classroom research since the early 1980s. There have been new methodological developments, to be sure, but more impressive has been the wide range of topics investigated in language classroom research. The traditional foci of classroom research listed above continue to be investigated, but other key topics have also appeared. Some of these issues, such as research on students' learning strategies (see, e.g., Chesterfield and Chesterfield 1985) have been influenced by second language acquisition research conducted outside of classrooms. Some are related to sociolinguistic research on contextualized forms of competence. For example, Rounds (1987) investigated the communication skills of non-native-speaking teaching assistants working in English in American universities. Other topics, such as those in the language awareness movement (see, e.g., van Lier 1995), are more closely related to developments in linguistics.

Three specific developments need to be mentioned: (1) investigations of teacher cognition, (2) the globalization of language classroom research, and (3) empirical studies of washback. We will briefly examine these areas, each of which has significance for language teachers worldwide.

CLASSROOM RESEARCH ON TEACHER COGNITION

Teacher cognition research investigates how teachers think about their work, what skilled decision making goes into effective teaching, and how novice teachers' thinking and teaching expertise develop over time. (See Wood 1996, for a review.)

Much of this research involves having teachers review data collected in their own classrooms by researchers. Then the teachers tell those researchers what they were thinking and what motivated their decision-making at the time. The procedure called *stimulated recall* (Gass and Mackey 2000) is often used in this research context. In stimulated recall, a researcher uses some record of an event to prompt the recollections of that event by someone who participated in it. The records, or data, can include audio or video recordings of the class, observers' fieldnotes, or transcripts of classroom interaction. The participants verbalize their recollections and the researchers record those recollections while the participants review the data. For example, Nunan (1996) and Johnson (1992a, 1992b) used the stimulated recall procedure in order to prompt in-service and preservice teachers to explain their mental processes during their lessons.

The topics of teacher cognition and development also have been accessed in classroom research through the use of teachers' journals. Sometimes the journals have been analyzed by people other than the teachers themselves. For example, Numrich (1996) analyzed the teaching journals kept by teachers-in-training who were enrolled in her practicum class. Pennington and Richards (1997) analyzed the teaching journals of five novice EFL teachers in Hong Kong. In other instances, the journals have been analyzed by the teachers who kept them—and thus provide us with examples of teacher research. These include Appel's (1995) booklength study based on a journal he kept for several years as he taught EFL in Germany. Brock, Yu, and Wong (1992) kept teaching journals of their university classes in Hong Kong and then read and discussed them together. Their report documents both their journal findings and what they learned by sharing their journals. Teacher decision making is a vast and important topic, and we are just beginning to understand its richness and complexity.

THE GLOBALIZATION OF LANGUAGE CLASSROOM RESEARCH

As indicated above, language classroom research has been conducted in a wide variety of contexts in recent years. In the early 1980s, much of the published research was done in Canada, Australia, the United Kingdom or the United States. This is no longer the case. For instance, teachers' concerns about working with large classes have emerged as an important topic with serious practical consequences in many regions. This issue has been investigated in Nigeria (Coleman 1989), Japan (LoCastro 1989), Indonesia (Sabander 1989), Pakistan (Shamim 1996), and South Africa (Stein and Janks 1996).

The language used by students and teachers during lessons, one of the early foci of language classroom research, has also been investigated (though not necessarily with action research or teacher research). These studies include research on code-switching in South African classrooms (Adendorff 1996); students' English use in Sri Lankan classrooms (Canagarajah 1993); the language choice in various situations in a French-English bilingual program in Quebec (Cleghorn and Genesee 1984); and the tasks performed in dual-language programs in Hungary (Duff 1995, 1996). The topic of washback illustrates this global trend quite well.

WASHBACK STUDIES IN LANGUAGE CLASSROOMS

Washback—loosely defined as the effects of testing on teaching and learning—has been studied in many parts of the world. Much of this classroom research was conducted by external observers rather than the teachers themselves.

In Sri Lanka, Wall and Alderson (1993) collected baseline data at the beginning of a three-year observational study. *Baseline data* refers to "information that documents the normal state of affairs [and] provides the basis against which we make comparative claims about how different or unusual the phenomena we have seen may be" (Allwright and Bailey 1991, p. 74). In the case of the washback studies, baseline data are usually collected before the implementation of a new test, so that the effects of that test on teaching and learning can be studied subsequently by collecting parallel data after the test has been used for some specific period of time.

Wall and Alderson's study involved classroom observers visiting English classes in five parts of Sri Lanka, over six rounds of observations, before and after a new national English test was implemented. They found that the new exam seriously influenced the content of English lessons, and also had some impact on how the Sri Lankan teachers designed their own in-class exams. However, it had very little influence on how they taught or how they graded their students' performance on tests.

The effects of Japanese university entrance examinations were studied by Watanabe (1996), who found some results very similar to those of Wall and Alderson. He observed two teachers, each of whom was teaching two test preparation courses. However, he found that the grammar-translation questions on the university entrance exams did not influence the two teachers in the same way. He felt that three factors promoted or inhibited washback in these cases: (1) the teachers' educational background and/or experience, (2) the teachers' different beliefs about what constituted effective teaching, and (3) the timing of the researcher's observations relative to the date of the upcoming exam.

In Israel, Shohamy, Donitsa-Schmidt, and Ferman (1996) conducted classroom research on the washback created by a new test of Arabic as a second language (ASL), as well as a new test of English as a foreign language (EFL). When the new ASL test was implemented, they observed that the teachers stopped covering new material and began to review intensively;

worksheets based on the previous year's ASL test replaced the textbooks; class activities became testlike and the atmosphere became tense. Once the test had been administered, these manifestations of washback stopped. In the case of the EFL test, which included an oral component, Shohamy et al. observed that the teachers increased the amount of class time spent on listening and speaking, using activities and tasks based on the EFL test. This study confirmed that washback at the very least influences what teachers emphasize in language classes.

Alderson and Hamp-Lyons (1996) observed the same two teachers as they taught regular ESL classes and Test of English as a Foreign Language (TOEFL) preparation classes in the United States. Among other things, their study found that the test preparation classes involved much more test taking, spent less time on pair work, entailed more teacher talk and less student talk, generated more metalanguage (talk about language), and elicited less laughter than the non-TOEFL classes.

In Hong Kong, Cheng (1997) observed the same secondary school English teachers working with two groups of students preparing for their school-leaving examinations—those slated to take the old exam and those who would take the new exam. The old exam included passages for the students to read aloud, while the new test included role plays and group discussions instead. In the new exam preparation classes, Cheng found that the teachers did not have students practice reading aloud, and that more time was spent on oral presentations and group discussions. She pointed out that the exam had changed the content of the courses, but had had a minimal impact on the teaching methods.

The existing classroom research studies on washback raise a number of interesting questions about how external tests influence teaching and learning. From what we have seen so far, tests seem to have considerable impact on what gets taught, but less influence on how that content is taught. Future research in this area is needed. To the best of my knowledge, none of the published classroom research on washback involves teacher research or the use of action research to investigate this important issue.

WHAT TOPICS HAVE BEEN INVESTIGATED BY TEACHERS DOING ACTION RESEARCH IN LANGUAGE CLASSROOMS?

As noted above, action research has seen a dramatic rise in popularity since 1980. The advent of action research as a legitimate approach to investigating phenomena in language classrooms has opened a wide range of new topics as well as promoting research by teachers who use this model.

Recently, a number of action research studies have been published in which language teachers (sometimes working alone, sometimes collaborating with others) have used the action research approach to investigate issues in their own classrooms. For example, Kebir (1994) studied adult language learners' communication strategies. A special edition of *Orbis Linguarum* edited by Michonska-Stadnik and Szulc-Kuparska (1997) documents a wide-scale action research investigation of learner independence in Poland. Chan (1996) looked at action research as a vehicle for professional development in Hong Kong. Also in Hong Kong, Tsui (1996) reported on a study in which several secondary school teachers in Hong Kong used action research to investigate their students' reticence to use English in the classroom. A study of Vygotskyan principles to promote interaction in a low-level ESL class was conducted by van Lier (1992). His work with the ESL learners resulted in discussion materials for use in his language teacher education courses, which fed back into the ESL class, and so on.

WHAT IS THE TEACHER'S ROLE IN LANGUAGE CLASSROOM RESEARCH?

The teacher's role in classroom research has grown tremendously (Allwright 1997; Nunan 1997). In the days when most research was experimental, investigations were typically conducted by outsiders to ensure objectivity in data collection and interpretation. Teachers were seen either as subjects in a particular study or as the implementers of the treatment in the experiment.

Now, however, there is a much more inclusive view of teachers as partners in the research enterprise, working in collaboration with researchers (see, e.g., Freeman's 1992 study of a secondary school French class). It is also not uncommon these days for teachers in our field to be producers, instead of consumers, of language classroom research (Crookes 1998; Freeman 1996). Pica (1997) has described the evolving relationship of language teaching and research as moving from coexistence to collaboration and complementarity. (See also Hudelson and Lindfors 1993.)

WHERE ARE WE NOW?

One clear development in the last few years is that there are now many methodological resources available to teachers and others who wish to conduct language classroom research. In addition to the action research references cited above, there are many texts and articles available about classroom research in general. For example, Allwright and Bailey (1991) wrote an introduction to both the topics and the methods of classroom research for language teachers. Brown (1985b) compared the diary study approach with participant observation in language classroom research. Brumfit and Mitchell (1990) and Bailey (1998a) reviewed a number of classroom research projects. Gass and Mackey (2000) provided step-by-step guidance and clear examples for researchers, including teacher researchers, who wish to use the stimu-lated recall procedure. Samway (1994) provided suggestions for teachers about how to record data while they are actually teaching. Freeman (1998), Johnson (1998, 1999), Nunan (1991b), Tsui (1995), and van Lier (1988, 1990) have all discussed how to investigate language classroom interaction.

One sign of professional maturity is the willingness of a field to critique its own work. In recent years a number of articles and books have been written which question the procedures used in classroom research or which identify problematic issues (see, e.g., Bailey 1991 and Seliger 1983). Schachter and Gass (1996) have edited an interesting collection of articles which candidly discuss the sorts of problems that arise in doing classroom research. Many of these resources would be helpful to language teachers who wish to get started on their own classroom research.

WHY SHOULD TEACHERS GET INVOLVED IN LANGUAGE CLASSROOM RESEARCH?

Why should teachers bother to get involved in action research, or any form of classroom research for that matter? Doesn't it take time to conduct such studies? Doesn't research require discipline and specialized training to carry out? The answer is yes, certainly. In addition, in many situations, teachers are not given financial or strategic support, release time, or even recognition for conducting research. Allwright (1997) has addressed some of these concerns. Also, Allwright and Lenzuen (1997) have described an approach called "exploratory teaching," which is related to action research but keeps the teaching central while allowing teachers to raise and answer important questions about their work in language classrooms.

There are still good reasons for teachers to conduct language classroom research, however. The processes involved in data collection and analysis can help them discover patterns (both positive and negative) in their interactions with students. They can discover interesting new puzzles and answers, both of which can energize their teaching. By reading or hearing accounts of other people's research, they can get new ideas for teaching and for their investigations, as well as becoming better connected with the profession at large. And by sharing the results of their own research (at conferences, in publications, in staff room lunch talks, and so on), they can get feedback from other teachers and learn from their experiences.

In closing, I want to quote three sentences from McPherson's action research report, which was summarized on pages 491–492 of this chapter. The first two sentences I wish to highlight follow:

> This action research project played a major role in helping *me* to understand the learning issues involved *in my class* and in developing systematic ways to investigate and address them. As a research method, action research was flexible enough to allow *me* to change the focus of *my* investigation from developing and trialing language learning materials and activities to addressing issues of difference and diversity (1997, p. 61).

I have added my own emphasis in these two sentences to stress the situated, localized nature of McPherson's research as well as what she herself gained from working on the project. The third sentence, below, provides an apt closing to this chapter, but also perhaps a great beginning regarding how to think about action research, teacher research, and classroom research in general. After she finished her study, McPherson concluded,

> The events that occurred forced me to remember that in the classroom there is more to learning a language than learning language (p. 60).

DISCUSSION QUESTIONS

1. In your understanding, how do language classroom research, teacher research, and action research differ from one another? How do they differ from other forms of research with which you may be familiar (for instance, library research or the scientific method)?
2. What are the advantages and disadvantages of language teachers conducting research in their own classrooms? What are the advantages and disadvantages of outsiders conducting research in language classrooms?
3. What are three topics of interest to you as a teacher which have been investigated in language classroom research to date? Why are they of particular interest?
4. *Washback* has been defined as the effects of testing on language teaching and learning. Have you ever experienced washback, either as a teacher or as a language learner? What were the circumstances? What was the test and how did it influence your teaching or learning?
5. If you had been able to do classroom research on the washback situation discussed in Question 4, what data would you have collected? What do you think the data would have shown you?

SUGGESTED ACTIVITIES

1. Tape record two or three consecutive lessons in the same language class. These tapes can provide baseline data. Listen to the tapes and write down three to five questions that arise about the interaction in the class.
2. Think of some ways that you could go about answering these questions by collecting additional data. How would your data collection procedures differ if you (a) were teaching the class, or (b) were observing someone else teaching the class?
3. If you are currently teaching, plan the initial steps of an action research project that you could conduct in your own class. Keep in mind that your goals may change as you work through the action research cycle of planning, acting, observing, reflecting, and replanning for the next iteration. Discuss your initial plans with a colleague or fellow student.
4. Keep a diary of your own language teaching (or language learning) for a set period of time for several days running—for instance, for a period of two weeks. Don't reread your diary entries until the predetermined period is over. What patterns emerge in the behaviors and attitudes documented in your diary? How could these issues be investigated further?

5. If you are currently teaching or doing your practice teaching, ask a trusted colleague or fellow student to observe you teaching a lesson and take notes on the interaction. What issues emerge from the observation that you were unaware of as the teacher? How could you and an observer investigate these issues further?

FURTHER READING

If you would like to learn more about action research, these books by Burns and Wallace are clear sources of information:

Burns, A. 1998. *Collaborative Action Research for English Teachers.* Cambridge: Cambridge University Press.

Wallace, M. J. 1998. *Action Research for Language Teachers.* Cambridge: Cambridge University Press.

Allwright and Bailey provides a user-friendly general introduction to language classroom research for teachers and preservice teachers.

Allwright, D., and K. M. Bailey. 1991. *Focus on the Classroom: An Introduction to Classroom Research for Language Teachers.* Cambridge: Cambridge University Press.

Nunan's book has many excellent ideas and clear examples for teachers who wish to begin classroom investigations of their own.

Nunan, D. 1989. *Understanding Language Classrooms: A Guide for Teacher-initiated Action.* New York: Prentice Hall.

Freeman's and Johnson's books are ideal starting places. They include examples of teacher research as well as teachers' comments on doing research.

Freeman, D. 1998. *Doing Teacher Research: From Inquiry to Understanding.* Boston, MA: Heinle & Heinle Publishers.

Johnson, K. E. 1999. *Understanding Language Teaching: Reasoning in Action.* Boston, MA: Heinle & Heinle Publishers.

Reflective Teaching in ELT

JOHN M. MURPHY

Murphy's chapter introduces several intriguing pathways for long-term professional growth. It features tools to learn more about who we are as teachers (including students' perceptions) through such procedures as five-minute papers, teacher-assessment surveys, student focus groups, retrospective field notes, and non-supervisory peer feedback. The chapter also highlights purposes of reflective teaching and topics explored by reflective teachers.

INTRODUCTION

Gaining teaching experience, participating in teacher-development courses, thinking about and discussing published scholarship, attending conferences, consulting colleagues, and getting to know students better are but some of the many ways that English language teachers can grow as professionals. This chapter adds to these resources by introducing ways for teachers to look inward, both within themselves and within the courses they offer, to access information and inspiration about their efforts in language classrooms. The chapter's purpose is to serve as an introduction to reflective teaching. For those interested in learning more about this vibrant tradition in the field of English language teaching (ELT), the section titled "Further Reading" provides an annotated listing of sources that served as the chapter's conceptual grounding.

One of the more intriguing characteristics that distinguishes adults from children is that adults have an increased capacity for self-reflective thought (Kohlberg 1981, Mezirow 1981). This is not to say that children are incapable of self-reflection or of learning through introspective means. Parents know that children, especially adolescents, can be highly self-reflective. Yet in comparison with younger people, adults possess greater capacities in this area. The challenge is to put such capacities to more productive use.

As a language teacher, have you ever finished all of your teaching for the day only to find your mind racing with thoughts about a lesson recently completed? This is a recurring experience for me, especially when returning home from work on public transportation. While others seated around me seem to be reading newspapers, staring into space, or calmly chatting with friends, my mind often races with classroom images, including insights, puzzles, second guesses, resolutions, and plans for the future. During such moments I find myself responding with a full range of emotion that includes not only excitement, joy, inspiration, and reassurance but also more troubling moments of boredom, annoyance, and even disappointment in myself. There are occasions when something particularly intriguing might find its way into subsequent plans for teaching but unless I take the step of writing them down, such insights tend to dissipate as the evening continues. This chapter explores ways to help ensure that such moments serve productive purposes.

PURPOSES OF REFLECTIVE TEACHING

The purposes of reflective teaching are three-fold: (1) to expand one's understanding of the teaching-learning process; (2) to expand one's repertoire of strategic options as a language teacher; and (3) to enhance the quality of learning opportunities one is able to provide in language classrooms. To these ends, those interested in reflective teaching take steps to deepen awareness of teaching and learning behaviors by working to improve their abilities to:

- Gather information on whatever is taking place within a language course
- Examine such information closely in an effort to better understand what they collect
- Identify anything puzzling about the teaching-learning process
- Build awareness and deepen understanding of current teaching and learning behaviors
- Locate and collaborate with others interested in processes of reflective teaching
- Pose and refine questions tied to one's teaching that are worth further exploration
- Locate resources that may help to clarify whatever questions are being posed
- Make informed changes in teaching, even if only modest changes
- Document changes in teaching-learning behaviors and responses
- Continue such efforts over time and share emerging insights with others

DEFINITION OF TERMS

Richards and Lockhart (1994) define reflective teaching as an approach to second language (L2) classroom instruction in which current and prospective teachers "collect data about teaching, examine their attitudes, beliefs, assumptions, and teaching practices, and use the information obtained as a basis for critical reflection" about their efforts in language courses (p. 1). They posit five basic assumptions:

- An informed teacher has an extensive knowledge base about teaching
- Much can be learned about teaching through self-inquiry
- Much of what happens in teaching is unknown to the teacher
- Teaching experience alone is insufficient as a basis for continuing development
- Critical reflection can trigger a deeper understanding of teaching

Why would we spend the time and energy it takes to develop understandings through reflective teaching? We may find the answer by considering both our continuing needs as teachers and, even more importantly, the needs of the language learners we serve. What the five assumptions cited above share is that reflective teachers are capable of learning from, and further developing, their personal understandings and explanations of life within language classrooms. A central reason to be interested in reflective teaching "is to gain awareness of our teaching beliefs and practices" and to learn "to see teaching differently" (Gebhard and Oprandy 1999, p. 4). A rationale to support reflective teaching certainly includes such insights, but it also extends beyond them. In addition to the reasons cited thus far, an integral part of reflective teaching is to learn to take action, when possible, on whatever we might be learning about ourselves as teachers and about students' responses, for the purpose of enhancing the quality of learning opportunities we are able to provide in our classrooms. For us as language teachers, taking action might involve exploring instructional innovations, trying out alternatives, and modifying—or even breaking—routines in teaching based upon what we learn.

TOPICS EXPLORED BY REFLECTIVE TEACHERS

To examine some of the topics typically explored by reflective teachers, we first need to acknowledge that each language course is unique. English language teaching and language learning are processes embedded within complex arrays of dynamic and socially interactive events. Early stages of reflective teaching begin with a classroom teacher's desire to better understand the dynamics of a single language course as it is being experienced by a group of learners and their teacher. This is not to say that reflective teaching cannot extend beyond the scope of a single course; at later stages it often does. But as a place to begin, most teachers find an individual course to be the most useful place to initiate what eventually becomes systematic efforts at reflective teaching. Some general topic areas reflective teachers often explore are: (1) communication patterns in the classroom; (2) teacher decision making; (3) ways in which learners apply knowledge; (4) the affective climate of the classroom, (5) the instructional environment; and (6) a teacher's self-assessment of growth and development as a professional.

Reflection Break #1

In addition to these six general areas, what are some other areas you think reflective teachers who work in ELT settings might profitably explore? Alternatively, what might be some specific examples of the six areas listed above?

Communication Patterns in the Classroom
Teachers who are interested in patterns of communication in language classrooms often explore classroom management issues such as, Who is doing what during lessons? As the teacher, am I the sole source of power and control? Do learners sometimes have an impact on what takes place? Classroom communication patterns is one of the more common topics explored by reflective teachers. Most of us are interested in better understanding how communications between everyone present in the classroom may influence teaching and learning processes. For example, a teacher might examine recurring features within the instructional routine to better understand students' learning preferences. A teacher interested in communication patterns might ask if lessons usually begin and end in the same way. With video support, it is possible to divide a language lesson into a series of manageable segments for analysis. Multiple viewing reveals how lessons begin (openings which tend to be broadly focused), introductions to specific activities (setting things up, giving directions, clarifying, providing support for what is to follow), core lesson segments (individual activities that tend to reflect preplanned teaching decisions), ways in which the teacher and the class move from one activity to another (transitions between lesson segments), how lesson segments are sequenced (pre-, core-, and post-activity phases), how students respond to teacher feedback, and the teacher's way of drawing a lesson to a close (calling for attention, assigning homework, previewing upcoming events). Most language lessons feature identifiable segments straddled by transitions from one segment to another. An interesting way to increase understanding of current ways of teaching is to gather information on how you structure, pace, and sequence lesson segments. By generating an audio or video recording of their teaching, for example, and then moving between macro- and microlevel examinations of whole lessons, reflective teachers can begin to better understand such features. Close review of their ways of teaching leads many teachers to then consider ways of manipulating lesson segments, and some of the features embedded with them, to increased effect.

Lesson Participant Interactions Another helpful topic to explore is to examine more specific patterns of learner-to-learner and teacher-to-learner(s) interactions in the classroom. Who speaks to whom, how often, in what sequence, and for how long? How are speaking turns distributed? Is the teacher the only one who controls their distribution? How are topics and shifts in topic development introduced? What are some of the ways in which learners take the floor as speakers in the midst of classroom communications? Are there learners who are relatively more or less participatory during particular lesson phases? Do patterns of communication in the classroom provide opportunities for learners to take the initiative?

Teacher Decision Making This area for exploration includes a vast, and as yet poorly understood, dimension of language teaching. Acts of language teaching spring from sources within us that include our cognitive and emotional responses to external classroom events. Because all of us depend upon knowledge, values, and beliefs about teaching and learning in order to function as teachers in the classroom, our internal understandings and expectations contribute to our teaching decisions and behaviors. Specialists sketch an intriguing territory of teacher decision making which Richards and Lockhart (1994) divide into pre-, during-, and post-lesson decisions. In the case of during-lesson decisions, teachers have very little time to follow through on what they decide to do since the process unfolds in collaboration with—and in front of—a group of learners. At such moments, a teacher's decisions may seem nearly instantaneous although they are informed by the teacher's background and previous experiences.

Communication patterns in classrooms, lesson participant interactions, and teacher decision making are just a few of the topics often explored by reflective teachers. A more complete listing would include learning to identify and explore:

■ The teacher's ways of giving instructions, responding to students' errors, providing feedback, using language, introducing new teaching strategies, encouraging language use beyond the classroom, identifying and attending to learners' needs, working with reluctant learners, responding to students' errors

■ Learners' ways of requesting clarifications, responding to feedback, applying knowledge, using language, interacting with their peers, responding to changes in teaching, using learning strategies

■ Even more general topics such as the affective climate of the classroom, debilitative and facilitative anxiety, cultural considerations, the instructional environment, the physical setup of the classroom, textbooks and other resources, student-generated materials, resources beyond the classroom

The above list illustrates the kinds of topics that all language teachers are interested in learning more about but that reflective teachers take deliberate action to explore.

Reflection Break #2

Generate a list of topics related to your own teaching that you think would be worth learning more about. See if you can come up with at least four examples not mentioned in the preceding section. Once your list is complete, compare it to that of one or more other language teacher(s). How might you set about increasing your understanding of at least some of the topics of interest to you?

TOOLS FOR REFLECTIVE TEACHING/GATHERING INFORMATION

Just as there are many topics to be explored by reflective teachers, there are also many different ways to gather information. I refer to ways of gathering information included in this section as *tools* in a positive sense since these are the "tools of the trade" that growing numbers of reflective teachers depend upon to explore the teaching-learning process. Teachers use different tools to access different sorts of information. By combining two or more tools over the span of an entire course, a teacher gains access to alternative vantage points. Though space limitations permit only a few tools to be featured in this chapter, Table 1 depicts a more comprehensive listing of some of the major tools reflective teachers use. Unless otherwise indicated, resources for learning more about them are featured in the "Further Reading" section. Expanding on Table 1, I discuss five tools that should be especially useful to teachers interested in becoming more involved in processes and procedures of reflective teaching. These tools are: five-minute papers, formative teacher assessment surveys, student focus groups, retrospective field notes, and formative feedback from peers.

FIVE-MINUTE PAPERS

Regular use of five-minute papers is a direct way of finding out how learners are perceiving and responding to our efforts as teachers. A few minutes before the end of the lesson, the teacher asks everyone to take out a sheet of paper and to write responses to one or two open-ended prompts such as: (1) What is the one thing you are likely to remember from today's class? (2) What was the most confusing concept we covered? (3) Is there anything you would like to know more about? (4) Is there anything you think I should be doing differently? Learner responses to such questions are especially useful if the teacher emphasizes that their purpose is to provide formative feedback on how the course is going. In many ELT courses teachers are able to

Table 1. Some Tools of Reflective Teaching: Ways of Gathering Information

- ■ Formative feedback from learners
  - Five-minute papers
  - Teacher assessment surveys
  - Questionnaires
  - Dialogue journals
  - Written assessments
  - Student focus groups

- ■ Formative feedback from other teachers
  - Peer collaborations (Murphy 1992)
  - "Case" interviews
  - Field notes and classroom ethnographies
  - Dialogue with a supervisor (Master 1983)
  - Observation schedules
  - Score charts
  - Classroom observation (Wajnryb 1992)

- ■ Self-generated sources of information
  - Retrospective field notes
  - Teaching journals and teaching logs
  - Classroom diagrams and maps
  - Lesson plans and lesson reporting
  - Audio recordings
  - Video recordings
  - Transcript analysis
  - Protocol analysis
  - Stimulus recall

- ■ Course descriptions (Graves 2000; Murphy and Byrd in press)

- ■ Summative feedback from learners at the end of the course

- ■ Action research (See Bailey's chapter in this volume)

ask students to compose five-minute papers in English. In settings where it is possible, students might be given the option of writing five-minute papers in their first language(s). Though five-minute papers take time away from the regular part of a lesson, using them at the end of class can better inform a teacher's post-lesson decisions. When introducing them for the first time, I explain to students that:

- ■ Their names should not appear on their papers (their writings will be kept in confidence).

- ■ When reading the papers I will *not* be looking at things like grammar, spelling, or vocabulary choice but only for the ideas they convey.

- ■ As their teacher I will be reading for the purpose of improving my teaching in the course and not to evaluate their progress.

Invariably, I find something of value in what students have to say. I will occasionally ask a colleague to read the papers first, and then discuss with me the gist of students' comments. Involving someone else is a small step toward gaining access to an outside perspective on my work. As well as providing an opportunity to talk about my teaching with another teacher, it helps to ensure I will be responsive to what students have to say. Experience with five-minute papers over the past few years has taught me that a teacher's sense of timing is essential since using them can be overdone. If students are asked to compose them too often, they lose interest and may even begin to resent being asked to do so. In courses that meet two or three times a week, I find that once every two or three weeks is often enough. Using them wisely can serve as vivid reminders to students that their responses to the course are valued and given serious attention.

FORMATIVE TEACHER ASSESSMENT SURVEYS:

A complement to five-minute papers is to schedule several surveys of students' perceptions of how well the course is going. These might be included in the course syllabus on the first day of class so students will know from the start that their impressions will be valued, when their impressions will be solicited, and what the survey will include. Some advantages of formative assessment surveys are that they can be clearly structured in advance, it is easy to keep students' comments anonymous, a lot of information can be gathered at one time, and the procedure may be carried out at regular intervals. One option is to implement such surveys three times during the span of an entire course. For example, I

work in an ESL setting where the length of courses I teach is 15 weeks. I gather formative assessment information through student surveys after the third, eighth, and thirteenth weeks of class. A survey early in the course serves as a window into students' initial responses to the course. By the eighth week their impressions are even better informed since learners are beyond the midpoint and have had ample opportunities to develop understandings and impressions of both the course and my role as their teacher. These first two surveys are the ones that directly impact on my teaching decisions in the section of the course students are taking. Though I also find a student survey in the thirteenth week to be useful, at this point the course is coming to a close and students' comments will have more of an impact on future iterations of the course.

When using formative teacher assessment surveys, a practical strategy is to place at the very end of the course syllabus a copy of the first survey sheet to be collected. By positioning it at the end, students only have to detach the first survey sheet on the appropriate day to complete it and hand it in. I arrange the second survey sheet (eighth week) as the second-to-last page in the syllabus, with the third one (thirteenth week) immediately before the second. The following is an illustration of a formative teacher assessment survey I recently included in the syllabus for a high-intermediate level ESL Oral Communication course I offer.

Formative Feedback (1st of 3) to the Instructor

Please complete and place in a stack on the front desk at the end of our 8th day of class, Wednesday, September XXX. (Alternatively, you are welcome to place it in my mailbox in the main office.)

Directions: Please <u>do not</u> sign your name. We are three weeks into the course. This is a time for some formative feedback from you as a course participant. You are welcome to use both sides of this page.
Thanks.

1   What are some features of the course that you think are working out pretty well (features you would like to see continued for the remainder of the course)?

2.   What are some possible changes you would like to see incorporated into the course from this point forward?

Another option is to follow similar procedures but to use a format that involves less writing by providing a list of items to which students can respond on an easily accessible scale, such as:

| Yes, I agree. | I agree somewhat. | No, I do not agree. |

Illustrations of sample items to include are:

In general, the textbooks, materials, and assignments in this course:[1]

- are interesting and useful
- are at the right level
- help me to practice and improve my language skills
- require the right amount of homework

In general, the teacher of this course:

- presents well-organized lessons
- speaks in a way that is clear and easy to understand
- is knowledgeable about the subjects we cover
- answers my questions well
- grades assignments and tests fairly
- makes good use of class time
- returns work (that I hand in) on time
- gives me individual help when I need it (or when I ask for it)
- encourages me to do my best
- relates well to students
- provides appropriate opportunities for me to participate in class

A final survey item might ask: *If you were in a conversation with a friend, would you recommend taking a course from this teacher? Why or why not?*

Reflection Break #3

Have you ever had an opportunity to receive learner feedback on your teaching? If so, what did you learn from the experience? If not, do you think such sources of information might be useful? Would you expect the quality of learner feedback to vary depending upon learners' cultural backgrounds? If so, what could you do to compensate for cultural differences?

STUDENT FOCUS GROUPS

The use of student focus groups is a simple idea, yet one underutilized in our field. It is more involved than five-minute papers or student surveys and takes careful planning. Beyond the field of language teaching, focus groups are becoming increasingly familiar in many walks of life, including advertising and politics. In language teaching, student focus groups engage either all members of a class or a subset of learners in a discussion of how a course is going. Though either the classroom teacher or a colleague-consultant may serve as focus group discussion leader, I prefer asking a colleague to perform this role. Some options are as follows. Make arrangements for a colleague you trust, and with whom you have a constructive working relationship, to serve as the focus group facilitator. I deliberately avoid working with a supervisor or program administrator at such times since student focus groups work best when they are not being used for formal evaluative purposes. I try to time my use of the procedure for a period in the course when things seem to be going relatively well (or at least normally). Invite your colleague to visit the class for a lesson during which you will not be present but for which students have been prepared in advance. As agreed upon with the class, your colleague's role is to lead the whole class in a discussion of broad topics such as:

- How is the course going?
- What do you like about the course (or the teacher)?
- What are your least favorite things?
- Does the course textbook—or other instructional material—seem helpful?
- What are some characteristics of the teacher's instructional style that work well?
- What are some characteristics you find to be less helpful?
- Do assessment procedures seem fair?
- What are some of the ways in which the course might be improved?

The facilitator could distribute a handout listing the above questions or he or she might use a copy of the teacher assessment survey from the preceding section. Students can then pick and choose their preferred topics for discussion. Prior to the day of the focus group and at the start of the actual discussion, students need to be assured that their comments will be kept in confidence. The facilitator's role is to listen carefully and empathetically, keep the discussion on track, and take notes (when possible) on what students have to say.

When the class is finished, the facilitator composes a written report (*not* to be used for formal evaluation purposes) that provides a synopsis for the teacher of the students' suggestions for the course. No names should appear in the report; it needs to be phrased to protect students' identities. Once it is completed, the visiting colleague gives the classroom teacher a copy and makes arrangements to discuss what took place.

A very effective situation for those interested in student focus groups is to build toward a reciprocal peer arrangement in which two teachers may serve as the discussion facilitator for each other's classes. Ideally, a mutually supportive collaboration evolves between teachers that could develop over time. One modification to the focus groups is to avoid involving the whole class, but to discuss the focus group process with them and ask for only a few members of the class (e.g., 20–25 percent) to volunteer to participate. In this option, students choose whether to participate. Many language teachers find the kind of information revealed as a result of student focus groups to be tremendously helpful for fine-tuning their planning decisions and increasing awareness of their strengths as well as areas they could improve.

RETROSPECTIVE FIELD NOTES

A less intrusive way to gather information on teaching is to document your understandings and explanations of what you are doing in the course through retrospective field notes. The word *retrospective* signals that such field notes are not generated during lessons but only after a lesson has finished. Since acts of teaching are complex and keep teachers incredibly busy, a teacher's field notes ideally should be generated immediately following the lesson. The idea is to find a private place to write after the lesson is over. It takes discipline to compose retrospective field notes

on a regular basis and it is important to start writing soon after the end of a class (for example, within 30–60 minutes). If too much time elapses, our memories of classroom events quickly fade. The activity is similar to keeping a personal journal or diary, with the difference that retrospective field notes focus on course-related events. To produce them, the teacher writes about whatever is fresh in his or her memory. General guidelines are to try to keep track of classroom issues that seem relevant to the lesson recently completed and to treat field notes as an ethnographer treats raw data. Reflective teachers using this procedure save their notes over time, review them on a regular basis, and look for what their notes may reveal about recurring patterns. After you have reworked your notes by deleting or modifying anything that might be personally uncomfortable, a colleague might be invited to read them and discuss whatever concerns you about a course. Retrospective field notes can become a valuable source of information about one's understandings and a richly textured record of one's explanations of teaching over time. Some general ways to frame fieldnotes are to respond to questions about yourself as a teacher, the teaching process, students in the class, the learning process, or anything tied to the dynamics of the lesson itself. A way to get started with retrospective field notes, and a useful task to return to whenever you have too little to write about, is to spend time generating a list of questions you might be able to use as writing prompts in the future.

Reflection Break #4

Collaborate with someone else (a pre- or in-service teacher) to produce a list of five to eight questions you could use as prompts for composing retrospective field notes. Plan them so each writing prompt targets different dimensions of classroom teaching and learning.

FORMATIVE FEEDBACK FROM PEERS

There are many ways in which a teacher may collaborate with others to gain a deeper understanding and awareness of the teaching-learning process. I have previously mentioned that colleagues may be consulted when examining materials such as five-minute papers, retrospective field notes, or survey responses. A classic way of gaining access to formative feedback is to invite a peer—that is, another language teacher whose opinion you respect—to visit one or more of your classes. For purposes of reflective teaching, such visits should be planned to be different from the kinds of observations carried out by supervisors (see Murphy 1992).

In setting up a peer's non-supervisory visit to the classroom, it is important to discuss and clarify the visitor's purpose in advance. Any potential visitor will have preconceptions, attitudes, and beliefs about what constitutes legitimate purposes for visiting another teacher's class. Some of these attitudes and beliefs may be compatible with your own, and others may not be. Along with many other educators, Fanselow (1988) points out that the primary purpose for observing another person teach is to gather descriptive information on what takes place during the lesson. This purpose is crucially important. Afterward, any information gathered may be examined, analyzed, discussed, or even ignored, but if some sort of record of what took place is never produced, meaningful discussions of teaching are less likely. A starting point to prepare for a classroom visit from a peer is for both parties to be aware of the importance of staying attentive, interested in the lesson, and open-minded. Though some visitors may be able to gather useful information by merely observing what takes place, visitor's recollections are more reliable and tend to be more helpful as starting points for discussion once the lesson is over if the visitor has written things down. When clarifying the purpose for a peer visit, I emphasize my interest in engaging in discussions of teaching that are tied to descriptive information the visitor is able to gather during the lesson.

Currently I am involved in a project that includes interviewing six pairs of classroom teachers who are in the process of developing relationships as peer-visitors to each other's classrooms. My purpose is to identify procedures that seem to be working for these teachers. All of them have been involved in reciprocal peer-observation of

teaching activities on multiple occasions. The following is a synthesis of some of the recurring themes the teachers have mentioned. The ideas and suggestions presented are not intended as prescriptions for other teachers to follow. For one thing, the number of teachers I am working with is small and what we are learning about peer visits to classrooms cannot necessarily be generalized to other settings. However, my work with these and other teachers convinces me that it is possible to develop reciprocally enriching relationships between teacher-colleagues for such purposes. A way to begin may be to review the advice offered below and to use it as a prompt for discussing and clarifying whatever your own preferences might be as either a "visiting" or "visited" teacher. I begin with comments from the perspective of a teacher who is being visited by one of his or her peers. This section is followed by comments from the perspective of a "visiting" teacher.

The "Visited" Teacher

■ The [peer] teacher coming to visit my class and I always set time aside to discuss the purpose for the classroom visit ahead of time.

■ A couple of classes prior to the day of the actual visit, I explain to students that someone will be coming to observe the class. If I try to explain it to the class once the visitor is in the room, it's too late. Whenever I spring things like this on students without preparing them, they act differently and the visitor ends up not really seeing a normal class.

■ When I ask a friend to visit my class, I already have a couple of things in mind I would like some feedback on. To make more efficient use of our time, I prepare a list in advance of what's been puzzling me and then we discuss each of the items together. During the initial conversation, I often find that the visitor's comments and questions help clarify what some of my concerns about the course might be. Together we rearrange the list of items in what we eventually settle upon as their order of priority to me.

■ During this initial conversation, we also arrange a time to meet in order to discuss the lesson afterward. I prefer to schedule our post-visit conversation for a couple of days after the actual class. Even though the visitor is a colleague whose opinions and insights I respect, we both find that we need time to be able to figure out what we want to discuss. Experiences as both a "visiting" and "visited" teacher have taught me that visitors have more useful things to say if they have a couple of days to think over what took place during the lesson. Though a few brief exchanges sometimes are inevitable prior to the time we have arranged in advance, I find scheduled conversations to be more helpful. When we get together, it is a time when both of us are better prepared to focus on what we have learned from the experience.

- I usually assume, or sometimes we will even agree in advance, that my colleague's conversation opener will be something very general that is intended to get me talking about what I remember from the class. A useful way for our discussion to begin is if my colleague says something like, "Well, what do you remember from the lesson?" Or "How do you think it went?" In anticipation, I use the time between the lesson visited and the day of our follow-up conversation to focus on what I remember. I also review the list of topics for discussion we settled upon in advance and give careful consideration to what I think the lesson might have revealed about them.

- Though I try to be forthcoming in response to my colleague's attempts to get me talking about the lesson, I am more interested in looking for opportunities to learn about what the visitor noticed. I try to be patient and listen carefully whenever my collaborator has something to say.

The "Visiting" Teacher

- When we talk in anticipation of the classroom visit, I try to figure out just what it is my colleague would like me to look for. It is easier to sort things out if he or she gives me some ideas for things to look for. Otherwise, I might end up responding to something of little practical value to the teacher.

- I ask things such as where in the room I should try to sit, whether or not the teacher will be comfortable if I take notes, how long I should stay, what I should do if small-group activities are used, and how I should respond if learners ask me direct questions.

- I prefer it if students are aware of why I am there but it's better if the teacher has made my purpose clear to students prior to the day of my being in the classroom.

- If my colleague introduces me at the beginning of the class it's OK, though I am more comfortable in my role as the visitor if the time spent introducing me is short and kept low-key. The more attention called to me, the less I am able to watch and observe what would normally be taking place during the lesson. Ideally, the teacher will have prepared students ahead of time so that a time-consuming explanation for why I am there is unnecessary.

- I am very careful to arrive a few minutes before the class begins. Ideally, I like to arrive well before very many of the students. If possible I find a seat at the back of the room, off to one side, and wait for everyone else to arrive.

- Though other visitors may find them useful, I never bring electronic recording devices or observation schedules with me. Since I am going to be present in the classroom, I make an effort to limit the materials I bring to the kinds of things learners normally work with during language lessons (such as a pen and paper). I stay alert, observe carefully, and try to take written notes as unobtrusively as I can.

- Since one of my purposes is to call as little attention to myself as possible, I find ways to appear to be busy as students are entering the room. My preferred strategy is to have a book I really am interested in reading open in front of me. As students arrive to class, what they see if they glance in my direction is someone reading a book. I keep the book open and continue reading (sometimes I am just pretending to read) up until the start of the class. Soon after the lesson begins, I quietly close the book and put it aside. At this point I find it easier to watch, listen, and gather information more directly.

- I find it essential to take notes on what I see happening during the lesson. My notes may seem messy but I am trying to write down dispassionate, non-judgmental descriptions of classroom events. If I notice that I am writing down an opinion or suggestion, I place brackets around it to remind me that such comments are different from my primary purpose. Eventually, my opinions and suggestions may end up being helpful as part of our subsequent discussions but I need a way to keep these separate and clearly identified for purposes of later review.

- Though taking notes is important, complications sometimes arise. If I notice that some students are paying an inordinate degree of attention to what I am doing, I suspend taking notes and simply watch and listen. I can always resume it later in the lesson. If for some reason notetaking is impossible, once the class is over I find a quiet place to begin writing down my memories of the lesson as well as I can.

- Sometimes students address me directly. When they do, I respond to what they say while trying to be as brief as possible.

- Occasionally, the teacher will ask me to participate in some sort of an activity with students. I follow the teacher's cue and become part of the activity while keeping my eye on the process of what is happening.

- A few hours after the lesson is over, or the next day, I spend about an hour reviewing my notes, elaborating what they include, and relating what seem to be important pieces of information to the themes the "visited" teacher and I agreed upon as possible topics for discussion. I also create a list of some additional ideas and points I would like to discuss with the teacher.

- When we have a chance to discuss the lesson, I focus on what took place, what the teacher and students were doing, things I might have learned, and any personal beliefs about the teaching-learning process I noticed being reinforced, further extended, or challenged. I prioritize the items for discussion we agreed upon in advance. I also look for opportunities to relate the class I visited to my own experiences in teaching. In this part of the discussion I often find myself saying things such as, "When you were doing X, Y, or Z as part of the lesson, it reminded me of things that I do, too." Comments that reveal connections to my own teaching are important since they help us build collaborative discussions relevant to both of our experiences.

Reflection Break #5

Design a list of suggestions and guidelines you would like to follow in order to collaborate with another language teacher in ways similar to those discussed in this section. Include guidelines for both a "visited" and a "visiting" teacher. Are there any topics mentioned above that would *not* be of particular concern to you? Are there any topics left unmentioned that you would like to see given more attention?

TWO UNDERLYING CONCERNS

Now that we have examined some topics and tools, it is important to acknowledge two fundamental challenges facing those interested in processes of reflective teaching: the search for multiple perspectives, and the question of learner involvement.

The Search for Multiple Perspectives

To become more involved in processes of reflective teaching, a language teacher needs to ask, How can I begin to see and examine my classroom efforts so that others might be able to see and examine them? Access to multiple perspectives makes it more likely that we will attain deeper understanding of our work. The search for multiple perspectives relates to two essential stages of reflective teaching: gathering information (the data collection stage) and making sense of what we find (the interpretation stage).

In the first stage, reflective teachers find ways of gathering information on teaching and learning that include outsider perspectives. As a result of our immersion within the process of language teaching, we are often too close to recognize our strengths and weaknesses. By way of illustration, most of us are somewhat surprised the first time we view a video recording of our teaching. In response to a video recording, we might notice ourselves thinking such things as: "Oh, my voice sounds terrible! That's not what I sound like." "Is that what I really look like?" "Why am I walking around so much (or so little)?" "No wonder students are having trouble following my directions; I really wasn't very clear." A video recording of teaching-in-action brings to the fore evidence of how others may view us. Recordings sometimes surprise us because they are serving as an *estrangement device*. An estrangement device is any tool we might use to gain an outsider's perspective on what we may be doing in the classroom. Anthropologists refer to such a vantage point as an *etic* perspective (an outsider's view).

To complement the inclusion of etic perspectives within the reflective teaching process, it is useful to gather information from course participants as well. Because learners are participants in the process, their vantage points represent *emic* perspectives. Just as an anthropologist might search for ways to learn about the perceptions and understandings of the members of another culture, reflective teachers depend upon learners' perceptions and understandings. Freeman (1998) explains the importance of the search for multiple perspectives succinctly: etic perspectives provide us with information on "what outsiders see" while emic perspectives provide information on "what insiders know" (p. 70). Figure 1 summarizes etic versus emic distinctions that we can apply to either the collection or examination of classroom information.

The need for multiple perspectives challenges reflective teachers to find ways of gathering information on teaching-learning processes not only through their own perceptions and understandings, but also through those of learners who are participating in the course, and through colleagues' perceptions.

The Question of Learner Involvement

In connection with emic perspectives, a second set of questions for reflective teachers to ask is, Do I want to involve learners in my efforts as a reflective teacher, and if so, to what degree? There are many ways to collect information about what goes on within courses we teach. A distinction we can make is between ways that are "less intrusive" as opposed to those that are relatively "more intrusive" with respect to their potential impacts on learners' classroom experiences. Less intrusive means of gathering information depend upon little or no involvement from learners. Teachers interested in less intrusive means do their best to avoid direct impact on inside-the-classroom events. For instance, a teacher might gather information about teaching on a daily basis but only after the completion of individual lessons. To do so, some teachers keep private teaching journals of which learners remain unaware. Other non-intrusive options

etic	emic
outsider's view	insider's view
participant understandings	consultant understandings
what outsiders see	what insiders know
teacher-peers' and colleagues' perceptions	classroom teacher's and learners' perceptions

Figure I. Continuum of Vantage Points for Either the Collection or Interpretation of Information on Teaching-Learning Processes

are, after a lesson has ended, to compose field notes of what happened inside the classroom only, or to look back on completed lessons through other retrospective procedures such as "lesson reporting." (A lesson report is similar to a lesson plan but with the following twist: lesson reports are generated following, not preceding, a lesson. By composing, saving, and reviewing them over time, a teacher is able to produce a substantive record of teaching that can be shared and discussed with others.) Through adoption of such nonintrusive procedures it is possible for teachers to gain considerable information about the teaching process without involving learners.

Even with less intrusive procedures, reflective teachers are able to incorporate multiple perspectives into their efforts by inviting colleagues whose opinions they respect to review and discuss whatever information the teacher is able to gather from the classroom. Two or more teachers might collaborate to review a video or audio recording of teaching, transcripts of lesson segments, journal entries, samples of student work, or students' responses to a survey questionnaire on how the course is going. Some of these options feature learner participation to some degree. A teacher might, for example, arrange for a lesson to be videotaped for later review. If a video camera is in the room, the teacher has already taken a step in the direction of involving learners. The presence of any recording device in a classroom inevitably has some impact on lesson events. Of course, as a classroom teacher, you can lessen such impacts by taking steps ahead of time to familiarize students with whatever might be the procedure you would like to follow. You can: (1) discuss what you are planning to do, (2) ask for learners' permissions, (3) take time at an earlier point in the course to introduce whatever the procedure or recording device might be, and/or (4) include it as a part of normal classroom routine. In the example of video cameras, some suggestions are to work with as small a camera as possible, position it in the back of the room—or at least out of students' direct lines of vision—and involve one or more members of the class in its operation. There are many approaches to second language instruction that already feature recording devices as a standard part of the teaching routine. In such classrooms, learners may perceive a teacher's use of recording equipment as perfectly normal and part of what they have already come to anticipate from the course. The point is to be aware of the potential impacts of such procedures and to make informed decisions on what you, your colleagues, and your students might consider to be (un)acceptable levels of learner involvement in reflective teaching procedures.

Table 2 provides a synopsis of several issues discussed in this section by featuring a matrix of two intersecting continua for gathering information on teaching.

Though far from a comprehensive list of options and possibilities explored by reflective teachers, Table 2 is intended to provide a synopsis of this chapter: procedures in *quadrant A* combine outsiders' perspectives with relatively more intrusive means of gathering information on teaching. *Quadrant D* is just the opposite, since these procedures tap into insiders' perspectives through somewhat less intrusive means. *Quadrant B* is weighted toward outsider perspectives through less intrusive means. With the procedures in *quadrant C,* the teacher involves course participants in sharing what they think about the course in ways that may impact students' learning experiences to varying degrees. Anyone interested in learning more about the processes and procedures of reflective teaching may refer to Table 2 as a reminder of its possibilities. Teachers might set as a professional development goal exploring one or more of the options listed in each of its four quadrants. As we continue to learn more about these and other pathways to reflective teaching, as well as the particular topics we would like to explore within the language courses we teach, this chapter can remind us of the rewards of self-discovery, the importance of multiple perspectives, and the potentially facilitating impacts of learners' and colleagues' contributions to our efforts.[2]

Table 2. Two-way Matrix for Gathering Information

	More Intrusive	Less Intrusive
E T I C	**(A)** * videotaping (video + audio) * video- (or audio-) taping for the first time * large, bulky video camera at the front of the room * learners participate in analyzing video recordings of lessons during class time * trained observer inside the classroom * in-class observer is someone unknown to learners * in-class observer takes notes or completes an observation schedule live in the classroom * a supervisor gathers information on teaching for formal assessment-of-teaching purposes	**(B)** * audiotaping (only) * video- (or audio-) taping for the fifth time * camera is small or out of sight * learners participate in analyzing video recordings of lessons only after a course has ended * trained observer watches video recording of lesson * in-class observer is someone learners know and are comfortable with * in-class observer watches and listens, tries to blend into the background, composes field notes only after the lesson has ended * teacher gathers information on teaching through self-initiated collaborations with peers/colleagues
E M I C	**(C)** * students compose journals in which they discuss their experiences as learners in the course and how they perceive the course * teacher conducts student focus groups * frequent student interviews * whole class, inside-the-classroom discussions of learners' perceptions and preferences while the course is in process * student focus group with whole class participating * teacher serves as focus group facilitator * students complete several instructor assessment forms at different points in the course (formative) * five-minute papers, frequent and on a regular basis * stimulated recall while the course is in process * teacher and learners collaborate to gather information on the teaching-learning process together	**(D)** * teacher keeps a diary or personal journal * teacher engages in lesson reporting * a third party conducts student focus groups in which learners' comments are kept anonymous * infrequent student interviews * outside-of-class discussions with individual learners of their perceptions and preferences while the course is in process * student focus group with only some class members participating * teacher-colleague serves as focus group facilitator * students complete a single end-of-term instructor assessment form (summative) * transcripts generated for discourse analysis of lesson events * stimulated recall only after the course is over * teacher gathers information on teaching while working alone [may collaborate with colleague(s)]

DISCUSSION QUESTIONS

1. Imagine you have reached the midpoint of a course in which you have been conscientious in trying to be an effective teacher. Nevertheless, you notice that many of the students seem disinterested in the course. How could you find out what some of the problems might be?

2. You are teaching an intermediate-level course focused on enhancing oral communication abilities in an English-dominant part of the world. The twenty-five students in the course come from Afghanistan, China, Colombia, Ivory Coast, Japan, Korea, Mexico, Russia, and Turkey. Compared to other members of the class, you notice that a majority of the Asian students seem very

reluctant to participate in class. What could you do to explore why this is so? How could you get them to be more involved?

3. You are teaching several sections of an ESL course housed within a continuing education program located in a major city in an English-dominant part of the world. The entry-level course you offer is designed for recent immigrants. Over the past several years you have come to realize that students mainly use their first languages outside the classroom. A complication is that the city encompasses many ethnic neighborhoods that provide easy access to a significant number of community services and businesses in the languages represented by the members of the class. Since students have demonstrated their reluctance, what can you do to encourage students to apply what they are studying in the course to their life experiences outside the classroom?

4. You have been hired by a large and well-organized language program which places significant emphasis on the role and importance of formal evaluations of teaching. While interviewing for the position, the search committee made clear that the primary purpose for supervisory classroom observation is quality control with respect to teaching. All teachers in the program are observed two to three times per term by a trained supervisor who is one of several "master teachers" on the faculty. You fortunately feel confident as a classroom teacher and your background is very compatible with the program's instructional focus. However, in addition to the kind of feedback supervisors may be able to provide, you are interested in learning more about your teaching through self-initiated means. Discuss with a partner some other things you might do to learn more about your teaching from both "etic" and "emic" perspectives.

5. You are teaching EFL in a secondary school setting in a non-English-dominant part of the world (you may substitute some other ELT setting depending upon whatever learner population and settings are most familiar to you). You are very excited about a series of new teaching procedures you are testing out

in the classroom. How can you document that constructive changes are taking place in the course as you are offering it? Who could you involve and what specifically would you want them to do?

SUGGESTED ACTIVITIES

1. Make arrangements to consult two or more practicing language teachers. Ask if they have ever heard of traditions such as reflective or exploratory teaching. (Be aware that some teachers use different terms and phrases for similar concepts.) Try to discover if they have ever been involved in such efforts. If they have, gather as much information as you can on how their efforts have made a difference in their teaching. If they have not, try to find out what might be some of the other things they do to grow and develop as language teachers.

2. Make arrangements to meet with a classroom teacher immediately following (or soon after) a lesson he or she has just taught. Try to arrange a time when the two of you may work uninterrupted for at least 30 minutes. Once together, interview the teacher on what the lesson was like. Begin by asking open-ended prompts such as, What were you planning to teach? How did things turn out? Was there anything unexpected that happened? Were there any complications? and so forth. As long as the teacher you observed consents in advance, consider tape-recording the interaction for later review. If you are serving as a classroom teacher, follow similar procedures while collaborating with someone else who is willing to interview you.

3. Imagine you are interested in producing a video recording of someone else's class in a language program with which you are familiar. How would you secure the teacher's permission? How would you approach him or her? What would you say? How would you put the teacher at ease? For this task you do not have to follow through with actually producing such a recording. Your charge is to generate guidelines for doing so if you ever have an

opportunity in the future. What are likely to be some of the classroom teacher's and learners' concerns? How would you address them? How would you suggest that learners be prepared? What are some of the steps you would follow on the day of the recording? What would you do with the recording once it was completed?

4. For this activity you need to place yourself in the position of a language learner. If you had a language teacher who was interested in reflective teaching, how would you want the teacher to involve you in such efforts?. After referring back to Table 2, make a list of the kinds of things you would be willing to do. Also, think of a specific language class you either are teaching now or some other course in which you were once a language learner. From the perspective of a learner in that course, what would be some of the topics you think would be worthy ones for the teacher to explore? As a learner in the class, what contributions would you be willing to make?

 FURTHER READING

The following are arranged in a recommended order for reading. The first two focus specifically on the tradition of reflective teaching. Each of the remaining three texts provides invaluable support for reflective teaching but also extends beyond this tradition by encouraging classroom language teachers to become explorers and researchers in their own classrooms.

Richards, J. C., and C. Lockhart. 1994. *Reflective Teaching in Second Language Classrooms.* New York: Cambridge University Press.
Certainly the most accessible, and probably the best, introduction to reflective teaching in the field of ELT.

Gebhard, J., and R. Oprandy. 1999. *Language Teaching Awareness: A Guide to Exploring Beliefs and Practices.* New York: Cambridge University Press.
An excellent resource for those interested in learning more about reflective teaching. The co-authors focus on building awareness of teaching through self-initiated means and help teachers to become more aware of their own teaching beliefs, attitudes, and practices.

Nunan, D. 1989b. *Understanding Language Classrooms: A Guide for Teacher-initiated Action.* Englewood Cliffs, NJ: Prentice Hall.
One of the earliest introductions to exploratory teaching, action research, and what we now call reflective teaching in the field of ELT. Provides an impressive survey of topics and tools that continues to be of interest to reflective teachers. Also serves as an accessible introduction to language classroom research for those who do not have specialist training in research methods.

Allwright, D., and K. Bailey. 1991. *Focus on the Language Classroom: An Introduction to Classroom Research for Language Teachers.* New York: Cambridge University Press.
The authors define the aims and principles of classroom research and are especially informative in their reviews of data collection and analysis procedures, how to get started, what to investigate, quantitative versus qualitative issues, and research findings. The two chapters devoted to affective considerations (titled "receptivity") are especially valuable.

Freeman, D. 1998. *Doing Teacher Research: From Inquiry to Understanding.* New York: Heinle & Heinle.
Similar to the purpose and scope of Nunan (1989b) and Allwright and Bailey (1991), this more recent book encompasses but also pushes beyond contemporary developments in reflective teaching by focusing on the intersection of teaching and research in our field.

ENDNOTES

1 The items presented here are adapted from an unpublished "Student Formative Assessment of Instructor" form developed in Georgia State University's Intensive English program by Sharon Cavusgil and Alan Forsyth in 1999.

2 I would like to acknowledge the invaluable contributions of Patricia Byrd and Barbara Hegyesi as this chapter's preliminary readers. Any remaining shortcomings are my own.

Second Language Assessment[1]

ANDREW D. COHEN

In "Second Language Assessment," Cohen considers key issues in the construction of assessment instruments. Beginning with a theoretical framework for types of instruments and types of items, he gives guidelines for reviewing or constructing tests, as well as giving insights into the types of items possible. Approaches to testing reading comprehension are provided, with sample approaches to other skills included in an appendix.

INTRODUCTION

Assessment is perhaps one of the least understood areas of language teaching and learning. Students and teachers alike cringe when they hear the word "testing." Students see tests as a threat to their competence, because they are afraid that they will not perform well. Teachers often do not like to construct tests, and are not altogether satisfied with the results when they do. They are also suspicious of the standardized, professionally designed tests because they are not always sure what these tests are actually trying to measure.

In a survey of EFL teachers and students in Israeli public schools, Shohamy (1985) found a variety of misuses of tests, of which the following are just a sampling:

- tests were used as punishment—e.g., because no one did the homework.
- tests were administered instead of teachers' giving instruction.
- the tests were the only measure for grading.
- tests did not reflect what was taught.
- the tests were returned with a lack of corrections or explanations.
- the tests reflected only one testing method.
- there was a lack of teacher confidence in their own tests.
- students were not adequately trained to take the tests.
- there was a substantial delay in returning the tests.

Although the survey was conducted some years ago and in an EFL, rather than an ESL context, many of the points ring true for current L2 classrooms all over the world. Given the above list, it is no wonder that both students and teachers are suspicious of tests. Fortunately, in recent years there has been a growing interest in improving the situation. For example, two recently published volumes are geared toward demonstrating how language assessment can be aligned more closely with authentic, real-world tasks; one is devoted to new ways of classroom assessment with testimonials from scores of practicing teachers (Brown 1998) and another focuses exclusively on language performance assessments (Norris et al. 1998).

A more constructive view of language testing exists when (a) testing is seen as an opportunity for interaction between teacher and student, (b) students are judged on the basis of the knowledge they have, (c) the tests are intended to help students improve their skills, (d) the criteria for success on the test are clear to students, (e) students receive a grade for their performance on a set of tests representing different testing methods (not just one), (f) the test takers are trained in how to take tests—especially those involving unfamiliar formats, (g) the tests are returned promptly, and (h) the results are discussed (Shohamy 1985). In a recent volume on the power of tests, Shohamy (2000) proposes critical agendas for democratizing and limiting the power of tests and protecting the rights of test takers.

This chapter will consider some key issues in the construction of language assessment instruments. It is intended to better equip the ESL/ EFL teacher both to understand and scrutinize tests prepared by others and to design their own means of assessment such that they and their students will be satisfied. Beginning with a theoretical framework for types of language assessment instruments and types of items, this chapter should help teachers determine just what kind of test they are constructing or reviewing, as well as give them insights into the types of items that are involved. What follows next is a discussion of approaches to testing reading comprehension, as illustrative of the factors to be considered in assessing any of the language skills. A discussion of approaches to testing the other skills—listening, speaking, and writing—is given in the appendix to this chapter. The chapter concludes with a discussion of test construction issues and test-taking strategies.

THEORETICAL FOUNDATIONS

Types of Language Assessment Instruments

In order to properly construct an assessment instrument, it is helpful to have some explicit notion of what is being measured and how it might be labeled. An elaborate way to describe language assessment instruments is according to their primary function—that is, for administrative, instructional, or research purposes (Jacobs et al. 1981). In fact, the same test could conceivably be used for twelve different purposes: five administrative purposes (assessment, placement, exemption, certification, promotion), four instructional purposes (diagnosis, evidence of progress, feedback to the respondent, evaluation of teaching or curriculum), and three research purposes (evaluation, experimentation, knowledge about language learning and language use). The average test is not intended to be used for more than several purposes, and the major split is often between *proficiency* tests intended for administrative purposes and *achievement* tests for assessment of instructional outcomes.

A distinction in testing is made between *norm-referenced* and *criterion-referenced assessment* as well. A test can be used, for example, to compare a respondent with other respondents, whether locally (e.g., in a class), regionally, or nationally. Classroom, regional, or national norms[2] may be established to interpret just how one student compares with another. A test can also be used to see whether a respondent has met certain instructional objectives or criteria, hence the term "criterion-referenced" assessment.

The seminal efforts by Canale and Swain (1980), and Canale (1983b) to operationalize Hymes' (1972) *communicative competence* has provided another set of criteria for describing tests. Tests are seen as tapping one or more of the four components making up the construct of communicative competence—namely, grammatical, discourse, sociolinguistic, and strategic competence. *Grammatical competence* encompasses "knowledge of lexical items and of rules of morphology, syntax, sentence-grammar semantics, and phonology" (Canale and Swain 1980, p. 29). *Discourse competence* is the ability to connect sentences in stretches of discourse and to form a meaningful whole out of a series of utterances. *Sociolinguistic competence* involves knowledge of the sociocultural rules of language.[3] *Strategic competence* refers to "the verbal and nonverbal communication strategies that may be called into action to compensate for breakdowns in communication due to performance variables or due to insufficient competence" (*ibid.*, p. 30).

While Canale and Swain's *strategic competence* put the emphasis on "compensatory" strategies, that is, strategies used to compensate or remediate for a lack in some language area, the term has come to take on a broader meaning. Bachman (1990) has broken down *strategic competence* into three components: an assessment component whereby the respondents set communicative goals, a planning component whereby the respondents retrieve the relevant items from language ability and plan their use, and an execution component whereby the respondents implement the plan.

Classifying an Item

Tests usually consist of a series of items. An item is a specific task to perform, and can assess one or more points or objectives. For example, an item may test *one* point, such as the meaning of a given vocabulary word, or *several* points, such as an item which tests the ability to obtain facts from a passage and then make inferences based on those facts. Likewise, a given objective may be tested by a series of items. For example, there could be five items all testing one grammatical point, say, tag questions. Items of a similar kind may also be grouped together to form *subtests* within a given test.

The Skill Tested

The language skills that we test include listening and reading, the more receptive skills, and speaking and writing, the more productive skills. Nonverbal skills can be both receptive (e.g., interpreting someone else's gestures) and productive (making one's own gestures).

The Nature of the Item

Items can be more discrete or more integrative in nature, just as they can be more objective or subjective. A completely discrete-point item would test simply one point or objective, while an integrative item would test more than one point or objective at a time. Sometimes an integrative item is really more a procedure than an item, as in the case of a free composition which could test a number of objectives.

The objectivity of an item refers to the way it is scored. A multiple-choice item, for example, is objective in that there is usually only one right answer. A free composition may be more subjective in nature if the scorer is not looking for any one right answer, but rather for evidence of a series of features, including, say, creativity, style, cohesion and coherence, grammar, and mechanics.

The Intellectual Operation Required

Items may call for different levels of intellectual effort (Valette 1969, after Bloom, ed. 1956). They can test for the following intellectual levels:

(a) knowledge retrieval (bringing to mind the appropriate material); (b) comprehension (understanding the basic meaning of the material); (c) application (applying the knowledge of the elements of language and comprehension to how they interrelate in the production of a correct oral or written message); (d) analysis (breaking down a message into its constituent parts in order to make explicit the relationships between ideas, including tasks such as recognizing the connotative meanings of words and correctly processing a dictation, and making inferences); (e) synthesis (arranging parts so as to produce a pattern not clearly there before, such as effectively organizing ideas in a written composition); and (f) evaluation (making quantitative and qualitative judgments about material). It is thought that these levels demand increasingly greater cognitive control as one moves from knowledge to evaluation. It may be that effective performance at more advanced levels, such as synthesis and evaluation, would call for more advanced control of the second language.

The Tested Response Behavior

Items can test different response behavior. Respondents may be tested for accuracy in pronunciation or grammar. Likewise, they could be assessed for fluency, for example, without concern for grammatical correctness. Aside from accuracy and fluency, they could also be assessed for how quickly they can produce a response.

As noted above, there has been an increased concern for developing measures of performance, that is, measures of the ability to perform real-world tasks, with criteria for successful performance based on a needs analysis for the given task (Brown 1998; Norris et al. 1998). Such tasks might include "comparing credit card offers and arguing for the best choice" or "making the most of a dating service." At the same time that there is a call for tasks that better reflect the real world, there is a commensurate concern for more *authentic* language assessment. At least one study, however, notes that the differences between authentic and pedagogic written and spoken texts may not be readily apparent, even to an audience specifically looking for differences

(Lewkowicz 1997). In addition, test takers may not necessarily concern themselves with task authenticity in a test situation. Test familiarity may be the overriding factor.

Characteristics of Respondents

Items can be designed to cater to populations with certain characteristics. Bachman and Palmer (1996) group these into four categories: personal characteristics (age, sex, and native language), topical knowledge that test takers bring to the situation, their affective schemata, and their language ability (pp. 64–78). With regard to the age variable, for example, a recent review suggests that educators need to revisit this issue and perhaps conceive of new ways to assess age-related differences in language ability (Marinova-Todd et al. 2000). With regard to language ability, both Bachman and Palmer (1996) and Alderson (2000) detail the many types of knowledge that respondents may need to draw on to perform well on a given item or task: world knowledge and culturally specific knowledge, knowledge of any necessary grammar, knowledge of different oral and written text types, knowledge of the subject matter or topic, and knowledge of how to perform well on the given task.

Item-Elicitation Format

The format for elicitation of the item has to be determined. An item can have a spoken, written, or visual stimulus, as well as any combination of the three. Thus, while an item or task may ostensibly assess one skill, it may also be testing some other as well. So, for example, a "listening" sub-test in which respondents answer oral questions by means of written multiple-choice responses is testing *reading* as well as listening.[4]

Item-Response Format

The item-response format can be fixed, structured, or open-ended. Those with a fixed format include true/false, multiple-choice, and matching items. Those which call for a structured format include ordering (where, for example, respondents are requested to arrange words to make a sentence, and several orders are possible), duplication—both written (e.g., dictation) and oral (e.g., recitation, repetition, mimicry), identification (e.g., explaining the part of speech of a form), and completion. Those calling for an open-ended format include composing—both written (e.g., creative fiction, expository essays) and oral (e.g., a speech)—as well as other activities, such as free oral response in role-playing situations.

Elements of Language to be Assessed

Finally, as noted above with reference to communicative competence, items can test for grammatical, discourse, and sociolinguistic competence, as well as for whatever strategic competence respondents draw on when they lack the required competence. *Grammatical competence,* here includes phonology, morphology, syntax, knowledge of lexical items and semantics (Canale and Swain 1980, p. 29), as well as matters of mechanics (spelling, punctuation, capitalization, and handwriting).

Advances in assessment have brought relatively untapped elements of language into assessment measures. Thus, for example, language assessment may now include more finely tuned assessment of specific purpose tasks (see Douglas 2000) and of vocabulary (see Read 2000), more sophisticated computer-based assessment (Dunkel 1999), as well as assessment of cross-cultural pragmatics (see Hudson et al. 1995; Brown in press). With regard to pragmatics, expertise is accumulating in the assessment of speech acts such as complaining, apologizing, requesting, and so forth. Additionally, the assessment field is becoming more sensitive to the use of the target language in specific, often technical contexts; the field is taking assessment of second language vocabulary knowledge beyond simplistic measures to better assess the depth and breadth of lexical control; and testers are pursuing research and development projects to provide us with not only computer-assisted assessment measures but computer-adaptive ones as well (see Chalhoub-Deville 2000).

ASSESSING LANGUAGE SKILLS

One way of contrasting different approaches to language assessment has been to distinguish between the testing of discrete language items and a more integrative or global assessment of language. Another more recent dichotomy exists between traditional or standard means of assessment and alternative means, such as the use of portfolios, journals, logs, conferences, and utilizing both self-assessment and peer assessment, as well as teacher assessment (see Brown 1998).

The following discussion of reading assessment is intended to reflect more current thinking about testing. The appendix contains examples of approaches to testing other skills.

Methods of Testing Reading Comprehension

Reading comprehension items or procedures require that learners use a certain type or types of reading, comprehend at a certain level or combination of levels of meaning, enlist a certain comprehension skill(s), and do all of this within the framework of a certain testing method(s). In this section, we will look at some of the choices available to the test constructor and at considerations of concern to the test user.

Types of Reading

Items and procedures can be written so that they implicitly or explicitly call for a given type of reading. For example, a respondent can be given a lengthy passage to read in a limited time frame such that the only way to handle it successfully is to skim[5] or to scan,[6] depending on the task. A further distinction has been made between scanning and "search reading," the latter being when the respondent is scanning without being sure about the form that the information will take (i.e., whether it will be a word, phrase, sentence, passage, and so on) (Pugh 1978, p. 53). A respondent could also be given a passage to read receptively.[7] Yet another approach is to have respondents read responsively, such that the written material prompts them to reflect on some point or other,

and then possibly respond in writing. Testing formats in which questions are interspersed within running text may cater to such an approach if the questions stimulate an active dialogue between the text and the reader.

The type of reading task is raised here because it would appear to be neglected at times in the process of test construction. In other words, reading items and tasks are sometimes constructed without careful consideration as to how the respondent is to read them. It may even be of benefit for the test constructor to indicate explicitly to the respondent the type of reading expected. For example, a certain item could be introduced by the following:

> Read the following text through rapidly (i.e., skim it) in order to get the main points. There will not be time to read the text intensively. When you have completed this reading, answer the questions provided—without looking back at the text. You will have ten minutes for the exercise.

Level of Meaning

A test item or procedure can tap comprehension at one of four levels of meaning or at several levels simultaneously: grammatical meaning, propositional meaning, discoursal meaning, and writer's intent (adapted from Nuttall 1982). Note, however, that these categories are presented as a heuristic, rather than as a hierarchy of discrete levels. *Grammatical meaning* deals with the meanings that words and morphemes have on their own. *Propositional meaning* refers to the meaning that a clause or sentence can have on its own— i.e., the information that the clause or sentence transmits. This meaning is also referred to as its "informational value." *Discoursal meaning* relates to the meaning a sentence can have only when in context. This meaning is also referred to as its "functional value." *Writer's intent* concerns the meaning that a sentence has only as part of the interaction between writer and reader. This is the meaning that reflects the writer's feelings and attitudes and the intended effect of the writing upon the reader.

The level of meaning that has perhaps gotten the most attention in the literature in recent years is the discoursal one, especially the reader's perception of rhetorical functions conveyed by text. For example, an item may overtly or covertly require a respondent to identify where and how something is being defined, classified, exemplified, or contrasted with something else. Often such "discourse functions" are signaled by connectors or "discourse markers." Nonetheless, uninformed or un-alert readers may miss these signals—words or phrases such as "unless," "however," "thus," "whereas," and the like. Research has shown that such markers need not be subtle to cause reading problems. Simple markers of sequential points ("first," "also," and "finally") as well as more subtle markers may be missed by a reader (see Cohen et al. 1979).

Actually, a level that is worthy of more attention by teachers and other test constructors is that of writer's intent, especially *author's tone*. It would appear that non-native respondents are slow to perceive humor, for example. Some years ago, an ESL Placement Test at a large university included a humorous passage about a man who turns to the lady sitting next to him at a fancy banquet and informs her that he thinks the current speaker has nothing to say and should sit down. She asks if he knows who she is. When he says "no," she informs him that she is the speaker's wife. Then he asks her if she knows who he is. When she says "no," he says, "Good!" and gets up and leaves. The passage had a multiple-choice item inquiring whether the text was (a) serious, (b) sad, (c) humorous, or (d) cynical. Most of the 700 respondents responded that it was serious. This example would suggest that respondents may not be operating at the appropriate cultural/pragmatic level when they perform certain tasks on tests.

Comprehension Skill

A test constructor and user must be aware not only of levels of comprehension but also of individual skills tested by reading comprehension questions at one or more such levels of meaning. Alderson (1987) offered a taxonomy which included: (1) the ability to recognize words and phrases of similar and opposing meaning; (2) identifying or locating information; (3) discriminating elements or features within context; the analysis of elements within a structure and of the relationship among them—e.g., causal, sequential, chronological, hierarchical; (4) interpreting of complex ideas, actions, events, relationships; (5) inferencing—deriving conclusions and predicting the continuation; (6) synthesis; and (7) evaluation. We note that this taxonomy omits the reader–writer relationship—e.g., the author's distance from the text and the level of participation in the text that the author requires of the reader. With this taxonomy, as with others, the boundaries between skills are assumed to be discrete when, in reality, they may not be.

Testing Method

Besides considering the type of reading to be performed, the desired levels of meaning, and the comprehension skills to be tapped, the test constructor or user needs to give careful thought to the testing method. The challenge is to maximize the measurement of the trait—i.e., the respondent's ability—while minimizing the reactive effects of the method. In order to do this, it is useful to be informed about the options for testing with each method and what these options yield. We will look at some of the innovative methods for testing reading: the cloze and the C-test, computerized adaptive testing, and communicative tests of reading comprehension. (Testing of summarization skills is discussed in the appendix.)

The Cloze and the C-Test

The origins of the cloze test date back farther than many would think—to 1897, in fact. At that time, Ebbinghaus proposed a series of tests that had one- or two-word deletions, rational deletion, and partial deletion from the beginning or end of words (Ebbinghaus 1897). There has been a controversy concerning the cloze test as to whether filling in cloze items is not just a matter of perceiving local redundancy but, rather, involves an awareness of the flow of discourse across sentences and paragraphs (Oller 1979; Oller and Jonz 1994). Chávez-Oller et al. (1985) found research evidence, for instance, that cloze was sensitive to constraints *beyond* 5 to 11 words on either side of a blank. Nonetheless, the results from various research studies would suggest that traditional fixed-word deletion is more of a microlevel completion test (a measure of word- and sentence-level reading ability) than a macrolevel measure of skill at understanding connected discourse (see, for example, Alderson 1983; Klein-Braley 1981).

As an alternative to the fixed-word deletion, researchers turned to the *gap-filling procedure* (Alderson 2000), originally referred to as the *rational-deletion cloze*. In the gap-filling procedure, words are deleted according to predetermined, primarily linguistic criteria, often stressing the area considered to be underrepresented, namely, macrolevel discourse links (Levenston et al. 1984). Research by Bachman (1985) with EFL university students found that the rational-deletion cloze or gap-filling procedure sampled many more inter-sentence boundaries and somewhat more inter-clausal boundaries within the same sentence than did the fixed-ratio cloze. Bachman concluded that the gap-filling procedure was a better measure of the reading of connected discourse, but that the question still remained as to whether such tests "in fact measure the components of language proficiency hypothesized by the deletion criteria" (*ibid.*, 1985, p. 550)—that is, the flow of discourse across sentences and paragraphs within a text.

A suggested alternative to the cloze test—namely, the C-test—was proposed by Klein-Braley and Raatz (Klein-Braley and Raatz 1984; Raatz 1985). In this procedure, the second half of every other word is deleted, leaving the first and the last sentence of the passage intact. A given C-test consists of a number of short passages (maximum 100 words) on a variety of topics. This alternative eliminates certain problems associated with cloze, such as choice of deletion rate and starting point, representational sampling of different language elements in the passage, and the inadvertent assessment of written production as well as reading. With the C-test, being given a clue (half the word) serves as a stimulus

for respondents to find the other half. The following is one passage within a C-test (Raatz 1985, p. 17):

> Pollution is one of the big problems in the world today. Towns a_____ cities a_____ growing, indu_____ is gro_____ and t_____ population o_____ the wo_____ is gro_____. Almost every_____ causes poll_____ in so_____ way o_____ another. T_____ air i_____ filled wi_____ fumes fr_____ factories a_____ vehicles, a_____ there i_____ noise fr_____ airplanes a_____ machines. Riv _____, lakes, a_____ seas a_____ polluted b_____ factories and by sewage from our homes.

At present it would appear that the C-test may well be a more reliable and valid means of assessing what the cloze test assesses, but as suggested above, it is still not clear to what extent it tests more than microlevel processing. Because half the word is given, students who do not understand the macro-context may still be able to mobilize their vocabulary skills adequately to fill in the appropriate word without engaging in higher-level processing.

Computerized Adaptive Testing (CAT)

Computerized adaptive testing (CAT) of reading comprehension implies an approach to testing whereby the selection and sequence of items depends on the pattern of success and failure experienced by the respondent. Most commonly, if the respondent succeeds on a given item, one of greater difficulty is presented, but if the respondent experiences failure, then an easier item is presented. The testing continues until sufficient information has been gathered to assess the particular respondent's ability. At present, such tests are mostly limited to objective formats, such as multiple-choice.

Among the advantages of CAT are the following: individual testing time may be reduced; frustration and fatigue are minimized; boredom is reduced; test scores and diagnostic feedback may be provided immediately; test security may be enhanced (since it is unlikely that two respondents would receive the same items in the same sequence); record-keeping functions are improved; and information is readily available for research purposes (Larson and Madsen 1985; Madsen 1986).

The main disadvantage is that CAT presumes that one major language factor or underlying trait is being measured at a time. Such an assumption runs counter to the existing theories of reading comprehension, which encompass multiple dimensions, such as world knowledge, language and cultural background, type of text, and reading styles (Canale 1986b). The line of development that Canale proposed for CAT was that it should move from simply mechanizing existing product-oriented reading comprehension item types to the inclusion of more process-oriented, interactive tasks that can be integrated into broad and thematically coherent language use/learning activities, such as "intelligent tutoring systems."[8] Dunkel (1999) points out some of the challenges this innovative approach to assessment presents, including the special psychometric and technical issues peculiar to CAT as opposed to traditional or paper-and-pencil tests. There are still major issues in the design of evaluative criteria for assessing the reliability, validity, and utility of L2 CATs (see Chalhoub-Deville 2000), as well as complexities involved in interpreting CAT scores.

Communicative Tests of Reading Comprehension

For years attention has been paid to so-called communicative tests—usually implying tests dealing with speaking. More recently, efforts have been made to design truly communicative tests of other language skills as well, such as reading comprehension. Canale (1984) points out that a good test is not just one which is valid, reliable, and practical in terms of test administration and scoring, but rather one that is acceptable— that is, accepted as fair, important, and interesting by test takers and test users.[9] Also, a good test has feedback potential, rewarding both test takers and test users with clear, rich, relevant, and generalizable information. Canale suggests that acceptability and feedback potential have often

been accorded low priority, thus explaining the curious phenomenon of multiple-choice tests claiming to assess oral interaction skills.

Some approaches to communicative testing were in part an outgrowth of Canale and Swain's theoretical framework presented above (Canale and Swain 1980). The particular variety of communicative test that they dealt with has been referred to as a "storyline" test, a test with a thematic line of development. In such a test, a common theme runs throughout in order to assess the effects of context. The basis for such an approach is that the respondents learn as they read on, that they double back and check previous content, and that the ability to use language in conversation or writing depends in large measure on the skill of picking up information from past discussion and using it in formulating new strategies (Low 1986).

Swain (1984), for example, developed a storyline test of French as a foreign language for high school French immersion students. The test consisted of six tasks around a common theme, "finding summer employment." There were four writing tasks (a letter, a note, a composition, and a technical exercise) and two speaking tasks (a group discussion and a job interview). The test was designed so that the topic would be motivating to the students and so that there would be enough new information provided in order to give the tasks credibility. Swain provided the respondents with sufficient time, suggestions as to how to do the test, and clear knowledge about what was being tested. There was access to dictionaries and other reference material, and opportunity for students to review and revise their work. Swain's main concern was to "bias for best" in the construction of the test—to make every effort to support the respondents in doing their best on the test.[10]

Brill (1986), for example, had 32 ninth-grade Hebrew speakers complete a communicative storyline test which included five tasks dealing with membership in a youth group. The tasks included writing a letter as a response to a friend interested in the youth movement the respondent belonged to, presenting questions to the group leader to get more information on the movement, preparing an announcement about the movement to post on bulletin boards, writing out a telephone request for information on how a local foundation could aid the movement, and writing out a telephone response to an invitation by a political group to join a demonstration of theirs. After completing the tasks, the students were then asked to compare their experience on this test and on the traditional multiple-choice one they had taken previously. They almost unanimously endorsed the communicative test as preferable because it was more creative, allowed them to express their opinions, was more interesting, taught them how to make contact with others, and investigated communication skills in addition to reading comprehension. For these reasons, they felt that it provided a truer measure of their competence than did the traditional test.

Canale (1985) viewed communicative tests such as those described above as "proficiency-oriented achievement tests" and offered five reasons supporting this view.

1. Such tests put to use what is learned. There is a transfer from controlled training to real performance.
2. There is a focus on the message and the function, not just on the form.
3. There is group collaboration as well as individual work, not just the latter.
4. The respondents are called upon to use their resourcefulness in resolving authentic problems in language use, as opposed to demonstrating accuracy in resolving contrived problems at the linguistic level.
5. The testing itself is more like learning, and the learners are more involved in the assessment.

(For sample items testing listening, speaking, and writing, see the Appendix.)

TEST CONSTRUCTION AND ADMINISTRATION

Inventory of Objectives

Test constructors first make an inventory of the objectives that they want to test. This involves distinguishing broad objectives from more specific ones and important objectives from trivial ones. Test items and procedures are then developed to assess these objectives either separately or along with other objectives. Varying the type of items or procedures testing a particular objective, as well as the difficulty, helps distinguish one student's grasp of the area covered by the objectives from that of another student. As said at the outset, there is currently a premium put on the use of multiple testing techniques in order to obtain a more representative sampling of a learner's language behavior.

The number of test items or procedures used to measure any given objective depends on several things. First, is the test intended to assess *mastery* of the objectives or simply some degree of attainment? If mastery is being assessed, there should be a large enough sample of items to allow its measurement. For example, including only one item on tag questions is unlikely to indicate to the testers that the respondent has a firm grasp of tag questions. But if the testers do not have the testing time to allow for, say, three items on tag questions, then they should at least be aware that they are not really testing for mastery. A respondent's correct answer on one item could be a result of guessing. Testers usually do not have the time to cover all the objectives they would like to, so instead they must satisfy themselves with a sampling.

If the test is designed for use in a course, then the objectives covered might be those most emphasized in the course and those of greatest value for the students as well. As previously mentioned, testers may need to resist the temptation to include difficult items of marginal importance simply because they differentiate between the better and poorer achievers.

Constructing an Item Bank

It is suggested that potential test items and procedures be selected and stored in an item bank. Before the advent of computer applications and sophisticated statistical procedures for processing items, test constructors would keep file cards of items. The use of computers allows for more rapid and more efficient handling of those kinds of items that lend themselves to computer applications. Whether computerized or not, an item bank would benefit from descriptive information on each item or procedure, such as the following:

1. the skill or combination of skills tested;
2. the language element(s) involved;
3. the item-elicitation and item-response formats;
4. instructions on how to present the item;
5. the section of the book or part of the course that the item relates to (if applicable);
6. the time it took to write the item (which gives an estimate of the time needed to prepare a series of such items for a test).

It is presumed that any item entered in the bank has been piloted on sample groups and reviewed. An item may seem easy or well written when it is generated but may exhibit glaring inadequacies upon later inspection.

Test Format

One basic issue of test format is whether the test progresses to increasingly more difficult items or whether easy and difficult items and procedures are interspersed. There are arguments on both sides. If items grow increasingly more difficult, the respondents may give up after a while and not attempt items after they encounter the first one that stumps them. Yet if respondents experience failure too frequently at the outset of a test because of difficult items, they may be discouraged from attempting the remainder of the items in a section. Thus, there may be a psychological advantage to pacing the items so that they become progressively more difficult. A compromise is to start the test with relatively easy items and then start interspersing easy and difficult items.

Another issue of format relates to multiple-choice items. Such items lend themselves to guessing. Increasing the number of alternatives (from, say, three to four) decreases the likelihood of getting the item right by chance alone. There is a 33 percent chance of getting a three-choice item right by guessing, and a 25 percent chance of guessing correctly on a four-choice item. This of course assumes that all choices are equally attractive to the respondent who does not know the answer to the item.

Instructions

The instructions should be brief and yet explicit and unambiguous. Examples may help, but on the other hand may hinder if they do not give the whole picture and become a substitute for reading the instructions. Respondents may need training in how to take a particular kind of test. For example, a research study demonstrated that supplying respondents with suggested strategies in the test instructions for summarizing foreign-language texts may have a beneficial effect on the respondents' knowing how to read the text and how to prepare a summary of it (Cohen 1993). In other words, more elaborated instructions may serve to ensure that the respondents do the task as intended by the test constructor. (Sample instructions for how to summarize can be found in the appendix, under "Assessing the Interaction of Reading and Writing.")

In addition, the respondents should be informed as to whether guessing incorrectly counts against them. They should also know the value of each item and section of the test. Finally, the time allowed for each subtest and/or for the total test should be announced. If speed is a factor for a subtest, the respondents should be made aware of this. Many years ago, Harris (1969) admonished teachers not to use timed tests that left more than 10 to 15 percent of the group behind. Perhaps in today's educational climate (see Shohamy 2000), we would not want to leave any students behind.

Scoring

If an objective is tested by more than one item—say, five items—then it is possible to speak of mastery of the objective, at least according to that means of measuring it. (Again, the importance of using multiple measures of the same objectives is stressed.) If Juan gets four of the five items right, he has displayed 80 percent mastery of that objective, according to the test. The test may have a series of such items. If Juan's test performance is stated only in terms of his mastery of objectives, then the test is being used for criterion-referenced evaluation. What constitutes mastery of an objective is a difficult question to answer.

Is it having four out of five items correct on that objective? What about three out of five? Further, what constitutes notable achievement? It could be that mastery of a certain objective reflects far more learning than mastery of another. For this reason, items covering one objective may be weighted more than items covering other objectives. For example, three questions asked after presentation of a lecture on a tape may count more than ten short-answer multiple-choice reading or grammar items. Weighting also involves consideration of the ease of the task and the time spent on it.

The test constructor has to consider how long it will take to score particular types of items, as well as the easiest procedure for scoring (e.g., automated scoring by an optical scanner or computer scoring vs. hand scoring). The more objective the scoring is for a particular item, the higher the scorer reliability is likely to be (i.e., the likelihood that two different scorers would come up with the same score for a particular respondent's test). For example, the scoring of a multiple-choice test would be considered more objective than that of an essay test, where the scorer's subjectivity plays more of a role.

Reliability

The reliability of a test concerns its precision as a measuring instrument. Reliability asks whether a test given to the same respondents a second time would yield the same results. At least three crucial factors relating to test reliability have been identified.

Test Factors. Test factors include the extent of the sampling of the objective, the degree of ambiguity of the items and restrictions on freedom of response (e.g., being given more specific and thus constraining topics for compositions), the clarity and explicitness of the instructions, the quality of the layout, the familiarity that the respondents have with the format, and the length of the total test, with longer tests being more reliable (Hughes 1989).

These test factors contribute to the likelihood that performance on one item on a test will be consistent with performance on another item, producing a test with greater *internal consistency*.

One measure of internal consistency is that of split-halves reliability, which calls for correlating the odd-numbered items on the test with the even-numbered ones. Other measures of internal consistency, such as Kuder-Richardson Formulas 20 and 21, call for more complex calculations (see Bachman 1990, pp.172–178). For the purpose of classroom testing, a reliability coefficient of .70 and up is good. Higher reliability coefficients would be expected of standardized tests used for large-scale administration (.80 or better). A perfect coefficient is 1.0.

The reliability of *ratings* is also an important test factor. Considerations include the nature of the scoring key in terms of detail and clarity, the training of scorers, and the number of scorers (Bachman 1990, pp. 178–183; Reed and Cohen 2000). In recent years, sophisticated statistical procedures using generalizability theory and multifaceted Rasch analysis have been employed to take into account the nature of the task being rated and the person doing the rating in determining the reliability of ratings (McNamara 1996). Verbal protocol studies have also been conducted to determine the extent to which raters of compositions, for instance, adhere to the rating schedule being used (e.g., Hamp-Lyons 1989).

Situational Factors The manner in which the examiner presents the instructions, the characteristics of the room (comfort, lighting, acoustics), outside noises, and other factors can have a bearing on how well the respondents perform on the test.

Individual Factors These include (a) transient factors, such as the physical and psychological state of mind of the respondent (motivation, rapport with examiner), and (b) stable factors, such as mechanical skill, IQ, ability to use English, and experience with such tests.

Validity

Validity refers to whether the test actually measures what it purports to measure. Thus, the test must be reliable before it can be valid. Assuming that the test is producing a reliable measure of something, the questions are then: What is that something?, and, Is it what the test is supposed to be measuring?

Face Validity This aspect of validity refers to whether the test *looks* as if it is measuring what it is supposed to. For this reason, Low (1985) referred to it as "perceived validity." For example, a test that measures a respondent's own English pronunciation by assessing his or her rating of another's pronunciation of English may not be readily accepted as a valid measure, nor may filling in blanks on a cloze test seem a valid way to assess reading skills. To many test takers, such measures appear to be too indirect. The fact that these measures are indirect may confuse and distract the respondent. Another example is that a test's title may be misleading. A test entitled "Pragmatic Syntax Measure," for instance, may actually deal more with morphology than with syntax and may use stilted grammar-book English rather than the language of everyday situational interactions, as one would expect of a truly pragmatic measure.

Content Validity. This type of validity refers to the adequacy of sampling of content or objectives in a test. Sometimes even commercial tests constructed by experts fail to state what objectives are being covered in the test and which items specifically are testing each of these objectives. Valette (1977, p. 46) notes, "For the language teacher, the degree of test validity is not derived from a statistical analysis of test performance, but from a meticulous analysis of the content of each item and of the test as a whole."

Criterion-Related Validity. A test can be validated by seeing how closely respondents' performance on specific sets of objectives on a total test parallels their performance at the same time or in the future on another test which is thought to measure the same or similar activities.

1. *Concurrent Validity:* Validation is concurrent if test results are compared with results from another test given at about the *same time.* For example, a teacher may wish to see how students' performance on a test that he or she constructed compares with students' performance on some criterion measure of reading obtained from a commercial test of reading.
2. *Predictive Validity:* Validity is predictive if test results are compared with results from another test or another type of measure obtained at a *later date.* For example, a lan-

guage aptitude test may be validated by a test of a student's achievement in the language class in which the student was placed on the basis of the aptitude test.

Construct Validity. This form of validity refers to the degree to which scores on a measure permit inferences about underlying traits. In other words, it examines whether the test is a true reflection of the theory of the trait being measured, in this case, language. Language assessment experts like Shohamy advise teachers to keep asking themselves whenever they construct a test "whether the tasks and items on the test are actually a reflection of what it means to know a language and to avoid those items which test something different than actual language knowledge" (Shohamy 1985, p. 74).

Convergent Validity. Validity in testing a given construct, such as listening comprehension, may be attained by testing the same phenomenon in a variety of different ways. The classroom teacher can practice this kind of validation. The discussion of item types presented earlier in this chapter (and in the appendix) provides a number of techniques for testing the same objectives differently. Varying the item-elicitation and item-response formats, as well as the discreteness and integrativeness of the items, can produce items testing the same objectives in different ways.

Item Analysis

Piloting the Test. If time and resources permit, then sound testing practice includes piloting the test on a population similar to that for which it is designed. The pilot administration provides the test constructor with feedback on the items and procedures. On timed subtests, pilot respondents can be instructed to mark how far they got when the time ran out and then to go ahead and complete the test so that there is feedback on all the items in the test.

Item Difficulty. Item difficulty refers to the proportion of correct responses to a test item. A test which aims to differentiate among respondents should have items which, say, 60 to 80 percent of the respondents answer correctly. (If 15 out of 20 respondents answer an item correctly, the item difficulty is 75 percent.) If the purpose of the test is to determine whether nearly all students have achieved the objectives of a course, on the other hand, then the proportion of correct responses should be 90 percent or better.

Item Discrimination The item discrimination index tells how well an item performs in separating the better students from the poorer ones. For a procedure to calculate the index, see Cohen (1994). The index is intended to distinguish respondents who know the most or have the skills or abilities being tested from those who do not. Knowledge of the material is determined by the respondent's performance on the total test (i.e., all subtests combined).

Test Revision

If an item has a difficulty coefficient of lower than 60 percent or higher than about 80 percent, and if the discrimination coefficient is below .30, then the item should probably be revised or eliminated. It is difficult to select or reject borderline items. Especially if the item analysis is performed on a small sample, just one or two responses added or deleted will change the index considerably. There may be justification for leaving an overly easy item in the test if, for example, it is a lead-off item used to give students encouragement to continue. Also, *where* an item appears in a test may affect performance on it. For example, students may do best on the items in the *middle* of an exam, after they have warmed up to the test and before fatigue sets in. Multiple-choice items can be improved by examining the percent of respondents who selected each choice. If some distractors draw no responses or too many, then they should be omitted or altered. This task requires both rigor and intuition. For instance, it may be necessary to change the syntax or vocabulary of a distractor, or perhaps its semantic thrust. In piloting an item, it is possible to ask the respondents what their rationale was for choosing a particular distractor instead of the correct answer to arrive at the best set of choices.

Ideally, the results of item analysis would be added to the information available on each item in the test constructor's item bank. If a particular test item comes under challenge by respondents or other examiners, it is useful to be able to check its item analysis information. Perhaps it will turn out to be a borderline item that should not have been included in the test.

Test Administration Checklist

The following checklist applies primarily to the administering of classroom tests and is intended as suggestive, not prescriptive. The "should"s of test administration will vary according to the testing situation.

1. The room should have adequate ventilation or heat, light, and acoustics.
2. If a tape recorder is to be used, it should be set up and tested in advance to make sure that it works well.
3. The test administrator should assume an affable but stern posture. A few smiles help to put the respondents at ease but the sternness is necessary to make it clear that cheating is not allowed—unless cooperative effort among respondents is an integral part of the particular test or a portion of it.
4. The time that the exam begins and the total time remaining for the test and/or subtests should be written on the blackboard.
5. If the instructions are to be read aloud, they should be read slowly with no departure from the established wording. If questions arise, the tester can use paraphrasing but should not add anything substantive to the instructions (Harris 1969).

Test-Taking Strategies

The strategies that respondents use in taking tests have implications both for the issue of test validity and "bias for best." Tests that are relied upon to indicate the readers' comprehension level may produce misleading results because of numerous techniques that readers have developed for obtaining correct answers on such tests without fully or even partially understanding the text. As Fransson (1984) so aptly puts it, respondents may not proceed via the text but rather around it. In effect, there are presumptions held by test constructors and administrators as to what is being tested, and there are the actual processes that test takers go through to produce answers to questions and tasks. The two may not necessarily be one and the same. The strategies the respondents are using may be detrimental to their overall performance, or at least not as helpful as other strategies.

Mentalistic measures using verbal report have helped determine how respondents actually take reading comprehension tests as opposed to how they might be expected to take them (Cohen 1984; 1994, pp. 130–136). Studies calling on respondents to provide immediate or delayed retrospection as to their test-taking strategies regarding reading passages with multiple-choice items have, for example, yielded the following results:

1. Although the instructions ask students to read the passage before answering the questions, students have reported either reading the questions first or reading just part of the article and then looking for the corresponding questions.
2. Although advised to read all alternatives before choosing one, students stop reading the alternatives as soon as they have found one that they decide is correct.
3. Students use a strategy of matching material from the passage with material in the item stem and in the alternatives, and prefer this surface-structure reading of the test items to one that calls for more in-depth reading and inferencing.
4. Students rely on their prior knowledge of the topic and on their general vocabulary.

From these findings and others, a description is emerging of how respondents actually answer test questions. Unless trained to do otherwise, they may use the most expedient means of responding, such as relying more on their previous experience with seemingly similar formats than on a close reading of the task at hand. Thus, when given a passage to read and summarize, they may perform the task the same way they did their last summary task, rather than paying attention to what is called for in the current one. Often this strategy works, but on occasion the particular task may require subtle or major shifts in response behavior in order for the test taker to perform well.

There appears to be a further insight to be gained from the test strategy literature, namely, that indirect testing formats—that is, those which do not reflect real-world tasks (e.g., multiple-choice, cloze)—may prompt the use of strategies solely for the purpose of coping with the test format. More direct formats such as summarizing a text may be freer of such added testing effects. However, as long as the task is part of a test, students are bound to use strategies they would not use under non-test conditions. It is largely the responsibility of test constructors and of those who administer such tests to be aware of what their tests are actually measuring. Verbal report techniques can assist the test developer and user in obtaining such information.[11]

Insights about the way in which respondents go about performing different testing tasks can be used to make informed decisions as to (1) the choice of testing format, (2) the choice and wording of instructions, and (3) the value and feasibility of coaching the respondents in how to take language tests. Work by O'Malley (1986) and others has already made use of such research findings in designing training modules for learning test-taking skills.

DISCUSSION QUESTIONS

1. Can you think of times when, as a student of a second or foreign language, one or more of the abuses of languages tests were "inflicted" upon you? Which ones? What was your reaction at the time? As a teacher of language, have you ever "perpetrated" any of those abuses yourself? What would be the appropriate remedies?
2. Identify and describe at least one test that you or a colleague used for an administrative, instructional, or research purpose. Was an instrument ever used for assessment in more than one of the three categories? If so, explain.
3. What does it mean to say that an item may test for points that are not consistent with the test constructor's objective(s) for that item? How would this be discovered and how might it be remedied?

SUGGESTED ACTIVITIES

1. Take an ESL/EFL test—either your own or someone else's—and review it, using the review checklist of questions provided below:

   a. Instructions

   (1) Are the instructions for each section clear? Do all the items in a section fit the instructions for that section?

   (2) Is the vocabulary in the instructions and in the items at the desired level of difficulty (or too hard—particularly in the instructions section)?

   (3) Are there good examples of how to complete each section (where applicable)?

   (4) In structured or open-ended sections, do the instructions indicate the approximate length of the response that is to be made?

   (5) If the test is timed, or timed in certain sections, is the timing realistic?

   (6) Are the respondents informed in the instructions as to whether the section is timed and how long they will have?

   (7) Do the instructions indicate the value of the particular section with respect to the overall test score? Is the overall value of the test clear to the intended respondents? Do they know what the purpose of the test is?

   (8) Is the method of administering the test/quiz carefully established (i.e., so that someone else would administer the test exactly as you would, if you were not able to give it or intended others to administer it)?

   b. Content

   (1) (with reference to achievement tests) Is the test adequately covering the instructional objectives for the course? Is it testing material *not* taught/learned in the course? (Remember that a good test should reveal gaps in the instructor's teaching as well as in the students' learning.)

   (2) Is the test testing the desired receptive/productive language skills? Has the test adequately isolated the desired skill (if this is what it purports to do)?

   (3) Does the content of the test cover the intended aspects of communicative competence (grammatical, discourse, and sociolinguistic competence)? Is the test intending to

   get at *mastery* of a set (or sampled subset) of objectives or simply some level of attainment of these objectives? Is the actual test consistent with the expressed design?

   (4) Is only one register (formal, casual, intimate) or dialect (standard or nonstandard) considered correct in one or all sections of the test? Are the respondents aware of this (refer to the "Instructions" section above)? If the intent is to keep the language "conversational" in, say, short-answer listening comprehension items, do the items reflect this intent?

   (5) Might some or many items be testing more points than you thought originally (if you constructed the test)? If so, would it help to simplify these items or procedures to give greater prominence to exactly the points intended to be measured?

   (6) Did you write any of your sentences as "linguistic curiosities" in an effort to test certain lexical and/or structural points (e.g., "My brother has something beautiful and I have nothing ugly") from Rivers 1981, p. 376)?

   (7) Does the test have the right title, or might it mislead both the respondents and potential test administrators and interpreters of the results?

   c. Item Format and Test Layout

   (1) Is the test as a whole too long or too short? (If too short, it may not be reliable.)

   (2) Is one objective or another being tested too much or too little? (Over-testing may start giving away the answers and under-testing may not give enough diagnostic information.)

   (3) Are the items which test the same objective worded and spaced in a way that one item does not provide a giveaway for the others?

   (4) Are any items or sections clearly too difficult or too easy to answer? (Of course, item analysis helps answer this question. The difficulty of an item is often hard to determine on an *a priori* basis.)

   (5) Have the correct true/false and multiple-choice responses been adequately randomized so as not to set up a response pattern (e.g., all T/F items should not be "true" and all M-C items should not have either "b" or "c" as the correct answer)?

(6) Are the items paced so that even the poorest student will experience at least a modicum of success at the outset?

(7) Are the item response formats the most appropriate ones for what you want to test (e.g., would matching be a more efficient means of testing vocabulary, say, than completion or multiple-choice, or would you wish to use several formats)?

(8) Is the item stimulus format appropriate (e.g., should the stimulus be audiotaped, rather than written, or should both modalities be used)?

(9) How good is the layout?

(a) Is the technical arrangement of the items on the printed page easy to follow (e.g., are the multiple-choice alternatives horizontal or vertical, in the sentence itself, or to one side)?

(b) Is the spacing between and within items adequate?

(c) If the test has been photocopied, is the print legible?

(10) Have the items been adequately reviewed by other native speakers (and non-natives, if possible) to eliminate poor distractors and deceptive or confusing items?

d. Scoring

(1) Have the methods for scoring the test or grading a procedure or section been adequately determined?

(2) Are the items and/or sections weighted appropriately in scoring—that is, do the weightings coincide with your notions about the most important objectives, the ones given the most emphasis in the class, the most useful elements?

2. Drawing on the suggestions in this chapter concerning testing reading comprehension, design a test of reading comprehension and write several sample items for it. Then review this test using the checklist in Activity I.

3. Devise a way to test for strategic competence in test taking. Then try it out on a small group of respondents and discuss the results with others.

FURTHER READING

Alderson, J. C., C. Clapham, and D. Wall. 1995. *Language Test Construction and Evaluation.* New York: Cambridge University Press.

This book focuses on the design of tests for administration primarily to larger groups of respondents. It offers tips on item writing, listing the pitfalls of formats such as multiple-choice. It covers all phases of test construction, from piloting to reporting of scores.

Bailey, K. M. 1998b. *Learning About Language Assessment: Dilemmas, Decisions, and Directions.* Boston, MA: Heinle & Heinle Publishers.

This volume discusses the value of different approaches to assessment, including testimonials from teachers who have had success with one or another approach. Test types discussed include dictation, cloze, C-tests, dictocomps and strip stories, role plays and performance tests, and writing samples and portfolios.

Brown, J. D., ed. 1998. New *Ways of Classroom Assessment.* Alexandria, VA: TESOL.

The book offers ESL teachers ideas for everyday classroom assessment activities which provide a way of observing or scoring students' performances and giving feedback on the effectiveness of the learning and teaching involved. Included are examples of alternative ways of assessing the four skills such as through portfolios, journals, logs, and student-teacher conferences. It also provides examples of self-assessment and peer assessment such as through oral and written book reports, and examples of alternative groupings for assessment.

Hamp-Lyons, L., and W. Condon. 2000. *Assessing the Portfolio: Principles for Practice, Theory, and Research.* Cresskill, NJ: Hampton Press.

The volume provides an overview of and framework for portfolio-based assessment of writing, discusses its application in college writing programs (for natives and non-natives), and provides a research agenda. The authors first focus on the learner variables that can be included in a portfolio (e.g., to what extent does the learner reveal information about him/herself versus what is taught in school?), then on the teacher, next on the assessor, and finally on the program.

McNamara, T. 2000. *Language Testing.* Oxford: Oxford University Press.

This brief volume defines what a language test is and relates the different types from the most discrete-point to the most integrative, pragmatic, and communicative, in terms of their communicative value. It is timely and refreshingly open in its handling of issues.

ENDNOTES

1 This is an updated version of a chapter with a similar title, appearing in M. Celce-Murcia, ed. (1991), *Teaching English as a Second or Foreign Language*, New York: Newbury House/HarperCollins (pp. 486–506).

2 Sometimes teachers speak of using a "curve," which simply means that they evaluate a student's performance in comparison with that of other students in the same class or in other classes.

3 See the appendix, under "Assessing Speaking Skills," for a distinction between sociocultural and sociolinguistic competence or ability.

4 It would be possible to avoid this by having the multiple-choice alternatives also presented orally.

5 Overall rapid inspection with periods of close inspection.

6 Locating a specific symbol or group of symbols—e.g., a date, a name of a person or place, a sum of money.

7 Discovering accurately what the author seeks to convey.

8 In intelligent tutoring systems, the computer diagnoses the students' strategies and their relationship to expert strategies, and then generates instruction based on this comparison.

9 This position is an endorsement of the need to take into account "perceived validity" (Low 1985), as discussed in the chapter under "validity."

10 The point here is that such cases of bias can be viewed as a good thing—as intentional bias. The aim would be to set up tasks that test-takers will be motivated to participate in, such as those that approximate real-life situations (Spolsky 1985).

11 For more on verbal report as a research tool, see Cohen 1998, pp. 34–39, 49–61.

APPENDIX

Example Test Items for Measuring Listening, Vocabulary, Speaking, and Writing Skills

As pointed out in Cohen (1994, Ch. 6), it is possible to combine different item-elicitation formats (i.e., oral, written, nonverbal, or a combination) and item-response formats (likewise oral, written, or nonverbal) in order to generate items. For this reason, lists of sample items in testing books may appear repetitious. For instance, a listening item and a reading item may actually have the same item stimulus (e.g., a written question) and differ only with respect to the way the multiple-choice responses are presented—orally, in the case of the listening item and in writing in the case of the reading item.

This appendix provides a brief sampling of some types of items that may be of benefit in testing, depending upon what is needed.

Assessing Listening Skills

Discrimination of Sounds

a. The respondent indicates which vowel sound of three is different from the other two. (Taped stimulus): (1) sun (2) put (3) dug; (response choices): (a) 1 *(b) 2 (c) 3.

b. These sounds could be in sentence context. (Taped stimulus): (1) It's a sheep. (2) It's a sheep. (3) It's a ship. (Response choices): (a) 1, (b) 2 *(c) 3.

Intonation

a. The respondent is to indicate whether two phrases have the same intonation. (Taped stimulus): You're coming?/ You're coming. (Response choices): (a) same, *(b) different

b. The respondent must determine the meaning of the phrase from the intonation. (Taped stimulus): Good morning! (Response choices): (a) happy to see employee, *(b) annoyed that the employee is late to work

Listening for Grammatical Distinctions

The respondent has to listen carefully for inflectional markers—for example, the respondent must determine whether the subject and verb are in the singular or the plural. (Taped stimulus): The boys sing well. (Response choices): (a) singular, *(b) plural, (c) same form for singular and plural.

Listening for Vocabulary

The respondent performs an action in response to a command (e.g., getting up, walking to the window) or draws a picture according to oral instructions (e.g., coloring a picture a certain way, sorting a set of objects according to instructions).

Auditory Comprehension

a. The respondent indicates whether a response to a question is appropriate. (Taped stimulus): How're you gonna get home? At about 3:30 P.M. (Response choices): (a) appropriate, *(b) inappropriate

b. The respondent hears a statement and must indicate the appropriate paraphrase for the statement. (Taped stimulus): What'd you get yourself into this time? (Response choices): (a) What are you wearing this time? (b) What did you buy this time? *(c) What's your problem this time?

c. The respondents listen in on a telephone conversation between two people and at appropriate times must indicate what they would say if they were one of the speakers in the conversation. (Taped stimulus): Mother: Well, Mary, you know you were supposed to call me last week. Mary: I know, Mom, but I got tied up. Mother: That's really no excuse. Mary: (Response choices): (a) Yes, I'll call him. *(b) You're right. I'm sorry. (c) I've really had nothing to do.

d. The respondent hears a lecture, with all the false starts, filled pauses, and other features that make it different from oral recitation of a written text. After the lecture, there are taped multiple-choice, structured, or open-ended questions to be responded to in writing on the answer sheet.

e. Dictation can serve as a test of auditory comprehension if it is given at a fast enough pace so that it is not simply a spelling test. As Bailey notes, "[D]ictation is really a family of related procedures that can be systematically altered (by manipulating the stimulus material, the task posed, the learners' response, and/or the scoring criteria) to meet different assessment purposes" (1998b, p. 20). Bailey offers the partial dictation and the graduated dictation as alternatives to a full dictation. In the first, parts of the text are already on the page. In the second, the size of the phrase groups between pauses is gradually increased. In addition, the length of the pauses and the speed at which the phrase groups are read can be varied.

Assessing Vocabulary

a. Respondents receive sets of six words and three meanings and are instructed to choose the right word to go with each meaning. They are to write the number of that word next to its meaning (Nation 1990):

1. apply
2. elect   _____ choose by voting
3. jump   _____ become like water
4. manufacture _____ make
5. melt
6. threaten

b. Respondents receive a long list of words (e.g., 100) and are to indicate whether they know their meaning. The list consists of both real and imaginary words (nonexistent words which the respondent could not possibly know) (Meara and Buxton 1987):

Check the words you know the meaning of, e.g., ✔ milk

gathering	forecast	wodesome
loyalment	flane	crope
dismissal	sloping	bluck
enclose	rehearsion	turmoil

c. Contextualized vocabulary: Respondents are asked to indicate what a word means within the context of a given passage. The response could be open-ended or multiple-choice—e.g., What does *delinquent* mean in line 7?

(Open-ended response): _____ .
(Multiple-choice response):
(a) naughty (b) haughty
(c) sinful   *(d) irresponsible

Assessing Speaking Skills

Good practice calls for using varied measures of speaking, such that for each learner more than one type of speaking is tapped (e.g., reporting in the L2 the contents of an article read in the native language, participating in group discussion on a common and possibly controversial theme, taking part in role play, and lecturing).

Then it would be important to establish which speech functions are to be assessed in each type of interaction (e.g., reporting: ability to state the main ideas and express an opinion about them; discussion: arguing; role play: appropriate execution of the necessary speech acts—requesting, complaining, apologizing, complimenting). Cohen (1994, Ch. 8) provides scales for rating communicative language ability in terms of sociocultural, sociolinguistic, and grammatical ability, respectively. The *sociocultural* scale assesses the appropriateness of the strategies selected for realizing speech acts in a given context, taking into account (1) the culture involved, (2) the age and sex of the speakers, (3) their social class and occupations, and (4) their roles and status in the interaction.

The scale for *sociolinguistic* ability is intended to assess the use of linguistic forms to express the intent of the speech act (e.g., regret in an apology, grievance in a complaint, the objective of a request, or the refusal of an invitation). For example, when a student carrying coffee bumps into a professor, spilling it on the professor's dress, "Sorry!" would probably constitute an inadequate apology. This category assesses the speakers' control over the actual language forms used to realize the speech act (e.g., "sorry," "excuse me," "very sorry," "really sorry"), as well as their control over register or formality of the utterance from most intimate to most formal language.

The *grammaticality* scale deals with how acceptably words, phrases, and sentences are formed and pronounced in the respondents' utterances. The focus is both on clear cases of errors in form, such as the use of the present perfect for an action completed in the past (e.g., "We have had a great time last night at your house"), as well as on matters of style (e.g., the learner uses a passive verb form in a context where a native would use the active form: "The CD was lost" vs. "I lost your CD"). Major errors might be considered those that either interfere with intelligibility or stigmatize the speaker. Minor errors would be those that neither get in the way of the listener's comprehension nor annoy the listener to any extent. Thus, getting the tense wrong in "We have had a great time last night at your house" could be viewed as a minor error, whereas producing "I don't have what to say" by translating directly from the appropriate Hebrew language (for "I really have no excuse") could be considered a major error since it is not only ungrammatical but also could stigmatize the speaker as rude and unconcerned, rather than apologetic.

Assessing the Interaction of Reading and Writing

An example of a test of reading and writing is that of summarizing. Summarization tests are complex in nature. The reading portion entails identifying topical information, distinguishing superordinate from subordinate material, and identifying redundant and trivial information. Writing up of summary entails selecting of topical information (or generating it if it is not provided), deleting trivial and redundant information, substituting superordinate material, and restating the test so that it is coherent and polished (Brown and Day 1983; Kintsch and van Dijk 1978).

Given the lack of clarity that often accompanies such tasks, it may be useful to give specific instructions as to how to go about the summarization task. For example:

Instructions on How to Read
- Read to extract the most important points—for example, those constituting topic sentences signaled as crucial by the paragraph structure: points that the reader of the summary would want to read.
- Reduce information to superordinate points.
- Avoid redundant information—points will be taken off.

Instructions on How to Write
- Prepare in draft form and then rewrite.
- Link points smoothly.

- Exact length of summary (e.g., 10 percent of original test, so 75 words for 750-word text)
- Write in your own words.
- Be brief.
- Write legibly.

It may also be beneficial to give raters specific instructions as to how to assess the summaries:

- Check to see whether each important point is included (points that were agreed upon by a group of experts in advance).
- Check to ensure that these points are linked together by the key linking/integrating elements appearing on the master list.
- Points will be taken off for each irrelevant point.
- Points will be taken off for illegibility.

Assessing Written Expression

Perhaps the main thing to be said about the testing of written expression is that it is a poor substitute for repeated samplings of a learner's writing ability while not under the pressure of an exam situation. The current process-oriented approach to writing suggests that it is unnatural for a learner to write a draft of a composition and submit it for a grade. Instead, learners prepare multiple drafts that are reviewed both by peers (in small groups) and by the teacher at appropriate times. Hence, if writing is to be assessed on a test, it would be important to provide the learners with specific guidelines as to the nature of the task. For example:

> Your boss has asked you to rough out an argument for why the factory employees should not get longer coffee breaks. Try to present your arguments in the most logical and persuasive way. Do not worry about grammar and punctuation at this point. There is no time for that now. Just concern yourself with the content of your ideas, their organization, and the choice of appropriate vocabulary to state your case.

It is also important for the person assessing the writing to pay attention only to those aspects of the task that learners were requested to perform.

Furthermore, the field of L2 writing has embraced the use of *portfolios* whereby the students prepare a series of compositions (possibly including the various drafts of each as well). Each entry may represent a different type of writing—for instance, one could be a narrative or descriptive or expressive piece, the second a formal essay, and the third an analysis of a prose text. Hence, the portfolio represents multiple measures of the students' writing ability. (For more on portfolios, see Hamp-Lyons and Condon 2000.)

Keeping Up to Date as an ESL or EFL Professional

JOANN (JODI) CRANDALL

Crandall's chapter identifies a number of strategies and resources for continuing professional development. The strategies include participating in professional associations, serving on curriculum development or textbook selection committees, researching classroom issues and practice, and working collaboratively with professionals from other fields. Also discussed are relevant journals, clearinghouses/centers, publishers, and Internet resources.

"That's the best part of teaching— the learning."

(An experienced teacher serving as a Peace Corps volunteer in Kiribati)

INTRODUCTION

Though you may be about to complete or may have recently completed a program to prepare you as an English as a second or foreign language teacher and you've learned a lot about theories of teaching and learning, language acquisition and development, the structure of English, approaches and techniques for teaching and testing language skills and proficiency, and cross-cultural communication and have had the opportunity to read about, discuss, and research a number of specific topics related to second and foreign language teaching and learning—this is only a beginning. If you have been able to teach during your program, you know how much more you learn when you can test out what you have been reading and thinking about. That testing and learning will now become a part of your daily routine. It was a wise person who said that teaching is lifelong learning. It's that learning ("the best part of teaching") which motivates many English language professionals to keep teaching when the benefits from other jobs would otherwise draw them away. Completing an academic program is really only the beginning of a lifelong quest to better understand our students, ourselves, our discipline, and the approaches and techniques we can use to help others to become competent users of English.

A number of resources are available to stimulate new ideas and to help us reconsider old ideas or practices. You have undoubtedly used many of these during your TESOL program. They will become even more important when you find yourself in settings where there are fewer colleagues to share concerns and ideas with on a regular basis than when you were a student. Some of the ways in which you can continue to grow as a teacher and become a better-informed ESL professional include:

- Participating in professional associations concerned with the teaching of English or other foreign languages, including attending local, national, or international conferences.
- Subscribing to journals and regularly reading periodicals about language teaching and learning and related fields.
- Placing your name on mailing lists of major ESL/EFL textbook publishers and information clearinghouses or resource centers.
- Offering to review texts for publishers or journals.
- Participating in electronic (e-mail) discussion groups and using the Internet to access language teaching and learning websites and electronic journals.
- Serving on textbook selection committees in your ESL program.

- Working on curriculum or textbook development teams in your ESL program.
- Attending or giving in-service workshops and seminars for teachers.
- Participating in summer institutes or special graduate programs to augment and update your knowledge and skills.
- Researching issues in your own classroom or participating in research projects that will enable you to work with colleagues from your own and other institutions who are engaged in analyzing issues relevant to your classroom.
- Working collaboratively with professionals in other fields.
- Being mentored by experienced colleagues and then becoming a mentor to novice teachers or those who are new to your institution or program.

PROFESSIONAL ASSOCIATIONS AND ORGANIZATIONS

Professional associations and organizations offer an excellent means of keeping in touch with others in the same field. They provide a number of formal and informal channels (publications, conferences, seminars, workshops, and committees) to learn what others in similar contexts are thinking and doing and to share insights and ideas from your own experience. Most also offer a number of professional development opportunities on the Internet and the World Wide Web, such as electronic discussion groups, online seminars or workshops, and e-mail question and answer services. While attending conferences or seminars in person may provide opportunities for interacting with many colleagues, increasingly it is possible to have that interaction without leaving home, through the Internet and other technology. These associations also publish a range of materials, including newsletters, journals, teacher reference books, and student texts or other materials, each of which provides a different way of keeping informed about new research, materials, or issues in the field. Most associations also host conferences, both at a national and more local level. These conferences offer multiple avenues

for professional growth. Plenary addresses often discuss emerging questions; papers analyze research results; workshops introduce techniques or strategies; and book exhibits provide an opportunity to examine new student and teacher resource texts. They also offer opportunities for informal conversation with others who share similar interests or concerns, often leading to long-term professional correspondence and friendship.

There is perhaps no single experience with more potential for educating and refreshing a professional than an international English language teaching conference. But even at a smaller, national, regional, or local level, these organizations and conferences are a great resource, sometimes providing information or assistance that is of more immediate use, since professionals in the same geographic area are likely to share similar concerns. Professional associations usually also offer ongoing programs of professional development through summer institutes, short courses, and seminars, scheduled so that teachers and others who are working are able to attend. Opportunities to participate in these professional development seminars from one's home, another institution, or through distance education are also increasing. These seminars, institutes, and workshops can all help revive a teacher who is feeling burned out from the daily stress of classroom teaching.

Through a professional association, you can also become more actively involved in improving the profession: in helping to set standards for instruction, in developing criteria for evaluating programs, or in recognizing exemplary research or practice. Most organizations also have a number of special interest groups which communicate regularly through publications, e-mail, or conferences about specific aspects of the profession—for example, the use of computers or video in teaching, the teaching of specific skills or specific levels, and the different roles of English language teaching professionals, such as materials development or program administration.

But reading others' work, listening to what others are learning or doing, or taking courses is also only a beginning. You need to try out your ideas by presenting something you have learned through your experience, perhaps giving a poster session where you display the results of an action research project you have undertaken in your class or participating in an informal "swap shop" or "what works" session where you join several colleagues in sharing teaching techniques that you have found particularly effective. The more actively you participate, the more the professional association will offer you and the more you will learn.

While there are many professional associations of interest to English language teaching professionals, the following are among the largest and most important (unless noted otherwise, all organizations listed are in the United States):

Teachers of English to Speakers of Other Languages (TESOL)

700 South Washington Street, Suite 200
Alexandria, VA 22314

Phone: (703) 836-0774
Fax: (703) 836-7864
E-mail: info@tesol.org
Website: http://www.tesol.org

TESOL publishes *TESOL Matters* (the organization's newsletter, with an excellent calendar of upcoming conferences), *TESOL Journal* (a practice-oriented magazine, including "Tips from the Classroom"), *TESOL Quarterly* (a research journal), a number of special-interest newsletters, and a range of teacher reference texts. It also maintains an extensive website. In addition to an annual conference, which draws about 10,000 English language teaching professionals, the organization also sponsors professional development seminars and academies and articulates standards for English language teaching in diverse contexts. Members can participate in 20 Interest Sections, with new ones forming as new interests emerge. There are also more than 90 TESOL Affiliates around the world, representing major metropolitan areas, states, provinces, regions, and countries. These "local" language-teaching organizations are also important sources of information, often sponsoring conferences, professional development seminars, publications fairs, and job lists, offering teachers an opportunity to link up with colleagues teaching in similar contexts. Many affiliates also publish newsletters, journals such as the *CATESOL Journal*, published by the California Association of Teachers of English to Speakers of Other Languages, and working papers, such as those published by the Washington, DC TESOL (WATESOL) affiliate.

International Association of Teachers of English as a Foreign Language (IATEFL)

3 Kingsdown Chambers
Whitstable, Kent CT5 2FL   UK

E-mail: iatefl@compuserve.com
Website: http://www.iatefl.org

This UK-based professional organization hosts an annual conference, usually held in conjunction with one of the 70 national professional organizations associated with IATEFL. The 14 Special Interest Groups also jointly sponsor an annual symposium, often in conjunction with the British Council. IATEFL members receive reduced rates on a number of professional journals, including the *ELT Journal, Modern English Teacher,* and *English Teaching Professional*. IATEFL also makes available teacher reference texts, some of which consist of papers from past IATEFL conferences. The website provides an extensive conference calendar, as well as news of the association.

International Association of Applied Linguistics (AILA)

c/o American Association for Applied Linguistics (AAAL)
PO Box 21686
Eagan, MN 55121-0686

Phone: (952) 953-0805
Fax: (952) 431-8404
E-mail: aaaloffice@aaal.org
Website: http://www.aaal.org
AILA Website: http://www.brad.ac.uk/acad/aila

AILA is an international association made up of national associations of applied linguists. Because it has no fixed secretariat, the easiest way to find out about AILA is through a national affiliate such as the American Association for Applied Linguistics (AAAL) or through the AILA website. AILA hosts a World Congress on Applied Linguistics in a different country every 3 years, providing an excellent opportunity to become acquainted with research and practice in more than 30 areas in applied linguistics. In addition, the association publishes *AILA News* and the *AILA Review* (thematic occasional papers). AAAL, the U.S. affiliate, convenes an annual conference, with a number of plenary speakers and colloquia on a range of topics in applied linguistics. It also publishes the *AAALetter* (available at the website) with notices about conferences, issues of concern to applied linguists, and a membership directory, as well as a directory of graduate programs in applied linguistics in North America. It also maintains an electronic mailing list for posting job notices and other information.

National Association for Bilingual Education (NABE)

1030 15th Street, NW, Suite 470
Washington, DC 20005-1503

Phone:	(202) 898-1829
Fax:	(202) 789-2866
E-mail:	NABE@nabe.org
Website:	http://www.nabe.org

Focusing on the education of language minority students in the United States, NABE offers a number of services of interest to ESL and EFL language professionals, including an extensive website, where back issues of the *Bilingual Research Journal* and *NABE News* (the association's newsletter) are archived. Among NABE's 18 Special Interest Groups are ones focused on Early Childhood, Elementary, Adult/Vocational or Higher Education, Global Education, Critical Pedagogy, and Information Technology. There is also a Special Interest Group for Parents.

NAFSA: Association of International Educators

1307 New York Avenue, NW, 8th Floor
Washington, DC 20005-4701

Phone:	(202) 737-3699
Fax:	(202) 737-3657
E-mail:	inbox@nafsa.org
Website:	http://www.nafsa.org

With a focus on international exchange of scholars to and from the United States, this association (formerly the National Association for Foreign Student Advisers) includes among its members directors of international programs, educational advisers and admissions officers, and ESL teachers and program administrators, working principally in higher education. The association hosts a national and several regional conferences, publishes *International Educator* (a quarterly newsletter), and provides an electronic news service which keeps members current on legislation and policy discussions, as well as more routine news of the association.

Linguistic Society of America (LSA)

1325 18th Street, NW, Suite 211
Washington, DC 20036-6501

Fax:	(202) 835-1717
E-mail:	lsa@lsadc.org
Website:	http://www.lsadc.org

An association principally of theoretical and descriptive linguists, LSA publishes the journal *Language* and the *LSA Bulletin,* convenes an annual scholarly meeting, sponsors summer institutes, and offers a number of journals at reduced rates to members. Its website provides an extensive listing of publishers, journals, and other information of interest to ESL/EFL language teaching professionals.

While participation in language and linguistics professional associations might seem an obvious source of professional growth, what may be less obvious is the role that related professional organizations can play in helping to broaden and deepen one's understanding of language teaching and learning. For example, attending a conference of reading or writing professionals or reading a journal concerned with cross-cultural communication or curriculum development can offer insights relevant to ESL/EFL teaching. Participating in a related professional organization can bring the insights of that field to one's own teaching and also bring together professionals who have much to share and learn from each other. With expanding linguistic and cultural diversity in national populations and increased study or use of English as an instructional medium for some portion of education in many countries of the world, links with other professional associations will become increasingly important for English language teaching professionals. These organizations exist in many parts of the world. In the United States, the International Reading Association (800 Barksdale Road, Newark, DE 19711; http://www.reading.org), the National Council of Teachers of English (1111 Kenyon Road, Urbana, IL 61801; http://www.ncte.org), The American Council on the Teaching of Foreign Languages (6 Executive Plaza, Yonkers, NY 10701; http://www.actfl.org), and the Association for Supervision and Curriculum Development (1793 Beauregard Street, Alexandria, VA 22314; http://www.ascd.org) all provide publications, conferences, and professional development opportunities relevant to ESL and EFL professionals. Their websites, as well, are excellent sources of information about topics of relevance to ESL and EFL professionals. Most of these organizations also have regional, state, or local affiliates that provide a means of developing professional relationships or collaborations with those closer to home.

PROFESSIONAL JOURNALS

Another way to keep current is to read and respond to journals in the field (some of which are published by the professional associations discussed above) and to submit comments, book reviews, and articles to them. Because the number of journals relevant to the teaching and learning of language continues to grow, only major, representative ones are described below. In the section on Electronic Resources, a number of websites are provided which can lead you to other journals of interest. Many of these journals also provide some portion of their current or past issues online. If you are unable to locate paper copies of these journals, you may be able to access at least portions of them through their websites.

Annual Review of Applied Linguistics (ARAL)
Cambridge University Press
110 Midland Ave.
Port Chester, NY 10573-4930
Or

Shaftesbury Road
Edinburgh Building
Cambridge CB2 2RU   UK
Website: http://uk.cambridge.org/journals

An annual, thematic issue with invited contributions, ARAL provides a comprehensive, up-to-date review of research and practice in an area of applied linguistics. Each article gives a critical summary of one topic, followed by an annotated bibliography of key references and a list of other references of interest. A broad range of topics is covered, including language teaching and testing, literacy, and language policy.

Applied Language Learning
Defense Language Institute, Foreign Language Center
Presidio of Monterey, CA 93944-5006
Website: http://di–www.army.mil/pages/
journal/all98-09.pdf

Published semi-annually by the Defense Language Institute Foreign Language Center and Presidio of Monterey, this journal focuses on the application of research from a number of fields to language teaching methods and techniques, curriculum and materials, testing and evaluation, and other concerns related to language professionals.

Applied Linguistics
Oxford University Press
Great Clarendon Street
Oxford OX2 6DP   UK
Or
2001 Evans Road
Cary, NC 27513
E-mail: journal.info@oup.co.uk
Website: http://www.oup.co.uk/journals

Published in cooperation with the American and British Associations for Applied Linguistics and the International Association of Applied Linguistics, this journal includes theoretical and research articles discussing first and second language acquisition, language teaching and testing, bilingualism and bilingual education, discourse analysis, and other topics of interest to applied linguists in diverse fields. Book reviews are also included.

ELT Journal

Oxford University Press
Great Clarendon Street
Oxford OX2 6DP   UK
Or
2001 Evans Road
Cary, NC 27513
E-mail: journal.info@oup.co.uk
Website: http://www3.oup.co.uk/eltj/

Formerly the *English Language Teaching Journal,* the *ELT Journal* "seeks to bridge the gap between the everyday practical concerns of the ELT professional and related disciplines such as education, linguistics, psychology, and sociology." In addition to reviews of new publications and articles relating theory to classroom practice, *ELTJ* reviews a "key concept in ELT" yearly, providing a synthesis and suggesting avenues for further reading. Key concepts have included deductive and inductive language learning, learner training, learning strategies, and project work.

English for Specific Purposes

Elsevier Science
P.O. Box 945
New York, NY 10159-0945
Or
The Boulevard, Langford Lane
Kiddington, Oxford OX5 1GB   UK
E-mail: usinfo-f@elsevier.com
Website: http://www.elsevier.com

Known formerly as the *ESP Journal,* this quarterly is the major source of information about research, program design, materials, teacher education, and other issues in the teaching of English for Specific Purposes around the world, including content-based language instruction and vocational ESL. Also has reviews of text materials and scholarly books on topics of interest to ESP professionals.

English Teaching Forum

301 4th Street, SW, Room 312
Washington, DC 20547
Website: http://exchanges.state.gov/forum/

While intended for teachers of English outside the United States and distributed by US embassies around the world, the *Forum* is a major source of information on practical issues in language teaching and teacher education for ESL/EFL professionals in the United States, especially those interested in international perspectives on language teaching and learning. The *Forum* occasionally publishes thematic issues and regularly includes practical discussions of innovative teaching techniques. Ordering information and back issues are available on-line at the address listed.

ESL Magazine

Bridge Press
220 McKendree Avenue
Annapolis, MD 21401
E-mail: eslmagazine@compuserve.com
Website: http://www.eslmag.com

A relative newcomer, this practical magazine includes articles about teaching in a variety of contexts (mostly second language) and instructional approaches and techniques especially for the K–12 teacher. Some articles are available on its website.

Issues in Applied Linguistics

Department of Applied Linguistics and TESL
UCLA
3300 Rolfe Hall, P.O. Box 951531
Los Angeles, CA 90095-1531
E-mail: ial2@humnet.ucla.edu
Website: http://www.humnet.ucla.edu/
             humnet/TESLAL/ial

Published by the graduate students in applied linguistics at UCLA, this journal focuses on new departures and cross-disciplinary applied linguistic research in areas such as discourse analysis, sociolinguistics, language acquisition, language education, and language assessment. Book reviews of teacher references and student texts are also frequently included.

Journal of Second Language Writing

Ablex Corporation
c/o Elsevier Science
P.O. Box 945
New York, NY 10159-0945
Or
The Boulevard, Langford Lane
Kiddington, Oxford OX5 1GB   UK
E-mail: usinfo-f@elsevier.com
Website: http://www.elsevier.com

This journal features theoretically grounded reports of research and discussion of issues central to second and foreign language writing and writing instruction, including characteristics and attitudes of L2 writers, features of their texts, and readers' responses to and evaluation of their writing in a variety of contexts.

Language Learning

Blackwell Publishers
350 Main Street
Malden, MA 02148
Or
P.O. Box 805
108 Cowley Road
Oxford OX4 1FH   UK
Website:
http://www.blackwellpublishers.co.uk/

A "journal of research on language studies," *Language Learning* includes research and theoretical articles on child, second, and foreign language acquisition and learning, language education, bilingualism, literacy, pragmatics, and culture, as well as book reviews, notes, and announcements. It also provides an annual supplement to subscribers in either the Best of Language Learning Series or Language Learning Monograph Series. While directed primarily to language researchers, it also includes articles of interest to language teachers.

Language Teaching

Cambridge University Press
110 Midland Ave.
Port Chester, NY 10573-4930
Or
Edinburgh Building
Shaftesbury Road
Cambridge CB2 2RU   UK
Website: http://uk.cambridge.org/journals

Language Teaching abstracts articles in applied linguistics, language studies, foreign languages, and ESL/EFL teaching from journals published in several languages, with particularly comprehensive coverage of European scholarship. Of special interest is the feature summary article, which presents a state-of-the-art overview of some important area in the field, such as learner strategies, motivation, or bilingual education. Also published is an annual research review that identifies trends in language teaching and learning from the previous year.

Language Testing

Arnold Publishers
Journal Department
338 Euston Road
London NW1 3BH   UK
Website: http://arnoldpublishers.com/

Language Testing is an international journal concerned with issues of testing and assessment of first, second, and foreign languages and is of interest to researchers and practitioners in ESL and EFL testing. Articles and research reports discuss testing theory and procedures and their practical implications. Also included are book and test reviews.

Modern Language Journal

Blackwell Publishers
350 Main Street
Malden, Massachusetts 02148
Or
P.O. Box 805
108 Cowley Road
Oxford OX4 1JF   UK
Website: http://www.blackwellpublishers.co.uk

MLJ focuses on foreign languages, but has articles on ESL as well. A range of research, review, and response articles is included, as well as publication and media reviews, a calendar of events, and news.

Reading in a Foreign Language

International Education Centre
University College of St. Mark and St. John
Derriford Road
Plymouth PL6 8BH   UK

This journal focuses on research and instructional issues related to reading in a second or foreign language.

Studies in Second Language Acquisition

Cambridge University Press
110 Midland Ave.
Port Chester, NY 10573-4930
Or

Edinburgh Building
Shaftesbury Road
Cambridge CB2 2RU   UK
Website: http://uk.cambridge.org/

Each year, one issue of SSLA is devoted to a particular theme. The other two issues are concerned with theoretical and research topics in second and foreign language acquisition and learning.

TESOL Journal

700 South Washington Street, Suite 200
Alexandria, VA 22314
E-mail: info@tesol.org
Website: http://www.tesol.org/

The *Journal* publishes articles on teacher research, teaching techniques, and issues of importance to classroom teachers working directly with ESL/EFL students. Also included are classroom tips, materials reviews, and a special section on websites and technology in language teaching. Special issues devoted to themes such as secondary school students or content-based language instruction.

TESOL Quarterly

700 South Washington Street, Suite 200
Alexandria, VA 22314
E-mail: info@tesol.org
Website: http://www.tesol.org/

TESOL Quarterly publishes scholarly articles of interest to researchers, teacher educators, curriculum developers, and teachers of English around the world. It also publishes book reviews, lengthier review articles, book notices, and brief research reports and summaries. A special feature is a forum for debate on issues that have been raised previously in the journal.

World Englishes

Blackwell Publishers
350 Main Street
Malden, MA 02148
Or
108 Cowley Road
Oxford OX4 1JF   UK
Website: http://www.blackwellpublishers.co.uk/

As the of variety of Englishes increases, so does the interest in studying them in their cultural and sociolinguistic contexts. This journal focuses on the study and teaching of these "World Englishes," with an international perspective on language, literature, and methodology of English language teaching. The Comments/Replies and Open Forum sections encourage lively discussion of the issues.

Other periodicals that deserve mentioning include *TESOL Matters* (the newsletter of the TESOL association, which provides information on meetings, conferences, legislation, and publications of interest to ESL/EFL professionals); *Cross Currents* (a journal which is particularly concerned with cross-cultural issues in English language teaching); the *RELC Journal* (a publication of the SEAMEO Regional Language Centre in Singapore, which focuses on language teaching and learning in Southeast Asia); the *JALT Journal* and *The Language Teacher* (publications of the Japan Association of Language Teachers, the latter offering thematic issues dealing with special topics in English and other foreign language teaching); the *TESL Reporter* (a slim journal with timely suggestions for ESL/EFL classroom teachers); the *Canadian Modern Language Review* (a journal with parallel articles in English and French concerned with language teaching and learning); *TESL Talk* (a "journal for teachers of ESL," especially those working with immigrants and refugees, published by the Ministry of Citizenship in Toronto, Canada); *English Teaching Professional* (a new, practical quarterly magazine intended primarily for classroom teachers of English in secondary schools); *Reading in a Foreign Language* (with a focus on research and practice in second and foreign language reading); and *Language Teaching Research* (which publishes both quantitative and qualitative research related to teaching of second and foreign languages [including English], with topics such as materials design, methodology, teaching of specific skills, and languages for specific purposes).

In addition, associations of professionals in the fields of reading, writing, foreign languages, teacher education, and curriculum development publish journals and magazines of relevance to

English language teaching. For example, the International Reading Association publishes *Reading Research Quarterly*, with theoretical articles and reviews of research of interest to reading researchers; the *Journal of Adolescent and Adult Literacy* (previously the *Journal of Reading*) focuses on theoretical and practical articles which are relevant to ESL/EFL literacy teachers at secondary school or adult levels; and *The Reading Teacher*, for elementary school teachers. The National Council of Teachers of English, with an ESL Assembly at its annual conference, publishes journals on writing with increasing discussion of second language issues, including *Research in the Teaching of English, Teaching English in the Two-Year College,* and *College Composition and Communication*. The Association for Supervision and Curriculum Development publishes *Educational Leadership,* the single magazine for keeping current on programmatic and political issues confronting public school education in the United States, with recent issues focusing on multiple intelligences, technology in teaching, and constructivist teaching. *Foreign Language Annals,* published by the American Council on the Teaching of Foreign Languages, is intended for foreign language administrators, researchers, and teachers in the United States, but contains theoretical, practical, and policy-oriented articles of interest to English language teaching professionals.

PUBLISHERS AND CLEARINGHOUSES

To keep current on student textbooks, teacher reference materials, audiovisual materials, and software, you will want to have your name or the name of your educational institution added to the mailing lists of the major ESL/EFL and applied linguistics publishers and information clearinghouses so that you can receive regular mailings of their catalogs or current materials and services. Many publishers also provide a list and description of their publications online. You can consult the websites listed below to see what materials and other services (e.g., newsletters, answers to questions, or lists of local marketing representatives) are provided.

The expanding role of English as an international or additional language has led to the development of an unprecedented quantity of English language teaching texts and reference materials, published by a wide range of publishers. It is impossible to list them all here. What follows is a representative list of those that produce diverse types of ELT publications. Readers of a former edition of this chapter will note that many of the previously listed publishers are now part of larger publishing houses. Since the former publishing imprints are still in distribution, I have listed them under their new publisher.

The majority of addresses provided below are for the United States and United Kingdom. Most publishers also maintain offices and distribution centers in a number of countries. If you work outside the United States and the United Kingdom, consult the publisher through its website or by mail for information about publication distribution closer to home.

CAMBRIDGE UNIVERSITY PRESS
40 West 20th Street
New York, NY 10011
Or
The Edinburgh Building
Cambridge CB2 2RU   UK
Website: http://uk.cambridge.org/journals

HEINEMANN
Eurospan Group
3 Henrietta Street
London WC2 8 LU   UK
Website: http://www.heinemann.com/

HEINLE & HEINLE PUBLISHERS
(publishers of Heinle & Heinle and Newbury House)
Division of Thomson Learning, Inc.
25 Thomson Place
Boston, MA 02110
Website: http://www.heinle.com
            http://www.thomsonlearning.com

HOUGHTON MIFFLIN COMPANY
222 Berkley Street
Boston, MA 02116
Website: http://www.hmco.com

JOSSEY-BASS
350 Sansome Street
San Francisco, CA 94104
Website: http://www.josseybass.com

LAWRENCE ERLBAUM ASSOCIATES, INC.
10 Industrial Avenue
Mahwah, NJ 07430-2262
Website: http://www.erlbaum.com
                  http://www.mheducation.com

McGRAW HILL COMPANIES
1221 Avenue of the Americas
New York, NY 100202
Website: http://www.mcgraw-hill.com

MULTILINGUAL MATTERS
Frankfurt Lodge, Clevedon Hall
Clevedon BS21 7HH   UK
Website: http://www.multilingual-
                  matters.com

NATIONAL TEXTBOOK COMPANY (NTC)
4255 West Touhy Avenue
Lincolnwood, IL 60712-1975
Website: http://www.ntc-school.com

OXFORD UNIVERSITY PRESS
ESL Department
198 Madison Avenue
New York, NY 10016
Website: http://www.oup-usa.org/esl
Or
English Language Teaching Division
Great Clarendon Street
Oxford OX2 6DP   UK
Website: http://www.oup.uk/

PEARSON EDUCATION
(Publishers of Longman, Prentice Hall Regents,
Scott Foresman, and Addison-Wesley)
10 Bank Street, Suite 900
White Plains, NY 10606-1951
Or
Edinburgh Gate
Harlow
Essex CM20 2JE   UK
Website: http://www.longman-elt.com

UNIVERSITY OF MICHIGAN PRESS
839 Greene Street, Box 1104
Ann Arbor, MI 48106-1104

Website: http://www.press.umich.edu/esl

Two other publishers/book distributors also
fill orders for books from other publishers:

ALTA BOOK CENTER PUBLISHERS
14 Adrian Court
Burlingame, CA 94010
Website: http://www.altaesl.com

DELTA SYSTEMS CO., INC.
1400 Miller Parkway
McHenry, IL 60050-7030
Website: http://www.delta-systems.com

There are also three major e-commerce sites for
book orders that can provide information about
current (and some out-of-print) books:
       http://www.amazon.com
       http://www.barnesandnoble.com
       http://www.borders.com

CLEARINGHOUSES

A number of information clearinghouses can
provide timely information and answers to questions that may arise as you work in the ESL/EFL
field. Some of these, such as the Educational
Resources Information Center (ERIC) system,
are long-standing; others develop as the need
for them arises, only to dissolve when the issues
are no longer as pressing or when funding is no
longer available. You will want to ask to be
placed on regular or electronic mailing lists and
to consult their websites for further information.
Also be on the lookout for new clearinghouses or
centers that may arise. Some of the most useful
include the following:

ERIC CLEARINGHOUSE ON LANGUAGES
AND LINGUISTICS (ERIC/CLL)
Center for Applied Linguistics
4646 40th Street, NW
Washington, DC 20016-1859

E-mail: eric@cal.org
Website: http://www.cal.org/ericcll

ERIC/CLL is one of 16 US-government funded
educational clearinghouses. Its major objective is

to make available to practitioners and researchers current information and resources on topics related to language teaching and learning, or more broadly, to applied linguistics. It abstracts and summarizes articles from journals, conference presentations, and other sources and inputs these into a computerized database to which all the clearinghouses contribute. It is possible to search the database online or to have searches conducted by the clearinghouse. Searches conducted for previous clients are available as well. ERIC/CLL also publishes the *ERIC/CLL News Bulletin* (a quarterly electronic newsletter), *Language Link,* Resource Guides, Digests, and "Q & As" which synthesize answers to questions frequently asked of clearinghouse personnel. Many of these are available at its extensive website, which also contains a list of "Internet Resources for Teachers of English as a Second Language" and another for teachers of foreign languages. An adjunct clearinghouse, the National Clearinghouse for ESL Literacy Education, disseminates answers to questions on topics related to adolescent and adult literacy, workplace and worker education, and other topics related to adult second language education. For information about other ERIC Clearinghouses and system-wide services, see the website: www.accesseric.org.

CENTER FOR APPLIED LINGUISTICS (CAL)
4646 40th Street, NW
Washington, DC 20016

E-mail: info@cal.org
Website: http://www.cal.org

The mission of CAL is "to promote and improve the teaching and learning of languages, identify and solve problems related to language and culture, and serve as a resource for information about language and culture." CAL carries out research, analysis, and dissemination of information, design and development of instructional materials, technical assistance, teacher education, and policy analysis in a range of areas, including second, foreign, and heritage language education. It operates a number of clearinghouses and technical assistance centers (including the ERIC Clearinghouse), and collaborates with a range of educational institutions in conducting research,

providing technical assistance, and disseminating information.

CENTRE FOR INFORMATION ON LANGUAGE TEACHING AND RESEARCH (CILT)
20 Bedfordbury
London WC2N 4LB   UK

E-mail: library@cilt.org.uk
Website: http://www.cilt.org.uk

Housed in London, but with links to centers throughout the United Kingdom, CILT collects and disseminates information on all aspects of modern languages and the teaching of modern languages. It houses a resource library, with an extensive collection of books, periodicals, and language teaching materials of all types (texts, visual aids, software, videos, etc.), supports research, organizes courses and conferences, and answers questions by e-mail and on-site. The website has an extensive set of helpful links.

MODERN LANGUAGE CENTRE
Ontario Institute for Studies in Education
252 Bloor Street West
Toronto, Ontario M5S 1V6   Canada

Website: http://www.oise.utoronto.ca/MLC

The Modern Language Centre at the University of Toronto offers courses, hosts seminars and colloquia, conducts research, and disseminates information on curriculum, instruction, and policies for second, foreign, and minority languages, with particular reference to English and French in Canada, but also to other languages and settings. Its library has one of the most extensive collections of language education materials in Canada.

NATIONAL CENTRE FOR ENGLISH LANGUAGE TEACHING AND RESEARCH (NCELTR)
Macquarie University
North Ryde NSW 2109   Australia

E-mail: nceltr@mq.edu.au
Website: http://www.nceltr.mq.edu.au

NCELTR's mission is to provide leadership and promote excellence in English language education through innovative and high quality research, professional development programs, publications, resources support, and English language courses.

NCELTR, in partnership with the Institute for Education at La Trobe University, also houses the Adult Migrant English Program Research Centre, providing research and professional development for Australia's adult migrant programs.

NATIONAL CLEARINGHOUSE FOR BILINGUAL EDUCATION (NCBE)
George Washington University
Center for the Study of Language and Education
2121 K Street, NW, Suite 260
Washington, DC 20037

E-mail: askncbe@ncbe.gwu.edu
Website: http://www.ncbe.gwu.edu

NCBE focuses on policy and practice in the education of language minority students in the United States. It offers a website that is easy to navigate, with links to numerous professional resources. It also has an online newsletter (with back issues archived) that provides timely information on legislative debates, new policy, funding opportunities, and other information of interest to those teaching linguistically and culturally diverse students, principally in the United States.

SEAMEO REGIONAL LANGUAGE CENTRE (RELC)
30 Orange Grove Road
Singapore 258352   Republic of Singapore

E-mail: admin@relc.org.sg
Website: http://www.relc.org.sg

A regional educational project of the Southeast Asian Ministers of Education Organization (SEAMEO), RELC is a center for research and information dissemination "dedicated to language teacher education," with special attention to Southeast Asian contexts. RELC offers courses (on-site and by distance), publications (including the *RELC Journal*), and an annual thematic conference on a state-of-the-art question in language teaching, the proceedings of which it publishes. It maintains one of the best libraries and information centers in applied linguistics in the world.

RESEARCH CENTRE ON MULTILINGUALISM
Brussels University K.U.B.
Vrijheidslaan 17
B-1080 Brussels   Belgium

Website: http://www.kubrussel.ac.be/centra/ovmeng.html

Focusing on language contact and language conflict in multilingual settings, the Research Centre on Multilingualism carries out research, convenes conferences, coordinates and disseminates information, and publishes a series (*Plurilingua*) on contact linguistics.

INTERNET RESOURCES: WEBSITES, E-MAIL DISCUSSION GROUPS, AND ONLINE PUBLICATIONS

The Internet has created global access for professional development through e-mail, electronic lists (e-mail discussion groups), and the World Wide Web, where accessing one website may lead to scores of other interesting sites linked to it. Most associations, publishers, journals, clearinghouses, and other resources have made it possible to get at least some of the information traditionally available in print or through personal visits by accessing a website or subscribing to e-mail or a list. Electronic journals and newsletters are also becoming increasingly available, published by research institutes, educational institutions, professional associations, and the like; many of these can be easily downloaded or printed for future access. The online format also supports the dissemination of more time-bound information such as notices of conferences, employment opportunities, and political issues, and promotes interaction through related e-mail or discussion groups. Even if you have only limited access to resource centers, libraries, journals, or colleagues, the Internet can provide much of the information you need.

Websites

Attempts to categorize websites are doomed to failure because most language and linguistics websites have multiple audiences, foci, and purposes. What follows, then, is a representative sample of the vast world of websites available for ESL/EFL language teaching and learning. Those with the greatest number and diversity of lists and links are listed first.

http://alt.venus.co.uk/VL/AppLingBBK/welcome.html

This site is a good general web resource in applied linguistics, with lists of conferences, dissertations, and theses in applied linguistics, societies and associations, publishers, and ESL/EFL electronic mailing lists, many with links to other sites.

http://www.linguistlist.org

This extensive and easily-navigated list includes a conference calendar and calls for papers, more than nine pages of linguistic associations with links, an extensive list of journals with descriptions and subscription information, information on subscribing to a number of electronic discussion groups (listservs), and a host of other resources for language educators.

http://www.eslcafe.com

Possibly the best-known site for ESL/EFL, Dave's ESL Cafe has numerous pages of Quizzes, Quotes, Slang, Idioms, Discussion Forums, and Chat Central, of interest to students, and sections such as The Web Guide and the Job Center, of interest to teachers. Special discussion lists are also available on this site.

http://owl.english.purdue.edu

Purdue University's Online Writing Lab offers a wealth of materials on general writing concerns, professional writing, writing across the curriculum, Power Point presentations, and online writing resources.

http://www.esl-lab.com

Randall's Cyber Listening Lab has an impressive amount of listening material for students, including general and academic listening quizzes, longer conversations, and short listening exercises.

http://members.tripod.com/~towerofenglish

ESL students can practice their English as they roam through the various rooms of the Tower of English, including the Study Hall, the Game Room, the Movie Theater, the Post Office, the Debate Hall, and the Library.

http://www.thinkquest.org/

ThinkQuest, an annual international contest, invites students between 12 and 19 years of age to create information-rich, web-based educational tools and materials. Past submissions are available for viewing at this site.

http://us.imdb.com/

The Internet Movie Database site offers a wealth of information on movies and is very popular among students and teachers alike.

http://www.gutenberg.net/

The goal of Project Gutenberg is to create digital versions of important books. The list of books already online is lengthy.

http://www.oup.co.uk/elt/magazine/worksh/worksh.html

This site offers a variety of information and hands-on teaching materials, many of them designed for use with Oxford University Press's textbook series and other materials, such as the *Oxford Learner's Dictionary of English Idioms*.

http://www.library.ubc.ca/ejour

This site has links to hundreds of electronic journals on the web. It is excellent for those with little confidence in or knowledge of electronic research. It is an electronic library, with links to the most important journals available on the web.

http://www.gsu.edu/~wwwesl/jegw/index2.htm

This site seeks to promote discussion of topics that have not been discussed elsewhere and to serve as a forum for the publication of previously unpublished research articles and book reviews, principally relating to grammar theory and pedagogy.

http://llt.msu.edu

This site focuses on computer-assisted language learning and teaching, including on-line publication of articles on current research.

http://www.kyoto-su.ac.jp/information/tesl-ej/index.html

This site is an electronic journal for teachers of English as a second or foreign language, TESL-EJ.

http://www.aitech.ac.jp/~iteslj

At this site is the *Internet TESL Journal,* an electronic journal for ESL and EFL teachers.

www.google.com

This is one of the most "intelligent" search engines. It ranks each hit based on the number of links to it. It can help locate publishers, journals, libraries, and other resources on an immense array of topics.

E-mail Lists/Electronic Discussion Groups

A number of e-mail lists or electronic discussion groups of interest to ESL/EFL professionals exist. They are an excellent place to get quick response to questions from colleagues with similar experiences. Many also discuss teaching materials, provide suggestions for other places to search, and maintain archives of previous articles which can be searched. Regional, national, and international lists all exist. The following provides a sample of the international lists, with instructions on how to subscribe to them. For each, the e-mail address is provided, followed by what should be typed in the body of the message. (Do not type anything else.)

CALL-ED

An e-mail discussion list for teacher trainers and educators interested in computer-assisted language learning.

> Majordomo@coe.missouri.edu
> Subscribe call-ed

LINGUIST

A major resource for all areas of theoretical and applied linguistics.

> Listserv@tamvm1.tamu.edu
> Subscribe linguist Your first name Your last name

NIFL-ESL

One of several lists of the National Institute for Literacy, this list focuses on issues in literacy theory and practice for adult second language learners in a variety of contexts.

> Listproc@literacy.nifl.gov
> Subscribe NIFL-ESL Your first name Your last name

SLART-L

An e-mail discussion list on second language acquisition of interest to researchers and teachers

> Listserv@cunyvm.cuny.edu
> Subscribe SLART-L Your first name Your last name

TESL-L

With 20,000 members, this is one of the most extensive lists. After subscribing, you may want to narrow your list to one of the sub-lists (K–12, Jobs, CALL, etc.) TESL-L also has substantial archives of prior discussions that can be searched.

> Listserv@cunyvm.cuny.edu
> Subscribe TESL-L Your first name Your last name

MATERIALS REVIEW, SELECTION COMMITTEES, AND CURRICULUM DEVELOPMENT TEAMS

Publishers and journal editors are continually in need of professionals to review manuscripts, teacher reference books, or student texts and materials. Publishers routinely require evaluation of textbooks or other materials by outside reviewers before publishing them. If you wish to serve as a reviewer, contact the publishers, usually through their ESL/EFL editors, or contact book review editors of newsletters or journals to let them know of your interest. Indicate the skill, level, or focus that you are particularly interested in and your qualifications, and you may find yourself regularly keeping up to date, since you may be reading new books or manuscripts even before they are published. An additional benefit of writing reviews for journals is that you usually are sent the book for your own professional library. To get started, you may want to write reviews for a newsletter or a publication of a local affiliate of one of the professional associations discussed above. You may soon find that you are being sent books for review on a regular basis, keeping you current and enhancing your own library.

Text and materials selection committees of your program or textbook adoption committees for local, state, or regional educational agencies offer another source of professional growth. These committees usually request copies of several relevant, new publications from a number of publishers from which the committee makes their final selections. By participating in these committees, you have an opportunity to keep current on the kinds of techniques and strategies that are included in the latest ESL/EFL materials and to enrich your own teaching, lesson planning, and materials writing projects. You are also likely to broaden your circle of English language teaching colleagues and to benefit from their unique educational backgrounds and experiences.

You may find, after reviewing manuscripts and books and serving on materials selection committees, that you want to create materials or books of your own or serve as a member of a curriculum writing team, preparing new materials. In the process of researching, developing, and field-testing these materials, you will learn a great deal about current practice in ESL/EFL classrooms and will undoubtedly adapt some of your own teaching accordingly. You will also have the benefit of working with other professionals, so that you can learn from each other as you collaborate on the writing project.

WORKSHOPS, SEMINARS, INSTITUTES, ACADEMIES, AND GRADUATE PROGRAMS

Naturally, one of the best ways of keeping up to date is to participate in local, state, national, or international in-service workshops or seminars, some of which are now being provided by distance learning. These continuing education programs may be sponsored by a professional association, a university-based teacher education program, a resource or technical assistance center, or by a department or ministry of education. They may offer graduate credit or help lead to employment advancement. Of equal importance, they

offer a forum for sharing problems and potential solutions, as well as ways of expanding one's teaching repertoire or identifying areas of potential classroom-based research. While you may begin participating as a learner, over time, you are likely to find yourself increasing your contributions to the discussion, participating as a member of a colloquium or panel, or leading one of the professional development programs yourself. You may also find yourself becoming part of a teacher research group, sharing your findings with colleagues in both your own and other communities.

Deserving special mention are the summer professional development institutes for students and teachers that are hosted by a variety of professional associations and universities. It is possible to enroll in intensive, short courses with English language teaching colleagues from many parts of the world, learning from them as well as from the instructor, in what is usually an informal, collaborative learning experience. The opportunity to participate in one of these intensive programs should not be missed: you are likely to emerge from the experience feeling renewed as a professional and reassured that you have chosen the right profession. You will also undoubtedly meet professional colleagues with whom you will correspond or collaborate for many years to come.

RESEARCH AND COLLABORATIVE PROJECTS

The more you teach, the more likely you are to begin asking questions about your own classroom, learners, or teaching practice. These questions can serve as the basis of a series of ongoing research projects of your own. Consider keeping a teaching journal or diary in which you record some of the "episodes" in your classes and some of your emerging insights about yourself, your teaching, or your students. This journal may highlight some areas for research, beginning, perhaps, with studying the progress or problems of a few students in your classes. You might want to see how a change in your own approach to teaching (for example, substituting some extensive reading for the intensive reading in your syllabus; introducing electronic discussion in your writing class; involving students in projects in your conversation class; or developing thematic units based on the students' other academic classes) affects your students' motivation or proficiency. You may also want to become part of a larger research group or project that is investigating questions of interest to you. You can identify potential research collaborators or ongoing research projects by contacting educational institutions or centers near you or by talking with colleagues at conferences. You might be surprised to learn that some university researchers have difficulty identifying teachers with whom to collaborate or classrooms with which to work; they are likely to welcome your interest in some kind of joint project, one that will have as its objectives something that can be applied to your classroom or your particular teaching situation (see Bailey's chapter in this volume).

Other interesting and broadening collaborations can occur within your own educational institution. Learning what is expected of students and what kinds of materials and instructional techniques are used in the teaching of natural and social sciences, mathematics, or technical and professional fields can provide you with ideas for including more academic or professional content and discourse in your ESL/EFL classroom. Similarly, the science, mathematics, social science, technical, or professional instructors may become more sensitive to the nature of the discourse demands of their disciplines when they talk or work with you or observe your classes. Collaborations such as these are valuable at elementary, secondary, or tertiary levels, and across the curriculum, especially where English is used as a textbook or instructional medium. A brief exchange in the hall about a particular student or assignment can grow into ongoing collaborative research, curriculum development, or even team teaching, all of which are likely to be professionally rewarding experiences. You may also want to link up with the testing and assessment teams in your institution or at a local, state, or national level, helping to develop or field-test new items or tests, and more important, bringing the classroom teacher's perspective to educational assessment (see Cohen's chapter in this volume). This is especially important when the tests are intended for students who are proficient (or native) users of the language and your students, who are only learning the language, are expected to pass them. Parents and community members can also be potential collaborators in your research and teaching.

The increasing availability of e-mail and electronic discussion groups makes it possible for long-distance collaborations. You may want to link up with an English language teacher or program in another city or country and use this as a basis for some of your instruction. Students can write to e-mail pals; groups can work on a variety of research and writing projects; or classes can conduct mini-ethnographies on aspects of their communities that are of interest to the other class, perhaps compiling an introductory guide to each others' schools or communities.

COACHING AND MENTORING NEW TEACHERS

During your first years as a teacher, it will be very helpful if you can find an experienced colleague who can provide you with guidance and advice, someone to act as a sounding board as you think through challenging situations or students. You may want to observe that teacher's classes or discuss homework or grading policies with him or her. As you become more experienced, you are likely to notice the challenges facing new colleagues and to remember how you felt early in your assignment or career. Offer to mentor beginning teachers or colleagues new to your institution. Meeting regularly with them, inviting them to observe your classes, co-teaching with them, or helping with paperwork, policies, or procedures can not only alleviate some of their burden, but also illuminate some of your own growth as a professional, helping you to articulate more clearly your own teaching assumptions and practice. Ongoing coaching and mentoring is also likely to highlight areas of your own teaching that you may want to research or lead you to search for instructional materials or reference works on topics that you may not have considered previously.

CONCLUSION

Completing a TESL/TEFL program is the beginning of a lifetime of professional growth. Teaching is, in itself, a continual growth experience, since one really "learns" something only when asked to explain or teach it to others. Students are often our best teachers, and you will learn from new students each term. If you have the opportunity of teaching different courses, grades, or levels or of adding a new role or responsibility as a tester, program administrator, resource center coordinator, or mentor, you will find that your understanding of the field and of your own practice will continue to grow. There are many ways in which being an ESL or EFL teacher is a growth experience. The suggestions offered here are only a few of the ways to keep up to date.

ENDNOTE

Updating this chapter while on leave in Kiribati (a small country of islands in the Central Pacific, where one Internet service is my major link to the academic and professional world) has heightened my appreciation of the value of online resources for English language teaching professionals and also of the important role that colleagues in more resource-rich environments can play for those without access to academic libraries, receipt of journals or other serial publications, or opportunities to engage in discussions with many colleagues. A number of people helped in updating this chapter. Silvio Avendano, Caitlin James, Mora Hockstein, Heather Williams, and Jeanne Yacoubou (undergraduate and graduate students at UMBC) tracked down addresses, phone numbers, websites, and other information that eluded me. In addition, Neil Anderson, Dora Johnson, Christine Meloni, Joy Reid, and Dick Tucker all made important suggestions of publications, websites, or other resources to include, and my brother, Robert Crandall, and niece, Margaret Crandall, also provided a great deal of long-distance help. My thanks to all of them.

DISCUSSION QUESTIONS

1. This chapter has discussed a number of ways in which ESL and EFL professionals can keep current in the field. Which are you already doing? Which do you think will be most helpful to you?
2. Are there other ways of "keeping up to date" that are not included in this chapter? Get together with colleagues who are enrolled in a TESOL program and see if you can identify other sources of information or means of sharing ideas that are not discussed here.
3. Why is it important to belong to a professional association in your field? What kinds of professional development opportunities do they offer? If you cannot belong to one of these associations, are there other ways in which you can benefit from their services?
4. Why do you think that it is so difficult for teachers to keep current in their fields? What are some of the factors that might affect your ability to keep up to date?
5. What kinds of resources for professional development are available through the Internet or e-mail? How might you involve your students in this?

SUGGESTED ACTIVITIES

1. Even if you are not a member, attend one of the international, national, or local conventions or meetings of one of the ESL/EFL professional associations. Try to attend some plenary (large group) sessions, some papers and workshops, and the book exhibits. If there are poster sessions where colleagues informally share their teaching ideas or research, spend some time there, talking with colleagues and getting ideas for related posters that you might develop to share with colleagues back home. Allow yourself time to get to know some of your colleagues by attending social activities, engaging in informal discussion groups, or spending time at the poster sessions.

2. Visit an information clearinghouse or center in your area or visit online or write to one described in this chapter. Find out about the services they provide and the publications they offer. Have your name added to any mailing lists (including electronic lists) they maintain.

3. Develop a form letter to send to publishers, describing your background and interests as an ESL/EFL professional. Leave enough room so that you can type in the name and address of the publisher. Then mail this letter to a number of publishers. If you send the letter to the attention of the ESL/EFL Editor, this letter can serve both to get your name added to their English language-teaching mailing list and also to indicate your interest in serving as a manuscript or materials reviewer.

4. Choose three of the journals listed in this chapter to examine more closely. What articles are included? What kinds of columns or information does the journal provide? Who is the intended audience? Do you think the journal will be useful to you? In what ways? Share your findings with a colleague.

5. Make a list of individuals or groups with whom you might collaborate and indicate some of the ways in which you might work together or share ideas about language teaching and learning.

 **FURTHER READING**

Crandall, J. A. 2000. Language teacher education. *Annual Review of Applied Linguistics* 20: 34–55.

Freeman, D., series ed. *Teacher Source Series*. Boston, MA: Heinle & Heinle Publishers.

Underhill, A., series ed. *The Teacher Development Series*. Oxford: Heinemann.

Warschauer, M., H. Schetzer, and C. Meloni. 2000. *Internet for English Teaching*. Alexandria, VA: TESOL.

References

Abercrombie, D. 1968. Paralanguage. *British Journal of Disorders of Communication* 3: 55–59.

Abraham, R., and R. Vann. 1987. Strategies of two learners: A case study. In *Learner strategies in language learning,* edited by A. L. Wenden and J. Rubin. New York: Prentice Hall.

ACTFL proficiency guidelines. 1988. Yonkers, NY: American Council on the Teaching of Foreign Languages.

Acton, W. 1984. Changing fossilized pronunciation. *TESOL Quarterly* 18(1): 71–85.

Adair-Hauck, B., L. Willingham-McLain, and B. Youngs. 1999. Evaluating the integration of technology. *CALICO Journal* 17(2): 273–305.

Adaskou, K., D. Britten, and B. Fahsi. 1989. Cultural content in a secondary English course for Morocco. *ELT Journal* 44(1): 3–10.

Adendorff, R. D. 1996. The functions of code switching among high school teachers and students in KwaZulu and implications for teacher education. In *Voices from the language classroom: Qualitative research on language education,* edited by K. M. Bailey and D. Nunan. New York: Cambridge University Press.

Adger, C., D. Christian, and O. Taylor, eds. 1999. *Making the connection: Language and academic achievement among African American students.* McHenry, IL: Center for Applied Linguistics/Delta Systems.

Adger, C., and J. Peyton. 1999. Enhancing the education of immigrant students in secondary school: Structural challenges and directions. In *So much to say: Adolescents, bilingualism, and ESL in the secondary school,* edited by C. Faltis and P. Wolfe. New York: Teachers College Press.

Adult Migrant Education Service. 1993. *Certificate in spoken and written English.* Sydney, New South Wales: Adult Migrant Education Service.

Aebersold, J. A., and M. L. Field. 1997. *From reader to reading teacher: Issues and strategies for second language classrooms.* New York: Cambridge University Press.

Alberta Education. 1997. *English as a second language.* Edmonton, Canada: Alberta Education.

Alderson, J. C. 1983. The cloze procedure and proficiency in English as a foreign language. In *Issues in languages testing research,* edited by J. W. Oller, Jr. New York: Newbury House.

_____. 1987. *Innovation in language testing: Can the micro-computer help? Special report no. 1: Language testing update.* Lancaster, UK: Institute for English Language Education, University of Lancaster.

_____. 2000. *Assessing reading.* New York: Cambridge University Press.

Alderson, J. C., C. Clapham, and D. Wall. 1995. *Language test construction and evaluation.* New York: Cambridge University Press.

Alderson, J. C., and L. Hamp-Lyons. 1996. TOEFL preparation courses: A study of washback. *Language Testing* 13(3): 280–297.

Alexander, L. G., R. Kingsbury, and J. Chapman. 1978. *Take a stand.* New York: Longman.

Aljaafreh, A., and J. Lantolf. 1994. Negative feedback as regulation and second language learning in the zone of proximal development. *Modern Language Journal* 78(4): 465–483.

Allan, D. 1991. Tape journals: Bridging the gap between communication and correction. *ELT Journal* 45: 61–66.

Allen, V. F. 1983. *Techniques in teaching vocabulary.* New York: Oxford University Press.

Allwright, D. 1983. Classroom-centered research on teaching and learning: A brief historical overview. *TESOL Quarterly* 17(2): 191–204.

_____. 1990. *Autonomy in Language Pedagogy.* (CRILE Working Paper No. 6.) Lancaster, UK: Centre for Research in Education, University of Lancaster.

_____. 1997. Quality and sustainability in teacher-research. *TESOL Quarterly* 31(2): 368–370.

Allwright, D., and K. M. Bailey. 1991. *Focus on the classroom: An introduction to classroom research for language teachers.* Cambridge: Cambridge University Press.

Allwright, D., and R. Lenzuen. 1997. Exploring practice: Work at the Cultura Inglesa, Rio de Janeiro, Brazil. *Language Teaching Research* 1(1): 71–79.

Allwright, R W. 1981. What do we want teaching materials for? *ELT Journal* 36(1): 5–18.

American Association for Applied Linguistics (AAAL). 1996. *AAAL resolution on the role and status of languages in the US.* Eagan, MN: AAAL. (Also on the web at http://www.aaal.org/pages/resolutions.html)

_____. 1997. *AAAL resolution on the application of dialect knowledge to education.* Eagan, MN: AAAL. (Also on the web at http://www.aaal.org/pages/resolutions.html)

American Association for the Advancement of Science. 1993. *Benchmarks for science literacy: Project 2061.* New York: Oxford University Press.

American Council on the Teaching of Foreign Languages. 1996. *Standards for foreign language learning.* Yonkers, NY: American Council on the Teaching of Foreign Languages.

American Educational Research Association. 2000. Position statement of the American Educational Research Association concerning high-stakes testing in pre-K–12 education. *Educational Researcher* 29 (8): 24–25.

Anderson, A., and T. Lynch. 1988. *Listening.* Oxford: Oxford University Press.

Anderson, J., and J. Fincham. 1994. Acquisition of procedural skills from examples. *Journal of Experimental Psychology* 20: 1322–1340.

Anderson, J. R. 1982. Acquisition of cognitive skill. *Psychological Review* 89(4): 369–406.

_____. 1985. *Cognitive psychology and its implications.* 2d ed. New York: W. H. Freeman.

_____. 1990. *Cognitive psychology and its implications.* 3d ed.. New York: W. H. Freeman.

_____. 1993. Problem-solving and learning. *American Psychologist* 48: 35–44.

_____. 1995. *Learning and memory: An integrated approach.* New York: Wiley.

Anderson, N. 1999. *Exploring second language reading: Issues and strategies.* Boston, MA: Heinle & Heinle.

Anderson, R. 1996. Research foundations to support wide reading. In *Promoting reading: Views on making reading materials accessible to increase literacy levels,* edited by V. Greaney. Newark, DE: International Reading Association.

Anthony, E. M. 1963. Approach, method, and technique. *ELT Journal* 17(2): 63–67.

Appel, J. 1995. *Diary of a language teacher.* Oxford: Heinemann English Language Teaching.

Ariew, R. 1982. The textbook as curriculum. In *Curriculum, competence, and the foreign language learner,* edited by T. V. Higgs. Skokie, IL: National Textbook Company.

Arva, V., and P. Medgyes. 2000. Native and non-native teachers in the classroom. *System* 24(3): 1–18.

Asher, J. 1969. The total physical response approach to second language learning. *Modern Language Journal* 53(1): 3–17.

_____. 1977. *Learning another language through actions: The complete teacher's guidebook.* Los Gatos, CA: Sky Oak Productions.

_____. 1996. *Learning another language through actions: The complete teacher's guidebook.* 5th ed. Los Gatos, CA: Sky Oak Productions.

Ashworth, M. 1985. *Beyond methodology.* Cambridge: Cambridge University Press.

Aston, G. 1993. The learner's contribution to the self-access centre. *ELT Journal* 47(3): 219–227.

Auerbach, E. 1986. Competency-based ESL: one step forward or two steps back? *TESOL Quarterly* 20(3): 411–429.

_____. 1992. *Making meaning, making change: Participatory curriculum development for adult ESL literacy.* McHenry, IL: Center for Applied Linguistics/Delta Systems.

_____. 1996. *Adult ESL/literacy from the community-to the community: A guidebook for participatory literacy training.* Mahwah, NJ: Lawrence Erlbaum.

Auerbach, E. with B. Barahona, J. Midy, F. Vaquerano, A. Zambrano, and J. Arnaud. 1996. *From the community to the community: A guidebook for participatory literacy training.* Mahwah, NJ: Lawrence Erlbaum.

August, D., and K. Hakuta, eds. 1997. *Improving schooling for language-minority students: A research agenda*. Washington, DC: National Academy Press.

Ausubel, D. 1968. *Educational psychology: A cognitive view*. New York: Holt, Rinehard and Winston.

Avery, P., and S. Erlich. 1992. *Teaching American English pronunciation*. Oxford: Oxford University Press.

Bachman, L. F. 1985. Performance on cloze tests with fixed-ratio and rational deletions. *TESOL Quarterly* 19(3): 535–556.

_____. 1990. *Fundamental considerations in language testing*. Oxford: Oxford University Press.

Bachman, L. F., and A. Palmer. 1996. *Language testing in practice*. Oxford: Oxford University Press.

Bader, M. J. 2000. Choosing CALL software: Beginning the evaluation process. *TESOL Journal* 9(2): 18–22.

Bahns, J. 1993. Lexical collocations: A contrastive view. *ELT Journal* 47(1): 56–63.

Bailey, K. M. 1985. Classroom-centered research on language teaching and learning. In *Beyond basics: Issues and research in TESOL*, edited by M. Celce-Murcia. Rowley, MA: Newbury House.

_____. 1991. Diary studies of classroom language learning: The doubting game and the believing game. In *Language acquisition and the second/foreign language classroom* (Anthology Series 28), edited by E. Sadtono. Singapore: SEAMEO Regional Language Center.

_____. 1998a. Approaches to empirical research in instructional language settings. In *Learning foreign and second languages: Perspectives in research and scholarship*, edited by H. Byrnes. New York: Modern Language Association of America.

_____. 1998b. *Learning about language assessment: Dilemmas, decisions, and directions*. Pacific Grove, CA: Heinle & Heinle.

Bailey, K. M., and D. Nunan, eds. 1996. *Voices from the language classroom*. Cambridge: Cambridge University Press.

Bailey, K. M., and L. Savage, eds. 1994. *New ways in teaching speaking*. Alexandria, VA: TESOL.

Bailey, N., C. Madden, and S. Krashen. 1974. Is there a "natural sequence" in adult second language learning? *Language Learning* 21: 235–243.

Baker, C. 1996. *Foundations of bilingual education and bilingualism*. 2d ed. Clevedon, UK: Multilingual Matters.

Bame, J. E. 1995. Building formal information schema. In *New ways in teaching listening*, edited by D. Nunan and L. Miller. Alexandria, VA: TESOL.

Barber, C. L. 1966. Some measurable characteristics of modern scientific prose. *Contributions to English syntax and phonology*. Stockholm: Almquist and Wiksell. Reprinted in Swales, 1988.

Bargfrede, A. 1996. *Don't hang up yet: NNS negotiation of telephone closings*. Unpublished Master's thesis, Pennsylvania State University.

Barlow, M. 1999. *Monoconc*. Athelstan Publishers. Concordancing software.

Bates, L., J. Lane, and E. Lange. 1993. *Writing clearly: Responding to ESL compositions*. Boston, MA: Heinle & Heinle.

Baugh, J. 2000. *Beyond Ebonics: Linguistic pride and racial prejudice*. New York: Oxford University Press.

Beall, P., and S. Nipp. 1979. *Wee sing children's songs and fingerplays*. Los Angeles: Price Stern Sloan.

_____. 1981. *Wee sing and play: Musical games and rhymes for children*. Los Angeles: Price Stern Sloan.

_____. 1982. *Wee sing silly songs*. Los Angeles: Price Stern Sloan.

_____. 1989. *Wee sing fun 'n folk*. Los Angeles: Price Stern Sloan.

_____. 1990. *Wee sing sing-alongs*. Los Angeles: Price Stern Sloan.

Beck, I., M. G. McKeown, R. L. Hamilton, and L. Kucan. 1997. *Questioning the author: An approach for enhancing student engagement with text*. Newark, DE: International Reading Association.

Becker, A. 2000. *Citizenship for refugee elders: Issues and options in test preparation*. Washington, DC: Catholic Legal Immigrant Network, Inc.

Becker, J. P., and S. Shimada, eds. 1997. *The open-ended approach: A new proposal for teaching mathematics*. Reston, VA: National Council of Teachers of Mathematics.

Beckett, G. 1999. *Project-based instruction in a Canadian secondary school's ESL classes: Goals and evaluations*. Ph.D. diss., University of British Columbia.

Beisbier, B. 1994. *Sounds great: Book 1*. Boston, MA: Heinle & Heinle.

_____. 1995. *Sounds great: Book 2*. Boston, MA: Heinle & Heinle.

Belasco, S. 1971. The feasibility of learning a second language in an artificial unicultural situation. In *The psychology of second language learning: Papers from the Second International Congress of Applied Linguistics, Cambridge, 8-12 September 1969*, edited by P. Pimsleur and T. Quinn. London: Cambridge University Press.

Benesch, S. 1993. ESL, ideology, and the politics of pragmatism. *TESOL Quarterly* 27: 705–717.

_____. 1996. Needs analysis and curriculum development in EAP: An example of a critical approach. *TESOL Quarterly* 30(4): 723–738.

Benz, C., and K. Dworak. 2000. *Tapestry: Listening and speaking 1*. Boston, MA: Heinle & Heinle.

Bereiter, C., and M. Scardamalia. 1993. *Surpassing ourselves: An inquiry into the nature and implications of expertise*. Chicago: Open Court Press.

Berkenkotter, C., and T. Huckin. 1995. *Genre knowledge in disciplinary communities*. Hillsdale, NJ: Lawrence Erlbaum.

Berne, J. 1998. Examining the relationship between L2 listening research, pedagogical theory, and practice. *Foreign Language Annals* 32: 170–190.

Bernhardt, E. 1991. *Reading development in a second language: Theoretical, empirical, and classroom perspectives*. Norwood, NJ: Ablex.

Bhatia, V. J. 1993. *Analyzing genre: Language use in professional settings*. London and New York: Longman.

Bialystok, E. 1990. *Communication strategies: A psychological analysis of second-language use*. Oxford, UK: Blackwell.

Bialystok, E., and K. Hakuta. 1994. *In other words: The science and psychology of second-language acquisition*. New York: Basic Books.

Biber, D. 1988. *Variation across speech and writing*. Cambridge: Cambridge University Press.

_____. 1994. An analytic framework for register studies. In *Sociolinguistic perspectives on register*, edited by D. Biber and E. Finnegan. Oxford: Oxford University Press.

Biber, D., S. Conrad, and R. Reppen. 1998. *Corpus linguistics: Investigating language structure and use*. Cambridge: Cambridge University Press.

Blair, R. N., ed. 1982. *Innovative approaches to language teaching*. Rowley, MA: Newbury House.

_____. 1991. Innovative approaches. In *Teaching English as a second or foreign language*, edited by M. Celce-Murcia. New York: Newbury House.

Blaxton, T. A. 1989. Investigating dissociations among memory systems: Support for a transfer appropriate processing framework. *Journal of Experimental Psychology: Learning, Memory and Cognition* 15: 657–668.

Bley-Vroman, R. 1988. The fundamental character of foreign language learning. In *Grammar and second language teaching*, edited by W. Rutherford and M. Sharwood Smith. New York: Newbury House.

Block, D. 1996. A window on the classroom: Classroom events viewed from different angles. In *Voices from the language classroom: Qualitative research on language education*, edited by K. M. Bailey and D. Nunan. New York: Cambridge University Press.

Bloomfield, L. 1933. *Language*. New York: Holt, Rinehart, and Winston.

Bloom, B. S., ed. 1956. *Taxonomy of educational objectives: The classification of educational goals*. Handbook I: Cognitive domain. New York: Longmans, Green, & Co.

Board of Education in the City of New York. 1997. *New standards performance standards: English language arts, English as a second language, Spanish language arts*. New York: Board of Education of the City of New York.

Bolinger, D. 1986. *Intonation and its parts*. Palo Alto: Stanford University Press.

Bond, G., and R. Dykstra. 1997. The cooperative research program in first-grade reading instruction. *Reading Research Quarterly* 32(4): 348–427.

Boni, M. B. 1947. *Fireside book of folk songs*. New York: Simon and Schuster.

Borg, S. 1999. The use of grammatical terminology in the second language classroom: A qualitative study of teachers' practices and cognitions. *Applied Linguistics* 20(1): 95–126.

Boswood, T., ed. 1997. *New ways of using computers in language teaching*. Alexandria, VA: TESOL.

Bowen, J. D. 1975. *Patterns of English pronunciation*. Rowley, MA: Newbury House.

Bowen, J. D., H. Madsen, and A. Hilferty. 1985. *TESOL techniques and procedures*. New York: Newbury House.

Bowen, T., and L. Marks. 1992. *The pronunciation book: Student-centered activities for pronunciation work*. London: Longman.

Braddock, R., R. Lloyd-Jones, and L. Schoer. 1983. *Research in written composition*. Champaign, IL: National Council of Teachers of English.

Braine, G., ed. 1999. *Non-native educators in English language teaching*. Mahwah, NJ: Lawrence Erlbaum.

Brazil, D., M. Coulthard, and C. Johns. 1980. *Discourse, intonation, and language teaching*. London: Longman.

Breen, M. P. 1985. The social context for language learning—a neglected situation? *Studies in Second Language Acquisition* 7(1): 135–158.

Breen, M. P., and C. Candlin 1980. The essentials of a communicative curriculum in language teaching. *Applied Linguistics* 1(1): 89–112.

Breiner-Sanders, K. E., P. Lowe, Jr., J. Miles, and E. Swender. 2000. ACTFL proficiency guidelines: Speaking (Revised 1999). *Foreign Language Annals* 33(1): 13–17.

Brill, H. 1986. *Developing a communicative test of reading comprehension and determining its effectiveness*. Unpublished manuscript. Jerusalem, Israel: School of Education, Hebrew University.

Brindley, G. 1984. *Needs analysis and objective setting in the Adult Migrant Education Service*. Sydney, Australia: Adult Migrant Education Service.

———. 1990. The role of needs analysis in adult ESL programme design. In *The second language curriculum*, edited by R. K. Johnson. Cambridge: Cambridge University Press.

———. 1991. Becoming a researcher: Teacher-conducted research and professional growth. In *Language acquisition and the second/foreign language classroom* (Anthology Series 28), edited by E. Sadtono. Singapore: SEAMEO Regional Language Center.

Brinton, D. M. 2000. Out of the mouths of babes: Novice teacher insights into content-based instruction. In *Content-based college instruction*, edited by L. F. Kasper. Mahwah, NJ: Lawrence Erlbaum.

Brinton, D. M., J. Frodesen, C. Holten, L. Jensen, and L. Repath-Martos. 1997. *Insights 2: A content-based approach to academic preparation*. White Plains, NY: Longman.

Brinton, D. M., J. Goodwin, and L. Ranks. 1994. Helping language minority students read and write analytically: The journey into, through, and beyond. In *With different eyes: Insights into teaching language minority students across the disciplines*, edited by F. Peitzman and G. Gadda. New York: Longman.

Brinton, D. M., and C. Holten. 1997. Into, through, and beyond: A framework to develop content-based material. *Forum* 35(4): 10–21.

Brinton, D. M., and L. Jensen. In press. Appropriating the adjunct model: English for academic purposes at the university level. In *Content-based instruction: Case studies in TESOL practice series*, edited by J. Crandall and D. Kaufman. Alexandria, VA: TESOL.

Brinton, D. M., and C. LaBelle. 1997. Using Internet resources to teach pronunciation. *Speak Out! Newsletter of the IATEFL Pronunciation Special Interest Group*, 21, 54–60.

Brinton, D. M., L. Jensen, L. Repath-Martos, J. Frodesen, and C. Holten. 1997. *Insights 1: A content-based approach to academic preparation*. White Plains, NY: Longman.

Brinton, D. M., and P. Master, eds. 1997. *New ways in content-based instruction*. Alexandria, VA: TESOL.

Brinton, D. M., M. A. Snow, and M. B. Wesche. 1989. *Content-based second language instruction*. Boston, MA: Heinle & Heinle.

Brisk, M. E. 1998. *Bilingual education: From compensatory to quality schooling*. Mahwah, NJ: Lawrence Erlbaum.

———. 2000. *Quality bilingual education: Defining success*. (LAB Working Paper No. 1.) Providence, RI: Northeast and Islands Regional Educational Laboratory.

Britten, D. 1985. Teacher training in ELT. *Language Teaching* 18(2): 112–118; 18(3): 220–238.

Britton, B. K., A. Woodward, and M. Binkley, eds. 1993. *Learning from textbooks: Theory and practice*. Hillsdale, NY: Lawrence Erlbaum.

Brobow, D. G., and A. Collins, eds. 1975. *Representation and understanding*. New York: Academic Press.

Brock, C. A. 1986. The effects of referential questions on ESL classroom discourse. *TESOL Quarterly* 20(1): 47–60.

Brock, M. N., B. Yu, and M. Wong. 1992. "Journaling" together: Collaborative diary-keeping and teacher development. In *Perspectives on second language teacher development*, edited by J. Flowerdew, M. N. Brock and S. Hsia. Hong Kong: City University of Hong Kong.

Brookes, A., and P. Grundy. 1998. *Beginning to write: Writing activities for elementary and intermediate learners*. Cambridge: Cambridge University Press.

Broukal, M. 1994. *Weaving it together. Book 3*. Boston, MA: Heinle & Heinle.

Brown, A. L., and J. D. Day. 1983. Macrorules for summarizing in texts: The development of expertise. *Journal of Verbal Learning and Verbal Behaviour* 22(1): 1–14.

Brown, C. 1985a. Requests for specific language input: Differences between older and younger adult language learners. In *Input in second language acquisition*, edited by S. Gass and C. Madden. Rowley, MA: Newbury House.

———. 1985b. Two windows on the classroom world: Diary studies and participant observation differences. In *On TESOL '94: Brave new world for TESOL*, edited by P. Larson, E. L. Judd, and D. S. Messerschmitt. Alexandria, VA: TESOL.

Brown, G. 1987. Twenty-five years of teaching listening comprehension. *English Teaching Forum* 25(1): 11–15.

Brown, G., and G. Yule. 1983a. *Discourse analysis*. Cambridge: Cambridge University Press.

———. 1983b. *Teaching the spoken language: An approach based on the analysis of conversational English*. Cambridge: Cambridge University Press.

Brown, G., K. Currie, and J. Kenworthy. 1980. *Questions of intonation*. London: Croom Helm.

Brown, H. D. 1994. *Teaching by principles: An interactive approach to language pedagogy*. Englewood Cliffs, NJ: Prentice Hall Regents.

———. 1998. *New vistas: Getting started*. Upper Saddle River, NJ: Prentice Hall Regents.

Brown, J. D. 1995. *The elements of language curriculum*. Boston, MA: Heinle & Heinle.

———, ed. 1998. *New ways of classroom assessment*. Alexandria, VA: TESOL.

———. In press. Pragmatic tests: Different purposes, different tests. In *Pragmatics in language teaching*, edited by G. Kasper and K. R. Rose. Cambridge: Cambridge University Press.

Brumfit, C., and K. Johnson. 1979. *The communicative approach to language teaching*. Oxford: Oxford University Press.

Brumfit, C., and R. Mitchell, eds. 1990. *Research in the language classroom: ELT Documents, 133*. London: Modern English Publications and British Council.

Burger, S., M. Wesche, and M. Migneron. 1997. "Late, late immersion": Discipline-based second language teaching at the University of Ottawa. In *Immersion education: International perspectives*, edited by R. K. Johnson and M. Swain. Cambridge: Cambridge University Press.

Burns, A. 1995. Teacher-researchers: Perspectives on teacher action research and curriculum renewal. In *Teachers voices: Exploring course design in a changing curriculum*, edited by A. Burns and S. Hood. Sydney: NCELTR, Macquarie University.

———. 1999. *Collaborative action research for English language teachers*. Cambridge: Cambridge University Press.

Burstein, J., K. Kukich, S. Wolff, C. Lu, and M. Chodorow. 1998. *Computer analysis of essays*. Available at http://www.ets.org/research/ncmefinal.pdf

Burt, M., M. Dulay, and M. Finocchiaro. 1977. *Viewpoints in English as a second language*. New York: Regents.

Burton, D. 1982. Conversation pieces. In *Literary texts and language study*, edited by R. Carter and D. Burton. London: Edward Arnold.

Bush, M. D., and R. M. Terry, eds. 1997. *Technology-enhanced language learning*. Lincolnwood, IL: National Textbook Company.

Bush, V. 1945. As we may think. *The Atlantic Monthly* 176(1): 101–108.

Buttjes, D., and M. Byram. 1991. *Mediating languages and cultures*. Clevedon, UK: Multilingual Matters.

Bygate, M., A. Tonkyn, and E. Williams. 1994. *Grammar and the language teacher*. Hemel Hempstead, UK: Prentice Hall International.

Byram, M. 1997. *Teaching and assessing intercultural communicative competence*. Clevedon, UK: Multilingual Matters.

Byram, M., and C. Morgan. 1994. *Teaching and learning language and culture*. Clevedon, UK: Multilingual Matters.

Byrd, P., and J. Reid. 1998. *Grammar in the composition classroom: Essays on teaching ESL for college-bound students*. Boston, MA: Heinle & Heinle.

Byrne, D. 1988. *Teaching writing skills*. London: Longman

Byrne, J., and A. Waugh. 1982. *Jingle bells*. Oxford: Oxford University Press.

Cahnmann, M. 1998. Over thirty years of language-in-education policy and planning: Potter Thomas Bilingual School in Philadelphia. *Bilingual Research Journal* 22: 65–81.

California Department of Education. 1999. *English language development standards.* Sacramento: California Department of Education.

California State Department of Education, Office of Bilingual Bicultural Education. 1981. *Schooling and language minority students: A theoretical framework.* Sacramento: Evaluation, Dissemination and Assessment Center, California State University, Los Angeles.

Campbell, C. 1998. *Teaching second language writing: Interacting with text.* Pacific Grove, CA: Heinle & Heinle.

Canagarajah, A. S. 1993. Critical ethnography of a Sri Lankan classroom: Ambiguities in student opposition to reproduction through ESOL. *TESOL Quarterly* 27(4): 601–625.

———. 1999. Interrogating the "native speaker fallacy": Non-linguistic roots, non-pedagogical results. In *Non-native educators in English language teaching*, edited by G. Braine. Mahwah, NJ: Lawrence Erlbaum.

Canale, M. 1983a. From communicative competence to communicative language pedagogy. In *Language and communication*, edited by J. Richards and R. Schmidt. London: Longman.

———. 1983b. On some dimensions of language proficiency. In *Issues in language testing research*, edited by J. W. Oller, Jr. Rowley, MA: Newbury House.

———. 1984. Considerations in the testing of reading and listening proficiency. *Foreign Language Annals* 17(4): 349–357.

———. 1985. *Proficiency-oriented achievement testing.* Toronto: Franco-Ontarian Centre and Curriculum Department, Ontario Institute for Studies in Education.

———. 1986. The promise and threat of computerized adaptive assessment of reading comprehension. In *Technology and language testing*, edited by C. W. Stansfield. Washington, DC: TESOL.

Canale, M., and M. Swain. 1980. Theoretical bases of communicative approaches to second language testing and teaching. *Applied Linguistics* 1(1): 1–47.

Candlin, C. 1978. *Teaching of English: Principles and an exercise typology.* London: Langenscheidt-Longman.

Candlin, C., G. Carter, M. Legutke, V. Samuda, and S. Hanson. 1988. *Experimental learning: Theory into practice.* Paper presented at the 22nd Annual TESOL Convention, Chicago, IL.

Candlin, C., and D. Murphy, eds. 1987. *Language learning tasks.* (Lancaster Practical Papers in English Language Education Vol. 7.) Englewood Cliffs, NJ: Prentice Hall International.

Carlisi, K., and S. Christie. 2000. *Tapestry: Listening and speaking 3.* Boston, MA: Heinle & Heinle.

Carr, W., and S. Kemmis. 1986. *Becoming critical: Education, knowledge and action research.* London: Falmer.

Carrell, P., and J. C. Eisterhold. 1983. Schema theory and ESL reading pedagogy. *TESOL Quarterly* 17(4): 553–574.

———. 1988. Schema theory and ESL pedagogy. In *Interactive approaches to second language reading*, edited by P. Carrell, J. Devine, and D. Eskey. Cambridge: Cambridge University Press.

Carroll, J. B., ed. 1956. *Language, thought and reality: Selected writings of Benjamin Lee Whorf.* New York: Wiley.

Carroll, S., and M. Swain. 1993. Explicit and implicit negative feedback: An empirical study of the learning of linguistic generalizations. *Studies in Second Language Acquisition* 15(3): 357–386.

Carroll, W. M. 1997. Brief report: Results of third-grade students in a reform curriculum on the Illinois state mathematics test. *Journal for Research in Mathematics Education* 28(2): 237–242.

Carson, J. G., and I. Leki, eds. 1993. *Reading in the composition classroom: Second language perspectives.* Boston, MA: Heinle & Heinle.

Carson, J. G., and G. L. Nelson. 1994. Writing groups: Cross-cultural issues. *Journal of Second Language Writing* 5(1): 1–19.

Carter, B., and H. Thomas. 1986. "Dear brown eyes": Experiential learning in a project-oriented approach. *English Language Teaching Journal* 40(3): 196–204.

Carter, R. 1996. Look both ways before crossing: Developments in the language and literature classroom. In *Language, literature, and the learner*, edited by R. Carter and J. McRae. London: Addison Wesley Longman.

———. 1998. *Vocabulary: Applied linguistics perspectives.* 2d ed. London: Routledge.

Carter, R., and M. McCarthy. 1995. Grammar and the spoken language. *Applied Linguistics* 16(2): 141–158.

———. 1988. Developments in the teaching of vocabulary. In *Vocabulary and language teaching*, edited by R. Carter and M. McCarthy. London: Longman.

Celce-Murcia, M. 1979. Language teaching aids. In *Teaching English as a second or foreign language*, edited by M. Celce-Murcia and L. McIntosh. Rowley, MA: Newbury House.

———. 1980. Language teaching methods from the ancient Greeks to Gattegno. *Mextesol Journal* 4(4): 2–13.

———. 1981. New methods in perspective. *Practical English Teaching* 2(1): 9–12.

———. 1985. Making informed decisions about the role of grammar in language teaching. *TESOL Newsletter* 29(1): 9–12.

———. 1991a. Discourse analysis and grammar instruction. *Annual Review of Applied Linguistics* 11: 135–151.

———. 1991b. Language teaching approaches: An overview. In *Teaching English as a second or foreign language*, edited by M. Celce-Murcia. Boston, MA: Heinle & Heinle.

———, ed. 1991c. *Teaching English as a second or foreign language.* 2d ed. New York: Newbury House/HarperCollins.

Celce-Murcia, M., D. Brinton, and J. Goodwin. 1996. *Teaching pronunciation: A reference for teachers of English to speakers of other languages.* New York: Cambridge University Press.

Celce-Murcia, M., Z. Dörnyei, and S. Thurrell. 1995. Communicative competence: A pedagogically motivated model with content specifications. *Issues in Applied Linguistics* 6: 5–35.

Celce-Murcia, M., and S. Hilles. 1988. *Techniques and resources in teaching grammar.* New York: Oxford University Press.

Celce-Murcia, M., and D. Larsen-Freeman. 1999. *The grammar book: An ESL/EFL teacher's course.* 2nd ed. Boston, MA: Heinle & Heinle.

Celce-Murcia, M., and L. McIntosh, eds. 1979. *Teaching English as a second or foreign language.* Rowley, MA: Newbury House.

Chalhoub-Deville, M., ed. 2000. *Studies in language testing 10: Issues in computer-adaptive testing of reading proficiency.* Cambridge: Cambridge University Press.

Chambers, F. 1997. Seeking consensus in coursebook evaluation. *ELT Journal* 51(1): 29–35.

Chamot, A. U. 1995. Learning strategies and listening comprehension. In *A guide for the teaching of second language listening*, edited by D. Mendelsohn and J. Rubin. San Diego, CA: Dominie Press.

Chamot, A. U., S. Barnhardt, P. El-Dinary, and J. Robbins. 1996. Methods for teaching learning strategies in the foreign language classroom. In *Language learning strategies around the world: Cross-cultural perspectives*, edited by R. Oxford. Manoa, HI: University of Hawaii Press.

Chamot, A. U., and J. M. O'Malley. 1994. *The CALLA handbook: Implementing the cognitive academic language learning approach.* Reading, MA: Addison-Wesley.

———. 1996. Implementing the cognitive academic language learning approach (CALLA). In *Language learning strategies around the world: Cross-cultural perspectives*, edited by R. Oxford. Manoa, HI: University of Hawaii Press.

Chan, M. 1987. *Phrase by phrase.* Englewood Cliffs, NJ: Prentice Hall Regents.

Chan, Y. H. 1996. Action research as professional development for ELT practitioners. *Working Papers in ELT and Applied Linguistics* 2(1): 17-28. Hong Kong: Hong Kong Polytechnic University.

Chang, H. 1990. *Newcomer programs: Innovative efforts to meet the educational challenges of immigrant students.* San Francisco, CA: California Tomorrow.

Chastain, K. 1988. *Developing second language skills: Theory and practice.* 3d ed. San Diego: Harcourt Brace Jovanovich.

Chaudron, C. 1977. A descriptive model of discourse in the corrective treatment of learners' errors. *Language Learning* 27(1): 29–46.

———. 1982. Vocabulary elaboration in teachers' speech to L2 learners. *Studies in Second Language Acquisition* 4: 170–180.

———. 1988. *Second language classrooms: Research on teaching and learning.* Cambridge: Cambridge University Press.

Chaudron, C., and J. C. Richards. 1986. The effect of discourse markers on the comprehension of lectures. *Applied Linguistics* 7(2): 112–127.

Chavez-Oller, M. A., T. Chihara, K. A. Weaver, and J. W. Oller, Jr. 1985.

When are cloze items sensitive to constraints across sentences? *Language Learning* 35(2): 181–206.

Chela Flores, B. 1998. *Teaching English rhythm: From theory to practice.* Caracas, Venezuela: Fondo Editorial Tropykos.

_____. 2000. *Teaching rhythm: Recognizing and overcoming difficulties.* Paper presented at the Annual TESOL Convention, Vancouver, Canada.

Cheng, L. 1997. How does washback influence teaching? Implications for Hong Kong. *Language and Education* 11(1): 238–254.

Chesterfield, R., and K. B. Chesterfield. 1985. Natural order in children's use of second language learning strategies. *Applied Linguistics* 6(1): 45–59.

Chomsky, N., and M. Halle. 1968. *The sound pattern of English.* New York: Harper and Row.

Chomsky, N. 1957. *Syntactic structures.* The Hague: Mouton.

_____. l965. *Aspects of the theory of syntax.* Cambridge: MIT Press.

Christian, D. 1996. Two-way immersion education: Students learning through two languages. *Modern Language Journal* 80(1): 66–76.

Christian, D., C. L. Montone, K. J. Lindholm, and I. Carranza. 1997. *Profiles in two-way immersion education.* McHenry, IL: Center for Applied Linguistics/Delta Systems.

Christison, M. A., and S. K. Bassano. 1995. Action research: Techniques for collecting data through surveys and interviews. *CATESOL Journal* 8(1): 89–103.

Ciborski, J. 1995. Using textbooks with students who cannot read them. *Remedial and Special Education* 16(2): 90–102.

Cisneros, S. 1995. Eleven. In *Voices in literature,* edited by M. L. McCloskey and L. Stack. Boston, MA: Heinle & Heinle.

Claire, E. 1998. *ESL teacher's activities kit.* Englewood Cliffs, NJ: Prentice Hall.

Clark, C., and M. Lampert. 1986. The study of teacher thinking: Implications for teacher education. *Journal of Teacher Education* 37(4): 27–31.

Clark, H., and E. Clark. 1977. *Psychology and language.* New York: Harcourt, Brace, and Jovanovich.

Clark, J. 1987. *Curriculum renewal in school foreign language learning.* Oxford: Oxford University Press.

Clarke, D. F., and I. S. P. Nation. 1980. Guessing the meanings of words from context: Strategy and techniques. *System* 8(3): 211–220.

Cleghorn, A., and F. Genesee. 1984. Languages in contact: An ethnographic study of interaction in an immersion school. *TESOL Quarterly* 18(4): 595–625.

Cloud, N., F. Genesee, and E. Hamayan. 2000. *Dual language instruction: A handbook for enriched education.* Boston, MA: Heinle & Heinle.

Coady, J., and T. Huckin, eds. 1997. *Second language vocabulary acquisition.* Cambridge: Cambridge University Press.

CobuildDirect. n.d. Concordancer and collocation software samplers. Available at: http://titania.cobuild.collins.co.uk/direct_info.html

Cohen, A. D. 1984. On taking language tests: What the students report. *Language Testing* 1(1): 70–81.

_____. 1993. The role of instructions in testing summarizing ability. In *A new decade of language testing research,* edited by D. Douglas and C. Chapelle. Arlington, VA: TESOL.

_____. 1994. *Assessing language ability in the classroom.* 2d ed. Boston, MA: Heinle & Heinle.

_____. 1998. *Strategies in learning and using a second language.* New York: Longman

Cohen, A. D., H. Glasman, P. R. Rosenbaum-Cohen, J. Ferrara, and J. Fine. 1979. Reading English for specialized purposes: Discourse analysis and the use of student informants. *TESOL Quarterly* 13(4): 551–564.

Cohen, A. D., and K. Scott. 1996. A synthesis of approaches to assessing language learning strategies. In *Language learning strategies around the world: Cross-cultural perspectives,* edited by R. Oxford. Manoa, HI: University of Hawaii Press.

Cohen, A. D., and S. J. Weaver. 1998. Strategies-based instruction for second language learners. In *Learners and Language Learning,* edited by W. A. Reyandya and G. M. Jacobs. Anthology Series 39. Singapore: SEAMEO Regional Language Center.

Cohen, A. D., S. J. Weaver, and T. Y. Yi. 1995. *The impact of strategies-based instruction on speaking a foreign language.* Research Report. Minneapolis, MN: National Foreign Language Research Center.

Coleman, A. 1929. *Teaching of modern foreign languages in the United States.* New York: Macmillan.

Coleman, H. 1989. *Large classes in Nigeria.* (Project Report No. 6.) Leeds, UK: Lancaster-Leeds Language Learning in Large Classes Research Project.

Coleman, J. 1992, March. Project-based learning, transferable skills, information technology and video. *Language Learning Journal* 5: 35–37.

Collier, V. 1989. How long? A synthesis of research on academic achievement in a second language. *TESOL Quarterly* 23: 509–531.

Collins COBUILD English Dictionary. 1995. 2d ed. London: HarperCollins.

Conrad, S. 1996. Investigating academic texts with corpus-based techniques: An example from biology. *Linguistics and Education* 8: 299–326.

Cook, G. 2000. *Language play, language learning.* New York: Oxford University Press.

Cook, V. 1999. Going beyond the native speaker in language teaching. *TESOL Quarterly* 33(2): 185–209.

Corder, S. P. 1967. The significance of learner's errors. *IRAL* 5: 161–169.

_____. 1988. Pedagogic grammars. In *Grammar and second language teaching: A book of readings,* edited by W. E. Rutherford and M. S. Smith. New York: Newbury House.

Cornett, C. 1983. *What you should know about teaching and learning styles.* Bloomington, IN: Phi Delta Kappa.

Cotton, W. 1968. *On behalf of adult education: A historical examination of the supporting literature.* Boston, MA: Center for the Study of Liberal Education for Adults.

Coxhead, A. 2000. A new academic word list. *TESOL Quarterly* 34(2): 213–238.

Crandall, J. A. 1998. Collaborate and cooperate: Teacher education for integrating language and content instruction. *Forum* 36(1): 2-9.

_____. 2000. Language teacher education. *Annual Review of Applied Linguistics* 20: 34–55.

Crandall, J. A., and Peyton, J., eds. 1993. *Approaches to adult ESL literacy instruction.* McHenry, IL: Center for Applied Linguistics/Delta Systems.

Crawford, J. 1992. *Hold your tongue: Bilingualism and the politics of "English only."* Reading, MA: Addison-Wesley.

_____. 1998. Language politics in the U.S.A.: The paradox of bilingual education. *Social Justice* 25(3): 50–69.

_____. 1999. *Bilingual education: History, politics, theory, and practice.* 4th ed. Los Angeles, CA: Bilingual Educational Services.

Cray, E. 1988. Why teachers should develop their own materials. *TESL Talk* 18(1): 69–81.

Cricket. Peru, IL: Carus Publishing.

Crittenden, J. 1978. *English with solo.* Oxford: Oxford University Press.

Crookes, G. 1986. *Task classification: A cross-disciplinary review.* (Technical Report No. 4.) Manoa, HI: Center for Second Language Classroom Research, Social Science Research Institute, University of Hawaii.

_____. 1989. Planning and interlanguage development. *Studies in Second Language Acquisition* 11(4): 367–383.

_____. 1993. Action research for second language teachers—it's not just teacher research. *Applied Linguistics* 14(2): 130–143.

_____. 1998. On the relationship between second and foreign language teachers and research. *TESOL Journal* 7(3): 6–11.

Crookes, G., and C. Chaudron. 1991. Guidelines for classroom language teaching. In *Teaching English as a second or foreign language,* edited by M. Celce-Murcia. Boston, MA: Heinle & Heinle.

Crookes, G., and S. M. Gass. 1993a. *Tasks in a pedagogical context: Integrating theory and practice.* Clevedon, UK: Multilingual Matters.

_____. 1993b. *Tasks in language learning: Integrating theory and practice.* Clevedon, UK: Multilingual Matters.

Crookes, G., and K. A. Rulon. 1988. Topic and feedback in native-speaker/non-native speaker conversation. *TESOL Quarterly* 22(4): 675–684.

Crotchett, K. 1997. *A teacher's project guide to the Internet.* Portsmouth, NH: Heinemann.

Crystal, D. 1997. *English as a global language.* Cambridge: Cambridge University Press.

Csikszentmihalyi, M. 1990. *Flow: The psychology of optimal experience.* New York: HarperCollins.

Cumming, A. 2000. *ESL/EFL writing instruction for adults in 6 countries: Experienced instructors' conceptualizations of their curricula, instruction, and assessment practices.* Paper presented at the American Association for Applied Linguistics Annual Conference, Vancouver, Canada.

Cummins, J. 1976. The influence of bilingualism on cognitive growth: A synthesis of research findings and explanatory hypotheses. *Working Papers on Bilingualism* 9: 1–43.

_____. 1979. Cognitive/academic language proficiency, linguistic interdependence, the optimum age question and some other matters. *Working Papers on Bilingualism* 19: 121–129.

_____. 1981. The role of primary language development in promoting success for language minority students. In *Schooling and language minority students: A theoretical framework*. Los Angeles, CA: Evaluation, Dissemination and Assessment Center, California State University.

_____. 1991. Interdependence of first- and second-language proficiency in bilingual children. In *Language processing in bilingual children*, edited by E. Bialystok. New York: Cambridge University Press.

_____. 1999. Beyond adversarial discourse: Searching for common ground in the education of bilingual students. In *Annual editions: Teaching English as a second language 99/00*, edited by I. A. Heath and C. J. Serrano. Guilford, CT: Dushkin/McGraw-Hill.

Curran, C. A. 1976. *Counseling-learning in second-language learning*. East Dubuque, IL: Counseling Learning Publications.

Current, R. N., ed. 1967. *The political thought of Abraham Lincoln*. Indianapolis and New York: The Bobbs-Merrill Company.

Curtain, H., and C. A. Pesola. 1994. *Language and children: Making the match*. 2d ed. White Plains, NY: Longman.

Dadour, E. S., and J. Robbins. 1996. University-level studies using strategy instruction to improve speaking ability in Egypt and Japan. In *Language learning strategies around the world: Cross-cultural perspectives*, edited by R. Oxford. Manoa, HI: University of Hawaii Press.

Dalton, C., and B. Seidlhofer. 1994. *Pronunciation*. Oxford: Oxford University Press.

Daoud, A., and M. Celce-Murcia. 1979. Selecting and evaluating a textbook. In *Teaching English as a second or foreign language*, edited by M. Celce-Murcia and L. McIntosh. New York: Newbury House.

Darley, B., and J. Latane. 1973. Bystander apathy. In *Urbanman: The psychology of urban survival*, edited by J. Helmer and N. Edington. New York: The Free Press.

Dauer, R. 1993. *Accurate English: A complete course in pronunciation*. Englewood Cliffs, NJ: Prentice Hall Regents.

Davies, A. 1991. *The native speaker in applied linguistics*. Edinburgh: Edinburgh University Press.

_____. 1996. *What second language learners can tell us about the native speaker: Identifying and describing exception*. Paper presented at the annual meeting of the American Association of Applied Linguists, Chicago, IL.

Davis, P., and M. Rinvolucri. 1988. *Dictation: New methods, new possibilities*. Cambridge: Cambridge University Press.

Day, R. R., ed. 1993. *New ways in teaching reading*. Alexandria, VA: TESOL.

Day, R. R., and J. Bamford. 1998. *Extensive reading in the second language classroom*. Cambridge: Cambridge University Press.

De Beaugrande, R. 1985. Sentence combining and discourse processing: In search of a general theory. In *Sentence combining: A rhetorical perspective*, edited by D. Daiker, A. Kerek and M. Morenberg. Carbondale, IL: Southern University Press.

DeKeyser, R. 1998. Beyond focus on form: Cognitive perspectives on learning and practicing second language grammar. In *Focus on form in classroom second language acquisition*, edited by C. Doughty and J. Williams. New York: Cambridge University Press.

Denes, P., and E. Pinson. 1963. *The speech chain*. Bell Telephone Laboratories, Inc.

Dentler, R., and A. Hafner. 1997. *Hosting newcomers: Structuring educational opportunities for immigrant children*. New York: Teachers College Press.

DePaola, T. 1988. *Tomi Paola's book of poems*. New York: G. P. Putnam's Sons.

Deterding, D. H., and G. R. Poedjosoedarmo. 1998. *The sounds of English: Phonetics and phonology for English teachers in southeast Asia*. Singapore: Prentice Hall.

Dewey, J. 1916. *Democracy and education: An introduction to the philosophy of education*. New York: MacMillan.

_____. 1938. *Experience and education*. New York: MacMillan.

_____. [1938] 1948. *Experience and education*. New York: MacMillan.

_____. [1956] 1990. *The school and society: The child and the curriculum*. Chicago: The University of Chicago Press.

Dickerson, W. 1989. *Stress in the speech stream*. Urbana, IL: University of Illinois Press.

Dickerson, W. 1994. Empowering students with predictive skills. In *Pronunciation pedagogy and theory: New views, new directions*, edited by J. Morley. Alexandria, VA: TESOL.

Diffily, D. 1996. The project approach: A museum exhibit created by kindergartners. *Young Children* (January): 72–75.

Dillard, J. T. 1978. Bidialectal education: Black English and standard English in the United States. In *Case studies in bilingual education*, edited by B. Spolsky and R. Cooper. Rowley, MA: Newbury House.

Dixon, C., and D. Nessel. 1983. *Language experience approach to reading and writing*. Hayward, CA: Alemany Press.

Donato, R. 1994. Collective scaffolding in second language learning. In *Vygotskian approaches to second language research*, edited by J. Lantolf and G. Appel. Norwood, NJ: Ablex.

Donato, R., and D. McCormick. 1994. A sociocultural perspective on language learning strategies: The role of mediation. *Modern Language Journal* 78: 453–464.

Dörnyei, Z. 1995. On the teachability of communication strategies. *TESOL Quarterly* 29: 55–85.

_____. 1997. Psychological processes in co-operative language learning: Group dynamics and motivation. *The Modern Language Journal* 81(4): 482–493.

Dörnyei, Z., and S. Thurrell. 1994. Teaching conversation skills intensively: Course content and rationale. *ELT Journal* 48: 40–49.

Doughty, C., and T. Pica. 1984. Information gap tasks: Do they facilitate second language acquisition? *TESOL Quarterly* 20: 305–325.

Doughty, C., and J. Williams, eds. 1998a. *Focus on form in classroom second language acquisition*. Cambridge: Cambridge University Press.

_____. 1998b. Pedagogical choice in focus on form. In *Focus on form in classroom second language acquisition*, edited by C. Doughty and J. Williams. New York: Cambridge University Press.

Douglas, D. 2000. *Assessing language for specific purposes*. Cambridge: Cambridge University Press.

Dreyer, C., and R. Oxford. 1996. Learning strategies and other predictors of ESL proficiency among Afrikaans-speakers in South Africa. In *Language learning strategies around the world: cross-cultural perspectives*, edited by R. Oxford. Manoa, HI: University of Hawaii Press.

Duber, J. n.d. Grammar Web Quiz #1. Available at: http://www.sirius.com/~dub/CALL/grammar1.html.

Dubin, F., and E. Olshtain. 1986. *Course design*. Cambridge: Cambridge University Press.

Dudley-Evans, T., and M. J. St. John. 1998. *Developments in English for specific purposes: A multi-disciplinary approach*. Cambridge: Cambridge University Press.

Duff, P. A. 1986. Another look at interlanguage talk: Taking task to task. In *Talking to learn: Conversation in second language acquisition*, edited by R. R. Day. Rowley, MA: Newbury House.

_____. 1995. An ethnography of communication in immersion classrooms in Hungary. *TESOL Quarterly* 29(3): 505–537.

_____. 1996. Different languages, different practices: Socialization of discourse competence in dual-language school classrooms in Hungary. In *Voices from the language classroom: Qualitative research on language education*, edited by K. M. Bailey and D. Nunan. New York: Cambridge University Press.

Dulay, H., and M. Burt. 1973. Should we teach children syntax? *Language Learning* 23: 245–258.

Dunkel, P. A. 1999. Considerations in developing or using second/foreign language proficiency computer-adaptive tests. *Language Learning and Technology* 2(2): 77–93.

Dunn, R., and Griggs, S. 1988. *Learning styles: Quiet revolution in American schools*. Reston, VA: National Association of Secondary School Principals.

Eastman, J. K. 1991. Learning to listen and comprehend: The beginning stages. *System* 19: 179–188.

Ebbinghaus, H. 1897. Über eine neue Methode zür Prüfung geistiger Fähigkeiten und ihre Anwendung bei Schulkindern. In *Zeitschrift für Psychologie und Physiologie der Sinnesorgane*, edited by S. Exner et al. Leipzig: Barth.

Echevarria, J., and A. Graves. 1998. *Sheltered content instruction: Teaching English-language learners with diverse abilities*. Boston, MA: Allyn and Bacon.

Echevarria, J., M. Vogt, and D. J. Short. 2000. *Making content comprehensible for English language learners: The SIP Model*. Des Moines, IA: Allyn and Bacon.

Edelhoff, C. 1981. Theme-oriented English teaching: Text-varieties, media, skills and project work. In *The communicative teaching of English: Principles and an exercise typology*, edited by C. N. Candlin. London: Longman.

Edge, J., and K. Richards, eds. 1993. *Teachers develop teachers research: Papers on classroom research and teacher development*. Oxford: Heinemann International.

Edge, J., and S. Wharton. 1998. Autonomy and development: Living in the materials world. In *Materials development in language teaching*, edited by B. Tomlinson. Cambridge: Cambridge University Press.

Ediger, A., and C. Pavlik. 2000. *Reading connections: Intermediate*. New York: Oxford University Press.

Educational Testing Service. 1996. *Test of written English guide*. 4th ed. Princeton, NJ: Educational Testing Service.

Edwards, H. P., M. B. Wesche, S. Krashen, R. Clement, and B. Kruidenier. 1984. Second language acquisition through subject matter learning: A study of sheltered psychology classes at the University of Ottawa. *Canadian Modern Language Review* 41: 268–282.

Egbert, J., and E. Hanson-Smith, eds. 1999. *CALL environments: Research, practice, and critical issues*. Alexandria, VA: TESOL.

Ehrman, M. 1996. *Second language learning difficulties: Looking beneath the surface*. Thousand Oaks, CA: Sage.

Ehrman, M., and R. Oxford. 1989. Effects of sex differences, career choice, and psychological type on adults' language learning strategies. *Modern Language Journal* 73: 1–13.

_____. 1990. Adult language learning styles and strategies in an intensive training setting. *Modern Language Journal* 74: 311–326.

Elbow, P. 1973. *Writing without teachers*. New York: Oxford University Press.

Elley, W. B. 1991. Acquiring literacy in a second language: The effect of book-based programs. *Language Learning* 41: 375–411.

Elley, W., and F. Mangubhai. 1983. The impact of reading on second language readers. *Reading Research Quarterly* 19: 53–67.

Ellis, N. 1998. Emergentism, connectionism, and language learning. *Language Learning* 48(4): 631–644.

_____. 1999. Cognitive approaches to SLA. *Annual Review of Applied Linguistics* 19: 22–42.

Ellis, N., and R. Schmidt. 1997. Morphology and longer-distance dependencies: Laboratory research illuminating the A in SLA. *Studies in Second Language Acquisition* 19(2): 145–171.

Ellis, R. 1985. Teacher-pupil interaction in second language development. In *Input in second language acquisition*, edited by S. Gass and C. Madden. Rowley, MA: Newbury House.

_____. 1989. Classroom learning styles and their effect on second language acquisition: A study of two learners. *System* 17: 249–262.

_____. 1994. *The study of second language acquisition*. Oxford: Oxford University Press.

_____. 1997. *Second language research and language teaching*. Oxford: Oxford University Press.

_____. 1998. Teaching and research: Options in grammar teaching. *TESOL Quarterly* 32(1): 39–60.

Emig, J. 1971. *The composing process of twelfth graders*. Urbana, IL: National Council of Teachers of English.

England, L., and C. U. Grosse. 1995. *Speaking of business*. Boston, MA: Heinle & Heinle.

Enright, D. S. 1991. Supporting children's English language development in grade-level and language classrooms. In *Teaching English as a second or foreign language*, edited by M. Celce-Murcia. New York: Newbury House.

Enright, D. S., and P. Rigg. 1986. Introduction to *Children and ESL: Integrating perspectives*, edited by P. Rigg and D. S. Enright. Washington, DC: TESOL.

Erteschik-Shir, N. 1979. Discourse constraints on dative movement. In *Syntax and semantics: Volume 12. Discourse and syntax*, edited by T. Givón. New York: Academic Press.

Eustace, G. 1996. Business writing—some aspects of current practice. *English for Specific Purposes* 15: 53–56.

Eyraud, K., G. Giles, S. Koenig, and F. L. Stoller. 2000. The word wall approach: Promoting L2 vocabulary learning. *English Teaching Forum* 38: 2–11.

Eyring, J. 1989. *Teacher experiences and student responses in ESL project work instruction: A case study*. Ph.D. diss., University of California, Los Angeles.

Eysenck, M., and M. Keane. 1995. *Cognitive psychology: A student's handbook*. East Sussex, UK: Psychology Press.

Faerch, C. 1986. Rules of thumb and other teacher-formulated rules in the foreign language classroom. In *Learning, teaching and communication in the foreign language classroom*, edited by G. Kasper. Aarhus, Denmark: Aarhus University Press.

Faltis, C., and S. Hudelson. 1994. Learning English as an additional language in K-12 schools. *TESOL Quarterly* 23(3): 457–468.

Falvey, M. 1995. *Inclusive and heterogeneous schooling*. Baltimore, MD: Paul H. Brookes Publishing.

Fanselow, J. 1988. "Let's see": Contrasting conversations about teaching. *TESOL Quarterly* 22(1): 113–130.

Ferguson, C. A. 1982. Foreword to *The other tongue: English across cultures*, edited by B. B. Kachru. Oxford: Pergamon Press.

Ferris, D. 1997. The influence of teacher commentary on student revision. *TESOL Quarterly* 31(2): 315–339.

_____. 1999. The case for grammar correction in L2 writing classes: A response to Truscott. *Journal of Second Language Writing* 8: 1–11.

Ferris, D., and J. Hedgcock. 1998. *Teaching ESL composition: Purpose, process and practice*. Mahwah, NJ: Lawrence Erlbaum.

Ferris, D., S. Pezone, C. R. Tade, and S. Tinti. 1997. Teacher commentary on student writing: Descriptions and implications. *Journal of Second Language Writing* 6(2): 155–182.

Ferris, D., and T. Tagg. 1996a. Academic oral communication needs of EAP learners: What subject-matter instructors actually require. *TESOL Quarterly* 30(2): 31–55.

_____. 1996b. Academic listening/speaking tasks for ESL students: Problems, suggestions, implications. *TESOL Quarterly* 30(2): 297–317.

Field, J. 1998. Skills and strategies: Towards a new methodology for listening. *ESL Journal* 52: 110–118.

Figueroa, J., L. Walker, M. Varon, and H. Johnson. 1988. Division of adult and occupational education 1986-87. Annual report. Los Angeles: Los Angeles Unified School District.

Fish, H. 1989. Playing with plays: Increasing student involvement with dramatic texts. In *Literature and the learner: Methodological approaches* [ELT Document 130], edited by C. Carter, R. Walker, and C. Brumfit. Hong Kong: Modern English Publications and the British Council.

Fishman, J. A. 1982. The sociology of English as an additional language. In *The other tongue: English across cultures*, edited by B. B. Kachru. Oxford: Pergamon Press.

Flashner, V. E. 1987. *An exploration of linguistic dichotomies and genres in the classroom language of native and nonnative English speaking children*. Ph.D. diss., University of California, Los Angeles.

Flowerdew, J., ed. 1994. *Academic listening: Research perspectives*. Cambridge: Cambridge University Press.

Floyd, P., and P. Carrell. 1987. Effects on ESL reading of teaching cultural content schemata. *Language Learning* 37: 89–108.

Foley, B. H. 1994a. *Listen to me! Beginning listening, speaking and pronunciation*. 2d ed. Boston, MA: Heinle & Heinle.

_____. 1994b. *Now hear this! High beginning listening, speaking and pronunciation*. 2d ed. Boston, MA: Heinle & Heinle.

Foley, K. S. 1993. Talking journals. *TESOL Journal* 3(1): 37–38.

Foster, P. 1998. A classroom perspective on the negotiation of meaning. *Applied Linguistics* 19(1): 1–23.

Fotos, S. 1993. Consciousness raising and noticing through focus on form: Grammar task performance versus formal instruction. *Applied Linguistics* 14: 385–407.

_____. 2001. Structure-based interactive tasks for the EFL grammar learner. In *New perspectives on grammar teaching in second language classrooms*, edited by E. Hinkel and S. Fotos. Mahwah, NJ: Lawrence Erlbaum.

Fotos, S., and R. Ellis 1991. Communicating about grammar: A task-based approach. *TESOL Quarterly* 25(4): 605–628.

Fowler, R. 1986. *Linguistic criticism*. Oxford: Oxford University Press.

Fragiadakis, H. K., and V. Maurer. 2000. *Tapestry listening and speaking 4*. Boston, MA: Heinle & Heinle.

Fransson, A. 1984. Cramming or understanding? Effects of intrinsic and extrinsic motivation on approach to learning and test performance.

In *Reading in a foreign language*, edited by J. C. Alderson and A. H. Urquhart. London: Longman.

Freedman, A., and P. Medway. 1994. *Learning and teaching genre*. Portsmouth, NH: Heinemann/Boynton-Cook.

Freeman, D. 1992. Collaboration: Constructing shared understandings in a second language classroom. In *Collaborative language learning and teaching*, edited by D. Nunan. Cambridge: Cambridge University Press

_____. 1996. Redefining the relationship between research and what teachers know. In *Voices from the language classroom: Qualitative research on language education*, edited by K. M. Bailey and D. Nunan. New York: Cambridge University Press.

_____. 1998. *Doing teacher research: From inquiry to understanding*. Boston, MA: Heinle & Heinle.

_____, ed. 2001. *Teacher Source series*. Boston, MA: Heinle & Heinle.

Freeman, R. D. 1998. *Bilingual education and social change*. Clevedon, UK: Multilingual Matters.

Freire, P. 1970a. *Pedagogy of the oppressed*. New York: Continuum.

_____. 1970b. *Cultural action for freedom*. Cambridge, MA: Harvard Educational Review.

_____. 1998. *Pedagogy of freedom: Ethics, democracy, and civic courage*. Lanham, MA: Rowman and Littlefield.

Fried-Booth, D. 1982. Project work with advanced classes. *ELT Journal* 36(2): 1–8.

_____. 1986. *Project work*. Oxford: Oxford University Press.

Fries, C. 1945. *Teaching and learning English as a foreign language*. Ann Arbor: University of Michigan Press.

Frodesen, J., and J. Eyring. 2000. *Grammar dimensions: Form, meaning and use, Book 4*. Boston, MA: Heinle & Heinle.

Fry, E. B. 2000. *Reading drills*. Lincolnwood, IL: National Textbook Company.

Fujimoto, D. 2000. Looking ahead to international standards. *TESOL Matters* 10(1): 9.

Fulwiler, T., ed. 1987. *The journal book*. Portsmouth, NH: Heinemann.

Gaer, S. 1995. Cookbook project. In *Virtual connections*, edited by M. Warschauer. Honolulu: University of Hawaii Press.

_____. 1998. Less teaching and more learning. *Focus on Basics* [on-line serial] 2, Issue D (December). Hostname: harvard.edu Directory

Gagné, R., and K. Medsker. 1996. *The conditions of learning*. Fort Worth, TX: Harcourt Brace.

Gaies, S. J. 1982. NS-NNS interaction among academic peers. *Studies in Second Language Acquisition* 5(1): 74–81.

Gairns, R., and S. Redman. 1986. *Working with words: A guide to teaching and learning vocabulary*. Cambridge: Cambridge University Press.

Galyean, B. 1977. A confluent design for language teaching. *TESOL Quarterly* 11(2): 143–155.

Garvie, E. 1990. *Story as vehicle: Teaching English to young children*. Clevedon, UK: Multilingual Matters.

Gass, S. M. 1997. *Input, interaction and the second language learner*. Mahwah, NJ: Lawrence Erlbaum.

Gass, S. M., and A. Mackey. 2000. *Stimulated recall methodology in second language research*. Mahwah, NJ: Lawrence Erlbaum.

Gass, S. M., A. Mackey, M. J. Alvarez-Torres, and M. Fernández-García. 1999. The effects of task repetition on linguistic output. *Language Learning* 49(4): 549–581.

Gass, S. M., and Varonis, L. 1985. Task variation and non-native/non-native negotiation of meaning. In *Input and second language acquisition*, edited by S. M. Gass and C. G. Madden. Rowley, MA: Newbury House.

Gatbonton, E., and Segalowitz, N. 1988. Creative automatization: Principles for promoting fluency within a communicative framework. *TESOL Quarterly* 22(3): 473–492.

Gattegno, C. 1972. *Teaching foreign languages in schools: The silent way*. New York: Educational Solutions.

_____. 1976. *The common sense of teaching foreign languages*. New York: Educational Solutions.

Gebhard, J. 1996. *Teaching English as a foreign or second language*. Ann Arbor: University of Michigan Press.

Gebhard, J., and R. Oprandy. 1999. *Language teaching awareness: A guide to exploring beliefs and practices*. New York: Cambridge University Press.

Geddes, M., and G. Sturtridge. 1979. *Listening links*. London: Heinemann.

Genesee, F. 1987. *Learning through two languages: Studies of immersion and bilingual education*. Cambridge, MA: Newbury House.

_____. 1994. Introduction to *Educating second language children*, edited by F. Genesee. New York: Cambridge University Press.

_____, ed. 1999. *Program alternatives for linguistically diverse students*. (Educational Practice Report No. 1.) Washington, DC: Center for Research on Education, Diversity, and Excellence/Center for Applied Linguistics.

Gersten, B. F., and N. Tlusty. 1998. Creating international contexts for cultural communication: Video exchange projects in the EFL/ESL classroom. *TESOL Journal* 7(6): 11–16.

Gertzman, A. 1988. Using Foxfire-type project in the ESL classroom: From the cuckooo's nest to worldview and beyond. *Hands-On* 32: 33–44.

Gianelli, M. C. 1997. Thematic units: Creating an environment for learning. In *The content-based classroom: Perspectives on integrating language and content*, edited by M. A. Snow and D. M. Brinton. New York: Longman.

Gilbert, E. N., and C. L. Mallows. 1984. *A history of engineering and sciences in the Bell System: Communication Sciences 1925-1980*. AT&T Bell Laboratories.

Gilbert, J. 1987. Pronunciation and listening comprehension. In *Current perspectives on pronunciation* (pp.29–39), edited by J. Morley. Washington, DC: TESOL.

Gilbert, J. 1993. *Clear speech*. 2d ed. New York: Cambridge University Press.

_____. 1994. Intonation: A navigation guide for the listener (and gadgets to help teach it). In *Pronunciation pedagogy and theory: New views, new directions*, edited by J. Morley. Alexandria, VA: TESOL.

_____. 1995. Pronunciation practice as an aid to listening comprehension. In *A guide for the teaching of second language listening*, edited by D. Mendelsohn and J. Rubin. San Diego, CA: Dominie Press.

_____. 2001. *Clear speech from the start*. New York: Cambridge University Press.

Gill, M. M., and P. Hartmann, P. 2000. *Tapestry listening and speaking 2*. Boston, MA: Heinle & Heinle.

Gillespie, M. 1994. *Native language literacy instruction for adults: Patterns, issues, and promises*. Washington, DC: National Clearinghouse for ESL Literacy Education/National Center on Adult Literacy.

_____. 1996. *Learning to work in a new land: A review and sourcebook for vocational and workplace ESL*. Washington, DC: Center for Applied Linguistics.

Giltrow, G., and M. Valiquette. 1994. Genre and knowledge: Students' writing in the disciplines. In *Learning and teaching genre*, edited by A. Freedman and P. Medway. Portsmouth, NH: Heinemann/Boynton-Cook.

Gimenez, J. C. 2000. Business e-mail communication: Some emerging tendencies in register. *English for Specific Purposes* 19: 237–252.

Givón, T. 1998. The functional approach to grammar. In *The new psychology of language: Cognitive and functional approaches to language structure*, edited by M. Tomasello. Mahwah, NJ: Lawrence Erlbaum.

Gomes de Matos, F. 2000. TESOLers as textbook evaluators: An interdisciplinary checklist. *BRAZ-TESOL Newsletter* June: 16–18.

Gomez, E. 2000. A history of the ESL Standards for pre-K–12 students. In *Implementing the ESL standards for pre-K–12 students in teacher education*, edited by M. A. Snow. Alexandria, VA: TESOL.

Gottlieb, M. 2000. Standards-based, large-scale assessment of ESOL students. In *Implementing the ESL standards for pre-K–12 students through teacher education*, edited by M. A. Snow. Alexandria, VA: TESOL

Gouin, F. 1880;1882. *L'art d'enseigner et d'etudier les langues*. Paris: Librairie Fischbacher.

Gower, R. 1986. Can stylistic analysis help the EFL learner to read literature? *ELT Journal* 40(2): 125–130.

Grabe, W. 1991. Current developments in second language reading research. *TESOL Quarterly* 25(3): 375–406.

_____. 1997. Discourse analysis and reading instruction. In *Functional approaches to written text: Classroom applications*, edited by T. Miller. Washington, DC: United States Information Agency.

_____. 1999a. Reading research and its implications for reading assessment. In *Fairness and validation in language assessment: Selected papers from the 19th Language Testing Research Colloquium, Orlando, Florida*, edited by A. J. Kunnan. Cambridge: Cambridge University Press.

_____. 1999b. Developments in reading research and their implications for computer-adaptive reading assessment. In *Issues in computer-adaptive testing of reading proficiency* (Studies in Language Testing 10), edited by M. Chalhoub-deVille. Cambridge: Cambridge University Press.

————. 2001. Reading writing relations: Theoretical perspectives and instructional practices. In *Reading and writing relations in L2 contexts*, edited by D. Belcher and A. Hirvela. Ann Arbor: University of Michigan Press.

Grabe, W., and R. B. Kaplan. 1996. *Theory and practice of writing*. New York: Longman.

Grabe, W., and F. L. Stoller. 1997. Content-based instruction: Research foundations. In *The content-based classroom: Perspectives on integrating language and content*, edited by M. A. Snow and D. M. Brinton. New York: Longman.

————. In press. *Teaching and researching reading*. New York: Addison Wesley Longman.

Graddol, D. 1997. *The future of English?* London: The British Council.

Graham, C. 1978. *Jazz chants*. New York: Oxford University Press.

————. 1979. *Jazz chants for children*. New York: Oxford University Press.

————. 1986. *Small talk*. New York: Oxford University Press.

————. 1988. *Jazz chant fairy tales*. New York: Oxford University Press.

————. 1993. *Grammarchants: More jazz chants*. New York: Oxford University Press.

————. 1994. *Mother Goose jazz chants*. New York: Oxford University Press.

Graham, C., and S. Aragones. 1991. *Rhythm and role play*. Studio City, CA: JAG Publications.

Grant, L. 2000. *Toward discourse level pronunciation: Activities for speaking and listening*. Paper presented at the Annual TESOL Convention, Vancouver, Canada.

————. 2001. *Well said: Pronunciation for clear communication*. 2d ed. Boston, MA: Heinle & Heinle.

Grate, H. G. 1987. *English pronunciation exercises for Japanese students*. New York: Regents.

Graves, K. 2000. *Designing language courses: A guide for teachers*. Boston, MA: Heinle & Heinle.

————, ed. 1996. *Teachers as course developers*. Cambridge: Cambridge University Press.

Graves, M. F. 2000. A vocabulary program to complement and bolster a middle-grade comprehension program. In *Reading for meaning: Fostering comprehension in the middle grades*, edited by B. M. Taylor, M. F. Graves, and P. van den Brock. Newark, DE: International Reading Association.

Green, C. F., E. R. Christopher, and J. Lam. 1997. Developing discussion skills in the ESL classroom. *ELT Journal* 51: 135–143.

Green, J., and R. L. Oxford. 1995. A closer look at learning strategies, L2 proficiency, and gender. *TESOL Quarterly* 29: 261–297.

Grellet, F. 1996. *Writing for advanced learners of English*. Cambridge: Cambridge University Press.

Grice, P. H. 1975. Logic and conversation. In *Syntax and semantics: Vol. 3 Speech acts*, edited by P. Cole and J. L. Morgan. New York: Academic Press.

Grognet, A. G. 1997. Integrating employment skills in adult ESL instruction. ERIC Q&A. Available at: http://www.cal.org/ncle/DIGESTS/EskillsQA.htm.

Grosjean, F. 1982. *Life with two languages: An introduction to bilingualism*. Cambridge, MA: Harvard University Press.

Gueye, M. 1990, July. One step beyond ESP: English for development purposes (EDP). *English Teaching Forum* 28(3): 31–34.

Gunderson, L. 1991. *ESL literacy instruction*. Englewood Cliffs, NJ: Regents/Prentice Hall.

Guthrie, J. T., A. Wigfield, J. L. Metsala, and K. E. Cox. 1999. Motivational and cognitive predictors of text comprehension and reading amount. *Scientific Studies of Reading* 3: 231–256.

Habermas, J. 1970. Toward a theory of communicative competence. *Inquiry* 13: 360–375.

Hafernik, J. J., D. Messerschmidt, and S. Vandrick. 1996. What are IEP's really doing about content? *Journal of Intensive English Studies* 10: 31–47.

Hagen, S. 2000. *Sound advice: A basis for listening*. 2d ed. White Plains, NY: Pearson Education.

Haines, S. 1989. *Projects for the EFL classroom*. Edinburgh: Thomas Nelson and Sons.

Hairston, M. 1982. The winds of change: Thomas Kuhn and the revolution in the teaching of writing. *College Composition and Communication* 33(1): 76–88.

Hakuta, K. 1986. *Mirror of language: The debate on bilingualism*. New York: Basic Books.

Hale, G., C. Taylor, B. Bridgeman, J. Carson, B. Kroll, and R. Kantor. 1996. *A study of writing tasks assigned in academic degree programs*. TOEFL Research Report No. 54. Princeton, NJ: Educational Testing Service.

Hall, J. 1995. (Re)creating our worlds with words: A sociohistorical perspective of face-to-face interaction. *Applied Linguistics* 16(2): 206–232.

Halliday, M. A. K. 1970. Language structure and language function. In *New horizons in linguistics*, edited by J. Lyons. Harmondsworth, UK: Penguin.

————. 1973. *Explorations in the functions of language*. London: Edward Arnold.

————. 1975. *Learning how to mean*. New York: Elsevier.

————. 1978. *Language as social semiotic: The social interpretation of language and meaning*. Baltimore, MD: University Park Press.

————. 1985. *Spoken and written language*. Deakin, Australia: Deakin University Press.

————. 1994. *An introduction to functional grammar*. 2d ed. London: Edward Arnold.

Halliday, M. A. K., and R. Hasan. 1976. *Cohesion in English*. London: Longman.

Hamayah, E. V. 1995. Approaches to alternative assessment. In *Annual review of applied linguistics, 15. A survey of applied linguistics*, edited by W. Grabe et al. New York: Cambridge University Press.

Hamayan, E. 1994. Language development of low-literacy students. In *Educating second language children*, edited by F. Genesee. Cambridge: Cambridge University Press.

Hamp-Lyons, L. 1989. Raters respond to rhetoric in writing. In *Interlingual processes*, edited by H. W. Dechert and M. Raupach. Tubingen: Gunter Narr.

Hamp-Lyons, L., and W. Condon. 2000. *Assessing the portfolio: Principles for practice, theory, and research*. Cresskill, NJ: Hampton Press.

Hancock, M. 1995. *Pronunciation games*. Cambridge: Cambridge University Press.

Harklau, L., K. M. Losey, and M. Siegel, eds. 1999. *Generation 1.5 meets college composition*. Mahwah, NJ: Lawrence Erlbaum.

Harley, T. 1995. *The psychology of language: From data to theory*. East Sussex, UK: Psychology Press.

Harmer, J. 1991. *The practice of English language teaching*. Harlow, UK: Longman.

————. 1998. *How to teach English*. Harlow, UK: Longman.

Harris, D. P. 1969. *Testing English as a second language*. New York: McGraw-Hill.

Hartnett, D. 1985. Cognitive style and second language learning. In *Beyond basics: Issues and research in TESOL*, edited by M. Celce-Murcia. New York: Newbury House.

Hartwell, P. 1985. Grammar, grammars, and the teaching of grammar. *College English* 47: 105–127.

Hawkins, B. 1988. *Scaffolded classroom interaction and its relation to second language acquisition for language minority children*. Ph.D. diss., University of California, Los Angeles.

————. 1996. Reexamining instructional paradigms for K–12 second language learners. *The CATESOL Journal* 9(2): 21–54.

Heald-Taylor, G. 1991. *Whole language strategies for ESL students*. San Diego, CA: Dominie Press.

Hedge, T. 1988. *Writing*. Oxford: Oxford University Press.

————. 1993. Key concepts in ELT: Fluency. *ELT Journal* 47: 275–276.

Henrichsen, L., B. Green, A. Nishitani, and C. Bagley. 1999. *Pronunciation matters: Communicative, story-based activities for mastering the sounds of North American English*. Ann Arbor: University of Michigan Press.

Henriksen, B. 1988. Udvikling af sprogelevers pragmatiske bevidsthed: Et pædagogisk forsøg i gymnasiets engelskundervisning. In *Sproglig bevidsthed* (Copenhagen studies in bilingualism, vol. 7), edited by E. Hansen. Copenhagen.

Henry, J. 1994. *Teaching through projects*. London: Kogan Page.

Herman, M., and Sacks, P. 1977. *Tell me how to spell*. Tel Aviv: University Publishing Projects.

Herron, C., and Tomasello, M. 1988. Learning grammatical structures in a foreign language: modeling versus feedback. *The French Review* 61(6): 910–922.

Heubert, J., and R. Hauser, eds. 1999. *High stakes: Testing for tracking, promotion, and graduation*. Washington, DC: National Academy Press.

Hewings, M., and S. Goldstein. 1998. *Pronunciation plus: Practice through interaction.* Cambridge: Cambridge University Press.

Higgs, T. V., and R. Clifford. 1982. The push toward communication. In *Curriculum, competence, and the foreign language teacher,* edited by T. V. Clifford. Lincolnwood, IL: National Textbook Company.

Hill, J., and M. Lewis, eds. 1997. *Dictionary of selected collocations.* Hove, UK: Language Teaching Publications.

Hilles, S. 1991. Access to universal grammar in second language acquisition. In *Point counterpoint: Universal grammar in the second language,* edited by L. Eubank. Amsterdam: John Benjamins.

Hilleson, M. 1996. I want to talk to them but I don't want them to hear: An introspective study of second language anxiety in an English-medium school. In *Voices from the language classroom: Qualitative research on language education,* edited by K. M. Bailey and D. Nunan. New York: Cambridge University Press.

Hillocks, G., Jr. 1986. *Research on written composition: New directions for teaching.* Urbana, IL: ERIC Clearinghouse.

Hinkel, E. 1994. Native and nonnative speakers' pragmatic interpretations of English texts. *TESOL Quarterly* 28(2): 353–376.

_____. 1996. When in Rome: Evaluations of L2 pragmalinguistic behaviors. *Journal of Pragmatics* 26(1): 51–70.

_____. 1999. *Culture in second language teaching and learning.* Cambridge: Cambridge University Press.

Hoffman, C. 1991. *An introduction to bilingualism.* London: Longman.

Holec, H. 1979. *Autonomy and foreign language learning.* Strasbourg: Council of Europe.

Holliday, A. 1994. *Appropriate methodology and social context.* Cambridge: Cambridge University Press.

Holten, C. 1997. Literature: A quintessential content. In *The content-based classroom: Perspectives on integrating language and content,* edited by M. Snow and D. Brinton. New York: Longman.

Holten, C., and J. Marasco. 1998. *Looking ahead: Mastering academic writing, Book 4.* Boston, MA: Heinle & Heinle.

Hones, D. F. 1999. U.S. Justice? Critical pedagogy and the case of Mumia Abu-Jamal. *TESOL Journal* 8(4): 27–33.

Hornberger, N., L. Harsch, B. Evans, and M. Cahnmann. 1999. Language education of language minority students in the United States. *Working Papers in Educational Linguistics* 15(1): 1–92. Philadelphia, PA: University of Pennsylvania Graduate School of Education.

Hornberger, N., and E. Skilton-Sylvester. 2000. Revisiting the continua of biliteracy: International and critical perspectives. *Language and Education* 14(2): 96–122.

Horowitz, D. 1986. What professors actually require: Academic tasks for the ESL classroom. *TESOL Quarterly* 20(3): 445–462.

Hovanesian, S. 1999. Building community through family: Family web page and quilt project. In *Learners' lives as curriculum: Six journeys to immigrant literacy,* edited by G. Weinstein. McHenry, IL: Delta Systems.

Howatt, A. P. R. 1984. *A history of English language teaching.* Oxford: Oxford University Press.

Huang, Z. 1999. The impact of globalisation on English in Chinese universities. In *English in a changing world,* edited by D. Graddol and U. H. Meinhof. Oxford: English Book Company and AILA.

Hudelson, S. 1984. Kan yu ret an rayt en Ingles: Children become literate in English as a second language. *TESOL Quarterly* 18(2): 221–238.

_____, ed. 1993. *Teacher resource guide for ESL.* Thousand Oaks, CA: Corwin Press.

_____. 1994. Literacy development of second language children. In *Educating second language children,* edited by F. Genesee. Cambridge: Cambridge University Press.

Hudelson, S. J., and J. W. Lindfors. 1993. *Delicate balances: Collaborative research in language education.* Urbana, IL: National Council of Teachers of English.

Hudson, T., E. Detmer, and J. D. Brown. 1995. *Developing prototypic measures of cross-cultural pragmatics.* (Technical Report No. 7.) Honolulu, HI: Second Language Teaching and Curriculum Center, University of Hawaii at Manoa.

Hughes, A. 1989. *Testing for language teachers.* Cambridge: Cambridge University Press.

Hughes, R., and M. McCarthy. 1998. From sentence to discourse: Discourse grammar and English language teaching. *TESOL Quarterly* 32(2): 263–287.

Hughey, J. B., D. R. Wormuth, V. F. Hartfiel, and H. L. Jacobs. 1983. *Teaching ESL composition: Principles and techniques.* New York: Newbury House.

Hulstijn, J. H. 1997. Mnemonic methods in foreign language vocabulary learning. In *Second language vocabulary acquisition,* edited by J. Coady and T. Huckin. Cambridge: Cambridge University Press

Hurst, M. 1985. *Do teachers know what student want to learn? A needs assessment of adult students of English as a second language.* Ph.D. diss., University of Southern California.

Hutchinson, T. 1991. *Introduction to project work.* Oxford: Oxford University Press.

Hutchinson, T., and A. Waters. 1987. *English for specific purposes.* Cambridge: Cambridge University Press.

Hyland, K. 1998. *Hedging in scientific research articles.* Amsterdam/ Philadelphia: John Benjamins.

Hymes, D. 1971. Competence and performance in linguistic theory. In *Language acquisition: Models and methods,* edited by R. Huxley and E. Ingram. London: Academic Press

_____. 1972. On communicative competence. In *Sociolinguistics: Selected readings,* edited by J. P. Pride and J. Holmes. Harmondsworth, UK: Penguin.

_____. 1996. *Ethnography, linguistics, narrative inequality.* Bristol, PA: Taylor and Francis.

Illés, É. 1991. Correspondence. *ELT Journal* 45(1): 87.

Ilyin, D., and T. Tragardh, eds. 1978. *Classroom practices in adult ESL.* Washington, DC: TESOL.

Isaac, A. 1995. *Evaluating an integrated approach to teaching spoken fluency to second language learners.* Master's thesis, The University of Melbourne, Australia.

Iwataki, S. 1981. Preparing to teach in adult education programs. In *On TESOL '80: Building bridges: Research and practice in teaching English as a second language,* edited by J. C. Fischer, M. A. Clark, and J. Schachter. Washington, DC: TESOL.

Jacobs, H. L., S. A. Zingraf, D. R. Wormuth, V. F. Hartfiel, and J. B. Hughey. 1981. *Testing ESL composition: A practical approach.* New York: Newbury House.

Janzen, J., and F. L. Stoller. 1998. Integrating strategic reading in L2 instruction. *Reading in a Foreign Language* 12: 251–269.

Jenkins, J. 1998. Which pronunciation norms and models for English as an International Language? *ELT Journal* 52(2): 119–126.

Jerald, M., and R. Clark. 1983. *Experiential language teaching techniques: Resources handbook number 3.* Brattleboro, VT: Pro Lingua.

Johns, A. M. 1980. Cohesion in written business discourse: some contrasts. *ESP Journal* 1: 35–44.

_____. 1987. The language of business. *Annual Review of Applied Linguistics* 7: 3–17.

_____. 1997. *Text, role, and context: Developing academic literacies.* Cambridge: Cambridge University Press.

Johns, A. M., and T. Dudley-Evans. 1991. English for specific purposes: International in scope, specific in purpose. *TESOL Quarterly* 26(2): 297–314.

Johns, T. 1989. Whence and whither classroom concordancing? In *Computer applications in language learning,* edited by T. Bongaerts, P. de Haan, S. Lobbe and H. Wekker. Dordrecht, The Netherlands: Foris.

_____. 1994. From printout to handout: Grammar and vocabulary teaching in the context of data-driven learning. In *Perspectives on pedagogical grammar,* edited by T. Odlin. New York: Cambridge University Press.

Johnson, D., and R. Johnson. 1985. The internal dynamics of cooperative-learning groups. In *Learning to cooperate, cooperating to learn,* edited by R. Slavin et al. New York: Plenum Press.

Johnson, J. S., and E. L. Newport. 1989. Critical period effects in second language learning: The influence of maturational state on the acquisition of English as a second language. *Cognitive Psychology* 21: 60–99.

Johnson, K. 1983. *Now for English* (Course and activity Books 1, 2, 3). Surrey, UK: Thomas Nelson.

Johnson, K. E. 1992a. Learning to teach: Instructional actions and decisions of preservice ESL teachers. *TESOL Quarterly* 26(3): 507–535.

_____. 1992b. The instructional decisions of pre-service English as a second language teachers: New directions for teacher preparation programs. In *Perspectives on second language teacher development,* edited by

J. Flowerdew, M. Brock and S. Hsia. Hong Kong: City University of Hong Kong.

_____. 1998. *Teachers understanding teaching.* Boston, MA: Heinle & Heinle.

_____. 1999. *Understanding language teaching: Reasoning in action.* Boston, MA: Heinle & Heinle.

Johnson, P. 1999. *A history of the American people.* New York: Harper Perennial.

Johnson, R. K., and M. Swain, eds. 1997. *Immersion education: International perspectives.* Cambridge: Cambridge University Press.

Joiner, E. 1997. Teaching listening: How technology can help. In *Technology enhanced learning*, edited by M. D. Bush and R. M. Terry. Lincolnwood, IL: National Textbook Company.

Judd, E. L. 1978. Vocabulary teaching and TESOL: A need for re-evaluation of existing assumptions. *TESOL Quarterly* 12: 71–76.

Kachru, B. B. 1985. Standards, codification and sociolinguistic realism: The English language in the Outer Circle. In *English in the world: Teaching and learning the language and literature*, edited by R. Quirk and H. G. Widdowson. Cambridge/London: Cambridge University Press/The British Council.

_____. 1992. World Englishes: Approaches, issues and resources. *Language Teaching* 25(1): 1–14.

Kagan, S. 1986. Cooperative learning and sociocultural factors in schooling. In *Beyond language: Social and cultural factors in schooling language minority students.* Sacramento: California State Department of Education.

Kaplan, M. 1997. Learning to converse in a foreign language: The reception game. *Simulation and Gaming* 28(2): 149–163.

Kappra, R. 2000. How to integrate SCANS competencies into CALL, ESL, or computer literacy classes. *CATESOL News* 14 and 17.

Kasper, G. 1985. Repair in foreign language teaching. *Studies in Second Language Acquisition,* 7(2): 200–215.

Kasper, L. F. 1993. The keyword method and foreign language vocabulary learning: A rationale for its use. *Foreign Language Annals* 26: 244–251.

_____, ed. 2000. *Content-based college instruction.* Mahwah, NJ: Lawrence Erlbaum.

Kato, F. 1996. *Results of an Australian study of strategy use in learning Japanese Kanji characters.* Unpublished manuscript, University of Sydney, Australia.

Katz, A. 1996. Teaching style: A way to understand instruction in language classrooms. In *Voices from the language classroom: Qualitative research on language education*, edited by K. M. Bailey and D. Nunan. New York: Cambridge University Press.

_____. 2000. Changing paradigms for assessment. In *Implementing the ESL standards for pre-K–12 students through teacher education*, edited by M. A. Snow. Alexandria, VA: TESOL.

Ke, C. 1996. An empirical study on the relationship between Chinese recognition and production. *The Modern Language Journal* 80(3): 340–349.

Kealey, J., and D. Inness. 1997. *Grammar-focused shenigames.* Brattleboro, VT: Pro Lingua.

Kearsey, J., and S. Turner. 1999. Evaluating textbooks: The role of genre analysis. *Research in Science and Technological Education* 17(1): 35–44.

Kebir, C. 1994. An action research look at the communication strategies of adult learners. *TESOL Journal* 4(1): 28–31.

Keefe, J. W. 1979. Learning style: An overview. In *Student learning styles: Diagnosing and prescribing programs*, edited by J. W. Keefe. Reston, VA: National Association of Secondary School Principals.

Kelly, L. G. 1969. *Twenty-five centuries of language teaching.* Rowley, MA: Newbury House.

Kemmis, S., and McTaggart, K. 1982. *The action research planner.* Victoria, Australia: Deakin University.

Kemmis, S., and McTaggart, R. 1989. Action research. *IATEFL Newsletter* 102: 2–3.

Kern, R. 1998. Technology, social interaction, and FL literacy. In *New ways of teaching and learning: Focus on technology and foreign language education*, edited by J. Muyskens. Boston, MA: Heinle & Heinle.

Kilpatrick, W. H. 1918. *The project method: The use of the purposeful act in the educative process.* New York: Teachers College, Columbia University.

Kincheloe, J. L. 1991. *Teachers as researchers: Qualitative inquiry as a path to empowerment.* London: The Falmer Press.

Kinsella, K. 1997. Moving from comprehensible input to "learning to learn" in content-based instruction. In *The content-based classroom:*

Perspectives on integrating language and content, edited by M. A. Snow and D. M. Brinton. New York: Longman.

Kintsh, W., and T. A. van Dijk. 1978. Toward a model of text comprehension and production, *Psychological Review* 85(5): 363–394.

Kirsch, I., A. Jungeblut, L. Jenkins, and A. Kolstad. 1993. *Adult literacy in America: A first look at the results of the National Adult Literacy Survey.* Washington, DC: U.S. Department of Education, National Center for Educational Statistics.

Klein-Braley, C. 1981. *Empirical investigations of cloze tests: An examination of the validity of cloze tests as tests of general language proficiency in English for German university students.* Ph.D. diss., University of Duisburg, West Germany.

Klein-Braley, C., and U. Raatz. 1984. A survey of research on the C-test. *Language Testing* 1(2): 134–146.

Knowles, M. 1976. Contract learning. In *Materials and methods in continuing education*, edited by C. Klevins. Canoga Park, CA: Klevins.

Knowles, M., and C. Klevins. 1976. History and philosophy of continuing education. In *Materials and methods in continuing education*, edited by C. Klevins. Canoga Park, CA: Klevins.

Kohlberg, L. 1981. *Essays on moral development.* San Francisco: Harper and Row.

Kohonnen, V. 1992. Experiential language learning: Second language learning as cooperative learner education. In *Collaborative language learning and teaching*, edited by D. Nunan. Cambridge: Cambridge University Press.

Kolb, D. 1984. *Experiential learning: Experience as the source of learning and development.* Englewood Cliffs, NJ: Prentice Hall.

Kovalik, S. with Olsen, K. 1997. *ITI: The model: Integrated thematic instruction.* 3d ed. Kent, WA: Books for Educators.

Kramsch, C. 1993. *Context and culture in language teaching.* Oxford: Oxford University Press.

_____. 1997. The privilege of the non-native speaker. *Publications of the Modern Language Association of America* 112(3): 359–369.

Krashen, S. D. 1978. The monitor model for second-language acquisition. In *Second language acquisition and foreign language teaching*, edited by R. Gingras. Washington, DC: Center for Applied Linguistics.

_____. 1981. *Second language acquisition and second language learning.* Oxford: Pergamon Press.

_____. 1982. *Principles and practice in second language acquisition.* Oxford: Pergamon Press.

_____. 1984. Immersion: Why it works and what it has taught us. *Language and Society* 12: 61–64.

_____. 1987. Applications of psycholinguistic research to the classroom. In *Methodology in TESOL: A book of readings*, edited by M. H. Long and J. C. Richards. New York: Newbury House.

_____. 1999. *Condemned without a trial: Bogus arguments against bilingual education.* Portsmouth, NH: Heinemann.

Krashen, S. D., R. C. Scarcella, and M. H. Long, eds. 1982. *Child-adult differences in second language acquisition.* Rowely, MA: Newbury House.

Krashen, S. D., and T. D. Terrell. 1983. *The natural approach: Language acquisition in the classroom.* New York: Pergamon Press.

Kress, G. 1985. *Linguistic processes in sociocultural practice.* Oxford: Oxford University Press.

Kroll, B. In press. An overview of the second language writing classroom. *Odense Working Papers in Language and Communication.*

Krueger, M., and F. Ryan, eds. 1993. *Language and content: Discipline- and content-based approaches to language study.* Lexington, MA: D.C. Heath.

Ku, P. N. 1995. *Strategies associated with proficiency and predictors of strategy choice: A study of language learning strategies of EFL students at three educational levels in Taiwan.* Ph.D. diss., Indiana University, Bloomington.

Kuhlman, N., and D. E. Murray. 2000. Changing populations, changing needs in teacher preparation. In *Implementing the ESL standards for pre-K–12 students in teacher education*, edited by M. A. Snow. Alexandria, VA: TESOL.

Kuhn, T. S. 1970. *The structure of scientific revolutions.* Chicago: University of Chicago Press.

Kusano H. K. In press. Zen and the Art of ELT. In *Communicative language teaching in translation: Contexts and concerns in teacher education*, edited by S. J. Savignon.

Ladybug: The Magazine for Young Children. Peru, IL: Carus Publishing.

Lambert, W. E., R. C. Gardner, H. C. Barik, and E. Tunstall. 1963.

Attitudinal and cognitive aspects of intensive study of a second language. *Journal of Abnormal and Social Psychology* 66(4): 358–368.

Lane, J., and E. Lange. 1999. *Writing clearly: An editing guide.* 2d ed. Boston, MA: Heinle & Heinle.

Lange, D. L. 1990. A blueprint for a teacher development program. In *Second language teacher education,* edited by J. C. Richards and D. Nunan. Cambridge: Cambridge University Press.

Lantolf, J. 2000. Second language learning as a mediated process. *Language Teaching* April: 79–96.

Lantolf, J. P., and G. Appel, eds. 1994. *Vygotskian approaches to second language research.* Norwood, NJ: Ablex.

Lapkin, S., ed. 1998. *French as a second language in Canada: Recent empirical studies.* Toronto: Toronto University Press.

Larimer, R. E., and L. Schleicher, eds. 1999. *New ways in using authentic materials in the classroom.* Alexandria, VA: TESOL.

Larsen-Freeman, D. 1986. *Techniques and principles in language teaching.* Oxford: Oxford University Press.

_____. 1991. Consensus and divergence on the content, role, and process of teaching grammar. In *Georgetown University roundtable on languages and linguistics 1991. Linguistics and language pedagogy: The state of the art,* edited by J. E. Alatis. Washington, DC: Georgetown University Press.

_____. 1995. On the teaching and learning of grammar: Challenging the myths. In *Second language acquisition theory and pedagogy,* edited by F. Eckman, D. Highland, P. Lee, J. Mileham, and R. Rutkowski Weber. Mahwah, NJ: Lawrence Erlbaum.

_____. 1997. Chaos/Complexity science and second language acquisition. *Applied Linguistics* 18(2): 141–165.

_____. 2000a. Grammar: Reasons and rules working together. *ESL Magazine* January/February: 10–12.

_____. 2000b. *Techniques and principles in language teaching.* 2d ed. New York: Oxford University Press.

_____. 2001. *Teaching language: From grammar to grammaring.* Boston, MA: Heinle & Heinle.

Larson, J. W., and H. S. Madsen. 1985. Computerized adaptive language testing: Moving beyond computer assisted testing. *CALICO Journal* 2(3): 32–36.

Laufer, B. 1986. Possible changes in attitude towards vocabulary acquisition. *International Review of Applied Linguistics* 24(1): 69–75.

Law, B., and M. Eckes. 2000. *The more-than-just-surviving handbook: ESL for every classroom teacher.* 2d ed. Winnipeg, Canada: Peguis Publishers.

Lazaraton, A. 1996. Interlocutor support in oral proficiency interviews: The case of CASE. *Language Testing* 13: 151–172.

Lazaraton, A., and P. F. Skuder. 1997, March. *Evaluating dialogue authenticity in ESL speaking texts.* Paper presented at the 31st Annual TESOL Convention, Orlando, FL.

Lea, M. R., and B. Street. 1999. Writing as academic literacies: Understanding textual practices in higher education. In *Writing: Texts, processes and practices,* edited by C. N. Candlin and K. Hyland. New York: Longman.

Lebauer, R. S. 2000. *Learn to listen, listen to learn: Academic listening and note-taking.* 2d ed. White Plains, NY: Pearson Education.

Lee, C. 1996. *Native speaker.* Berkeley: Berkeley Publishing Group.

Lee, J. S., and B. McChesney. 2000. Discourse rating tasks: A teaching tool for developing sociocultural competence. *ELT Journal* 54: 161–168.

Legutke, M. 1984. Project airport. Part I. *Modern English Teacher* 4: 10–14.

_____. 1985. Project airport. Part II. *Modern English Teacher* 12: 28–31.

Legutke, M., and H. Thomas. 1991. *Process and experience in the language classroom.* Harlow, UK: Longman.

Leinhardt, G., and J. G. Greeno. 1986. The cognitive skill of teaching. *Journal of Educational Psychology* 78(2): 75–95.

Leki, I. 1990. Potential problems with peer responding in ESL writing classes. *CATESOL Journal* 3(1): 5–19.

_____. 1992. *Understanding ESL writers: A guide for teachers.* Portsmouth, NJ: Boynton/Cook Heinemann.

Lemke, J. L. 1993. *Talking science: Language, learning, and values.* Norwood, NJ: Ablex.

Leshinsky, J. G. 1995. *Authentic listening and discussion for advanced students.* Upper Saddle River, NJ: Prentice Hall Regents.

Lester, R. B. 1994. Cocktail party. In *New ways in teaching speaking,* edited by K. M. Bailey and L. Savage. Alexandria, VA: TESOL.

Levenston, E. A., R, Nir, and S. Blum-Kulka. 1984. Discourse analysis and the testing of reading comprehension by cloze techniques. In *Reading for professional purposes,* edited by A. K. Pugh and J. M. Ulijn. London: Longman.

Levin, L. 1972. *Comparative studies in foreign language teaching.* Stockholm: Almquist and Wiksell.

Levinson, S. 1983. *Pragmatics.* Cambridge: Cambridge University Press.

Levis, J. 2000. *Bridging the gap between controlled and spontaneous speech.* Paper presented at the Annual TESOL Convention, Vancouver, Canada.

Lewin, K. 1946. Action research and minority problems. *Journal of Social Issues* 2: 34–46.

Lewis, M. 1993. *The lexical approach.* Hove, UK: Language Teaching.

_____. 1997. *Implementing the lexical approach.* Hove, UK: Language Teaching.

Lewkowicz, J. A. 1997. Authentic for whom? Does authenticity really matter? In *Current developments and alternatives language assessment: Proceedings of LTRC 96,* edited by A. Huhta, V. Kohonen, L. Kurki-Suonio, and S. Luoma. Jyväskylä, Finland: University of Jyväskylä and University of Tampere.

Lightbown, P. 1998. The importance of timing in focus on form. In *Focus on form in classroom second language acquisition,* edited by C. Doughty and J. Williams. New York: Cambridge University Press.

Lim, P., and W. Smalzer. 1995. *Noteworthy: Listening and notetaking skills.* Boston, MA: Heinle & Heinle.

Linguistic Society of America. 1996. LSA Statement on Language Rights. Washington, DC: Linguistic Society of America. (Also on the web at http://www.lsadc.org/web2/lgright.htm)

Little, D. 1991. *Learner autonomy 1: Definitions, issues, and problems.* Dublin: Authentik.

_____. 1994. Words and their properties: Arguments for a lexical approach to pedagogical grammar. In *Perspectives on pedagogical grammar,* edited by T. Odlin. New York: Cambridge University Press.

Littlewood, W. 1981. *Communicative language teaching.* Cambridge: Cambridge University Press.

Liu, D. 1999. Training non-native TESOL students: Challenges for TESOL teacher education in the West. In *Non-native educators in English language teaching,* edited by G. Braine. Mahwah, NJ: Lawrence Erlbaum.

Liu, J. 1999. Non-native-English-speaking professionals in TESOL. *TESOL Quarterly* 33(1): 85–102.

Llanas, A., and E. Taylor. 1983. *Sunrise 1.* Surrey, UK: Thomas Nelson.

LoCastro, V. 1989. *Large size classes: The situation in Japan.* (Project Report No. 5.) Leeds, UK: Lancaster-Leeds Language Learning in Large Classes Research Project.

Long, M. H. 1980a. *Input, interaction, and second language acquisition.* Ph.D. diss., University of California, Los Angeles.

_____. 1980b. Inside the "black box": Methodological issues in research on language teaching and learning. *Language Learning* 30(1): 1–42. Reprinted in *Classroom oriented research in second language acquisition,* edited by H. W. Seliger and M. H. Long. Rowley, MA: Newbury House, 1983.

_____. 1983. Does second language instruction make a difference? A review of research. *TESOL Quarterly* 17(3): 359–382.

_____. 1985. The design of classroom second language acquisition: towards task-based language teaching. In *Modeling and assessing second language acquisition,* edited by K. Hyltenstam and M. Pienemann. London: Multilingual Matters.

_____. 1990. Maturational constraints on language development. *Studies in Second Language Acquisition* 12: 251–285.

_____. 1991. Focus on form: A design feature in language teaching methodology. In *Foreign language research in cross-cultural perspective,* edited by K. de Bot, R. Ginsberg and C. Kramsch. Amsterdam: John Benjamins.

Long, M. H., L. Adams, M. McLean, and F. Castanos. 1976. Doing things with words: Verbal interaction in lockstep and small-group classroom situations. In *On TESOL '76,* edited by R. Crymes and J. Fanselow. Washington, DC: TESOL.

Long, M. H., C. Brock, G. Crookes, C. Deicke, L. Potter, and S. Zhang. 1984. *The effect of teachers' questioning patterns and wait-time on pupil participation patterns in public high school classes in Hawaii for students of limited English proficiency.* (Technical Report No. 1.) Honolulu, HI: University of Hawaii, Center for Second Language Classroom Research, Social Science Research Institute.

Long, M. H., and G. Crookes. 1987. Intervention points in second language classroom processes. In *Patterns of classroom interaction in Southeast Asia*, edited by B. Das. Singapore: RELC.

_____. 1993. Units of analysis in syllabus design-the case for task. In *Tasks in a pedagogical context: Integrating theory and practice*, edited by G. Crookes and S. M. Gass. Clevedon, UK: Multilingual Matters.

Long, M. H., S. Inagaki, and L. Ortega. 1998. The role of implicit negative feedback in SLA: Models and recasts in Japanese and Spanish. *The Modern Language Journal* 82(3): 357–371.

Long, M. H., and P. Porter. 1985. Groupwork, interlanguage talk, and second language acquisition. *TESOL Quarterly* 19(2): 207–227.

Long, M. H., and J. Richards, eds. 1987. *Methodology in TESOL*. Rowley, MA: Newbury House.

Long, M. H., and P. Robinson. 1998. Focus on form: Theory, research, and practice. In *Focus on form in classroom second language acquisition*, edited by C. Doughty and J. Williams. New York: Cambridge University Press.

Long, M. H., and C. Sato. 1983. Classroom foreigner talk discourse: Forms and functions of teachers' questions. In *Classroom-oriented research in second language acquisition*, edited by H. W. Seliger and M. H. Long. New York: Newbury House.

Lorenz, E. B., and M. Met. 1988. *What it means to be an immersion teacher*. Rockville, MD: Office of Instruction and Program Development, Montgomery County Public Schools.

Loschky, L., and R. Bley-Vroman. 1993. Grammar and task-based methodology. In *Tasks and language learning: Integrating theory and practice*, edited by G. Crookes and S. M. Gass. Clevedon, UK: Multilingual Matters.

Low, G. D. 1985. Validity and the problem of direct language proficiency tests. In *Lancaster practical papers in English language education*, Vol. 6, edited by J. C. Alderson. Oxford: Pergamon Press.

_____. 1986. Storylines and other developing contexts in use-of-language test design. *Indian Journal of Applied Linguistics* 12: 15–38.

Lozanov, G. 1978. *Suggestology and outlines of suggestopedy*. New York: Gordon and Breach Science.

Lozanov, G. 1982. Suggestion and suggestopedy. In *Innovative approaches to language teaching*, edited by R. W. Blair. New York: Newbury House.

Lucas, T. 1997. *Into, through, and beyond secondary school: Critical transitions for immigrant youths*. McHenry, IL: Center for Applied Linguistics/Delta Systems.

Lucas, T., and A. Katz. 1994. Reframing the debate: The roles of native languages in English-only programs for language minority students. *TESOL Quarterly* 28(3): 537–561.

Lucas-Uygun, J. 1994. Secret audio pals. In *New ways in teaching speaking*, edited by K. M. Bailey and L. Savage. Alexandria, VA: TESOL.

Lynch, T. 1983. *Study listening*. Oxford: Oxford University Press.

_____. 1996. *Communication in the language classroom*. Oxford: Oxford University Press.

Lyster, R. 1998a. Recasts, repetition, and ambiguity in L2 classroom discourse. *Studies in Second Language Acquisition* 20(1): 51–81.

_____. 1998b. Negotiation of form, recasts, and explicit correction in relation to error types and learner repair in immersion classrooms. *Language Learning* 48(2): 183–218.

Lyster, R., and L. Ranta. 1997. Corrective feedback and learner uptake: Negotiation of form in communicative classrooms. *Studies in Second Language Acquisition* 19(1): 37–66.

Ma, L. 1999. *Knowing and teaching elementary mathematics: Teachers' understanding of fundamental mathematics in China and the United States*. Mawah, NJ: Lawrence Erlbaum.

Mach, T., and F. L. Stoller. 1997. Synthesizing content on a continuum. In *New ways in content-based instruction*, edited by D. Brinton and P. Masters. Alexandria, VA: TESOL.

Macias, A. 2000. Workforce education, perspectives on border issues. *Journal of Borderlands Studies* 15(2).

MacIntyre, P. D., and K. A. Noels. 1996. Using social psychological variables to predict the use of language learning strategies. *Foreign Language Annals* 29: 373–386.

Mackey, W. 1978. A typology of bilingual education. In *Bilingual schooling in the United States*, 2d ed., edited by T. Andersson and M. Boyer. Austin, TX: National Educational Laboratory.

MacWhinney, B. 1997. Second language acquisition and the competition model. In *Tutorials in bilingualism: Psycholinguistic perspectives*, edited by A. M. B. de Groot and J. F. Kroll. Hillsdale, NJ: Lawrence Erlbaum.

Madsen, H. S. 1986. Evaluating a computer-adaptive ESL placement test. *CALICO Journal* 4(2): 41–50.

Maley, A., and A. Duff. 1978. *Drama techniques in language learning*. Cambridge: Cambridge University Press.

_____. 1989. *The inward ear: Poetry in the language classroom*. Cambridge: Cambridge University Press.

Maley, A., and S. Moulding. 1979. *Learning to listen*. Cambridge: Cambridge University Press.

Marinova-Todd, S. H., D. B. Marshall, and C. E. Snow. 2000. Three misconceptions about age and L2 learning. *TESOL Quarterly* 34(1): 9–34.

Markee, N. 2000. *Conversation analysis*. Mahwah, NJ: Lawrence Erlbaum.

Markee, N. P. 1994. Toward an ethnomethodological respecification of second-language studies. In *Research methodology in second-language acquisition*, edited by E. E. Tarone, S. M. Gass and A. D. Cohen. Mahwah, NJ: Lawrence Erlbaum.

Marshall, B. 1997a. How can ESL teachers respond to welfare reform? *Learning a Living*. Sacramento, CA: Author

_____. 1997b. Keeping learner empowerment on the agenda: How ESL teachers can respond to welfare reform. *CATESOL News* 14, 16, 18, and 22.

Maslow, A. 1962. *Towards a psychology of being*. Princeton, NJ: Van Nostrand.

Mason, A. 1994. By dint of: Student and lecturer perceptions of lecture comprehension strategies in first-term graduate study. In *Academic listening: Research perspectives*, edited by J. Flowerdew. Cambridge: Cambridge University Press.

Master, P. 1983. The etiquette of observing. *TESOL Quarterly* 17: 497–501.

Matsuda, P. 1998. Situating ESL writing in a cross-disciplinary context. *Written Communication* 15(1): 99-121.

_____. 1999. Composition studies and ESL writing: A disciplinary division of labor. *College Composition and Communication* 50(4): 699–721.

Matsumoto, K. 1989. An analysis of a Japanese ESL learner's diary: Factors involved in the L2 learning process. *JALT Journal* 11: 167–192.

Matsunobu, J. 1983. *Discourse and rhetoric in graduate business lectures: A comparative study*. Paper presented at the 17th Annual TESOL Conference, Toronto, Canada.

McAlpin, J. 1980. *The magazine picture library*. London: George Allen and Unwin.

McCaleb, S. P. 1994. *Building communities of learners: A collaboration among teachers, students, families and community*. New York: St. Martin's Press.

McCarthy, B. 1994. *Grammar drills: What CALL can and cannot do*. Paper presented at the EUROCALL Meeting, Karlsruhe, Germany. (ERIC Doc. No. ED 38 20 22).

McCarthy, M. 1984. A new look at vocabulary in EFL. *Applied Linguistics* 5: 12–22.

_____. 1998. *Spoken language and applied linguistics*. Cambridge: Cambridge University Press.

McCloskey, M. L., and L. Stack. 1993. *Voices in literature*. Boston, MA: Heinle & Heinle.

McGroarty, M. 1998. *Partnerships with linguistic minority communities*. (TESOL Professional Paper No. 4.) Alexandria, VA: TESOL.

_____. In press. Evolving influences on language policy. In *Language policies in education: Critical issues*, edited by J. Tollefson. Mahwah, NJ: Lawrence Erlbaum.

McGroarty, M., and S. Scott. 1993. *Workplace ESL instruction: Varieties and constraints*. Washington, DC: National Clearinghouse for ESL Literacy Education. (ERIC Doc. No. ED 367 190)

McIntire, R. D. 1988. *Study of the instructional impact on adults enrolled in English as a second language classes with respect to employment*. Ph.D. diss., Santa Barbara University.

McKay, S. 1982. Literature in the ESL classroom. *TESOL Quarterly* 16(4): 529–536.

_____. 2000. English language learners and educational investments. In *New immigrants in the United States*, edited by S. McKay and S. L. Wong. Cambridge: Cambridge University Press.

_____. In press. It's certainly been nice to see you: Using plays to develop sociolinguistic competence. *Guidelines*.

McKeon, D., and K. D. Samway. 1993. Common threads, common bonds. In *Common threads of practice: Teaching English to children around the world*, edited by K. D. Samway and D. McKeon. Arlington, VA: TESOL.

McLaughlin, B. 1987. *Theories of second language acquisition.* London: Edward Arnold.

McLaughlin, B., T. Rossman, and B. McLeod. 1983. Second language learning: An information-processing perspective. *Language Learning* 33: 135–158.

McLaughlin, D. 1992. *When literacy empowers: Navajo language in print.* Albuquerque: University of New Mexico Press.

McLean, J. 1995. *Improving education through action research: A guide for administrators and teachers.* Thousand Oaks, CA: Corwin Press.

McNamara, T. 1996. *Measuring second language performance.* Harlow, UK: Longman.

_____. 2000. *Language testing.* Oxford: Oxford University Press.

McPherson, P. 1997. Action research: Exploring learner diversity. *Prospect: A Journal of Australian TESOL* 12(1): 50–62.

Meara, P. 1981. Vocabulary acquisition: A neglected aspect of language learning. In *Cambridge language teaching surveys 3,* edited by K. Kinsella. Cambridge: Cambridge University Press.

_____. 1995. The importance of a early emphasis on L2 vocabulary. *The Language Teacher* 19(2): 8–10.

Meara, P., and B. Buxton. 1987. An alternative to multiple-choice vocabulary tests. *Language Testing* 4(2): 2–154

Medgyes, P. 1994. *The non-native teacher.* Basingstoke, UK: Macmillan.

_____. 1999a. Language training in teacher education. In *Non-native educators in English language teaching,* edited by G. Braine. Mahwah, NJ: Lawrence Erlbaum.

_____. 1999b. *The non-native teacher.* 2d ed. Ismaning, Germany: Hueher Verlag.

Mee, C., and N. Moi, eds. 1999. *Language instructional issues in Asian class-rooms.* Newark, DE: International Development in Asia Committee of the International Reading Association.

Mellon, J. 1969. *Transformational sentence combining: A method for enhancing the development of syntactic fluency in English composition.* Urbana, IL: National Council of Teachers of English.

Mendelsohn, D. 1995. Applying learning strategies in the second/foreign language listening comprehension lesson. In *A guide for the teaching of second language listening,* edited by D. Mendelsohn and J. Rubin. San Diego, CA: Dominie Press.

Mendelsohn, D., and J. Rubin, eds. 1995. *A guide for the teaching of second language listening.* San Diego, CA: Dominie Press.

Merrifield, J. 1998. *Contested ground: Performance accountability in adult basic education.* (Report No. 1.). National Center for the Study of Adult Learning and Literacy.

Met, M. 1998. Curriculum decision-making in content-based second language teaching. In *Beyond bilingualism: Multilingualism and multilingual education,* edited by J. Cenoz and F. Genesee. Clevedon, UK: Multilingual Matters.

_____. 1999. *Content-based instruction: Defining terms, making decisions.* NFLC Report, January. Washington, DC: National Foreign Language Center.

Mey, J. 1993. *Pragmatics: An introduction.* Oxford: Blackwell.

Meyers, C., and S. Holt. 1998. *Pronunciation for success.* Burnsville, MN: Aspen Productions.

Mezirow, J. 1981. A critical theory of adult learning and education. *Adult Education* 32(1): 3–24.

Michonska-Stadnik, A., and M. Szulc-Kurpaska, eds. 1997. *Action research in the lower Silesia cluster colleges: Developing learner independence.* A special edition of Orbis Linguarum. Legnica, Poland: Nauczycielskie Kolegium Jezkw Obcych and the British Council.

Miller, S. 2000. *Targeting pronunciation.* Boston, MA: Houghton Mifflin.

Minsky, M. L. 1975. A framework for representing knowledge. In *The psychology of computer vision,* edited by P. H. Winston. New York: McGraw Hill.

Miramontes, O., A. Nadeau, and N. Commins. 1997. *Restructuring schools for linguistic diversity: Linking decision making to effective programs.* New York: Teachers College Press.

Mitchell, R. 2000. Applied linguistics and evidence-based classroom practice: The case of foreign language grammar pedagogy. *Applied Linguistics* 21(3): 281–303.

Mitoma, D., and K. Son. 1999. Sequencing information competence skills in an ESL program. *The CATESOL Journal* 11(1): 123–136.

Mohan, B. A. 1986. *Language and content.* Reading, MA: Addison-Wesley.

Mollica, A. S. 1979. Print and non-print materials: Adapting for class-room use. In *Building on experience: Building for success,* edited by J. K. Phillips. Skokie, IL: National Textbook Company.

Montone, C., and M. Loeb. 2000. *Implementing two-way immersion programs in secondary schools.* (Educational Practice Report No. 5.) Washington, DC: Center for Research on Education, Diversity, and Excellence/Center for Applied Linguistics.

Morgan, J., and M. Rinvolucri. 1983. *Once upon a time.* Cambridge: Cambridge University Press.

Morley, J. 1972. *Improving aural comprehension.* Ann Arbor: University of Michigan Press.

_____. 1979. *Improving spoken English.* Ann Arbor: University of Michigan Press.

_____. 1984. *Listening and language learning in ESL.* Englewood Cliffs, NJ: Prentice-Hall.

_____. 1985. Listening comprehension: Student-controlled modules for self-access self-study. *TESOL Newsletter* 19(6): 1, 32–33.

_____. 1992. *Extempore speaking practice.* Ann Arbor: University of Michigan Press.

_____. 1995. Academic listening comprehension instruction: Models, principles, and practices. In *A guide for teaching second language listening,* edited by D. Mendelsohn and J. Rubin. San Diego, CA: Dominie Press.

_____. 1999a. Current perspectives on improving aural comprehension. *ESL Magazine* 2(1): 15–19.

_____. 1999b. New developments in speech/pronunciation instruction. *As We Speak . . .* (Newsletter of the TESOL Speech/Pronunciation Interest Section) 2(1): 1–5.

Morris, C. 1939. *Foundations of a theory of signs.* Chicago: Chicago University Press.

Moskowitz, G. 1978. *Caring and sharing in the foreign language class: A sourcebook on humanistic techniques.* Rowley, MA: Newbury House.

Moss, D., and C. Van Duzer. 1998. Project-based learning for adult English language learners. ERIC Digest, National Clearinghouse for ESL Literacy Education. (ERIC Doc. No. EDO-LE-98-07)

Mullins, P. 1992. *Successful English language learning strategies of students enrolled in the faculty of arts, Chulalongkorn University, Bangkok, Thailand.* Ph.D. diss., United States International University, San Diego, CA.

Munby, J. 1978. *Communicative syllabus design.* Cambridge: Cambridge University Press.

Murdoch, G. 1994. Language development in teacher training curricula. *ELT Journal* 48(3): 253–259.

Murphey, T. 1997. Content-based instruction in an EFL setting: Issues and strategies. In *The content-based classroom: Perspectives on integrating language and content,* edited by M. A. Snow and D. M. Brinton. New York: Longman.

Murphy, J. 1992. An etiquette for the nonsupervisory observation of L2 classrooms. *Foreign Language Annals* 25(3): 215–225.

Murphy, J., and H. Byrd. In press. *Understanding the courses we teach: Local perspectives on English language teaching.* Ann Arbor: University of Michigan Press.

Murphy, J. M. 1991. Oral communication in TESOL: Integrating speaking, listening, and pronunciation. *TESOL Quarterly* 25(1): 51–75.

Murphy, T. 1992. *Music and song.* Oxford: Oxford University Press.

Musumeci, D. 1997. *Breaking tradition: An exploration of the historical relationship between theory and practice in second language teaching.* New York: McGraw Hill.

Nagle, S. J., and S. L. Sanders. 1986. Comprehension theory and second language pedagogy. *TESOL Quarterly* 20(1): 9–26.

Naiman, N., M. Fröhlich, H. H. Stern, and A. Todesco. 1975. *The good language learner.* Toronto: Ontario Institute for Studies in Education.

Nash, A., ed. 1999. *Civic participation and community action sourcebook.* New England Literacy Resource Center.

Nash, A., A. Cason, L. McGrail, and R. Gomez-Sanford. 1992. *Talkin shop.* Center for Applied Linguistics. McHenry, IL: Delta Systems.

Nation, I. S. P. 1990. *Teaching and learning vocabulary.* Boston, MA: Heinle & Heinle.

National Clearinghouse for ESL Literacy Education. 1998. *Research agenda for adult ESL.* Washington, DC: Center for Applied Linguistics.

National Council of Teachers of English. 1982. *NCTE position statement on TESOL and bilingual education.* Urbana, IL: National Council of Teachers of English.

_____. 1997. *Standards for the English language arts*. Urbana, IL: National Council of Teachers of English.

National Council of Teachers of Mathematics. 2000. *Principles and standards for school mathematics*. Reston, VA: National Council of Teachers of Mathematics.

National Languages and Literacy Institute of Australia. 1993. *ESL development: Language and literacy in schools: Vol. 1. Teacher's volume*. Canberra, Australia: National Languages and Literacy Institute of Australia.

National Literacy Summit. 2000. *From the margins to the mainstream: An action agenda for literacy*. Washington, DC: National Literacy Summit.

Nattinger, J. R. 1988. Some current trends in vocabulary teaching. In *Vocabulary and language teaching*, edited by R. Carter and M. McCarthy. London: Longman.

Nattinger, J. R., and J. S. DeCarrico. 1992. *Lexical phrases and language teaching*. Oxford: Oxford University Press.

Neisser, U. 1967. *Cognitive psychology*. New York: Appleton, Century, Crofts.

Nelson, G., with J. Burns. 2000. Managing information for writing university exams in American history. In *Sustained content teaching in academic ESL/EFL*, edited by M. Pally. Boston, MA: Houghton Mifflin.

Nelson, G., and T. Winters. 1993. *Operations in ESL*. Brattleboro, VT: Pro Lingua.

Nesbit, T. 1997. Michela Stone. In *Life at the margins: Literacy, language and technology in everyday life*, edited by J. Merrifield, M. B. Bingman, D. Hemphill, and K. B. deMarrais. New York: Teacher's College Press.

Nevo, D. L., L. Weinbach, and N. Mark. 1987. *Final report on the pilot research on the evaluation of achievement in writing in elementary schools*. Tel Aviv, Israel: Tel Aviv University.

Newmark, G. and E. Diller. 1964. Emphasizing the audio in the audio-lingual approach. *Modern Language Journal* 48(1): 18–20.

Nicholson, T., and A. Tan. 1999. Proficient word identification for comprehension. In *Learning to read: Beyond phonics and whole language*, edited by G. B. Thompson and R. Nicholson. New York: Teachers College Press.

Nida, E. 1953. Selective listening. *Language Learning: A Journal of Applied Linguistics* 4(3/4): 92–101.

_____. 1982. Learning by listening. In *Innovative approaches to language teaching*, edited by R. Blair. Rowley, MA: Newbury House.

Nilsen, D. L. F., and A. P. Nilsen. 1987. *Pronunciation contrasts in English*. Englewood Cliffs, NJ: Prentice Hall Regents.

Nixon, T., and F. Keenan. 1997. *Citizenship preparation for adult ESL learners*. Washington, DC: National Clearinghouse for ESL Literacy Education. (ERIC Doc. No. EDO-LE-97-04)

Noll, M. 1997. *American accent skills: Books 1 and 2*. Oakland, CA: Ameritalk Press.

Nord, J. R. 1981. Three steps leading to listening fluency: A beginning. In *The comprehension approach to foreign language instruction*, edited by H. Winitz. Rowley, MA: Newbury House.

Norris, J. M., J. D. Brown, T. Hudson, and J. Yoshioka. 1998. *Designing second language performance assessments*. (Technical Report No. 18.) Honolulu, HI: Second Language Teaching and Curriculum Center, University of Hawaii Press.

Norris, J., and L. Ortega. 2000. Effectiveness of L2 instruction: A research synthesis and quantitative meta-analysis. *Language Learning* 50(3): 417–528.

Northern California Grantmakers. 1998. *New citizens vote!* San Francisco, CA: Northern California Citizenship Project.

Norton, B. 1997. Language, identity, and the ownership of English. *TESOL Quarterly* 31(3): 409–429.

Numrich, C. 1995. *Consider the issues*. White Plains, NY: Pearson Education.

_____. 1996. On becoming a language teacher: Insights from diary studies. *TESOL Quarterly* 30(1): 131–151.

Nunan, D. 1988a. *Syllabus design*. Oxford: Oxford University Press.

_____. 1988b. *The learner-centered curriculum*. New York: Cambridge University Press.

_____. 1989a. *Designing tasks for the communicative classroom*. Cambridge: Cambridge University Press.

_____. 1989b. *Understanding language classrooms: A guide for teacher-initiated action*. Englewood Cliffs, NJ: Prentice Hall.

_____. 1990. Action research in the language classroom. In *Second language teacher education*, edited by J. C. Richards and D. Nunan. Cambridge: Cambridge University Press.

_____. 1991a. *Language teaching methodology*. London: Prentice Hall.

_____. 1991b. Methods in second language classroom-oriented research. *Studies in Second Language Acquisition* 13(2): 249–274.

_____. 1991c. *The learner-centered curriculum*. Cambridge: Cambridge University Press.

_____, ed. 1992. *Collaborative language learning and teaching*. Cambridge: Cambridge University Press.

_____. 1993a. Challenges in EFL classrooms. *TESOL Matters* August-September.

_____. 1993b. Action research in language education. In *Teachers develop teachers research: Papers on classroom research and teacher development*, edited by J. Edge and K. Richards. Oxford: Heinemann International.

_____. 1995. Closing the gap between learning and instruction. *TESOL Quarterly* 29(1): 133–158.

_____. 1996. Hidden voices: Insiders' perspectives on classroom interaction. In *Voices from the language classroom: Qualitative research on language education*, edited by K. M. Bailey and D. Nunan. New York: Cambridge University Press.

_____. 1997a. Does learner strategy training make a difference? *Lenguas Modernas* 24: 123–142.

_____. 1997b. Developing standards for teacher-research in TESOL. *TESOL Quarterly* 31(2): 365–367.

_____. 1999a. *Go for it! Student book 1*. Boston, MA: Heinle & Heinle.

_____. 1999b. *Second language teaching and learning*. Boston, MA: Heinle & Heinle.

Nunan, D., and L. Miller, eds. 1995. *New ways in teaching listening*. Alexandria, VA: TESOL.

Nuttall, C. 1982. *Teaching reading skills in a foreign language*. London: Longman.

Nyikos, M., and R. L. Oxford. 1993. A factor-analytic study of language learning strategy use: Interpretations from information processing theory and social psychology. *Modern Language Journal* 77(1): 11–23.

Ochs, E., and B. Schieffelin. 1995. The impact of socialization on grammatical development. In *The handbook of child language*, edited by P. Fletcher and B. MacWhinney. Cambridge, MA: Blackwell.

Odlin, T. 1994. *Perspectives on pedagogical grammar*. New York: Cambridge University Press.

O'Haver, Tom 1995. How to make a web page. Available at: http://www.wam.umd.edu/~toh/HowToMakeAWebPage.html

Oja, S. N., and L. Smulyan. 1989. *Collaborative action research: A developmental approach*. London: The Falmer Press.

Oller, J. W., Jr. 1979. *Language tests at school*. London: Longman.

Oller, J. W., Jr., and J. Jonz. 1994. *Cloze and coherence*. Lewisburg, PA: Bucknell University Press.

Olshtain, E., and A. Cohen. 1991. Teaching speech act behavior to non-native speakers. In *Teaching English as a second or foreign language*, edited by M. Celce-Murcia. Boston, MA: Newbury House.

Olshtain, E., T. Feuerstein, M. Schcolnik, and B. Zerach. 1970. *English for speakers of Hebrew: Pre-reader workbook*. Tel Aviv: University Publishing Projects.

_____. 1998. *Beginners' file one: Book and workbook*. Tel Aviv: University Publishing Projects.

O'Malley, J. M. 1986. *Test-taking strategies for ESL students*. Rosslyn, VA: International Research Associates.

O'Malley, J. M., and A. U. Chamot. 1990. *Learning strategies in second language acquisition*. Cambridge: Cambridge University Press.

O'Malley, J. M., A. U. Chamot, and L. Kupper. 1989. Listening comprehension strategies in second language acquisition. *Applied Linguistics* 10: 418–437.

O'Malley, J. M., A. U. Chamot, G. Stewner-Manzanares, L. Küpper, and R. Russo. 1985. Learning strategies used by beginning and intermediate ESL students. *Language Learning* 35: 21–46.

O'Malley, J. M., A. U. Chamot, and C. Walker. 1987. Some applications of cognitive theory to second language acquisition. *Studies in Second Language Acquisition* 9: 287–306.

O'Malley, J. M., and L. Valdez Pierce. 1996. *Authentic assessment for English language learners*. Reading, MA: Addison-Wesley.

O'Neill, R. 1982. Why use textbooks? *ELT Journal* 36(2): 104–111.

Opie, I., and P. Opie. 1959. *The lore and language of schoolchildren.* Oxford: Oxford University Press.

Opitz, M. 1998. *Literacy instruction for culturally and linguistically diverse students.* Newark, DE: International Reading Association.

Ortega, L. 1999. Planning and focus on form in L2 oral performance. *Studies in Second Language Acquisition* 21(1): 109–148.

Orton, J., R. Swart, A. Isaac, and C. Thompson. 1995. *The rhythm of language.* Melbourne, Australia: The Department of Language and Literacy, The University of Melbourne. Videocassette.

Ovando, C. J., and V. P. Collier. 1998. *Bilingual and ESL classrooms: Teaching in multicultural contexts.* 2d ed. Boston, MA: McGraw-Hill.

Oxford, R. L. 1988. *Strategy inventory for language learning (SILL).* Version 4.0 February 1987. (adapted version 6.0 for EFL/ESL by M. Nyikos, K. Nyikos, R. Oxford.)

_____. 1990. *Language learning strategies: What every teacher should know.* New York: Newbury House.

_____. 1996a. *Language learning strategies around the world: Cross-cultural perspectives.* Manoa, HI: University of Hawaii Press.

_____. 1996b. Personality type in the foreign or second language classroom: Theoretical and empirical perspectives. In *Understanding literacy: Personality preferences in rhetorical and psycholinguistic contexts,* edited by A. Horning and R. Sudol. Creskill, NJ: Hampton Press.

_____. 1999a. *Language learning strategies in the context of autonomy.* Synthesis of Findings from the International Invitational Conference on Learning Strategy Research. New York: Teachers College, Columbia University.

_____. 1999b. Relationships between learning strategy use and language proficiency in the context of learner autonomy and self-regulation. In *Learner autonomy as a central concept of foreign language learning,* edited by L. Bobb. Special issue of *Revista Canaria de Estudios Ingleses* 38: 109–126.

Oxford, R. L., and N. Anderson. 1995. State of the art: A crosscultural view of language learning styles. *Language Teaching* 28: 201–215.

Oxford, R. L., and M. E. Ehrman. 1995. Adults' language learning strategies in an intensive foreign language program in the United States. *System* 23: 359–386.

Oxford, R. L., C. Judd, and J. Giesen. 1998. *Relationships among learning strategies, learning styles, EFL proficiency, and academic performance among secondary school students in Turkey.* Unpublished manuscript, University of Alabama.

Oxford, R. L., and B. L. Leaver. 1996. A synthesis of strategy instruction for language learners. In *Language learning strategies around the world: Cross-cultural perspectives,* edited by R. Oxford. Manoa, HI: University of Hawaii Press.

Padgett, G. 1994. An experiential approach: Field trips, book publication, video production. *TESOL Journal* 3(3): 8–11.

Paikeday, T. M. 1985. *The native speaker is dead!* Toronto: Paikeday Publishing.

Pally, M., ed. 2000. *Sustained content teaching in academic ESL/EFL: A practical approach.* Boston, MA: Houghton Mifflin.

Palmer, H. 1917. *The scientific study and teaching of languages.* Yonkers-on-Hudson, NY: World Book Company.

Park, G. 1994. *Language learning strategies: Why do adults need them?* Unpublished manuscript, University of Texas at Austin.

Parker, R. E. 1993. *Mathematical power: Lessons from a classroom.* Portsmouth, NH: Heinemann.

Park-Oh, Y. Y. 1994. *Self-regulated strategy training in second-language reading: Its effects on reading comprehension, strategy use, reading attitudes, and learning styles of college ESL students.* Ph.D. diss., University of Alabama.

Parks, S., and H. Black. 1990. *Organizing thinking: Graphic organizers.* Book I. Pacific Grove, CA: Critical Thinking Press and Software.

_____. 1992. *Organizing thinking: Graphic organizers.* Book II. Pacific Grove, CA: Critical Thinking Press and Software.

Patthey-Chavez, G. G., and D. R. Ferris. 1997. Writing conferences and the weaving of multi-voiced texts in college composition. *Research in the Teaching of English* 31(1): 51–90.

Paulston, C. B. 1974. Linguistic and communicative competence. *TESOL Quarterly* 8: 347–362.

Pawley, A., and F. Syder. 1983. Two puzzles for linguistic theory: Nativelike selection and nativelike fluency. In *Language and communication,* edited by J. Richards and R. Schmidt. London: Longman.

Peck, S. 1978. Child-child discourse in second language acquisition. In *Second language acquisition,* edited by E. Hatch. Rowley, MA: Newbury House.

_____. 1980. Language play in child second language acquisition. In *Discourse analysis in second language research,* edited by D. Larsen-Freeman. Rowley, MA: Newbury House.

_____. 1995. Learning styles and elementary school ESL. In *Learning styles in the ESL/EFL classroom,* edited by J. Reid. Boston, MA: Heinle & Heinle.

Pelavin Research Center and American Institutes for Research. 1999. "What Works" study for adult ESL literacy students: Revised research design.

Penfield, J. 1987. *The media: Catalysts for communicative language learning.* Reading, MA: Addison-Wesley.

Pennington, M. C. and J. C. Richards. 1997. Reorienting the teaching universe: The experience of five first-year English teachers in Hong Kong. *Language Teaching Research* 1(2): 149–178.

Peregoy, S., and O. Boyle. 1997. *Reading, writing, and learning in ESL.* 2d ed. New York: Longman.

Pérez, B., and M. Torres-Guzman. 1992. *Learning in two worlds: An integrated Spanish/English biliteracy approach.* New York: Longman.

Perls, F., R. E. Hefferline, and P. Goodman. 1951. *Gestalt therapy: Excitement and growth in the human personality.* New York: Dell.

Perros, D. 1993. Unpublished observation report. California State University, Northridge.

Peterson, P. W. 1997. Knowledge, skills, and attitudes in teacher preparation for content-based instruction. In *The content-based classroom: Perspectives on integrating language and content,* edited by M. A. Snow and D. M. Brinton. New York: Longman.

Peyton, J. K., and L. Reed. 1990. *Dialogue journal writing with nonnative English speakers: A handbook for teachers.* Alexandria, VA: TESOL.

Phillips, S. 1993. *Young learners.* Oxford: Oxford University Press.

Phillipson, R. 1992. *Linguistic imperialism.* Oxford: Oxford University Press.

Piaget, J. 1967. *Six psychological studies.* New York: Vintage Books.

Pica, T. 1994. Questions from the language classroom: Research perspectives. *TESOL Quarterly* 28: 49–79.

_____. 1997. Second language teaching and research relationships: A North American view. *Language Teaching Research* 1(1): 48–72.

Pica, T., and C. Doughty. 1985. Input and interaction in the communicative language classroom: A comparison of teacher-fronted and group activities. In *Input and second language acquisition,* edited by S. M. Gass and C. G. Madden. Rowley, MA: Newbury House.

Pica, T., R. Kanagy, and J. Falodun. 1993. Choosing and using communication tasks for second language instruction and research. In *Tasks and language learning: Integrating theory and practice,* edited by G. Crookes and S. M. Gass. Clevedon, UK: Multilingual Matters.

Pica, T., F. Lincoln-Porter, D. Paninos, and J. Linnell. 1996. Language learners' interaction: How does it address the input, output, and feedback needs of language learners? *TESOL Quarterly* 30(1): 59–84.

Pica, T., R. Young, and C. Doughty. 1987. The impact of interaction on comprehension. *TESOL Quarterly* 21(4): 737–758.

Pienemann, M. 1989. Is language teachable? Psycholinguistic experiments and hypotheses. *Applied Linguistics* 10: 52–79.

Pienemann, M., and M. Johnston. 1987. Factors influencing the development of language proficiency. In *Applying second language acquisition research,* edited by D. Nunan. Adelaide: National Curriculum Resource Centre.

Piepho, H. E. 1974. *Kommuicative kompetence als übergeornete lernziel des Englischunterrichts.* Dornburg-Frickhofen, West Germany: Frankonius.

Piepho, H. E., and L. Bredella, eds. 1976. *Contacts: Integriertes Englischlehrwerk für klassen 5-10.* Bochum, West Germany: Kamp.

Pike, K. 1959. Language as particle, wave, and field. *Texas Quarterly* 2: 37–54.

Pinker, S. 1994. *The language instinct.* Harmondsworth, UK: Allen Lane.

Pittman, G. 1963. *Teaching structural English.* Brisbane, Australia: Jacaranda Press.

Plays. Wisconsin: Kalmbach Publishing Co.

Ponsot, M., and R. Deen. 1982. *Beat not the poor desk: Writing: What to teach, how to teach it and why.* Montclair, NJ: Boyton/Cook.

Porter, D., and J. Roberts. 1987. Authentic listening activities. In *Methodology in TESOL,* edited by M. Long and J. Richards. Rowley, MA: Newbury House.

Postovsky, V. A. 1974. Effects of delay in oral practice at the beginning of second language learning. *Modern Language Journal* 58(3): 229–239.

———. 1978. Why not start speaking later? In *Viewpoints in English as a second language*, edited by M. Burt, H. Dulay, and M. Finocchiaro. New York: Regents.

Prator, C. H., with M. Celce-Murcia. 1979. An outline of language-teaching approaches. In *Teaching English as a second or foreign language*, edited by M. Celce-Murcia and L. McIntosh. Rowley, MA: Newbury House.

Pressley, M. 1998. *Reading instruction that works.* New York: Guilford Press.

Pressley, M., with C. B. McCormick. 1995. *Advanced educational psychology for educators, researchers, and policymakers.* New York: HarperCollins.

Pressley, M., and Associates. 1990. *Cognitive strategy instruction that really improves children's academic performance.* Cambridge, MA: Brookline Books.

Preston, D. 1981. Ethnography of TESOL. *TESOL Quarterly* 15: 105–116.

Price-Machado, D. 1998. *Skills for success.* New York: Cambridge University Press.

Prince, E. 1990. *Write soon! A beginning text for ESL writers.* New York: Maxwell Macmillan.

Pugh, A. K. 1978. *Silent reading.* London: Longman.

Pulvermüller, F., and J. Schumann. 1994. Neurobiological mechanisms of language acquisition. *Language Learning* 45: 681–734.

Purpura, J. 1997. An analysis of the relationships between test takers' cognitive and metacognitive strategy use and second language test performance. *Language Learning* 42(2): 289–325.

———. 1999. Learner characteristics and L2 test performance. In *Language learning strategies in the context of autonomy: Synthesis of findings from the international invitational conference on learning strategy research*, edited by R. L. Oxford. New York: Teachers College, Columbia University.

Raatz, U. 1985. Tests of reduced redundancy: The C-test, a practical example. *Fremdsprachen in Hochschule.* Bochum, West Germany: AKS-Rundbriefe 13-14: 14–19.

Raimes, A. 1985. What unskilled ESL students do as they write: A classroom study of composing. *TESOL Quarterly* 19(2): 229–258.

———. 1991. Out of the woods: Emerging traditions in the teaching of writing. *TESOL Quarterly* 25(3): 407–430.

———. 1998. Teaching writing. In *Foundations for second language teaching*, edited by W. Grabe. Annual Review of Applied Linguistics, Vol. 18. New York: Cambridge University Press.

Ray, B., and C. Seely. 1998. *Fluency through TPR storytelling.* 2d ed. Berkeley, CA: Command Performance.

Redman, S., and R. Ellis. 1989. *A way with words: Book I.* Cambridge: Cambridge University Press.

Read, J. 2000. Assessing vocabulary. Cambridge: Cambridge University Press.

Reed, D. J., and A. D. Cohen. 2000. Revisiting raters and ratings in oral language assessment. In *Experimenting with uncertainty: Language testing essays in honour of Alan Davies*, edited by C. Elder, A. Brown, E. Grove, K. Hill, N. Iwashita, T. Lumley, T. McNamara, and K. O'Loughlin. Cambridge: Cambridge University Press.

Reid, J. 1987. The learning style preferences of ESL students. *TESOL Quarterly* 21(1): 87–111.

———, ed. 1995. *Learning styles in the ESL/EFL classroom.* Boston, MA: Heinle & Heinle.

———. 1998. Learning styles and grammar teaching in the composition classroom. In *Grammar in the composition classroom*, edited by P. Byrd and J. Reid. Boston, MA: Heinle & Heinle.

Reid, J., and B. Kroll. 1995. Designing and assessing effective classroom writing assignments for NES and ESL students. *Journal of Second Language Writing* 4(1): 17–41.

Reves, T., and P. Medgyes. 1994. The non-native English speaking EFL/ESL teacher's self-image: An international survey. *System* 22(3): 353–367.

Richards, J. C. 1983. Listening comprehension: Approach, design, procedure. *TESOL Quarterly* 17(2): 219–239.

———. 1984. The secret life of methods. *TESOL Quarterly* 18(1): 7–23.

———. 1985. *The context of language teaching.* Cambridge: Cambridge University Press.

———. 1990. *The language teaching matrix.* Cambridge: Cambridge University Press. (Chapter Three: "Designing Instructional Materials for Teaching Listening Comprehension.")

———. 1995. *Basic tactics for listening.* New York: Oxford University Press.

———. In press. *Second language curriculum development.* Cambridge: Cambridge University Press.

Richards, J. C., and C. Lockhart. 1994. *Reflective teaching in second language classrooms.* New York: Cambridge University Press.

Richards, J. C., and T. S. Rodgers. 1986. *Approaches and methods in language teaching: A description and analysis.* New York: Cambridge University Press.

———. 1987. Method, approach, design, and procedure. In *Methodology in TESOL: A book of readings*, edited by M. H. Long and J. C. Richards. New York: Newbury House.

Rickford, J., and A. Rickford. 1995. Dialect readers revisited. *Linguistics and Education* 7: 107–128.

Rigg, P. 1986. Reading in ESL: Learning from kids. In *Children and ESL: Integrating perspectives*, edited by P. Rigg and D. S. Enright. Alexandria, VA: TESOL.

Rigg, P., and V. Allen. 1989. Introduction to *When they all don't speak English: Integrating the ESL student into the regular classroom*, edited by P. Rigg and V. Allen. Urbana, IL: National Council of Teachers of English.

Riggenbach, H. 1999. *Discourse analysis in the language classroom, Volume 1: The spoken language.* Ann Arbor: University of Michigan Press.

Rinvolucri, M., and P. Davis. 1995. *More grammar games: Cognitive, affective, and movement activities for EFL students.* Cambridge: Cambridge University Press.

Rivera, K. 1999. Popular research and social transformation: A community-based approach to critical pedagogy. *TESOL Quarterly* 33(3): 485–500.

Rivers, W. 1966. Listening comprehension. *Modern Language Journal* 50(4): 196–204.

———. 1981. *Teaching foreign language skills.* 2d ed. Chicago: University of Chicago Press.

Robinson, P. 1996. Learning simple and complex second language rules under implicit, incidental, enhanced, and instructed conditions. *Studies in Second Language Acquisition* 18(1): 27–68.

———. 2000. Task complexity, cognitive resources, and second language syllabus design. In *Cognition and second language instruction*, edited by P. Robinson. New York: Cambridge University Press.

Rogers, C. 1991. *On becoming a person.* Boston, MA: Houghton Mifflin.

Rogers, C. V., and F. W. Medley. 1988. Language with a purpose: Using authentic materials in the foreign language classroom. *Foreign Language Annals* 21: 467–478.

Roithmeier, W., and S. J. Savignon. In press. The potential of computer mediated communication for CLT: Socially constructed knowledge and conflict avoidance. *Applied Linguistics.*

Rooks, G. 1988. *The non-stop discussion workbook.* 2d ed. New York: Newbury House.

———. 1994. *Let's start talking.* Boston, MA: Heinle & Heinle.

Rose, M. 1989. *Lives on the boundary.* New York: Free Press.

Rosen, N. G., and L. Sasser. 1997. Sheltered English: Modifying content delivery for second language learners. In *The content-based classroom: Perspectives on integrating language and content*, edited by M. A. Snow and D. M. Brinton. New York: Longman.

Rosenblatt, L. 1978. *The reader, the text, the poem.* Carbondale, IL: Southern Illinois University Press.

Rost, M. 1990. *Listening in language learning.* New York: Longman.

———. 1994. On-line summaries as representations of lecture understanding. In *Academic listening: Research perspectives*, edited by J. Flowerdew. Cambridge: Cambridge University Press.

Rost, M., and S. Ross. 1991. Learner use of strategies in interaction: Typology and teachability. *Language Learning* 41: 235–273.

Rost, M., and M. Uruno. 1995. *Basics in listening: Short tasks for listening development.* Singapore: Pearson Education Asia.

Rostand, E. 1897. *Cyrano de Bergerac: A play in five acts*, translated by Gladys Thomas and Mary F. Guillemard. Project Gutenberg. English text available at: ftp://metalab.unc.edu/pub/docs/books/gutenberg/etext98/cdben10.zip

French text available at: ftp://metatab.unc.edu/pub/docs/books/gutenberg/etext98/cdbfr10.zip

Rothstein, R. 1998. *The way we were? The myths and realities of America's student achievement.* New York: The Century Foundation Press.

Rounds, P. L. 1987. Characterizing successful classroom discourse for NNS teaching assistant training. *TESOL Quarterly* 21(4): 643–671.

References

569

Rowe, M. B. 1969. Science, soul, and sanctions. *Science and Children* 6(6): 11–13.

Rubin, J. 1975. What the "good language learner" can teach us. *TESOL Quarterly* 9(1): 41–51.

———. 1994. A review of second language listening comprehension research. *The Modern Language Journal* 78: 199–221.

———. 1995. The contribution of video to the development of competence in listening. In *A guide for the teaching of second language listening*, edited by D. Mendelsohn and J. Rubin. San Diego, CA: Dominie Press.

Rulon, K. A., and J. McCreary. 1986. Negotiation of content: Teacher fronted and small-group interaction. In *Talking to learn: Conversation in second language acquisition*, edited by R. R. Day. Rowley, MA: Newbury House.

Rumelhart, D. 1980. Schemata: The building blocks of cognition. In *Theoretical issues in reading comprehension*, edited by R. J. Spiro, B. C. Bruce, and W. F. Brewer. Hillsdale, NJ: Lawrence Erlbaum.

Rutherford, W. E. 1987. *Second language grammar: Learning and teaching*. London: Longman.

Rutherford, W. E. 1988. Functions of grammar in a language-teaching syllabus. In *Grammar and second language teaching*, edited by W. E. Rutherford. New York: Newbury House.

Rutherford, W. E., and M. Sharwood Smith, eds. 1988. *Grammar and second language teaching: A book of readings*. New York: Newbury House.

Ryan, F., and M. Krueger, eds. 1993. *Language and content: Discipline- and content-based approaches to language study*. Lexington, MA: D.C. Heath.

Rymes, B. 1997. Second language socialization: A new approach to second language acquisition research. *Journal of Intensive English Studies* 11: 143–155.

———. 1996. Rights to advise: Advice as an emergent phenomenon in student-teacher talk. *Linguistics and Education* 8: 409–437.

Rymes, B., and D. Pash. 2000. Questioning identity: The case of one second language learner. Paper presented at the American Association for Applied Linguistics Annual Conference, Vancouver, Canada.

Sabander, J. 1989. *Language learning in large classes in Indonesia.* (Project Report No. 9.) Leeds, UK: Lancaster-Leeds Language Learning in Large Classes Research Project.

Safadi, M. 1992. Correspondence. *TESOL Matters* December/January: 7.

Samimy, K. K. 1997. A review on the non-native teacher. *TESOL Quarterly* 31(4): 815–817.

Samimy, K. K., and J. Britt-Griffler. 1999. To be a native or non-native speaker: Perceptions of "non-native" students in a graduate TESOL program. In *Non-native educators in English language teaching*, edited by G. Braine. Mahwah, NJ: Lawrence Erlbaum.

Samuels, S. J., N. Schermer, and D. Reinking. 1992. Reading fluency: Techniques for making decoding automatic. In *What research has to say about reading instruction*, 2d ed., edited by S. J. Samuels and A. E. Farstrup. Newark, DE: International Reading Association.

Samway, K. D. 1994. But it's hard to keep fieldnotes while also teaching. *TESOL Journal* 4(1): 47–48.

Santos, T. 2001. The place of politics in second language writing. In *On second language writing: Collected papers from the Purdue University symposium on second lnguage writing*, edited by T. Silva and P. Matsuda. Mahwah, NJ: Lawrence Erlbaum.

Saroyan, W. 1984. Out of order. In *At the door: Selected literature for ESL students*, edited by S. McKay and D. Pettit. Englewood Cliffs, NJ: Prentice-Hall.

Sasser, L., and B. Winningham. 1991. Sheltered instruction across the disciplines: Successful teachers at work. In *With different eyes: Insights into teaching language minority students across the disciplines*, edited by F. Peitzman and G. Gadda. White Plains, NY: Longman.

Sato, K. In press. CLT and teacher education: Teacher context, beliefs, and practices. In *Communicative language teaching in translation: Contexts and concerns in teacher education*, edited by S. J. Savignon. New Haven: Yale University Press.

Savignon, S. J. 1972. *Communicative competence: An experiment in foreign language teaching.* Philadelphia, PA: Center for Curriculum Development.

———. 1974. Teaching for communication. In *Voix et visages de la France: Level 1 Teachers' Guide* by R. Coulombe, R. J. Barré, C. Fostle, N. Poulin, and S. Savignon. Chicago: Rand-McNally. Reprinted in *English Teaching Forum* 16 (1978): 2–5, 9.

———. 1983. *Communicative competence: Theory and classroom practice.* 2d ed. Reading, MA: Addison-Wesley.

———. 1997. *Communicative competence: Theory and classroom practice.* New York: McGraw Hill.

———, ed. In press. *Communicative language teaching in translation: Contexts and concerns in teacher education.* New Haven: Yale University Press.

Saville-Troike, M. 1989. *The ethnography of communication.* Oxford: Blackwell.

Sawada, T. 1997. Developing lesson plans. In *The open-ended approach: A new proposal for teaching mathematics*, edited by J. Becker and S. Shimada. Reston, VA: National Council of Teachers of Mathematics.

Scarcella, R. 1996. Secondary education in California and second language research: Instructing ESL students in the 1990s. *CATESOL Journal* 9(1): 129–151.

Scarcella, R., and R. Oxford. 1992. *The tapestry of language learning: The individual in the communicative classroom.* Boston, MA: Heinle & Heinle.

Schachter, J. 1986. Three approaches to the study of input. *Language Learning* 36(2): 211–225.

Schachter, J., and M. Celce-Murcia. 1977. Some reservations concerning error analysis. *TESOL Quarterly* 11(4): 441–449.

Schachter, J., and S. Gass, eds. 1996. *Second language classroom research: Issues and opportunities.* Mahwah, NJ: Lawrence Erlbaum.

Schane, S. 1970. Linguistics, spelling and pronunciation. *TESOL Quarterly* 4(2): 137–141.

Schank, R. C. 1975. The structure of episodes in memory. In *Representation and understanding*, edited by D. G. Brobow and A. Collins. New York: Academic Press.

Schank, R. C., and R. Abelson. 1977. *Scripts, plans, goals, and understanding: An inquiry into human knowledge structures.* Hillsdale, NJ: Lawrence Erlbaum.

Schecter, S. 1984. *Listening tasks for intermediate students of American English.* Cambridge: Cambridge University Press.

Schinke-Llano, L. 1993. On the value of a Vygotskian framework for SLA theory and research. *Language Learning* 43: 121–129.

Schleppegrell, M. 1998. Grammar as resource: Writing a description. *Research in the Teaching of English* 32(2): 182–211.

———. 2000. *Challenges of the science register for ESL students: Interpersonal and intertextual meanings.* Paper presented at the Conference on Advanced Literacy, University of California, Davis, February 18.

Schmidt, R. W. 1990. The role of consciousness in second language learning. *Applied Linguistics* 11(2): 17–46.

———, ed. 1995. *Attention and awareness in foreign language learning.* (Technical Report No. 9.) Honolulu, HI: University of Hawaii, Second Language Teaching and Curriculum Center.

Schmidt, R. W., and S. N. Frota. 1986. Developing basic conversational ability in a second language: A case study of an adult learner of Portuguese. In *Talking to learn: Conversation in second language acquisition*, edited by R. R Day. Rowley, MA: Newbury House.

Schmitt, N. 1997. Vocabulary learning strategies. In *Vocabulary: Description, acquisition, and pedagogy*, edited by N. Schmitt and M. McCarthy. Cambridge: Cambridge University Press.

———. 2000. *Vocabulary in language teaching.* Cambridge: Cambridge University Press.

Schmitt, N., and D. Schmitt. 1995. Vocabulary notebooks: Theoretical underpinnings and practical suggestions. *English Language Teaching* 49(2): 133–143.

Schmuck, R. 1985. Learning to cooperate, cooperating to learn: Basic concepts. In *Learning to cooperate, cooperating to learn*, edited by R. Slavin, et al. New York: Plenum Press.

Schnailberg, L. 1966. On assignment: Portraits of passage. *Education Week*, November 27, 1996, pp. 34–41.

Schoonen, R., J. Hulstijn, and B. Bossers. 1998. Metacognitive and language specific knowledge in native and foreign language reading comprehension: An empirical study among Dutch students in grades 6, 8, and 10. *Language Learning* 48: 71–106.

Schumann, J. 1994. Where is cognition? Emotion and cognition in second language acquisition. *Studies in Second Language Acquisition* 16(2): 231–242.

———. 1997. *The neurobiology of affect in language.* Malden, MA: Blackwell. (Also available as a special supplement to *Language Learning* 48.)

Schwandt, T. 1994. Constructivist, interpretivist approaches to human inquiry. In *Handbook of qualitative research*, edited by N. K. Denzin and Y. S. Lincoln. Thousand Oaks, CA: Sage.

Scollon, R., and S. W. Scollon. 1995. *Intercultural communication*. Oxford: Blackwell.

Scott, W. A., and L. Ytreberg. 1990. *Teaching English to children*. New York: Longman.

Seely, C., and E. Romijn. 1998. *TPR is more than commands—at all levels*. Berkeley, CA: Command Performance Language Institute.

Segalowitz, N., and E. Gatbonton. 1994. *Assessing the acquisition of second language fluency and determining input conditions for its promotion*. Paper presented at the Second Language Research Forum, Montreal.

Seidlhofer, B. 1995. Pronunciation awareness: A focus on appropriateness rather than correctness: Some thoughts on pronunciation in teacher education. *Speak Out!* Newsletter of the IATEFL Pronunciation Special Interest Group. No. 6, 12–16. England: IATEFL.

Seidlhofer, B. 1996. It is an undulating feeling: The importance of being a non-native teacher of English. *Views* 5(3-4): 63–80.

Seliger, H. W. 1983. The language learner as linguist: Of metaphors and realities. *Applied Linguistics* 4: 179–191.

Selinker, L. 1972. Interlanguage. *IRAL* 10: 209–231.

Semke, H. 1980. German café-theater: A venture in experiential learning. *Foreign Language Annals* 13(2): 137–138.

Shamim, F. 1996. In or out of the action zone: Location as a feature of interaction in large ESL classes in Pakistan. In *Voices from the language classroom: Qualitative research on language education*, edited by K. M. Bailey and D. Nunan. New York: Cambridge University Press.

Sharwood Smith, M. 1993. Input enhancement in instructed SLA: Theoretical bases. *Studies in Second Language Acquisition* 15(2): 165–179.

Shaw, P. A. 1996. Voices for improved learning: The ethnographer as co-agent of pedagogic change. In *Voices from the language classroom: Qualitative research on language education*, edited by K. M. Bailey and D. Nunan. New York: Cambridge University Press.

Shepard, L. 2000. The role of assessment in a learning culture. *Educational Researcher* 29(7): 4–14.

Shih, M. 1998. ESL writers' grammar editing strategies. *College ESL* 8(2): 64–86.

Shohamy, E. 1985. *A practical handbook in language testing for the second language teacher* (prepublication version). Tel Aviv, Israel: School of Education, Tel Aviv University.

_____. 2000. *The power of tests: A critical perspective of the uses of language tests*. Harlow, UK: Longman.

Shohamy, E., S. Donitsa-Schmidt, and I. Ferman. 1996. Test impact revisited: Washback effect over time. *Language Testing* 13(3): 298–317.

Short, D. J. 1994. Expanding middle school horizons: Integrating language, culture, and social studies. *TESOL Quarterly* 23: 581–608.

_____. 1997. Reading and 'riting and . . . social studies: Research on integrated language and content in secondary classrooms. In *The content-based classroom: Perspectives on integrating language and content*, edited by M. A. Snow and D. M. Brinton. New York: Longman.

_____. 2000. Using the ESL standards for curriculum development. In *Implementing the ESL standards for pre-K-12 students through teacher education*, edited by M. A. Snow. Alexandria, VA: TESOL.

Short, D., N. Cloud, E. Gomez, E. Hamayan, S. Hudelson, and J. Ramirez. 1997. *ESL standards for pre-K-12 students*. Alexandria, VA: TESOL.

Siegel, J. 1999. Stigmatized and standardized varieties in the classroom: Interference or separation? *TESOL Quarterly* 33(4): 701–728.

Silberstein, S. 1994. *Techniques and resources in teaching reading*. New York: Oxford University Press.

Silva, T. 1993. Toward an understanding of the distinct nature of L2 writing: The ESL research and its implications. *TESOL Quarterly* 27(4): 657–677.

Silva, T., and P. Matsuda, eds. 2001. *On second language writing*. Mahwah, NJ: Lawrence Erlbaum.

Simpson, P. 1997. *Language through literature*. London: Routledge.

Sinclair, J. 1984. The teaching of oral communication. *Speech and Language Learning* (Nagoya, Japan: Center for Foreign Language Education and Research) 10:1–11.

_____. 1991. *Corpus, concordance, collocation*. Oxford: Oxford University Press.

Sinclair, J., and G. Fox. 1990. *Collins COBUILD English grammar*. London: Collins.

Sinclair, J., and A. Renouf. 1988. A lexical syllabus for language learning. In *Vocabulary and language teaching*, edited by R. Carter and M. McCarthy. London: Longman.

Singer, M. 1998. *Perception and identity in intercultural communication*. Yarmouth, ME: Intercultural Press.

Skehan, P. 1989. *Individual differences in second-language learning*. London: Edward Arnold.

_____. 1996. A framework for the implementation of task-based instruction. *Applied Linguistics* 17(1): 38–62.

_____. 1998a. *A cognitive approach to language processing*. Hong Kong: Oxford University Press.

_____. 1998b. Task-based instruction. *Annual Review of Applied Linguistics* 18: 268–286.

Skierso, A. 1991. Textbook selection and evaluation. In *Teaching English as a second or foreign language*, 2d ed., edited by M. Celce-Murcia. New York: Newbury House/HarperCollins.

Skinner, B. F. 1957. *Verbal behavior*. New York: Appleton-Century-Crofts.

Slavin, R., S. Sharan, R. Hertz-Lazarowitz, C. Webb, and R. Schmuck, eds. 1985. *Learning to cooperate, cooperating to learn*. New York: Plenum Press.

Smith, S. W., ed. 1992. *English-as-a-second language model standards for adult education programs*. Sacramento, CA: Department of Education.

Snow, M. A. 1997. Teaching academic literacy skills: Discipline faculty take responsibility. In *The content-based classroom: Perspectives on integrating language and content*, edited by M. A. Snow and D. M. Brinton. New York: Longman.

_____. 1998. Trends and issues in content-based instruction. *Annual Review of Applied Linguistics* 18: 243–267.

Snow, M. A., and D. M. Brinton. 1988. Content-based language instruction: Investigating the effectiveness of the adjunct model. *TESOL Quarterly* 22(4): 553–574.

_____, eds. 1997. *The content-based classroom: Perspectives on integrating language and content*. New York: Longman.

Snow, M. A., and L. D. Kamhi-Stein. 1997. Teaching academic literacy skills: A new twist on the adjunct model. *Journal of Intensive English Studies* 11: 93–108.

_____. In press. Teaching and learning academic literacy through Project LEAP. In *Content-based instruction: Case studies in TESOL practice series*, edited by J. Crandall and D. Kaufman. Alexandria, VA: TESOL.

Snow, M. A., M. Met, and F. Genesee. 1989. A conceptual framework for the integration of language and content in second/foreign language instruction. *TESOL Quarterly* 23: 201–217.

Sokmen, A. J. 1997. Current trends in teaching second language vocabulary. In *Vocabulary: Description, acquisition, and pedagogy*, edited by N. Schmitt and M. McCarthy. Cambridge: Cambridge University Press.

Somerville, M. 1997. Workplace literacy and power: preliminary investigations. *Literacy and Numeracy Studies: An International Journal in the Education and Training of Adults* 7: 89–102.

Soto, L. D. 1997. *Language, culture, and power: Bilingual families and the struggle for quality education*. Albany: State University of New York Press.

Souillard, A. 1989. Visuals for practicing oral and aural skills with science and technology students. *English Teaching Forum* 27(3): 24–27.

Spada, N., and P. Lightbown. 1993. Instruction and the development of questions in the L2 classroom. *Studies in Second Language Acquisition* 15(2): 205–221.

Spargo, E. 1989. *Timed readings: Fifty 400-word passages with questions for building reading*. 3d ed. Lincolnwood, IL: Jamestown.

_____. 1998. *Timed readings plus: Twenty-five two-part lessons with questions for building reading speed and comprehension*. Lincolnwood, IL: Jamestown.

Sperling, D. 1998. *Dave Sperling's Internet guide*. Englewood Cliffs, NJ: Prentice Hall Regents.

_____. n.d. Prepositions I Quiz. Dave's ESL Cafe: Quizzes. Available at: http://www.pacificnet.net/~sperling/quiz/prep1.html

Spiro, R. J., B. C. Bruce, and W. F. Brewer, eds. 1980. *Theoretical issues in reading comprehension*. Hillsdale, NJ: Lawrence Erlbaum.

Spolsky, B. 1985. *Intentional and unintentional bias*. Unpublished manuscript. Ramat Gan, Israel: English Department, Bar-Ilan University.

St. John, M. J. 1987. Writing processes of Spanish scientists publishing in English. *English for Specific Purposes* 6: 113–120.

Stahl, S. A. 1999. *Vocabulary development*. Cambridge, MA: Brookline Books.

Stahl, S. A., and S. J. Vancil. 1986. Discussion is what makes semantic maps work in vocabulary instruction. *Reading Teacher* 40(1): 62–67.

Steffensen, M., and C. Yoag-Dev. 1984. Cultural knowledge and reading. In *Reading in a foreign language*, edited by C. Alderson and A. Urquhart. New York: Longman.

Stein, P., and H. Janks. 1996. Collaborative teaching and learning with large classes: A case study from the University of Witwatersrand. *Perspectives in Education* 17(1): 99–116.

Stein, S. 1997. *Equipped for the future: A reform agenda for adult literacy and lifelong learning*. Washington, DC: National Institute for Literacy.

Stempleski, S., and B. Tomalin. 1990. *Video in action: Recipes for using video in language teaching*. New York: Prentice Hall.

Stengel, E. 1930. On learning a new language. *International Journal of Psychoanalysis* 20: 471–479.

Stern, D. A. 1991. *Breaking the accent barrier: American sound and style for all speakers of English as a second language*. Los Angeles, CA: Video Language Products. Videocassette.

Stern, H. H. 1983. *Fundamental concepts of language teaching*. Oxford: Oxford University Press.

Stern, S. 1980. Drama in second language learning from a psycholinguistic perspective. *Language Learning* 30(1): 77–97.

Stevens, V. 1993. Concordances as enhancements to language competence. *TESOL Matters* 2 (6):11.

Stevick, E. W. 1971. *Adapting and writing language lessons*. Washington, DC: Foreign Service Institute.

_____. 1976. *Memory, meaning and method: Some psychological perspectives on language learning*. New York: Newbury House.

_____. 1980. *Teaching languages: A way and ways*. New York: Newbury House.

_____. 1989. *Success with foreign languages*. New York: Prentice Hall.

_____. 1990. *Humanism in language teaching: A critical perspective*. Oxford: Oxford University Press.

_____. 1998. *Working with teaching methods: What's at stake?* Boston, MA: Heinle & Heinle.

Stewart, E. 1972. *American cultural patterns: A cross-cultural perspective*. Yarmouth, ME: Intercultural Press.

Stewart, E., and M. Bennett. 1991. *American cultural patterns: A cross-cultural perspective*. Yarmouth, ME: Intercultural Press.

Stoller, F. L. 1993. Developing word and phrase recognition exercises. In *New ways in teaching reading*, edited by R. Day. Alexandria, VA: TESOL.

_____. 1994a. Developing a focused reading lab for L2 students. *Reading in a Foreign Language* 10: 33–53.

_____. 1994b. Making the most of a newsmagazine passage for reading skills development. *English Teaching Forum* 32: 2–7.

_____. 1997. Project Work: A means to promote language content. *English Teaching Forum* 35(4):2–9 and 37

Stoller, F. L., and W. Grabe. 1997a. A six T's approach to content-based instruction. In *The content-based classroom: Perspectives on integrating language and content*, edited by M. A. Snow and D. M. Brinton. New York: Longman.

_____. 1997b. Content-based instruction: Research foundations. In *The content-based classroom: Perspectives on integrating language and content*, edited by M. A. Snow and D. M. Brinton. New York: Longman.

Stotsky, S. 1997. *State English standards: An appraisal of English language arts/reading standards in 28 states*. Eric Document Reproduction Service. (ERIC Doc. No. ED 420 879).

Stoynoff, S. 1996. Resources in language testing and assessment. *TESOL Quarterly* 30(4): 781–786.

Strevens, P. 1977. *New orientations in the teaching of English*. Oxford: Oxford University Press.

_____. 1987. Interaction outside the classroom. In *Interactive language teaching*, edited by W. Rivers. Cambridge: Cambridge University Press.

_____. 1988a. ESP after twenty years: A re-appraisal. In *ESP: State of the art*, edited by M. Tickoo. Singapore: SEAMEO Regional Language Centre.

_____. 1988b. Language learning and language teaching: Towards an integrated model. In *Linguistics in context: Connecting observation and understanding: Lectures from the 1985 LSA/TESOL and NEH Institute*, edited by D. Tannen. Norwood, NJ: Ablex.

Strickland, D. 1998. What's basic in beginning reading? *Educational Leadership* March: 6–10.

Stubbs, M. 1995. Collocations and semantic profiles: On the cause of trouble with quantitative studies. *Functions of Language* 2(1): 1–33.

Suidan, L., J. K. Badenhoop, E. D. Glendening, and F. Weinhold. 1995. Common textbook and teaching misrepresentation of Lewis structures. *Journal of Chemical Education* 72(7): 583–593.

Susser, B. 1994. Process approaches in ESL/EFL writing instruction. *Journal of Second Language Writing* 3(1): 31–47.

Swain, M. 1984. Large-scale communicative language testing: A case study. In *Initiatives in communicative language teaching*, edited by S. J. Savignon and M. S. Berns. Reading, MA: Addison-Wesley.

_____. 1985. Communicative competence: Some roles of comprehensible input and comprehensible output in its development. In *Input in second language acquisition*, edited by S. M. Gass and C. G. Madden. New York: Newbury House.

Swain, M. 1988. Manipulating and complementing context teaching to maximize second language teaching. *TESL Canada Journal* 6(1): 68–83.

_____. 1993. The output hypothesis: Just speaking and writing aren't enough. *The Canadian Modern Language Review* 50: 158–164.

_____. 2000. The output hypothesis and beyond: Mediating acquisition through collaborative dialogue. In *Sociocultural theory and second language learning*, edited by J. P. Lantolf. Oxford: Oxford University Press.

Swain, M., and S. Lapkin. 1995. Problems in output and the cognitive processes they generate: A step towards second language learning. *Applied Linguistics* 16(3): 371–391.

_____. 1998. Interaction and second language learning: Two adolescent French immersion students working together. *The Modern Language Journal* 82(3): 320–327.

Swain, M., and B. Smith, eds. 2001. *Learner English*. 2d ed. Cambridge: Cambridge University Press.

Swales, J. M. 1980. ESP: The textbook problem. *The ESP Journal* 1(1): 11–23.

_____. 1988. *Episodes in ESP: A source and reference book on the development of English for science and technology*. New York: Prentice-Hall.

_____. 1990. *Genre analysis: English in academic and research settings*. Cambridge: Cambridge University Press.

Swales, J. M., and C. B. Feak. 1994. *Academic writing for graduate students: Essential tasks and skills*. Ann Arbor: University of Michigan Press.

Swan, M., and C. Walter. 1984. *The Cambridge English course*. Cambridge: Cambridge University Press.

Sweet, H. 1899. *The practical study of languages*. (Reprinted.) London: Oxford University Press.

Syed, Z. 1997. *Technology and experiential learning: Building a sense of community*. Paper presented at the Annual TESOL Convention, Orlando, FL.

Tajino, A., and Y. Tajino. 2000. Native and non-native: What can they offer? *ELT Journal* 54(1): 3–11.

Tang, G. M. 1992. The effects of graphic representation of knowledge structures on ESL reading comprehension. *Studies in Second Language Acquisition* 14: 177–195.

_____. 1997. Teaching content knowledge and ESL in multicultural classrooms. In *The content-based classroom: Perspectives on integrating language and content*, edited by M. A. Snow and D. M. Brinton. New York: Longman.

Tannen, D. 1988. *Linguistics in context: Connecting observation and understanding: Lectures from the 1985 LSA/TESOL and NEH institutes*. Volume 24 in the series *Advances in discourse processes*. Norwood, NJ: Ablex.

Tarone, E. 2000. Getting serious about language play: Language play, interlanguage variation and second-language acquisition. In *Social and cognitive factors in second language acquisition: Selected proceedings of the 1999 SLRF*, edited by B. Swierzbin, F. Morris, M. E. Anderson, C. A. Klee, and E. Tarone. Somerville, MA: Cascadilla Press.

Tarone, E., S. Dwyer, S. Gillette, and V. Icke. 1981. On the use of the passive in two astrophysics journal papers. *The ESP Journal* 1: 123–140.

Tarone, E., and Kuehn, K. 2000. Negotiating the social services oral intake interview: Communicative needs of nonnative speakers of English. *TESOL Quarterly* 34: 99–126.

Teachers of English to Speakers of Other Languages (TESOL). 1992. *TESOL statement on the role of bilingual education in the education of children in the United States*. Alexandria, VA: TESOL.

_____. 1997. *ESL standards for pre-K–12 students*. Alexandria, VA: TESOL.

_____. In press. *Adult ESL language and literacy instruction: A vision and action agenda for the 21st century.* Alexandria, VA: TESOL.

Tharp, R. G., and R. Gallimore. 1988. *Rousing minds to life: Teaching, learning, and schooling in school context.* Cambridge: Cambridge University Press.

Thomas, J. 1983. Cross-cultural pragmatic failure. *Applied Linguistics* 4(2): 91–112.

Thomas, R. J., L. A. Bird, and J. Grover. 1992. *Serving vocational ESL students.* Washington, DC: American Association of Community Colleges.

Tillitt, B., and M. N. Bruder. 1985. *Speaking naturally: Communication skills in American English.* New York: Cambridge University Press.

Tinajero, J. V., and A. Schifini. 1997. *Into English!* Carmel, CA: Hampton-Brown.

Tobin, K. 1987. The role of wait time in higher cognitive level learning. *Review of Educational Research* 57(1): 69–95.

Tomasello, M. 1998. Introduction to *The new psychology of language: Cognitive and functional approaches to language structure,* edited by M. Tomasello. Mahwah, NJ: Lawrence Erlbaum.

Tomasello, M., and C. Herron. 1988. Down the garden path: Inducing and correcting overgeneralization errors in the foreign language classroom. *Applied Psycholinguistics* 9(3): 237–246.

_____. 1989. Feedback for language transfer errors. *Studies in Second Language Acquisition* 11(4): 384–395.

Tomlinson, B., ed. 1998. *Materials development in language teaching.* Cambridge: Cambridge University Press.

Toukomaa, P., and T. Skutnabb-Kangas. 1976. *Teaching migrant children's mother tongue and learning the langue of the host country in the context of the socio-cultural situation of the migrant family.* Helsinki, Finland: The Finnish National Commission for UNESCO.

Trosset, C. 1986. The social identity of Welsh learners. *Language in Society* 13: 165–192.

Truscott, J. 1996. The case against grammar correction in L2 writing classes. *Language Learning* 46: 327–369.

Tsui, A. B. M. 1995. *An introduction to classroom interaction.* London: Penguin.

_____. 1996. Reticence and anxiety in second language learning. In *Voices from the language classroom: Qualitative research on language education,* edited by K. M. Bailey and D. Nunan. New York: Cambridge University Press.

Tyler, R. 1949. *Basic principles of curriculum and instruction.* Chicago: University of Chicago Press.

Underhill, A., series ed. *The teacher development series.* Oxford: Heinemann.

Underhill, N. 1987. *Testing spoken language: A handbook of oral testing techniques.* Cambridge: Cambridge University Press.

Ur, P. 1984. *Teaching listening comprehension.* Cambridge: Cambridge University Press.

_____. 1988. *Grammar practice activities: A practical guide for teachers.* New York: Cambridge University Press.

_____. 1996. *A course in language teaching: Practice and theory.* Cambridge: Cambridge University Press.

Ur, P., and A. Wright. 1992. *Five-minute activities: A resource book for language teachers.* New York: Cambridge University Press.

Urquhart, A. H., and C. Weir. 1998. *Reading in a second language: Process, product, and practice.* London and New York: Longman.

U.S. Department of Labor. 1993. *The secretary's commission on achieving necessary skills.* Washington, DC: U.S. Department of Labor.

Valcárcel, M., C. Chaudron, M. Verdú, and J. Roca. 1985. Adaptations to COLT and a developing system of activity types. In *COLT: Coding Conventions and Applications,* edited by N. Spada and M. Fröhlich. Sydney, Australia: National Centre for English Language Teaching and Research.

Valdés, G. 1995. The teaching of minority languages as academic subjects: Pedagogical and theoretical challenges. *The Modern Language Journal* 79(3): 299–328.

_____. 1996. *Con respecto.* New York: Teacher's College Press.

Valdés, G., and R. Figueroa. 1994. *Bilingualism and testing: A special case of bias.* Norwood, NJ: Ablex.

Vale, D., with A. Feunteun. 1995. *Teaching children English: A training course for teachers of English to children.* New York: Cambridge University Press.

Valette, R. 1969. *Directions in foreign language testing.* New York: Modern Language Association.

Valette, R. 1977. *Modern language testing.* 2d ed. New York: Harcourt Brace Jovanovich.

Van den Branden, K. 2000. Does negotiation of meaning promote reading comprehension? A study of multilingual primary school classes. *Reading Research Quarterly* 35(3): 426–443.

Van Duzer, C., and R. Berdan. 2000. Perspectives on assessment in adult ESOL instruction. In *Annual review of adult learning and literacy,* edited by J. Comings, B. Barner, and C. Smith. San Francisco, CA: Jossey-Bass Publishers.

van Ek, J. A. 1976. *The threshold level for modern language learning in schools.* London: Council of Europe, Longman.

van Lier, L. 1988. *The classroom and the language learner: Ethnography and second language classroom research.* London: Longman.

_____. 1990. Classroom research in second language acquisition. *Annual Review of Applied Linguistics* 10: 73–186.

_____. 1992. Not the nine o'clock linguistics class: Investigating contingency grammar. *Language Awareness* 1(2): 91–108.

_____. 1994. Action research. *Sintagma* 6: 31–37.

_____. 1995. *Introducing language awareness.* London: Penguin.

Van Patten, B. 1996. *Input processing and grammar instruction in second language acquisition.* Norwood, NJ: Ablex.

Vandergrift, L. 1998. Constructing meaning in L2 listening: Evidence from protocols. In *French as a second language in Canada: Recent empirical studies,* edited by S. Lapkin. Toronto: Toronto University Press.

Vaughan-Rees, M. 1991. Rhymes and rhythm. *Speak Out!* Special issue. Newsletter of the IATEFL Pronunciation Special Interest Group.

Venezky, R. L. 1970. *The structure of English orthography.* The Hague: Mouton.

Vygotsky, L. [1934] 1962. *Thought and language,* translated by E. Hanfman and G. Vakar. Cambridge, MA: MIT Press.

_____. 1978. *Mind in society: The development of higher psychological processes.* Cambridge, MA: Harvard University Press.

Wada, M., ed. 1994. *The course of study for senior high school: Foreign languages* (English version). Tokyo: Kairyudo.

_____. In press. Teacher education for ELT innovation in Japan. In *Communicative language teaching in translation: Contexts and concerns in teacher education,* edited by S. J. Savignon. New Haven, CT: Yale University Press.

Wajnryb, R. 1992. *Classroom observation tasks.* New York: Cambridge University Press.

Wall, D., and J. C. Alderson. 1993. Examining washback: The Sri Lankan impact study. *Language Testing* 10(1): 41–69.

Wallace, M. J. 1998. *Action research for language teachers.* Cambridge: Cambridge University Press.

Walmsley, S. A. 1994. *Children exploring their world: Theme teaching in elementary school.* Portsmouth, NH: Heinemann.

Wang, C. C. 2000. *A sociolinguistic profile of English in Taiwan: Social context and learner needs.* Ph.D. diss., The Pennsylvania State University.

_____. In press. Innovative teaching in EFL contexts: The case of Taiwan. In S. J. Savignon (Ed.): *Communicative language teaching in translation: Contexts and concerns in teacher education,* edited by S. J. Savignon. New Haven: Yale University Press.

Warschauer, M. 1995. *E-mail for English teaching.* Alexandria, VA: TESOL.

_____. 1997. Computer-mediated collaborative learning: Theory and practice. *Modern Language Journal* 81(4): 470–481.

Warschauer, M., H. Schetzer, and C. Meloni. 2000. *Internet for English teaching.* Alexandria, VA: TESOL.

Watanabe, Y. 1996. Does grammar translation come from the entrance examination? Preliminary findings from classroom-based research. *Language Testing* 13(3): 318–333.

Watson-Gegeo, K. 1988. Ethnography in ESL: Defining the essentials. *TESOL Quarterly* 22(4): 575–592.

Weaver, C. 1972. *Human listening: Processes and behavior.* New York: Bobbs-Merrill.

_____. 1994. *Reading process and practice.* 2d ed. Portsmouth, NH: Heinemann.

Weinstein, G. 1997. From problem-solving to celebration: Discovering and creating meanings through literacy. *The Canadian Modern Language Review* 54(1): 28–47.

_____. 1998. *Family and intergenerational literacy in multilingual communities.* ERIC Q&A. Washington, DC: National Clearinghouse on ESL Literacy Education.

References

_____, ed. 1999. *Learners' lives as curriculum: Six journeys to immigrant literacy.* McHenry, IL: Delta Systems.

Weinstein, G., A. Whiteside, and N. Gibson. In press. Collisions on the road to citizenship: "Thanks to God I passed." In *Case studies in community partnerships*, edited by A. Auerbach. Alexandria, VA: TESOL.

Wenden, A. L., and J. Rubin. 1987. *Learner strategies in language learning.* Englewood Cliffs, NJ: Prentice-Hall.

Wergrzecka-Kowalewski, E. 1997. Content-based instruction: Is it possible in high school? In *The content-based classroom: Perspectives on integrating language and content*, edited by M. A. Snow and D. M. Brinton. New York: Longman.

Wesche, M. B. 1987. Communicative testing in a second language. In *Methodology in TESOL: A book of readings*, edited by M. H. Long and J. C. Richards. New York: Newbury House.

Wesche, M. B., and D. Ready. 1985. Foreigner talk in the university classroom. In *Input in second language acquisition*, edited by S. M. Gass and C. G. Madden. New York: Newbury House.

West, M. 1941. *Learning to read a foreign language.* London: Longman.

_____. 1953. *A general service list of English words.* London: Longmans, Green & Co.

_____. 1960. *Teaching English in difficult circumstances.* London: Longman.

White, R. V., ed. 1995. *New ways in teaching writing.* Alexandria, VA: TESOL.

Whitehead, A. N. 1929. *The aims of education.* New York: Macmillan.

Widdowson, H. G. 1975. *Stylistics and the teaching of literature.* London: Longman.

_____. 1978. *Teaching language as communication.* Oxford: Oxford University Press.

_____. 1981. English for specific purposes: Criteria for course design. In *English for academic and technical purposes: Studies in honor of Louis Trimble*, edited by L. Selinker, E. Tarone, and V. Hanzeli. Rowley, MA: Newbury House.

_____. 1983. *Learning purpose and language use.* Oxford: Oxford University Press.

_____. 1988. Grammar, nonsense and learning. In *Grammar and second language teaching: A book of readings*, edited by W. E. Rutherford and M. Sharwood Smith. New York: Newbury House.

_____. 1992. *Practical stylistics: An approach to poetry.* Oxford: Oxford University Press.

_____. 1994. The ownership of English. *TESOL Quarterly* 29(2): 377–389.

Wilkins, D. 1976. *Notional syllabuses.* Oxford: Oxford University Press.

Willing, K. 1988. *Learning styles in adult migrant education.* Melbourne, Australia: Research Series, National Curriculum Resource Centre: Adult Migrant Education.

Willis, D. 1990. *The lexical syllabus.* London: HarperCollins.

Winitz, H., ed. 1981. *The comprehension approach to foreign language instruction.* New York: Newbury House.

Winston, P. H., ed. 1975. *The psychology of computer vision.* New York: McGraw Hill.

Wong, M. S. 1994. Two-minute conversations: "If I were . . ." In *New ways in teaching speaking*, edited by K. M. Bailey and L. Savage. Alexandria, VA: TESOL.

Wood, D., J. Bruner, and G. Ross. 1976. The role of tutoring in problem solving. *Journal of Child Psychology and Psychiatry* 17: 89–100.

Woods, D. 1996. *Teacher cognition in language teaching: Beliefs, decision-making and classroom practice.* Cambridge: Cambridge University Press.

Woodward, T., and S. Lindstrom. 1995. *Planning from lesson to lesson: A way of making lesson planning easier.* Harlow, UK.

Wright, A. 1976. *Visual materials for the language teacher.* London: Longman.

_____. 1989. *Pictures for language learning.* Cambridge: Cambridge University Press.

_____. 1995. *Storytelling with children.* New York: Oxford University Press.

Wrigley, H. 1998. Knowledge in action: The promise of project-based learning. *Focus on Basics* [on-line serial], 2, Issue D (December). Hostname: Harvard.edu Directory: 1998/wrigley.htm

_____. 1993. *Innovative programs and promising practices in adult ESL literacy.* Washington, DC: National Clearinghouse on Literacy Education.

Wrigley, H., and G. Guth. 2000. *Bringing literacy to life: Issues and options in adult ESL.* San Mateo, CA: Aguirre International.

Yalden, J. 1983. *The communicative syllabus: Evolution, design, and implementation.* Oxford: Pergamon Press.

Yamamoto, H. 1994. Seventeen syllables. In *Seventeen syllables*, edited by K. K. Cheng. New Brunswick, NJ: Rutgers University Press.

Yee, V., and M. Wagner. 1984. *Teacher talk: The structure of vocabulary and grammar explanations.* Unpublished manuscript, University of Hawaii, Honolulu.

Young, L., K. Thearling, S. Skieno, A. Robison, S. Omohundro, B. Mel, and S. Wolfram. 1988. In the year 2000. In *Self, literacy, technology, and society: Confronting the issues*, edited by G. E. Hawisher and C. Selfe. Englewood Cliffs, NJ: Prentice Hall.

Yun, M. 1998. *House of the winds.* New York: Interlink Books. Interview on NPR Weekend Edition, Sunday, Nov. 15.

Zak, H., and T. Dudley-Evans. 1986. Features of word omission and abbreviation in telexes. *ESP Journal* 5: 59–71.

Zamel, V. 1985. Responding to student writing. *TESOL Quarterly* 19(1): 79–102.

_____. 1987. Recent research on writing pedagogy. *TESOL Quarterly* 21(4): 697–715.

Zentella, A. C. 1997. *Growing up bilingual: Puerto Rican children in New York.* Malden, MA: Blackwell Publishers.

Zhang, S. 1995. Reexamining the affective advantage of peer feedback in the ESL writing class. *Journal of Second Language Writing* 4(3): 209–222.

Zimmerman, B. J., and M. M. Pons. 1986. Development of a structured interview for assessing student use of self-regulated learning strategies. *American Educational Research Journal* 23: 614–628.

Zimmerman, C. B. 1997. Historical trends in second language vocabulary instruction. In *Second language vocabulary acquisition*, edited by J. Coady and T. Huckin. Cambridge: Cambridge University Press.

Index

Index

Thearling, K., 477
Think-aloud procedure, 220
Think-aloud techniques, 365
Thinking learning style, 361
Thomas, H., 333, 334, 335, 336, 337, 338, 339, 340, 341
Thomas, J., 448
Thomas, R. J., 52
Thought groups, 119
Threshold hypothesis, 376–377
Threshold level of language ability, 15
Tillitt, B., 105
Time frame shifts, 239
Timed readings, 197
Tinajero, J. V., 141
Tlusty, N., 113
Tobin, K., 40
TOEFL, 100, 112, 495
Tomalin, B., 474
Tomasello, M., 41, 257, 270, 271, 283, 492
Tomlinson, B., 30, 424
Tone, 76, 96
    tonic syllable, 133n
Tonkyn, A., 265
Top-down processing, 14
    listening, 74–75, 76, 88, 89, 91, 93, 94, 96–97, 99
    pronunciation, 119. See also Approaches
Torres-Guzmán, M., 351
Toukomaa, P., 376, 377
Toyota Families for Learning, 174
TPR (Total Physical Response), 6, 88, 143, 145, 147, 148, 334, 364
    TPR—storytelling, 146, 147, 149
Tragardh, T., 398
Transactional language, 73–75, 76, 82
Transactional Strategies Instruction (TSI), 195
Trosset, C., 387, 397, 399n
Truscott, J., 229, 244
Tsui, A. B. M., 495, 496
Turner, S., 419
Tyler, R., 55

U.S. Adult Education Act, 186, 398
U.S. copyright code, 128
U.S. Department of Labor, 398
U.S. National Literacy Act, 186, 398
U.S. Office of Education, 386
Underhill, A., 552
Underhill, N., 111, 115
United States Congress, 173, 174
Universal grammar, 269
Universal order for language acquisition, 274
Uptake, 41, 234
Ur, P., 78, 82, 84, 140, 145, 146, 149, 266, 403, 405, 408, 424, 474
Urquhart, A. H., 153, 203
Uruno, M., 93, 94, 95

Valcárcel, M., 33, 42n,
Valdés, G., 171, 175, 346, 350, 356n
Valdez Pierce, L., 168
Vale, D., 140
Valette, R., 517, 526
Valiquette, M., 50
Van den Branden, K., 155, 166
van Dijk, N/A, 533
Van Duzer, C., 181
Van Ek, J. A., 15, 76
van Lier, L., 490, 493, 495, 496
Van Patten, B., 257
Vancil, S., 288
Vandergrift, L., 91, 101
Vandrick, S., 307
Vann, R., 363
Varonis, L., 37
Vaughan-Rees, M., 126
Venesky, R. L., 208, 209
Verdú, M., 42n
VESL (Vocational ESL), 43, 45, 48, 49

cluster VESL, 51
occupational-specific VESL, 51
on-site English courses, 47
preemployment and workplace program goals, 176
preemployment VESL, 51
pre-workplace classes, 176
workplace VESL, 52
Videotaping, 107, 109, 113, 127–129, 133n
    drama, 127
    exchanges, 109, 113
    for pronunciation teaching, 127, 128–129, 133n
    of speeches, 107
Viëtor, W., 4
Visual learning, 140
Vocabulary, 7, 78, 87, 107, 146, 285–299
    book flood approach, 289
    building, 203
    collocations, 292
    development, 192–193
    explicit learning of, 286–289
    guessing meaning from context, 290–291
    historical overview, 285–286
    implicit learning of, 289–290
    instruction, 201
    keyword method, 291
    knowledge, 154
    learning strategies, 290–294
    meaning associations, 288
    mnemonic devices, 291
    other learner strategies, 291
    semantic associations, 292–293
    semantic mapping, 288
    syntactic collocation types, 293
    teaching techniques and activities, 288–289
    use of computers in vocabulary teaching, 288
    use of corpus studies, 294–295
    vocabulary network, 288
    vocabulary notebooks, 29
    word families, 287, 289
    word set grids, 289. See also Teacher
Vogt, M., 315
von Humboldt, A., 4
Vowels, 122–123
    chart, 137
    orthography, 209
    phonetic symbols, 136. See also Spelling
Vygotsky, L., 269, 304, 335, 373–374, 381
Vygotskyan principles, 495

Wada, M., 13
Wagner, M., 32
Wait-time, 39–40
Walker, D., 30, 38
Wall, D., 494, 530
Wallace, M. J., 491, 498
Walmsley, S. A., 306
Walter, C., 61
Wang, C. C., 14, 24
Warschauer, M., 337, 488, 552
Washback, 494–495, 497
Watanabe, Y., 494
Waters, A., 49
Watson-Gegeo, K., 397, 399n
Waugh, A., 143
Weaver, C., 70, 157, 161
Weaver, K. A., 521
Weaver, S. J., 363
Websites, 547–549
Wegrzecka-Kowalewski, E., 308
Weinbach, L., 211
Weinhold, F., 419
Weinstein, G., 171, 174, 175, 178, 180, 181, 185, 214, 392
Weir, C., 153, 203
Welfare reform, 174
Wenden, A. L., 78, 437, 461
Wesche, M. B., 306, 308, 309, 318n, 395, 459, 474n
West, M., 5, 38, 42n

West, W., 287
White, R. V., 232
Widdowson, H. G., 47, 58, 61, 234, 251, 319, 320, 321, 322, 328, 431
Wilkins, D., 55, 61, 76
Williams, E., 265
Williams, J., 31, 233, 256, 266, 268, 273
Willing, K., 277
Willinham-McLain, L., 337
Willis, D., 297
Winningham, B., 376
Winters, T., 260, 476
Wolfram, S., 477
Wong, M. S., 110, 493
Wood, D., 374, 493
Woodward, A., 419
Woodward, T., 408
Word-learner processes, 192
Workshops, 549–550
World Congress on Applied Linguistics, 538
World Englishes, 26
Wormuth, D. R., 516
Wright, A., 145, 473, 474, 475
Wrigley, H. S., 178, 181, 185
Writing, 7, 153, 207–248
    academic, 219–232
    composition, L1 vs. L2, 220–221, 230, 232n, 233–234
    conferencing, 228, 246
    controlled composition, 220
    curriculum, 221–222
    discovery approach, 226
    emotive writing tasks, 212–213
    freewriting, 224
    goal of course, 223
    grammar in, 233–248
    guided writing, 240–244
    heuristic devices (prewriting), 224, 232n
    history of teaching, 219–221
    matching for mechanics of writing, 211, 215
    mechanics of, 207–217
    personal writing, 226
    prewriting activities, 223–224, 242–243
    process vs. product, 220–221, 234
    quickwriting, 224
    responding to, 227
    rhetorical patterns, 226
    school-oriented writing tasks, 213
    science writing, 238, 240–241
    scoring—of writing placement tests, 222
    speed writing, 224
    tasks, 212–213
    wet ink writing, 224
    See also Assessment; Audio recordings;
        Beginning-level student; Business
        English; Children; Culture and cultural
        background; Curriculum; Dialogue
        journals; Errors; Feedback; Grammar;
        Reading; Spelling; Strategies; Tasks

Yamamoto, H., 329
Yedlin, J., 476
Yee, V., 32
Yoshioka, J., 515, 518
Young, L., 477
Young, R., 459
Youngs, B., 337
Ytreberg, L., 140, 148
Yu, B., 493
Yule, G., 73, 84, 111
Yun, M., 22

Zak, H., 50
Zamel, V., 227, 230
Zentella, A. C., 355n
Zhang, S., 229
Zimmerman, B. J., 285, 363
Zone of proximal development, 304, 335, 382